EUROPEAN YEARBOOK ON HUMAN RIGHTS 2018

This publication is supported by

AUSTRIAN
HUMAN RIGHTS INSTITUTE

EIUC
European Inter-University
Centre for Human Rights
and Democratisation

Ludwig Boltzmann Institute
Human Rights

EUROPEAN YEARBOOK ON HUMAN RIGHTS 2018

Edited by
Wolfgang BENEDEK
Philip CZECH
Lisa HESCHL
Karin LUKAS
Manfred NOWAK

Cambridge – Antwerp – Chicago

Vienna

Intersentia Ltd
Sheraton House | Castle Park
Cambridge | CB3 0AX | United Kingdom
Tel.: +44 1223 370 170 |
Fax: +44 1223 370 169
Email: mail@intersentia.co.uk
www.intersentia.com | www.intersentia.co.uk

NWV Verlag GmbH
Seidengasse 9/OG 2/TOP 2.4
A-1070 Vienna
Tel.: +43 1 796 35 62-24 |
Fax: +43 1 796 35 62-25
Email: office@nwv.at
www.nwv.at

Distribution for the UK and Ireland:
NBN International
Airport Business Centre, 10 Thornbury Road
Plymouth, PL6 7PP
United Kingdom
Tel.: +44 1752 202 301 | Fax: +44 1752 202 331
Email: orders@nbninternational.com

Distribution for the USA and Canada:
Independent Publishers Group
Order Department
814 North Franklin Street
Chicago, IL 60610
USA
Tel.: +1 800 888 4741 (toll free) | Fax: +1 312 337 5985
Email: orders@ipgbook.com

Distribution for all other countries:
Intersentia Publishing nv
Groenstraat 31
2640 Mortsel
Belgium
Tel.: +32 3 680 15 50 | Fax: +32 3 658 71 21
Email: mail@intersentia.be

European Yearbook on Human Rights 2018
© The editors and contributors severally 2018

The editors and contributors have asserted the right under the Copyright, Designs and Patents Act 1988, to be identified as authors of this work.

No part of this book may be reproduced, stored in a retrieval system, or transmitted, in any form, or by any means, without prior written permission from Intersentia, or as expressly permitted by law or under the terms agreed with the appropriate reprographic rights organisation. Enquiries concerning reproduction which may not be covered by the above should be addressed to Intersentia at the address above.

Artwork on cover: © cienpies/vectorstock

ISBN (NWV) 978-3-7083-1244-6
ISBN (Intersentia) 978-1-78068-706-3
D/2018/7849/103
NUR 828

British Library Cataloguing in Publication Data. A catalogue record for this book is available from the British Library.

Scientific Advisory Board

Kalliope Agapiou-Josephides (Nicosia), Veronique Arnault (Brussels), Heiner Bielefeldt (Erlangen), Bojko Bučar (Ljubljana), Emmanuel Decaux (Paris), Koen De Feyter (Antwerp), Olivier De Schutter (Leuven), Andrew Drzemczewski (Strasbourg), Horst Fischer (Brussels), Jenny Goldschmidt (Utrecht), Felipe Gomez (Bilbao), Jonas Grimheden (FRA, Vienna), Gábor Halmai (Florence), Thomas Hammarberg (former CoE Commissioner for Human Rights), Enver Hasani (Pristina), Kirsten Hastrup (Copenhagen), Walter Kälin (Bern), Dzidek Kedzia (President, EIUC Board), Matthias C. Kettemann (Frankfurt), Renate Kicker (Graz), Morten Kjærum (Lund), Rumyana Kolarova (Sofia), Josip Kregar (Zagreb), Eva Maria Lassen (Copenhagen), Jean-Paul Lehners (Luxembourg), Paul Lemmens (Judge, ECtHR, Leuven), Peter Leuprecht (Montréal), Lauri Mälksoo (Tartu), Carmen Marquez-Carrasco (Sevilla), Fabrizio Marrella (Venice), Iulia Moțoc (Judge, ECtHR, Bucarest), Michael O'Flaherty (Director FRA, Vienna), Margot O'Salomon (LSE, London), Maria Teresa Pizzaro Beleza (Lisbon), Allan Rosas (Judge, ECJ), William Schabas (Middlesex), Alexander Sicilianos (Judge, ECtHR), Markku Suksi (Abo Akademi University), Engelbert Theuermann (Vienna), George Ulrich (Secretary General, EIUC), Mark Villiger (Judge, ECtHR), Knut Vollebæk (Oslo), Ineta Ziemele (Riga).

EDITORS' PREFACE

Dear readers,

The year 2017 has been a difficult one for regional human rights protection in Europe. The Council of Europe (CoE) was put under financial stress by the suspension of the Russian financial contributions and the reduction of those from Turkey; the European Union (EU) was struggling with reforming its migration policy and proceeding with the crisis concerning the rule of law in Poland; and the Organization for Security and Cooperation in Europe (OSCE) under Austrian chairmanship, only after very difficult political negotiations, appointed three key positions, among them the director of the Office of Democratic Institutions and Human Rights (ODIHR) and the Representative on Freedom of the Media.

All this and much more is analysed in the new *European Yearbook on Human Rights 2018* (EYHR). While the struggle for human rights and the critical review of topical human rights challenges have been at the core of the EYHR from its inception, the Yearbook itself underwent some important changes last year. From 2018 onwards, the EYHR will be published by Intersentia, which means that all contributions are now subject to a double-blind review procedure. This allows us not only to ensure the high academic standard of the EYHR, but to improve it still further. It should be noted that we, the editorial team, when selecting the final contributions pay attention not only to the highest academic standard and gender balance, we also believe in 'academic diversity', encouraging, in particular, excellent young scholars to submit their contributions and publish them alongside renowned academics in the field of human rights. Additionally, we consider the mutual informing between academia and practice as crucial to reflect in a comprehensive way on human rights developments in Europe. Accordingly, as in previous years and complementary to academic debates, the EYHR 2018 provides the reader with first-hand information from the inside of relevant institutions on the developments in the field of human rights protection in Europe in 2017.

As in past years, the *European Yearbook* remains structured around current human rights challenges that the European institutions, namely EU, the CoE and the OSCE have been particularly confronted with in the year 2017. Additionally, there is one 'Topic of the Year' and a part on 'Other issues'. Finally, the EYHR 2018 includes nine book reviews of recent publications in fields relevant to human rights developments in Europe 2017.

Editors' Preface

As 'Topic of the Year' we, the editors, chose the ongoing rule of law, democratic and fundamental rights crisis in Poland. Coinciding with the EU Commission launching an infringement procedure against Poland regarding the Polish Law on the Supreme Court, Professor Mirosław Wyrzykowski, a renowned former judge of the Polish constitutional tribunal and academic, describes in his contribution, 'The Vanishing Constitution', the three acts of the dramatic constitutional crisis in Poland and provides a detailed and insightful account of the legal changes introduced which challenge the rule of law and the protection of fundamental human rights principles in Poland.

The next part of the book on human and fundamental rights developments in the EU is introduced by a review of the relevant jurisprudence of the Court of Justice of the European Union (CJEU) by Eva Radlgruber and Hans-Peter Folz. While the CJEU has dealt with a variety of important fundamental rights issues, its approach in 2017 seemed to remain ambivalent, leaving room for improvements, *inter alia*, in the field of asylum.

Migration and asylum have clearly been decisive topics in Europe 2017. Hence, the EYHR 2018 includes in total six related contributions, three of them in the EU section. First, Danaé Coquelet's contribution on resettlement and human rights is dedicated to the specific case of Syrian refugees resettled from Lebanon to Belgium. In her contribution, Coquelet not only analyses the findings from her field study on the expectations of Syrian refugees in Lebanon vis-à-vis Belgium as a resettlement country; she also analyses the Belgian resettlement scheme from a human rights perspective, touching upon crucial issues that might undermine the integration progress of resettled refugees.

Resettlement is considered one of the last remaining legal channels for people in need of protection to reach the EU where the closing of migratory routes, the establishment of extraterritorial asylum centres and the enhanced migration control cooperation with third states dominate the discussions about the future direction of the Common European Asylum System (CEAS). In light of thousands of people losing their lives in the Mediterranean, the physical access to protection and the meaning of the latter has been a topic of concern not only for the Member States (MS) and the European Commission. In 2017, the CJEU in *X and X v Belgium* and *A.S. v Slovenian Republic* and *Khadija Jafari and Zainab Jafari* had the opportunity to rule on the humanitarian visa for refugees and the deviation of common rules of the CEAS under extreme circumstances. However, as Lisa Heschl and Alma Stankovic find in their contribution, 'The Decline of Fundamental Rights in CJEU Jurisprudence after the 2015 "Refugee Crisis"', the Court missed opportunities in 2017 to provide a basis for changing the rules of the CEAS but rather contributed to the continuance of fundamental right breaches people seeking protection face on their dangerous journeys to the EU. The CJEU's judgments are thereby in line with the securitisation approach dominating the discourse on migration and asylum in the EU.

Editors' Preface

As already mentioned, the physical access to the territory of the EU and its MS was a major topic of discussion in 2017 and still ranks high on the European agenda. In its Conclusions of 28 June 2018 the European Council reaffirmed the need to increase cooperation with third states and called on the Commission and the Council to explore the concept of regional disembarkation platforms.[1] The Council Conclusions support the externalisation strategies the EU and its Member States promoted in recent years. Hence, Mathilde Duhaâ's contribution 'The EU Migration Crisis and the Human Rights Implications of the Externalisation of Border Control', could not be more topical, providing the reader with an analysis of the human rights problems accompanying the EU-Turkey 'deal' and the operations of the European Coast Guard Agency.

While migration and asylum clearly shaped the discussion in the EU, other important fundamental and human rights developments in the EU in 2017 require our attention. In 2017 the Commission's mid-term review of the 'Framework for National Roma Integration Strategies up to 2020' took place. Gregor Fischer in his contribution asks 'Does the EU Framework for Roma Integration Promote the Human Rights of Romani Persons in the Union?'. In order to provide answers, Fischer supplements his analysis of the state of the implementation of the Framework with a case study on Austria to reveal factual and legal shortcomings of the European and national strategies for enhancing Romani equality at the local level.

While the results of the mid-term evaluation of the Framework for National Roma Integration Strategies were published in early 2018, no comparable document has been made publicly available for the evaluation of the EU Guidelines on the promotion and protection of freedom of religion or belief adopted in 2013. Adina Portaru thus dedicates her contribution to the question whether in the dawn of its 5th anniversary the implementation of the Guidelines is lagging behind and whether the EU itself is respecting its commitments in the area of freedom of religion and belief.

In the last contribution of the EU section, Theodor Rathgeber shifts the perspective and analyses the stabilising role of the EU within the UN Human Rights Council (HRC), which finds itself in 'troubled waters'. Not only did the US in June 2018 withdraw from the Council, the latter is also confronted with severe financial constraints and ongoing criticism of its political bias. The EU in 2017 has played a substantial and stabilising role in the activities of the HRC as Rathgeber shows by using the case of Syria as an example.

From the EU level, the EYHR now turns to relevant human rights developments at the CoE level. As in the previous Part, the CoE Part begins

---

[1] European Council Conclusions, 28 June 2018, Press Release, 421/18, 29.06.2018, available at http://www.consilium.europa.eu/en/press/press-releases/2018/06/29/20180628-euco-conclusions-final/, last accessed 18.07.2018.

with a review of the jurisprudence of the European Court of Human Rights (ECtHR) 2017 by Stefan Kieber. Although 2017 saw a reduction of the number of pending applications to the lowest level since 2004, the Court is still confronted with a massive workload, challenging its effective functioning. In order to prevent a deadlock hanging like the sword of Damocles over the Court, David Reichel and Jonas Grimheden suggest a better understanding of the structural issues contributing to the Court's situation by examining human rights violations found by the Court from a statistical perspective. While statistical records of the case law of the Court are accessible through the HUDOC database, Reichel and Grimheden focus on repetitive cases deriving from structural and common problems at the national level and the techniques the Court has developed to address them.

One approach to reduce the workload of the Court is to increase and deepen the dialogue between the highest national courts and the ECtHR since dialogue will smooth the cooperation between the ECtHR and domestic judges, thus enhancing mutual understanding and eventually reducing future cases. Lize R. Glas in her contribution, however, analyses the legal boundaries of such a deepened dialogue about a Strasbourg judgment from different perspectives, namely the perspective of the Court and the domestic perspective of eleven domestic legal orders.

The *Yukos* case is the best example that there is a need to strengthen the dialogue between the ECtHR and national highest courts. Kanstantsin Dzehtsiarou's and Filippo Fontanelli's contribution deals with the finding of the Russian Constitutional Court that the implementation of the *Yukos* judgment of the ECtHR was incompatible with the Russian Constitution and the judgment impossible to execute.

Whereas the relationship between the ECtHR and national courts is of crucial importance, its relationship with the CJEU is decisive for the unity of human rights protection in Europe since both may have to deal with comparable human and fundamental rights violations. In order to ensure the coherence and consistency between the CJEU and the ECtHR, Article 52(3) Charter of Fundamental Rights of the European Union (CFREU) foresees that the CJEU is bound by the interpretation of case law by the ECtHR for corresponding rights in the ECtHR. Joyce De Coninck in her contribution 'The Impact of ECtHR and CJEU Judgments on the Rights of Asylum Seekers in the European Union: Adversaries or Allies in Asylum?' argues, however, that in the highly politicised field of migration, a lack of coherence in the judgments of the two Courts can be found. Ultimately, the divergencies could detrimentally affect the principles of legal certainty and legitimate expectations of those seeking relief before either of the Courts, as well as the effectiveness of protection and ultimately, the institutional legitimacy of both Courts.

Elspeth Guild and Vladislava Stoyanova also dedicate their contribution to the field of migration. However, they approach current discussions about the arrival of migrants through a different human rights lens, namely from the perspective of the right to leave any country. More concretely, they examine the right to leave a state under international and European human rights law and question the legality of various efforts to make the right to leave any country dependent on a right of entry to another country.

The next contribution, by Mathieu Leloup, shifts the focus in the field of migration to the most vulnerable: children. In times where children are separated from their parents and detained in special facilities, Leloup's approach to revitalise the principle of the best interests of the child in expulsion cases is of crucial importance. Of similar topicality is the contribution of Claudia V. Elion dealing with the relationship between religious extremism and human rights in the case law of the ECtHR and the tensions between counter-terrorism measures and human rights.

The last contribution in the CoE part, by Agnieszka Szklanna, concerns questions related to the delays in implementation of ECtHR judgments. While CoE members have an obligation to execute the judgments of the ECtHR and the Committee of Ministers is in charge of supervising this execution, there are still some 7,500 cases that the Committee of Ministers is currently supervising. Szklanna in her contribution focuses on the implementation of ECtHR judgments related to electoral issues due to their political and legal importance.

While before 2014 the OSCE's death was proclaimed on a regular basis, in particular, its Special Monitoring Mission (SMM) to Ukraine and its election monitoring missions worldwide contributed to the recovery of its reputation and weight at the international level. Nevertheless, despite this general revival of the OSCE, in the area of fundamental freedoms and human rights, its human dimension is still struggling to maintain its relevance. Jean P. Froehly in his contribution reviews the reform process of the human dimension mechanism and recommends a comprehensive reform proposal including a new 'OSCE Human Dimension Implementation Review Mechanism' (IRM).

As has been mentioned above, the EYHR aims to bring together academics with experts from the field. The subsequent contribution by Christian Strohal complements the article by Froehly providing an insight to the developments of the human dimension in 2017 from the view of the Austrian chairmanship. When Austria took over the chairmanship from Germany in 2017, the OSCE participating states had been unable to agree on human dimension decisions for three years in a row. Strohal in his contribution provides an overview of the challenges the Austrian chairmanship faced and the results that have been achieved, allowing for a rather more positive outlook and better prospects for the human dimension of the OSCE than for calls proclaiming the 'end of human rights'.

One of the achievements of the Austrian chairmanship was the appointment of a new director of ODHIR after lengthy political negotiations. ODHIR provides support, assistance and expertise to participating States and civil society to promote democracy, rule of law, human rights, tolerance and non-discrimination. However, new communication technologies and techniques challenge the way international institutions and organisations communicate about human rights and fundamental freedoms. Katarzyna Gardapkhadze and Gareth Davies in their contribution discuss the urgent need and possible ways for international organisations to communicate more effectively, to be able to show to ordinary people that human rights and fundamental freedoms are indispensable in their lives, and thereby to strengthen public support for those rights and freedoms.

Modern technologies and new ways of communications were also crucial for the topics of the subsequent two articles on the rise of populism and the #MeToo movement. Ajla van Heel and Jacopo Leone in their contribution use four case studies on Italy, France, Poland and the Netherlands to assess the impact populist parties and their agendas have on gender equality and women's rights across the OSCE region. They compare the political agendas and narratives of populist parties in the selected countries on gender equality and women's rights issues, with the aim of identifying consistent patterns, possibly highlighting concerns and recommendations to be taken into consideration in future efforts to promote more inclusive and equal democratic societies. Ewa Sapiezynska and Johanna Pruessing subsequently dedicate their contribution to #MeToo and how a digital social movement can give agency to the victims and impact the structural level. Their focus is thereby on the impact the #MeToo campaign has had on women's human rights in the OSCE region, both *de facto* and *de jure*.

The EYHR deals with human rights developments within the major European institutions. However, room is also given to human rights protection at the national level. In the final part dedicated to 'Other Issues', Monika Mayerhofer sheds light on the national human rights protection framework in Ukraine, by focusing on the role of the Ukrainian Parliament Commissioner for Human Rights as a complementary instrument to foster human rights at the national level.

The editors of the Yearbook representing the three Austrian human rights centres and the European Inter-University Centre for Human Rights and Democratisation (EIUC) in Venice would like to acknowledge the crucial financial support of EIUC to this publication. We further would like to thank the ODIHR and the EU Fundamental Rights Agency for the excellent cooperation and the submission of contributions by their collaborators. A double-blind review process requires a lot of commitment; accordingly, we would like to express our gratitude to all reviewers within and beyond the Scientific Advisory Board for their valuable work. The review process was organised by Lisa Heschl and Philip Czech, who deserve special thanks. Many thanks go further to Reinmar Nindler, who was in charge of the book reviews and to Manuela Rusz, who took care of the formatting and harmonisation of the articles. Without their precious help, the EYHR 2018 would not have been possible in the same form. Finally, particular thanks go to Tom Scheirs and Rebecca Moffat from Intersentia for their cooperation in publishing this volume.

We hope that reading this Yearbook, which is unique in its focus and vocation, will not only help to better understand the rich landscape of the European regional human rights system but will also stimulate discussion and critical thinking about human rights developments, eventually encouraging some readers to submit contributions to the next edition of the European Yearbook on Human Rights.

Graz, Salzburg, Venice, Vienna – June 2018
Wolfgang Benedek, Philip Czech, Lisa Heschl,
Karin Lukas and Manfred Nowak

CONTENTS

Editors' Preface vii
List of Abbreviations xix
List of Contributors xxiii

PART I. TOPIC OF THE YEAR

The Vanishing Constitution
    Mirosław WYRZYKOWSKI 3

PART II. EU

The Court of Justice of the European Union and Human Rights in 2017
    Hans-Peter FOLZ and Eva RADLGRUBER 47

Understanding Resettlement Through the Prism of Human Rights:
A Case Study on the Resettlement in Belgium of Syrian Refugees
from Lebanon
    Danaé COQUELET 75

The Decline of Fundamental Rights in CJEU Jurisprudence
after the 2015 'Refugee Crisis'
    Lisa HESCHL and Alma STANKOVIC 103

The EU Migration Crisis and the Human Rights Implications
of the Externalisation of Border Control
    Mathilde DUHAÂ 135

Does the EU Framework for Roma Integration Promote the Human Rights
of Romani Persons in the Union?
    Gregor FISCHER 167

The EU Guidelines on Freedom of Religion or Belief at Their Fifth
Anniversary: Implementation Lagging Behind?
    Adina PORTARU 193

Human Rights Council in Troubled Waters: The EU as a Stabilising Factor
    Theodor RATHGEBER 211

PART III. CoE

The Jurisprudence of the European Court of Human Rights in 2017
Stefan KIEBER 229

A Decade of Violations of the European Convention on Human Rights:
Exploring Patterns of Repetitive Violations
David REICHEL and Jonas GRIMHEDEN 267

The Boundaries to Dialogue with the European Court of Human Rights
Lize R. GLAS 287

Unprincipled Disobedience to International Decisions: A Primer
from the Russian Constitutional Court
Kanstantsin DZEHTSIAROU and Filippo FONTANELLI. 319

The Impact of ECtHR and CJEU Judgments on the Rights of Asylum
Seekers in the European Union: Adversaries or Allies in Asylum?
Joyce DE CONINCK. 343

The Human Right to Leave Any Country: A Right to be Delivered
Elspeth GUILD and Vladislava STOYANOVA 373

Some Reflections on the Principle of the Best Interests of the Child
in European Expulsion Case Law
Mathieu LELOUP 395

Salafism in Europe: A Legal and Political Analysis of Human Rights
and Security
Claudia V. ELION 419

Delays in the Implementation of ECtHR Judgments: The Example of Cases
Concerning Electoral Issues
Agnieszka SZKLANNA 445

PART IV. OSCE

Enhanced Structure and Geographical Balance: Reforming the OSCE's
Human Dimension Meetings
Jean P. FROEHLY 467

The Crisis of the International Protection of Human Rights
and the Geopolitical OSCE Perspective: 'The End of Human Rights',
'Shooting the Messenger' or Strengthening Cooperation?
Christian STROHAL 481

How Multilateral Organisations can Communicate Better about
Human Rights
    Katarzyna GARDAPKHADZE and Gareth DAVIES 495

Rising Populism and its Impact on Women's Rights: Selected Cases
from the OSCE Region
    Ajla van HEEL and Jacopo LEONE 521

The Impact of #MeToo on Women's Rights in the OSCE Region
    Ewa SAPIEZYNSKA and Johanna PRUESSING........................ 543

PART V. OTHERS

The Role of the Ukrainian Parliament Commissioner for Human Rights
in the Field of Equality and Non-Discrimination
    Monika MAYRHOFER... 573

PART VI. BOOK REVIEWS

Katja S. Ziegler, Elizabeth Wicks and Loveday Hodson (eds.): The UK
and European Human Rights – A Strained Relationship?
    Christian BREITLER 599

Emily Reid: Balancing Human Rights, Environmental Protection and
International Trade – Lessons from the EU Experience
    Moritz DEINHAMMER 601

Nicole Bürli: Third-Party Interventions before the European Court
of Human Rights
    Philipp Alexander DILLINGER 605

Stijn Smet and Eva Brems (eds.): When Human Rights Clash at the
European Court of Human Rights – Conflict or Harmony?
    Christina SEEWALD 607

Violeta Moreno-Lax: Accessing Asylum in Europe, Oxford Studies
in European Law
    Ulrike BRANDL... 609

Mark Dawson: The Governance of EU Fundamental Rights
    Amaia AZKORRA CAMARGO and Sara VASSALO AMORIM 613

Philip Leach: Taking a Case to the European Court of Human Rights,
4th Edition
    Florian HASEL... 615

Sionaidh Douglas-Scott and Nicholas Hatzis (eds.): Research Handbook on EU Law and Human Rights
    Melanie Helene SCHINAGL 619

Lauri Mälksoo and Wolfgang Benedek (eds.): Russia and the European Court of Human Rights – The Strasbourg Effect
    Reinmar NINDLER 621

Index 623

LIST OF ABBREVIATIONS

ACPO	Association of Chief Police Officers
AFSJ	Area of Freedom, Security and Justice
AG	Advocate General
CCJE	Consultative Council of European Judges
CDA	Christian Democratic Appeal
CEAS	Common European Asylum System
CEDAW	Convention on the Elimination of All Forms of Discrimination against Women
CERD	Convention on the Elimination of All Forms of Racial Discrimination
CESCR	Committee on Economic, Social and Cultural Rights
CETA	Comprehensive Economic and Trade Agreement
CFR/CFREU	Charter of Fundamental Rights of the European Union
CFSP	Common Foreign and Security Policy
CGRS	Commissioner General for Refugees and Stateless Persons
CJEU	Court of Justice of the European Union
CLAHR	Committee on Legal Affairs and Human Rights
CM	Committee of Ministers
CoE	Council of Europe
CoI	Commission of Inquiry
CoM	Committee of Ministers
COMECE	Catholic Church in the EU
ComRC	Committee on the Rights of the Child
CORE	IFSH's Centre for OSCE Research
COREPER	Committee of the Permanent Representatives of the Governments of the Member States to the EU
CPRSI	Contact Point for Roma and Sinti Issues
CRC	UN Convention on the Rights of the Child
CRPD	Convention on the Rights of Persons with Disabilities
CSCE	Conference on Security and Co-operation in Europe
CSO	Civil Society Organisation
CSW	Commission on the Status of Women
CT	Constitutional Tribunal
DRC	Democratic Republic of Congo
DSB	Dispute Settlement Body

EASO	European Asylum Support Office
EAW	European Arrest Warrant
EBCG	European Border and Coast Guard
EC	European Commission
ECHR	European Convention on Human Rights
ECI	European Citizens Initiative
ECJ	European Court of Justice
ECtHR	European Court of Human Rights
EEAS	European External Action Service
EIDHR	European Instrument for Democracy and Human Rights
ENCJ	European Network of Councils for the Judiciary
ENNHRI	European Network of National Human Rights Institutions
ENF	Europe of Nations and Freedom Group
EO's	European Ombudsman's
EP	European Parliament
EPHA	European Public Health Alliance
ERRC	European Roma Rights Centre
EU	European Union
EUNAVFOR MED	European Union Naval Force Mediterranean
FN	Front National
FoRB	Freedom of Religion or Belief
FRA	European Union Agency for Fundamental Rights
FSM	Five Star Movement
FTFs	Foreign Terrorist Fighters
GA	General Assembly
GANHRI	Global Alliance of National Human Rights Institutions
GATT	General Agreement on Tariffs and Trade
GBV	Gender Based Violence
GCRS	Office of the Commissioner General for Refugees and Stateless Persons
GL	Greenleft
GNA	Government of National Accord
GRC	Geneva Convention relating to the Status of Refugees
GRECO	Group of States Against Corruption
HCNM	High Commissioner on National Minorities
HDIM	Human Dimension Implementation Meeting
HDS	Human Dimension Seminar
HIV	Human Immunodeficiency Virus
HJIL	Heidelberg Journal of International Law
HRA	Human Rights Act
HRVP	High Representative of the Union for Foreign Affairs and Security Policy

HRC	UN Human Rights Council
HRW	Human Rights Watch
ICTJ	International Center for Transitional Justice
IDP	Internally Displaced Person
IEI	Inter-Ethnic Initiative for Human Rights
IFSH	Institute for Peace Research and Security Policy at the University of Hamburg
IOM	International Organisation for Migration
IRM	OSCE Human Dimension Implementation Review Mechanism
IS/ISIS	Islamic State
LGBTIQ	Lesbian, Gay, Bisexual, Transgender, Intersex, Queer
LIBE Committee	European Parliament's Committee on Civil Liberties, Justice and Home Affairs
LNA	Libyan National Army
LRI	Local reception initiative
LTV visa	Visa with limited territorial validity
MOAS	Migrant Offshore Aid Station
MoU	Memorandums of Understanding
MS	Member States
NGO	Non-Governmental Organisation
NHRI	National Human Rights Institution
NRCP(s)	National Roma Contact Point(s)
NRISs	National Roma Integration Strategies
OCP	Occupational Health Psychology
ODIHR	OSCE Office for Democratic Institutions and Human Rights
OHCHR	Office of the United Nations High Commissioner for Human Rights
OSCE	Organization for Security and Cooperation in Europe
PACE	Parliamentary Assembly of the Council of Europe
PC	Permanent Council
PEP	Protected Entry Procedures
PKK	Kurdistan Workers' Party
PNR	Passenger Name Record
PSWC	Public Social Welfare Centre
PvdA	Labour Party (PvdA)
PVV	Party for Freedom
RAINN	Rape, Abuse and Incest National Network
RCC	Russian Constitutional Court
RCD	Reception Conditions Directive
RFOM	Representative on the Freedom of the Media
RLDC	Revue Lamy de Droit Civil

SBC	Schengen Border Code
SHDIM	Supplementary Human Dimension Implementation Meetings
SMM	Special Monitoring Mission in Ukraine
SP	Socialist Party
SRL	Syrian refugees in Lebanon
TEU	Treaty on European Union
TFEU	Treaty on the Functioning of the European Union
TTIP	Transatlantic Trade and Investment Partnership
UDHR	Universal Declaration of Human Rights
UK	United Kingdom
UN	United Nations
UNDP	United Nations Development Programme
UNGA	United Nations General Assembly
UNHCR	United Nations High Commissioner for Refugees
UNODC	United Nations Office for Drugs and Crime
UNOG	United Nations Office at Geneva
UNSC	United Nations Security Council
UNSMIL	United Nations Support Mission in Libya
UPR	Universal Periodic Review
US(A)	United States of America
VCLT	Vienna Convention on the Law of Treaties
VLAP	Action Plan on Visa Liberalisation
VVD	People's Party for Freedom and Democracy
WHO	World Health Organization
WTO	World Trade Organization

LIST OF CONTRIBUTORS

Wolfgang BENEDEK
Wolfgang Benedek is Professor Emeritus at the Institute of International Law and International Relations and former Director of the European Training and Research Centre for Human Rights and Democracy of the University of Graz (UNI-ETC). He is a regular lecturer at the Vienna Diplomatic Academy and the European Master Programmes on Human Rights and Democratisation in Venice and Sarajevo. His main research interests include human rights, human development and human security, on which he has published substantially. He is the managing co-editor of this Yearbook.

Danaé COQUELET
Danaé Coquelet works as an attaché for the Belgian Federal Agency for the Reception of Asylum Seekers (Fedasil). She obtained a master's degree from the European Inter-University Centre for Human Rights and Democratisation (EIUC) and specialised in migration and gender. She previously collaborated with UNHCR and OHCHR and worked on topics such as female leadership, gender-based violence and refugee resettlement. In 2017, she joined the Saint Joseph University of Beirut to conduct extensive research on the resettlement in Belgium of Syrian refugees from Lebanon.

Philip CZECH
Philip Czech holds a Dr iur and a Dr phil degree. Since 2002, he has been a researcher at the Austrian Institute for Human Rights, which became a department of the University of Salzburg in 2014. He is the editor of the *Newsletter Menschenrechte*, a periodical reporting in German on the current case law of the European Court of Human Rights. He is mainly engaged with publishing and teaching in the field of fundamental rights, especially with the case law of the ECtHR and its transposition in Austria.

Gareth DAVIES
Gareth Davies is the editor at the OSCE Office for Democratic Institutions and Human Rights (ODIHR). He was previously the editor at the European Council on Foreign Relations (ECFR). He holds an M. phil in Race, Ethnicity and Conflict from Trinity College Dublin and a BA (hons) in English Literature from the University of York.

Joyce DE CONINCK

Joyce De Coninck is an academic assistant and PhD candidate at the Ghent European Law Institute at Ghent University. Prior to her current position, Joyce conducted research at the Department of Criminology, Criminal Law and Social Law at Ghent University for FreSsco – an EU mandated project concerning free movement of persons and social security coordination. In addition, Joyce was a junior associate at Pappas and Associates in Brussels. Her PhD research focuses on the responsibility of the European Union for human rights violations in the field of asylum and migration, particularly in view of the parallel applicability of (international) human rights regimes.

Mathilde DUHAÂ

Mathilde Duhaâ currently works as a human rights trainee at the Delegation of the European Union to the United Nations in New York. She holds a master's degree in International Relations and Crisis Management from the Institut d'Etudes Politiques de Toulouse and a European master's degree in Human Rights and Democratisation (EMA) from the European Inter-University Centre for Human Rights and Democratisation (EIUC) in Venice. Prior to completing her EMA, she worked as an advocacy assistant with Amnesty International and undertook internships with several other NGOs. Her research interests include migration and border control, human security and the EU governance system.

Kanstantsin DZEHTSIAROU

Kanstantsin Dzehtsiarou is a senior lecturer in law at the University of Liverpool. His research interests are spread between interpretation of the European Convention on Human Rights, reform of the European Court of Human Rights, administration of international justice, comparative and constitutional law. As an expert he collaborates with the Council of Europe, the United Nations Development Programme, OSCE and others.

Claudia V. ELION

Claudia V. Elion works at the Council of Europe on the topics of financing of terrorism and money laundering. She obtained her master's degree in Human Rights and Democratisation at the European Inter-University Centre of Human Rights and Democratisation in Venice, Italy and the Université de Strasbourg in France. For her interdisciplinary master's thesis she concentrated on the issue of Salafism in Europe.

Gregor FISCHER

Gregor Fischer earned his law degree at the University of Graz in 2016 and is a legal researcher at the European Training and Research Centre for Human Rights and Democracy of the University of Graz (UNI-ETC). In his research, he focuses on non-state actors' human rights obligations, human rights and sports, the human rights situations of Romani communities in Europe and the (de-)radicalisation of societies.

Hans-Peter FOLZ

Hans-Peter Folz is Professor of European Law and International Law and Head of the Institute of European Law at the University of Graz. His main research interests include the legal framework for human rights protection in Europe through the ECHR and the EU Charter of Fundamental Rights, the relationship between different instruments of human rights protection in Europe, as well as questions relating to the institutional law of the European Union. He has published extensively on these topics. He recently authored the commentary on the EU Charter of Fundamental Rights and Article 6 TEU for the second, revised edition of C. Vedder and W. Heintschel von Heinegg (eds.), *Europäisches Unionsrecht* (Nomos Publishing House 2018).

Filippo FONTANELLI

Filippo Fontanelli is a senior lecturer in international law at the Law School of the University of Edinburgh. He is a co-rapporteur of the ILA Committee on the procedural reform of international courts and tribunals, a consultant for the Italian Government on investment arbitration and a fellow of the Scottish Parliament information centre on matters of international trade.

Jean P. FROEHLY

Jean P. Froehly is Head of the Economic Section at the German Embassy in Moscow. He was previously Head of the Director's Office and Senior Political Advisor to Director Michael Georg Link at the OSCE Office for Democratic Institutions and Human Rights (ODIHR) in Warsaw from 2014 to 2017 and continued as a policy advisor in ODIHR until June 2018. Before joining the German Federal Foreign Service in 2002, he was a senior research fellow at the German Council on Foreign Relations (DGAP). He graduated from the Institut d'Etudes Politiques de Paris (Sciences Po).

Katarzyna GARDAPKHADZE

Katarzyna Gardapkhadze is First Deputy Director at the OSCE Office for Democratic Institutions and Human Rights (ODIHR). She was previously Head of the Human Rights Department at ODIHR. She has a university education in psychology (University of Gdansk, Faculty of Social Science), 30 years of professional experience from across the OSCE region, and expertise in strategic and change management.

Lize R. GLAS

Lize R. Glas is Assistant Professor of European Law at Radboud University, the Netherlands. Her research centres on how the European Court of Human Rights functions through its procedure and in combination with other actors (for example, the Committee of Ministers and the CJEU) and how (procedural) reform affects the applicant.

Jonas GRIMHEDEN

Jonas Grimheden holds a PhD and is Senior Policy Manager at the European Union's human rights advisory body for human rights within the EU, the Agency for Fundamental Rights (FRA) in Vienna, Austria. Previously heading FRA's access to justice work, he has been with the Agency since 2009. He is a specialist in international human rights law with focus of work placed on justice, business and human rights, indicators, and monitoring mechanisms.

Elspeth GUILD

Elspeth Guild is Jean Monnet Professor ad personam at Queen Mary University of London and Radboud University, the Netherlands. She is co-author of E. Guild, S. Grant, and C.A. Groenendijk (eds.) *Human Rights of Migrants in the 21st Century* (Routledge 2017). Her research on the human right to leave a country was carried out for the Odysseus Academic Network for Legal Studies on Immigration and Asylum in Europe conference February 2018.

Lisa HESCHL

Lisa Heschl is a post-doctoral research and teaching fellow at the European Training and Research Centre on Human Rights and Democracy at the University of Graz (UNI-ETC). She received her PhD in law from the University of Graz and holds a European master's degree in human rights and democratisation (EMA). Her research focuses on the European migration and asylum policy and legislation, the extraterritorial application of international and European refugee and human rights law and its relation to European border policies. Her most recent publication is, L. Heschl, *Protecting the Rights of Refugees beyond European Borders: Establishing Extraterritorial Responsibilities* (Intersentia 2018).

Stefan KIEBER

Stefan Kieber is Senior Scientist at the Austria Institute for Human Rights at the University of Salzburg. His main research fields are human rights in general, the case law of the ECtHR and the implementation of international (human rights) obligations in national law. He is also Chief Editor of the academic journal *Newsletter Menschenrechte*.

Mathieu LELOUP

Mathieu Leloup is a PhD candidate at the University of Antwerp and an assistant in administrative and constitutional law. He holds a master's degree in law from the University of Antwerp and a master's degree in human rights and democratisation from the European Inter-University Centre. His main areas of interest are human rights law, constitutional law and administrative law.

Jacopo LEONE

Jacopo Leone holds an MSc in International and European Politics from the University of Edinburgh. He has been working as a political analyst for over eight years in the field of democracy assistance and governance, with a strong focus on parliamentary strengthening, political party assistance, anti-corruption, public integrity, and civil society development. He is currently working as a Democratic Governance Officer at the OSCE Office for Democratic Institutions and Human Rights (ODIHR), providing analyses of political developments and delivering assistance to OSCE participating States on democratic governance issues. Before joining ODIHR, he worked, among others, for the OSCE Mission in Kosovo, NATO, the European Union Institute for Security Studies (EUISS) and the European Parliament.

Karin LUKAS
Karin Lukas holds an LLM in Gender and the Law (American University), an EMA in human rights and democratisation (University of Padova) and a PhD in Legal Studies (University of Vienna). She is a senior researcher and Head of Department at the Ludwig Boltzmann Institute of Human Rights. In January 2011 she joined the European Committee of Social Rights (ECSR) of the Council of Europe and has been Vice-President since 2017. She has been a consultant for various national and international organisations. Her work in the field of human rights has particularly centred on women's rights, development cooperation and business and economic, social and cultural rights. Her most recent publication, *Corporate Accountability*, explored the effectiveness of non-judicial grievance mechanisms. She currently works on the issue of economic, social and cultural rights in Europe.

Monika MAYRHOFER
Monika Mayrhofer holds a PhD and is a senior researcher at the Department Asylum, Anti-Discrimination and Diversity at the Ludwig Boltzmann Institute of Human Rights in Vienna, Austria. Her research focuses on equality and anti-discrimination, the European human rights system and mobility in the context of climate change.

Manfred NOWAK
Manfred Nowak is Professor for International Human Rights at the University of Vienna, where he is the Scientific Director of the Vienna Master of Arts in Human Rights and Co-Director of the Ludwig Boltzmann Institute of Human Rights. Since 2016, he also serves as Secretary General of the European Inter-University Center for Human Rights and Democratisation (EIUC) in Venice. In October 2016, he was appointed as an independent expert leading the UN Global Study on Children Deprived of Liberty. He formerly taught at various prestigious universities, such as Utrecht, Lund, Stanford and the Graduate Institute in Geneva, and has published more than 600 books and articles in this field. He has carried out various expert functions for the UN, the Council of Europe, the EU and other intergovernmental organisations. Most importantly, he served for many years in various functions as UN Expert on Enforced

Disappearances (1993–2006), as one of eight international judges in the Human Rights Chamber for Bosnia and Herzegovina in Sarajevo (1996–2003), and as UN Special Rapporteur on Torture (2004–2010).

Adina PORTARU
Adina Portaru works as Legal Counsel for ADF International in Brussels, a legal organisation defending religious freedom at the international institutions. Prior to joining ADF International, Adina worked in academic research at Maastricht University in the Netherlands and at the European Training and Research Centre for Human Rights and Democracy in Austria. Adina earned an LLM in law and globalisation from Maastricht University, and a doctorate in law at Karl Franzens University in Austria. Her thesis assesses how the European Court of Human Rights and the UN Human Rights Committee interpret freedom of religion and belief.

Johanna PRUESSING
Johanna Pruessing works as a project assistant in the human rights defenders programme at the OSCE Office for Democratic Institutions and Human Rights (ODIHR) in Warsaw. She is a trained anthropologist and holds a master's degree in politics and security from the School of Slavonic and East European Studies of University College London (UCL) and a master's degree from the Higher School of Economics (HSE) in Moscow. Johanna has a long-standing professional and academic interest in women's rights and gender equality.

Eva RADLGRUBER
Eva Radlgruber is a lawyer at the office of records of the Regional Administrative Court of Styria, Austria. Prior to that, she was a teaching and research assistant at the Institute of European Law at the University of Graz. Her research focuses, *inter alia*, on the framework of human rights protection in Europe, as well as on institutional questions of the European Union. She is a PhD candidate at the University of Graz and currently completing her dissertation on secessionist movements in the European Union.

Theodor RATHGEBER
Theodor Rathgeber is a political scientist and holds a PhD from the Free University of Berlin. He is a lecturer at the Universities of Kassel and Düsseldorf, Germany, on human rights, international law and development policies, with a focus on indigenous and minority rights, and is a freelance consultant on the same subjects. He is observer to the HRC assigned by the German NGO network Forum Human Rights. He has published a series of articles on the Human Rights Council and contributed to the EYHR since its inception.

David REICHEL
David Reichel holds a PhD and is a researcher at the European Union Agency for Fundamental Rights (FRA). He works on statistics and surveys and is

responsible for managing FRA's work concerning artificial intelligence, big data and fundamental rights. He is a specialist in the analysis of international statistics and has published numerous articles, working papers and book chapters on issues related to migration and integration, citizenship and human rights.

Ewa SAPIEZYNSKA
Ewa Sapiezynska holds a PhD in social science from Universidad de Chile and works as Human Rights Officer at the OSCE Office for Democratic Institutions and Human Rights (ODIHR). The ODIHR's programme she represents, 'Human Rights, Gender and Security', has gender-based violence in the OSCE region as one of its main topics. Sapiezynska has published on media sociology and has worked extensively on gender issues in Norway and Poland as well as in Chile, Colombia, Guatemala, Mexico and Nicaragua.

Alma STANKOVIC
Alma Stankovic is a project researcher and PhD candidate at the Institute of International Law and International Relations and University of Graz, where her work focuses on transnational governance, human rights, migration, and refugee law. She previously worked as a practising attorney for high level NGOs, including the Clinton Foundation in New York and Public Counsel Law Center in Los Angeles, where she conducted legal advocacy, policy development, and litigation on behalf of immigrants and persons living in poverty.

Vladislava STOYANOVA
Vladislava Stoyanova holds a PhD and is Ragnar Söderberg Associate Senior Lecturer at the Faculty of Law, Lund University, Sweden. Her research interests are in the area of international public law, human rights law, migration and refugee law. She is the author of *Human Trafficking and Slavery Considered. Conceptual Limits and States' Positive Obligations in European Law* (Cambridge University Press 2017). Research for her article in this book was partially conducted while Dr. Stoyanova was a visiting scholar at the Bonavero Institute of Human Rights, University of Oxford. She would like to thank Cathryn Costello, Annelen Micus, Kate O'Reagan, Stefan Theil and Zoe Davis-Heaney for their support during her stay in Oxford.

Christian STROHAL
Ambassador Christian Strohal is an Austrian diplomat with a long career in multilateral work, including Permanent Representative to the Organization for Security and Cooperation in Europe (OSCE) in Vienna and the UN Office in Geneva where he held, *inter alia*, the positions of Chairman of the Governing Bodies of the IOM and Vice-President of the Human Rights Council. Previously, he was Director of the Office for Democratic Institutions and Human Rights (ODIHR) of the OSCE. Earlier functions include Ambassador for the 1993 Vienna World Conference on Human Rights, Director for Human Rights at the

Austrian Ministry for Foreign Affairs and Ambassador to Luxembourg. He was educated at the universities of Vienna and Geneva and the LSE, holding a Dr iur from Vienna, lecturing regularly at different institutions.

Agnieszka SZKLANNA

Agnieszka Szklanna, Dr, adwokat, MA (College of Europe-Natolin), is Secretary to the Committee on Legal Affairs and Human Rights, Parliamentary Assembly of the Council of Europe. Agnieszka studied law and applied linguistics at the Warsaw University. Since 2003, she has been a staff member of the Council of Europe (previously as a legal officer in the Registry of the European Court of Human Rights and then in the Department for the Execution of ECtHR Judgments). She lectured at Warsaw University, Faculty of Law (1999–2003), and at the Strasbourg University, Political Studies Institute (2012–2015), and regularly publishes on issues of ECtHR system, legal protection of aliens, relations between the European Union and the Council of Europe.

Ajla VAN HEEL

Ajla van Heel's work focuses on advancing gender equality and women's political participation. She led and contributed to the development of a number of publications and practical knowledge tools on gender equality in parliaments, political parties, and national human rights institutions. Prior to joining the OSCE, she worked with the International Organisation for Migration (IOM) and United Nations Development Programme (UNDP), mainly on combating trafficking in women and girls in the Western Balkans. Ms. van Heel holds a bachelor degree in international affairs from Princeton University and a master's degree in human rights from the University of Bologna.

Mirosław WYRZYKOWSKI

Mirosław Wyrzykowski is Professor of the University of Warsaw (ret.) and Human Rights Chair of the Faculty of Law and Administration. He was a judge of the Polish Constitutional Tribunal from 2001–2010. Furthermore, from 2011–2015, he was President of the Legal Sciences Committee of the Polish Academy of Science.

PART I
TOPIC OF THE YEAR

THE VANISHING CONSTITUTION

Mirosław Wyrzykowski

1. The Context of the Constitutional Crisis 4
2. The Drama's First Act 6
3. Antigone in Warsaw 7
4. 'Standard' Unconstitutionality 11
5. The Drama's Second Act 12
6. Symptoms and Phenomena of Excluding the Constitutional Tribunal from the Constitutional System of Government 15
7. The Constitution Modified by the Statute 15
8. The Drama's Third Act: Court Packing of the Supreme Court. 16
9. The Drama's Fourth Act: Compliment of the Political Control Over the Judiciary. 21
10. Legislation Violating the Freedoms and Rights of the Individual 23
    10.1. Data Protection. 23
    10.2. Freedom of Assembly 25
    10.3. Civil Service 27
11. International Reaction to Violation of Rule of Law 28
12. 'Clear Risk of Serious Breach of the Rule of Law': Use of Article 7(1) of the TEU 34
13. Change of the Constitutional System by Non-Constitutional Methods: Rule of Law and Sovereignty of the State 39
14. How to Solve the Crisis? 42

ABSTRACT

In Poland, the constitutional crisis continues. The crisis was initiated in autumn 2015 by the combination of three elements: resolutions of the Parliament infringing the law, the President of the Republic and the President of the Council of Ministers. The constitutional crisis concerned the election by the Parliament of three judges of the Constitutional Tribunal to replace the judges already duly elected, the President's refusal to swear in the original three judges of the

Constitutional Tribunal and the refusal of the Prime Minister to publish the judgments of the Constitutional Tribunal. The Acts passed in 2015 and 2016 regulate the Constitutional Tribunal in a way that is to be considered as violating the Constitution. The Constitutional Tribunal lost its role as the guardian of the Constitution. Further, the Parliament, in violation of the Constitution, made changes in the organisation and structure of the Supreme Court, *inter alia*, forcing more than 30% of the judicial membership into early retirement or interrupting the constitutionally-guaranteed six–year term of office of the First President of the Supreme Court. Furthermore, the new regulation regarding the National Council of the Judiciary has encroached on the term of office of the Council's judicial members. Moreover, this reform set in motion a process of politicisation of the Council because its new judicial membership was appointed by the Parliament and not – as formerly required – by the assemblies of judges of particular judicial orders. These, as well as many other regulations, indicate a process of a 'hostile takeover' of the constitutional order by changing the constitutional order through ordinary legislation: the parliamentary majority does not have the qualified majority required to formally change the Constitution of the Republic of Poland. The regulations discussed above violate the basic tenets of the rule of law and have become the subject of an unequivocally negative reaction of international organisations and authorities (the European Union (EU), the Council of Europe (CoE), and the United Nations (UN)) as well as associations representing general and constitutional courts.

1. THE CONTEXT OF THE CONSTITUTIONAL CRISIS

It is somewhat puzzling that there should be a phenomenon of a social movement protecting the constitutional order after the Constitution of the Republic of Poland has been in force for 20 years. The phenomenon arose suddenly and puzzles lawyers, political scientists, political analysts, Polish-language linguists, as well as historians of ideas and contemporary historians. The origin of the phenomenon can be pinned down easily to the well-known constitutional crisis concerning the very essence of constitutional review regulated by the Constitution in as much as the election of judges of the Constitutional Tribunal was concerned.

The matter concerned the election of judges of the Constitutional Tribunal to vacancies available at the end of 2015. Under the Act on the Constitutional Tribunal of 25 June 2015, the Sejm, a lower chamber of the Parliament, elected three judges who were to fill the vacancies available in November and two judges who were to fill vacancies available in December. The election of judges made, as the Sejm's 7th term was due to expire, was subject to constitutional review. The Constitutional Tribunal stated that the election was constitutional in respect of three judges elected to vacancies available in November and was unconstitutional in respect of two judges elected to vacancies available only in December; the judges elected to take posts in December 2015 were elected 'just in case' whereas the new Parliament was competent to make the election.[1]

Before the Constitutional Tribunal was able to make a pronouncement, however, the constitutional crisis was already in the air. It was fanned by events of ever-increasing constitutional magnitude. All the events have one thing in common, namely the violation of the rule of law by the constitutional authorities of the state. The violations can be easily enumerated. The first unconstitutional deed was the decision of the Sejm of the 7th term to open the election of the judges to vacancies only in December 2015 – a violation of constitutional law as has been ascertained by the Constitutional Tribunal. The second deed was the refusal to take oath from three judges of the Constitutional Tribunal who were duly elected to fill vacancies available in November 2015 since the President of the Republic of Poland does not enjoy the privilege of refusing to swear in judges of the Constitutional Tribunal and thus thereby violated the Constitution. As the Sejm does not have the power of voiding resolutions of the Sejm of the previous term, the third violation of the rule of law was that the newly elected Sejm of the 8th term adopted a resolution to the effect of voiding the election of all five judges of the Constitutional Tribunal made by the Sejm of the previous term. It is to be noted that the Constitutional Tribunal not only considered the Sejm's election of three 'November' judges to be effective and constitutional but also indicated that the election of two additional 'December' judges was void and thus obligated the newly-elected Sejm to proceed and make the election to vacancies available in December. The Sejm's resolutions were not only *praeter legem* in respect of the Constitutional Tribunal's analysis of the issue. They also violated the Constitution by expiring the term of office of three judges duly elected by the Sejm of the previous term to November vacancies whereas the expiration of the term of office of the judge of the Constitutional Tribunal is a matter regulated by statute that the resolution of the Sejm somehow 'substituted'. The fourth violation of the rule of law was electing judges of the Constitutional Tribunal in respect of three vacancies made available in November despite the fact that the Constitutional Tribunal explicitly made the decision that proceedings be stayed pending its judgment. The fifth violation of the rule of law was swearing in the three 'substitute' judges of the Constitutional Tribunal by the President of the Republic. There was some contrast in respect of the refusal of swearing in the three judges who were duly elected by the Sejm of the previous term: the oath ceremony was precipitous – it took place late at night, three hours after the Sejm's election of the substitute three judges was announced.

---

[1] M. Wyrzykowski, 'Bypassing the Constitution or Changing the Constitutional Order Outside the Constitution', in A. Szmyt and B. Banaszak (eds.), *Transformation of Law Systems in Central, Eastern and South-Eastern Europe in 1989-2015, Liber Amicorum in Honorem Prof. Dr. Dres. H.C. Rainer Arnold*, Gdańsk University Press, 2016, pp. 175–176.

2. THE DRAMA'S FIRST ACT

The events concerning the election of judges of the Constitutional Tribunal that took place in October and November 2015 were politically and constitutionally dramatic; they should not, however, overshadow other events contributing to the constitutional crisis. In parallel to the actions aimed at creating irreversible factual changes in the composition of the Constitutional Tribunal, the Sejm enacted a new statute on the Constitutional Tribunal. The Act amending the Act on the Constitutional Tribunal of 18 November 2015 was ultimately voided by the Constitutional Tribunal (K35/15).[2] Among other matters, it regulated the term of office of the President and the Vice-President of the Constitutional Tribunal (implicitly providing for the expiration of the term of office of the judges who exercised those functions), it provided for a 30-day term for taking oath by judges elected by the Sejm (implicitly providing for the term of office to begin with the decision by the President of the Republic to swear in the judge elected by the Sejm as opposed to beginning with the election by the Sejm). The amendment also provided for new candidates to be elected thus implicitly providing for nominating judges in excess of the number of the Constitutional Tribunal (i.e. 15).

The judgment of the Constitutional Tribunal is to be immediately and unconditionally published by the President of the Council of Ministers. This obligation arising under Article 190.2 of the Constitution of the Republic of Poland was violated by the Prime Minister. The Prime Minister refused to publish the judgment of the Constitutional Tribunal based on the argument that the decision of the President of the Constitutional Tribunal assigning judges to the case was illegal and thus the judgment was to be considered 'null and void'. The refusal to publish the judgment deepened the constitutional crisis. The obligation to publish the judgment of the Constitutional Tribunal is unqualified and the publication should be ordered immediately upon receipt of the judgment. It is important to note that the Prime Minister's pronouncement was tantamount to usurping the power of reviewing the legality of the judgment. The President of the Council of Ministers obviously cannot aspire to have such powers because the executive cannot have the power of annulling judgments of the judicial branch within the constitutional order of things. Based on

---

[2] L. GARLICKI, 'Die Ausschaltung des Verfassungsgreichtshofes in Polen?' (Disabling the Constitutional Court in Poland?), in A. SZMYT and B. BANASZAK (2016), *Transformation of Law Systems, supra* note 1, p. 69; T.T. KONCEWICZ, 'Bruised, but not dead (yet): The Polish Constitutional Court has spoken', *VerfBlog*, 10.12.2015, available at https://verfassungsblog.de/bruised-but-not-dead-yet-the-polish-constitutional-court-has-spoken-2, last accessed 26.06.2018; T.T. KONCEWICZ, '"Court-packing" in Warsaw: The Plot Thickens', *VerfBlog*, 18.12.2015, available at https://verfassungsblog.de/court-packing-in-warsaw-the-plot-thickens, last accessed 25.06.2018.

a motion filed by a citizen, the public prosecutor-initiated proceedings in respect of the violation of the duties of office by the Prime Minister; the Prime Minister published the judgment of the Constitutional Tribunal under pressure of potential criminal accountability. It turned out that the refusal to publish was an act of testing the limits of the powers of the executive in relation to the Constitutional Tribunal. The Prime Minister would later refuse to publish two more judgments of the Constitutional Tribunal in respect of statutes that purported to regulate the status of the Constitutional Tribunal.

3. ANTIGONE IN WARSAW

As the constitutional crisis unfolded, it was further deepened by the adoption of the Act of 22 December 2015 amending the Act on the Constitutional Tribunal that was dubbed somewhat derisively 'repair restructuring'.

It is important to recall that the very essence of the amendment can be ascertained as introducing the following modifications of the mechanism of constitutional review. The amendment (a) provided for a new requirement in respect of making resolutions by the General Assembly of Judges of the Constitutional Tribunal by stipulating that such resolutions be made by a two-thirds supermajority with at least 13 judges present; (b) required that constitutional review be considered in full court with at least 13 judges participating in all cases initiated by a motion. It provided for the obligation to consider cases on a first-come-first-served basis and introduced the obligation to hold court hearings at the earliest three months after the parties to proceedings have been notified of the date of the hearing and at the earliest six months after the parties to proceedings have been notified of the date of the hearing in cases considered by a full court; (c) introduced a qualified majority voting requirement of two-thirds for cases decided in full court; (d) required the reassignment of cases pending before the Constitutional Tribunal and thus provided for the cases pending to be reconsidered anew; (e) provided for the power of the President of the Republic and/or the Minister of Justice to initiate disciplinary proceedings in respect of judges of the Constitutional Tribunal; (f) provided for the penalty of expiration of term of office of the judge of Constitutional Tribunal and transferring the power to dismiss the judge onto the Sejm with the President of the Republic and the Minister of Justice wielding the power of initiating the proceedings concerning the termination of the term of office of the judge of the Constitutional Tribunal; (g) transferred the power of declaring the expiration of the term of office of the judge of the Constitutional Tribunal from the General Assembly of Judges of the Constitutional Tribunal and the President of the Constitutional Tribunal onto the Sejm; (h) purported to deregulate the disciplinary accountability in respect to facts predating taking of office. The amendment's wholesale reach further modified the procedure and time-frame of nominating candidates in election of judges of the Constitutional Tribunal, abrogated the chapter regulating proceedings before the Constitutional Tribunal in the situation of emergency where the President of the Republic is unable to report his or her inability of discharge the duties of the office. Its ambitions were symbolically stated by providing for immediate effect of the amendment upon publication.

The amendment contained a number of obvious consequences for the Polish constitutional order. It also, however, contained a number of surreptitious consequences. The latter included the devices that seemingly precluded – as a matter of seeming impracticality – the constitutional review of the amendment itself. That would have fundamental consequences for the constitutional order. The legal scheme of the amendment in this respect can be broken down to the following elements: (1) The statute entered into force on the date of publication, which precluded constitutional review before its entry into force; (2) in the case that constitutional review was initiated after entry into force of the amendment, the amendment's procedural regulations would be at the same time subject to review and the very basis of such review; and consequently (3) considering the irreversibility of procedural vices of the Constitutional Tribunal's judgments it was essential that any constitutional problems concerning the legal basis of the judgment be addressed before the regulations are applied; (4) at the date of the initiation of the procedure the Constitutional Tribunal was composed of only 12 judges; and (5) the Constitution unequivocally stipulates that the Constitutional Tribunal's judgments are made by simple majority voting as opposed to the supermajority requirement of the amendment.[3]

If the amendment took effect as it was adopted by the Parliament, the Constitutional Tribunal would be in fact eliminated from the governmental system set up by constitutional law, endowing the constitutional court its rightful role as the guardian of the Constitution. The Constitutional Tribunal thus sought to neutralise the effects of the amendment by accommodating the model of proceedings that would be capable of neutralising the proclaimed intention of the Parliament to 'extinguish' – as it was common to 'technically' say at the time – the Constitutional Tribunal.

The Constitutional Tribunal thus decided that it would proceed on the basis of applicable provisions of the Constitution as well as the provisions of the Act on the Constitutional Tribunal as amended by the December 2015 amendment with the exception of a number of specific provisions.

The following principles allowed the Constitutional Tribunal to proceed with constitutional review of the Act amending the Act on the Constitutional

---

[3] T.T. Koncewicz, 'The Polish Constitutional Crisis and "Politics of Paranoia"', *VerfBlog*, 11.03.2016, available at https://verfassungsblog.de/the-polish-constitutional-crisis-and-politics-of-paranoia, last accessed 25.06.2018.

Tribunal of 22 December 2015.[4] The fundamental premise of the Constitutional Tribunal's stance consisted in the principle that the Constitutional Tribunal is obligated to discharge its institutional duties, which include reviewing constitutionality of statutes regulating its very operation. This principle was particularly important in respect of a statute that could violate the very essence of constitutional review. It was not unimportant that the statute could influence the constitutional review in cases pending before the Constitutional Tribunal. Further, the Constitutional Tribunal considered it important that the object of constitutional review should be neither the basis of proceedings nor the basis of the final judgment of the Constitutional Tribunal. It so happened that Constitutional Tribunal was obligated to review the constitutionality of the Act of 25 June 2015 on the Constitutional Tribunal as amended by the amendment of 22 December 2015 and the same act regulated its operation. This possibility was rejected based on the prediction that any judgment voiding parts of the Act subject to review would potentially void the constitutional review itself and thus the judgment would self-referentially be based on unconstitutional legal precepts. The Constitutional Tribunal emphasised that the procedural vices of its judgments were not subject to review and thus were irreversible so to speak. It was therefore essential that any constitutional problems with the legal foundation of its operation were addressed before the provisions of the Act as amended were effectively applied.

It was uncontested that the Parliament brought about conditions that precluded normal constitutional review of the statute regulating the Constitutional Tribunal (the amendment seemingly precluded technically such review) and the Constitutional Tribunal thus took the unprecedented decision to proceed regardless of such conditions. The extraordinary character of the situation brought about by the Parliament and the President of the Republic (who did not see fit to initiate preventive constitutional review proceedings before the 22 December 2015 amendment was promulgated) required an extraordinary reaction of the Constitutional Tribunal. It seems that resorting to Article 195.1 was a fitting response in this situation. Article 195.1 stipulates that 'Judges of the Constitutional Tribunal, in the exercise of their office, shall be independent and subject only to the Constitution'. It thus explicitly allows the Constitutional Tribunal to proceed by refusing to apply statutory norms in certain circumstances.

Consistently enough, the Constitutional Tribunal considered it proper to proceed with the proceedings based on applicable provisions of the Constitution of the Republic as well as the Act on the Constitutional Tribunal as amended

---

[4] For an excellent analysis of the case see T.T. KONCEWICZ, 'Of Institutions, Democracy, Constitutional Self-defence and the Rule of Law: The Judgments of the Polish Constitutional Tribunal in Cases K 34/15, K 35/15 and beyond', (2016) 53(6) *Common Market Law Review*, p. 1753ff.

by the 22 December 2015 Amendment with the exception of a number of its enumerated provisions. First, the Constitutional Tribunal excepted the provisions that purported to regulate proceedings and could be applicable in the case. The Constitutional Tribunal stated that 'it is unacceptable that the same provisions of the statute should be the basis and the object of constitutional review at the same time'. Furthermore, the Constitutional Tribunal performed an analysis of the legal and factual situation at the date of hearing. It was stated that the full court is composed of 12 judges of the Constitutional Tribunal. The analysis ran as follows:

> if [...] the Constitutional Tribunal is obligated to hand down a judgment when a number of its judges are not competent to participate in the judgment as the consequence of inaction of a state authority other than the Constitutional Tribunal but all the judges competent to participate in the judgment in fact participate, then such a panel of judges is to be considered as sitting in 'full court'.[5]

The Constitutional Tribunal's remark concerning 'inaction of a state authority other than the Constitutional Tribunal' referenced the refusal of the President of the Republic to swear in three judges of the Constitutional Tribunal who were duly elected by the Sejm of the previous term to take seats available in November 2015.

Finally, the Constitutional Tribunal refused to apply the provision that required that cases be considered on a first-come-first-served basis as well as the provision that required that hearings be held three or six months after notification of all parties to the proceedings; those provisions were considered to factually preclude constitutional review of the statute. The Constitutional Tribunal also 'dis-applied' the statutory requirement of a supermajority of two-thirds and applied the *lex superior* principle providing for the simple majority as governing judicial decision-making by the Constitutional Tribunal (Article 190.5 of the Constitution of the Republic of Poland).

The Constitutional Tribunal thus was caught up in a situation that is parallel to the situation of *Antigone chez Sophocles*.[6] Antigone disobeyed the order of Creon that forbid burying Polynices. Violating the order of the ruler, Antigone relied on the divine law requiring that the dead be buried. In the Polish constitutional crisis, Creon's order was represented by the statute enacted by

---

[5] Polish Constitutional Court, Case K 47/15, 03.12.2015.
[6] M. Wyrzykowski, 'Antigone in Warsaw', in M. Zubik (ed.), *Human Rights in Contemporary World. Essays in Honor of Professor Leszek Garlicki*, Wydawnictwo Sejmowe 2017, p. 378; L. Garlicki (2016), 'Die Ausschaltung des Verfassungsgreichtshofes in Polen?', *supra* note 2, p. 70; different opinion see B. Banaszak, 'The Main Principles of the Reform of the Polish Constitutional Tribunal in December 2015: A Comparative Approach', in A. Szmyt and B. Banaszak (2016), *Transformation of Law Systems supra* note 1, p. 41.

the Parliament that contravened the Constitution by obstructing constitutional review of the very statute. To counteract the unconstitutional enactment by the Parliament, the Constitutional Tribunal relied on the essence of the Constitution and its specific applicable provisions. The Constitutional Tribunal applied the Constitution as the highest law of the land in order to neuter statutory regulation conceived of and enacted in order to subvert the constitutional order of the Polish Republic through paralysing the mechanism of constitutional review of legislation.[7]

4. 'STANDARD' UNCONSTITUTIONALITY

The Constitutional Tribunal's judgment was devastating for the amendment itself and for the Parliament. The Constitutional Tribunal voided all but one provision of the amendment as well as declared the statute unconstitutional on the grounds of flagrant and gross violation of legislative procedure. The violation of a legislative procedure was that the first reading of the statute took place only two days after the bill was introduced as opposed to seven days required from the date the bill is published and duly distributed among the Members of Parliament. Secondly, whilst the first reading of the statute took place at the sitting of the Sejm, it was modified beyond its original contents at the sitting of the Legislative Committee after the first reading and at the second reading. In fact, the bill was only subject to two readings by the Sejm and the constitutional requirement of three readings was thus violated. Thirdly, the Marshall of the Sejm failed to abide by the requirement of filing a motion for the opinion of the Legislative Committee after negative opinions on the draft legislation were filed. Fourthly, the second reading of the bill took place on the very same day the Legislative Committee filed its report on the bill, as opposed to seven days required after a report was filed. Fifthly, the Sejm failed to abide by the requirement of consultation with authorities and bodies concerned with the bill (i.e. the National Council of the Judiciary, the Supreme Court and the NGOs). Those bodies were not in a position to present their opinion with respect to provisions introduced between the first and second readings of the bill contravening the Constitution. The sixth point concerned the expediency of legislative procedure contravening the principle of diligent and comprehensive consideration of bills intervening in the system of government of the Republic. Finally, the Constitutional Tribunal pointed out that the procedural vices of the amendment of 18 November 2015 were

---

[7] A. ŚLEDZIŃSKA-SIMON, 'Paradoxes of Constitutionalisation: Lessons from Poland', *VerfBlog*, 30.03.2016, available at https://verfassungsblog.de/paradoxes-of-constitutionalisation-lessons-from-poland, last accessed 26.06.2018.

specifically addressed in the judgment of the Constitutional Tribunal of 9 December 2015 (K35/15) and were not only replicated but indeed aggravated to the degree requiring the amending statute to be abrogated on procedural grounds. At this point it is proper to note that the Constitutional Tribunal stated that 'the proceedings in the Sejm in as much as they failed to take into account the results of constitutional analysis presented in the judgment Case Call No. K 35/15 that was known during the legislative proceeding as well as to take account of problems concerning constitutionality of specific provisions corroborate the hypothesis that the legislature proceeded consciously and purposefully in contravention of the principle of action on the basis and within the limits of law'.[8]

The list of all these procedural improprieties, including the entry into force of the statute on the day of publication, makes one think that the Parliament managed to reach the very opposite of the standard of proper legislation while legal scholars and the case law of the Constitutional Tribunal have been working hard to define the parameters of 'proper' legislation.

5. THE DRAMA'S SECOND ACT

The saga does not end here. The Constitutional Tribunal was not spared further developments. On 22 July 2016, the Parliament adopted a new statute governing the Constitutional Tribunal, of which parts were subject to constitutional review.[9] It was somewhat striking – having regard to legislative practice of the Parliament of the new term – that the new statute should provide for a fortnight of *vacatio legis*. The Constitutional Tribunal had thus a cleaner shot at reviewing the constitutionality of this piece of legislation after the case was initiated by parliamentary opposition.[10] The following parts were declared unconstitutional:

- The obligation to consider cases in full court of 15 judges if three judges so required within 14 days of receipt of the copies of constitutional complaints,

---

[8] For the most comprehensive study see P. RADZIEWICZ and P. TULEJA (eds.), *Konstytucyjny spór o granice zmian organizacji i zasad działania Trybunału Konstytucyjnego (czerwiec 2015–marzec 2016)*, *(The Constitutional Dispute on the limits of Amendment of Organisations and Principles of Activity of the Constitutional Tribunal (June 2015–March 2016)*, Wolters Kluwer, Warsaw 2017.

[9] Act on the Constitutional Tribunal, *Journal of Laws* No. 1157 (hereinafter referred to as the '2016 Act on CT').

[10] W. SADURSKI, 'How Democracy Dies (in Poland): A Case Study of Anti-Constitutional Populist Backsliding', Legal Studies Research Paper No. 18/01, Sydney Law School, The University of Sydney, 17.01.2018, p. 17ff, available at http://ssrn.com/abstract=3103491, last accessed 25.06.2018.

constitutional review requests or preliminary reference requests.[11] The Constitutional Tribunal declared this regulation unconstitutional in as much as it was inconsistent with the constitutional principle of effectiveness of the operation of public authorities (the request could be filed by judges who were not assigned to the case, was unrelated to the substantial issues of the case and was arbitrary in that no justification was required to accompany the request), the principle of diligence of the operation of state authorities (subversion of the principle that full court consideration of cases is the exception rather than the rule) and the principle of effectiveness of the operation of state authorities (the provision coupled with the obligation to consider cases on the first-come-first-served basis and the requirement that full court be composed of 13 judges could translate into considering all cases in full court, which would impede the Constitutional Tribunal in performing its constitutional review function).

- The obligation to consider all abstract review requests to the Constitutional Tribunal on the first-come-first-served basis.[12] The underlying intention of this regulation was clear enough: the new obligation was to create a lag in consideration of new legislation that could be subject to constitutional review on the request of the parliamentary opposition or state authorities competent to be guardians of the Constitution and legality of legislation. The Constitutional Tribunal stated that this provision violated the principle of a democratic state ruled by law, the principle of separation of powers, the principle of independence of the judicial branch and the principle of the constitutional status of the Constitutional Tribunal.
- The obligation to suspend a judgment until the Public Prosecutor-General or its representative is present at the hearing in cases where the statute provides for such participation.[13] In case the Public Prosecutor-General was absent at a hearing, the Constitutional Tribunal would not be able to proceed with the case and would be obligated to schedule a new hearing. Making the competence of the Constitutional Tribunal conditional on the behaviour of the Public Prosecutor-General could frustrate constitutional review in full court. It must be noted that the Public Prosecutor-General is the Minister of Justice, i.e. a politician of special characteristics. This regulation violates the principle of separation of powers, the principle of independence of the judicial branch and the system of government powers of the Constitutional Tribunal.
- The right of veto of a group of judges in respect of the anticipated substance of the ruling of the Constitutional Tribunal in cases considered in full court. The veto powers vested in a group of judges would result in postponing the

---

[11] Article 26.1(1)(g) of the 2016 Act on CT.
[12] Article 38.3–6 of the 2016 Act on CT.
[13] Article 66.6 of the 2016 Act on CT.

hearing by three months and another three months in case of a consecutive veto.[14] The unconstitutionality of the provision is a result of the violation of the system of the government function of the Constitutional Tribunal, the violation of the right to have a case considered by a court without undue delay and the violation of the principle of effectiveness and diligence of state authorities. The provision of statute paralleled the right of three judges to require a case to be considered by the full court and thus allowed for arbitrary interference with the independence of judges assigned to the case and their powers to declare the cases particularly problematic assigning the case to full court proceedings. According to the Constitutional Tribunal, this construct attempted to institutionalise the 'judicial minority' within the Constitutional Tribunal based on the procedural guarantees developed in parliamentary law but did not correspond to the function of the Constitutional Tribunal as an authority of the judicial branch and to the individual status of the judge of the Constitutional Tribunal.

- The powers of the President of the Constitutional Tribunal to assign to divisions judges who were sworn in by the President of the Republic but have not been competent to discharge judicial duties to the date of the coming into force of the act.[15] This provision concerned the status of the three judges elected by the Sejm of the new term to replace the judges elected by the Sejm of the previous term to vacancies available in November 2015. While latter were not sworn in by the President of the Republic, the former were even though there were no vacancies to fill. The Constitutional Tribunal recalled its judgment in the case K 34/15, where it was stated that the three judges were duly elected by the Sejm of the previous term and thus filled the vacancies available in October 2015. This regulation was therefore secondarily unconstitutional.

The process of excluding the Constitutional Tribunal from effective constitutional review translated normatively into three other statutes enacted in November and December 2016, namely the Act of 30 November 2016 on the Organization and Rules of Procedure before the Constitutional Tribunal, the Act of 30 November 2016 on the Status of the Judges of the Constitutional Tribunal and the Act of 13 December 2016 – provisions introducing the Act on the Organization and Rules of Procedure before the Constitutional Tribunal and the Act on the Status of the Judges of the Constitutional Tribunal. The legislative disorderliness created a situation whereby in the period between 20 December 2016 and 3 January 2017 there were no statutory grounds for the Constitutional Tribunal to undertake judicial functions (the Act on the

---

[14] Article 68.5–7 of the 2016 Act on CT.
[15] Article 90 of the 2016 Act on CT.

Constitutional Tribunal of 22 July 2016 expired on 20 December 2016 and the new Act only took effect on 3 January 2017).[16]

6. SYMPTOMS AND PHENOMENA OF EXCLUDING THE CONSTITUTIONAL TRIBUNAL FROM THE CONSTITUTIONAL SYSTEM OF GOVERNMENT

As far as it concerns the functioning of the Constitutional Tribunal, the dramatic decrease in the number of applications, constitutional complaints and preliminary reference ruling requests received by the Tribunal is an expression of the constitutional crisis. In the period 2015–2017, the number of cases decreased from 623 to 282, and the number of judgments decreased from 173 to 88. In the first quarter of 2018, only nine cases were registered. Therefore, by forecasting the first-quarter trends, it can be estimated that in the whole year only 40 new cases will be pending before the Constitutional Tribunal; this would mean that there would be fewer than three cases per one judge per year.[17]

Repeated changes to its regulatory framework of the constitutional court resulted in the unprecedented disruption of its functioning and effectiveness. The dysfunctionalities mainly resulted from regulations requiring the appointment of panels composed of a new number of judges, the appointment of new presiding judges in pending cases, transferring cases previously qualified for the hearing to be resolved at a closed session and transferring the cases assigned to a closed meeting decision to court hearing.

7. THE CONSTITUTION MODIFIED BY THE STATUTE

With regard to the statute of the constitutional court, the meaning of direct application of constitutional law in constitutional reviews of statutory regulations is not relevant. The mechanism of changing the constitutional order by statute, on the other hand, is relevant and can be used whenever the ruling coalition has a majority in Parliament but does not have the super majority required for amending the Constitution. By way of statute, the Parliament for instance

---

[16] BATORY FOUNDATION, 'Analiza działalności orzeczniczej Trybunału Konstytucyjnego w latach 2014–1017', Analysis of the judicial activity of the Constitutional Tribunal in the years 2014–2017, 2018, available at http://www.batory.org.pl/upload/files/Programy%20 operacyjne/Odpowiedzialne%20Panstwo/Raport%20ZEP%20o%20funkcjonowaniu%20TK. pdf, last accessed 26.06.2018.

[17] For the statistics see the homepage pf the Constitutional Court at www.trybunal.gov.pl / sprawy w Trybunale, last accessed 16.07.2018.

modified the constitutional model of civil service. The Parliament degraded the constitutional authority of the National Council of Radio Broadcasting and Television by transferring the bulk of its essential competences to the newly established Council of National Media. Furthermore, the Parliament intentionally sought to extinguish the term of office of the First President of the Supreme Court under the pretence of lowering the retirement age of Supreme Court judges (superannuation) and the revision of the structure of the Supreme Court. Interestingly, the latter initiative was vetoed politically but not constitutionally by the President of the Republic.[18]

8. THE DRAMA'S THIRD ACT: COURT PACKING OF THE SUPREME COURT

The next phase of remodelling Poland's constitutional order in the judicial sphere concerned the regulation of the Supreme Court.[19] The Supreme Court is the highest authority of the judicial branch whose powers break down into four areas.[20] First, it is the administrator of justice guaranteeing the legality and uniformity of the application of laws by the courts of general jurisdiction ('common courts') and the army courts by hearing appeals, taking resolutions on certain aspects of laws and by extraordinarily reviewing final court judgments with the aim of implementing the rule of law and social justice. Secondly, it considers disciplinary cases within the scope of the statute. Thirdly, the Supreme Court is not only competent to consider appeals regarding national elections and adjudicates upon their validity and the validity of elections to the European Parliament. It also considers appeals concerning the validity of national referenda including constitutional referenda also adjudicate upon their validity. Fourthly, the Supreme Court has the competence to give opinion on bills and drafts of other normative instruments that will be applied by the courts and that regulate the courts as well as give opinion on other bills that bear on matters within the powers of the Supreme Court.

While some of the provisions of the Act on the Supreme Court are only subject to doubts as to their constitutionality, some regulations indeed

---

[18] M. Wyrzykowski (2015), 'Bypassing the Constitution or Changing the Constitutional Order Outside the Constitution', *supra* note 1, p. 164ff.
[19] T.T. Koncewicz, 'Farewell to the Separation of Powers – On the Judicial Purge and the Capture in the Heart of Europe', *VerfBlog*, 19.07.2017, available at https://verfassungsblog.de/farewell-to-the-separation-of-powers-on-the-judicial-purge-and-the-capture-in-the-heart-of-europe, last accessed 26.06.2018.
[20] Article 1 of the Act of 8 December 2017 on the Supreme Court, Journal of Laws 2018, item 5 (hereinafter referred to as the 'Act on the Supreme Court').

manifestly and unashamedly violate the Constitution as will be illustrated subsequently:[21]

The first example concerns the superannuation of judges of the Supreme Court as the age of retirement has been lowered. A Judge of the Supreme Court retires (or goes into the reserve as it is technically called) on the day he or she turns 65.[22] This is a statutory obligation and not a right to retire. Previous regulations foresaw the retirement at the age of 70 if the judge's term of office was not set but also allowed for the judge to continue in office. The modification of the age of retirement of the judges who have acquired subjective rights constitutes a violation of the constitutional principle of the democratic state ruled by law (Article 2 of the Constitution) with a special emphasis on the principle of protection of acquired rights and the foreseeability of the actions of state authorities. Truly, the legislator has the power to specify the age of retirement. Its power is, however, circumscribed by the limits of its regulatory freedom. In the given case, this means that, in order to be constitutional, the regulation should provide for transitory measures guaranteeing that judges who hold their office are able to continue their professional activity according to the regulations applicable at the date of commencement of their term of office. New regulations would only apply to judges nominated after the new regulation concerning lower age of superannuation takes effect.

It is a drastic violation of the Constitution to retire all judges of the Supreme Court who served on the Chamber for the Army without any possibility to continue their professional activities in another chamber of the Supreme Court or in another court.[23]

It is worth noting that the Act of 22 June 2017, which was ultimately prevented by the President's veto, provided for all and every judge of the Supreme Court to be retired. This would have amounted to a total clearing of the personal substrate of the Supreme Court. However, this policy has also inspired the new statute but has only been implemented partially since the lowering of the age of retirement only concerns about 36% of the judges of the Supreme Court.[24] On 2 August 2018, the Supreme Court sent five questions to the CJEU seeking its preliminary ruling with regard to interpretation of judicial independence and impartiality as principles of EU law and the prohibition of discrimination based on age.[25]

---

[21] W. SADURSKI, 'Judicial "Reform" in Poland: The President's Bills are as Unconstitutional as the Ones he Vetoed', *VerfBlog*, 28.11.2017, available at https://verfassungsblog.de/judicial-reform-in-poland-the-presidents-bills-are-as-unconstitutional-as-the-ones-he-vetoed, last accessed 26.06.2018.
[22] Article 37.1 of the Act on the Supreme Court.
[23] Article 111.3 of the Act on the Supreme Court.
[24] Article 111.1 of the Act on the Supreme Court.
[25] An English translation of the questions referred to the CJEU is available at https://www.iustitia.pl/en/118-information/2469-decision-the-polish-supreme-court-iii-uzp-4-18-2-august-2018, last accessed 06.09.2018.

The second example of a violation of the Constitution concerns the termination of the term of office of the First President of the Supreme Court. According to Article 183.3 of the Constitution, '[t]he First President of the Supreme Court shall be appointed by the President of the Republic for a 6-year term of office from amongst candidates proposed by the General Assembly of the Judges of the Supreme Court'. The new Act on the Supreme Court lowers the age of retirement of the judges of the Supreme Court to 65 years. Thereby, the term of office of the First President of the Supreme Court is to be collaterally shortened by two years under the pretence of implementing a new system of retirement at the Supreme Court. The judge who holds the office of the First President of the Supreme Court turned 65 before the Act took effect. Similarly, to the situation of all judges as described above, a new system of retirement must ensure that the term of office of the First President of the Supreme Court is not unduly shortened. Regardless of age, the office of the First President of the Supreme Court should only expire as provided by the Constitution, namely after six years.[26]

Another example of a violation of the Constitution concerns the authorities of the executive – including the President and the Prime Minister – namely the mechanism of consent for the prolongation of employment of the superannuated judge. Upon turning 65, a judge can file a statement with the First President of the Supreme Court (and within three months following the statute enters into force) stating that he or she wishes to continue in office which has to be accompanied by a statement by a doctor that his or her health allows holding the office of a judge. In such a case, the President of the Republic can – but is in no way obligated to – express his consent for the continuation in office of a superannuated judge of the Supreme Court. Furthermore, the consent of the President is not an official act falling within the powers enumerated as the President's prerogatives. Thus, it is necessary that the consent is countersigned by the Prime Minister. Accordingly, the composition of the Supreme Court is determined by the two most important authorities of the dualist executive. This regulation violates Article 179 of the Constitution which stipulates that '[j]udges shall be appointed for an indefinite period by the President of the Republic on the motion of the National Council of the Judiciary'. This regulation further violates Article 144 of the Constitution in as much as it regulates the prerogatives of the President. It is therefore clear that the regulation is an example of a violation of the fundamental constitutional principle of the separation of powers and the principle of independence of the judicial branch.

Similar problems relate to the new construct of new sections of the Supreme Court, i.e. the Chamber for Extraordinary Supervision and Public Affairs and the Disciplinary Chamber.

---

[26] W. SADURSKI (2017), 'How Democracy Dies (in Poland)', *supra* note 10, p. 40ff.

The Act on the Supreme Court is an example – one among many others – of the statute modifying the contents and meaning of a constitutional provision that has a safeguarding character.[27] The Chamber for Extraordinary Supervision and Public Affairs has a wide margin of competence including considering cases of extraordinary applications, cases concerning appeals in elections and appeals in cases concerning the validity of the national referendum and the constitutional referendum as well as adjudicating on the validity of elections and referenda. It furthermore considers other cases within the scope of public law, including cases concerning the protection of free competition, energy, telecommunications, railroad transportation law as well as appeals of decisions of the President of the National Council of Radio Broadcasting and Television and appeals concerning the undue delay in proceedings before courts of general jurisdiction, military courts and the Supreme Court.[28] This Chamber therefore deals with the most important issues concerning elections, the structure of the electronic media market as well as strategic and military investments.

Another novelty that prompts constitutional doubts concerns the introduction of an extraordinary appeal. The extraordinary appeal can challenge any final judgment if it is considered necessary for the implementation of the rule of law and social justice. Cases decided in the past could be filed[29] within five years of the date that the judgment becomes final and valid. With regard to new cases finally adjudicated, such an appeal can be filed within five years of the date the judgment became final or within one year if cassation appeal had been filed.[30]

It is obvious that there is not only a clear interference with the stability of court decisions and a departure from the principle of protection of the rights of the party winning proceedings terminated by a court ruling. The inclusion of such an extraordinary appeal clearly endangers the legal certainty of Court decisions and can be considered as (negative) precedent in modern European legal orders. There is a sizeable risk that the extraordinary appeal is an instrument of deformalising the legal system:

> [C]onsidering its very wide scope and that it will be decided by the persons selected according to the principles described, it can become a way of undermining the

---

[27] T.T. Koncewicz (2017), 'Farewell to the Separation of Powers', *supra* note 19.
[28] Article 26 of the Act on the Supreme Court.
[29] Extraordinary appeal may be submitted by the General Prosecutor, the Ombudsman and, within the scope of its jurisdiction, the President of the General Prosecutor's Office, the Ombudsman for Children, the Patient's Rights Ombudsman, Chairman of the Financial Supervision Commission, Financial Ombudsman and the President of the Office of Competition and Consumer Protection (Article 89.3 of the Act on the Supreme Court).
[30] Article 89.3 of the Act on the Supreme Court.

principle of legal certainty, a tool for verifying judgments, which for political rather than substantive reasons do not correspond to the political actors' aspirations and wishes.[31]

It is significant in this regard that the judges of the Chamber of Labour, Social Security and Public Affairs, which was competent of some of the matters currently reserved to the Chamber of Extraordinary Supervision and Public Affairs, are not integrated within the new Chamber. Just like the Disciplinary Chamber, the Chamber of Extraordinary Supervision and Public Affairs will be composed of newly appointed judges of the Supreme Court and there is no hint of respecting the judicial experience in the highest judicial body developed by the former judges of the Supreme Court.

Even though it is not essential for the purposes of this analysis, it should be noted that the Disciplinary Chamber of the Supreme Court also gives rise to concerns. While, in particular, the question of the disciplinary accountability of judges and also representatives of other legal professions (prosecutors, lawyers, legal advisors) would require a separate analysis, it should be noted that this Chamber, established as an independent chamber of the Supreme Court, has – in comparison with other chambers – structural, personal as well as financial autonomy. The First President of the Supreme Court will not have any authority over matters decided by the Disciplinary Chamber of the Supreme Court. Considering the changes concerning the National Council of the Judiciary as an essential element of the appointment of judges, it should be pointed out that the legislative and executive powers obtained allows for unprecedented possibilities of shaping the composition of the highest disciplinary court. The Supreme Court Act could be called without a risk of error an act on the disciplinary liability of judges and other legal professions and the Supreme Court. Apart from the mechanism of appointing disciplinary prosecutors and determining the adjudication panels, the law uses concepts whose root is 'discipline' over 580 times: disciplinary proceedings, disciplinary spokesman and disciplinary court. The chilling effect – or even intimidation – is a guaranteed side-effect of the regulation.

Additionally, a Supreme Court judge adjudicating within the Disciplinary Chamber receives a 40% higher remuneration than the basic salary and the functionary allowance of the judge in other chambers of the Supreme Court.[32] This shocking regulation was justified by the special circumstances that a judge is prohibited from taking another job or taking additional employment

---

[31] The attack on the courts was deliberate planned and effective. STEFAN BATORY FOUNDATION, 'Report of the Team of Legal Experts at the Stefan Batory Foundation on the consequences of legislative activities for the judiciary in Poland in 2015–2018', 28.02.2018, available at http://www.batory.org.pl/en/news, last accessed 27.06.2018.
[32] Article 48.7 of the Act on the Supreme Court.

(except for scientific or didactic work). It is interesting, however, that this prohibition applies to all judges of the Supreme Court.[33]

All this must be considered in perspective of the actual scale of disciplinary delinquencies committed by legal professionals. In 2016, the Supreme Court received a total of 196 cases (62 disciplinary cases concerning judges of the Supreme Court and other courts of general jurisdiction, and the rest concerning other legal professions).[34]

The opinion of the Supreme Court on the bill on the Supreme Court submitted by the President of the Republic of Poland, which became the binding law indicates a major problem with the legislation. The scope of competence of the Chamber for Extraordinary Supervision and Public Affairs and the Disciplinary Chamber as well as their structure and personal composition indicates that we are not dealing with chambers equivalent to other chambers of the Supreme Court, but with 'supra-chambers', or rather separate and independent courts which were only formally seated within the structure of the Supreme Court. It has thus been stated that:

> [b]oth the Chamber for Extraordinary Supervision and Public Affairs and the Disciplinary Chamber, from the point of view of the tasks entrusted to them, competences, constitutional structure and relations with other Chambers of the Supreme Court, the First President of the Supreme Court or the College of the Supreme Court are completely new and separate courts, and such courts are not mentioned in the Constitution of the Republic of Poland as courts competent to participate in the administration of justice.[35]

9. THE DRAMA'S FOURTH ACT: COMPLIMENT OF THE POLITICAL CONTROL OVER THE JUDICIARY

The newly established mechanism for selecting the composition of the National Council of the Judiciary also manifestly violates the Constitution.[36] The National Council of the Judiciary is a constitutional authority entrenched constitutionally to safeguard the independence of courts and judges

---

[33] Article 44 of the Act on the Supreme Court.
[34] See Information on the Supreme Court activity in 2006, pp. 202–203, available in Polish at http://www.sn.pl/osadzienajwyzszym/Dzialalnosc_SN/Dzialalnosc_SN_2016.pdf, last accessed 16.07.2018.
[35] Activities of the First President of the Supreme Court in the Field of the Protection of the Rule of Law in Poland in the Years 2015–2017, Warsaw 2017, p. 224; T.T. KONCEWICZ (2017), 'Farewell to the Separation of Powers', *supra* note 19.
[36] W. SADURSKI, 'Bad Response to a Tragic Choice: the Case of Polish Council of the Judiciary', *VerfBlog*, 16.04.2018, available at https://verfassungsblog.de/bad-response-to-a-tragic-choice-the-case-of-polish-council-of-the-judiciary, last accessed 26.06.2018.

(Article 186.1 of the Constitution). Its competence encompasses proposing candidates for the position of judges for an indefinite period by the President of the Republic (Article 179 of the Constitution). The National Council of the Judiciary's membership includes three categories of persons: on the one hand there are those whose membership derives from the provisions of constitutional law (i.e. the First President of the Supreme Court, the Minister of Justice, the President of the Supreme Administrative Court and a member designated by the President of the Republic); a further four members are elected by the Sejm from the Members of the Sejm; two members are Senators elected by the Senate; and lastly, 15 members are judges of the Supreme Court, courts of general jurisdiction, administrative courts and military courts. The model entrenched by the Constitution rested on the unspoken premise that those members are duly elected by respective general assemblies of judges of the courts indicated by the Constitution. This implemented the idea that the National Council of the Judiciary should represent all the respective branches of the governmental system.

The amendment to the Act on the National Council of the Judiciary destroyed this constitutional structure, depriving the judges of the right to choose their own representatives in the Council and assigning the Sejm the power to choose 15 Council members who are judges. This means that, contrary to the Constitution, instead of four members, the Sejm elects 19 Council members. In total, the legislature elects 21 members, the executive branch is represented by two members (the Minister of Justice and the President's representative) and two judges are members of the Council under constitutional provisions (the First President of the Supreme Court and the President of the Supreme Administrative Court). The judges, as an independent and separate authority, are deprived of the competence to elect their representatives to the Council.

The second violation of the Constitution is the shortening of the constitutionally determined four-year term of the Council members elected from among the judges (Article 187.3 of the Constitution). The term of office of the National Council of the Judiciary members elected among judges is to last only until the day preceding the beginning of the new members' term of office.[37] It is significant that this regulation does not apply to deputies and senators and the President's representative who are members of the Council, clearly demonstrating the intentions of the statute's sponsors to fully politicise the new composition of the Council.[38]

The Sejm has elected 15 judges as members of the Council, but also violated the Constitution in this respect, because among the selected judges

---

[37] However, not longer than for 90 days from the date of entry into force of the Act, unless it ceased earlier in connection with the expiry of the term of office.

[38] W. SADURSKI (2018), 'Bad Response to a Tragic Choice', *supra* note 36.

(there were only 18 candidates to 15 seats), there are no judges of the Supreme Court and military courts as required by the Constitution.

10. LEGISLATION VIOLATING THE FREEDOMS AND RIGHTS OF THE INDIVIDUAL

There are two parallel and concerning developments undertaken by the political forces represented in the Parliament and the government: on the one hand the mechanism of rule of law, independence of judiciary and instruments of protections of rights and freedoms of individuals are step by step undermined and demolished; on the other individual rights and freedoms are also continuously further restricted.

10.1. DATA PROTECTION

One example of the restriction of individual's freedoms and rights is a newly introduced regulation within the Act of 15 January 2016 amending the Police Act and certain other acts (Journal of Laws of 2016, item 147). While its title suggests otherwise, the Act does not amend certain but in fact all laws regulating the status and functioning of special services in the state.[39] Contrary to the declarations included in the justification, the Act not only does not implement the guidelines contained in the Constitutional Tribunal's judgment of 30 July 2014 (K 23/11)[40] concerning the protection of individual freedoms and rights and the application of proportionate means of interference in freedom and rights, but rather runs counter the spirit of the judgment by

---

[39] See the questioned provisions of: Act of 6 April 1990 on the Police (Official Journal 2011, No 11, item 287); Act of 12 October 1990 on the Border Guard (Official Journal 2011, No 116, item 675); Act of 28 September 1991 on Tax Audit (Official Journal 2011, No 41, item 214); Act of 24 August 2001 on the Military Police and Military Authorities Responsible for Maintaining Order and Discipline (Official Journal 2013, No 568, item 675); Act of 24 May 2002 on the Internal Security Agency and the Foreign Intelligence Agency (Official Journal 2011, No 116, item 675); Act of 9 June 2006 on the Military Counter-Intelligence Service and the Military Intelligence Service (Official Journal 2014, item 253); Act of 9 June 2006 on the Central Anti-Corruption Bureau (Official Journal 2012, item 621); Act of 27 August 2009 on the Customs Service (Official Journal 2013, item 1404).

[40] Printed in OTK ZU 7A/2014, item 80. The case concerned the catalogue of data on the individual, collected via electronic means in the course of operational surveillance as well as data destruction requirements. The Constitutional Tribunal issued a judgment with regard to seven joined applications submitted by the Polish Ombudsman and the Public Prosecutor-General. The said applications concerned provisions on carrying out operational surveillance activities and disclosing communications data to the Police, the Border Guard, the Military Police, authorities responsible for tax audits, the Internal Security Agency, the Military Counter-Intelligence Service, the Central Anti-Corruption Bureau as well as – and that only regarded disclosing communications data – the Customs).

violating constitutional and international standards of individual rights to an unprecedented degree.

The amendment of the Police Act gave state police agencies access to Internet data, including the communication content, under court orders (up to three months but without a requirement of necessity or proportionality)[41] or to metadata even without court orders.[42]

The reservations voiced by the Ombudsman concern several fundamental issues. First, there is no time limit on a disproportionately long period of operational control. Operational control may be extended beyond the basic time-frame if – during the application of the supervision – new circumstances have arisen that are essential for preventing or detecting an offence, or for establishing the perpetrators and obtaining evidence of the offence.[43] The court may issue further resolutions on the extension of operational control for successive periods of time, the total length of which may not exceed 12 months.[44] Secondly, the Act provides for the limitation of professional secrecy based on the obligation to use materials covered by professional secrecy or related to the function to be admitted to court in criminal proceedings; it provides the legal basis to summon and hear persons obliged to confidentiality in respect to the obligations of a notary, attorney, legal advisor, tax advisor, a medic, journalist or statistician.[45] Thirdly, the police and special services have obtained the right to gather data from online services, not just telecommunications, mail or comparable transmissions and can also process such data without the knowledge and consent of the person concerned. In other words, the police and other law enforcement services obtained the right to use and extract unlimited data from the Internet, other forms of telecommunications and postal data.[46]

Another violation of constitutional standards is the lack of effective control of data processing. The only control carried out by the court consists in analysing bi-annual reports that the services present to the court. The rather toothless character of this form of follow-up control based only on statistic information and not on the content is further highlighted by the fact that in most cases the competent court for the control will be, due to the seat of the special services, the single district court in Warsaw.

---

[41] Article 19 of the statute of 6 April 1990 on the Police as amended (Journal of Laws 2017, item 2067).
[42] Article 20c of the statute of 6 April 1990 on the Police as amended.
[43] See Article 19 para 6–6a of the statute of 6 April 1990 on the Police as amended (Journal of Laws 2017, item 2067).
[44] See Article 19 para 9 of the statute of 6 April 1990 on the Police as amended (Journal of Laws 2017, item 2067).
[45] See Article 19 para 15f–15h of the statute of 6 April 1990 on the Police as amended (Journal of Laws 2017, item 2067).
[46] See Article 19 para 20–20cb of the statute of 6 April 1990 on the Police as amended (Journal of Laws 2017, item 2067).

Furthermore, constitutional and international norms are violated because of the lack of obligation to notify the person monitored retrospectively.

The most important regulations indicated above violate constitutional principles and norms concerning the essence of a democratic state of law, freedom of economic activity, human dignity, the right to defence in criminal proceedings, the right to privacy, the right not to disclose information, freedom and protection of communication secrets and also violate the right to a fair trial established in Article 6 and the right to respect for private life as defined in Article 8 European Convention on Human Rights (ECHR) and the right to respect for private life and communication (Article 7) and the right to the protection of personal data (Article 8) of the Charter of Fundamental Rights of the European Union.

The Ombudsman withdrew his motion from the Constitutional Tribunal saying that there was no chance for independent and substantial control of constitutionality by this Tribunal due to the irregular and more than doubtful composition of the bench.

10.2. FREEDOM OF ASSEMBLY

One of the new Parliament's legislative efforts concerned the amendment to the Act on Assemblies introducing a new type of gathering defined as 'cyclical assemblies'. The idea behind this special type of cyclical assemblies stems from monthly assemblies of a mixed (intentional) religious and political character held every 10th of the month to commemorate the victims of the plane crash in Smolensk that happened on 10 April 2010 in which the political elite died, including the then President of the Republic of Poland. The celebrations have been called the 'Smolensk monthiversary'.[47]

Cyclical assemblies are assemblies organised by the same organiser in the same place or on the same route at least four times a year according to a schedule or at least once a year if they are organised during state or national holidays. In the past three years, such gatherings even if not taking the form of assemblies, took place several times and aimed at, in particular, commemoration of momentous events significant for the history of the Republic of Poland. The above-mentioned definition of a cyclical assembly fully corresponds to monthly assemblies: the 'Smolensk monthiversaries' took place monthly during

---

[47] A monthly recurring date of a past event, especially one of historical, national, or personal importance; a celebration commemorating such a date; the English term's origin is attributed to French *mensiversaire* coined from *mēnsis* ('month') + *vertere* ('to turn') on the model of *anniversaire* [*annus* ('year') + *vertere* ('to turn')]. Smolensk is the place where a plane crashed with 96 people on board, including the elite of the Polish political, military, cultural milieu, as well as the President of Poland, members of the parliament, ministers, etc.

a period of over four years before the adoption of the Act and were justified by the organisers as a form of commemoration of an event important for the history of Poland. The decision of the local government authority provides the basis for organising such assemblies for three years, whereby these assemblies are privileged in such a way that they have statutory precedence. At the same time and in the same place there is a ban on organising other gatherings.

In the face of this regulation constitutional reservations have been raised, in particular, concerning the violation of the principle of equality. Filing a motion with the Constitutional Tribunal under the preventive control procedure, the President of the Republic of Poland pointed out that 'there is nothing in Article 57 of the Constitution to differentiate the situation of assemblies applying the criterion of their frequency' and stated that 'the entry into force of regulations governing proceeding of periodically organized gatherings will seriously weaken guarantees of the constitutional freedom of assembly and will introduce a state of legal uncertainty for those who wish to make use of this freedom'. The procedural regulations that are negatively evaluated in the President's position concern – among other matters – the operation of the Act with retrospective effect (application of a new regulation regarding assemblies about which the organisation's intention was made before the amending Act came into force) and lack of possibility to challenge a replacement order issued by the local government administration authority on the prohibition of gathering in the event of failure by the municipal authority to issue a decision prohibiting the assembly based on the premise of the cyclic assembly.

Whilst it might seem that the arguments were convincing in that they established that the regulation violated the Constitution as well as Article 11 ECHR, the Constitutional Tribunal found no constitutional fault with the legislation (Kp 1/17, judgment of 16 March 2017). It should be highlighted though, that the majority at the Constitutional Tribunal was made up of the judges who were elected by the Sejm in November 2015, including the judges whose status was questionable; all four judges who were elected before that date filed a dissident opinion. They, *inter alia*, pointed out that abstractly understood national and historical values shall not be recognised as constitutionally legitimate justification for absolute priority of assemblies on *de facto* governmental character. Despite the fact that the judgment does not directly refer to the constitutional identity, it gives a clear signal of the change in the Tribunal case law. First, the core of the justification was based on national values on high importance for Homeland and its history. Secondly, the Tribunal did not carry the full proportionally and equality tests out. Thirdly, the Tribunal accepted the absolute priority of the only one type of assemblies and automatically excluded right to contremanifestation. Article 57 of the Constitution does not authorise the Parliament to specify an abstract hierarchy of assemblies due to its national or historical aim.

10.3. CIVIL SERVICE

With regard to civil servants, a violation of the Constitution relates to the exchange of persons employed in the organisational structures of the state. The unconstitutional exchange of people employed in the organisational structures of the state may be considered as another piece in the puzzle of the hostile takeover of the constitutional order as will be shown below.[48]

The first example is the exchange of human resources employed in the civil service. By adopting the Act amending the Act on the Civil Service and certain other Acts on 30 December 2015 (Journal of Laws of 2016, item 34), the Parliament of the current term has made major changes to the constitutional model of the civil service. The Act applies to higher positions in the civil service and its effects concern several hundred people holding key positions within the government administration.

The new model of the civil service introduced by the amendment to the Civil Service Act that has been implemented within the foreseen 30 days from the date of the amendment's entry into force, is based on five basic principles that can be considered the constitutional 'cardinal sins' of the adopted system of shaping the civil service. First, open and competitive recruitment for higher positions in the civil service was replaced by nomination. The new regulation replaced the system of highest level of employment protection and stability with the lowest level of protection against dismissal or change of employment conditions. Secondly, the eligibility requirements for applying for higher positions in the civil service have been drastically reduced. The requirement of at least six years of service, including at least three years of managerial seniority in units of the public finance sector (in the case of applying for the post of general director of the office), and the requirement of at least three years of service, including at least one year in the post, have been abolished. The requirement of managerial or two-year experience in an independent position in public finance sector in the case of applying for another post has been abolished. The amendment to the Civil Service Act abolished the requirement of having any professional experience by persons appointed for higher positions in the civil service. Thirdly, the eradication of competitive recruitment procedures means that it is impossible to control access to the civil service on an equal basis. The mechanism verifying the correctness of the constitutional requirement to fill senior positions in the civil service in a way that guarantees professional, reliable, impartial and politically neutral performance of the state's tasks has been simply eradicated. Fourthly, the right of citizens to be informed

---

[48] See also M. WYRZYKOWSKI (2015), 'Bypassing the Constitution or Changing the Constitutional Order Outside the Constitution', *supra* note 1, p. 160ff.

about vacant higher positions in the civil service was eliminated. Information on vacancies is currently not publicly available and will be open to only a very small group of party nomenclature. The principles of openness, transparency and equality used to be fundamental to the selection procedures to the civil service. Fifthly, the constitutional principle of legal certainty and legal security of an individual is violated by the regulation providing for the termination of employment relations with all persons occupying higher positions in the civil service after 30 days from the date of entry into force of the Act, if new terms of employment or pay are not offered before the expiry of that period. The statutory termination of the relationship of appointment is an unprecedented act of arbitrariness of the legislator confirming its legislative constitutional nihilism.

The indicated regulations grossly violate constitutional principles and norms, in particular the principle of the rule of law, including the protection of acquired rights and citizens' trust in the state and the law (Article 2 of the Constitution); the right of Polish citizens to access public services on equal terms (Article 60 of the Constitution); constitutional rules governing the civil service and the requirement of the elements of professionality, reliability, impartiality and political neutrality in the performance of the tasks of the state (Article 153.1 of the Constitution) and the principle of proportionality of legal regulation (Article 31.3 of the Constitution). Although the group of deputies and the Commissioner for Citizens' Rights submitted applications to the Constitutional Tribunal requiring constitutional review of the indicated regulations, the Tribunal has not considered the case for more than two years (K 6/16).

11. INTERNATIONAL REACTION TO VIOLATION OF RULE OF LAW

Legislation regarding the Constitutional Tribunal, the Supreme Court, the courts of general jurisdiction, the National Council of the Judiciary and the prosecutor's office have been subject to analyses and assessments by international organisations and institutions, both at the European and the universal (UN) level.

The European Commission for Democracy through Law (the Venice Commission) upon invitation by the Polish government, criticised the statute amending the Act on the Constitutional Tribunal passed on 22 December 2015. It was particularly concerned about those provisions determining that, as a general rule, the Tribunal considered cases in full court composed of at least 13 out of 15 judges; taking decisions by a two-thirds majority instead of a simple majority; examining applications in the order in which they were submitted to the court; termination of a judge's term of office by the Sejm (and not, as before, by the Tribunal) or the power of the President of the Republic of Poland and the Minister of Justice to institute disciplinary proceedings against the judges of the Constitutional Tribunal.[49]

The Commission stated that: 'the amendment of 22 December 2015 affecting the effectiveness of the Constitutional Tribunal would have endangered not only the rule of law, but also the functioning of the democratic system' and that 'these amendments, notably when taken together, could lead to a serious slow-down of the activity of the Tribunal and could make it ineffective as a guardian of the Constitution'.[50] Moreover, at the outset of the constitutional crisis, the Venice Commission stated in its opinion:

> Crippling the Tribunal's effectiveness will undermine all three basic principles of the Council of Europe: democracy – because of an absence of a central part of checks and balances; human rights – because the access of individuals to the Constitutional Tribunal could be slowed down to a level resulting in the denial of justice; and the rule of law – because the Constitutional Tribunal, which is a central part of the Judiciary in Poland, would become ineffective. Making a constitutional court ineffective is inadmissible and this removes a crucial mechanism which ensures that potential conflicts with European and international norms and standards can be resolved at the national level without the need to have recourse to European or other subsidiary courts, which are overburdened and less close to the realities on the ground.[51]

Finally, the Venice Commission indicated:

> A refusal to publish judgment 47/15 of 9 March 2016 would not only be contrary to the rule of law, such an unprecedented move would further deepen the constitutional crisis triggered by the election of judges in autumn 2015 and the Amendments of 22 December 2015. Not only the Polish Constitution but also European and international standards require that the judgments of a Constitutional Court be respected. The publication of the judgment and its respect by the authorities are a precondition for finding a way out of this constitutional crisis.[52]

The second opinion of the Venice Commission, prepared on the motion of the Secretary General of the CoE, concerned the Law on the Constitutional Tribunal of 22 July 2016 and was in line with its previous opinion stating that: '[...] numerous other provisions of the adopted Act would considerably delay and obstruct the work of the Tribunal and make its work ineffective, as well as undermine its independence by exercising excessive legislative and executive

---

[49] VENICE COMMISSION, Opinion on Amendments to the Act of 25 June 2015 on the Constitutional Tribunal of Poland adopted by the Venice Commission at its 106th Plenary Session (Venice, 11–12 March 2016), CDL-AD(2016)001.
[50] Ibid., para. 137.
[51] Ibid., para. 138.
[52] Ibid., para. 143.

control over its functioning'. These concern notably: (1) the sequence rule and scope of the exceptions to it, which do not allow sufficient flexibility for the work of the Tribunal (Article 38); (2) the referral of a case to the full bench without the possibility for the other judges to reject the referral (Article 26); (3) the postponement of a case for up to six months upon request by four judges, which lacks justification and could easily be abused to delay delicate cases (Article 68); (4) the provision allowing the dully notified Prosecutor-General to block a hearing of the Tribunal by his or her absence, which both delays and politicises the functioning of the Tribunal (Articles 30 and 61); (5) the suspension of all institutional cases for six months followed by re-registration, which would delay the work of the Tribunal on important pending cases, and the requirement that other cases be terminated within one year (Articles 83–87); and (6) lack of flexibility to reduce the time before a hearing in certain categories of cases (Article 61).[53] The Venice Commission concludes that:

> individually and cumulatively, these shortcomings show that instead of unblocking the precarious situation of the Constitutional Tribunal, the Parliament and Government continue to challenge the Tribunal's position as the final arbiter of constitutional issues and attribute this authority to themselves. They have created new obstacles to the effective functioning of the Tribunal instead of seeking a solution on the basis of the Constitution and the Tribunal's judgments, and have acted to further undermine its independence. By prolonging the constitutional crisis, they have obstructed the Constitutional Tribunal, which cannot play its constitutional role as the guardian of democracy, the rule of law and human rights.[54]

Besides the Council of Europe's Venice Commission, concerns about the developments in Poland were also raised within the European Union. Therefore, the European Commission with reference to the Communication 'A new EU Framework to Strengthen the Rule of Law' analysed the constitutional situation in Poland in the period November 2015–July 2016 stressing the regulations concerning the Constitutional Tribunal.[55] The Commission highlighted the

---

[53] Ibid., p. 123.
[54] VENICE COMMISSION, Opinion, *supra* note 55, p. 128.
[55] EUROPEAN COMMISSION, A new EU Framework to strengthen the Rule of Law, COM(2014) 158 final, 11.03.2014. See also L. PECH and K.L. SCHEPPELE, 'Poland and the European Commission, Part I: A Dialogue of the Deaf?', *VerfBlog*, 03.01.2017, available at https://verfassungsblog.de/poland-and-the-european-commission-part-i-a-dialogue-of-the-deaf, last accessed 26.06.2018; L. PECH and K.L., SCHEPPELE, 'Poland and the European Commission, Part II: Hearing the Siren Song of the Rule of Law', *VerfBlog*, 06.01.2017, available at https://verfassungsblog.de/poland-and-the-european-commission-part-ii-hearing-the-siren-song-of-the-rule-of-law, last accessed 26.06.2018 and L. PECH and K.L. SCHEPPELE, 'Poland and the European Commission, Part III: Requiem for the Rule of Law', *VerfBlog*, 03.03.2017, available at https://verfassungsblog.de/poland-and-the-european-commission-part-iii-requiem-for-the-rule-of-law, last accessed 26.06.2018.

systemic threat to the rule of law and recommends that the Polish authorities: (1) implement fully the judgments of the Constitutional Tribunal of 3 and 9 December 2015 which requires that the three judges that were lawfully nominated in October 2015 by the previous legislature can take up their function of judge in the Constitutional Tribunal, and that the three judges nominated by the new legislature without a valid legal basis do not take up the post of judge without being validly elected; (2) publish and implement fully the judgments of the Constitutional Tribunal of 9 March 2016 and its subsequent judgments and ensure that the publication of future judgments is automatic and does not depend on any decision of the executive or legislative power; (3) ensure that any reform of the Law on Constitutional Tribunal (CT) respects the judgments of the CT and takes the opinion of the Venice Commission fully into account; ensure that the effectiveness of the CT as a guarantor of the Constitution is not undermined by requirements, whether separately or through their combined effect, such as those referred above; (4) ensure that the CT can review the compatibility of the new law adopted on 22 July on the CT before its entry into force and publish and implement fully the judgment of the CT in that respect; and (5) refrain from actions and public statements which could undermine the legitimacy and efficiency of the CT.[56]

In the a consecutive Recommendation[57] the Commission recommends the implementation of the previous Recommendations and recommends further that the Polish authorities take the following actions: (1) to restore the independence and legitimacy of the Constitutional Tribunal as guarantor of the Polish Constitution by ensuring that its judges, its President and its Vice-President are lawfully elected and appointed and by implementing fully the judgments of the Constitutional Tribunal of 3 and 9 December 2015 which requires that the three judges that were lawfully nominated in October 2015 by the previous legislature can take up their function of judge in the Constitutional Tribunal, and that the three judges nominated by the new legislature without a valid legal basis no longer adjudicate without being validly elected; (2) to publish and implement fully judgments of the Constitutional Tribunal of 9 March 2016, 11 August 2016 and 7 November 2016; (3) to ensure that the law on the National Council of Judiciary, the Law on Ordinary Courts Organizations and the law on the Supreme Court do not enter into force and that the law on the National School of Judiciary is withdrawn or amended in order to ensure

---

[56] EUROPEAN COMMISSION, Commission Recommendation of 27.7.2016 regarding the rule of law in Poland, C(2016)5703 final, 27.07.2016.

[57] EUROPEAN COMMISSION, Commission Recommendation of 26.7.2017 regarding the rule of law in Poland complementary to Commission Reccomendations (EU) 2016/1374 and (EU) 2017/146, C (2017) 5320 final, 26.07.2017, para. 53.

its compliance with the Constitution and European standards on judicial independence; (4) refrain from any measure interfering with the tenure of the Supreme Court judges and their functions; (5) ensure that any justice reform upholds the rule of law and complies with EU law and the European standards on judicial independence and is prepared in close cooperation with the judiciary and all interested parties; and (6) refrain from actions and public statements which could undermine further the legitimacy of the Constitutional Tribunal, the Supreme Courts the ordinary courts, the judges, individually or collectively, or the judiciary as a whole.

In the next Recommendation[58] concerning especially the Supreme Court and the National Council of Judiciary the Commission recommends that the Polish authorities take appropriate action to address the systemic threat to the rule of law as a matter of urgency. In particular, the Commission recommends that the Polish authorities take the following actions with regard to the newly adopted laws in order to ensure their compliance with the requirements of safeguarding the independence of the judiciary, of separation of powers and of legal certainty as well as with the Polish Constitution and European standards on judicial independence: (1) to ensure that the law on the Supreme Court is amended so that a lowered retirement age for the current Supreme Court judges does not apply and that the discretionary power of the President of the Republic to prolong the active judicial mandate of the Supreme Court judges and remove the extraordinary appeal procedure is removed; (2) to ensure that the law on the National Council for the Judiciary is amended so that the mandate of judges-members of the National Council for the Judiciary is not terminated and the new appointment regime is removed in order to ensure election of judges-members by their peers; (3) refrain from actions and public statements which could undermine further the legitimacy of the Supreme Court, the ordinary courts, the judges, individually or collectively, or the judiciary as a whole.

In addition, the Commission recalls that none of the following actions, recommended in its Recommendation of 26 July 2017, relating to the Constitutional Tribunal, the law on Ordinary Courts Organization and the law on the National School of Judiciary have been taken and therefore reiterates its recommendation to take the following actions: (1) to restore the independence and legitimacy of the Constitutional Tribunal as guarantor of the Polish Constitution by ensuring that its judges, its President and its Vice-President are lawfully elected and appointed and by implementing fully the judgments of the Constitutional Tribunal of 3 and 9 December 2015 which require that

---

[58] EUROPEAN COMMISSION, Commission Recommendation of 20.12.2017 regarding the rule of law in Poland complementary to Commission Recommendations (EU) 2016/1374, (EU) 2017/146 and (EU) 2017/1520, C (2017) 9050 final, 20.12.2017.

the three judges that were lawfully nominated in October 2015 by the previous legislature can take up their function of judge in the Constitutional Tribunal, and that the three judges nominated by the new legislature without a valid legal basis no longer adjudicate without being validly elected; (2) to publish and implement fully the judgments of the Constitutional Tribunal of 9 March 2016, 11 August 2016 and 7 November 2016; (3) to ensure that the law on Ordinary Courts Organization and on the National School of Judiciary is withdrawn or amended in order to ensure its compliance with the Constitution and European standards on judicial independence; specifically, the Commission recommends in particular: to remove the new retirement regime for judges of ordinary courts, including the discretionary power of the Minister of Justice to prolong their mandate; to remove the discretionary power of the Minister of Justice to appoint and dismiss Presidents of courts; and to remedy decisions already taken; and (4) to ensure that any justice reform upholds the rule of law and complies with EU law and the European standards on judicial independence and is prepared in close cooperation with the judiciary and all interested parties.[59]

The Commission underlines that the loyal cooperation which is required amongst the different state institutions in rule of law related matters is essential to find a solution for the present situation. The Commission also encourages the Polish authorities to implement the opinions of the Venice Commission on the law on the National Council for the Judiciary, the law on the Ordinary Courts Organization and the law on the Supreme Court as well as to seek the views of the Venice Commission on any new legislative proposal aiming to reform the justice system in Poland.[60] The Commission invites the Polish Government to solve the problems identified in this Recommendation within three months of receipt of this Recommendation, and to inform the Commission of the steps taken to that effect.[61]

This Recommendation was issued at the same time as the reasoned proposal presented by the Commission in accordance with Article 7(1) Treaty on European Union (TEU) regarding the rule of law in Poland.[62] The Commission repeated that is ready, in close consultation with the European Parliament and the Council, to reconsider that reasoned proposal, should the Polish authorities implement the recommended actions set out in the present Recommendation within the time prescribed.

---

[59] Commission Recommendation of 20.12.2017, *supra* note 58, pp. 46–48.
[60] Ibid., para. 49.
[61] Ibid., para. 50.
[62] D. KOCHENOV, L. PECH and K.L. SCHEPPELE, 'The European Commission's Activation of Article 7: Better Late than Never?', *VerfBlog*, 23.12.2017, available at https://verfassungsblog.de/the-european-commissions-activation-of-article-7-better-late-than-never, last accessed 26.06.2018.

12. 'CLEAR RISK OF SERIOUS BREACH OF THE RULE OF LAW': USE OF ARTICLE 7(1) OF THE TEU

Despite repeated efforts, for almost two years, to engage the Polish authorities in a constructive dialogue in the context of the Rule of Law Framework, the Commission concluded on 20 December 2017 that there is a clear risk of a serious breach of the rule of law in Poland.[63] The Commission is therefore proposing to the Council to adopt a decision under Article 7(1) of the Treaty on European Union. The Commission stated that over a period of two years, the Polish authorities have adopted more than 13 laws affecting the entire structure of the justice system in Poland, impacting the Constitutional Tribunal, Supreme Court, ordinary courts, National Council for the Judiciary, prosecution service and National School of Judiciary. The common pattern is that the executive and legislative branches have been systematically enabled to politically interfere in the composition, powers, administration and functioning of the judicial branch. The Recommendation clearly sets out a set of actions that need to be taken by the Polish authorities to address its concerns. The Polish authorities are invited, *inter alia*, to:[64]

- Amend the Supreme Court law, not apply a lowered retirement age to current judges, remove the discretionary power of the President to prolong the mandate of Supreme Court judges, and remove the extraordinary appeal procedure, which includes a power to reopen final judgments taken years earlier;
- Amend the law on the National Council for the Judiciary, to not terminate the mandate of judges-members, and ensure that the new appointment regime continues to guarantee the election of judges-members by their peers;
- Amend or withdraw the law on Ordinary Courts Organization, to remove the new retirement regime for judges including the discretionary powers of the Minister of Justice to prolong the mandate of judges and to appoint and dismiss Presidents of courts;
- Restore the independence and legitimacy of the Constitutional Tribunal, by ensuring that its judges, President and Vice-President are lawfully elected and by ensuring that all its judgments are published and fully implemented;
- Refrain from actions and public statements which could further undermine the legitimacy of the judiciary.

---

[63] EUROPEAN COMMISSION, Reasoned proposal in accordance with the Article 7(1) of the Treaty on European Union regarding the rule of law in Poland. Proposal for a Council decision on the determination of a clear risk of a serious breach by the Republic of Poland of the rule of law, COM(2017) 835 final, 20.12.2017.
[64] Ibid.

For the first time in the history of the European Union, the European Commission adopted a proposal presented to the Council of the European Union for a decision on the determination of a clear risk of a serious breach by the Republic of Poland to the rule of law. Article 2 of the proposed decision suggests that the Council recommends that the Republic of Poland take the following actions within three months after notification of this Decision: (1) to restore the independence and legitimacy of the Constitutional Tribunal as guarantor of the Polish Constitution by ensuring that its judges, its President and its Vice-President are lawfully elected and appointed, by implementing fully the judgments of the Constitutional Tribunal of 3 and 9 December 2016 which require that the three judges that are lawfully nominated in October 2015 by the previous legislature can take up their function of judge in the Constitutional tribunal, and that the three judges nominated by the new legislature without a valid basis no longer adjudicate without being validly elected; (2) to publish and implement fully the judgments of the Constitutional Tribunal of 9 March 2016, 11 August 2016 and 7 November 2016; (3) to ensure that the law on the Supreme Court, the law on Ordinary Courts Organization, the law on the National Council for the Judiciary and the law on the National School of Judiciary are amended in order to ensure their compliance with the requirements relating to the independence of the judiciary, the separation of powers and legal certainty; (4) to ensure that any justice reform is prepared in close cooperation with the judiciary and all interested parties, including the Venice Commission; and (5) to refrain from actions and public statements which could undermine further the legitimacy of the Constitutional Tribunal, the Supreme Court, the ordinary courts, the judges, individually or collectively, or the judiciary as a whole.

Additionally, the Commission also decided to refer the Polish Government to the European Court of Justice for breach of EU law, concerning the Law on the Ordinary Courts and, specifically, the retirement regime it introduces.[65] The Commission's key legal concern identified in this law relates to the discrimination based on gender due to the introduction of a different retirement age for female judges (60 years) and male judges (65 years). This is contrary to Article 157 of the Treaty on the Functioning of the European Union (TFEU) and Directive 2006/54 on gender equality in employment. In its referral to the European Court of Justice, the Commission will also raise the linked concern that the independence of Polish courts will be undermined by the fact that the Minister of Justice (now, after the amendment of the law, the President of Poland, being also the executive authority) as it has been given a discretionary

---

[65] EUROPEAN COMMISSION, 'Rule of Law: Commission launches infringement procedure to protect the independence of the Polish Supreme Court', Press release, 02.07.2018, available at http://europa.eu/rapid/press-release_IP-18-4341_en.htm, last accessed 06.09.2018.

power to prolong the mandate of judges which have reached retirement age (see Article 19(1) TEU in combination with Article 47 of the EU Charter of Fundamental Rights).

The serious problems related to the described developments also raised the concern whether the change of the Polish judiciary system, especially from the perspective of independence of judiciary and the European standards of rule of law, may have an impact on cooperation of the jurisdictions of the member states of the EU.[66] Accordingly, the European Commission stated that in one of its recommendations that the perception of the rule of law standards and independency of judiciary may influence, for example, the cooperation in the field of European Arrest Warrant.[67]

And as a matter of fact, it happened. The High Court of Ireland in 2018 expressed its concerns with regard to the execution of a European Arrest Warrant against Artur Celmar and his extradition to Poland due to rule of law concerns and the judicial reforms underway in Poland and referred the case to the CJEU asking

> a/ Is the *Aranyosi and Caldararu* test, which relies upon principles of mutual trust and mutual recognition, the correct test to apply where the High Court, as an executing judicial authority under the Framework Decision, has found that the common value of the rule of law set out in Article 2 TEU has been breached in Poland?
>
> b/ If the test to be applied is whether the requested person is at real risk of a flagrant denial of justice, does the High Court, as an executing judicial authority, have to revert to the issuing judicial authority for any further necessary information about the trial that this requested person will face, where the High Court has found that there is a systemic breach to the rule of law in Poland?[68]

---

[66] K.L. SCHEPPELE and L. PECH, 'What is Rule of Law Backsliding?', *VerfBlog*, 02.03.2018, available at https://verfassungsblog.de/what-is-rule-of-law-backsliding, last accessed 25.06.2018.

[67] T.T. KONCEWICZ, 'The Consensus Fights Back: European First Principles Against the Rule of Law Crisis (part 1)', *VerfBlog*, 05.04.2018, available at https://verfassungsblog.de/the-consensus-fights-back-european-first-principles-against-the-rule-of-law-crisis-part-1, last accessed 26.06.2018; T.T. KONCEWICZ, 'The Consensus Fights Back: European First Principles Against the Rule of Law Crisis (part 2)', *VerfBlog*, 05.04.2018, available at https://verfassungsblog.de/the-consensus-fights-back-european-first-principles-against-the-rule-of-law-crisis-part-2, last accessed 26.06.2018.

[68] See High Court, Record No. 2013 EXT 295, Record No. 2014 EXT 8, Record No. 2017 EXT. 291 between the Minister for Justice and Equality Applicant and Artur Celmer, respondent; judgment of Ms. Justice Donnelly delivered on 12.03.2018. See CJEU, *Minister for Justice and Equality v LM*, C-216/18 PPU, 25.07.2018, ECLI:EU:C:2018:586. On 25 July 2018 the CJEU delivered the judgement crucial for the principles of mutual trust and the mutual recognition of decisions and the question whether European Member States could make judgments about the legitimacy and fundamental rights compliance, in particular the right to a fair trial in one another's courts. Importantly, while the CJEU recognised the possibility to suspend extraditions to another Member State because of possible violations of the rule of law, it introduced a rather high bar for the test to be applied. The Court in answering the questions of the High Court of Irleand in para. 79 stated: 'Article 1(3) of Council Framework Decision

The convergence of views of the European Commission and the Venice Commission on the state of the rule of law in Poland does not exhaust the general disapproval of the problem as expressed by various international authorities and organisations as well as by international associations of judges and lawyers.

Similar critical opinions were expressed, for example, by the Parliamentary Assembly of the Council of Europe on new threats to the rule of law in Poland. The Parliamentary Assembly expressed its concern about the legislation adopted in Poland, in particular, the risk to the independence of the judiciary and the division and balance of powers.[69] In much the same vain, the European Parliament not only expressed its concern about the rule of law and democracy in Poland[70] but also adopted the resolution concerning the initiation by the European Commission of the procedure under Article 7(1) TEU.[71]

In a letter to the Polish Prime Minister, the Council of Europe Human Rights Commissioner expressed his concern about the rule of law, the independence of the judicial branch, as well as the negative impact of the degradation of the rule of law on the protection of human rights in Poland.[72] The Group of States

---

2002/584/JHA of 13 June 2002 on the European arrest warrant and the surrender procedures between Member States, as amended by Council Framework Decision 2009/299/JHA of 26 February 2009, must be interpreted as meaning that, where the executing judicial authority, called upon to decide whether a person in respect of whom a European arrest warrant has been issued for the purposes of conducting a criminal prosecution is to be surrendered, has material, such as that set out in a reasoned proposal of the European Commission adopted pursuant to Article 7(1) TEU, indicating that there is a real risk of breach of the fundamental right to a fair trial guaranteed by the second paragraph of Article 47 of the Charter of Fundamental Rights of the European Union, on account of systemic or generalised deficiencies so far as concerns the independence of the issuing Member State's judiciary, that authority must determine, specifically and precisely, whether, having regard to his personal situation, as well as to the nature of the offence for which he is being prosecuted and the factual context that form the basis of the European arrest warrant, and in the light of the information provided by the issuing Member State pursuant to Article 15(2) of Framework Decision 2002/584, as amended, there are substantial grounds for believing that that person will run such a risk if he is surrendered to that State.' For an analysis of the judgment see W. VAN BALLEGOOIJ and P. BÁRD, 'The CJEU in the Celmer case: One step forward, two steps back for upholding the rule of law within the EU', *VerfBlog*, 29.07.2018, available at https://verfassungsblog.de/the-cjeu-in-the-celmer-case-one-step-forward-two-steps-back-for-upholding-the-rule-of-law-within-the-eu/, last accessed 06.09.2018.

[69] PARLIAMENTARY ASSEMBLY – COUNCIL OF EUROPE (PACE), New threat to the rule of law in Council of Europe member states: selected examples, Resolution 2188(2017), 11.10.2017.

[70] European Parliament Resolution of 15 November 2017 on the situation of the rule of law and democracy in Poland (2017/2931(RSP)).

[71] European Parliament Resolution on the Commission decision to activate Article 7(1) TEU as regards the situation in Poland (2018/2541(RSP)).

[72] COUNCIL OF EUROPE, 'Poland has a duty to preserve judicial independence', N. MUIŽNIEKS, the Council of Europe Commissioner for Human Rights, 17.07.2017, available at https://www.coe.int/en/web/commissioner/-/poland-has-a-duty-to-preserve-judicial-independence?desktop=true, last accessed 26.06.2018, recently in a letter

Against Corruption (GRECO), another authority operating within the Council of Europe, expressed the view that the reforms of the judiciary undermine the standards applicable to the mechanisms controlling corruption.[73]

Further, concerns related to the standards of the independence of the judiciary were expressed by the UN Special Rapporteur on the Independence of Judges and Lawyers. The latter stated that the newly-adopted Act on the Supreme Court and the Act on the National Council of the Judiciary raised fundamental reservations from the point of view of international standards.[74] UN Human Rights Committee stresses that Poland should ensure respect for and protection of the integrity and independence of the Constitutional Tribunal and its judges and ensure the implementation of its judgments as well as urges the Polish government to immediately publish officially all the judgments of the Tribunal and refrain from introducing measures that obstruct its effective functioning and ensure a transparent and impartial process of the appointment of its members and security of tenure, which meets all requirements of quality domestic and international law.[75]

Furthermore, the Office for Democratic Institutions and Human Rights (ODIHR) has repeatedly criticised the changes of Polish legislation made since autumn 2015. This institution's critical remarks pertained to limiting the immunity of the Ombudsman[76] and new regulations regarding the Supreme Court, the National Council of the Judiciary and changes to other acts.[77]

---

addressed to the Polish Prime Minister, Letter to Mr Mateusz-Morawiecki, the Prime-Minister of the Republic of Poland, 06.02.2018, available at https://www.coe.int/en/web/commissioner/-/commissioner-concerned-about-human-rights-backsliding-in-poland, last accessed 26.06.2018, or available at https://rm.coe.int/letter-to-mr-mateusz-morawiecki-prime-minister-of-the-republic-of-pola/1680784182, last accessed 26.06.2018.

[73] COUNCIL OF EUROPE, 'Poland: Judicial reforms violate anti-corruption standards, say Council of Europe experts', Newsroom, GRECO, 29.03.2018, available at https://www.coe.int/en/web/greco/-/poland-judicial-reforms-violate-anti-corruption-standards-say-council-of-europe-experts, last accessed 26.06.2018.

[74] UN, Report of the Special Rapporteur on the independence of judges and lawyers on his mission to Poland, UN Doc. A/HRC/38/38/Add.1, 05.04.2018.

[75] HUMAN RIGHTS COMMITTEE, 'Concluding observations in the seventh periodic report of Poland adopted 31 October 2016', available at https://www.rpo.gov.pl/sites/default/files/CCPR_C_POL_CO_7_25815_E.pdf, last accessed 26.06.2018.

[76] OSCE/ODIHR, 'Final Opinion on the Draft Act Amending the Act on the Commissioner for Human Rights of Poland based on an unofficial English translation of the Draft Act commissioned by the OSCE Office for Democratic Institutions and Human Rights', Opinion-Nr.: NHRI-POL/282/2016 [AlC], 16.02.2016, available at https://www.osce.org/odihr/223436?download=true, last accessed 26.06.2018.

[77] OSCE/ODIHR, Final Opinion on Draft Amendments to the Act on The National Council of the Judiciary and Certain Other Acts of Poland based on an unofficial English translation of the Draft Act commissioned by the OSCE Office for Democratic Institutions and Human Rights, Opinion-Nr.: JUD-POL/305/2017-Final [AlC/YM], 05.05.2017, available at https://www.osce.org/odihr/315946?download=true, last accessed 26.06.2018.

Finally, the convergence of critical opinions about the rule of law in Poland is also visible in the opinions of organisations of judges such as the European Network of Councils for the Judiciary (ENCJ)[78] as well as the Consultative Council of European Judges (CCJE).[79]

13. CHANGE OF THE CONSTITUTIONAL SYSTEM BY NON-CONSTITUTIONAL METHODS: RULE OF LAW AND SOVEREIGNTY OF THE STATE

The intensity of unconstitutionality of the legislator's actions in respect of the constitutional position of the Constitutional Tribunal, and – later – in respect of the judicial branch and freedom and rights of the individual, as described above, must raise some fundamental questions. These questions concern the problem of change of the state-system by non-constitutional methods, the validity of basic democratic principles expressed in Parliament's powers for such legislative acts as well as the sense of legal security and the status of the individual in relation to the individual's freedoms and rights and the guarantees of their enforcement.[80] The scale of the negative consequences of the changes effectuated is thus connected with considerations of the ease of their implementation by the parliamentary majority. It is to be noted that the conclusions of the Venice Commission emphasise – in the context of the paralysis of the Constitutional Tribunal – the functional relationship of the rule of law, democracy and human rights.[81]

The beginnings of the constitutional crisis in Poland in autumn 2015 were a result of the actions of the constitutional organs of the state, in particular, the

---

[78] ENCJ, 'Opinion of the ENCJ Executive Board on the request of the Krajowa Rada Sądownictwa of Poland', available at www.encj.eu/images/stories/pdf/Members/rfc_krs_pl_opinion_encj_eb_30_1_2017_final.pdf, last accessed 26.06.2018; concerning the National Judicial Council see ENCJ, Opinion of the ENCJ Executive Board on the adoption of the amendments to the law on the Krajowa Rada Sądownictwa of Poland, 05.12.2017, available at https://www.encj.eu/images/stories/pdf/Members/krs_pl_opinion_encj_eb_5_dec_2017.pdf, last accessed 26.06.2018.

[79] COUNCIL OF EUROPE, 'Statement as Regards the Situation on the Independence of the Judiciary in Poland', Consultative Council of European Judges (CCJE), CCJE(2017)9, 10.11.2017, available at https://rm.coe.int/statemenet-as-regards-the-situation-on-theindependence-of-the-judiciar/1680765391, last accessed 26.06.2018.

[80] K.L. SCHEPPELE and L. PECH, 'Didn't the EU Learn That These Rule-of-Law Interventions Don't Work?', *VerfBlog*, 09.03.2018, available at https://verfassungsblog.de/didnt-the-eu-learn-that-these-rule-of-law-interventions-dont-work, last accessed 26.06.2018.

[81] M. MATCZAK, 'Some Thoughts on Authoritarian Backsliding', *VerfBlog*, 27.12.2017, available at https://verfassungsblog.de/some-thoughts-on-authoritarian-backsliding, last accessed 26.06.2018. K.L. SCHEPPELE and L. PECH, 'What is Rule of Law Backsliding?', *VerfBlog*, 02.03.2018, available at https://verfassungsblog.de/what-is-rule-of-law-backsliding, last accessed 26.06.2018.

Parliament and the President, that were inconsistent with the Constitution and statutes. This initial situation evolved into a 'state of war' with the constitution. An attack on the Constitutional Tribunal is an attack on the Constitution. The dynamics the unconstitutional actions of political actors unfolded over the time as a supranational rather than merely an internal affair of Poland. Both the European Union and the Council of Europe, and then UN agencies, recognised that in Poland the rule of law was seriously violated, and since the rule of law and the principles of democracy and human rights are so closely interrelated a violation of the rules underpinning the system of the organised European constitutional space is given.

It is worth restating that the constitutional crisis concerns the essence of the statehood of the Republic of Poland because it concerns the essence of the sovereignty of the Polish state. On 20 May 2016, the Sejm of the Republic of Poland adopted a resolution 'on the defence of the sovereignty of the Republic of Poland and the rights of its citizens'. On the eve of the follow-up European Commission meeting on the state of the rule of law in Poland, the Sejm declared that the Republic of Poland was a sovereign and democratic state of law in accordance with the Constitution and stated that 'in recent times there have been violations of the sovereignty of our state, undermining the principles of democracy, legal order and social peace in Poland. The starting point for such actions is the issue of a political dispute over the Constitutional Tribunal'.[82] The Sejm called on the government to 'oppose all actions against the sovereignty of the state' and stated that it was the government's duty to defend the 'national interest and the constitutional order in the Polish Commonwealth'.[83]

In relation to the latter statement, it is impossible to resist the sense of a saddening *déjà vu*. In its modern understanding, sovereignty is a legal state not overruling the Constitution but existing within the constitution's very framework. The sovereignty of a nation in a constitutional state is not limited. What is limited is the power of the sovereign's representatives, elected on the basis of the applicable law for a definite period of time determined by the Parliament's term of office. This power of the representatives is limited because it is to be exercised on the basis, within and in accordance with the constitution. It might be added that what binds the legislator is both the constitution's letter and spirit, as the latter may enlighten the representatives of the sovereign.

The concept of sovereignty expressed in the resolution of the Sejm refers to the concept of uniformity of state power identified until the 20th century as the sole representative of the will of the sovereign; the role of the statute was the unmistakable expression of the sovereign's will. Under this theory, the sovereign could not be wrong and the Parliament, as the sole representative

---

[82] See http://www.monitorpolski.gov.pl/MP/2016/466, last accessed 16.07.2018.
[83] Ibid.

of sovereign's will, cannot err either. The recognition of the idea of a balanced government reflecting the principle of the division of powers and the mechanism of constitutional review of legislation as the corollary of the implementation of the powers of the Parliament was a response to the experience of the tragic system of government of the recent past. The return to the concept presented in the Sejm's resolution expresses the idea of an unbalanced and unsustainable – one might add unlimited – government as an expression of one of the many deep political conflicts regarding, *inter alia*, the 'institutional framework for the protection of democratic relations against themselves'.[84]

There is a paradox in that exercising sovereignty outside the scope of the Constitution is self-destructive because it undermines its own legitimacy as the result of the violation of the constitution. We are dealing with the de-legitimisation of the system by violating the law and, in particular, violation of constitutional norms. Also, from an internal perspective, and not only from the perspective of international law, 'sovereignty is a concept that protects the state and it not just the expression of the state's allegedly unlimited power'.[85]

If the authorities of a state do not respect their constitutional order, protected by effective and effectual mechanisms with violations entailing sanctions, it is reasonable to suspect (as a matter of a hypothesis) that the same state will also disregard international obligations spelling much weaker enforcement and compliance mechanism. The concept of sovereignty expressed in the resolution of the Sejm undermines Poland's position within the international community because it undermines (negates or challenges) the principles underpinning both the constitutional and the international legal order.

The actions of the Parliament of the current term indicate the weakness of the self-defence system of the constitutional order against a hostile takeover.[86] The political element does not respect the basics of the social contract. The social contract was concluded between the society and those who come to exercise its power by approving the Constitution of the Republic of Poland in a constitutional referendum. The social contract was unilaterally broken with the false argument that the 'sovereign', with mere 18% of the population voting for the winning coalition in 2015, granted legitimacy for unlimited changes to

---

[84] J. ZALEŚNY, The Parliament as the Supreme and only True Authority [Parlament władzą najwyższą i jedyną prawdziwą], *Dziennik Gazeta Prawna* Daily, No. 230, D7. 29, 29.11.2016. The author superbly and synthetically reconstructs the concept of the system of government espoused by the authors of the policy of 'good change' of the constitutional order without changing the Constitution of the Republic of Poland.

[85] J. KRANZ, The Concept of Sovereignty in Contemporary International Law [Pojęcie suwerenności we współczesnym prawie międzynarodowym], Dom Wydawniczy Elipsa, Warsaw 2015, p. 50.

[86] M. MATCZAK, 'Poland: From Paradigm to Pariah? Facts and Interpretations of Polish Constitutional Crisis', available at https://papers.ssrn.com/sol3/papers.cfm?abstract_id=3138541, last accessed 26.06.2018.

the legal system, including changes to the constitutional order. The principle of *pacta sunt servanda* has given way to the *rebus sic stantibus* argument, as false but effective as it is. What is striking is that the electoral program of the victorious coalition did not ever cover this declaration of war on the constitution.

14. HOW TO SOLVE THE CRISIS?

An increasingly serious constitutional crisis has been growing over the past two years. But every crisis comes to an end.[87] In the political arena, there are calls for a solution to the political crisis. It is stated that a constitutional compromise is possible and that it could have a fundamental constitutional effect. The resolution of this kind of crisis cannot, however, be achieved through a constitutional compromise.

Are there any conclusions to be drawn or proposals to be made?

First, liberal democracy, but also the idea of an open society, has to recognise and respect the inviolability of the constitutional legal order. The Constitution is not only a guarantee of individual and community rights, it is also a fundamental moral idea. Secondly, the crisis caused by political decisions – actions and omissions – can be resolved correctly if such efforts take the Constitution as the starting point of all such efforts. The constitutional crisis cannot be solved outside the constitutional framework or even against the constitution. Thirdly, the constitutional crisis, as I indicated, had its source in the abuse of power by state authorities. An abuse of the law cannot be maintained through changes to the constitution. This would open the way to creating a permanent constitutional crisis as a mechanism for constitutional amendments. This should be avoided because there will always be parliamentary majorities that do not have the qualified majority required to take the road of a formal constitutional amendment. Fourthly, the crisis may be an opportunity. However, for the Constitution it is a weak opportunity. It is a *sui generis* test of the Constitution. However, the Constitution, the Constitutional Tribunal, the Supreme Court, the National Council of the Judiciary, the court system, the freedoms and rights of the individual are the victims of the crisis and they are too valuable for the state and society to be subject to such testing. The Constitution sets the limits of the political compromise that could resolve the constitutional crisis. Fifthly, the constitutional democracy model allows for an optimal compromise. An optimal compromise is characterised by maximal benefits and minimal loss. This means that the solution to the constitutional crisis should strengthen modern constitutionalism, i.e. the concept of a system

---

[87] M. WYRZYKOWSKI (2015), 'Bypassing the Constitution or Changing the Constitutional Order Outside the Constitution', *supra* note 1, p. 175.

of government where freedom, democracy, rule of law and individual rights are entrenched and thrive.

However, any discussion about the premises and methods of solving the constitutional crisis must consider the state of affairs as starting point for a return to the idea of democracy and the rule of law. This will not be the state of destruction, as to scope and depth, that I outlined in this article. The process of destruction continues, and one can expect that its dynamics will grow. It appeared to be easy to abolish the constitutional guarantees of democracy, the rule of law and the rights of the individual. They seemed inviolable due to their sound and systemic functions but were subjected to a stress test where they proved non-resilient as violations of law entailed no sanction. Because the basic bolts holding the system of enforcement of the Constitution have been removed, further changes in Polish legislation can be expected. This means that a balance sheet of the destruction can only be made when new political actors take the power and have the resolution to respect the constitutional order, democracy, the rule of law and the rights of the individual. Only this will mark the day that could be dubbed the 'day after'.

Only then and only according to the circumstances will it be possible and necessary to propose methods and ways of restoring constitutional democracy. There is no doubt, however, that the model to be adopted will integrate a model of transitional justice. In 1989, the Polish model for resolving political conflict known as the 'Round Table' became a model for transition processes in the countries of Central and Eastern Europe (post-Soviet states). It was the source of pride and satisfaction. The satisfaction was political, legal, economic and ethical because it was a process of moving away from political, social and economic slavery to democracy, rule of law and individual rights. When it is possible to make an inventory of the constitutional state of the country, it will be possible to propose a name of the state of affairs that will be the beginning of the path to the return to the standards of modern constitutionalism. The correctness of the diagnosis will be the premise of the correctness of the methods fit to restore those standards.

PART II
EU

THE COURT OF JUSTICE OF THE EUROPEAN UNION AND HUMAN RIGHTS IN 2017

Hans-Peter Folz and Eva Radlgruber

1. The Right to Asylum. 48
   1.1. The Refugee Status 49
   1.2. Humanitarian Visa. 51
2. The Right to Hold a European Citizens' Initiative 54
   2.1. Minority Safepack 54
   2.2. TTIP: The *Efler* Case 55
   2.3. The *Anagnostakis* Case. 56
   2.4. Conclusion 57
3. Data Protection: *Opinion 1/15* 58
   3.1. Background. 58
   3.2. The Legal Basis of the PNR Agreement. 59
   3.3. The Merits of the PNR Agreement. 60
   3.4. Conclusion 62
4. Non-Discrimination. 62
   4.1. Religion: Headscarf Ban in the Work Place 62
       4.1.1. The *Achbita* Judgment 63
       4.1.2. The *Bougnaoui* Judgment. 64
       4.1.3. Conclusion. 65
   4.2. Age: The *Fries* Case 65
5. Rule of Law 66
   5.1. Judical Protection against Restrictive Measures:
        The *Rosneft* Case. 66
       5.1.1. Background 67
       5.1.2. The Judgment. 68
       5.1.3. Conclusion. 69
   5.2. Judicial Protection against Measures of Administrative
        Cooperation 70
   5.3. *Nulla Poena Sine Lege* and the Protection of EU Financial
        Interest. 72
6. Conclusion. 74

ABSTRACT

In 2017, the Court of Justice of the European Union (CJEU) delivered several highly important judgments and opinions in the field of human rights law. The present article aims to provide an overview of this jurisprudence. It considers the most important cases in the fields of asylum law, the right to hold a European Citizens' Initiative, data protection, non-discrimination, and the rule of law. Following a summary of each case discussed, it analyses the relevant aspects concerning human rights protection. The article finally concludes that the case law of the CJEU in the field of human rights law remains ambivalent. While some cases show further improvement in protecting the individual, other cases still show a strong tendency of relying on a utilitarian approach to human rights.

1. THE RIGHT TO ASYLUM

The Right to Asylum under Article 18 of the EU Charter of Fundamental Rights[1] (CFR) is of immense practical importance as the Common European Asylum System (CEAS) is still struggling with the consequences of the refugee crisis of 2015.[2] The jurisprudence of the European Court of Justice (ECJ) in 2017 on the matter has also clarified issues that are of general importance for EU human rights law and doctrine.

---

[1] See C. THIELE, 'Art 18 GRC', in M. PECHSTEIN, C. NOWAK and U. HÄDE (eds.), *Frankfurter Kommentar EUV GRC AEUV*, Band I, Mohr Siebeck, Tübingen 2017, pp. 1258ff rec. 1ff.

[2] See generally S. PEERS, 'Volume 3: EU Asylum Law', in S. PEERS, V. MORENO-LAX, M. GARLICK et al. (eds.), *EU Immigration and Asylum Law (Text and Commentary): Second Revised Edition*, Brill Nijhoff, Leiden 2015; D. THYM, 'Schnellere und strengere Asylverfahren – Die Zukunft des Asylrechts nach dem Beschleunigungsgesetz', (2015) 34(23) *NVwZ*, pp. 1625–1633; H.-J. PAPIER, 'Asyl und Migration als Herausforderung für Staat und EU', (2016) 69(33) *NJW*, pp. 2391–2396; D. DREYER, 'Europäische Gerichte als Akteure einer individualrechtlich orientierten Asylpolitik', (2014) 34(10) *ZAR*, pp. 359–365; W. KANTHER, 'Verfassungsrechtliche Vorgaben zur europäischen Asylpolitik', (2018) 51(2) *ZRP*, pp. 47–49; A. PEUKERT, C. HILLGRUBER and U. FOERSTER et al., 'Einreisen lassen oder zurückweisen? Was gebietet das Recht in der Flüchtlingskrise an der deutschen Staatsgrenze?', (2016) 36(4) *ZAR*, pp. 131–136; H.O. ZINELL, 'Die "Flüchtlingskrise", die Rechtsprechung des EuGH und die "Gefährder"', (2018) 39(3) *VBlBW*, pp. 89–97; A. WIECKHORST, 'Rechts – und verfassungswidriges Regierungshandeln in der sog. Flüchtlingskrise', (2016) 25(8) *ThürVBl*, pp. 181–189; T. KINGREEN, 'Mit gutem Willen und etwas Recht: Staatsrechtslehrer in der Flüchtlingskrise', (2016) 71(18) *JZ*, pp. 887–890; D. THYM and K. HAILBRONNER, 'Grenzenloses Asylrecht? Die Flüchtlingskrise als Problem europäischer Rechtsintegration', (2016) 71(15–16) *JZ*, pp. 753–763; S. FONTANA, 'Verfassungsrechtliche Fragen der aktuellen Asyl-und Flüchtlingspolitik im unions- und völkerrechtlichen Kontext', (2016) 35(11) *NVwZ*, pp. 735–742; S. F. NICOLOSI, 'Going Unnoticed? Diagnosing the Right to Asylum in the Charter of Fundamental Rights of the European Union', (2017) 23(1–2) *European Law Journal*, pp. 94–117; CJEU (ECJ), *Majid Shiri v Bundesamt für Fremdenwesen und Asyl*, Case C-201/16, 25.10.2017, ECLI:EU:C:2017:805.

1.1. THE REFUGEE STATUS

Many systems of human rights protection have a general concept that individuals responsible for acts of persecution and violations of human rights should not benefit from fundamental rights and freedoms themselves. Enemies of freedom should not benefit from fundamental rights while they are trying to subvert them. At the very least, the rights of the enemies of human rights can be restricted more severely than those of other beneficiaries. Thus, Article 17 of the European Convention on Human Rights (ECHR) contains a prohibition of abuse of rights, which makes it clear that the ECHR may not be interpreted as allowing any act aimed at the destruction of the rights guaranteed in the Convention. In the same vein, Article 1 section F of the 1951 Geneva Convention relating to the Status of Refugees (CSR51) states that the provisions of the Convention shall not apply to any person who is guilty of acts contrary to the purposes and principles of the United Nations (UN).[3] The CFR, however, does not contain a similar clause. The EU acts constituting the CEAS incorporate the CSR51 exception from the refugee status into EU law.[4] Consequently, individuals seeking international protection in the EU do not qualify as refugees if they have committed acts contrary to the purposes and the principles of the UN.

In the *Lounani* case,[5] the individual asking for protection had been a leading member of an Islamist terrorist organisation. He had been sentenced by Belgian courts to six years in prison. However, in his application for refugee status he argued that he had not perpetrated violent acts of terrorism himself.

---

[3] Convention relating to the Status of Refugees (adopted 28 July 1951), 189 UNTS 137, 1951 Refugee Convention.

[4] Council Directive 2004/83 EC of 29 April 2004 on minimum standards for the qualification and status of third country nationals or stateless persons as refugees or as persons who otherwise need international protection and the content of the protection granted, OJ L 304/12, 30.04.2004; Art. 12 para. 2: 'A third country national or a stateless person is excluded from being a refugee where there are serious reasons for considering that: (a) he or she has committed a crime against peace, a war crime, or a crime against humanity, as defined in international instruments drawn up to make provision in respect of such crimes; (b) he or she has committed a serious non-political crime outside the country of refuge prior to his or her admission as a refugee; which means the time of issuing a residence permit based on the granting of refugee status; particularly cruel actions, even if committed with an allegedly political objective, may be classified as serious non-political crimes; (c) he or she has been guilty of acts contrary to the purposes and principles of the United Nations as set out in the Preamble and Article 1 and 2 of the Charter of the Unites Nations.'; Art. 12 para. 3: 'Paragraph 2 applies to persons who instigate or otherwise participate in the commission of the crimes or acts mentioned therein.'; now: Directive 2011/95/EU of the European Parliament and of the Council of 13 December 2011 on standards for the qualification of third-country nationals or stateless persons as beneficiaries of international protection, for a uniform status for refugees or for persons eligible for subsidiary protection, and for the content of the protection granted, OJ L 337/9, 20.12.2011.

[5] CJEU (ECJ), *Lounani*, Case C-573/14, 31.01.2017, ECLI:EU:C:2017:71.

Instead, he had provided logistical support and recruitment for the organisation. The Belgian Conseil d'État felt the need to refer the case to the ECJ under Article 267 of the Treaty on the Functioning of the European Union (TFEU) and asked whether acts, such as the ones committed in the main proceedings, could be considered as sufficient to trigger the exception from refugee status.

In its judgment the ECJ makes it clear from the outset, that EU norms must be interpreted in the light of the CSR51, since this convention constitutes the cornerstone of the international regime for refugee protection.[6] The exclusion from refugee status foreseen by EU law corresponds in essence to the exclusion clause in the CSR51.[7] The reasoning of the EU Directive 2004/83 even expressly refers in Recital 22 to acts of terrorism as contrary to the purposes and principles of the UN. Furthermore, the UN Security Council (UNSC) has decided in binding resolutions under Chapter VII of the UN Charter that acts, such as financing, planning, preparation as well as any other form of support must be considered as acts contrary to the purposes and principles of the UN.[8] The UNSC expressly made it clear that the concept of acts contrary to the purposes and principles of the UN could not be confined to acts, methods and practices of terrorism, in the sense of direct involvement in violent acts.[9] The fight against terrorism required a far wider range of measures, including the denial of safe haven and the prosecution of persons suspected of financing, planning, preparing or committing terrorist acts.[10] If the EU legislature had wanted to deviate from this wide concept, it could have easily done so by expressly narrowing down the scope of activities that would disqualify an asylum seeker from refugee status.[11]

The Court still had to deal with the question what level of personal involvement in terrorist acts was necessary in order to disqualify an individual from refugee status. It finds that the UNSC resolutions also sought to prevent activities such as the recruitment, organisation, transportation or equipment of individuals engaging in transnational terrorism. Consequently, the exclusion

---

[6] Ibid., paras. 41–42.
[7] See H.-P. FOLZ, 'Art 18 GRC', in C. VEDDER and W. HEINTSCHEL VON HEINEGG (eds.), *Europäisches Unionsrecht, EUV/AEUV/GRCh/EAGV, Handkommentar*, 2. Auflage, Nomos, Baden-Baden 2018, p. 1351, rec. 5.
[8] See e.g. UNSC Resolution 1377 (2001): 'The Security Council [...] [s]tresses that acts of international terrorism are contrary to the purposes and principles of the Charter of the United Nations, and that the financing, planning and preparation of as well as any other form of support for acts of international terrorism are similarly contrary to the purposes and principles of the Charter of the United Nations[.]'
[9] See e.g. UNSC Resolution 2178 (2014): 'Member States shall [...] prevent and suppress the recruiting, organizing, transporting or equipping of individuals who travel to a State other than their States of residence or nationality for the purpose of the perpetration, planning, or preparation of, or participation in, terrorist acts or the providing or receiving of terrorist training, and the financing of their travel and of their activities[.]'
[10] CJEU (ECJ), *Lounani*, supra note 5, paras. 45–48.
[11] Ibid., paras. 52–53.

clause cannot be confined to the actual perpetrators of terrorist acts but could extend equally to supporting activities such as recruitment. However, the national authorities may apply the exception clause only after undertaking an assessment of the specific facts for each individual case. Membership in the leadership of a terrorist organisation and logistical support, such as the forgery of passports as well as the assistance to volunteers to travel to other states, would justify the exclusion of refugee status.[12]

The outcome of the *Lounani* case is to be welcomed. Any other result would be hard to imagine, much less to accept. As the UNSC has decided under Chapter VII of the UN Charter ever since 9/11, international terrorism is a threat to international peace and security. The granting of refugee status to leading members of terrorist groups would seriously undermine any effort in the fight against terrorism. Equally, the exclusion from refugee status is well justified. Simply because a member of a terrorist group has not committed terrorist acts himself, does not mean he has no blood on his hands. Those seeking asylum, however, should come with clean hands.[13]

Nevertheless, the insistence of the Court on an assessment of all the relevant facts in each and every individual case points to a problem of continually evolving practical importance. Ever since the refugee crisis of 2015, an increasing number of asylum seekers admit to having been involved in the activities of terrorist organisations. However, they claim to have acted under duress, trying to save themselves or others from persecution. There is still a wide range of involvement whether voluntary or involuntary that raises the question of an application of the exclusion clause. Consequently, it seems unlikely that the *Lounani* judgment will be the last word of the ECJ on the matter.

1.2. HUMANITARIAN VISA[14]

One of the major contributions of the European Court of Human Rights (ECtHR) in Strasbourg to Human Rights Law doctrine is the concept of Positive Obligations.[15] Even if a fundamental right is phrased as a prohibition addressed to the state, preventing the state from interfering with the rights of the individual, sometimes this right will have a further dimension.[16] A fundamental

---

[12] Ibid., paras. 68–75.
[13] Maxim; see 'The Meaning of "Clean Hands" in Equity', (1922) 35(6) *Harvard Law Review*, pp. 754–757.
[14] CJEU (ECJ), *X and X v État belge*, Case C-638/16 PPU, 07.03.2017, ECLI:EU:C:2017:173.
[15] See A. MOWBRAY, *The Development of Positive Obligations under the European Convention on Human Rights by the European Court of Human Rights*, Hart, Oxford 2004.
[16] E. BREMS and J. GERARDS (eds.), *Shaping Rights in the ECHR: The Role of the European Court of Human Rights in Determining the Scope of Human Rights*, Cambridge University Press, Cambridge 2014.

right may impose positive obligations on the state, forcing it to take active steps in order to safeguard the rights of individuals against the encroachment by others or by other states. Another strand of human rights law doctrine is the concept of construing ordinary statute law in light of higher ranking human rights law.[17] Ordinary statute law is construed in conformity with human rights as to avoid a conflict between two sets of norms.[18] The ingenuity of the argument in the *Humanitarian Visa* case lies in connecting these two different strains of thought.

Syrian citizens travelled from Syria to Lebanon and submitted applications for humanitarian visas at the Belgian embassy in Beirut. They wanted to obtain visas on the basis of the EU Visa Code,[19] which would enable them to enter legally into Belgium and to apply for asylum there. The Belgian authorities rejected the application since the requirements of the EU Visa Code were not met. The applicants clearly wished to stay for a longer period in the EU, whereas the EU Visa Code allowed for a maximum stay of 90 days only. The applicants challenged this refusal before the administrative courts in Belgium and they expressly relied on positive obligations under EU human rights law. The EU Member States were held to be under a positive obligation to guarantee the right of asylum according to Article 18 of the CFR.[20] International protection in the EU would also be the only way to avoid the risk of inhuman treatment in the sense of Article 3 ECHR and Article 4 of the Charter. The Belgian Court referred the matter to the ECJ under Article 267 TFEU asking the Court whether a right to a humanitarian visa could be inferred from an interpretation of the Visa Code in the light of EU Fundamental Rights guaranteed by the Charter.

Adopting a very strict and narrow approach to the interpretation of the relevant EU secondary law, the Court found that the Visa Code did not apply to the kind of humanitarian visa which the applicants had in mind. The Visa Code had been adopted on the basis of Article 62 para. 2 lit. a and b (ii) of the pre-Lisbon EC Treaty. This legal base covered only visas for intended stays of no more than 90 days and therefore could not enable the EU legislature to provide for a humanitarian visa with a stay of potentially unlimited duration. Consequently, any application for a humanitarian visa would fall outside the scope of the EU Visa Code. In the view of the Court, this result was confirmed by the fact that there was a specific legal base for a humanitarian visa

---

[17] See A. MOWBRAY (2004), *The Development of Positive Obligations*, supra note 15.
[18] See C. BEZEMEK, *Grundrechte in der Rechtsprechung der Höchstgerichte*, Facultas, Vienna 2016, pp. 37–40.
[19] Regulation (EC) No 810/2009 of the European Parliament and of the Council of 13 July 2009 establishing a Community Code on Visas (OJ L 243, 15.09.2009), as amended by Regulation (EC) No 610/2013 of the European Parliament and of the Council of 26 June 2013, OJ L 182, 29.06.2013.
[20] See C. THIELE (2017), 'Art 18 GRC', supra note 1, pp. 1263–1264, rec. 11 f.

in Article 79 para. 2 lit. a TFEU. This Treaty base would allow regulation of the granting of long-term visas to third state nationals on humanitarian grounds. However, the EU legislature so far had not yet enacted such a legislative act, leaving the matter to national law. Since the Visa Code did not apply to the matter of humanitarian visas, the Member States were not bound by the CFR. They did not implement EU law in the sense of Article 51 para. 1 1st sentence of the Charter. The Court here expressly refers to its *Åkerberg Fransson*-jurisprudence.[21]

Since the Charter does not apply to the matter of humanitarian visas, there can be neither positive obligations resulting from its provisions nor can there be an interpretation of the Visa Code in the light of EU human rights.

The Court finds this result confirmed by that fact that the defining feature of the situation in this case is the difference in purpose of the application for a potentially long-term humanitarian visa if compared to a visa under the EU Visa Code. To conclude otherwise would mean allowing asylum seekers to apply for visa in order to obtain international protection in EU Member States. This, however, would run contrary to the purpose of the Visa Code, which did not intend to harmonise the law of international protection. Those acts of secondary law regulating international protection within the EU did not impose any such obligation on the Member States. On the contrary, they expressly excluded requests for diplomatic asylum from their scope of application.[22]

The result reached by the Court in the *Humanitarian Visa* case seems inevitable.[23] Any other outcome would have brought the CEAS to the brink of collapse. Far from benefiting individuals seeking protection in the EU, such a development would most likely have deepened the divide between the Member States and the EU. In addition to that, the reasoning by the Court manages to be persuasive. Indeed, the Court employs a strictly systematic and thorough method of interpretation which one would like to encounter more often in the jurisprudence of the Court. There is nevertheless one deficit in the line of reasoning. While the Court expressly refers to the *Åkerberg Fransson* judgment,[24] it neglects to mention the *Siragusa* judgment in which it had developed a list of criteria that would determine whether in a particular case the Charter would apply under Article 51 para. 1 1st sentence.[25] It is unclear whether the Court held a methodical assessment to be unnecessary or whether it sought to overrule *Siragusa*.

---

[21] CJEU (ECJ), *X and X v État belge*, supra note 14, paras. 40–45.
[22] Ibid., paras. 47–49.
[23] Diverging view in the Opinion of AG Mengozzi. See CJEU (ECJ), *X and X v État belge*, C-638/16 PPU, Opinion of AG Mengozzi, 07.02.2017, ECLI:EU:C:2017:93, paras. 71ff.
[24] See H.-P. Folz, 'The Court of Justice of the European Union and Human Rights in 2013–2014', in W. Benedek, F. Benoît-Rohmer, M.C. Kettemann et al. (eds.), *European Yearbook on Human Rights 15*, NWV/Intersentia, Graz/Antwerp 2015, pp. 109–111.
[25] See ibid., pp. 112–113.

One more aspect of the *Humanitarian Visa* judgment seems worthy of note. The ECJ insists that the matter of the humanitarian visa for the time being rests outside of the scope of application of secondary EU law. Consequently, the Member States retain the competence under Article 2 para. 2 TFEU to deal with the matter themselves. The granting of humanitarian visas lies within their discretion.

2. THE RIGHT TO HOLD A EUROPEAN CITIZENS' INITIATIVE

As reported last year,[26] the Right to a European Citizens' Initiative (ECI) according to Article 11 para. 4 TEU[27] is the only expression of the concept of direct democracy on EU level. Its introduction has raised high hopes among politically active Union citizens, who however fail to succeed more often than not. An increasing number of cases before EU courts demonstrate the limits of the ECI.

2.1. MINORITY SAFEPACK[28]

In 2013, a citizens' committee submitted a proposal for an ECI to the European Commission. The proposed ECI called for the protection of persons belonging to national and linguistic minorities, traditionally a highly controversial topic in many Member States. The committee had drafted a list of possible legal acts and corresponding legal bases in the Treaties, which in their view would have allowed the Commission to submit a set of formal proposals for legislation by the EU legislature. The Commission, however, refused to register the initiative. It argued that whereas a part of the proposed measures fell within the sphere of competence of the EU, others were not covered by the jurisdiction conferred on the Union under Article 5 para. 2 TEU. Since Regulation 211/2011[29] did not allow for a partial registration of a proposed initiative, the entire proposal was rejected. The committee sought

---

[26] See H.-P. FOLZ, 'The Court of Justice of the European Union and Human Rights in 2015–2016', in W. BENEDEK, M.C. KETTEMANN, R. KLAUSHOFER et al. (eds.), *European Yearbook on Human Rights 17*, NWV/Intersentia, Graz/Antwerp 2017, pp. 63–66.

[27] See S. HESELHAUS, 'Art 11 EUV', in M. PECHSTEIN, C. NOWAK and U. HÄDE (eds.), *Frankfurter Kommentar EUV GRC AEUV*, Band I, Mohr Siebeck, Tübingen 2017, pp. 418–430, rec. 54ff.

[28] CJEU (EGC), *Minority SafePack – one million signatures for diversity in Europe v Commission*, Case T-646/13, 03.02.2017, ECLI:EU:T:2017:59.

[29] Regulation (EU) No 211/2011 of the European Parliament and of the Council of 16 February 2011 on the citizens' initiative, OJ L 65/1, 11.03.2011.

annulment of the Commission's decision under Article 263 para. 4 TFEU before the EU General Court.[30]

In its judgment, the Court annulled the contested decision, finding the reasoning given by the Commission to be inadequate. In the view of the Court, the Commission should have indicated which of the measures that had been suggested in the proposal, were considered to be *ultra vires* and should have given reasons for such a legal opinion. Having failed to do so, the citizens' committee was not able to identify the potential defects in their proposal. They were prevented from contesting the merits of the Commission's assessment. For the same reason, the Court was not in a position to review the legality of the decision. The failure to provide a full statement of reasons also made it more difficult for the committee to submit a new revised proposal, which would have taken account of the Commission's concerns. Accepting such a result would run counter to the objective of the ECI, which is to encourage participation by citizens in the democratic life of the EU.[31]

2.2. TTIP: THE *EFLER* CASE[32]

In 2014, a citizens' committee had requested the Commission to register a proposal for an ECI that aimed at the cancellation of the mandate to negotiate the Transatlantic Trade and Investment Partnership (TTIP) with the United States and at refraining from the conclusion of the Comprehensive Economic and Trade Agreement (CETA) with Canada. The Commission issued a decision by which it refused to register the proposal, arguing that it would manifestly lack the powers necessary to forward such a proposal. The proposed measures would not be proposals for a legal act of the EU for the purpose of implementing the Treaties, as required by the wording of Article 11 para. 4 TEU.[33] The citizens' committee sought the annulment of the decision under Article 263 para. 4 TFEU before the General Court.[34]

In its judgment, the Court annulled the contested decision, refuting the opinion of the Commission that an international agreement, such as TTIP, could not be considered a legal act in the sense of Article 11 para. 4 TEU. In the view of the Court, the ECI pursued the objective to improve the democratic

---

[30] CJEU (EGC), *Minority SafePack – one million signatures for diversity in Europe*, supra note 28, paras. 8 ff.
[31] Ibid., paras. 32ff.
[32] CJEU (EGC), *Michael Efler v Commission*, Case T-754/14, 10.05.2017, ECLI:EU:T:2017:323; see J. BRAUNECK, 'TTIP, CETA, Brexit: Die Europäische Bürgerinitiative – ein Instrument der EU-Kommission?', (2017) 36(18) *NVwZ*.
[33] See S. HESELHAUS (2017), 'Art 11 EUV', supra note 27, pp. 418–430, rec. 54ff.
[34] CJEU (EGC), *Michael Efler*, supra note 32, paras. 1 ff.

functioning of the EU by granting every citizen a general right to participate in democratic life. This objective required a broader interpretation of the concept of legal act, one that would include a decision to open negotiations with third states aimed at the conclusion of an international agreement. Such an agreement would obviously seek an eventual modification of the EU legal order. Correspondingly, there was no conceivable valid reason to exclude the matter of opening or ending such negotiations from democratic debate. Neither would there be an inadmissible interference with an ongoing legislative procedure. An ECI would allow Union citizens to present in detail the questions raised in the initiative to the Commission, stimulating a democratic debate. This could not be considered an infringement of the principle of institutional balance. It is up to the Commission to decide whether or not it will accept an ECI. The Commission is only under an obligation to give its legal and political conclusions on a successful initiative, to communicate the action it intends to take and its reasons for taking or not taking that action.[35]

2.3. THE *ANAGNOSTAKIS* CASE[36]

As reported before,[37] the plaintiff, a Greek attorney at law, had asked the Commission to register a proposal aiming at the introduction of a principle of state necessity in EU law. Such principle would have allowed Member States to refuse repayment of state debts during an economic emergency. The Commission found that there was no appropriate legal basis for the enactment of corresponding secondary law and refused to register the Initiative. The plaintiff sought the annulment of the decision before the General Court under Article 263 para. 4 TFEU. The Court, however, rejected the claim, finding that indeed the Treaties did not provide the necessary legislative competence. The plaintiff appealed to the ECJ.[38]

In its judgment, the ECJ confirmed the judgment of the General Court. While the ECJ expressly accepts the importance of the ECI as a means for citizens to participate in the democratic life of the Union and stresses the need to give clear reasons for a refusal to register, here, the Commission had adequately explained its reasons. Therefore, the contested decision had provided a sufficient statement of reasons under Article 296 TFEU.[39]

---

[35] Ibid., paras. 21ff.
[36] CJEU (ECJ), *Anagnostakis v Commission*, C-589/15 P, 12.09.2017, ECLI:EU:C:2017:663.
[37] See H. P. FOLZ (2017), 'The Court of Justice of the European Union and Human Rights in 2015–2016', *supra* note 26, pp. 63–66.
[38] CJEU (ECJ), *Anagnostakis*, *supra* note 36, paras. 11–13.
[39] Ibid., paras. 22ff.

The ECJ confirms the view of the General Court that Article 122 para. 1 TFEU cannot be considered an adequate legal basis. This norm does not constitute an appropriate legal basis for financial assistance to member states facing a financial crisis. It cannot serve as a legal basis for the adoption of an EU measure that would allow a Member State to decide unilaterally not to repay all or part of its debt.[40]

Neither does Article 122 para. 2 TEU provide an appropriate legal basis in the view of the ECJ. Article 122 para. 2 TFEU cannot justify the introduction of a permanent and general mechanism for the abandonment of debt. Equally, the subject matter of Article 122 TFEU is solely the financial assistance granted by the Union and not by Member States. A principle of state necessity cannot be regarded as assistance granted by the Union. It would also cover not only debts owed to the Union, but debts owed to other natural and legal persons, both public and private.

The ECJ confirms the findings of the General Court on Article 136 TFEU as well. The role of the EU in the area of economic policy is restricted to the adoption of coordinating measures. The adoption of a legislative act authorising a member state not to repay its debt is not suited to strengthen the coordination of budgetary discipline. Instead, the introduction of such a principle would in fact result in replacing the free will of contracting parties with a legislative mechanism for the unilateral writing-off of sovereign debt.[41]

2.4. CONCLUSION

The jurisprudence of the EU courts shows that the Commission still tends to refuse to register proposals for ECIs – sometimes for good, more often for bad reasons. The impression is that the Commission is very much in favour of direct democracy in general, but not when it would place the Commission in an awkward position. This includes situations where the Commission would have to risk conflicts with the Member States if it actually accepted the proposal mandated by a successful initiative or where the Commission would be faced with a choice between antagonising third states or taking a decision unpopular within the Union itself. The judgments by the EU courts are to be welcomed because they show that the Commission must take the ECI seriously. On the other hand, the EU courts are also willing to respect the limits of EU competences under Article 5 para. 2 TEU.[42]

---

[40] Ibid., para. 31.
[41] Ibid., paras. 51 ff.
[42] See E. Pache, 'Art 5 EUV', in: M. Pechstein, C. Nowak and U. Häde (eds.), *Frankfurter Kommentar EUV GRC AEUV*, Band I, Mohr Siebeck, Tübingen 2017, pp. 201–217, rec. 17 ff.

3. DATA PROTECTION: *OPINION 1/15*

3.1. BACKGROUND

The European Court of Justice (ECJ) issued *Opinion 1/15*[43] on the draft agreement between Canada and the EU dealing with the Transfer of Passenger Name Record (PNR) data from the EU to Canada on 26 July 2017. It is noteworthy that this is the first time the ECJ has been called upon to give a ruling on the compatibility of a draft international agreement with the CFR.[44]

The PNR agreement was signed in 2014; the Council of the EU requested the European Parliament's (EP's) approval of the agreement. The draft agreement was referred to the ECJ by the EP under Article 218 para. 11 TFEU on 30 January 2015, in order to ascertain the compatibility of the envisaged agreement with EU primary law, and in particular, the compatibility with provisions guarding the respect for private life and the protection of personal data.

The envisaged agreement regulates the exchange and processing of PNR data between the EU and Canada. PNR data reveal passengers' personal information, such as the names of the air passengers, itinerary, and travel habits and preferences. It permits the systematic and continuous transfer of PNR data to a Canadian authority with a view to that data being used and retained, and possibly transferred subsequently to other authorities and to non-member countries, for the purpose of combating terrorism and other forms of serious transnational crime. The draft agreement provides for a data storage period of five years and further lays down certain requirements in relation to PNR data security and integrity.

Following the *Schrems* decision of the ECJ in 2015,[45] the adoption of the agreement proves to be of significant relevance as the Court held that the

---

[43] CJEU (ECJ), *Opinion 1/15*, Opinion of the Court pursuant to Article 218 para. 11 TFEU, 26.07.2017, ECLI:EU:C:2016:656.
[44] For a discussion see C. KUNER, 'International Agreements, Data Protection, and EU Fundamental Rights on the International Stage: Opinion 1/15, EU-Canada PNR', (2018) 55(3) *CMLRev*, pp. 857–882; A. VEDASCHI and C. GRAZIANI, 'PNR Agreements between fundamental rights and national security: Opinion 1/15', *European Law Blog*, 23.01.2018, available at http://europeanlawblog.eu/2018/01/23/pnr-agreements-between-fundamental-rights-and-national-security-opinion-115, last accessed 20.06.2018; L. WOODS, 'Transferring personal data outside the EU: Clarification from the ECJ?', *EU Law Analysis*, 04.08.2017, available at http://eulawanalysis.blogspot.co.at/2017/08/transferring-personal-data-outside-eu.html, last accessed 20.06.2018; S. SCHONHOFEN and A. HARDINGHAUS, 'CJEU has released Opinion on EU-Canada Passenger Name Record Agreement – What it means for international data transfer mechanisms', LEXOLOGY, 28.07.2017, available at https://www.lexology.com/library/detail.aspx?g=5c2feff6-8935-4fad-a12e-f72fd4272ffc, last accessed 20.05.2018; R. PRIEBE, 'EuGH beanstandet Fluggastdatenabkommen zwischen der EU und Kanada', (2017) 28(19) *EuZW*, pp. 762–766.
[45] CJEU (ECJ), *Schrems*, Case C-362/14, 06.10.2015, ECLI:EU:C:2015:650.

transfer of data to a third country is only possible, if the country ensures an adequate level of protection. The standard of an adequate level of protection can be assessed, according to the ECJ, by an adequacy decision of the European Commission, or alternatively, by international commitments in place between the EU and third-countries, e.g. such as the one examined by the Court in this decision.[46]

Given the nature of the draft agreement, it is not surprising that the focus of the Opinion lies on balancing liberty and security. In a realistic approach, the ECJ considers mass surveillance – at least in theory – tolerable, as a useful tool in prevention of terrorism. However, the Court clearly states the need for very strict rules regarding the implementation of such surveillance.

The Court found that the PNR agreement may not be concluded in its current form because several of its provisions are incompatible with Article 7 and 8 of the CFR and therefore the EU institutions will have to renegotiate the draft agreement with Canada.

The Opinion given by the Court can generally be divided into two parts, which are focused on the one hand on procedural aspects and on the other hand on substantive aspects. The former addresses the legal basis for the Council's decision on the signature of the agreement, while the latter deals with the merits of the draft agreements, especially the compatibility with the CFR.

3.2. THE LEGAL BASIS OF THE PNR AGREEMENT

First, the Court noted that the agreement fell within the EU's constitutional framework, and therefore, must comply with its constitutional principles. Although the ECJ did not state this expressly, this includes the respect for fundamental human rights.[47]

After dealing with questions of admissibility, the Court addressed the question of an appropriate legal base in the Treaty. In this context, the ECJ found that the draft agreement has two aims: safeguarding public security and safeguarding personal data.[48] The Court concluded that these two objectives are inseparably intertwined: whilst the need for a PNR agreement is the protection

---

[46] See H.-P. Folz (2017), 'The Court of Justice of the European Union and Human Rights in 2015–2016', *supra* note 26, pp. 81–84; L.-J. Wagner, 'Daheim ist`s am schönsten – Anmerkungen zum Urteil Schrems', 13.10.2015, available at http://www.juwiss.de/73-2015/, last accessed 20.06.2018; E. Radlgruber, 'Der EuGH als sicherer Hafen für den europäischen Datenschutz? Das Urteil des EuGH in der Rechtssache Schrems', (2016) 27(1) *JAP*, pp. 31–34; L. Marx and L. Wüstenhof, 'CJEU shuts down Safe Harbor for Transatlantic Data Transfer – Case C-362/14 Maximilian Schrems v. Data Protection Commissioner', (2015) 4(6) *EuCML*, pp. 242–246.
[47] CJEU (ECJ), *Opinion 1/15*, *supra* note 43, paras. 66ff.
[48] Ibid., para. 90.

of public security, the transfer of data can only be lawful if data protection rules apply.[49]

The ECJ held – contrary to what the Council claimed – that the decision could not be based on Article 82 para. 1 lit d TFEU, as none of the provisions of the draft agreement envisaged a facilitation of judicial cooperation. Further, the Canadian authority in charge of the PNR data is not a judicial authority, nor equivalent to it.[50] In accordance with the Council the Court went on to consider Article 87 para. 2 lit a TFEU as legal basis, as the draft agreement deals with police cooperation. Further, it should be based on Article 16 TFEU – the right to data protection – uniting the two aims of the draft agreement: the protection of public security and the protection of personal data.

3.3. THE MERITS OF THE PNR AGREEMENT

In the second part of *Opinion 1/15*, the Court performed a classic proportionality test: it assessed whether there is an interference with fundamental rights to privacy or data protection; whether such interference is justified in light of an objective of general interest; and whether such interference is proportional. Again, it is noteworthy, as mentioned above, that it is the first time that the ECJ has ruled on the compatibility of a draft international agreement with the CFR.

Looking at the issue of data protection the Court stated that the agreement was contrary to the rights guaranteed by Article 7 and Article 8 CFR.[51] The ECJ analysed each provision of the draft agreement to determine whether they were clear and precise enough to be limited to what is strictly necessary.

First, the Court found that certain headings of the agreement do not specify concerned data in a clear and precise manner.[52] Further, sensitive data (e.g. data revealing religious belief, ethnic origins, etc.) cannot be transferred to a third country such as Canada without a precise and particularly solid reason beyond that of public security. Notably, the prevention of terrorism is not considered sufficient reason to transfer sensitive data. The ECJ continues by stating that Directive (EU) 2016/681 ('PNR Directive')[53] prohibits the processing of sensitive data.

Second, while the agreement tried to limit the impact of automated decision-making, the Court found it problematic. It warned that databases

---

[49] Ibid., para. 94.
[50] Ibid., para. 103.
[51] See H.-P. FOLZ, 'Art 8 GRC', in C. VEDDER and W. HEINTSCHEL VON HEINEGG (eds.) (2018), *Europäisches Unionsrecht, supra* note 7, pp. 1333–1334, rec. 9.
[52] CJEU (ECJ), *Opinion 1/15, supra* note 43, paras. 157ff.
[53] Directive (EU) 2016/681 of the European Parliament and the Council of 27 April 2016 on the use of passenger name record (PNR) data for the prevention, detection, investigation and prosecution of terrorist offences and serious crime, OJ L 119/132, 04.05.2016.

with which data is crossed-checked should be reliable, up to date and limited to databases used by Canada in relation to the fight against terrorism and serious transnational crime.[54]

Next, the Court focused on definitions: in terms of the purposes for processing the data, the definition of terrorist offences and serious transnational crime were sufficiently clear. The agreement, however, says that PNR data can be processed, in exceptional circumstances, also for 'other purposes', which according to the ECJ is too vague.[55]

In line with its earlier case law, the Court went on to focus on the data retention mechanism contained by the draft agreement. Relying on its recent judgments in *Schrems*[56] and *Tele2*,[57] the ECJ reiterated that there must be a connection between the data retained and the objective pursued. This connection should be established by objective criteria, resulting in the existence of substantive and procedural conditions governing the use of data. When applying these principles to the draft agreement, several problems arise: first, the agreement allows for the data to be retained for five years from the moment of collection. While the data must be masked after 30 days, it is however still possible to unmask it afterwards. Secondly, the data can be retained and used before the arrival and after the departure of the passengers. While there is a plausible connection between the retention before the passengers' arrival, there is no clear connection between the retention and the objective pursued during the passengers' stay in Canada. The Court proposes that the use of such data should be subject to review by a court or an independent administrative body. As the agreement, however, does not provide for such a review, the use of data is not limited to what is strictly necessary.[58] Similar points were made, even more strongly, in relation to the use of PNR data after the passengers had left Canada. PNR data may be stored in Canada, however, when particular passengers present a risk of terrorism or serious transnational crime. It is remarkable though, that the ECJ did not address the envisaged retention period, contrary to what it had done in other judgments.[59]

Further, the agreement allows PNR data to be disclosed by the Canadian authority to other Canadian government authorities and to government authorities of third countries. The Court found that disclosure to Canadian authorities is not limited to what is strictly necessary because there is no

---

[54] CJEU (ECJ), *Opinion 1/15*, *supra* note 43, para. 172.
[55] Ibid., paras. 178–181.
[56] CJEU (ECJ), *Schrems*, *supra* note 45.
[57] CJEU (ECJ), *Tele 2 Sverige*, Case C-203/15, 21.12.2016, ECLI:EU:C:2016:970; see A. SANDHU, 'Die Tele 2 Entscheidung des EuGH zur Vorratsdatenspeicherung in den Mitgliedstaaten und ihre Auswirkungen auf die Rechtslage in Deutschland und in der Europäischen Union', (2017) 52(3) *EuR*, 453–469.
[58] CJEU (ECJ), *Opinion 1/15*, *supra* note 43, paras. 201–203.
[59] CJEU (ECJ), *Digital Rights Ireland*, Joined Cases C-293/12 and C-594/12, 08.04.2014, ECLI:EU:C:2014:238.

obligation to disclose in compliance with the conditions governing the use of data. Those conditions have been laid down in the Court's case law. In its decision *Tele2* the Court stated that the use of data must be subject to a prior review by a court or an independent administrative body.[60]

To ensure that the individuals' rights to access their data and to have data rectified is protected, according to the Court, passengers must be notified of the transfer of their PNR data to Canada and of its use as soon as that information is no longer liable to jeopardise the investigations of government authorities referred to in the draft agreement. The Court found the agreement in this respect to be deficient. While the ECJ accepted that the agreement provided passengers with a possible remedy, the agreement was deficient in that it did not guarantee in a sufficiently clear and precise manner that the oversight of compliance would be carried out by an independent authority, as required by Article 8 para. 3 CFR.

3.4. CONCLUSION

The Opinion of the Court gives rather specific and precise guidelines on how the agreement should be re-drafted, as it lays down the requirements that must be met when concluding agreements with third countries. The Court presents another step forward in the protection of privacy and data protection.

4. NON-DISCRIMINATION

4.1. RELIGION: HEADSCARF BAN IN THE WORK PLACE

The issue of Islamic headscarf has reached the ECJ through two preliminary references, *Achbita*[61] and *Bougnaoui*,[62] issued by Belgian and French Courts, respectively. On 14 March 2017, the Court upheld the banning of the visible display of any political, philosophical or religious sign in the workplace. The cases involved two female employees who were dismissed for refusing to remove their headscarves. Both cases concern the interpretation of genuine and determining occupational requirements and discrimination on the grounds of religion or belief.[63]

---

[60] CJEU (ECJ), *Opinion 1/15*, supra note 43, para. 202.
[61] CJEU (ECJ), *Samira Achbita, Centrum voor gelijkheid van kansen en voor racismebestrijding v G4S Secure Solutions NV*, C-157/15, 14.03.2017, ECLI:EU:C:2017:203.
[62] CJEU (ECJ), *Asma Bougnaoui, Association de défense des droits de l'homme (ADDH) v Micropole SA*, Case C-188/15, 14.03.2017, ECLI:EU:C:2017:204.
[63] See G. Davies, 'Achbita v G4S: Religious equality squeezed between profit and prejudice', *EUROPEAN LAW BLOG*, 06.04.2017, available at https://europeanlawblog.eu/tag/c%E2%

The first case – *Achbita* – was referred by the Court of Cassation in Belgium and deals with a Muslim woman who worked as receptionist for G4S. At the start of Ms. Achbitas' employment G4S had an unwritten rule that prohibited employees from wearing visible signs of political, philosophical or religious beliefs in the workplace. When Ms. Achbita informed her employer that she wanted to start wearing an Islamic headscarf, she was dismissed. The Court of Cassation then queried the interpretation of the EU directive on equal treatment in employment and occupation, by asking whether the prohibition on wearing an Islamic headscarf, which arises from general internal rules of a private undertaking, constitutes a direct discrimination.

The second case – *Bougnaoui* – concerns a French IT consultant who was requested to remove her headscarf after a customer complained. When Ms Bougnaoui refused to comply she also was dismissed. The French Court of Cassation went on to ask the Court, whether 'the willingness of an employer to take account of the wishes of a customer no longer to have the employer's services provided by a worker wearing an Islamic headscarf may be considered a "genuine and determining occupational requirement" within the meaning of Directive 78/2000/EC'.

Both applicants challenged their dismissal, claiming to be discriminated on the grounds of religion or belief contrary to Directive 78/2000/EC.[64]

4.1.1. The Achbita *Judgment*

In its judgment the Court found, that under the directive, the principle of equal treatment means that there is to be no direct or indirect discrimination whatsoever on the grounds of religion.[65] It went on to uphold that the directive does not include a definition of the term religion; however, the EU legislature referred to the ECHR and to the constitutional traditions common to the Member States.[66] Therefore, the concept of religion covers both the fact of having religious belief and the freedom to express that belief in public.[67]

        80%9115715-achbita, last accessed 20.06.2018; R. BANKEL, 'A Critical Commentary on the ECJ's Judgment in G4S v Achbita', *EJIL:Talk!*, 05.04.2017, available at https://www.ejiltalk.org/a-critical-commentary-on-the-ecjs-judgment-in-g4s-v-achbita, last accessed 20.06.2018; S. PEERS, 'Headscarf bans at work: explaining the ECJ rulings', *EU Law Analysis*, 14.03.2017, available at http://eulawanalysis.blogspot.com/2017/03/headscarf-bans-at-work-explaining-ecj.html last accessed 20.06.2017; E. BREMS, 'Analysis: European Court of Justice allows ban on religious dress in workplace', *IACL-AIDS BLOG*, 25.03.2017, available at https://iacl-aidc-blog.org/2017/03/25/analysis-european-court-of-justice-allows-bans-on-religious-dress-in-the-workplace, last accessed 20.06.2018.

64   Council Directive 2000/78/EC of 27 November 2000 establishing a general framework for equal treatment in employment and occupation, OJ L 303/16, 02.12.2000.
65   CJEU (ECJ), *Achbita*, *supra* note 61, para. 30.
66   Ibid., paras. 25–27.
67   Ibid., para. 28.

The ECJ continued and held that there was no direct discrimination, because 'the internal rule at issue [...] refers to the wearing of visible signs of political, philosophical or religious beliefs and therefore covers any manifestation of such beliefs without distinction. The rule must, therefore, be regarded as treating all workers of the undertaking in the same way by requiring them, in a general an undifferentiated way, to dress neutrally, which precludes the wearing of such signs'.[68]

The ECJ then considered the matter of indirect discrimination, which under Directive 78/2000/EC can be justified if the measure is objectively justified by a legitimate aim and if the means of achieving the aim are proportionate.[69]

The Court accepts a policy of political, philosophical or religious neutrality in relations with customers as a legitimate aim, linked to the freedom to conduct a business in Article 16 CFR. It went even further by considering the ban appropriate for the purpose of pursuing a policy of neutrality if the policy is 'genuinely pursued in a consistent and systematic manner'.[70]

The ECJ ruled that the ban of Islamic headscarves can be found strictly necessary if two conditions are met: first, it should cover only the employees who interact with customers. Secondly, a dismissal is allowed only if it is not possible to offer the applicant a post not involving any visual contact with customers.[71]

In short, the Court concluded that the prohibition of wearing an Islamic headscarf, which arises from an internal rule such as the one in question, does not constitute direct discrimination based on religion or belief within the meaning of the directive. By contrast, such a prohibition may constitute indirect discrimination, which may be justified by a legitimate aim.[72]

4.1.2. The Bougnaoui Judgment

In this case, where the headscarf ban was not part of a general neutrality policy but was based on client preference, the ECJ found a violation.[73]

The Court ruled that it was a case of direct discrimination on grounds of religion, which can only be justified in accordance with Article 4 para. 1 of the directive in case of a genuine and determine occupational requirement. According to the ECJ, the 'willingness of an employer to take account of the

---

[68] Ibid., para. 30.
[69] Ibid., paras. 33ff.
[70] Ibid., para. 39.
[71] Ibid., paras. 42–43.
[72] See E. BREMS, 'ECJ headscarf series (5): The Field in which Achbita will Land – A Brief Sketch of Headscarf Persecution in Belgium', 16.09.2016, available at https://strasbourgobservers.com/2016/09/16/ecj-headscarf-series-5-the-field-in-which-achbita-will-land-a-brief-sketch-of-headscarf-persecution-in-belgium, last accessed 20.06.2018.
[73] CJEU (ECJ), *Bougnaoui*, supra note 62.

wishes of a customer no longer to have the services of that employer provided by a worker wearing an Islamic headscarf cannot be considered a genuine and determining occupational requirement'.[74]

In summary, the Court concluded that in absence of any company rule, the mere desire of an employer to take into account the customers' wishes to ban religious symbols qualifies as direct discrimination.

4.1.3. Conclusion

Whilst the *Bouganaoui* case seems to be in line with the case law of the ECJ,[75] the *Achbita* judgment surprises and was criticised in literature.[76]

In general, the judgments mean that employers may ban employees from wearing headscarves, but only in certain cases. However, the cases only concern customer-facing employees, on the condition that the employer has a 'neutrality' policy. The weight given to a company's desire to promote neutral appearance seems a bit curious. Mainly, because it appears to contradict the ECtHR judgment in the case *Eweida and Others v the UK*.[77] The ECtHR held in that case, that it was a violation of the right to freedom of religion or belief when an employee was not allowed to wear a crucifix at work. The Court recognised that the employer's wish to protect a certain image could be regarded as a legitimate aim; it found that the national court put too much weight on this argumentation.

4.2. AGE: THE *FRIES* CASE[78]

Mr. Fries was employed as captain by Lufthansa until the end of October 2013 when he had reached the mandatory age limit of 65 years laid down in EU legislation for pilots of commercial aircrafts. He assumed that such age limit at issue constitutes a discrimination on grounds of age and infringes the freedom to choose an occupation.[79]

---

[74] Ibid., para. 41.
[75] CJEU (ECJ), *Centrum voor gelijkheid van kansen en voor racismebestrijding v Firma Feryn NV*, Case C-54/07, 10.07.2008, ECLI:EU:C:2008:397.
[76] See G. DAVIES (2017), 'Achbita v G4S', *supra* note 63; R. BANKEL (2017), 'A critical commentary', *supra* note 63; S. PEERS (2017), 'Headscarf bans at work', *supra* note 63; E. BREMS (2017), 'European Court of Justice allows ban on religious dress in workplace', *supra* note 63.
[77] ECtHR, *Eweida and others v the United Kingdom*, nos 48420/10, 59842/10, 51671/10 and 36516/10, 27.05.2013.
[78] CJEU (ECJ), *Werner Fries v Lufthansa CityLine GmbH*, Case C-190/16, 05.07.2017, ECLI:EU:C:2017:513.
[79] See H.-P. FOLZ, 'Art 21 GRC', in C. VEDDER and W. HEINTSCHEL VON HEINEGG (eds.) (2018), *supra* note 7, p. 1355, rec. 6.

The ECJ handed down its judgment on 5 July 2017 and acknowledged that the age limit set out under EC Regulation 1178/2011 is discriminatory but ruled that such a discrepancy in treatment is justified to protect aviation safety.

The Court ruled that it is an appropriate means of maintaining an adequate level of civil aviation safety to prohibit holders of a pilot's license who have attained the age of 65 from acting as pilot of aircraft engaged in commercial air transport.[80] It weighed the potential hardship suffered by pilots affected by the cap against benefits derived by society and concluded that the age limit was a proportionate restriction that was justified by safety objectives.

The ECJ further held that pilots are an essential element in the chain of actors in air navigation. In that context, adopting measures to ensure that only those persons having the necessary physical capabilities are authorised to pilot aircraft is essential for the purpose of minimising the risk of failures of human error.

Further, the Court acknowledged that the age limit did restrict Fries's freedom to choose an occupation but said the cap did not restrict him or other pilots over 65 from operating ferry flights without any passengers or cargo on board, or from working as an instructor or examiner on a board flight.

5. RULE OF LAW

5.1. JUDICAL PROTECTION AGAINST RESTRICTIVE MEASURES: THE *ROSNEFT* CASE

On 28 March 2017 the ECJ delivered the long-awaited judgment in the *Rosneft* case.[81] The Court decided in a preliminary ruling under Article 267 TFEU that restrictive measures adopted by the Council against Russian undertakings are valid. The judgment is of great significance, as it first, clarifies the scope of the Court's jurisdiction in the sphere of the EU's Common Foreign and Security Policy (CFSP), and secondly, it is an important precedent in the field of EU sanctions law in general.[82]

---

[80] CJEU (ECJ), *Werner Fries*, supra note 78, paras. 59ff.
[81] CJEU (ECJ), *Rosneft*, Case C-72/15, 28.03.2017, ECLI:EU:C:2017:236; see also CJEU (ECJ), *A and others v Minister van Buitenlandse Zaken*, Case C-158/14, 14.03.2017, ECLI:EU:C:2017:202.
[82] S.Ø. JOHANSEN, 'Judicial control of EU foreign policy: the ECJ judgment in Rosneft', *EU Law Analysis*, 29.03.2017, available at http://eulawanalysis.blogspot.co.at/2017/03/judicial-control-of-eu-foreign-policy.html, last accessed 20.06.2018; P. VAN ELSUWEGE, 'Judicial Review of the EU's Common Foreign and Security Policy: Lessons from the Rosneft case', *Verfassungsblog*, 06.04.2017, available at https://verfassungsblog.de/judicial-review-of-the-eus-common-foreign-and-security-policy-lessons-from-the-rosneft-case, last accessed 20.06.2018; T. HENZE and J. HAHN, 'Die Gemeinsame Außen- und Sicherheitspolitik der EU unter der Kontrolle des EuGH, Zum Urteil des EuGH in der Rs. Rosneft, C-72/15', (2017) 28(13)

5.1.1. Background

Since the Treaty of Lisbon, the Court has been entrusted with only a limited jurisdiction in relation to the CFSP. According to Article 24 para. 1 TFEU it 'shall not have jurisdiction with respect to these provisions [e.g. specific provisions on the CFSP enshrined in Chapter 2 TEU] with the exception of its jurisdiction to monitor compliance with Article 40 TEU and to review the legality of certain decisions as provided for by the second paragraph of Article 275 TFEU'. The latter provision further specifies that 'the Court shall have jurisdiction to monitor compliance with Article 40 TEU and to rule on proceedings, brought in accordance with the conditions laid down in the fourth paragraph of Article 263 of this Treaty, reviewing the legality of decisions providing for restrictive measures against natural or legal persons adopted by the Council on the basis of Chapter 2 of Title V of the Treaty on the European Union'. As has been argued, these provisions have made it possible for the Court, although within limits, to exercise judicial control with regard to certain CFSP acts. Literature calls Article 24 para. 1 second subparagraph TEU and Article 275 para. 2 TFEU, with its similar wording, 'claw-back' provisions, re-establishing jurisdiction of the Court in certain cases.[83]

The scope of this 'claw-back' clause is the key jurisdictional question in the *Rosneft* case: CFSP sanction regimes follow a specific structure, as they are enacted by using two separate legal instruments. In *Rosneft* these are, on the one hand, Decision 2014/512 – adopted on the basis of Article 29 TEU – concerning restrictive measures towards Russia's actions destabilising the situation in Ukraine. On the other hand, the implementation of that decision in the EU legal order, Regulation 833/2014. Recalling the Court's famous *Kadi* judgment, the ECJ leaves no doubt whatsoever that it must ensure the full review of legality of all acts adopted on the basis of the TFEU.[84]

In *Rosneft*, both the Decision and the accompanying Regulation were challenged. The question was whether the Court can assert jurisdiction and provide a court of a Member State with an interpretation of Union law in a case referred to it under Article 267 TFEU, when the subject matter is in regard with the CFSP.[85]

EuZW, pp. 506–511; J.M. HOFFMANN, 'Rechtsschutz gegen individualgerichtete Embargomaßnahmen in Vorabentscheidungsverfahren', (2018) 37(1–2) *NVwZ*, pp. 34–38; G. HAFNER, 'Völkerrechtliche Grenzen und Wirksamkeit von Sanktionen gegen Völkerrechtssubjekte', (2016) 76(2) *ZaöRV*, pp. 391–413.

[83] See e.g. P. VAN ELSUWEGE (2017), 'Judicial Review of the EU's Common Foreign and Security Policy', *supra* note 82.

[84] CJEU (ECJ), *Kadi and Al Barakaat International Foundation*, Joined Cases C-402/05 P and C-415/05 P, 03.09.2008, ECLI:EU:C:2008:461; see H.-P. FOLZ (2015), 'The Court of Justice of the European Union and Human Rights in 2013–2014', *supra* note 24, pp. 116–119.

[85] CJEU (ECJ), *Rosneft*, *supra* note 81.

AG Wathelet came to the conclusion that the Court did have jurisdiction to answer the question.[86] Whilst acknowledging the Court's jurisdiction in CFSP matters appears to be limited by Article 24 para. 1 TEU and Article 275 TFEU 'at first sight',[87] he skirted a narrow interpretation of Article 263 TFEU and its apparent lack of foresight of preliminary references.[88]

For the mentioned Article 24 para. 1 TEU and Article 275 TFEU, it can be assumed that there was a need for them to have the intended same effect. However, according to AG Wathelet, they are worded differently and thus might put out the 'false impression' of the Court not having jurisdiction. Hence, the two articles enable the Court to 'review the compliance with Article 40 TEU of all CFSP acts',[89] regardless of the way the question ends up at the Court.

5.1.2. The Judgment

Before going into matters of substance, the Court had to handle the question of jurisdiction. The Council had queried whether the questions referred by the national court could have been answered only in respect of the Regulation, rather than challenging the validity of the Decision, as the Decision constitutes an act of the CFSP and the Regulation does not.[90] The Court rejected this viewpoint, stating that it is solely up to the national courts to ask questions on the interpretation of EU law. The Court can, therefore, only not answer a reference when it fails to have a legal question in need of answering or is only a hypothetical question.[91]

Furthermore, the Court stated that only focusing on reviewing the legality of the Regulation, and not the questions asked as a whole would not be adequately answering the questions asked of it.[92] Moreover, despite the sharp distinction between a CFSP act and non-CFSP act, in order to impose a sanction within the EU legal order, the Court noted that they are inextricably tied. The fact how sanctions are imposed in the legal order is a perfect demonstration of the possibility of a close tied relationship between CFSP and non-CFSP legal bases, given the Court in *Kadi* said the link occurs[93] when it has been made explicit. In *Rosneft*, the Court, however, went on to state that even if the latter Regulation implementing a CFSP Decision was to be declared invalid, that would still

---

[86] CJEU (ECJ), *Rosneft*, Case C-72/15, Opinion of AG Wathelet, 31.05.2016, ECLI:EU:C:2016:381.
[87] Ibid., para. 39.
[88] Ibid., paras. 40ff.
[89] Ibid., para. 65.
[90] CJEU (ECJ), *Rosneft*, supra note 81, para. 48.
[91] Ibid., paras. 49ff.
[92] Ibid., para. 53.
[93] CJEU (ECJ), *Kadi and Al Barakaat International Foundation*, supra note 84, para. 202.

mean that a Member State was to conform to a CFSP Decision. Thus, in order to invalidate a Regulation following a CFSP Decision, the Court would have to have jurisdiction to examine that CFSP Decision.[94]

In a next step, the Court proceeded with answering substantive questions. The ECJ stated that Articles 19, 24 and 40 TEU, Article 275 TFEU and Article 47 CFR must be interpreted, as meaning that the Court has jurisdiction to give preliminary rulings on the validity of an act adopted on the basis of provisions relating to the CFSP.[95] The Court's assertion of its jurisdiction must, however, meet one of two conditions: First, it must relate to Article 40 TEU on the Court having the jurisdiction to determine the boundary between CFSP and non-CFSP in its border-patrolling role. Second, it involves the legality of restrictive measures against natural or legal persons.[96] This means that according to the Court, as far as the judicial review of restrictive measures against natural or legal persons is concerned, the coherence of the EU system of judicial protection is preserved and there is no difference in comparison to any other area of EU law.

Finally, the judgment contributes to the expanding case law regarding the EU's sanctions policy. The ECJ analysed all arguments brought forward by *Rosneft* carefully and rejected all claims with a reference to the Council's broad discretionary powers, especially in relation to issues of foreign and security policy.[97]

The Court further states that the level of detail of the CFSP decision does not affect its qualification as a non- legislative act. The exclusion of the right to adopt legislative acts in the area of the CFSP reflects the intention that policy should be subject to specific rules and procedures.[98]

The ECJ also confirms that the sanctions against Russian companies in relation to the Ukraine crisis can lawfully be adopted for the protection of essential EU security interests and for the maintenance of international peace and security.[99] The objective of maintaining peace and security further justifies the negative consequences for individual operators such as *Rosneft*.[100]

5.1.3. Conclusion

The Court's preliminary ruling in Rosneft is important in many respects. It upholds the coherence of the EU system of judicial protection as far as the

---

[94] CJEU (ECJ), *Rosneft*, supra note 81, para. 56.
[95] Ibid., para. 70.
[96] Ibid., para. 81.
[97] Ibid., paras. 82ff.
[98] Ibid., para. 91.
[99] Ibid., para. 113.
[100] Ibid., para. 150.

adoption of targeted sanctions is concerned and brings further legal clarity about the validity of those sanctions.

5.2. JUDICIAL PROTECTION AGAINST MEASURES OF ADMINISTRATIVE COOPERATION[101]

The Directive 2011/16/EU[102] on administrative cooperation in the field of taxation creates a system of administrative cooperation between the tax authorities of EU Member States. It allows one Member State to request another Member State for information that is foreseeably relevant to the collecting of taxes. The requested Member State directs a person, who is in possession of that information, to disclose the information and forwards it to the requesting Member State. The addressee of the information order does not have to be identical with the taxpayer under investigation. The interstate request is confidential; its content is to be treated as secret and must not be disclosed to the addressee of the information order.

During a review of the tax affairs of the French company Cofima, the French tax authorities sent a request for information to the Luxembourg tax authorities. The requested authority directed Berlioz, the parent company of Cofima, to provide the requested information. Berlioz complied in part, disclosing part of the required information. The company refused to divulge information that it did not deem relevant. In response, the Luxembourg tax authorities imposed on Berlioz a fine of €250,000. Berlioz contested the fine before the Luxembourg administrative court and sought the annulment of the decision. The court reduced the fine but held that it had no competence to annul the contested decision. On appeal, Berlioz argued that Article 47 CFR guaranteed a right to an effective remedy.[103] The Luxembourg administrative court referred the matter to the ECJ under Article 267 TFEU.

First, the ECJ found that by applying the mechanism provided by Directive 2011/16/EU, the Member States were implementing EU law, although the directive did not expressly foresee the imposition of financial fines. Consequently, the Member States were bound by the CFR under Article 51 para. 1. The Court went on to assess whether Article 47 of the Charter entitled the addressee of an information order to challenge the legality of that decision. Pointing to Article 19 para. 1 subpara. 2 TEU, the Court found that the obligation imposed

---

[101] CJEU (ECJ), *Berlioz Investment Fund SA v Directeur de l'administration des contributions directes*, Case C-682/15, 16.05.2017, ECLI:EU:C:2017:373.
[102] Council Directive 2011/16/EU of 15 February 2011 on administrative cooperation in the field of taxation and repealing Directive 77/799/EEC, OJ L 64/1, 11.03.2011.
[103] See H.-P. Folz, 'Art 47 GRC', in C. Vedder and W. Heintschel Von Heinegg (eds.) (2018), *supra* note 7, p. 1380, rec. 3.

on the Member States to provide effective remedies, corresponded to the guarantee under Article 47 CFR. The right to an effective remedy required the possible violation of a right under EU law. The Court recalled that the protection against arbitrary or disproportionate intervention by public authorities in the sphere of the private activities of any natural or legal persons amounted to a general principle of law, constituting a subjective right of the individual. This right could be invoked by a relevant person such as Berlioz, adversely affected by the information order. Thus, the addressee of an information order had a right to an effective remedy under Article 47 CFR.[104]

The ECJ then sought to find out whether the right to an effective remedy required that the addressee should be able to challenge the legality of the fine and whether such review would also include the information order and the original interstate request. The Court conceded that only a review of the legality of the information order and an incidental assessment of the interstate request enable the national courts to grant an effective remedy against the financial fine. The standard of review is, however, a very narrow one. The courts of the requested state are restricted to verify whether the information sought is not devoid of any foreseeable relevance to the investigation being carried out by the requesting authority. The Court recalled the principles underlying the system of administrative cooperation between EU Member States. This is founded on mutual trust and confidence, meant to ensure fast and efficient cooperation. The requested Member State must, in principle, trust the requesting authority and assume the legality of the request, since it does not generally have extensive knowledge on the law and facts in the case at hand. In particular, the requested authority cannot substitute its own assessment of the possible usefulness of the information sought. The judicial review therefore must also respect the requesting state's discretion.[105]

The final question raised by the Luxembourg administrative court concerned the right of access for the plaintiff to the original interstate request. The ECJ acknowledged that the equal right of access to relevant information was part of the guarantee to a fair trial. The principle of equality of arms implies that no party to a judicial proceeding is placed at a substantial disadvantage vis-à-vis its opponent. However, the Court holds that the rights of the defence may be restricted by the public interest. Therefore, it is sufficient if the deciding court has access to the interstate request. In order to establish the unlawfulness of the information order, it is necessary but sufficient to demonstrate that the requested information has no foreseeable relevance. Access to information contained in the interstate request is only necessary insofar as the Directive 2011/16/EU expressly provides it. If this information should prove inadequate,

---

[104] CJEU (ECJ), *Berlioz Investment Fund SA*, supra note 101, paras. 32–42.
[105] Ibid., paras. 44–59.

it would be up to the deciding court to provide additional information while taking due account of the confidentiality of that information.[106]

The Berlioz case demonstrates one particular aspect of EU law which makes the protection of Fundamental Rights in the EU more complicated than in national legal systems. Two or more Member States cooperate in the implementation of secondary EU law. By doing so, they interfere with the Fundamental Rights of Union citizens. The relevant acts of secondary law do not contain any provisions on the protection of individual rights nor do they provide for effective judicial remedies. In other words, individuals are treated as the object of administrative cooperation; fundamental rights are seen as an obstacle to a successful interstate cooperation. In addition to that, the responsibility for any interference with individual rights is in doubt. It is unclear whether responsibility lies with the requesting state, the requested state or the EU itself, given the fact that it provides the normative basis.

The Court here tries to balance the competing interests. It is to be welcomed that the ECJ safeguards the rights of the individual to a judicial remedy under Article 47 of the Charter.[107] However, whether this remedy will prove to be effective remains to be seen. The standard of the review of legality is extremely narrow and the treatment of the principle of a fair trial places a great burden on the national courts in each individual case. One might be tempted to think that the Court is primarily interested in upholding the principle of mutual trust and the functionality of administrative cooperation between Member States.

5.3. *NULLA POENA SINE LEGE* AND THE PROTECTION OF EU FINANCIAL INTEREST[108]

Two persons had been indicted for a serious case of VAT fraud in Italy. The Italian courts found that the prescription periods provided by Italian criminal law had lapsed and that the prosecution would be consequently time-barred. The ECJ, however, in its *Taricco* judgment had decided that under certain conditions the application of prescription rules under national criminal law would run counter to Article 325 TFEU. If prescription rendered the protection of EU financial interest ineffective, national courts would be under an obligation to disapply those national norms. The Italian Constitutional Court had serious doubts about the compatibility of this obligation that had been imposed on the national courts by the ECJ with the principle of *nulla poena sine lege*

---

[106] Ibid., paras. 90–101.
[107] See H.-P. FOLZ, 'Präambel GRC', in C. VEDDER and W. HEINTSCHEL VON HEINEGG (eds.) (2018), *supra* note 7, p. 1316, rec. 2.
[108] CJEU (ECJ), *M. A. S. and M. B.*, Case C-42/17, 05.12.2017, ECLI:EU:C:2017:936.

enshrined in Italian Constitutional Law, Article 7 ECHR and Article 49 of the CFR.[109] The Italian Constitutional Court pointed to the fact that in the Italian legal order prescription is considered as part of material criminal law. It referred the matter to the ECJ under Article 267 TFEU.

Recalling its earlier jurisprudence, the Court held that the Member States are under an obligation to provide criminal sanctions for serious cases of VAT fraud, which must be effective and deterrent. The application of prescription in such proceedings could jeopardise the protection of the EU financial interest. Such an infringement of Article 325 TFEU would impose a legal obligation on the national legislation to remedy the situation. The Court points out that a partial harmonisation had only taken place by the enactment of Directive 2017/1371 on the fight against fraud to the Union's financial interests by means of criminal law[110] and that the Italian Republic had been free to define criminal offences according to its own constitutional rules and discretion. This included the right to apply national standards of protection of fundamental rights, provided that such application did not compromise the primacy, unity and effectiveness of EU law.[111]

Nevertheless, Article 49 of the Charter would have to be observed by the Member States. By sanctioning VAT fraud, they implemented EU law in the sense of Article 51 para. 1 CFR and consequently were bound by the fundamental rights of the Charter. The principle that offences and penalties must be defined by law was also part of the general principles of law resulting from the common constitutional traditions of the Member States. In addition to that, the Court expressly refers to Article 52 para. 3 CFR making it clear that Article 49 CFR has the same meaning and scope as Article 7 ECHR. Summing up the relevant jurisprudence of the Strasbourg Court, the ECJ finds that provisions of criminal law must comply with certain conditions of accessibility and foreseeability as regards both the definition of the offence and the determination of the penalty. These requirements also applied in the Italian legal system for the limitation rules for criminal offences relating to VAT. Therefore, the national court would have to decide whether the non-application of prescription rules would lead to a situation of uncertainty. If the principle that the applicable law must be precise were breached, the national court would not be obliged to disapply the rules of prescription. Otherwise, persons could be thus made subject retroactively to conditions of criminal liability that were stricter than those in force at the time the infringement was committed.

---

[109] See H.-P. FOLZ, 'Art 49 GRC', in C. VEDDER and W. HEINTSCHEL VON HEINEGG (eds.) (2018), *supra* note 7, pp. 1386–1387, rec. 3.

[110] Directive 2017/1371 of the European Parliament and of the Council of 5 July 2017 on the fight against fraud to the Union's financial interests by means of criminal law, OJ L 198/29, 28.07.2017.

[111] CJEU (ECJ), *M. A. S. and M. B.*, *supra* note 108, paras. 34–47.

If the resulting application resulted in the impending impunity for acts of VAT fraud, it would be the responsibility of the national legislature to take the necessary steps.[112]

The judgment of the Court leaves an ambiguous impression. The reasoning followed by the Court offers many arguments. However, these do not add up to a coherent concept. It is not clear why the fact that Italian law sees prescription as part of material criminal law, should have a decisive influence on the outcome of the case. It would have made more sense if the Court had developed an autonomous concept of *nulla poena sine lege*, relying on the jurisprudence of the Strasbourg court.[113] Such a concept would have applied uniformly to all Member States.

However, we do not take issue with the result reached by the ECJ. The non-application of prescription in VAT fraud cases would have resulted in a situation of serious legal uncertainty undermining the rule of law. In addition to that, a possible difference of treatment, depending on whether a Member State would consider prescription as part of material criminal law or criminal procedure, would have led to arbitrariness. Therefore, the solution is to entrust the national legislature with the amendment of prescription rules. However, it should also be noted, that this means in effect a reversal of the *Taricco* judgment. If the Court decides to overrule its earlier jurisprudence, it should do so openly and in a transparent manner.

6. CONCLUSION

The jurisprudence of EU courts on human rights in 2017 shows further consolidation. Some judgments can be seen as a clear sign of commitment to the value of human rights protection, the protection of the individual as a value in itself. It is this value that shows the strength or weakness of a particular system of human rights protection. Even if to uphold this standard means to risk conflict with third states, even if it means taking politically unpopular decisions, the standard of protection provided by the courts shows the level of commitment to human rights. The judgments of EU courts show success and improvement as well as cases where a more utilitarian approach prevails. The impression given by the human rights jurisprudence of EU courts continues to be ambivalent, leaving room for further improvement.

---

[112] Ibid., paras. 52–61.
[113] On the relationship between prescription and *nulla poena sine lege* in the jurisprudence of the ECtHR see ECtHR, *Borcea v Romania*, no 55959/14, Decision of 22.09.2015, para. 64 and the case law cited therein. It should be noted that the ECtHR has considered but not decided the question whether the extension of an already lapsed prescription period could qualify as a breach of Article 7 ECHR – cf. ECtHR, *Coëme v Belgium*, no 32492/96 et al., 22.06.2000, para. 149.

UNDERSTANDING RESETTLEMENT THROUGH THE PRISM OF HUMAN RIGHTS

A Case Study on the Resettlement in Belgium of Syrian Refugees from Lebanon

Danaé Coquelet

1. Introduction 76
2. The Individual Factor: Expectations of Syrian Refugees from Lebanon.... 77
   2.1. Identifying Syrians' Expectations: Case Study and Methodology.... 77
   2.2. Resettlement Awareness 78
   2.3. Personal Expectations 79
       2.3.1. Security of Person, Education and Work: The Illusory Nature of the Traditional Dichotomisation................ 80
       2.3.2. Dignity in Forced Displacement: A Fundamental Dimension....82
   2.4. Expectations vis-à-vis Host Countries 84
   2.5. The Individual Factor: A Final Reflection..................... 86
3. The Legal Factor: Human Rights Approach to the Belgian Resettlement Scheme 87
   3.1. Compliance with Human Rights Standards 87
       3.1.1. Legal Framework Surrounding Resettlement 87
       3.1.2. Access to Housing and Healthcare 88
           3.1.2.1. Access to Housing 90
           3.1.2.2. Access to Healthcare 92
   3.2. Future Prospects: Towards More Violations of the Rights of Resettled Refugees? 94
       3.2.1. Civil Society Participation 94
           3.2.1.1. Specialised Actors 94
           3.2.1.2. Intermediaries 95
           3.2.1.3. Linguistic Mediators 95
           3.2.1.4. Facilitators for Access to Housing and Healthcare....96
           3.2.1.5. Lobbying Force................................ 98
       3.2.2. Non-Discrimination.................................... 99
   3.3. The Legal Factor: A Final Reflection 100
4. Conclusion.. 101

ABSTRACT

According to United Nations High Commissioner for Refugees (UNHCR), resettlement is one of the only three durable solutions for refugees. Despite the importance of this practice, little literature offers an in-depth analysis of its inherent challenges. Evidence shows that one of them is the existence of a gap between expectations in the pre-resettlement phase and reality in the post-resettlement phase. This article aims at shedding light on the resettlement practices of the State of Belgium in Lebanon from this particular perspective. Since 2013, Belgium has regularly carried out selection missions with the view to resettling Syrian refugees from Lebanon (SRL). The goal of the research is to highlight the root causes of the gap between their pre-resettlement expectations and their post-resettlement reality. It examines to what extent two factors – the individual factor and the legal factor – contribute to widening it. To this end, both qualitative and quantitative methods of research were used: 291 SRL were surveyed in Lebanon and a series of semi-structured interviews were conducted in Belgium with five resettlement actors (UNHCR, the Federal Agency for the Reception of Asylum Seekers (Fedasil), Commissioner General for Refugees and Stateless Persons (CGRS), Convivial, and Caritas) and ten resettled SRL. The article concludes that the root cause of the discrepancy is both individual and legal in nature: SRL develop unrealistic expectations, mostly due to a lack of knowledge about UNHCR's scheme and show low levels of satisfaction with the host country because the latter fails to acknowledge their vulnerability and adopt a human rights approach to resettlement.

1. INTRODUCTION

With thousands of applications submitted each year, the resettlement programme of the UNHCR is the largest worldwide. Resettlement is defined by UNHCR as 'the selection and transfer of refugees from a state in which they have sought protection to a third state which has agreed to admit them with permanent refugee status'.[1] For the most vulnerable, it is often a synonym for hope. After being selected for resettlement, refugees find themselves trapped between a painful past they wish to flee and a future they tend to idealise. A recurrent issue singled out by resettlement professionals is the gap between expectations in the pre-resettlement phase and reality in the post-resettlement phase. In the event that their expectations are not fulfilled, refugees show low levels of satisfaction with the host country, which has a direct influence on their integration process. In 2013, Belgium launched its first structural resettlement scheme and resettled 100 African refugees from the Great Lakes region.

---

[1] UNHCR, 'The UNHCR Resettlement Handbook', July 2011, p. 9, available at http://www.unhcr.org/46f7c0ee2.pdf, last accessed 09.05.2018.

Since then, the country's annual quota has been constantly revised upwards and reached a total of 1,100 refugees in 2017. The main focus of the programme was put on a new refugee population: Syrians. Lebanon, which is currently host to around 1.1 million Syrians, has become an attractive first country of asylum for Belgian authorities to carry out their selection missions. This article aims at shedding light on the root causes of the systematic gap between the expectations of Syrian refugees in Lebanon and their reality once resettled in Belgium. The analysis explores the influence of two factors – the individual factor and the legal factor – and the results should be read with the view to improve the quality of the Belgian resettlement programme.

2. THE INDIVIDUAL FACTOR: EXPECTATIONS OF SYRIAN REFUGEES FROM LEBANON

2.1. IDENTIFYING SYRIANS' EXPECTATIONS: CASE STUDY AND METHODOLOGY

Today, Lebanon is host to almost 1.1 million Syrian refugees.[2] Though all SRL are not eligible for it, resettlement with UNHCR is one of the few legal channels still available for them to travel abroad. The idea of being a potential resettlement beneficiary leads SRL to develop certain expectations. This section will raise two questions: can expectations of SRL be considered unrealistic? If so, do these hopes contribute to the creation of a gap between expectations and reality? Three main elements will be explored: resettlement awareness, personal expectations and expectations vis-à-vis resettlement countries.

Quantitative data collection was carried out by handing out a standard questionnaire in Arabic to a total of 291 SRL in April 2017. In order to obtain the most accurate and reliable data possible, both camp refugees and urban refugees were targeted. Refugees living in informal camps were surveyed in the Bekaa Valley: the Non-Governmental Organisation (NGO) Sawa for Development and Aid gave access to the Al-Dalhamia Camp; the NGO Salam Lebanese Association for Development Communication gave access to both camps and private houses located in Bar Elias, Taanayel and Haouch el Harimi. As for urban refugees in Beirut, the NGO Amel Association International opened the doors of two of its community centres: the Baajour Centre and the Haret Hreik Centre. Other urban refugees were surveyed in their homes in the Ras el Nabaa area.

---

[2] UNHCR, 'Syria Regional Refugee Response: Inter-Agency Information Sharing Portal', 2017, available at http://data.unhcr.org/syrianrefugees/country.php?id=122, last accessed 09.05.2017.

2.2. RESETTLEMENT AWARENESS

Resettlement awareness is considered high given that more than 80% of surveyed refugees said they had heard about UNHCR's resettlement programme. When carefully examined, results show that registration with UNHCR is a factor that influences refugees' awareness about resettlement: 84.6% of registered refugees were aware of the existence of a resettlement programme compared to only 68.5% of their non-registered peers. The place of residency is also an influential factor: camp refugees were on average more informed than urban refugees. Even though registration with UNHCR seems to have a positive impact on resettlement awareness, only 10.2% of surveyed refugees declared that they had been told about the programme by UNHCR's staff. Friends (45.2%) and the Internet, especially social media (35.7%), appeared to be the main sources of information. A number of camp refugees also mentioned that they had been told about the programme by an NGO. For instance, in the Bekaa Valley, refugees living in camps managed by Sawa for Development and Aid systematically answered positively when asked whether they had already heard of the possibility of being resettled. Most of them insisted that Sawa's staff had conducted information sessions about resettlement. This explains why figures show a higher level of resettlement awareness among camp refugees than among urban refugees. Being hosted in a camp managed by an NGO, refugees are exposed to more information as they are surrounded and taken care of by well-informed actors. On the contrary, their urban peers tend to be more isolated and, as a consequence, reachable with difficulty. Families met in the Bekaa Valley underlined the essential role played by Sawa in their camp: not only did Sawa inform about resettlement opportunities, but they also identified and referred vulnerable cases to UNHCR. This demonstrates that non-governmental actors are crucial intermediaries between refugees and UNHCR.

In its Resettlement Handbook, UNHCR stresses that 'an effective communication outreach programme is a key part of managing expectations'.[3] Evidence suggests that expectations tend to be amplified by rumours in communities, misunderstandings and a lack of information.[4] Under the current scheme, only refugees who satisfy UNHCR's criteria can be resettled and, though they might be encouraged to express their preferences, they are not able to choose their host country. As far as family reunification is concerned, UNHCR points out that 'family members and dependants seeking reunification

---

[3] UNHCR (2011), 'UNHCR Resettlement Handbook', *supra* note 1, p. 142.
[4] The Refugee Sponsorship Training Program, 'Managing Expectations: A Resource Kit for Refugee Sponsors', March 2013, p. 1, available at http://www.rstp.ca/wp-content/uploads/2014/03/expecttool2013.pdf, last accessed 09.05.2018.

with a resettled refugee may be considered for derivative status in accordance with their right to family unity'.[5] Relatives are expected to submit a claim for derivative refugee status and their application must be assessed and approved by both UNHCR and the resettlement country. Family reunification is not automatically granted. According to the survey, 20.7% of SRL believed that any refugee could be resettled and 52.4% of them did not know; 45% of them were convinced that they could choose their host country while 33.3% said they did not know. As to the statement 'Other members of my family can join me after my arrival', results are even more worrying: 54% of SRL ticked 'Yes' and 36.4% opted for 'I don't know', which suggests that fewer than 10% of refugees are aware of the additional conditions attached to the right to family reunification. In view of the results, it is self-evident that SRL lack basic knowledge about UNHCR's resettlement programme.

Despite the fact that most Syrians in Lebanon have heard about the possibility of being resettled, the functioning of UNHCR's resettlement programme remains vague for the great majority of them. UNHCR's awareness-raising strategies bear fruit to some extent but provide SRL with only a cursory knowledge of resettlement. Refugees tend to develop assumptions about submission categories, the possibility of choosing a resettlement country or the right to family reunification; their lack of in-depth knowledge about basic resettlement principles leads them to raise unrealistic expectations.

2.3. PERSONAL EXPECTATIONS

SRL also develop expectations directly linked to their personal situation. Traditionally, the search for a better future translates into a series of hopes. These expectations can be 'powerful in that they can motivate the refugees to do well if they are set high, and also cause disappointment and grief if they are not met'.[6] For the purpose of this analysis, the term 'expectations' will be understood as 'how the present and the future are framed based on past experiences, perceptions, emotions, imagination and desires – sometimes without a rational basis and with little available information'.[7] Syrians who found refuge in Lebanon face numerous hurdles on a daily basis; they were thus asked to identify a series of rights that they wished to fulfil through resettlement.

---

5   UNHCR (2011), 'UNHCR Resettlement Handbook', *supra* note 1, p. 79.
6   The Refugee Sponsorship Training Program (2013), 'Managing Expectations: A Resource Kit for Refugee Sponsors', *supra* note 4, p. 2.
7   Ibid.

2.3.1. Security of Person, Education and Work: The Illusory Nature of the Traditional Dichotomisation

The right to security of person (mentioned by 33.2% of respondents), the right to education (19.2%) and the right to work (13%) were identified as the main needs that could be satisfied through resettlement in a third country. Other rights such as the right to housing, the right to health, the right to asylum, the right to equality and non-discrimination, the right to reside, access to justice, freedom of thought, conscience and religion, and freedom of movement were also singled out.

The primacy of the right to security of person supports the idea that SRL's basic protection needs are not fulfilled. A Syrian refugee disclosed: 'I want safety, no fear of hunger and a future for my children. I want to get away from problems and wars. I dream of settling down and having a peaceful life.' Predictably, a significant number of refugees expressed other needs in relation to their legal status. For instance, issues such as the impossibility to be granted refugee status, the difficulty to obtain a residency permit or register children at birth, the obligation to have a sponsor and the lack of freedom of movement were mentioned. Also, SRL strongly emphasised difficulties regarding integration into the Lebanese society due to racism and discrimination. The following testimony gives an insight into this issue: 'I want security, a decent life and a better situation for my children and my family. I would also like us to stop living as victims of racism in Lebanon.' The right to education and the right to work emerged as the second and third priorities of SRL. The fact that SRL made mention of rights belonging to both civil and political rights and economic, social and cultural rights brings light to the debate surrounding their coexistence in the context of forced displacement.

By referring to education (19.2%) and work (13%), SRL demonstrated that economic, social and cultural rights are tangible. Due to the lack of international protection caused by the refusal of the State of Lebanon to ratify the 1951 Refugee Convention, many SRL are out of school or out of work. With 59% of school-aged SRL out of formal education,[8] human rights actors are warning that Syrian refugee children might be on the verge of becoming the next lost generation. With no legal access to the labour market, 71% of Syrian households are living under the poverty line, meaning on less than $4 a day.[9]

---

[8] UNHCR, '2017 March Statistical Dashboard', March 2017, available at http://data.unhcr.org/syrianrefugees/working_group.php?Page=Country&LocationId=122&Id=21, last accessed 09.05.2018.

[9] UNHCR, 'Livelihoods 2017 Quarter 1 Dashboard', 31.03.2017, available at http://data.unhcr.org/syrianrefugees/working_group.php?Page=Country&LocationId=122&Id=51, last accessed 09.05.2018.

Testimonies collected among SRL suggest that this lack of access to education and to the labour market makes SRL unable to fully develop their potential and rebuild a decent life. They are firmly convinced that economic, social and cultural rights are 'true rights, not mere aspirational targets'.[10] The traditional belief that economic, social and cultural rights should be progressively realised is questioned by their experience: they see these rights as a starting point rather than a distant goal. This echoes the view that economic, social and cultural rights are not social ideals but rather the basis for the 'equitable participation in the production and distribution of the values and resources' of the Lebanese society and the State of Lebanon must 'utilise its available resources maximally in order to redress social and economic imbalances and inequalities'.[11]

SRL also questioned the dichotomisation into two categories of rights, namely the International Covenant on Civil and Political Rights and the International Covenant on Economic, Social and Cultural Rights. Just like the 1948 Universal Declaration of Human Rights, SRL made no obvious distinction between civil and political rights and economic, social and cultural rights. Nor did they give one set of rights primacy over the other. Testimonies of SRL support Roosevelt's idea that 'necessitous men are not free men'[12] in the sense that all rights are interrelated and interdependent. Mower asserts that 'rights to certain opportunities and conditions are essential to enable an individual to enjoy a decent standard of living'.[13] Answers of SRL proved that they believe all rights are interactive, not sequential: 'I need freedom of thought first and the opportunity to work to secure a decent life.'; 'I need security, safety and an appropriate work with a suitable salary.' There is little doubt that, in the Lebanese context, socio-economic stability cannot be attained without individual freedoms and *vice versa*. The rights of SRL – be they civil and political or economic, social and cultural – are deeply connected and mutually reinforcing. The three priorities expressed by SRL (right to security of person, right to education and right to work) support's Shue's belief that there is a basic right to personal integrity, encompassing security and subsistence,[14] and that this right is both political and economic in nature.

---

[10] J. MAPULANGA-HULSTON, 'Examining the Justiciability of Economic, Social and Cultural Rights', (2002) 6(4) *The International Journal of Human Rights*, p. 29.
[11] Ibid., pp. 31–34.
[12] Roosevelt Institute, 'FDR's Second Bill of Rights: "Necessitous Men are not Free Men"', 01.11.2011, available at http://rooseveltinstitute.org/fdrs-second-bill-rights-necessitous-men-are-not-free-men, last accessed 09.05.2018.
[13] J. MAPULANGA-HULSTON (2002), 'Examining the Justiciability of Economic, Social and Cultural Rights', *supra* note 10, pp. 42–43.
[14] H. SHUE, *Basic Rights: Subsistence, Affluence, and U.S. Foreign Policy*, Princeton University Press, Princeton 1980, p. 158.

2.3.2. Dignity in Forced Displacement: A Fundamental Dimension

In addition to traditional rights, a high percentage of SRL made explicit references to another type of entitlements. For example, 33.2% of respondents referred to notions such as 'humanity', 'human being', 'human rights', 'respect', 'dignity' 'freedom' and 'decency': 'I want respect for each person as they are human beings and have the right to live in dignity and freedom.' Syrian refugees feel that their precarious situation in Lebanon deprives them from their right to live in dignity. This finding goes hand in hand with the conclusions of the International Center for Transitional Justice (ICTJ) report 'Not without Dignity: Views of Syrian Refugees in Lebanon on Displacement, Conditions of Return and Coexistence', indicating that most Syrians highly value the concept of 'dignity' (*karama* in Arabic). According to Karim El Mufti and Rim El Gantri, 'dignity was identified as a common loss, beginning with the very fact of their displacement by a war that has changed their lives forever'.[15] The two researchers insist that 'the humiliation and discrimination faced by refugees impacted on people who had been used to a certain social and economic level in Syria, despite a quasi-absence of civil and political rights'.[16]

Against the backdrop of the Syrian refugee crisis, the concept of dignity is of special interest. Indeed, dignity has long acquired recognition in Middle Eastern societies because it is deeply rooted in both Arabic and Islamic values. In Arab societies, the concept of dignity is taught to children in schools and largely depicted in Arab literature. For instance, the influential poet Antarah Ibn Shaddad wrote extensively about honour and self-esteem.[17] One of his famous verses read: 'Don't offer me life elixir with humiliation. Offer me rather a drink of colocynth with dignity.' From an Islamic point of view, dignity is a core principle as it appears in the Quran under various forms. A statement such as 'the upper hand is better than the lower one' shows how Islamic values exhort believers to 'provide for their needs and preserve their dignity'.[18] According to Surat al-Isra, verse 70, human dignity is bestowed on all humans by virtue of their creation by God: 'We have honoured [conferred dignity] on the descendants [progeny] of Adam, and we have carried [borne] them over land and sea, and provided for them sustenance out of the good things of life, and favoured them far above

---

[15] K. EL MUFTI and R. EL GANTRI, 'Not without Dignity: Views of Syrian Refugees in Lebanon on Displacement, Conditions of Return and Coexistence', 09.06.2017, p. 35, available at https://www.ictj.org/sites/default/files/ICTJ_Report_Syria_NotWithoutDignity.pdf, last accessed 09.05.2018.

[16] K. EL MUFTI and R. EL GANTRI (2017), 'Not without Dignity: Views of Syrian Refugees in Lebanon on Displacement, Conditions of Return and Coexistence', *supra* note 15, p. 35.

[17] Ibid.

[18] Ibid., pp. 35–36.

most of Our creation.'[19] Dignity is a 'God-given right that applies to all humans, irrespective of ethnicity, gender, religious belief, or other distinction'[20] and SRL are convinced their displacement deprived them of it.

The International Covenant on Civil and Political Rights stresses that 'rights *derive* from the inherent dignity of the human person'.[21] Human dignity is said to 'precede and justify human rights'.[22] This vision is coherent with the observation that the primary concern of SRL is to be recognised as human beings. They describe the need to enjoy traditional human rights as subordinate to the need to live in dignity. Allen Wood asserts that dignity is 'the capacity to think for oneself and direct one's own life with responsibility both for one's own well-being and for the way one's actions affect the rights and welfare of others'.[23] The reflections of SRL substantiate this theory. They perceive their lack of autonomy in the Lebanese society as a deprivation of human dignity: 'I want security, education and the feeling of being a human being who is capable of developing his or her community.' Furthermore, testimonies of SRL support Howard-Hassmann's theory that there are two kinds of human dignity rights:[24] a right to minimum absolute wealth – defined as the possibility to obtain a fair share of the economic resources of the community ('I want safety; I am harassed by the residents of the area. I cannot secure my daily necessities, I cannot secure permanent work and I spend more than what I earn.'); and a right to community (right of belonging) – defined as 'the need to feel secure in one's kinship or social system and in one's exercise of custom, ritual culture; the need to feel that those who have power have some legitimacy and are not arbitrary' ('I would like to go to any country that gives us the same rights as its citizens, a country where there is no racial or sectarian discrimination.').[25]

In conclusion, SRL believe that resettlement will ensure their enjoyment of the following rights: right to security of person, right to education, right to work, right to housing, right to health, right to asylum, right to equality and non-discrimination, right to reside, access to justice, freedom of thought, conscience and religion, and freedom of movement. These rights are core components of most national and international human rights laws. For instance,

---

[19] C. BASSIOUNI, *The Shari'a and Islamic Criminal Justice in Time of War and Peace*, Cambridge University Press, Cambridge 2014, p. 91.
[20] Ibid.
[21] International Covenant on Civil and Political Rights (adopted 16.12.1966, entered into force 23.03.1976) 999 UNTS 171 (ICCPR), Preamble.
[22] D. SCHROEDER, 'Human Rights and Human Dignity: An Appeal to Separate the Conjoined Twins', (2012) 15(3) *Ethical Theory and Moral Practice*, p. 325.
[23] A. WOOD, 'Human Dignity, Right and the Realm of Ends', 2007, p. 10, available at https://web.stanford.edu/~allenw/webpapers/keynote2007.doc, last accessed 09.05.2018.
[24] B. MOORE, cited in R.E. HOWARD-HASSMANN, 'The Full-Belly Thesis: Should Economics Rights Take Priority Over Civil and Political Rights? Evidence from Sub-Saharan Africa', (1983) 5(4) *Human Rights Quarterly*, p. 488.
[25] Ibid.

Belgium has a specific legislation regarding the treatment of aliens, is bound by relevant EU Law and is party to UN human rights instruments; the country is therefore under the obligation to safeguard the enjoyment of such rights for resettled refugees. Other resettlement countries, providing that they are bound by similar human rights provisions, are also expected to do so. As for human dignity, it was identified as a prerequisite for the compliance with refugees' rights in a context of forced displacement: human dignity is far from being a mere theoretical notion, it is a fundamental dimension of refugees' well-being. Accordingly, personal expectations of SRL as expressed in this section can be described as realistic.

2.4. EXPECTATIONS VIS-À-VIS HOST COUNTRIES

Expectations of SRL vis-à-vis a third party – the host country – were studied on the basis of age, gender and level of education. Results demonstrate how these variables affect the goals that refugees wish to pursue through resettlement. For instance, the younger the refugees are, the more concerned they are about their own future. Concerns about family are, for their part, amplified as the refugees' age increases. Refugees under 26 expressed their will to build a new life (57.2%) by emphasising that they wished to either get or finish their education in the hope of finding a job in the host country. Among refugees over 26, on the contrary, the number of SRL who prioritised the building of a new life dropped to 35.4%; a higher share of individuals said that they wished to find safety for their family and secure their children's future. Females saw security as their priority; males had a strong tendency to prioritise the building of a new life. Significant variations were also observed with regard to children: while 31.1% of women declared that their children's future was their main concern, only 18.8% of men did. These observations reveal the existence of pre-eminent gender-based patterns among the Syrian refugee population living in Lebanon. In decision-making, women are statistically more child-oriented[26] and risk-averse[27] than their male counterparts. As for the level of education, the more educated refugees are, the more knowledgeable they are about resettlement and the brighter they believe their integration prospects are in the host country.

Results also brought attention to a crucial dilemma: in order for integration in the post-resettlement phase to be successful, a reasonable balance must be

---

[26] K. PARKER, 'Women More than Men Adapt their Careers for Family Life', 01.10.2015, available at http://www.pewresearch.org/fact-tank/2015/10/01/women-more-than-men-adjust-their-careers-for-family-life, last accessed 09.05.2018.

[27] J.P. BYRNES et al., 'Gender Differences in Risk Taking: A Meta-Analysis', (1999) 125(3) *Psychological Bulletin*, p. 367.

kept between the responsibility of the host country to provide assistance and the necessity of welcomed refugees to show a high level of resilience. The following testimony shows how complementary these two components are:

> Yes, I know someone who was resettled in Canada. He was assisted by the government at the beginning. Then, he started working in the same field as in Syria and became an active member of the community. Today he is convinced he will achieve what he aspires to and make his dreams come true.[28]

On average, SRL are well aware of this dilemma: 85.7% of the refugees surveyed agreed with the statements 'life will be difficult when I arrive, I will have to solve problems by myself' and 'the government will do its best to help me in my everyday life'. Only, 14.4% of the panel believed that the government *must* help in their everyday life and only one in five refugees declared he would feel anger towards the host country if their expectations were not met in the post-resettlement phase. An important pattern emerged from answers: the less educated refugees are, the more they expect from the host country. That is, the level of education of a refugee is negatively correlated with their belief that the government is the main duty-bearer in resettlement. Figures show that while 55.6% of uneducated refugees opted for the answer 'the government must help me in my everyday life,' it was the case for only 23.6% of refugees who finished primary school, 8.5% of those who finished secondary school and only 7.3% of university graduates. When asked, uneducated refugees argued that if the government had deliberately chosen them to come, it was incumbent on them to guide newcomers until they were able to rebuild a new life abroad. In this regard, the Canadian Refugee Sponsorship Program stresses the difference between expectations and unrealistic expectations, the latter being identified as the main cause for the emergence of a 'sense of entitlement'.[29] Uneducated or poorly educated refugees hold the strong belief that they *deserve* something because they have already *earned it*; this sense of entitlement becomes counterproductive when it starts causing 'feelings of resentment, frustration and anger on the part of refugees'.[30] The primary goal of expectation management is to address conflicts arising from these mismatched expectations.

Besides, the image reflected by a resettlement country is of utmost importance: the more positive the image of a country is, the more attractive this country becomes for refugees. Among the refugee population surveyed, Canada was by far the most popular destination. Reasons invoked by the refugees are numerous. The presence of friends and relatives in the country is the leading

---

[28] Interview with a Syrian refugee (Bekaa Valley, Lebanon, March 2017).
[29] The Refugee Sponsorship Training Program (2013), 'Managing Expectations: A Resource Kit for Refugee Sponsors', *supra* note 4, p. 3.
[30] Ibid.

factor in the choice of a resettlement country. Other factors such as compliance with human rights standards, religious freedom, multiculturalism, language compatibility, education, safety, healthcare and willingness to help Syrians are also highly valued by SRL. Canada ranked first as it seems to offer a perfect combination of the aforementioned factors. SRL described Canada as being 'a country governed by the rule of law and that respects religious and cultural diversity'. It was also said to be 'democratic', 'free', 'peaceful' and 'not racist'; it was called a 'nation that respects human rights' and offers Syrians a chance to 'live in dignity'. Refugees believed that Canada provided 'high living standards', 'quality education' and 'good medical and psychological treatment'. One testimony read:

> Canada: I am looking for safety and it is a wonderful country in terms of treatment and humanity. Here, in Lebanon, I do not feel that I am ever considered a man […]. We are treated like the animals of the Lebanese forest, everyone is becoming hateful and people do not want us in their country. We became a bother, we became undesirable. I want to live proudly and I am tired of everything here.[31]

Interestingly, Prime Minister Justin Trudeau's open-door policy towards Syrian refugees was also mentioned as an encouraging factor. So far, Canada has resettled more than 40,000 Syrian refugees via UNHCR's scheme and its private sponsorship programme.[32] Trudeau has been increasingly vocal about his support for Syrians and his will to promote diversity within his country. Trudeau's actions went beyond the political sphere and transformed into a large-scale pro-refugee campaign. He personally welcomed Syrian families at the airport, publicly teared up over their stories or tweeted about Canada's openness. This pro-refugee communication strategy contributed to the creation of a deep emotional link with the Syrian population. In times when they feel abandoned by the international community, Syrians are sensitive to the willingness of a country to welcome them. The attractiveness of Canada for SRL illustrates the theory under which there is an obvious link between a country's image and its attractiveness as a resettlement destination.

2.5. THE INDIVIDUAL FACTOR: A FINAL REFLECTION

Resettlement was thoroughly examined from three different perspectives – resettlement awareness, personal expectations and expectations vis-à-vis host countries. Several conclusions can be drawn. On the one hand, even though

---

[31] Interview with a Syrian refugee (Bekaa Valley, Lebanon, March 2017).
[32] Government of Canada, '#WelcomeRefugees: Canada Resettled Syrian Refugees', 05.04.2018, available at https://www.canada.ca/en/immigration-refugees-citizenship/services/refugees/welcome-syrian-refugees.html, last accessed 09.05.2018.

most SRL are aware of the existence of a resettlement programme, they lack basic knowledge about its functioning. As a result, they are highly likely to develop unrealistic expectations vis-à-vis UNHCR's resettlement scheme. On the other hand, SRL set high expectations both for themselves and host countries. Personal expectations are in line with international refugee law and can therefore be described as fully realistic. In contrast, expectations vis-à-vis host countries vary according to the level of education of a refugee. The more uneducated a refugee, the more unrealistic their expectations become. In conclusion, the individual factor can have a negative influence on the level of satisfaction of a refugee. In the event that the refugee developed unrealistic expectations, he or she is extremely likely to be disappointed in the post-resettlement phase after discovering what he or she is legally entitled to.

3. THE LEGAL FACTOR: HUMAN RIGHTS APPROACH TO THE BELGIAN RESETTLEMENT SCHEME

3.1. COMPLIANCE WITH HUMAN RIGHTS STANDARDS

Compliance with human rights principles can have a true effect on refugees' satisfaction in the post-resettlement phase: reality can either exceed expectations or fall short of them. This section aims at understanding whether the Belgian resettlement scheme implemented in Lebanon is in line with core human rights principles. The goal of this assessment is to uncover whether refugees' satisfaction is low, which would certainly contribute to exacerbating the asymmetry between expectations and reality. A critical analysis will be carried out so as to underline the main shortcomings of the programme in terms of compliance with human rights. Qualitative data was collected through a series of interviews conducted in March 2017 with five resettlement actors – UNHCR, Fedasil, the CGRS, Convivial and Caritas – and ten resettled SRL. Though the main expectations identified by SRL were the right to security of person, the right to education and the right to work, attention will be focused on what resettled Syrians pointed at during the interviewing process in Belgium. Three elements – the legal framework surrounding resettlement, the access to healthcare and the access to housing – emerged as unsatisfactory. They will be examined in light of the human rights obligations of the State of Belgium.

3.1.1. Legal Framework Surrounding Resettlement

As of today, Belgium lacks a legal framework for resettlement. Resettled refugees fall under the legal regime provided by the Law of 15 December 1980 regarding entry, residence, settlement and removal of foreign nationals. Yet, neither the original legislation, nor its amended versions contain any specific provision regarding resettlement.³³ Every decision affecting resettlement activities is the result of a strictly political decision. The Cabinet of Theo Francken, the Belgian State Secretary for Asylum and Migration, is the only institution that lays down guiding principles for the Belgian resettlement policy. Due to this legal loophole, Belgium is not equipped with any mechanism of extraterritorial refugee status recognition. In accordance with the Law of 15 December 1980, refugee status determination can only be done in Belgium.³⁴ Both UNHCR's Bureau for Europe and CGRS see this issue as a legal constraint. As mentioned previously, applying for asylum upon arrival is nothing but a formality as refugees' claims were previously examined and accepted by CGRS following the selection mission in Lebanon. No interview on the substance of the asylum request will be conducted in Belgium.³⁵ Yet, this formality will soon constitute a major hurdle as the country's quota is regularly revised upwards. Geert Beirnaert, Policy Officer at CGRS, commented on this future difficulty:

> After their arrival, refugees still have to lodge an asylum request. It is certainly a disadvantage for us because we are working with groups that are increasingly bigger. We used to work with around 100 refugees per year and we are soon going to reach more than 1,000, around 600 Syrians from Turkey, 300 from Lebanon and 150 from Jordan. [...] Even if it is only a formality, it takes several days because the administrative path must be followed. [...]. Officially, we cannot take a decision before they set foot in Belgium, but de facto we have already given the green line.³⁶

3.1.2. Access to Housing and Healthcare

Belgium being a signatory to the International Covenant on Economic, Social and Cultural Rights, it is under the obligation to 'take steps [...] to the maximum of its available resources, with a view to achieving progressively the full realisation of the rights recognised in the [...] Covenant by all appropriate means'.³⁷ Article 11 of the Covenant lays out the right of everyone to an adequate standard of living, which includes housing; Article 12 guarantees the enjoyment

---

33   F. FISHER and S. PHILLMANN, 'Know Reset – Country Profile: Belgium', December 2012, p. 3, available at http://www.know-reset.eu/files/texts/00145_20130704132512_knowresetcountryprofilebelgium.pdf, last accessed 09.05.2018.
34   European Migration Network, 'Resettlement and Humanitarian Admission in Belgium', December 2016, p. 6, available at https://ec.europa.eu/home-affairs/sites/homeaffairs/files/02a_belgium_resettlement_study_en.pdf, last accessed 09.05.2018.
35   Ibid., p. 19.
36   Interview with Geert Beirnaert, Policy Officer, Office of the Commissioner General for Refugees and Stateless Persons (GCRS) (Brussels, Belgium, 27.03.2017).
37   International Covenant on Economic, Social and Cultural Rights (adopted 16.12.1966, entered into force 03.01.1976) 993 UNTS 3 (CESCR), Art. 2 para. 1.

of the highest attainable standard of physical and mental health for everyone.[38] Belgium also has obligations stemming from its belonging to the EU and the Council of Europe. At a European level, the rights to housing and health are recognised in the EU Charter of Fundamental Rights – Article 34(3) (social security and social assistance), Article 35 (healthcare) – and in the European Social Charter – Article 31 (right to housing), Article 13 (right to social and medical assistance).[39] Furthermore, even though the right to housing and the right to health are not directly enshrined in the European Convention on Human Rights, the recent jurisprudence of the European Court of Human Rights suggests that their applicability is increasingly relevant, especially in the field of asylum. For example, in *M.S.S. v Belgium*, the Court held that, after being sent back to Greece from Belgium, the applicant's living conditions reached the threshold to amount to a breach of Article 3 of the ECHR on the prohibition of torture and inhuman or degrading treatment or punishment.[40]

Attention must also be paid to Directive 2013/33/EU, which lays down the standards for the reception of applicants for international protection. General principles (11) and (18) of the Directive provide that EU Member States should maintain standards that 'suffice to ensure [applicants] a dignified standard of living' and reception should be specifically designed to meet their needs.[41] This particular Directive was transposed into the Belgian legislation in the Law of 12 January 2007 on the reception of asylum seekers and other categories of foreigners.[42] Due to the unusual way in which they were accepted into the country, resettled refugees fall in a legal loophole: they are placed in centres under the authority of Fedasil, just like regular asylum seekers, but are already recognised as refugees. Because they are not asylum seekers, Syrians arriving through the Belgian resettlement scheme do not directly fall under the scope of either the Reception Directive or the Law of 12 January 2007. Indeed, the Reception Directive covers only 'applicants of international protection in Member States';[43] the Law of 12 January 2007, for its part, applies exclusively to asylum seekers and their relatives, unaccompanied minors and families with

---

[38] Ibid., pp. 8–9.
[39] EU Agency for Fundamental Rights, 'Handbook on European Law Relating to Asylum, Borders and Immigration', June 2014, p. 180, available at http://fra.europa.eu/en/publication/2013/handbook-european-law-relating-asylum-borders-and-immigration, last accessed 09.05.2018.
[40] ECtHR, *M.S.S. v Belgium*, no 30696/09, 21.07.2011.
[41] Directive 2013/33/EU of the European Parliament and of the Council of 26 June 2013 laying down standards for the reception of applicants for international protection, OJ L 180/97, general principles (11) and (18).
[42] European Migration Network (2016), 'Resettlement and Humanitarian Admission in Belgium', *supra* note 34, p. 64.
[43] Directive 2013/33/EU of the European Parliament and of the Council of 26 June 2013 laying down standards for the reception of applicants for international protection, OJ L 180/99, Art. 1.

minors illegally residing in Belgium.[44] Their applicability will nevertheless be discussed hereunder as reception conditions are very similar for both resettled refugees and regular asylum seekers.

3.1.2.1. Access to Housing

Since the creation of the structural resettlement scheme in 2013, several changes occurred in the field of reception. Elisabeth Verniers and Roxanne Tremblay, Resettlement Project Coordinators respectively at NGOs Caritas and Convivial, explained that in 2013 and 2014, resettled refugees were first hosted for a period of six weeks in a Fedasil centre before being sent to a social house. The main partner was a Public Social Welfare Centre (PSWC).[45] In 2015, in the aftermath of the asylum crisis, the number of places available in Fedasil centres and social houses dropped sharply. It was agreed that resettled refugees would be first hosted in a Fedasil centre for a period of six weeks before being transferred to a local reception initiative (LRI) – a reception facility supervised by a PSWC in close collaboration with Fedasil.[46] Each LRI is usually composed of at least one social assistant and one educator; the LRI staff is in charge of providing daily administrative legal, social, psychological, medical support to newcomers.[47] The overlapping of the two systems created tensions among the resettled population. Roxanne Tremblay pointed out:

> In 2015, some Syrians were hosted in a LRI while others were still granted a social house by a partner PSWC. Of course, they were comparing their respective situations and they did not understand why one was offered accommodation for one year, why another one could choose freely where to reside […]. It caused tensions and even aggressiveness among resettled refugees.[48]

Consequently, Fedasil decided to harmonise the system. At present, resettled refugees are first hosted for six weeks in a Fedasil centre and then transferred for a period of six months to an LRI. They are then expected to find permanent housing.

---

[44] CIRÉ, 'Fiche pratique : l'accueil des bénéficiaires de la loi du 12 janvier 2007. Pratiques et évolutions', (n.d), available at http://www.lstb.be/pdf/2010-01-08-Fiche%20pratique-accueil-1.pdf, last accessed 09.05.2018.
[45] Fedasil, 'Resettlement Process', (n.d.), available at https://www.fedasil.be/en/resettlement/resettlement-process, last accessed 09.05.2018.
[46] CPAS Charleroi, 'Service ILA', (n.d.), available at https://www.cpascharleroi.be/index.php/aide-sociale/service-ila, last accessed 09.05.2018.
[47] CPAS Profondeville, 'Initiative Locale d'Accueil (I.L.A.)', (n.d), available at http://www.cpas-profondeville.be/services/initiative-locale-daccueil, last accessed 09.05.2018.
[48] Interview with Roxanne Tremblay, Resettlement Project Coordinator, Convivial (Brussels, Belgium, 27.03.2017).

Belgium complies with its core obligations with regard to the right to housing. Nonetheless, both resettled refugees and NGOs question the logic behind the housing system as implemented today and claim that a more human approach to housing should be envisioned. Most refugees being low-income individuals, they usually struggle to find decent housing. As of today, the main duty-bearer in the search of post-reception accommodation is not clearly defined. After the first six months, responsibility often becomes a bone of contention. Under the new LRI system, refugees must be proactive; theoretically, they are expected to find private accommodation with the help of the LRI staff. In practice, many resettled refugees turn to Caritas and Convivial to look for additional support as the two NGOs have experience and are better equipped – linguistically, amongst others – to respond to their needs. As demonstrated in March 2017 in a study carried out by the University of Ghent, the psychosocial well-being of resettled refugees is deeply challenged by the uncertainty surrounding access to accommodation in the post-reception phase.[49] Tensions arise, resettled refugees feel abandoned and NGOs and social services feel pressured.

Both NGOs and resettled refugees also underlined that the system is not optimal because it does not favour long-term solutions. Elisabeth Verniers, Resettlement Project Coordinator at Caritas, believes that the initial system in which a partner PSWC was involved for a duration of one year had virtues despite the fact that it gave refugees little scope for action. According to her, it favoured security and reduced stress:

> Under the system where we had a partner PSWC, they could not choose at all: if there was a house for 6 people in Mortsel, they were sent to Mortsel. They had no choice, but it also had one advantage. When refugees arrived in Belgium, they had no global understanding of the country, they didn't know the cities, and they didn't know where to settle down. In a way, they were happy to be provided with housing upon arrival and, after one year, we were helping them to find a permanent house.[50]

Many resettled refugees interviewed believed that because they had been selected by Belgian authorities, Belgium should provide long-term private accommodation upon arrival. This practice is common and highly successful in other resettlement countries – in Scandinavia, for instance. When refugees arrive, they are immediately transferred to private accommodation and the country's social services show greater flexibility regarding a future deadline for

---

[49] F. CAESTECKER and I. DERLUYN, 'Les expériences des réfugiés réinstallés en Belgique', Study or the Myria Centre Fédéral Migration, 2017, available at http://www.myria.be/files/170425_Les_exp%C3%A9riences_des_r%C3%A9fugi%C3%A9s_r%C3%A9install%C3%A9s__FINAL_FR.pdf, last accessed 17.05.2018, p. 9.
[50] Interview with Elisabeth Verniers, Resettlement Project Coordinator, Caritas (Brussels, Belgium, 29.03.2017).

departure, Elisabeth Verniers pointed out. In her view, such a system favours successful integration as refugees are given the chance to build a solid social network in the post-resettlement phase. She is convinced that the fragmentation of the Belgian housing system has a negative impact on resettled refugees' integration potential.

> Instead of facilitating integration, the system postpones it. Six weeks in a centre, six months in a LRI, then moving to another city [...] Kids are in school close to the centre, then close to the LRI, then parents are moving and the kids have to restart from scratch. If parents were on a waiting list for language classes and they move, they have to start all over again. It is a real waste of time.[51]

Finally, NGOs and resettled refugees assert that the Belgian accommodation policy is paradoxical: the country decides to take in vulnerable Syrians but is not equipped with a suitable housing system to welcome them. In Franck Caestecker and Ilse Derluyn's view, 'considering that Belgian authorities choose [...] to resettle vulnerable groups and that the need for protection is a major reason behind the selection of an individual, this vulnerability should be taken into account'.[52] In addition to assisting them in their search, authorities should be equipped with a system that ensures that they have access to healthcare and basic services such as language classes, social assistance, civic integration courses etc.[53] At present, it is rarely the case. Needless to say, hosting facilities have a strong influence on rights accessibility.[54]

3.1.2.2. Access to Healthcare

Even though Belgium guarantees *de jure* healthcare for resettled refugees, most of them enjoy a very limited access to it *de facto*. Admittedly, all refugees in Belgium face such a hurdle, but the case of resettled refugees raises particular concerns as many of them have been selected on the basis of their particular medical vulnerabilities. According to both Caritas and Convivial, the problem is triple.

First, in the post-resettlement phase, the proximity of medical institutions is not a primary concern during the search for permanent accommodation. Roxanne Tremblay, Resettlement Project Coordinator at Convivial, explained that, in many cases, finding suitable accommodation is already an achievement.

---

[51] Ibid.
[52] F. CAESTECKER and I. DERLUYN (2017), 'Les expériences des réfugiés réinstallés en Belgique', *supra* note 49, p. 80.
[53] Ibid., p. 11.
[54] S. FRANGUIADAKIS et al., *En quête d'asile : aide associative et accès au(x) droit(s)*, L.G.D.J., Paris 2004, p. 240.

Making sure that medical facilities are easily accessible comes second. Syrians resettled in Belgium in rural areas said they experienced very low access to health facilities. Secondly, poor language proficiency often prevents resettled refugees from having effective access to healthcare. Elisabeth Verniers, Resettlement Project Coordinator at Caritas, claimed:

> Another issue is guaranteeing access to healthcare [...]. Given that people speak only Arabic and do not speak Dutch or French, they are stuck. Many hospitals and doctors do not work with interpreters or are not really willing to make efforts in order to communicate with people who do not speak French or Dutch.[55]

She added that Caritas tried to solve this issue by setting up a network of informal interpreters:

> We try to find official interpreters but it is very difficult. In Caritas, we partner up with 'life experts', people who are refugees and who speak Arabic and French or Dutch but who do not have an educational background in interpretation. When they have to interpret for specialists, it becomes tricky [...]. But if we have no other solution, that's what we do. The best option is finding someone who studied interpretation and knows the specialised terminology.[56]

According to her, finding Arabic-speaking doctors can be a solution, but, once again, only refugees resettled in or around big cities have that opportunity. Arabic-speaking doctors are not likely to be found in small, isolated villages. During interviews, some Syrians mentioned that they often brought a bilingual friend along or called bilingual NGO workers when they attended medical appointments.

Thirdly, Belgium faces a shortage of institutions specialised in trauma linked to forced displacement. As a consequence, resettled refugees often end up being attended by non-specialised doctors in non-specific health institutions. Elisabeth Verniers summarised:

> Finding psychological care is a challenge. There are departments specialised in migration and migration-related trauma, but mostly in Brussels and other big cities. And they have very few places [...]. It's extremely complicated to find a facility that is easily accessible, affordable and adapted. A psychologist used to treating patients who are getting divorced is not suitable for a Syrian who was a victim of torture [...].[57]

---

[55] Interview with Elisabeth Verniers, Resettlement Project Coordinator, Caritas (Brussels, Belgium, 29.03.2017).
[56] Ibid.
[57] Ibid.

In other words, resettled refugees have *de jure* access to healthcare, which suggests that the country complies with its core obligations, but the current infrastructure clearly fails to ensure them effective access to it. Elisabeth Verniers insists that bilateral efforts must be made: it is essential to explain to resettled refugees how the Belgian system works and to raise awareness about their situation among healthcare professionals.

3.2. FUTURE PROSPECTS: TOWARDS MORE VIOLATIONS OF THE RIGHTS OF RESETTLED REFUGEES?

3.2.1. Civil Society Participation

In *En quête d'asile*, Franguiadakis, Jaillardon and Belkis assert that the level of participation of civil society is positively correlated with refugees' enjoyment of their rights. They highlight the difficulty of establishing a trustful relationship between grassroots associations and governmental agencies in a field that falls under the exclusive competence of the state.[58] They also warn that, in such a context, the scope of action of NGOs can be rapidly questioned and partnerships terminated.[59] This analysis strongly resonates with the most recent developments surrounding the Belgian resettlement programme. In January 2017, the Belgian resettlement scheme underwent a major change. It was agreed that Caritas and Convivial – the two NGOs in charge of resettled refugees' daily guidance in the post-resettlement phase – should be progressively discharged from their responsibilities. Their mandate consisted in providing personalised social guidance to resettled refugees for a period of up to two years to facilitate their integration into Belgian society. Caritas and Convivial will continue to follow refugees who arrived prior to January 2017 but will not be entrusted with any similar mission in the future. Fedasil and the LRI facilities now bear the entire responsibility for the welcoming of incoming resettled refugees. The termination of Caritas and Convivial's mandate raises questions as the two NGOs played a crucial role in the integration process of resettled refugees and facilitated their access to rights.

3.2.1.1. Specialised Actors

NGO workers and resettled refugees interviewed expressed strong concerns when asked about the quality of the post-resettlement guidance. Caritas and Convivial have long-term experience in the field of forced displacement, which

---

[58] S. FRANGUIADAKIS et al. (2004), *En quête d'asile : aide associative et accès au(x) droit(s)*, supra note 54, p. 238.
[59] Ibid.

makes them highly-qualified actors. LRI structures, on the contrary, are better described as mainstream social structures dealing with refugee-related matters. Roxanne Tremblay, Resettlement Project Coordinator at Convivial, explained:

> We are a true specialised actor. We have lawyers in case we face legal problems, we have family reunification experts. PSWC have no idea about this, for example. We can grant small loans and find alternative solutions. We know everything about refugee law; we know that in the municipality, they might have problems registering a new-born, acknowledging the validity of a marriage [...]. These are issues linked to the mere fact of being a refugee and, for that reason, we believe that specialised services are essential, at least for the most vulnerable.[60]

3.2.1.2. Intermediaries

Franguiadakis, Jaillardon and Belkis found out that 'associations play a fundamental role in accompanying asylum seekers, but also in acting as intermediaries between these individuals and government-led services'.[61] According Roxanne Tremblay, NGOs are indeed 'refugees' voice' for they act as a go-between. They make sure that refugees' needs are correctly expressed to LRIs and addressed by the latter. They enable LRIs to pass information over and remind them of their obligations: 'We follow up with the families, so we know them. During collective activities, people meet but also complain. We take these complaints to the PSWC and try to solve the issues.'[62]

3.2.1.3. Linguistic Mediators

In its Article 15, the Law of 12 January 2007 states:

> The Agency [Fedasil] or the partner ensures that the reception beneficiary has access to social interpretation and translation services as part of the rights and obligations they are entitled to under the present law. The Agency or the partner can establish partnerships with services or organisations specialised in social interpretation or translation.[63]

Caritas and Convivial fulfil the crucial role of linguistic mediator. When in a Fedasil centre, resettled refugees benefit from the same advantages as regular asylum seekers, which includes linguistic assistance. Later, once individuals – be they resettled refugees or regular asylum seekers – are transferred to an LRI, such

---

[60] Interview with Roxanne Tremblay, Resettlement Project Coordinator, Convivial (Brussels, Belgium, 27.03.2017).
[61] Ibid.
[62] Ibid.
[63] Belgian Law of 12.01.2007, Art. 15.

services become less common. Although, according to the law, LRIs are supposed to partner up with specialised institutions, this is rarely the case. So far, resettled refugees were privileged as they could rely on Caritas and Convivial. Roxanne Tremblay asserts that frustration often emerges on both sides: LRIs complain that refugees constantly fail to reach imposed targets while refugees report that the LRI's social assistant speaks to them in a language they do not understand. She commented: 'Services offered will be different. Needs will not be addressed in the same way by LRIs for a simple reason: how will people communicate? LRIs don't have either cultural mediators or interpreters.'[64]

3.2.1.4. Facilitators for Access to Housing and Healthcare

In the previous section, it was demonstrated that Caritas and Convivial facilitated a greater enjoyment of the rights to housing and health by increasing their accessibility for resettled refugees. With the removal of the NGOS from the post-resettlement process, there is no doubt that these two rights will be further jeopardised.

During the legal reception period – six weeks in a Fedasil centre and six months in a LRI – resettled refugees enjoy the same rights as regular asylum seekers. Their right to housing and to heath care are guaranteed respectively by Article 16 ('the reception beneficiary is hosted in a collective or individual reception facility') and Article 23 ('the reception beneficiary has a right to medical assistance required to live in human dignity') of the Law of 12 January 2007.[65] The law does not contain any provision concerning the period following the six-month stay in the LRI. Legally speaking, Belgium does not directly violate any right of resettled refugees by putting an end to the mandate of NGOs. However, from an ethical point of view, this choice is questionable on the following basis. Article 36 of the Law of 12 January 2007 provides that 'in order to fulfil the specific needs of vulnerable persons, for instance minors, unaccompanied minors, isolated parents with children, pregnant women, persons with disabilities, victims of human trafficking, victims of violence or torture or the elderly, the Agency or the partner establishes partnerships with specialised services or organisations'.[66] By stating in its legislation that some refugees are more vulnerable than other and by setting up a resettlement scheme specifically designed to alleviate their plight, Belgium implicitly recognises their inherent need for closer supervision. The previous system was in line with this reasoning as it foresaw long-term social assistance – during the first six months and beyond this legal reception period.

---

[64] Interview with Roxanne Tremblay, Resettlement Project Coordinator, Convivial (Brussels, Belgium, 27.03.2017).
[65] Belgian Law of 12.01.2007, Arts. 16 and 23.
[66] Ibid., Art. 36.

Under the International Covenant on Economic, Social and Cultural Rights, Belgium has the obligation to respect two key principles: progressive realisation and non-regression. Regressive steps must be understood as 'all of those acts, of omission or of commission on the part of the state, which deprives people of rights that they used to enjoy'.[67] In the meantime, Committee on Economic, Social and Cultural Rights (CESCR) General Comment No. 3 states that 'any deliberately retrogressive measure [...] would require the most careful consideration and would need to be fully justified'. It underpins that 'even in times of severe resources constraints whether caused by a process of adjustment, of economic recession or by other factors, the vulnerable members of society can and indeed must be protected'.[68] Applied to the Belgian case, these provisions suggest that neither the 2015 asylum crisis (budgetary constraints, lack of reception places, etc.), nor the need for a restructuring of the resettlement programme constituted a valid reason to set up an NGO-free scheme. Article 12 (d) of the Covenant highlights the importance of creating favourable conditions to guarantee access for all to basic rights.[69] General Comment No. 3 insists that it is incumbent upon States parties to strive to ensure the widest possible enjoyment of economic, social and cultural rights.[70] Because it cancels the possibility of relying on specialised assistance, the decision of Belgian asylum authorities assuredly causes resettled refugees to have lower access to the essential rights they used to enjoy, including basic healthcare or shelter.

Increasing the annual resettlement quota but all the while dismantling the support system involves risks. Peter O'Sullivan, UNHCR Resettlement Officer at the Bureau for Europe, confirmed that countries should undertake proper planning before implementing any new resettlement programme.

> That applies to every aspect of resettlement [...]. If those elements are not in place, then the programme will not be sustainable: refugees feel that they are not given the support that they need and they might feel the need to move on. It has happened that a country had resettled refugees and the refugees did not feel that they were receiving the support that they needed and they started to move to another member state because they believed that might get better support there.[71]

---

[67] International Network for Economic, Social & Cultural Rights, 'Progressive Realisation and Non-Regression', (n.d.), available at https://www.escr-net.org/resources/progressive-realisation-and-non-regression, last accessed 09.05.2018.
[68] CESCR, 'General Comment No. 3: The Nature of States Parties' Obligations (Article 2, para. 1, of the Covenant)', UN Doc E/1991/23, 14.12.1990, pp. 3–4.
[69] International Covenant on Economic, Social and Cultural Rights (adopted 16.12.1966, entered into force 3 January 1976) 993 UNTS 3 (CESCR), Art. 12 para. 2 (d).
[70] CESCR (1990), 'General Comment No. 3: The Nature of States Parties' Obligations (Article 2, para. 1, of the Covenant)', p. 4.
[71] Interview with Peter O'Sullivan, Resettlement Officer, UNHCR Bureau for Europe (Brussels, Belgium, 30.03.2017).

He also stressed that the involvement of civil society was key to the success and sustainability of a resettlement system. In UNHCR's view, NGOs play a pivotal role, especially in the post-resettlement phase:

> I think that is why it is so helpful to have NGOs involved in this because the government and government-supported services cannot always be there whereas NGOs, through volunteers for examples, can have that more day-to-day and hands-on support for refugees. Where this is lacking, refugees might feel lonely or abandoned to some extent. It is really, really important that they are given special support upon arrival, because they arrive with very particular needs, psychological trauma or medical issues, for example.[72]

Nordic countries, traditionally recognised by UNHCR as efficient resettlement countries, tend to favour the creation of support mechanisms tailored to the specific needs of resettled refugees with the view to maximising their chances of integration. Peter O'Sullivan gave the following example:

> The Nordic countries develop individual integration plans for refugees when they arrive. They sit down with them and they capture all of their skills, whether soft skills or hard skills (maybe they worked as a nanny or a welder or a technician) and ask what they wish to do in our country and they try to charter the plan that will assist them in attaining their goal.[73]

While most European countries are following suit, Belgium seems to opt for the opposite approach. Caritas and Convivial used to provide resettled refugees with daily support adapted to their specific needs; as of January 2017, no tailor-made supervision has been available.

3.2.1.5. Lobbying Force

Civil society organisations should remain a strong lobbying force that has the capacity to face up to the authority of the state; their role in the field of asylum should not 'come down to being the state's auxiliaries in charge of implementing public policies'.[74] So far, Belgian civil society served as a whistle-blower: it singled out the shortages of the resettlement policies while trying to maintain a good relationship with governmental asylum authorities. NGOs find themselves torn between their reception mission and their political activism.[75] Due to the 2017 reform, not only will Convivial and Caritas be limited in terms of actions,

---

[72] Ibid.
[73] Ibid.
[74] S. FRANGUIADAKIS et al. (2004), *En quête d'asile : aide associative et accès au(x) droit(s)*, supra note 54, p. 238.
[75] Ibid., p. 242.

but they will progressively disappear from the scheme. With their removal, the State of Belgium deliberately decided to get rid of the only partners that ensured monitoring beyond hands-on guidance.

3.2.2. Non-Discrimination

Article 3 of the Convention relating to the Status of Refugees states: 'The Contracting States shall apply the provisions of this Convention to refugees without discrimination as to race, religion or country of origin.' Belgium is one of the few countries that has consistently considered very diverse refugee populations for resettlement. The country imposes very flexible selection criteria and does not prioritise individuals on the basis of age, religion or health condition or others. Furthermore, unlike many of its peers, Belgium has never used any integration potential criterion – proficiency in one of the country's official languages or education level, for example – to select its resettled population.[76]

Nevertheless, since 2014, the proportion of Syrians resettled in Belgium has kept on increasing at the expense of other refugee populations. For 2017, an annual quota of 1,100 refugees was adopted. Beside around 100 Congolese, according to Geert Beirnaert, 'the country should welcome more than 600 Syrians from Turkey, 300 from Lebanon and 150 from Jordan'. Fedasil argues the decision is in line with UNHCR's policy. The UN agency indeed called upon states make sure that 10% of the Syrian refugee population could have access to resettlement by 2018.[77]

This new orientation based on country of origin raises questions as to whether the Belgian resettlement actors act in full respect of the non-discrimination provisions contained in the Convention relating to the Status of Refugees. A very similar question was addressed in 2015 at the European Parliament after a debate targeted the legal validity of accepting only Christian refugees under the voluntary resettlement and relocation schemes. On 18 February 2016, Dimitris Avramopoulos, EU Commissioner for Migration, Home Affairs and Citizenship, gave the following answer:

> [...] Under the Conclusions on resettlement of 20 July 2015 the Member States agreed to take account of specific priority regions for resettlement. Both Council Decisions on relocation state that Member States of relocation may indicate their preferences in relation to applicants with due respect to the principle of non-discrimination. Under these Decisions, preferences include qualifications, language skills or family, cultural

---

[76] European Migration Network (2016), 'Resettlement and Humanitarian Admission in Belgium', *supra* note 34, p. 37.
[77] UNHCR, 'UNHCR Projected Global Resettlement Needs 2017', June 2016, p. 50, available at http://www.unhcr.org/protection/resettlement/575836267/unhcr-projected-global-resettlement-needs-2017.html, last accessed 09.05.2018.

or social ties which may facilitate integration of applicants into Member States of relocation. However, the decisions make it clear that the expressed preferences are not a condition for relocation. The only ground on which Member States may refuse to relocate is where there are reasonable grounds for considering an applicant a danger to national security or public order [...].[78]

No case law has yet shed light on discrimination on the grounds of religion or country of origin in the context of resettlement. Only close monitoring of EU Member States' country-oriented resettlement schemes and European jurisprudence will reveal whether such practices can amount to a possible breach of the non-discrimination principle. Should Belgium decide to start resettling exclusively Syrians in the future, the question would become even more pressing. When asked about the new Belgian policy, Peter O'Sullivan, UNHCR Resettlement Officer at the Bureau for Europe, formulated UNHCR's view on the matter:

> [...] Our point of view is that yes, absolutely there are significant needs for Syrian refugee population, now there are a 4.9 million registered in the region, and they are in desperate need of pathways of admission to Europe, including resettlement, but at the same time, there are a number of other protracted refugee populations around the world, for example Congolese, Afghans, Iranians, Iraqis, Eritreans, Somalis, and that's the challenge for us in the European context: while we very much welcome the efforts towards providing resettlement opportunities and other pathways of admission for Syrians, it shouldn't be at the expense of other refugee populations globally.[79]

3.3. THE LEGAL FACTOR: A FINAL REFLECTION

The Belgian resettlement scheme was examined from a purely legal perspective. It was observed that the majority of SRL resettled in Belgium show high levels of satisfaction with the programme. Nonetheless, they expressed discontent regarding the right to housing and to healthcare in the immediate post-resettlement phase. Creating a long-term housing system and enhancing tailored-made assistance are two key measures that could efficiently improve their well-being in this respect. Though Belgium fulfils its core obligations under international law, its current resettlement system does not sufficiently take into consideration the vulnerability of Syrian refugees. The 2017 reform,

---

[78] European Commission, 'EU Relocation and Resettlement: EU Member States Urgently Need to Deliver', Press Release, IP/16/1343, 12.04.2016, available at http://europa.eu/rapid/press-release_IP-16-829_en.htm, last accessed 09.05.2018.

[79] Interview with Peter O'Sullivan, Resettlement Officer, UNHCR Bureau for Europe (Brussels, Belgium, 30.03.2017).

which stripped the NGOs Caritas and Convivial from their mandate, confirms this hypothesis. With the removal of NGOs from the post-resettlement process, it is highly likely that Syrians will be left with *de jure* rather than effective access to housing and healthcare. By implementing the 2017 reform, Belgium went one step further in not acknowledging the vulnerability of its resettled population. It should also be mentioned that the termination of the partnership with NGOs supposes a total lack of monitoring of the Belgian asylum authorities by civil society organisations, thus leaving the door open for future potential breaches of the rights of resettled refugees in the country. In other words, it is clear that the legal factor contributes to widening the gap between expectations and reality: Belgium's human rights approach to resettlement is insufficient, which causes a drop in the satisfaction of its Syrian resettled population.

4. CONCLUSION

This article studied the complexity of the gap between the expectations raised by Syrian refugees in Lebanon and their reality once resettled in Belgium through the UNHCR's resettlement scheme. Two factors – the individual factor and the legal factor – were identified as the potential root causes of this asymmetry and were successively explored.

First, expectations of Syrian refugees in Lebanon were examined through three channels: resettlement awareness, personal expectations and expectations vis-à-vis resettlement countries. With more than 80% of SRL aware of the existence of UNHCR's programme, resettlement awareness was deemed high. Yet, SRL showed a very cursory knowledge of conditions attached to the programme. Their personal expectations and expectations vis-à-vis resettlement countries were, on average, realistic. SRL expressed their desire to satisfy three particular needs through resettlement: the right to security of person, the right to education and the right to work. It should be emphasised that they also attributed great value to the concept of dignity: they believed that their precarious situation in Lebanon deprived them from their right to live a dignified life. Upon arrival, SRL expected to find quality education and healthcare. Disaggregated data highlighted the influence of a refugee's level of education: the less educated a refugee is, the higher his or her expectations become towards the host country.

Secondly, the Belgian resettlement scheme in Lebanon was analysed from a human rights angle. Even though Belgium does respect its core obligations under human rights law, improvement is needed. CGRS deplored the lack of a legal framework for resettlement while NGOs and refugees insisted that the current housing system was not optimal. Considering that Belgium decides to welcome vulnerable refugees, a long-term housing system should be put in place to favour security and reduce stress among the Syrian resettled population. The 2017 reform must also be closely monitored, especially due to the withdrawal of

Caritas and Convivial from the integration process. It was demonstrated that the two NGOs are specialised organisations acting as essential linguistic mediators and intermediaries between asylum authorities and resettled refugees; their workers also play a significant role in facilitating access to housing and healthcare for resettled Syrians. The termination of their mandate is thus likely to have a negative influence on refugees' effective access to the two aforementioned rights.

To conclude, the individual and the legal factors directly contributed to the creation of a gap between pre-resettlement expectations and post-resettlement reality. In Lebanon, the significant lack of knowledge of Syrian refugees led them to develop misconceptions about, for instance, conditions attached to family reunification. Increasing resettlement knowledge and focusing on expectation management are key to building realistic expectations in the pre-resettlement phase. As for the post-resettlement phase, the need to adopt a deeply human approach to resettled populations is pressing. By failing to recognise the inherent vulnerability of resettled refugees, Belgium is jeopardising the rights they are entitled to under international human rights law. Instead of reducing assistance, the country must guarantee that each and every resettled refugee is provided with long-term, tailor-made guidance, notably through the direct involvement of NGOs. The experience of resettled Syrians revealed that such guidance is, *de facto*, a leading factor in their satisfaction with the host country and, consequently, their willingness to integrate.

THE DECLINE OF FUNDAMENTAL RIGHTS IN CJEU JURISPRUDENCE AFTER THE 2015 'REFUGEE CRISIS'

Lisa HESCHL and Alma STANKOVIC

1. Introduction 104
2. The CEAS under Stress: Testing the Effectiveness of the Union's Rules....106
3. CJEU and the Crisis: Entrenching a Failing System and Creating New Tragedies 111
    3.1. Humanitarian Visa: *X and X v Belgium*....................... 113
        3.1.1. Background 113
        3.1.2. The European Legal Framework and Humanitarian Visa... 116
        3.1.3. *X and X v Belgium*................................. 118
        3.1.4. Implications for a Future EU Scheme on Humanitarian Visa 121
    3.2. Dublin Rules: *A.S.* and *Jafari* 123
        3.2.1. Background 123
        3.2.2. The Mutual Trust Doctrine and Fundamental Rights in the Context of the EU Asylum Law 125
        3.2.3. *Jafari* and *A.S.* 127
        3.2.4. Interpretation and Implications 130
4. Conclusion... 134

ABSTRACT

In the past, the Court of Justice of the European Union (CJEU) has been one of the driving forces ensuring the compliance of secondary acts adopted under the Common European Asylum System (CEAS) with fundamental rights issues. It even came to be considered a 'fundamental rights' Court, often taking a progressive stance in interpreting the relevant norms in light of the Charter of Fundamental Rights (CFREU) and other applicable human and refugee rights norms. While the Court has always been eager to demonstrate its legal integrity preventing second thoughts on its political independence, the proclaimed 'refugee crisis' of the last years with the surrounding political turmoil seems to have had an impact on the Court and its approach towards the protection of fundamental rights within the European Union (EU) as well. This article seeks to analyse two judgments *X and X* and *A.S. and Jafari* considered exemplary for the shift the CJEU has undergone in the last years. In both cases, the CJEU has had the opportunity to change the course of the CEAS ensuring its compliance with fundamental rights standards. However, as will be shown below, the Court in 2017 has adopted a conservative if not politically motivated approach to CEAS cases.

1. INTRODUCTION

When in 2015 more than one million people arrived at the shores of the EU,[1] policy makers were quick in proclaiming it a 'migration' or 'refugee crisis'. While 3,771 reported deaths in the Mediterranean and other related tragedies[2] triggered only modest expressions of condolences, the increasing numbers of people applying for asylum provoked a chain reaction with mostly emotional, populist and fear-induced policies adopted at the Member States (MS) level.[3] The crisis rhetoric surrounding the arrivals of people seeking international protection supported the renaissance of unilateral approaches, and soon those

---

[1] UNCHR, 'Over one million sea arrivals reach Europe in 2015', 2015, available online at http://www.unhcr.org/afr/news/latest/2015/12/5683d0b56/million-sea-arrivals-reach-europe-2015.html, last accessed 16.05.2018.

[2] UNHCR, *The Mediterranean Situation*, available at http://data2.unhcr.org/en/situations/mediterranean, last accessed 16.05.2018.

[3] Hungary has been particularly and consistently vocal on wishing to exclude asylum seekers from its territory and has taken political stances and created laws that have anti-immigrant objectives and intent. See e.g. L. BAYER, 'Hungary's "zero refugee' strategy"', *Politico*, 20.09.2016, available at https://www.politico.eu/article/hungary-zero-refugee-strategy-viktor-orban-europe-migration-crisis, last accessed 16.05.2018; L. DEARDEN, 'Hungarian parliament approves law allowing all asylum seekers to be detained', *Independent*, 07.03.2017, available at https://www.independent.co.uk/news/world/europe/hungary-parliament-asylum-seekers-detain-law-approve-refugees-immigration-crisis-arrests-border-a7615486.html, last accessed 16.05.2018; R. STAUDENMEIER, 'Hungary's Orban tells Germany: "You wanted the migrants, we didn't"', *Deutsche Welle*, 08.01.2018, available at http://www.dw.com/en/hungarys-orban-tells-germany-you-wanted-the-migrants-we-didnt/a-42065012, last accessed 16.05.2018. However, other countries had similar rhetoric. After initially warmly welcoming refugees, Austria's policies also turned populist, with the country's right wing party ultimately securing a coalition with the conservative party and becoming the ruling party in the last elections. See A. JAMIESON, 'Refugee Crisis: Austria Limits Asylum to 1.5 Percent of Population', *NBC News*, 20.01.2016, available at http://www.nbcnews.com/storyline/europes-border-crisis/refugee-crisis-austria-limits-asylum-1-5-percent-population-n500326, last accessed 16.05.2018; S. NASRALLA, 'Austria puts the squeeze on refugees with benefit cuts', *Reuters*, 04.10.2017, available at https://www.reuters.com/article/us-austria-elections-benefits-migrants/austria-puts-the-squeeze-on-refugees-with-benefit-cuts-idUSKCN1C90VF, last accessed 16.05.2018; R. HEINISCH, 'A Populist Victory in Austria', *Foreign Affairs*, 28.12.2017; 'Austria's conservatives and right-wing populists agree on coalition government', *Deutsche Welle*, 16.12.2017, available at http://www.dw.com/en/austrias-conservatives-and-right-wing-populists-agree-on-coalition-government/a-41818503, last accessed 16.05.2018.

arrivals became the stress test for the European project as a whole. With the temporary reintroduction of internal border controls by several MS,[4] the Union seemed to be rudely awakened from its Schengen dream, and the story of the ever-closer Union seemed to have come to an end. One reason why the Union was shaken to the core by the events of 2015 was that structural deficiencies of the CEAS surfaced and revealed that the EU is far from having accomplished a coherent set of norms in the field of asylum.[5] Only a short period after the second phase instruments had to be transposed into national laws, the EU found itself in a rather paradoxical if not schizophrenic situation. While the correct implementation of the CEAS rules had led to an overburdening of especially southern MS, their disregard in 2015 led to a perceived overburdening of northern MS such as Germany, Sweden, or Austria.

The CJEU became an important actor with regard to the CEAS. Although the Commission was rather quick to note and tackle both the solidarity issues among MS as well as the failure of implementing the CEAS rules correctly *inter alia* by initiating infringement cases against delinquent MS, national courts increasingly referred preliminary questions fundamental for the continuation of the CEAS to the CJEU seeking its judgment on the interpretation of secondary legislative acts. The political efforts to reform the CEAS have been not particularly fruitful and indeed have brought to light not just the extent of the discrepancies in solidarity and unity between the MS but also a certain drive to minimise the protection of fundamental and human rights of those seeking international protection. Accordingly, great hopes to change the current course of the CEAS have been placed on the CJEU, which was usually at the forefront of protecting the fundamental rights of all persons in the EU, including those seeking international protection. However, while in the past the CJEU was not afraid to rebuke the MS and EU efforts to diminish fundamental rights for the purpose of upholding the EU's migration and asylum policy, in 2017 it seemed to take a far more deferential stance, seemingly trading the protection of fundamental rights for the maintenance of a dysfunctional system, thereby taking on the role of a political actor challenging to a considerable extent its legal integrity. Before analysing the *X and X* and the *A.S.* and *Jafari* judgments, the subsequent section aims at contextualising them providing a background necessary to understand the dynamics and logic of the CEAS reflected in the CJEU's decision making.

---

4   For a full list of MS' notifications of the reintroduction of internal border controls see EUROPEAN COMMISSION, 'Temporary Reintroduction of Border Control', available at https://ec.europa.eu/home-affairs/what-we-do/policies/borders-and-visas/schengen/reintroduction-border-control_en, last accessed 16.05.2018.

5   See generally V. CHETAIL, 'The Common European Asylum System: Bric-à-brac or System?', in V. CHETAIL, P. DE BRUYCKER and F. MAIANI, *Reforming the Common European Asylum System. The New European Refugee Law*, Leiden/Boston, Brill Nijhoff 2016, pp. 3–38.

2. THE CEAS UNDER STRESS: TESTING THE EFFECTIVENESS OF THE UNION'S RULES

The CEAS from its inception has been framed as a means of migration control rather than a supplement to the Geneva Refugee Convention. Hence, the CEAS itself is not exclusively concerned with providing asylum; rather it attempts to fulfil various conflicting objectives. On the one hand, the humanitarian vocation[6] to provide those in need with protection concurs with the logic that the 'CEAS is a constituent part of the European Union's objective of progressively establishing an area of freedom, security and justice'.[7] Fulfilling the therewith tied aim to control the movement of asylum seekers within and across MS and to prevent the 'abuse' of domestic asylum systems by ordinary migrants, on the other hand, was meant as insurance to avoid the overburdening of any single MS's system. However, when the CEAS was being developed, its emphasis quickly shifted from this idea of a European protection system to a tool for migration control and the administering of refugee flows.[8] Therefore, the CEAS from its beginning was negotiated by the MS as a system to allocate responsibility for asylum applications lodged in the EU and to reduce the volume of refugees by establishing strict criteria to distinguish them from the rest, from those migrants who are neither economically wanted nor have a genuine right to a legal status. When the numbers of asylum applications reached their peak in 2015, it became clear, however, that the rules of the CEAS failed all these expectations.

---

[6] Art. 78(1) TFEU sets the direction for the need of a common asylum system in order to offer an appropriate status to any TCN and to ensure compliance with the obligation of *non-refoulement* and other human and refugee rights obligations. The CJEU has confirmed this pursuit in *Abdulla et. al v Germany*, joined cases C-175/08, C-176/08, C-178/08, C-179/08, 02.03.2010, ECLI:EU:C:2010:105, paras. 51–54.

[7] See common recital 2 of the Preambles of Directive 2011/95/EU of the European Parliament and of the Council of 13 December 2011 on standards for the qualification of third-country nationals or stateless persons as beneficiaries of international protection, for a uniform status for refugees or for persons eligible for subsidiary protection, and for the content of the protection granted (recast), OJ L 337, 20.12.2011 (hereinafter Qualification Directive); Directive 2013/32/EU of the European Parliament and of the Council of 26 June 2013 on common procedures for granting and withdrawing international protection (recast), OJ L 180, 29.06.2013 (hereinafter Asylum Procedures Directive 2013/33/EU of the European Parliament and of the Council of 26 June 2013 laying down standards for the reception of applicants for international protection (recast), OJ L 180, 29.06.2013 (hereinafter Reception Conditions Directive); and Regulation (EU) No 604/2013 of the European Parliament and of the Council of 26 June 2013 establishing the criteria and mechanisms for determining the Member State responsible for examining an application for international protection lodged in one of the Member States by a third-country national or a stateless person (recast), OJ L 180, 29.06.2013 (hereinafter Dublin III Regulation).

[8] V. Moreno-Lax, 'Life after Lisbon: EU Asylum Policy as a Factor of Migration Control', in D. Acosta Arcarazo and C. Murphy (eds.), *EU Security and Justice Law. After Lisbon and Stockholm*, Oxford/Portland, Hart Publishing 2014, p. 161.

While the MS blamed the underlying structure of the CEAS as an aggravating factor and resorted to unilateral national measures to regain control, the Commission lamented that the lacking implementation of the existing framework worsened the situation.[9] The approach by the Commission, namely that a mix of proper transposition of the provisions of the CEAS, their effective monitoring and uniform interpretation by the CJEU, and the consequential harmonisation of national asylum systems would equip MS with necessary means to respond to situations such as the one in 2015, seemed to fall short of the actual circumstances. Years and years of harmonisation have not aligned disparities between asylum practices in the MS. Therefore, the CEAS and, in particular, the responsibility-allocation rules of the Dublin III System continue to build on the false premise of a level playing asylum field.[10] Moreover, they continue to disregard asylum seekers' choices and preferences of countries of destination.[11]

The counter-productivity of this negligence became obvious in 2015. Asylum seekers tried to reach those countries in the EU arguably providing them with the highest level of protection. To avoid becoming subject to the allocation rules of the Dublin System, they often displayed disobedient behaviours, for example by lying about the route of their flight during asylum determination procedures, avoiding registration (even cutting off fingertips to avoid identity

---

[9] See e.g. EUROPEAN COMMISSION, European Agenda on Migration, COM(2015) 240 final, 13.05.2015, p. 12.

[10] An evaluation report by the Commission's DG on Migration and Home Affairs of the Dublin III Regulation in 2015 found as much, stating in relevant part: 'In addition to the inherent weaknesses, several challenges, which result from the interaction of Dublin with the broader context, also render achievement of its objectives more difficult. Despite harmonisation efforts of the CEAS, differences remain in the asylum procedures, reception conditions and integration capacity of EU Member States Several stakeholders emphasised that this undermines Dublin's core assumption that asylum applicants will receive equal consideration and treatment in whatever Member State they lodge their claim. The lack of a level playing field may further encourage secondary movements.' EUROPEAN COMISSION, 'Evaluation of the Dublin III Regulation', 04.12.2015, available at https://ec.europa.eu/home-affairs/sites/homeaffairs/files/what-we-do/policies/asylum/examination-of-applicants/docs/evaluation_of_the_dublin_iii_regulation_en.pdf, last accessed 16.05.2018. Nevertheless, the CJEU in particular retains the myth of a level playing field as noted below in section 3.

[11] There is a growing body of research into the issue of asylum destination choice. The reasons for choosing certain countries over others are manifold, and choices cannot be explained only by economic considerations or recognition rates. Determinants for choosing a country are, in particular, the presence of family and other social contacts, the level of xenophobia, geographical proximity, language ties, colonial links, etc. See e.g. M. McAuliffe and D. Jayasuriya, 'Do Asylum Seekers and Refugees Choose Destination Countries?, Evidence from large-scale surveys in Australia, Afghanistan, Bangladesh, Pakistan and Sri Lanka', (2016) 54(4) *International Migration*, pp. 44–59; E. Neumayer, 'Bogus Refugees?, The Determinants of Asylum Migration to Western Europe', (2005) 49(3) *International Studies Quarterly*, pp. 389–410; W.H. Moore and S.M. Shellman, 'Whither Will They Go?, A Global Study of Refugees' Destinations, 1965–1995', (2007) 51(4), *International Studies Quarterly*, pp. 811–834.

determinations), or going into hiding in order to avoid the implementation of Dublin transfer decisions.[12] As a reaction, the MS tried to find 'solutions' by either applying existing rules in a more coercive way, including taking fingerprints by force, or extending administrative detention for asylum seekers awaiting their transfers.[13] Or, recalling their sovereignty, MS refrained from applying the common rules, particularly the responsibility-allocation rules of the Dublin III Regulation. Instead, the MS took questionable unilateral measures, such as providing lower levels of protection[14] or even creating coercive and punitive measures in conflict with human rights.[15] The underlying rationale for MS was to lower their attractiveness and hence stem the influx of persons coming into their territory. The 1990s 'race to the bottom' was on again, and 'ad hoc' measures adopted by MS aimed at protecting national asylum systems

---

[12] M. DEN HEIJER, J. RIJPMA and T. SPIJKERBOER, 'Coercion, Prohibition, and Great Expectations: The Continuing Failure of the Common European Asylum System', (2016) 53 *Common Market Law Review*, p. 4.

[13] According to the Commission, 21 out of 31 MS (including Norway, Sweden and Iceland) frequently use detention in order to enforce Dublin transfers. See EUROPEAN COMMISSION, Proposal for a Regulation of the European Parliament and of the Council establishing the criteria and mechanisms for determining the Member State responsible for examining an application for international protection lodged in one of the Member States by a third-country national or a stateless person (recast), COM(2016) 270 final, 04.05.2016. In September 2017, the CJEU ruled in *Khir Amayry* on the time limits of 'Dublin detentions' and found that these have to be in strict accordance with the rule of law and fundamental and human rights. See CJEU, *Mohammad Khir Amayry v Migrationsverket*, C-60/16, 13.09.2017, ECLI:EU:C:2017:675.

[14] Some MS, such as Denmark, have purposefully lowered the benefit amount awarded to refugees or those eligible for subsidiary protections. See 'Denmark to slash benefits for asylum seekers in attempt to deter refugees', *The Guardian*, 01.07.2015, available at https://www.theguardian.com/world/2015/jul/01/denmark-slash-benefits-asylum-seekers-refugees, last accessed 16.05.2018. Others have instituted schemes that ensure protection only for a limited period of time or have passed laws that delay family reunification for those seeking protection. (e.g. AT – Änderung des Asylgesetzes 2005, des Fremdenpolizeigesetzes 2005 und des BFA-Verfahrensgesetzes, BGBl. I Nr. 24/2016; SE – Lag (2016:752) om tillfälliga begränsningar av möjligheten att få uppehållstillstånd i Sverige, Svensk författningssamling 2016:752). See also 'Regierung beschließt "Asyl auf Zeit"', *Kurier*, 26.01.2016, available at https://kurier.at/politik/inland/regierung-beschliesst-asyl-auf-zeit/177.262.265, last accessed 16.05.2018; D. BILEFSKY, 'Sweden Toughens Rules for Refugees Seeking Asylum', *New York Times*, 21.06.2016, available at https://www.nytimes.com/2016/06/22/world/europe/sweden-immigrant-restrictions.html, last accessed 16.05.2018.

[15] For example, Denmark has instituted a law that seizes the asylum seekers' property. See A. DAMON and T. HUME, 'Denmark adopts controversial law to seize asylum seekers' valuables', *CNN.com*, 26.01.2016, available at https://www.cnn.com/2016/01/26/europe/denmark-vote-jewelry-bill-migrants/index.html, last accessed 16.05.2018. Also, Denmark has attempted to discourage those helping refugees cross borders out of pure humanitarian impulse by criminalising them as human traffickers. M. CHRISTOPH, 'Punishing those who help refugees – "a perverse logic"', *Deutsche Welle*, 18.05.2017, available at http://www.dw.com/en/punishing-those-who-help-refugees-a-perverse-logic/a-38894477, last accessed 16.05.2018.

came not only at the cost of European Unity but also of the rule of law and fundamental rights. Yet, they seemed to *inter alia*[16] have had the MS's intended effect: Figures published by the European Asylum Support Office (EASO) show that the numbers of asylum applications in 2017 dropped by 43% compared to 2016.[17] The numbers of 2017 are now pretty much the same as they were before the crisis in 2014.[18]

With regard to the disobedience of EU secondary legislation, the reaction of the EU was admittedly swift, though its effectiveness is still to be determined. In 2015, the Commission opened 37 infringement cases[19] for the late transposition of the recast Asylum Procedures Directive and the recast Reception Conditions Directive. Further infringement procedures against MS for incorrect implementation and/or breaches of EU asylum legislation have been opened in particular against Greece for continuing deficiencies in its national asylum system[20] and against Hungary, whose new asylum legislation was considered to be in breach of the EU Asylum *acquis* and the Fundamental Rights Charter.[21] In addition, the practice of MS to refrain from registering migrants according to the Eurodac Regulation[22] to avoid responsibilities under the Dublin III Regulation was reason for the opening of infringement procedures against four MS.[23] In 2016, 66 new infringement cases were

---

[16] To reduce the pull-factor 'favourable-asylum-legislation' at the internal level has not been the only measure taken in order to reduce the numbers of people arriving. Instead, such measures at the internal level have been accompanied by a variety of external measures such as the cooperation with third states in the field of operational migration control measures. See e.g. L. HESCHL, *Protecting the Rights of Refugees Beyond European Borders – Establishing Extraterritorial Legal Responsibilities*, Intersentia, Antwerp/Oxford 2018.

[17] See EASO, 'EASO releases overview of 2017 EU+ asylum trends', Press Release, 01.02.2018, available at https://www.easo.europa.eu/news-events/press-release-easo-releases-overview-2017-eu-asylum-trends, last accessed 16.05.2018.

[18] See ibid.; see also EASO, Annual Report on the Situation of Asylum in the European Union 2014, July 2015, available at https://www.easo.europa.eu/sites/default/files/public/EASO-Annual-Report-2014.pdf, last accessed 16.05.2018, p. 7.

[19] EUROPEAN COMMISSION, Monitoring the application of European Union law, 2015 Annual Report, COM(2016) 463 final, 15.07.2016, p. 12.

[20] Ibid.

[21] Ibid.

[22] Regulation (EU) No 603/2013 of the European Parliament and of the Council of 26 June 2013 on the establishment of 'Eurodac' for the comparison of fingerprints for the effective application of Regulation (EU) No 604/2013 establishing the criteria and mechanisms for determining the Member State responsible for examining an application for international protection lodged in one of the Member States by a third-country national or a stateless person and on requests for the comparison with Eurodac data by Member States' law enforcement authorities and Europol for law enforcement purposes, and amending Regulation (EU) No 1077/2011 establishing a European Agency for the operational management of large-scale IT systems in the area of freedom, security and justice, OJ L 180/60 of 29 June 2013 (hereinafter Eurodac Regulation).

[23] EUROPEAN COMMISSION (2016), 2015 Annual Report, *supra* note 19, p. 12.

opened in the field of asylum.[24] Most of these infringement cases are still open, with the Commission closing only a few older cases in 2017.[25]

While most of the cases concern the implementation of the Asylum *acquis*,[26] prominent cases of infringement procedures also try to address the lack of solidarity among the MS in the field of asylum. For example, in June 2017, the Commission launched infringement procedures against the Czech Republic, Hungary and Poland for failing to comply with the emergency relocation scheme established in two Council Decisions in September 2015 foreseeing the mandatory intra-EU relocation of 160,000 asylum seekers from Italy and Greece.[27] In December 2017, the case was referred to the CJEU since the

---

[24] EUROPEAN COMMISSION, Commission Staff Working Document – Part I. Monitoring the application of European Union law 2016 annual Report, SWD(2017) 259 final, 06.07.2017, p. 65.

[25] A notable closure in 2016 was that of the infringement cases against Greece and Italy for incorrect implementation of the recast Eurodac Regulation. See EUROPEAN COMMISSION, 'Fact Sheet, December infringements package: key decisions', 08.12.2016, available at http://europa.eu/rapid/press-release_MEMO-16-4211_en.htm, last accessed 16.05.2018. A search of the EU Home Affairs Law database reveals that the closures seen in 2017 concerned much older cases arising before the crisis, from 2013 and 2014, against several southern European states regarding the Qualification Directive. Database available at https://ec.europa.eu/home-affairs/what-is-new/eu-law-and-monitoring_en, last accessed 16.05.2018.

[26] Most notably the Commission moved forward with the infringement procedures against Hungary concerning its asylum legislation. In May 2017, a formal notice was sent to Hungary requesting the Hungarian authorities to respond to the arguments of the Commission finding the Hungarian law in asylum in breach of the Asylum Procedures Directive (recast), the Reception Conditions Directive (recast) and the Return Directive (Directive 2008/115/EC). See EUROPEAN COMMISSION, 'Commission follows up on infringement procedure against Hungary concerning its asylum law', Press Release, IP/17/1285, 17.05.2017, available at http://europa.eu/rapid/press-release_IP-17-1285_en.htm, last accessed 17.05.2018. The formal opinion was followed in December 2017 by reasoned opinion by the Commission still finding that the Hungarian asylum legislation is in breach of the EU Asylum *acquis*. See EUROPEAN COMMISSION, 'Migration: Commission steps up infringement against Hungary concerning its asylum law', Press Release, IP/17/5023, 07.12.2017, available at http://europa.eu/rapid/press-release_IP-17-5023_en.htm, last accessed 17.05.2018. Closely related to the infringement procedure Hungary is facing due to its inconformity with the Asylum *acquis* is the infringement procedure the Commission initiated against Hungary in October 2017 concerning its NGO law which also poses disproportionate burdens on NGOs providing support to asylum seekers. In December 2017 Hungary was referred to the CJEU. See EUROPEAN COMMISSION, 'Infringements -European Commission refers Hungary to the Court of Justice for its NGO Law', Press Release, IP/17/5003, 07.12.2017, available at http://europa.eu/rapid/press-release_IP-17-5003_en.htm, last accessed 17.05.2018.

[27] COUNCIL OF THE EUROPEAN UNION, Decision (EU) 2015/1601 of 22 September 2015 establishing provisional measures in the area of international protection for the benefit of Italy and Greece, OJ L 248, 24.09.2015, and COUNCIL OF THE EUROPEAN UNION, Decision (EU) 2015/1523 of 14 September 2015 establishing provisional measures in the area of international protection for the benefit of Italy and of Greece, OJ L 239, 15.09.2015. Under the emergency relocation scheme which was only foreseen for two years and came to an end in September 2017 a total of 31,503 asylum seekers have been relocated. So far, a continuation of a relocation scheme is not foreseen since the numbers of arrivals, particularly in Greece, dropped because of the EU-Turkey deal by 96%. See EUROPEAN COMMISSION, Report to

three countries in question remained the only MS not having relocated asylum seekers from Italy or Greece.[28] Having been filed only recently, the cases are still open.

3. CJEU AND THE CRISIS: ENTRENCHING A FAILING SYSTEM AND CREATING NEW TRAGEDIES

While there has been slow progress on the legislative proposals for a new CEAS and the resolution of infringement cases is also still likely far down the line, the CJEU in 2017 became concerned with several cases important for the clarification of the relation between and compatibility of fundamental rights obligations of the Union and its MS and the continuation of the CEAS. Proponents of fundamental rights were particularly attentive to these opportunities, as in the past the CJEU has been a driving force in ensuring compliance of the implementation of the secondary legislative acts with fundamental rights leading to shifts in national practices or formal legislative changes.[29] While in its past jurisprudence the CJEU had often been attributed the role as 'fundamental rights' Court expanding progressively the scope of the CFREU,[30] in 2017, the upholding of a legal system in place, i.e. the CEAS, as dysfunctional as it might be, seemed to be more relevant for the Court. By its reluctance to provide a basis for changing the rules of the CEAS, it thereby contributed to the continuance of fundamental right breaches people seeking protection face on their dangerous journeys to the EU.

---

the European Parliament, the European Council and the Council – Progress report on the European Agenda on Migration: Relocation (Annex 6), COM(2017) 669 final, 15.11.2017.

[28] In September 2017, the CJEU had already dismissed an action brought by Slovakia and Hungary against the mandatory relocation scheme. See CJEU, *Slovak Republic and Hungary v Council*, Joined Cases C-643/15 and C-647/15, 9/6/2017, ECLI:EU:C:2017:631.

[29] The second phase instruments have been mainly shaped by the CJEU's jurisprudence. For the impact of the CJEU's judgments in practice see EUROPEAN COUNCIL ON REFUGEES AND EXILES, 'Preliminary Deference?, The impact of judgments of the Court of Justice of the EU in cases X.Y.Z., A.B.C. and Cimade and Gisti on national law and the use of the EU Charter of Fundamental Rights', 2017, available at http://s3.amazonaws.com/ecre/wp-content/uploads/2017/03/14102648/CJEU-study-Feb-2017-NEW.pdf, last accessed 16.05.2018.

[30] See S. CARRERA, M. DE SOMER and B. PETKOVA, 'The Court of Justice of the European Union as a Fundamental rights Tribunal. Challenges for the Effective Delivery of Fundamental Rights in the Area of Freedom, Security and Justice', CEPS Papers in Liberty and Security, 2012, available at https://www.ceps.eu/publications/court-justice-european-union-fundamental-rights-tribunal-challenges-effective-delivery, last accessed 16.05.2018. On the fundamental rights approach by the CJEU in asylum cases see S. VELLUTI, *Reforming the common European asylum system. Legislative developments and judicial activism of the European Courts*, Heidelberg, Springer 2014. See more critically G. DE BÚRCA, 'The Road Not Taken: The EU as a Global Human Rights Actor', (2011) 105(4) *American Journal of International Law*, pp. 649–693.

This article analyses judgments issued in 2017, *X and X v Belgium*, *A.S. v Slovenian Republic* and *Khadija Jafari and Zainab Jafari*, deemed crucial for the future course of the CEAS by the authors. Even if *Jafari* must be considered in light of the extraordinary circumstances in 2015 and *X and X* as a missed opportunity rather than a clear break by the CJEU with its previous stance, the Court's stressing of the maintenance of the existing rules of the CEAS is surprising. The selected judgments are thus exemplary for how the CJEU contributes to the upholding of a system that not only led to the disintegration of the EU but perpetuates large-scale fundamental rights violations.[31] The discussion of the judgments aims to show that the Court seems willing to align with the EU institutions and MS that times of crisis require robust measures even if that requires a bypassing of fundamental rights commitments in order to save an already failed system. While the balancing of tensions between legal certainty, i.e. upholding, in particular, the Dublin III rules, and fundamental rights is nothing unusual for courts, the analysed decisions have also to be considered in light of the ongoing renegotiations of the secondary legislative acts composing the CEAS.[32] The securitisation argument dominating current

---

[31] The judgments discussed are not the only controversial judgments concerning the responses to the 'migration crisis'. For instance, in February 2017, the CJEU, by a contested procedural move, discharged itself from reviewing the legality of the EU-Turkey deal. See GC, *NF v European Council*, joined Cases T-192/16, T-193/16 and T-257/16, 28.02.2017, ECLI:EU:T:2017:128. For a discussion of the *NF* case see J. BAST, 'Scharade im kontrollfreien Raum: Hat die EU gar keinen Türkei-Deal geschlossen?', *Verfassungsblog*, 03.03.2017, available at https://verfassungsblog.de/scharade-im-kontrollfreien-raum-hat-die-eu-gar-keinen-tuerkei-deal-geschlossen, last accessed 16.05.2017.

[32] See EUROPEAN COMMISSION, Towards a Reform of the Common European Asylum System and Enhancing Legal Avenues to Europe, COM(2016) 197 final, 06.04.2016; EUROPEAN COMMISSION, Proposal for a Regulation of the European Parliament and of the Council establishing the criteria and mechanisms for determining the Member State responsible for examining an application for international protection lodged in one of the Member States by a third-country national or a stateless person (recast), COM(2016) 270 final, 04.05.2016; EUROPEAN COMMISSION, Proposal for a Regulation of the European Parliament and of the Council on the European Union Agency for Asylum and repealing Regulation (EU) No 439/2010, COM(2016) 271 final, 04.05.2016; EUROPEAN COMMISSION, Proposal for a Regulation of the European Parliament and of the Council on the establishment of 'Eurodac' for the comparison of fingerprints for the effective application of [Regulation (EU) No 604/2013 establishing the criteria and mechanisms for determining the Member State responsible for examining an application for international protection lodged in one of the Member States by a third-country national or a stateless person], for identifying an illegally staying third-country national or stateless person and on requests for the comparison with Eurodac data by Member States' law enforcement authorities and Europol for law enforcement purposes (recast), COM(2016) 272 final, 04.05.2016; EUROPEAN COMMISSION, Proposal for a Regulation of the European Parliament and of the Council on standards for the qualification of third-country nationals or stateless persons as beneficiaries of international protection, for a uniform status for refugees or for persons eligible for subsidiary protection and for the content of the protection granted and amending Council Directive 2003/109/EC of 25 November 2003 concerning the status of third-country nationals who are long-term residents, COM(2016) 466 final, 13.07.2016; EUROPEAN COMMISSION, Proposal for a Regulation of the European Parliament and the Council establishing a common procedure

discussions about a European approach towards the reception of refugees and asylum seekers, the scope of protection people should have a right to, and the sharing of responsibilities among MS already seems to disregard fundamental rights obligations the EU and its MS have. The Court's judgments therefore might be considered as a signal embracing the approach that fundamental rights protection is secondary to the security of the EU even though it remains unclear what the latter entails and why people searching for protection may threaten it.

3.1. HUMANITARIAN VISA: *X AND X v BELGIUM*

3.1.1. Background

Since the beginning of 2015, more than 12,000 people have lost their lives while trying to cross the Mediterranean.[33] While legal channels to the EU for those seeking international protection are largely lacking, the secondary legislative acts adopted under the CEAS apply an explicit territorial outlook, suggesting that claims for international protection can only be made once the territory of an EU MS is reached.[34] The combination of a lack of possibilities of legal entry and the territorial notion of asylum in the EU spurs a downward spiral of fundamental rights violations and increasingly restrictive responses to migratory movements by the EU and its MS.

Possibilities for the creation of further avenues for legal access to the EU have been discussed on different levels and for different groups of people. Delivering the European Agenda on Migration, in June 2016 the Commission published a proposal to revise the Blue Card Directive[35] aimed at improving and facilitating access to the EU for highly skilled migrants.[36] The proposed revision of the Blue Card Directive forms part of the long-term strategy of the Commission to tackle the 'migration crisis', and applies to only a small group of migrants on

---

for international protection in the Union and repealing Directive 2013/32/EU, COM(2016) 467, 13.07.2016.

[33] See IOM, 'Missing Migrants', available at https://missingmigrants.iom.int, last accessed 16.05.2018.

[34] Both the Reception Conditions Directive and the Asylum Procedures Directive constrain applications for international protection to the borders, the territorial waters, and the transit zones of MS. See Art. 3(1) Asylum Procedures Directive, Art. 3(1) Reception Conditions Directive. The Dublin III Regulation only applies to applications made on the territory of MS, including applications made at the borders and in transition zones, whereas applications made in the territorial waters are not encompassed. See Art. 3(1) Dublin III Regulation.

[35] Council Directive 2009/50/EC of 25 May 2009 on the conditions of entry and residence of third-country nationals for the purposes of highly qualified employment, OJ L 155, 18.06.2009.

[36] See EUROPEAN COMMISSION, Proposal for a Directive of the European Parliament and of the Council on the conditions of entry and residence of third-country nationals for the purposes of highly skilled employment, COM(2016) 378 final, 07.06.2016.

the one side of the migration spectrum. For migrants on the other side of the migration spectrum, i.e. persons seeking international protection, short- and medium-term legal entry possibilities were discussed *inter alia* as 'Protected Entry Procedures' (PEP).

PEPs have been explored at the EU level since the beginning of the new millennium.[37] They allow a person in need of protection to approach a potential host state already outside its territory with a claim for international protection and to be granted a form of entry permit in case of a positive assessment of the claim for international protection, either final or preliminary, irrespectively.[38] The actual form of a PEP is defined at neither the national nor the EU level, and different MS have applied different approaches thereto. However, since extraterritorial asylum processing centres so far, despite increasing demand, have not reached a point beyond conceptual thought,[39] the primary PEP

---

[37] Following the Tampere Council Conclusions 1999, the Commission's Communication 'Towards a common asylum procedure and a uniform status, valid throughout the Union, for persons granted asylum' raised the possibility to adopt common 'policies on visas and external border controls to take account of the specific aspects of asylum', including 'facilitating the visa procedure in specific situations to be determined'. Furthermore, it promoted the idea of 'processing requests for protection directly in the region of origin' and developing resettlement schemes in order to facilitate the safe arrival of persons in need of protection in the EU. EUROPEAN COMMISSION, Communication from the Commission to the Council and the European Parliament. Towards a Common Asylum Procedure and a Uniform Status, Valid Throughout the Union, for Persons Granted Asylum, COM(2000) 755 final, 22.11.2000, p. 8. Similarly, in 2001 the Communication on a common policy on illegal immigration stressed that the fight against irregular migration must be conducted in a sensitive way balancing the rights of persons in need of protection with national interests. It recommended MS to make use of their discretion 'in allowing more asylum applications to be made from abroad or the processing of a request for protection in the region of origin and facilitating the arrival of refugees on the territory of the Member States by resettlement scheme.' COMMISSION OF THE EUROPEAN COMMUNITIES, Communication to the Council and the European Parliament on a common policy on illegal immigration, COM(2001) 672 final, 15.11.2001, p. 8.

[38] G. NOLL, *Study on the Feasibility of Processing Asylum Claims outside the EU against the Background of the Common European Asylum System and the Goal of a Common Asylum Procedure*, Study for the European Commission, 2002, p. 3. The EU later endorsed this definition see COMMISSION OF THE EUROPEAN COMMUNITIES, Communication to the Council and the Parliament – Towards more accessible, equitable and managed asylum systems, COM(2003) 315 final, 03.06.2003, p. 15.

[39] In 2003 the UK proposed for the first time at EU level to establish asylum processing centres in third countries, while Germany introduced in 2005 the idea of asylum centres in North Africa. For the full text of the UK's proposal 'New international approaches to asylum processing and protection', see STATEWATCH, 'UK Asylum Plan for 'Safe Havens': Full-text of Proposal and Reactions', 2003, available at http://www.statewatch.org/news/2003/apr/10safe.htm, last accessed 16.05.2018. For the German proposal see, 'Außenminister distanzieren sich von Schilys Asyl-Plänen', *Die Welt*, 04.10.2010, available at https://www.welt.de/print-welt/article344224/Aussenminister-distanzieren-sich-von-Schilys-Asyl-Plaenen.html, last accessed 16.05.2018. However, the idea of creating asylum processing centres, despite the support of various policy makers has not taken concrete forms so far. Such centres would require the establishment of a complex legal framework not only acceptable to all MS but also in

open for people seeking protection is resettlement. Since 2015, approximately 26,000 persons have been transferred directly to EU MS under either the respective Council Decision[40] or the EU Turkey Deal,[41] where they were admitted either on humanitarian grounds or as refugees.[42]

As a complementary tool to resettlement, humanitarian visas have been considered and discussed as an alternative PEP. Similar to resettlement, the underlying idea of a humanitarian visa is to provide persons seeking protection with the possibility to access the territory of a MS in a legal way to avoid people risking their lives and physical integrity by taking more dangerous journeys and the risk of exploitation by criminal smugglers and human traffickers. However, different from resettlement procedures, which are mostly facilitated by UNHCR and have a rather collective nature, a humanitarian visa would be issued by the host state directly at an embassy upon an individual application by the person in need of protection, following specific procedural rules. The humanitarian visa would, therefore, most likely become part of the general visa policy of the MS, providing people seeking international protection with an additional channel for reaching safety in a legal way. The EU's common list of countries whose citizens must be in possession of a valid visa in order to cross the EU's external borders in a legal way lists virtually all countries where people seeking for international protection are likely to come from.[43] People seeking

---

accordance with fundamental human and refugee rights principles the EU is bound by, in particular, the principle of *non-refoulement* and the right to asylum as it is also enshrined in Art. 18 CFREU.

[40] COUNCIL OF THE EUROPEAN UNION, Outcome of the 3405th Justice and Home Affairs Council Meeting, 11097/15, 20.07.2015, p. 5.

[41] COUNCIL OF THE EUROPEAN UNION, 'EU-Turkey statement', Press Release, 144/16, 18.03.2016, available at http://www.consilium.europa.eu/en/press/press-releases/2016/03/18/eu-turkey-statement/pdf, last accessed 17.05.2018.

[42] EUROPEAN COMMISSION, 'Resettlement and Legal Migration 2017', available at https://ec.europa.eu/home-affairs/sites/homeaffairs/files/what-we-do/policies/european-agenda-migration/20171207_resettlement_and_legal_migration_en.pdf, last accessed 16.05.2018. In order to overcome the ad hoc character of resettlement, the Commission in 2016 proposed a Union Resettlement Framework. See EUROPEAN COMMISSION, Proposal for a Regulation of the European Parliament and of the Council establishing a Union Resettlement Framework and amending Regulation (EU) No 516/2014 of the European Parliament and the Council, COM(2016) 468 final, 13.07.2016. Additionally, the Commission in September 2017 recommended that the MS not only to increase their resettlement pledges but also to make use of the funds available through the Asylum, Migration and Integration Fund. See EUROPEAN COMMISSION, Recommendation of 27.9.2017 on enhancing legal pathways for persons in need of international protection, C(2017) 6504, 27.09.2017, p. 6.

[43] Council Regulation (EC) No 539/2001 of 15 March 2001 listing the third countries whose nationals must be in possession of visas when crossing the external borders and those whose nationals are exempt from that requirement, OJ L 81, 21.3.2001. In its Art. 4, the common visa list does not provide for exemptions for persons in need of international protection. However, recital 8 of the Preamble provides that 'MS may exempt certain categories of persons from the visa requirement [...] in accordance with international law or custom'.

protection, however, are not able to meet visa requirements and might therefore be excluded from accessing the EU legally even though they might have a rightful claim to asylum. The humanitarian visa would hence secure the physical transfer and legal protection of people having a rightful claim to protection under EU asylum legislation and thus constitute an alternative to dangerous journeys resulting in the irregular crossing of European external borders. Regarding the procedural arrangements, most likely only the eligibility assessment would be conducted extraterritorially at the diplomatic representation of a state, while the final determination procedures could be conducted territorially upon the arrival in the territory of the MS.[44]

3.1.2. The European Legal Framework and Humanitarian Visa

The EU legislative order does not foresee for a humanitarian visa scheme *per se*. However, the Visa Code,[45] establishing the procedures and conditions for short-stay Schengen visas, allows for the possibility of granting a visa on humanitarian grounds in particular on the basis of two provisions. First, Article 19(4) Visa Code foresees that the admissibility requirements for a Schengen short-term visa can be waived on humanitarian grounds or for reasons of national interest. Secondly, Article 25(1)(a) Visa Code – the primary subject of analysis in this article – states that a visa with limited territorial validity (LTV visa)[46] shall be issued 'exceptionally' when the MS concerned 'considers it necessary on humanitarian grounds, for reasons of national interest, or because of international obligations'. In 2016, 98,173 LTV visas were

---

[44] In 2013 the National Committee on Refugees in Brazil passed a Resolution establishing a humanitarian visa regime for people affected by the Syrian war. The Resolution recognises that people fleeing the Syrian war will most likely not meet the visa requirements for entering Brazil in a regular way. Accordingly, the requirements are alleviated for people in need of protection who may apply for humanitarian visa at the embassies of five countries neighbouring Syria. Upon arrival in Brazil, asylum applications have to be submitted in order to determine the final status of the holders of the humanitarian visa. The scheme has been in force from 2013 for two years and has been prolonged in 2015 for two more years. See L. JUBILUT, C. SOMBRA MUIÑOS DE ANDRADE and A. DE LIMA MADUREIRA, 'Humanitarian visas: building on Brazil's experience', 2016, available at http://www.fmreview.org/community-protection/jubilut-andrade-madureira.html, last accessed 16.05.2018; UNHCR, 'UNHCR welcomes Brazil humanitarian visas for Syrians fleeing conflict', available at http://www.unhcr.org/news/briefing/2013/9/524574d39/unhcr-welcomes-brazil-humanitarian-visas-syrians-fleeing-conflict.html, last accessed 16.05.2018.

[45] Regulation (EC) No 810/2009 of the European Parliament and of the Council of 13 July 2009 establishing a Community Code on Visas (Visa Code), OJ L 243, 15.09.2009, (hereinafter Visa Code).

[46] Art. 2 Visa Code foresees different types of visas. First there is the 'uniform' visa valid on the entire territory of the MS; then there is the 'airport transit visa', which is valid for transit through the international transit areas of one or more airports of the Member States; and finally, there is the LTV visa, which is valid for the territory of one or more Member States but not all Member States.

issued by Schengen States in total.⁴⁷ However, in the statistics provided by the Commission there is no indication of the reasons for which they were issued. A study commissioned by the European Parliament's Committee on Civil Liberties, Justice and Home Affairs (LIBE Committee) in 2014 found that 16 MS in the past have used special schemes to issue humanitarian visas also for people seeking protection.⁴⁸

Despite the apparent recognition by MS that a humanitarian visa can be used to provide people in need of protection with legal venues of entry to the EU, there has been no understanding whether MS, under certain conditions, may be obliged to issue them. The Visa Code is also not clear about whether MS have an obligation to examine the possibility of issuing an LTV visa on humanitarian grounds or due to international obligations. Nor does it say anything about the relationship between the waiving of standard admissibility criteria on humanitarian grounds according to Article 19(4) Visa Code and the 'shall-provision' of Article 25(1) Visa Code obliging MS to issue an LTV visa when considered necessary.⁴⁹ The legally non-binding 'Handbook for Schengen Visa'⁵⁰ equally does not provide for further clarification on these issues. Instead, it only mentions some vague examples related to health rather than fundamental rights issues, allowing the MS a wide margin of interpretation in this regard.⁵¹

When in 2013 the CJEU ruled in *Koushkaki*⁵² that applicants for a Schengen visa have a right to a visa if they meet the necessary conditions, discussions about the consequences of this judgment for humanitarian visas for persons

---

47   EUROPEAN COMMISSION, 'Visa Policy', available at https://ec.europa.eu/home-affairs/what-we-do/policies/borders-and-visas/visa-policy_en, last accessed 16.05.2018.
48   U. IBEN JENSEN, *Humanitarian visas: option or obligation?*, Study for the LIBE Committee of the European Parliament, PE 509.986, 2014, pp. 43–49.
49   No specific procedures are foreseen in the Visa Code for lodging or processing an application for an LTV visa on humanitarian grounds or because of international obligations. Accordingly, the Visa Code does not spell out an obligation that MS are obliged to initiate an assessment of Art. 19 (4) or Art. 25 (1) Visa Code. For a more detailed analysis, see U. IBEN JENSEN, *Humanitarian visas, supra* note 48, pp. 21 et seq.
50   EUROPEAN COMMISSION, Commission Decision C(2010) 1620 final of 19.3.2010 establishing the Handbook for the processing of visa applications and the modification of issued visas and Commission Implementing Decision C (2011) 5501 final of 4.8.2011 amending Commission Decision No C (2010) 1620 final of 19 March 2010 establishing the Handbook for the processing of visa applications and the modification of issued visas, (hereinafter Handbook for Schengen Visa).
51   One example for 'humanitarian grounds' given by the Handbook for Schengen Visa, which would allow for disregarding the admissibility criteria is: A Philippine national urgently needs to travel to Spain where a relative has been victim of a serious accident. His travel document is only valid for one month beyond the intended date of return. See Handbook for Schengen Visa, para. 4.7., p. 38.
52   CJEU, *Koushkaki v Bundesrepublik Deutschland*, Case C-84/12, 19.12.2013, ECLI:EU:C:2013:862.

seeking international protection arose anew. In direct response to the judgment, many academics argued that the 'right to a visa' implicitly spelled out by the Court, applied by analogy to persons seeking international protection, would mean that the Visa Code obliges MS to issue an LTV visa if this follows from their human and refugee rights obligations.[53] In 2017, the CJEU finally got the opportunity to deal with the question whether states under certain conditions are obliged to issue humanitarian visas. The case *X and X v Belgium* concerned the clarification of the scope, meaning and objective of Article 25(1) Visa Code and the question whether MS would be bound by international refugee and EU fundamental rights law when examining applications for visa with limited territorial validity of persons seeking international protection.[54]

3.1.3. X and X v Belgium[55]

The case concerned a Christian family, which sought to flee the city of Aleppo due to its occupation by ISIS. Since all legal routes where closed, the family planned to travel to Belgium on an LTV visa ex Article 25(1) Visa Code and apply there for asylum upon arrival. When the Belgian authorities rejected their request, they appealed the negative decision. The Belgian Court of Appeal referred the case for a preliminary ruling on the interpretation of Article 25(1) Visa Code and the scope of application of EU law on applications for LTV visas in situations such as the one in the Belgian proceeding to the CJEU.[56]

---

[53] See e.g. S. Peers, 'Do potential asylum-seekers have the right to a Schengen visa?', *EU Law Analysis*, 20.01.2014, available at http://eulawanalysis.blogspot.co.at/2014/01/do-potential-asylum-seekers-have-right.html, last accessed 16.05.2018.

[54] For a more detailed analysis of the judgment, see e.g. K. Müller, 'Kein legaler Zugangsweg in die EU durch humanitäre Visa, Einordnung des Verfahrens "X und X gegen Belgien" in die Europäische Migrations- und Flüchtlingspolitik', (2017) 20(2) *ZEuS*, pp. 161–184; M. Ovádek, 'The CJEU on Humanitarian Visa: Discovering 'Un-Chartered' Waters of EU Law', *Verfassungsblog*, 13.03.2017, available at https://verfassungsblog.de/the-cjeu-on-humanitarian-visa-discovering-un-chartered-waters-of-eu-law, last accessed 16.05.2018; A. Romano and M. Helena Zoeteweij-Turhan, '"X and X v Belgium", The need for EU legislation on humanitarian visa', (2017) *Sui Generis*, pp. 68–84.

[55] P. Folz and E. Radlgruber, 'The Court of Justice of the European Union and Human Rights in 2017', see article in this book.

[56] The questions for preliminary ruling read: '(1) Do the international obligations referred to in Article 25(1)(a) of the Visa Code cover all the rights guaranteed by the Charter, including, in particular, those guaranteed by Articles 4 and 18, and do they also cover obligations which bind the Member States, in the light of the ECHR and Article 33 of the Geneva Convention? (2) (a) Depending on the answer given to the first question, must Article 25(1)(a) of the Visa Code be interpreted as meaning that, subject to its discretion with regard to the circumstances of the case, a Member State to which an application for a visa with limited territorial validity has been made is required to issue the visa applied for, where a risk of infringement of Article 4 and/or Article 18 of the Charter or another international obligation by which it is bound is established? (b) Does the existence of links between the applicant and the Member State to which the visa application was made (for example, family connections,

The judgment of the Court has not only been awaited with impatience but also with great expectations by both MS and the EU institutions on the one hand and civil society organisations on the other. While the former warned of 'fatal consequences' for the EU migration and asylum policy as a whole,[57] the latter hoped the judgment would effectively annul the Dublin rules and open new legal and above all safe ways for refugees to seek protection in the EU. The hopes of those criticising the lack of a humanitarian response to the proclaimed 'refugee crisis' were fuelled by the previous opinion of Advocate General (AG) Mengozzi. In his findings, he clearly favoured positive obligations of MS to issue a valid LTV visa where it must be believed that the refusal to issue a visa would directly result in the applicants being subjected to treatment contrary to the rights enshrined in the CFREU, in particular to Article 4 CFREU, the prohibition of torture.[58]

The Court, however, did not follow the AG's opinion. AG Mengozzi devoted considerable space in elaborating on the issues at stake, in particular the fundamental rights obligations of the EU.[59] The CJEU, in a short and rather formal judgment, instead decided to follow the arguments made by the Belgian government supported by the Commission and several MS and negated the application of not only the Visa Code but EU law as a whole on visa applications like the ones made by the applicants. The Court's main argument was that the application for a visa with the view to applying for asylum in Belgium and thereby for a residence permit with a validity of longer than 90 days would fall outside the scope of the Visa Code which covers only short-term visas. While the Visa Code has been adopted on the basis of Article 62(2)(b) EC treaty, the decision on applications for visas for an intended stay longer than three months remains in the competences of the MS, since no measures with regard to long-term visa have been adopted on the basis of Article 79(2)(a) Treaty on the Functioning of the European Union (TFEU) yet.[60] According to the Court, neither the Visa Code nor other provisions of EU law would govern the visa application made on humanitarian grounds by X and X but only national laws would do so.[61]

---

host families, guarantors and sponsors) affect the answer to that question? Questions 1 and 2 (a) will be the subject of the further analysis.' CJEU, *X and X v Belgium*, C-638/16 PPU, 07.03.2107, ECLI:EU:C:2017:173, paras. 40–45 (hereinafter *X and X*).

[57] See for instance the statement by the Czech Government, cited in CJEU, Opinion by AG Menozzi, *X and X v Belgium*, Case C-638/16 PPU, 07.02.2017, ECLI:EU:C:2017:93, para. 5 (hereinafter Opinion by AG Mengozzi). In total 14 governments made submissions.

[58] For an analysis of the opinion, see E. BROUWER, 'AG Mengozzi's conclusion in *X and X v Belgium* on the positive obligation to issue humanitarian visas A legitimate plea to ensure safe journeys for refugees', CEPS Policy Insights, (2017) 09, available at https://www.ceps.eu/system/files/PI2017-09_EB_VisaCode.pdf, last accessed 16.05.2018.

[59] CJEU, Opinion by AG Mengozzi, *supra* note 57, para. 6.

[60] CJEU, *X and X*, *supra* note 56.

[61] Ibid., para. 51.

The narrow view on the Visa Code by the Court is rather striking. The Court avoided answering the clear question by the Belgian Court whether MS are bound by the CFREU and other human and refugee rights obligations when considering visa applications in such situations. While AG Mengozzi elaborated extensively on the question whether the intention to apply for asylum in Belgium upon arrival would alter the nature and the purpose of a short-term visa with limited territorial validity according to Article 25(1) Visa Code,[62] the Court simply neglected the applicability of the Visa Code from the onset. It ignored the fact that the competent Belgian authorities actually classified, examined and processed the visa application by X and X under the Visa Code.[63] AG Mengozzi rightfully argued that the intention to apply for international protection upon arrival and therefore for a long-term residence could constitute a ground for refusal but would not exclude the applicability of the Visa Code and EU law *per se*.[64] By disregarding these arguments, the Court excused itself from looking into Article 25(1) Visa Code and the margin of interpretation MS should have with regard to applications for validity LTV visas on humanitarian grounds. Additionally, it ignored the fact that the Visa Code explicitly includes the basis for issuing humanitarian visas due to 'international obligations' opening the application of the *non-refoulement* obligations deriving from the CFREU. By arguing that the prospect of a subsequent asylum application would automatically transform the character of the short-term visa with limited territorial validity into a long-term visa not governed by EU law, the Court allows MS to circumvent humanitarian and international obligations as foreseen by the Visa Code itself and renders Article 25(1) Visa Code practically meaningless.

Furthermore, again deviating from the opinion by AG Mengozzi, the Court falls short of taking the broader obligations to '[…] offer […] appropriate status to any third-country national requiring international protection and ensuring compliance with the principle of *non-refoulement*' as prescribed by Article 78(1) TFEU into account when considering the case. With regard to the prohibition of *refoulement* this is even more perplexing since the Court itself, when justifying the urgent procedure according to Article 107 of the Rules of Procedures of the Court, acknowledged that 'the applicants […] were facing a real risk of being subjected to inhuman and degrading treatment'.[65] It is difficult to reconcile this clear finding of a situation of eventual human rights violations by the Court with its conclusion that based on EU law no positive obligations to issue a humanitarian visa can be established.

---

[62] See CJEU, Opinion by AG Mengozzi, *supra* note 57, paras. 50 et seq.
[63] CJEU, Opinion by AG Mengozzi, *supra* note 57, para. 49.
[64] Ibid., para. 50.
[65] CJEU, *X and X*, *supra* note 56, para. 33.

The Court thereby missed not only the opportunity to clarify the actual objective of Article 25(1) Visa Code and its relation to fundamental and refugee rights obligations of MS, it also missed the opportunity to set the course for a change in the CEAS as a whole. The Court embraced the continuance of, in particular, the rules of the Dublin system by remarking that applying the Visa Code and EU law on applications for a short-term visa in order to ultimately obtain international protection in the MS concerned would undermine 'the general structure of the system established by Regulation No 604/2013 [the Dublin III Regulation]'.[66] The Court underlines its argument by stressing the territorial outlook of the Procedures Directive only applying 'to applications for international protection made in the territory, including at the border, in the territorial waters or in the transit zones of the Member States, but not to requests for diplomatic or territorial asylum submitted to the representations of Member States'.[67] The Court's references to the CEAS are surprising since they are rather beside the point and go even against the questions referred by the Belgian Court. If it was about the extraterritorial applicability of EU law, then it was about the applicability of the CFREU on visa applications made ex Article 25(1) Visa Code at the diplomatic representations of the MS and not the applicability of the rules of the CEAS. The errant position of the Court suggests that the *X and X* judgement might be an expression of political opportunism by the Court and not so much about a legal contention of the issues at stake. This criticism is not about claiming that the CJEU should have ruled in favour of the applicants' right to a humanitarian visa. However, even if denying such a right, in light of a coherent application of EU law, the Court should have underpinned its decision to exclude the applicability of the Visa Code and EU law with a more substantive discussion about the scope of Article 25(1) Visa Code.

3.1.4. Implications for a Future EU Scheme on Humanitarian Visa

By neglecting the applicability of EU law on visa applications as in *X and X* the Court placed the ball in the MS and their national courts. While the application of the CFREU on such cases has been excluded, MS remain bound by the ECHR and international refugee law, in particular, the Geneva Refugee Convention and the prohibition of *refoulement* which should guide their decisions on applications for LTV visas on humanitarian grounds. The CJEU thereby follows the approach by MS reclaiming their sovereign rights to govern migration and asylum at the national level.

---

[66] Ibid., para. 48.
[67] Ibid., para. 50.

For the adoption of an EU wide humanitarian visa scheme *X and X* has been a major setback. In 2014, the Commission adopted a proposal aimed at reforming the Visa Code.[68] The proposal did not contain any changes to the framework of the humanitarian visa. The European Parliament (EP), however, seized the opportunity to push for enhanced possibilities to apply for a humanitarian visa directly at the embassies of MS. In a Resolution in 2016 on the situation in the Mediterranean, as part of its claim for a holistic approach to migration, the EP called for an amendment to the Visa Code including more specific provisions on the humanitarian visa.[69] To this end, a report by the LIBE Committee made some amendments to the Commission's proposal, with the view to elaborate on the already existing provisions related to the humanitarian visa in the Visa Code.[70] In its amendments, the EP suggests directly linking the humanitarian visa with applications for asylum, which, for the first time, would constitute a PEP based on an individual claim on the basis of EU law.[71] In line with this call, the EP furthermore suggested an amendment to lift the standard period of validity of short-term visa, i.e. 90 days in any 180 days, and allow for an extension for a period of 12 months for people in need of protection if the situation in the country of origin required it.[72] The position of the EP would take the EU clearly one step closer to a humane system based on the general principles of EU law to respect and protect fundamental rights as provided for in Articles 2 and 6 TEU. However, the Commission and the Council universally rejected the amendments proposed by the EP. Both argued that the Visa Code's objective was not to deal with migration but referred the issue of the humanitarian visa to the EU Resettlement Framework as the better forum for discussion.[73] *X and X* seemed to add the last nail in the coffin of a common EU-wide humanitarian visa scheme. Applauded by the Commission and the Council, the judgment stalled the discussions about amending the Visa Code with a view to include a humanitarian visa.[74] Even though *X and X* shed light on the lacuna of the

---

[68] EUROPEAN COMMISSION, Proposal for a Regulation of the European Parliament and of the Council on the Union Code on Visas (Visa Code) (recast), COM(2014) 164 final, 01.04.2014.
[69] EUROPEAN PARLIAMENT, Resolution of 12 April 2016 on the situation in the Mediterranean and the need for a holistic EU approach to migration, 2015/2095(INI), paras. 26–27.
[70] EUROPEAN PARLIAMENT COMMITTEE ON CIVIL LIBERTIES, JUSTICE AND HOME AFFAIRS, Report on the proposal for a Regulation of the European Parliament and of the Council on the Union Code on Visas (Visa Code) (recast), A8-0145/2016, 25.04.2016.
[71] Ibid., Amendment 95.
[72] Ibid., Amendment 96.
[73] See EUROPEAN PARLIAMENT, 'Humanitarian Visas – Amendment of the EU Visa Code', available at http://www.europarl.europa.eu/legislative-train/theme-towards-a-new-policy-on-migration/file-humanitarian-visas-%E2%80%93-amendment-of-the-eu-visa-code, last accessed 16.05.2018.
[74] See e.g. the formal answer by Mr Avramopoulos on behalf of the Commission to a parliamentary question on the EU's stance on humanitarian visa in light of the CJEU's

humanitarian visa at the interface of the EU's visa and asylum policy, it seems that the door to approach the issue from a humanitarian perspective was closed by the CJEU.

3.2. DUBLIN RULES: *A.S.* AND *JAFARI*

3.2.1. Background

The Dublin system harks back to the original Convention,[75] set up as a common means of allocating responsibility of asylum applications in the signatory countries; once the EU was formed, the Convention was reformulated into a piece of EU legislation, the Dublin II Regulation in 2003,[76] which was subsequently amended as the Dublin III Regulation in 2013. The purpose of the newest iteration is 'to ensure quick access to asylum procedures and the examination of an application on the merits by a single, clearly determined [MS]'.[77] The Regulation sets up the criteria by which the MS responsible is determined, the general rule being that the MS of first entry is the one responsible, with some exceptions.[78] If an applicant is found in another MS, that MS can transfer the applicant to the original state, though sovereignty rules permit the MS to accept responsibility for applications that are not technically theirs to consider.[79]

The problems of the Dublin system were quickly noted from a human rights perspective: first, the rules leave out the desires of the asylum seekers.[80]

---

judgement: 'The Commission notes also that, in accordance with the judgment in Case C-638/16 PPU of the Court of Justice of the European Union of 7 March 2017, to which the Honourable Member refers, the question raised by the Honourable Member does not fall within the scope of Union law, given that no measure has been adopted to date by the Union with regard to the conditions governing the issue by Member States of long-term visas and residence permits to third-country nationals on humanitarian grounds. The judgment is binding on the Union's institutions.' See EUROPEAN COMMISSION, Parliamentary Questions, E-002183/2017, 17.07.2017.

[75] Convention Determining the State Responsible for Examining Applications for Asylum Lodged in One of the Member States of the European Communities Dublin Convention (signed 15.06.1990) OJ C 254/1, 19.08.1997.

[76] Regulation (EC) No 343/2003 of the European Council of 18 February 2003 establishing the criteria and mechanisms for determining the member state responsible for examining an asylum application lodged in one of the member states by a third-country national, OJ L 50/1, 25.02.2003.

[77] EUROPEAN COMMISSION, 'Country responsible for asylum application (Dublin)', available at https://ec.europa.eu/home-affairs/what-we-do/policies/asylum/examination-of-applicants_en, last accessed 16.05.2018.

[78] Arts. 8–10 and 13 Dublin III Regulation.

[79] Art. 17 Dublin III Regulation.

[80] As noted previously, on research regarding the issue of taking asylum seekers' preferences, see e.g. M. MCAULIFFE and D. JAYASURIYA (2016), 'Do asylum seekers and refugees choose destination countries?', *supra* note 11, pp. 44–59; E. NEUMAYER (2005), 'Bogus Refugees?',

Aside from allowances made for minors[81] or those who already have family receiving protection in the EU,[82] applicants have no choice in the MS in which they are allowed to petition for international protection. Second, despite the harmonisation of rules for application, there is no harmonisation of recognition of status: a person who is accorded protection in one MS does not have any status in another MS; she must settle in the MS that granted protection and can travel through the EU only in a limited fashion.[83] The automaticity of the transfers is also conceptually problematic from the perspective of the issue of *non-refoulement*, though the by-now entrenched concept of safe third country has legitimised the transfers – unless the conditions in the original MS are too atrocious to safeguard fundamental rights. In its seminal case, *M.S.S. v Belgium*,[84] the European Court of Human Rights (ECtHR) essentially pointed out that the Dublin system does not take precedence over the MS's equally binding human rights obligations under the European Convention on Human Rights (ECHR) by holding that transfers from Belgium to Greece, when Belgium should have known that the reception conditions in Greece were so inadequate, would violate Article 3 of the ECHR.[85] This obligation, outside the scope of EU law, forced the MS between a rock and a hard place: on the one hand, they had to abide by the Dublin rules; on the other hand, they had to abide by their human rights obligations. This forced the CJEU to take up the issue and decide on it, and it came to a similar conclusion in the case of *N.S. v Secretary of State for the Home Department*,[86] though it did so on its own terms, as explained below.

---

supra note 11, pp. 389–410; W. H. MOORE and S. M. SHELLMAN (2007), 'Whither Will THEY Go?', *supra* note 11, pp. 811–834.

[81] Art. 8 Dublin III Regulation.
[82] Arts. 9–10 Dublin III Regulation.
[83] In 2013, Cyprus requested information within the Commission's European Migration Network (EMN) to what extent recognised refugees are able to move to and reside in other MS. Seventeen MS's EMN representatives responded, noting their countries' varying degrees of permission afforded. See EUROPEAN COMMISSION, 'Ad-Hoc Query on right of Recognised Refugees to travel in EU', 14.01.2014, available at https://www.udi.no/globalassets/global/european-migration-network_i/ad-hoc-queries/ad-hoc-query-on-right-of-recognised-regugees-to-travel-in-eu.pdf, last accessed 16.05.2018. Most EU MS are also party to the 1960 European Agreement on the Abolition of Visas for Refugees (ETS 31), which permits entry to refugees recognized in one party state entry up to 90 days in the other party states without the need for a visa. For a full list of signatories, see COUNCIL OF EUROPE, 'Chart of signatures and ratifications of Treaty 031', available at https://www.coe.int/en/web/conventions/full-list/-/conventions/treaty/031/signatures?p_auth=QFwBl7zO, last accessed 16.05.2018.
[84] ECtHR, *M.S.S. v Belgium and Greece* [GC], no 30696/09; 21.01.2011 (hereinafter M.S.S.).
[85] Ibid., paras. 359–360.
[86] CJEU, *N.S. v Secretary of State for the Home Department and M. E. and Others v Refugee Applications Commissioner and Minister for Justice, Equality and Law Reform*, Joined, Cases C-411/10 and C-439/10, 21.12.2011, ECLI:EU:C:2011:865 (hereinafter N.S.).

3.2.2. The Mutual Trust Doctrine and Fundamental Rights in the Context of the EU Asylum Law

One of the foundations of the Dublin system as it stands today is the doctrine of mutual trust, which is a general doctrine fundamentally underlying the entirety of the EU's functioning. In the field of asylum, under this doctrine, it is assumed that all MS have an equivalent and equally protective asylum system, 'presuming, therefore, that asylum seekers would not benefit from any advantage by having their application examined in a specific country'.[87] But as noted above, this notion was quickly challenged in the context of Dublin, since it seemed evident, even to the casual observer, that the states that form the outer border of the Union would always be more likely to get a greater number of applications than those that have no borders with third countries, leading to a greater burden on the former.[88] The biggest challenge to this idea came in the case of *N.S.*, in which the CJEU found that when there are substantial grounds for believing there are systemic deficiencies within a MS's asylum system that would result in inhuman or degrading treatment of asylum seekers, then the normally obligatory Dublin transfer to such as MS should not be undertaken as it would violate Article 4 of the CFREU.[89] While this ruling appears to dismantle the mutual trust doctrine, a close reading of the *N.S.* judgment shows that the Court actually upheld it; moreover, the CJEU stated plainly that due to the doctrine of mutual trust, there is no possibility that 'any infringement of a fundamental right by the Member State responsible will affect the obligations of other Member States to comply with [the Dublin II Regulation]'.[90] In essence, rather than giving asylum seekers an affirmative right to assert the violation of their fundamental rights, the CJEU created the systemic deficiency test as a rebuttal argument against the presumption of the doctrine of mutual trust.[91]

While the CJEU then went on to curb the procedural and substantive rights as to when the systemic deficiencies test applies,[92] it circled back to the question

---

[87] See C. RIZCALLAH, 'The Dublin system: the ECJ Squares the Circle Between Mutual Trust and Human Rights Protection', EU Law Analysis Blog, 20.02.2017, available at http://eulawanalysis.blogspot.mx/2017/02/the-dublin-system-ecj-squares-circle.html, last accessed 16.05.2018.

[88] Indeed, at the outset of her opinion to the *A.S.* and *Jafari* cases, AG Sharpston points out the flaw in the presumption underlying Dublin. See CJEU, Opinion of AG Sharpston in the cases C-490/16, *A.S. v Slovenia* and C-646/16, *Jafari*, 08.06.2017, paras. 1–3. For an analysis of the Opinion of AG Sharpston see S. SALOMON, 'Normality and Exception: The Advocate General's Opinion in A.S. and Jafari', *VerfBlog*, available at https://verfassungsblog.de/normality-and-exception-the-advocate-generals-opinion-in-a-s-and-jafari, last accessed 16.05.2018.

[89] CJEU, *N.S.*, supra note 86, para. 86.

[90] Ibid., para. 82.

[91] Ibid., *N.S.*, supra note 86, para. 81.

[92] In the case *Abdullahi*, the CJEU deemed it permissible for Austria to effect a transfer of an applicant to Hungary, since Hungary accepted responsibility for the application, even

of mutual trust in the case of *C.K. and Others v Slovenia* and came to a slightly different result.[93] The case concerned an asylum seeker family, the mother being pregnant and in bad health when the Slovenian government decided to effect a Dublin transfer to Croatia, which had no systemic deficiencies and which accepted responsibility for the application.[94] The family appealed on the grounds of the mother's health, and the Slovene court referred the case to the CJEU, with the major question being whether such individual circumstances required a MS to exercise the sovereignty clause of Article 17 of the Dublin III Regulation in order to prevent an Article 4 CFREU violation. The Court gave a qualified yes. In its judgment, the CJEU required that the MS assess the risk of a violation given individual circumstances that pointed to a risk[95] and that a transfer be suspended while the risk persisted.[96] Still, the Court did not make the exercise of the sovereignty clause mandatory,[97] leaving uncertainty as to what substantive rights an asylum seeker would have to compel the MS that is suspending the transfer to review the application substantively.[98] However, for a brief moment, the CJEU signalled that it weighed the protection of fundamental rights more heavily than a formulaic interpretation of EU law and the upholding of the Dublin system. But what the CJEU giveth, it taketh away. In the two cases of *Khadija Jafari and Zainab Jafari* and *A.S. v Slovenian Republic*, the Court confronted the issues of mutual trust and fundamental rights in the context of the 2015 events – and it sided decidedly with the doctrine of mutual trust, upholding the functioning of the Dublin system, at the expense of fundamental rights of asylum seekers.

---

though the applicant pleaded that the MS responsible is actually Greece, where there existed systemic deficiencies. See CJEU, *Shamso Abdullahi v Bundesasylamt*, C-394/12, 10.12.2013, ECLI:EU:C:2013:813. The Court specifically relied on the mutual doctrine reasons (paras. 52–53, 60), concluding that the only means to prevent the transfer is for the applicant to convincingly argue that systemic deficiencies exist in the MS that has taken on the responsibility for her application.

[93] CJEU, *C.K. v Supreme Court of Slovenia*, C-578/16 PPU, 16.02.2017, ECLI:EU:C:2017:127 (hereinafter C.K.).
[94] Ibid., para. 30.
[95] CJEU, *C.K.*, supra note 93, para. 76.
[96] Ibid., para. 84.
[97] Ibid., para. 96. In doing so, the Court reaffirmed its holding in *Puid*, where it plainly stated that 'a finding that it is impossible to transfer an asylum seeker to the Member State initially identified as responsible does not in itself mean that the Member State which is determining the Member State responsible is required itself, under Article 3(2) of the [Dublin II] Regulation, to examine the application for asylum.' CJEU, *Bundesrepublik Deutschland v Kaveh Puid*, C-4/11, 14.11.2013, ECLI:EU:C:2013:740, para. 37.
[98] For an excellent analysis on the significance of the *C.K.* case in relation to the mutual trust doctrine, see C. RIZCALLAH, 'The Dublin system', noted above. See also I. GOLDNER LANG, 'Human Rights and Legitimacy in the Implementation of EU Asylum and Migration Law', in S. VÖNEKY and G. NEUMAN (eds.) *Human Rights, Democracy, and Legitimacy in a World of Disorder*, Cambridge University Press, forthcoming in 2018.

3.2.3. Jafari *and* A.S.

The first of the two cases, *Jafari*, pertained to two Afghani sisters and their children, who had been among the many persons on the West Balkan route that were allowed to pass through Croatia and Slovenia on their way north without verification whether they fulfilled any formal requirements, such as those for a transit visa for example. Indeed, the Croatian government organised transport for the sisters to the Slovenian border.[99] Once in Slovenia, they were issued documents by the authorities noting their destinations as Austria and Germany, and on that same day, they entered Austrian territory and claimed asylum there.[100] The Austrian authorities' Dublin requests pursuant to Article 34 of the Dublin III Regulation were met with an answer from their Slovenian counterparts disclaiming any responsibility under the Regulation.[101] Shortly after, the Austrian authorities requested that Croatia take charge of the sisters' application as the MS responsible and rejected their asylum claims on those grounds.[102] The sisters went through the appellate process, and this led eventually to a referral by the Austrian Upper Administrative Court (Verwaltungsgerichtshof) to the CJEU with a multitude of convoluted and interlinked questions.

The *A.S.* case involved similar facts and issues: Having fled from his/her home country of Syria, AS went along the West Balkan Route, arriving in Croatia in 2016. As with the Jafari sisters, Croatian authorities made arrangements for AS to be transported to its border with Slovenia, from where s/he was then taken to the border between Slovenia and Austria.[103] However, since Austrian authorities refused AS entry, s/he lodged an asylum application with Slovenian authorities, who promptly invoked Article 21 of the Dublin III Regulation and requested that Croatia take charge of the application, which Croatia did.[104] In subsequently deciding not to examine AS's application, the Slovenian authorities specifically relied on Article 13(1) of Dublin III Regulation, since AS 'had irregularly crossed the Croatian border coming from a third country'.[105] After AS appealed the case, the Slovenian Supreme Court (Vrhovno sodišče) made a referral to the CJEU.[106]

---

[99] CJEU, *Khadija Jafari and Zainab Jafari v Bundesamt für Fremdenwesen und Asyl*, C-646/16, 26.07.2017, ECLI:EU:C:2017:586, para. 29 (hereinafter Jafari).
[100] Ibid., para. 30.
[101] Ibid., para. 31.
[102] Ibid., para. 32.
[103] CJEU, *A.S. v Republika Slovenija*, C-490/16, 26.07.2017, ECLI:EU:C:2017:585 paras. 14–15 (hereinafter A.S.).
[104] Ibid., paras. 15–17.
[105] Ibid., para. 18.
[106] Ibid., para. 19.

As with *Jafari*, the resulting referral was a set of interlinked questions; however, in both cases, underlying all the legal questions were two relatively simple yet crucial issues:

(1) whether the Croatian and Slovenian policies of 'waiving' the applicants through its territory constituted the issuance of a 'visa' under Article 2(m) and 12 of the Dublin III Regulation,[107] and
(2) whether the fact that the formalities for entry were not observed by Croatia and Slovenia meant that the applicants' entry and transit through these countries constituted an 'irregular crossing' within the meaning of Article 13(1) of the Dublin III Regulation, read in conjunction with the Schengen Border Code (SBC),[108] making Croatia indeed the MS responsible for their asylum applications.

In regard to the first question, the CJEU's answer was based on a straightforward reading of the Dublin III Regulation: the waiving through of persons without verifying the requirements did not mean the conferral of a visa. Although the Court noted that the Visa Code forms 'part of the context to be taken into account in interpreting Article 2(m) and Article 12 of the Dublin III Regulation, the fact remains that the concept of a "visa", within the meaning of [...] [the Dublin III] regulation, cannot be inferred directly from those acts and must be construed on the basis of the specific definition found in Article 2(m) and the general scheme of the [Dublin III] regulation'.[109] In that context, visa was defined specifically as 'act formally adopted by a national authority, not to mere tolerance [of presence],' and further the Court held that 'a visa is not to be confused with admission to the territory of a Member State, since a visa is required precisely for the purposes of enabling such admission'.[110] In light of that definition, the CJEU held that the Croatian policies did not constitute the issuance of a visa, regardless of the extenuating circumstances in 2015.[111]

---

[107] The issue of the existence of a 'visa' was more an issue in the *Jafari* case; however, the Court specifically noted its Jafari holding on the issue of visas in the A.S. judgment, which is why both issues are addressed together for both cases.
[108] Regulation (EC) No 562/2006 of the European Parliament and of the Council of 15 March 2006 establishing a Community Code on the rules governing the movement of persons across borders (Schengen Borders Code), OJ L 105/1 of 13 April 2006 (hereinafter Schengen Borders Code or SBC). The Schengen Borders Code has since been replaced by Regulation (EU) 2016/399 of the European Parliament and of the Council of 9 March 2016 on a Union Code on the rules governing the movement of persons across borders (Schengen Borders Code), OJ L 77/1 of 23 March 2016; however, the former SBC was still in force at the time of the events in the case, which is why the Court applied it rather than the new version. See CJEU, *Jafari*, *supra* note 99, para. 5.
[109] Ibid., para. 47.
[110] Ibid., para. 48.
[111] Ibid., para. 48; CJEU, *A.S.*, *supra* note 103, para. 37.

This argument by the CJEU was predictable, as the AG Sharpston pointed to this conclusion in her singularly detailed analysis.[112] However, on the second issue, the CJEU surprisingly diverged from the AG's opinion. In her opinion, AG Sharpston pointed out that the term 'irregularly crossed', referred to in Article 13 of the Dublin III Regulation, is not only not defined within the regulation itself,[113] she also notes that despite guidance from the Dublin Implementing Regulation and requirements of the Schengen Border Code, ultimately, the issue is a factual determination to be made by a MS: 'The references to elements of proof in Article 22(3) of the Dublin III Regulation and the Dublin Implementing Regulation clearly indicate that *whether there is an irregular entry in any particular case is primarily a question of fact* for the national authorities.'[114] The CJEU disagreed. Though it agreed with AG Sharpston that the term 'irregular crossing' is not defined by the relevant legal instruments,[115] it chose to interpret the concept's meaning and scope through consideration of the term's 'usual meaning, while also taking into account the context in which it occurs and the purposes of the rules of which it is part'.[116] In the Court's view, this meant that crossing the border 'without fulfilling the conditions imposed by the legislation applicable in the [MS] in question must necessarily be considered "irregular", within the meaning of Article 13(1) of the Dublin III Regulation,' and where the MS is subject to the rules of the SBC, that Code must be taken into account.[117] Here, the Court did allow for the argument, that a MS could suspend its own and the Schengen rules on account of its humanitarian reasons; however, such a suspension is not valid for the entirety of the Schengen Zone.[118] Hence, according to the Court, a derogation of the SBC entry requirements does not regularise the entry of a person,[119] and the person 'must be regarded as having "irregularly crossed" the border of that first Member State, within the meaning of Article 13(1) of the Dublin III Regulation, whether that crossing has been tolerated or authorised in breach of the applicable rules or authorised on humanitarian grounds and by derogation from the entry conditions in principle imposed on third-country nationals'.[120] That these

---

[112] CJEU, Opinion by AG Sharpston, *supra* note 88, paras. 145–154.
[113] Ibid., paras. 155 and 163. Note that AG Sharpston also points out that the terminology used is far from clear, though to this argument it is not ultimately decisive to her conclusion. Ibid, paras. 155–162.
[114] Ibid., para. 164. (emphasis in original). Using this standard, AG Sharpston creates a compelling argument why in these cases there was no irregular crossing. See below, section 3.2.4.
[115] CJEU, *Jafari*, *supra* note 99, para. 61; CJEU, *A.S.*, *supra* note 103, para. 38.
[116] CJEU, *Jafari*, *supra* note 99, para. 73.
[117] Ibid., paras. 74–75.
[118] Ibid., paras. 79–80.
[119] Ibid., para. 80.
[120] CJEU, *A.S.*, *supra* note 103, para. 39.

circumstances occurred during an intense situation such as the massive influx of persons in 2015 was irrelevant for the Court.[121]

3.2.4. Interpretation and Implications

The Court's ruling was a blow for supporters of fundamental rights in the asylum context. But, it was also concerning because the Court went through legal acrobatics to come to a solution that it appears to have been pre-determined: the upholding of the core of the Dublin System despite the high costs.[122] Some of these flawed legal arguments are evident in the Court's usage of the 'usual meaning' test in conjunction with the SBC as a guide for defining 'irregular crossing'. In doing so, the CJEU ignored a key component of AG Sharpston's opinion, especially in its *Jafari* judgment, namely that the MS in question, and particularly Croatia, did not merely tolerate the presence of the applicants – and those in the same situation as them – but that it actively assisted them in crossing over to Slovenia.[123] In her exposition on the purpose of the Dublin III Regulation, AG Sharpston correctly noted that the idea of irregular crossing applied to those persons who entered a MS illicitly, 'without that entry being approved (procedurally and substantively) by the competent authorities,' that entry not being condoned but due entirely to the 'failure' of the MS's vigilance in securing the external EU border.[124] In such a scenario, an irregular crossing is obvious, as is the responsibility of the MS who 'failed' to protect the EU border to now deal with said individual. However, as per AG Sharpston, in the applicants' scenario, the crossing of the applicants was not illicit within the meaning of the purpose of the Regulation: they entered with full knowledge and authorisation by the two MS, in the case of the Jafari sisters even being issued documents along the way. As a result, she concluded that where a MS 'actively facilitated both entry into and transit across territories,' such a crossing cannot be defined as irregular under Article 13(1) of the Dublin III Regulation.[125]

Moreover, the Court's application of the SBC provisions appears bizarre when juxtaposed with the results. Instead, the SBC provisions are logically more consistent with AG Sharpston's approach of letting the definition of whether an 'irregular crossing' within the meaning of Article 13 of the Dublin III Regulation exists be an evidentiary concern for the MS at issue. Doing so would lead to the logical conclusion that the applicants did not cross irregularly until they

---

[121] CJEU, *Jafari*, *supra* note 99, paras. 93–100; CJEU, *A.S.*, *supra* note 103, para. 40.
[122] That the Court was not always willing to pay the costs in the past is evidenced by its critical stance towards the Dublin system in other judgments, for instance in the above noted *N.S.* case.
[123] The Court did, however, use the word 'authorisation' in *A.S.* CJEU, *A.S.*, *supra* note 103, para. 39.
[124] CJEU, Opinion by AG Sharpston, *supra* note 88, para. 179.
[125] Ibid., paras. 176 and 184.

arrived in Austria (or at the Austrian border in the case of AS). As noted by the Court, the SBC specifically allows for the derogation from its requirements for humanitarian reasons for a specific MS. If the legal requirements of the SBC are waived by an MS, then logically any entry is not illegal according to the laws of that particular MS. That such a crossing should be not illegal but still irregular seems an odd proposition.[126] Instead, contrary to the CJEU's statement, it appears more logical that this derogation of the requirements means the MS *did* regularise the applicants' entry; it is only once they crossed or attempted to cross into another MS which has not suspended the SBC rules for humanitarian reasons that the crossing has become irregular. In this case, consistent with AG Sharpston's opinion, since both Croatia and Slovenia actively assisted the applicants in the entry and transit through their territories, a suspension of the SBC rules can be implied, and only when the applicants reached Austria was their crossing irregular within the meaning of the Dublin III Regulation.

While it is true that this conclusion is inconsistent with the overall scheme of the Dublin III Regulation since it would allow MS to free themselves of their Dublin responsibilities, as the CJEU noted,[127] AG Sharpston correctly pointed out that the Dublin system was not created to sustain situations such as the one presented in 2015, 'a situation of *authorised* border crossings by a mass inflow of potential applicants for international protection',[128] for whom the MS that form the external EU border could not possibly create humane reception conditions and take on their applications for international protection.[129] The type of humanitarian tragedies and the fundamental rights violations, especially those subject to the provisions of Article 4 of the CFREU (and implicitly also under Article 3 of the ECHR), that can occur when a MS's system is overloaded were more than visible in Greece throughout 2015 and 2016. While it is true that through its concurrent decision in *Mengesteab*,[130] the Court softened the blow to many asylum seekers who arrived in 2015 by imposing a three-month limit within which a Dublin transfer request needs to be processed,[131] it nevertheless set a precedent that continues to put the onus on MS on the EU's outer border, which in turn only shifts the risk of fundamental rights violations.[132] Namely,

---

[126] Note the issue of wording, mentioned above, as pointed out by AG Sharpston. CJEU, Opinion by AG Sharpston, *supra* note 88, paras. 155–162.
[127] CJEU, *Jafari*, *supra* note 99, para. 84.
[128] CJEU, Opinion by AG Sharpston, *supra* note 88, para. 189.
[129] Ibid., para. 183.
[130] CJEU, *Tsegezab Mengesteab v Bundesrepublik Deutschland*, Case C-670/16, 26.07.2017, ECLI:EU:C:2017:587 (hereinafter Mengestead). It should be noted, however, that the Jafari sisters ultimately did indeed get transferred to Croatia. See 'Afghan sisters deported from Austria after landmark EU ruling', BBC.com, 13.03.2018, available at http://www.bbc.com/news/world-europe-43393879, last accessed 16.05.2018.
[131] CJEU, *Mengesteab*, *supra* note 130, paras. 51–53.
[132] In the context of Croatia this is particularly concerning as there have been anecdotal reports by NGOs and individual asylum seekers of serious fundamental rights violations in the form

by requiring those MS to comply with the Dublin III Regulation even in exceptional circumstances, the Court essentially puts them in the position of 'choosing' when and which of its obligations they may violate in a future scenario similar to the one in 2015: either they can accept an inordinately high amount of asylum seekers, so overburdening their internal systems and then risking claims of Article 4 CFREU and Article 3 ECHR violations, or they can restrict entry into their countries, leaving the same people in border camps the likes of Idomeni, again potentially violating the rights guaranteed by Article 4 and Article 3, respectively, as well as their international obligations, such as the *non-refoulement* principle.[133] In short, what was needed in these cases, what AG Sharpston argued, was a pragmatic approach to an extraordinary situation. What the Court, in choosing to overlay the Dublin system over a very inapplicable situation, provided was a value judgment, that went against the core of its seminal cases on the issues of mutual trust and fundamental rights: it decided that a formulaic interpretation and the upholding of the Dublin system weighs more heavily than the concern for violations of fundamental rights of asylum seekers.

In doing so, the CJEU, as with the issue of humanitarian visas and the impact of the *X and X* decision, undercut efforts of those in the legislative branch that seek to reform the CEAS, and particularly the Dublin III rules, to be in greater conformity with the EU and MS's general obligation of respecting and protecting fundamental rights under Articles 2 and 6 TEU. The initial proposals for reform of the CEAS by the Commission in 2016 emphasised migration control, containing, for example, ideas to accelerate the process (and potential rejections) and impose an obligation on the MS to investigate whether an application is inadmissible on the grounds of the safe third country or safe country of origin concept within the Dublin procedures themselves, a notion that was sharply

---

of beatings and illegal seizure of valuables by local police of those seeking asylum, as well as apparent violations of *non-refoulement*, as asylum seekers claimed that Croatian officials engaged in tactics meant to prevent them from presenting an application for protection, from refusing to accept an application and instead summarily deporting them to simply pushing them back at the border. See e.g. HUMAN RIGHTS WATCH, 'Croatia: Asylum Seekers Forced Back to Serbia', 20.01.2017, available at https://www.hrw.org/news/2017/01/20/croatia-asylum-seekers-forced-back-serbia, last accessed 16.05.2018; N. RUJEVIC, 'Refugees in Serbia – stranded in a warehouse', *Deutsche Welle*, 17.01.2017, available at http://www.dw.com/en/refugees-in-serbia-stranded-in-a-warehouse/a-37167779, last accessed 16.05.2018. For a detailed report of the asylum process in Croatia including of the alleged incidents as reported by multiple agencies and NGOs and updated reports from 2018, see ASYLUM INFORMATION DATABASE/EUROPEAN COUNCIL ON REFUGEES AND EXILES, 'Country Report: Croatia', 31.12.2017, available at http://www.asylumineurope.org/sites/default/files/report-download/aida_hr_2017update.pdf, last accessed 16.05.2018.

[133] See I. GOLDNER LANG, 'Croatia and EU Asylum Law: Playing on the Sidelines of at the Centre of Events?', in V. STOYANEVA and E. KARAGEORGIOU (eds.), *The New Asylum and Transit Countries in Europe During and in the Aftermath of the 2015/2016 Crisis*, Brill, Leiden, forthcoming in 2018.

criticised by scholars and advocates of running afoul of international human rights and refugee law obligations.[134] Some of the more questionable ideas from the perspective of fundamental rights were tempered by counter-proposals of the EP, which took a more rights-oriented approach to reform,[135] which would have been greatly aided if the Court's opinion in these cases aligned more with the approach proposed by AG Sharpston. By not doing so, the leverage those voices in the legislative branch have now appears diminished,[136] and there continues to be a significant deadlock over the shape of the reforms among the legislative.[137]

---

[134] See S. PEERS, 'The Orbanisation of EU asylum law: the latest EU asylum proposals', *EU Law Analysis*, 06.05.2016, available at https://eulawanalysis.blogspot.co.at/2016/05/the-orbanisation-of-eu-asylum-law.html, last accessed 16.05.2018; C. KVORNING LASSEN, 'Reforming the Common European Asylum Policy (CEAS)', EUROPEUM Institute for European Policy – Policy Paper, 22.06.2017, p. 7, available at http://europeum.org/data/articles/ckl.pdf, last accessed 16.05.2018.

[135] For example, the EP's LIBE Committee proposals emphasised *inter alia* the need to ensure the rights of the child are respected in the cases of unaccompanied minors, family reunification, and the consideration of asylum seekers' preferences. The EP also stressed the need for solidarity and a humane resettlement and relocation scheme to ensure that the outer border MS do not have to bear the brunt of large-scale influxes in the future while preserving the ability of those seeking protection to obtain it. EUROPEAN PARLIAMENT – COMMITTEE ON CIVIL LIBERTIES, JUSTICE AND HOME AFFAIRS, EU asylum policy: reforming the Dublin rules to create a fairer system, Background Report, BKG/86/403, 19.10.2017, available at http://www.europarl.europa.eu/pdfs/news/expert/background/20171019BKG86403/20171019BKG86403_en.pdf, last accessed 16.05.2018. For an overview of the proposals from various EU institutions up to 2017, see EUROPEAN PARLIAMENT, 'Reform of the Common European Asylum System', available at http://www.europarl.europa.eu/legislative-train/theme-towards-a-new-policy-on-migration/file-reform-of-the-common-european-asylum-system, last accessed 16.05.2018; ASYLUM INFORMATION DATABASE/EUROPEAN COUNCIL ON REFUGEES AND EXILES, 'CEAS reform: State of play of negotiations on the Dublin IV Regulation', 30.11.2017, available at http://www.asylumineurope.org/news/30-11-2017/ceas-reform-state-play-negotiations-dublin-iv-regulation, last accessed 16.05.2018.

[136] In taking on the rotating Council Presidency in January 2018, Bulgaria's government signalled that the security concerns come first in the EU's reshaping of the Union's migration rules. BULGARIAN PRESIDENCY OF THE COUNCIL OF THE EUROPEAN UNION, 'Priorities – Security and Stability', available at https://eu2018bg.bg/en/53, last accessed 16.05.2018. Meanwhile, although the EP's LIBE Committee still maintains a human rights approach in its proposals, by for example inserting provisions allowing for free legal assistance and refusing to include Turkey as a safe third country, it did recently approve a new CEAS reform proposal that allows for accelerated process and rejection of applications without consideration of their substance *inter alia* in cases where the applicant comes from a 'safe third country' or 'has a "sufficient connection"' – such as previous residence – with a safe country where he or she may "reasonably be expected to seek protection"'. EUROPEAN PARLIAMENT – COMMITTEE ON CIVIL LIBERTIES, JUSTICE AND HOME AFFAIRS, 'MEPs support reforms to speed up assessment of asylum requests in the EU', Press Release, IPR/02/320, 25.04.2018, available at http://www.europarl.europa.eu/news/en/press-room/20180423IPR02320/meps-support-reforms-to-speed-up-assessment-of-asylum-requests-in-the-eu, last accessed 16.05.2018.

[137] Admittedly, it is the new rules on resettlement and relocation requested by the EU that are the greatest reason for deadlock: rules proposed to have a system in place have created significant opposition from the Eastern MS, while the newest proposals from Bulgaria to make

4. CONCLUSION

Despite the tragedies occurring in 2015, despite the legal complications that arose as a result of the so-called 'migration' crisis, the EU appears to be nevertheless immobile on how to handle such situations in the future. The legislative arm is still working on possible solutions, but the one most likely to align itself with fundamental rights – a process for issuing humanitarian visas – has been undercut both by the EC and Council as well as by the CJEU through its judgment in *X and X*. Similarly, while the EU is still struggling with reconfiguring the CEAS, sometimes with suggestions that pull the standards lower than they should, the aspect of the system that needs the greatest overhaul, the Dublin system, is not being reformed. Even though its faulty functioning is threatening the Union, the CJEU insists on entrenching it with the judgments in *Jafari* and *A.S.* and at the expense of fundamental rights.

The CJEU's stance is an odd one given its case law history. Though it often exhorted the supremacy of the EU law, when EU law came in conflict with fundamental rights, the CJEU tended to find ways to align and harmonise the two matters. It utterly failed to do so in these two cases. The judgment in *X and X* is particularly devastating, as it fails to address the substance of the matter at all, leaving the burden fully on the legislative arm to resolve the matter. Similarly, the Court's view in *Jafari* and *A.S.* that the regardless of even extreme circumstances, Dublin rules must be upheld, leaves little room in the future for change to the system from the judicial branch. In the process, these judgments embolden voices that seek to restrict fundamental rights, such as those opposing the humanitarian visa, and those who benefit from the outer MS having to carry the burden of the Dublin system, even when its application puts the whole Union under duress. Whether this was truly a political statement given the extraordinary circumstances or not, it is perceived as such by those who see the decisions as a sign that fundamental rights need not be considered as a primary concern in reshaping the CEAS. It can only be hoped that the CJEU finds its progressive stance again, once the 'crisis' has fully subsided.

---

reallocations voluntary are opposed by the Southern MS. See N. NIELSEN, 'EU states tackle Dublin asylum reform "line by line"', *euobserver*, 07.03.2018, available at https://euobserver.com/migration/141236, last accessed 16.05.2018; G. PARAVICINI and D. HERSZENHORN, 'Southern rim rebels against EU migration proposal', *Politico*, 05.05.2018, available at https://www.politico.eu/article/eu-migration-crisis-italy-spain-rebels-bulgaria-dublin-quotas-proposal, last accessed 16.05.2018.

THE EU MIGRATION CRISIS AND THE HUMAN RIGHTS IMPLICATIONS OF THE EXTERNALISATION OF BORDER CONTROL

Mathilde Duhaâ

1. Introduction: The EU Migration Crisis, a State of Play................. 136
2. The EU's Response: Towards the Externalisation of Border Management?... 139
3. Tackling Security Threats Whilst Upholding European Values: Principles vs. Realities 143
   3.1. The EU-Turkey Statement.................................... 146
   3.2. The European Border and Coast Guard Agency (EBCG) 151
   3.3. Reinvigorating Cooperation with Libya? 154
4. Conclusion... 163

ABSTRACT

In the context of the world's largest refugee crisis since World War II, the European Union (EU) has to cope with unprecedented numbers of arrivals at its external borders. In light of the weekly shipwrecks and drownings in the Mediterranean, European states decided to develop a common approach to the crisis, as they realised the upcoming months and years would be characterised by massive migration flows to the continent.

This article investigates the EU's response to the migration crisis focusing on migration as a policy area, especially with regards to border management and control of the European external borders. It will aim at critically assessing the human rights impact of the policies implemented since 2016, exploring the human rights consequences of the externalisation of the EU's migration management. As case studies, it will analyse three specific instruments introduced by the EU since March 2016: the EU-Turkey statement, the creation of the European Border and Coast Guard Agency and the establishment of a closer partnership with Libya.

To overcome the crisis, this research will assert that the EU needs to find a balance between its moral and legal obligations and its duty to ensure the safety of its citizens and the securing of its external borders. It will provide recommendations regarding the need for a genuine holistic approach, one that bridges security and human rights concerns. Extending the understanding of national security with human security approaches could help develop more comprehensive and effective migration management policies.

1. INTRODUCTION: THE EU MIGRATION CRISIS, A STATE OF PLAY

In the words of Dimitri Avramopoulos, European Commissioner for Migration, Home Affairs and Citizenship, 'the world finds itself facing the worst refugee crisis since the Second World War'.[1] In recent years, an unprecedented level of human mobility was recorded across the globe. The United Nations High Commissioner for Refugees (UNHCR) asserts that 65.6 million persons were displaced worldwide at the end of 2016, a staggering 22.5 million of whom were refugees.[2] Although the Global South continues to receive the largest share of them – with around 84% of the world's refugees hosted in developing countries[3] – migration flows to the EU have dramatically increased in recent years, with unprecedented numbers of arrivals at the European external borders. According to Eurostat, the statistical data office of the Union, over 1.26 million asylum requests were logged in 2015[4] amounting to the highest level ever recorded. Figures for the year 2016 reached over 1.20 million first-time applicants.[5] Another illustration of this phenomenon is the rise in the number of arrivals at the European borders: the count from the International Organisation for Migration (IOM) indicates that, between January and December 2017, land routes have seen 14,406 migrants whilst 172,362 arrived by sea, the vast majority of whom – namely 119,369 – landed on Italian shores.[6]

---

[1] D. AVRAMOPOULOS, 'A European Response to Migration: Showing solidarity and sharing responsibility', 14.08.2015, available at http://europa.eu/rapid/press-release_SPEECH-15-5498_fr.htm, last accessed 13.06.2018.
[2] UNCHR, 'Global Trends – Forced Displacement in 2016', 19.06.2017, available at http://www.unhcr.org/statistics/unhcrstats/5943e8a34/global-trends-forced-displacement-2016.html, last accessed 13.06.2018, p. 2.
[3] Ibid., p. 2.
[4] EUROSTAT, 'Record number of over 1.2 million first time asylum seekers registered in 2015', 04.03.2016, available at http://ec.europa.eu/eurostat/documents/2995521/7203832/3-04032016-AP-EN.pdf, last accessed 13.06.2018.
[5] EUROSTAT, 'Asylum in the EU Member States, 1.2 million first time asylum seekers registered in 2016', 16.03.2017, available at http://ec.europa.eu/eurostat/documents/2995521/7921609/3-16032017-BP-EN.pdf/e5fa98bb-5d9d-4297-9168-d07c67d1c9e1, last accessed 13.06.2018.
[6] IOM, 'Migration flows to Europe – 2017 Overview', January 2018, available at https://reliefweb.int/sites/reliefweb.int/files/resources/2017_Overview_Arrivals_to_Europe.pdf, last accessed 13.06.2018.

Consequently, the Mediterranean has become the most dangerous sea route[7] for refugees and migrants, 2016 being the deadliest year so far with more than 5,098 drownings at sea estimated.[8] In the absence of legal and safe pathways to Europe for people seeking international protection, and in light of increased borders restrictions throughout the EU with several Schengen states having temporarily reintroduced internal border checks,[9] 'many saw no alternative to undertaking dangerous journeys'[10] details the United Nations High Commissioner for Refugees' (UNHCR) Bureau for Europe. As expressed by the current UN High Commissioner for Refugees Filippo Grandi, 'for so many deaths to have occurred just in a matter of days and months is shocking and shows just how truly perilous these journeys are'.[11] Growing public pressure and media attention after the series of deadly shipwrecks of April 2015, near the Italian island of Lampedusa, and images of three-year-old Aylan Kurdi's body washed up on the Turkish beach of Bodrum on 2 September 2015[12] constituted a wakeup call for the EU Member States (MS) as they realised that the coming months and years will be characterised by coping with a massive influx of arrivals.

In the meantime, the several terrorist attacks carried out on European soil since January 2015 – principally in France, Belgium, Germany and the United Kingdom – resulted in increasing concerns regarding security at the national and EU levels. As clearly stated in the President Juncker's Political Guidelines[13]

---

[7] The IOM Missing Migrants project, which tracks disappearances of migrants along the different migratory routes around the globe, recorded a total of 7,763 migrants' estimated deaths worldwide in 2016. IOM, 'Migrant deaths and disappearances worldwide: 2016 analysis', Data Briefing Series, 08.03.2017, p. 2, available at https://publications.iom.int/system/files/pdf/gmdac_data_briefing_series_issue_8.pdf, last accessed 13.06.2018.

[8] IOM, 'Missing Migrants. Tracking deaths along migratory routes', 12.06.2018, available at https://missingmigrants.iom.int/mediterranean, last accessed 13.06.2018.

[9] The Schengen area, established in 1985, is an internal area of 26 European states where border control is abolished, and the free circulation of persons and goods is guaranteed. In accordance with Article 29 of the Schengen Borders Code (that allows for the reintroduction of temporary control in cases of serious threats to the internal security), Germany, Austria, Denmark, Norway and Sweden have reintroduced some internal border checks in the fall of 2015. EUROPEAN COMMISSION, 'Temporary reintroduction of border control', available at https://ec.europa.eu/home-affairs/what-we-do/policies/borders-and-visas/schengen/reintroduction-border-control_en, last accessed 13.06.2018.

[10] UNHCR, 'Desperate Journeys', February 2017, available at www.unhcr.org/58b449f54.pdf, last accessed 13.06.2018.

[11] UNHCR, 'Mediterranean death toll soars in first 5 months of 2016', 31.05.2016, available at www.unhcr.org/news/latest/2016/5/574db9d94/mediterranean-death-toll-soars-first-5-months-2016.html, last accessed 13.06.2018.

[12] H. SMITH, 'Shocking images of drowned Syrian boy show tragic plight of refugees', *The Guardian*, 02.09.2015, available at www.theguardian.com/world/2015/sep/02/shocking-image-of-drowned-syrian-boy-shows-tragic-plight-of-refugees, last accessed 13.06.2018.

[13] J.C. JUNCKER, 'A New Start for Europe: My Agenda for Jobs, Growth, Fairness and Democratic Change. Political Guidelines for the next European Commission', Strasbourg, 15.07.2014, p. 10, available at https://www.eesc.europa.eu/resources/docs/jean-claude-juncker---political-guidelines.pdf, last accessed 13.06.2018.

and the European Commission Agenda on Security,[14] the fight against terrorism lies at the top of the EU's priorities. In this context, migration has been increasingly framed as a transnational security threat and a generator of risk at the EU level. Indeed, since the beginning of the migration crisis, several European politicians have raised their voices to express concern about the migration-terrorism nexus, arguing that uncontrolled movements of people, combined with porous borders, pose a threat to their national security. Although Ben Emmerson, UN Special Rapporteur on Counter-terrorism and Human Rights, found little evidence of links between migration and increased terrorist threats in his 2016 report to the UN General Assembly,[15] nationalist and populist movements on the rise throughout the continent continue to exploit the crisis using such fears. The Hungarian Prime Minister, Victor Orbán, who back in March 2017 qualified migration as being 'the Trojan horse of terrorism',[16] is one of many examples.

This article will explore the EU's response to the migration crisis focusing on migration as a policy area, more precisely with regards to the management and control of the European external borders. It will aim at critically assessing the human rights impact of some of the EU policies and strategies in the field of border control, exploring the human rights consequences of the externalisation of the EU's migration management.[17] This research will ask in what ways, if any, does the EU's approach to externalisation of migration management reflect its own human rights standards. The aim of this article is to provide recommendations regarding the need for a holistic approach to the migration crisis, one that bridges both security and human rights concerns. Such an approach would not only aim at stemming the flows of arrivals but will address the underlying causes of migration that spurred people to leave their countries of origin in the first place. Extending the understanding of national security with human security approaches could help develop more comprehensive and effective migration management policies.

---

[14] EUROPEAN COMMISSION, The European Agenda on Security, COM(2015) 185 final, 28.04.2015.
[15] UN GENERAL ASSEMBLY, Report of the Special Rapporteur on the promotion and protection of human rights and fundamental freedoms while countering terrorism, UN Doc. A/71/384, 13.09.2016, p. 4.
[16] J. BRUNSDEN, 'Europe refugee policy is "Trojan horse of terrorism"', says Orban', *Financial Times*, 30.03.2017, available at https://www.ft.com/content/538b2a0a-154e-11e7-80f4-13e067d5072c, last accessed 13.06.2018.
[17] For a detailed analysis of the legal implications of externalisation strategies, see generally M. DEN HEIJER, *Europe and Extraterritorial Asylum*, Hart, Oxford/Portland 2012; T. GAMMELTOFT-HANSEN, *Access to Asylum. International Refugee Law and the Globalisation of Migration Control*, Cambridge University Press, New York 2011 or L. HESCHL, *Protecting the Rights of Refugees beyond European Borders: Establishing Extraterritorial Responsibilities*, Intersentia, Cambridge 2018.

As case studies, it will analyse three specific instruments introduced by the EU since March 2016 with the aim of reducing the migratory pressure at its external borders: the adoption and the implementation of the EU-Turkey statement, the creation of the European Border and Coast Guard Agency (EBCG) and the discussions around a potential partnership between the EU and Libya, telling examples of the EU's perception of the migration crisis through a security lens.

It will be argued that there are discrepancies between the EU stated principles and their translation into practice. Indeed, despite the Union's stated goal of developing and implementing a comprehensive migration policy addressing both security and human rights, recent developments relating to border management – the reintroduction of some internal Schengen Borders, cooperation with countries that hold dire human rights records, increased militarised presence in the Mediterranean to name but a few – show that security measures remain central in the way in which MS have decided to address the situation. It also demonstrates that the EU's response continues to be very much focused on strengthening border controls rather than having its MS acting in solidarity to protect the human rights and human security of migrants.

2. THE EU'S RESPONSE: TOWARDS THE EXTERNALISATION OF BORDER MANAGEMENT?

In its response to the crisis, the EU has developed several border management strategies articulated around two central objectives: securing and managing its external borders while saving lives and guaranteeing the human rights of migrants. These two main goals could appear to be contradictory at first sight. However, as claimed by Omar Grech and Monika Wohlfeld 'effective migration management and border management policies would address national security problems while enhancing the human security of migrants'.[18] In their article 'Managing Migration in the Mediterranean: Is the EU Failing to Balance State Security, Human Security, and Human Rights', they argue that 'this is arguably a rather complex task, and one at which Europe seems to be failing'.[19]

According to EU law, border control is a shared competence between the EU and its MS,[20] but states have the primary responsibility for the management and protection of their external borders. Additionally, in accordance with

---

[18] O. GRECH and M. WOHLFELD, 'Managing Migration in the Mediterranean: Is the EU Failing to Balance State Security, Human Security, and Human Rights?', in INSTITUTE FOR PEACE RESEARCH AND SECURITY POLICY AT THE UNIVERSITY OF HAMBURG (ed.), *OSCE Yearbook 2015*, Nomos, Baden-Baden 2016, p. 317.
[19] Ibid., p. 317.
[20] Article 4(2) Treaty on the Functioning of the EU (hereinafter TFEU).

the principle of state sovereignty, every individual Member State has the right to decide on the conditions of entry and stay on its own territory for third-state nationals.[21] However, to safeguard the existence of Schengen as an area abolishing internal border controls and ensuring the free movements of persons, external border management[22] must be effectively coordinated at the European level.

When adopting and implementing policies related to migrants and refugees, the EU and its MS ought to respect an entire set of human rights obligations. Refugees and migrants are rights-holders and therefore, entitled to the same universal human rights and fundamental freedoms as all other individuals, regardless of their legal status.[23] The human rights of migrants and refugees are enshrined in different international documents, such as the 1948 Universal Declaration of Human Rights[24] and subsequent UN human rights treaties,[25] as well as in the 1951 Geneva Convention relating to the Status of Refugees (GRC) and its 1967 Optional Protocol, cornerstone of the international refugee protection regime. These rights are also recognised in different European treaties: namely the 1953 European Convention for the Protection of Human Rights and Fundamental Freedoms (ECHR) and the 2000 Charter of Fundamental Rights of the EU (CFREU). Its Articles 18 and 19 are of particular interest when it comes to refugee protection as they relate to the right to asylum and protection in the event of removal, expulsion or extradition.

According to the Lisbon treaty, the concepts of solidarity and burden-sharing are the core principles of the EU migration policy. These values are underscored by Article 80 of Treaty on the Functioning of the European Union (TFEU) which stipulates that the EU migration and asylum policies 'shall

---

[21] P. BOELES, M. DEN HEIJER, G. LODDER and K. WOUTERS, *European Migration Law*, Intersentia, Cambridge 2014, p. 16.

[22] The IOM defines border management as followed: 'facilitation of authorised flows of persons, including business people, tourists, migrants and refugees, across a border and the detection and prevention of irregular entry of non-nationals into a given country. Measures to manage borders include the imposition by States of visa requirements, carrier sanctions against transportation companies bringing irregular migrants to the territory, and interdiction at sea. International standards require a balancing between facilitating the entry of legitimate travellers and preventing that of travellers entering for inappropriate reasons or with invalid documentation.' IOM, 'Key Migration Terms', available at www.iom.int/key-migration-terms, last accessed 14.06.2018.

[23] As reaffirmed in the UN General Assembly, New York Declaration for Refugees and Migrants, UN. Doc. A/RES/71/1, 03.09.2016.

[24] Universal Declaration of Human Rights, 217 A (III), 10.12.1948, Article 1.

[25] Such as the 1966 International Covenant on Civil and Political Rights (especially its Article 7 relating to the prohibition of torture and Article 12 on freedom of movement), the 1984 Convention against Torture and Other Cruel, Inhuman or Degrading Treatment of Punishment, or the 1989 Convention on the Rights of the Child.

be governed by the principle of solidarity and fair sharing of responsibility, including its financial implications, between the Member States'.[26]

The European Agenda on Migration[27] adopted in May 2015 has become the cornerstone of the EU's institutional framework in the field of migration and border control. As the key document summarising the EU policy, it sets out standards and priorities regarding migration management at the regional level. Emphasis is put on the need and urgency to develop a comprehensive European approach, combining both internal and external policies. Particular importance is given to the development of a multi-stakeholder and collective response that involves a wide range of actors such as 'member states, EU institutions, international organisations, civil society, local authorities and third countries' to mention but a few.[28] Meant to be a holistic document curbing migration challenges faced by the Union not only in the short term – with immediate measures being undertaken – but also in the long run, the agenda is articulated around four pillars: reducing incentives for irregular migration; border management: saving lives at sea and securing external borders; a strong common asylum policy and a new policy on legal migration.

With the European Agenda on Migration, EU countries recognised the need to develop a common European approach in order to tackle the migration crisis. As outlined in this core strategy document, no single European state has the capacity to face and tackle the migratory challenges on its own. This is why the Commission strongly advised MS to work towards finding solutions to the migratory pressure at the European level.[29]

The tension between the human rights of migrants and the securing of the European external borders has been closely monitored and scrutinised by human rights activists and academics since the very beginning of the crisis. Qualifying this situation as a 'migration crisis' is debated amongst human rights scholars and advocates preferring the use of the terms 'refugee crisis',[30] 'crisis of solidarity'[31] or 'crisis of reception'.[32] They argue that framing the

---

[26] TFEU, Article 80.
[27] EUROPEAN COMMISSION, A European Agenda on Migration, COM(2015) 240 final, 13.05.2015.
[28] Ibid., p. 2.
[29] Ibid., p. 2.
[30] AMNESTY INTERNATIONAL, 'Tackling the global refugee crisis: from shirking to sharing responsibility', 18.10.2016, available at www.amnesty.org/en/documents/document/?index Number=pol40%2f4905%2f2016&language=en, last accessed 14.06.2018.
[31] Statement made by B. KI-MOON, former UN Secretary General, 'Refugee Crisis about solidarity, Not Just Numbers, Secretary General Says at Event on Global Displacement Challenge', Press Release 15.04.2016, available at www.un.org/press/en/2016/sgsm17670.doc.htm, last accessed 14.06.2018.
[32] Statement made by A. GUTERRES, former UN High Commissioner for Refugees and current UN Secretary General, 'Statement by UN High Commissioner for Refugees, António Guterres on refugee crisis in Europe', UNHCR Press Release, 04.09.2015, available at www.unhcr.org/

phenomenon as such puts the emphasis on the danger posed by influx of people and neglects the vulnerabilities and personal experiences of migrants. Behind the notion of crisis is indeed the idea that one must cope with a phenomenon of exceptional dimension, with potentially damaging and harmful effects.

The qualification of crisis also relates to the concept of securitisation, elaborated by the Copenhagen School of Security Studies. Securitisation can be defined as the process by which a particular issue is socially constructed as a threat and transformed into a security concern, most of the time allowing for the use of extraordinary measures to deal with it. As argued by theorists from the Copenhagen School, 'the special nature of security threats justifies the use of extraordinary measures to handle them. The invocation of security has been the key to legitimising the use of force, but more generally it has opened the way for the state to mobilize, or to take special powers, to handle existing threats'.[33] In this way, issues initially apprehended as political, environmental, economic or human rights concerns in nature can become securitised, which means that some actors will define them as threats to security to legitimise the use of extraordinary measures.

Authors such as Barry Buzan, Ole Waever and Jef Huysmans argued that, since the 1990s, migration has become a policy issue penetrated by security discourses, which has had an impact on the type of response developed by the EU. As stated by Huysmans 'the development of security discourses and policies in the area of migration is often presented as an inevitable policy response'.[34] Khalid Koser explains that 'labelling any issue a security threat has implications in terms of the laws, norms, policies and procedures that become justified in response. In the migration context […] the label has been used to justify greater surveillance, detention, deportation and more restrictive policies'.[35] As for Didier Bigo, securitisation of migration is linked with the issue of politicisation.[36] Articulating and constructing migration first and foremost as a problem with security implications is a way for politicians to mobilise certain means to manage and respond to the threats, which enable them to then justify their own authority: 'the framing of the state as a body endangered by migrants is a political narrative activated for the purpose of political game.'[37]

---

news/press/2015/9/55e9459f6/statement-un-high-commissioner-refugees-antonio-guterres-refugee-crisis.html, last accessed 12.06.2018.

[33] B. BUZAN, O. WAEVER and J. DE WILDE, *Security, a New Framework for Analysis*, Lynne Rienner Publishers, Boulder/London 1998, p. 21.

[34] J. HUYSMANS, 'The European Union and the Issue of Migration', (2000) 38(5) *Journal of Common Market Studies (JCMS)*, p. 757.

[35] K. KOSER, 'When is Migration a Security Issue?', *Brookings*, 31 March 2011, available at www.brookings.edu/opinions/when-is-migration-a-security-issue, last accessed 12.06.2018.

[36] D. BIGO, 'Security and Immigration: toward a Critique of the Governmentality of Unease', (2002) 27 *Alternatives*, p. 65.

[37] Ibid., p. 68.

Anna Lindley elaborates further on the links between migration and crisis in the political and social discourses, stating that 'despite the relatively recent emergence of more nuanced and even celebratory accounts of mobility, the tendency to link migration with crisis in a strongly negative fashion remains deeply entrenched and vigorously persistent'.[38]

People on the move have indeed different and sometimes mixed motives: be it fleeing a conflict area, escaping persecution, searching for new economic prospects and better life opportunities; or due to the impact of climate change and natural disasters. Though a large number of people who have arrived in Europe since 2015[39] are entitled to refugee status or subsidiary protection under the criteria set forth in the 1951 Refugees Convention, migration flows are mixed, and economic migrants continue to make their way to Europe.

Therefore, in this article, the term migration will be based on the IOM's definition that one can consider as being the broadest and the most encompassing:

> the movement of a person or a group of persons, either across an international border, or within a State. It is a population movement, encompassing any kind of movement of people, whatever its length, composition and causes; it includes migration of refugees, displaced persons, economic migrants, and persons moving for other purposes, including family reunification.[40]

More precisely, this article will focus on irregular migrants who are 'foreign nationals whose migration status does not comply with the requirements of domestic immigration legislation and rules',[41] often perceived by European governments as a threat for European security.

3. TACKLING SECURITY THREATS WHILST UPHOLDING EUROPEAN VALUES: PRINCIPLES vs. REALITIES

The year 2016 can be considered as a turning point in the EU's response to the migration crisis: limiting numbers of arrivals was a priority for the EU and

---

[38] A. LINDLEY, *Crisis and Migration: Critical Perspectives*, Routledge, London/New York 2014, p. 1.
[39] T. JAULIN, 'Migrations en Méditerranée: la Crise de l'Asile', in (2016) 4 *Politique Etrangère*, available at https://interaffairs.ru/i/PE_4_2016_WEB.pdf, last accessed 12.06.2018, p. 31.
[40] IOM, 'Key Migration Terms', available at www.iom.int/key-migration-terms, last accessed 14.06.2018.
[41] AMNESTY INTERNATIONAL, 'A perfect storm – The failure of European policies in the Central Mediterranean', Report, 06.07.2017, available at www.amnesty.org/en/documents/eur03/6655/2017/en, last accessed 12.06.2018, p. 4.

policies of externalisation of migration control accelerated, with third countries being handed greater control. For Bill Frelick, director of the Refugee Rights Programme for Human Rights Watch (HRW), externalisation of migration can be defined as the 'extraterritorial State actions to prevent migrants, including asylum-seekers, from entering the legal jurisdictions or territories of destination countries or regions or of making them legally inadmissible without individually considering the merits of their protection claims'.[42] Keegan Williams and Alison Mountz explain that externalisation policies take various forms: they can consist in the interception of migrants, developing detention facilities in transit regions or developing bilateral arrangements for policing and repatriation, amongst others.[43]

These externalisation trends were already described in 2013 by François Crépeau, the UN Special Rapporteur on the human rights of migrants, who declared that 'through a range of sophisticated policies and programmes, European Union policy increasingly operates to ensure that border control no longer takes place at the physical borders of the European Union'.[44] When it comes more precisely to the externalisation of border control, Amnesty International's definition reads as follows: 'enlisting other countries to engage in punitive or preventive policies aiming at stopping irregular border crossings by refugees, asylum-seekers and migrants.'[45]

Behind this strategy of externalisation is a logic of deterrence and the idea that migration flows can be prevented. If the EU advances humanitarian arguments to justify these policies – saying such agreements are a way to drastically reduce the number of deaths at sea and a useful tool to deter smuggling networks – this tendency of outsourcing border management out of the EU remains of great concern when it comes to the impact of such a strategy on the human rights of migrants. Indeed, externalisation policies may increase the likelihood of human rights violations: by delegating its authority to other countries or stakeholders, the EU loses part of its ability to ensure that the human rights of migrants and refugees are effectively protected. Often, these third countries have fewer resources – as they might have a weaker

---

[42] B. FRELICK, 'The Impact of Externalisation of Migration Controls on the Rights of Asylum Seekers and other Migrants', (2016) 4(4) *Journal on Migration and Human Security*, p. 193.

[43] K. WILLIAMS and A. MOUNTZ, 'Rising Tide – Analysing the Relationship between Externalisation and Migrant Deaths and Boat Losses', in R. ZAIOTTI (ed.), *Externalising Migration Management: Europe, North America and the Spread of 'Remote Control' Practices*, Routledge, London/New York 2016, p. 32.

[44] UN HUMAN RIGHTS COUNCIL, Report of the Special Rapporteur on the human rights of migrants, Regional study: management of the external borders of the European Union and its impact on the human rights of migrants, UN Doc. A/HRC/23/46, 24.04.2013, para. 55.

[45] AMNESTY INTERNATIONAL, 'The human rights risks of external migration policies', 13.06.2017, available at https://www.amnesty.org/en/documents/pol30/6200/2017/en, last accessed 12.06.2018.

legal framework or a lower budget – available to protect the fundamental rights of migrants and refugees.[46] According to Sara Prestianni, international immigration policies researcher for ARCI Immigration and Migreurop, the problem with these practices of externalisation is that 'negotiations begin with third countries without first assessing the human rights standards in those places or the way local governments handle immigration issues'.[47] Examples of the potentially negative impact EU's externalisation policies have on migrants and refugees will be detailed in the different case studies.

'If chaos characterised the response of the EU and its member states in 2015, wrong-headed and rights abusing policies have defined 2016.'[48] This fierce criticism from Human Rights Watch outlines a paradox: while 2015 constituted the absolute record year in terms of arrivals, 2016 saw significantly fewer people coming to Europe but contained more deaths, despite the different measures undertaken by the EU. The death count of 5,098 people is a mere estimation based on the dead bodies fished out of the Mediterranean. This does not include those who drowned and whose bodies remain undiscovered at sea, a figure which is underestimated. According to Matteo de Bellis, Amnesty International's migration researcher: 'no matter how much money European governments invest in international aid projects purportedly intended to address the root causes of displacement, the reality is that EU leaders have so far largely favoured projects which create barriers for migration, and used international aid as leverage to get African governments to cooperate in their implementation'[49] such as the EU Trust Fund for Africa,[50] set up by the EU during the 2015 Valletta summit with the aim of tackling the root causes of migration from African countries.

The present section will closely examine – in a chronological order – three border management initiatives put in place in the EU since March 2016: the EU-Turkey statement, the European Border and Coast Guard Agency and the establishment of a closer partnership with Libya.

---

[46] B. FRELICK (2016), 'The impact of externalisation of migration controls on the rights of asylum seeks and other migrants', *supra* note 42.

[47] C. LOPEZ CURZI, 'The externalisation of European borders: steps and consequences of a dangerous process', *Open Migration*, 12.07.2016, available at https://openmigration.org/en/analyses/the-externalisation-of-european-borders-steps-and-consequences-of-a-dangerous-process, last accessed 12.06.2018.

[48] HRW, 'EU Policies Put Refugees at Risk – An Agenda to Restore Protection', 23.11.2016, available at www.hrw.org/news/2016/11/23/eu-policies-put-refugees-risk, last accessed 12.06.2018.

[49] AMNESTY INTERNATIONAL, 'A radical change is need to failing EU migration policy', 22.06.2017, available at www.amnesty.org/en/latest/news/2017/06/a-radical-change-is-needed-to-failing-eu-migration-policy, last accessed 12.06.2018.

[50] EUROPEAN COMMISSION, 'The EU Emergency Trust Fund for Africa', available at https://ec.europa.eu/europeaid/regions/africa/eu-emergency-trust-fund-africa_en, last accessed on 12.06.2018.

3.1. THE EU-TURKEY STATEMENT

As early as 2015, the European Commission developed a new 'hotspot approach' in its European Agenda on Migration. This approach was developed as a response to the pressure at the EU external borders, especially with the aim of assisting frontline states Italy and Greece, facing increasing numbers of arrivals. Hotspots were defined as follows: 'located at key arrival points in frontline Member States, hotspots are designed to inject great order into migration management by ensuring that all those arriving are identified, registered and properly processed.'[51] This hotspot approach has been subject to vehement criticism from non-governmental organizations (NGOs). Research from Amnesty International published in November 2016 concluded that its implementation did not alleviate pressure on frontline states and even led to violations of refugees and migrants' rights,[52] highlighting cases of ill-treatment and arbitrary detention in Italy. In April 2017, the EU Commission also alerted MS to the situation of children in migration,[53] especially unaccompanied minors, who are particularly vulnerable when they arrive in the hotspots.

Nonetheless, MS decided to increase their political and financial engagement with Turkey. A logical follow-up to the hotspot approach, the EU-Turkey statement[54] was signed on 18 March 2016 between the European heads of states and their Turkish counterpart to put an end to irregular migration flows departing from Turkey to Europe. It was presented by the European Commission as an effective way to prevent migrants from putting their lives at risk and to organise safe and legal pathways to Europe. Presenting externalisation policies as a way of protecting migrants, and not only as border control management tool, is a classic argument in favour of a security imperative.

As expressed in the text of the deal, key features of the agreement were that all new irregular migrants crossing from Turkey into the Greek islands, as of 20 March 2016, would be returned to Turkey; migrants arriving would be duly registered and any application for asylum would be processed individually by the Greek authorities, in cooperation with the UNHCR;

---

[51] EUROPEAN PARLIAMENT, 'On the frontline: the hotspot approach to managing migration', Study, May 2016, p. 8, available at http://www.europarl.europa.eu/RegData/etudes/STUD/2016/556942/IPOL_STU(2016)556942_EN.pdf, last accessed on 13.06.2018.

[52] AMNESTY INTERNATIONAL, 'Hotspot Italy – How EU's flagship approach leads to violations of refugee and migrant rights', 03.11.2016, available at www.amnesty.org/en/documents/eur30/5004/2016/en, last accessed 12.06.2018.

[53] EUROPEAN COMMISSION, The Protection of children in migration, COM(2017) 211 final, 12.04.2017.

[54] COUNCIL OF THE EUROPEAN UNION, 'EU-Turkey statement, 18 March 2016', Press Release 144/16, 18.03.2016, available at http://www.consilium.europa.eu/en/press/press-releases/2016/03/18/eu-turkey-statement/pdf, last accessed 14.06.2018.

for every Syrian being returned to Turkey from the Greek islands, another Syrian would be resettled from Turkey to the EU (1:1 mechanism), taking into account the UN vulnerability criteria. Finally, Turkey would take any necessary measures to prevent new sea or land routes for illegal migration opening from Turkey to the EU. In exchange for its efforts to accept the return of irregular migrants, Turkey would receive €6 billion from the EU, along with promises to facilitate visa liberalisation and re-energise discussions around EU accession.

Signing a deal with Turkey was controversial from the outset.[55] It raised the question of how to conclude partnerships with third countries, a strategy at the heart of the EU's externalisation approach. The Union argued that to build up a comprehensive response all stakeholders in the crisis must be involved: not only the different MS, institutions and agencies but also third countries. If this argument is deemed valid, there are questions which derive from it. How can it be ascertained that the states involved will respect human rights? Is the EU not relieving itself of some of its legal and moral obligations by focusing solely on stemming flows of migrants and preventing them from reaching its territory?

Numerous issues have arisen in response to these questions, especially regarding the principle of *non-refoulement*[56] and the prohibition of collective expulsions. One of the main concerns for NGOs and academics[57] was whether Turkey could be considered a safe third country for migrants and refugees. Being the largest host country in the world with around 2.9 million refugees,[58] Turkey has to cope with a great number of challenges, especially regarding access to lawful employment and education for refugees. It is important to note that Turkey has ratified the 1967 Optional Protocol relating to the Status of Refugees with a reservation related to the geographical limitation,[59] therefore non-Europeans

---

[55] For further legal analysis of the EU-Turkey deal, see M. GATTI, 'The EU-Turkey Statement: A Treaty that Violates Democracy' (Part 1 of 2), *EJIL: Talk!*, 18.04.2016, available at https://www.ejiltalk.org/the-eu-turkey-statement-a-treaty-that-violates-democracy-part-1-of-2, last accessed 12.06.2018.

[56] The principle of *non-refoulement* is the core principle of the 1951 Refugee Convention, laid out in its Article 33. It prohibits the sending of refugees to places where there is reasonable ground to think that they would face danger or persecution: 'where his [or her] life or freedom would be threatened on account of race, religion, nationality, membership of a particular social group or political opinion.' Reservations to Article 33 are not permitted by the treaty, therefore States parties cannot derogate from this *non-refoulement* obligation. The principle of *non-refoulement* is also enshrined in Article 78 para. 1 of the TFEU.

[57] S. PEERS and E. ROMAN, 'The EU, Turkey and the Refugee Crisis: What could possibly go wrong?', *EU Law Analysis*, 05.02.2016, available at http://eulawanalysis.blogspot.com/2016/02/the-eu-turkey-and-refugee-crisis-what.html, last accessed 14.06.2018.

[58] UNHCR, 'Figures at a Glance', 19.06.2017, available at www.unhcr.org/figures-at-a-glance.html, last accessed 12.06.2018.

[59] 'The instrument of accession stipulates that the Government of Turkey maintains the provisions of the declaration made under section B of article 1 of the Convention relating

are excluded from qualifying for refugee status in the country. Because of this geographical reservation, refugees from countries other than Syria, for instance those originating from Iraq or Afghanistan, cannot benefit from the same level of protection under the EU-Turkey deal, although their personal situation could make them benefit from such status under international law.

Furthermore, Turkish forces were also accused of deporting refugees back to Syria in violation of international law the same month the deal was signed with the EU.[60] The country also closed its border with Syria in April 2016, whilst Syrian camps were shelled by the regime, leaving thousands of people trapped outside of Turkey.[61]

The dire human rights record of Erdogan's presidency also remains an issue of concern. The attempted coup on 15 July 2016, terrorist attacks and ongoing armed clashes between the PKK (the Kurdistan Workers' Party) and government forces in the southeast show the situation in the country is unstable. 2016 and 2017 have been characterised by a serious crackdown on human rights, targeting especially human rights defenders and civil society activists, such as journalists, academics, judges, or members of the police, who were dismissed through the course of the last year and a half.[62] Additionally, the future of the deal remains very fragile due to growing tensions between Recep Tayyip Erdogan and several EU leaders, notably those of Germany and the Netherlands.[63] The risk that President Erdogan uses the refugee deal as a bargaining chip or a political lever remains: if EU MS denounce the increasingly authoritarian nature of his regime, he could call the agreement into question and threaten to open his country's gates to let migrants pass.

---

to the Status of Refugees, done at Geneva on 28 July 1951, according to which it applies the Convention only to persons who have become refugees as a result of events occurring in Europe, and also the reservation clause made upon ratification of the Convention to the effect that no provision of this Convention may be interpreted as granting to refugees greater rights than those accorded to Turkish citizens in Turkey'. UNHCR, Reservations and declarations to the 1967 Protocol relating to the Status of Refugees, New York, 31 January 1967 http://www.unhcr.org/protection/convention/4dac37d79/reservations-declarations-1967-protocol-relating-status-refugees.html, last accessed 17.06.2018.

[60] AMNESTY INTERNATIONAL, 'Turkey: illegal mass returns of Syrian refugees expose fatal flaws in EU-Turkey deal', 01.04.2016, available at www.amnesty.org/en/press-releases/2016/04/turkey-illegal-mass-returns-of-syrian-refugees-expose-fatal-flaws-in-eu-turkey-deal, last accessed 14.06.2018.

[61] HRW, 'Turkey: Open Border to Displaced Syrians Shelled by Government – No Escape for Thousands Fleeing Attacks on Border Camps', 20.04.2016, available at www.hrw.org/news/2016/04/20/turkey-open-border-displaced-syrians-shelled-government, last accessed 12.06.2018.

[62] AMNESTY INTERNATIONAL, 'Turkey 2016/2017', available at www.amnesty.org/en/countries/europe-and-central-asia/turkey/report-turkey, last accessed 12.06.2018.

[63] G. DARROCH, 'Netherlands "will pay the price" for blocking Turkish visit – Erdoğan', *The Guardian*, 12.03.2017, available at www.theguardian.com/world/2017/mar/12/netherlands-will-pay-the-price-for-blocking-turkish-visit-erdogan, last accessed 12.06.2018.

When evaluating the deal one year after its adoption, the EU qualified it as a 'game changer'.[64] In the 'Fifth Report on the Progress made in the implementation of the EU-Turkey Statement'[65] from March 2017, the Commission argued it was 'producing tangible results, despite the challenging circumstances. The number of crossing since the Statement continues to be substantially reduced and loss of life has been stemmed'.[66] UNHCR figures show that 'after March, the numbers crossing the sea to Greece from Turkey dropped drastically with arrivals in October 2016 almost 99% lower than in October 2015':[67] from an average of 6,828 arrivals a day in October 2015, numbers reached 43 a day in February 2017. Overall, since March 2016, the average of daily crossing in the Aegean Sea is around 80, which represents a 97% decrease in comparison with the situation before the EU-Turkey Statement was adopted.[68]

In terms of quantitative results, the deal incontestably had a deterrent effect on the number of arrivals via the Eastern Mediterranean route and can be deemed to be efficient if one focuses only on the drop in numbers. The implementation of the EU-Turkey deal went along with the closure of the Western Balkans route, Eastern European countries having reintroduced fences and tighter border control measures, making it harder for refugees to reach the Schengen zone's external borders. For the Commission, the fact that arrivals have decreased shows 'clearly that the business model of smugglers exploiting migrants and refugees can be broken'.[69] However, the situation on the ground is bit more complex.

No longer able to reach Europe through the Balkans, refugees find themselves trapped in Greek camps. There is some improvement with the registration rates at hotpots reaching 100% in early 2017 against 8% in October 2015[70] and increased support from the EU institutions and MS in order to alleviate the situation on the Greek islands, but much remains to be done.

---

[64] EUROPEAN COMMISSION, 'EU Turkey-statement, one year on', Factsheet, 17.03.2017, available at https://ec.europa.eu/home-affairs/sites/homeaffairs/files/what-we-do/policies/european-agenda-migration/background-information/eu_turkey_statement_17032017_en.pdf, last accessed 14.06.2018.

[65] EUROPEAN COMMISSION, 'Fifth Report on the Progress made in the implementation of the EU-Turkey Statement', 02.03.2017, available at http://www.refworld.org/docid/58b98ba54.html, last accessed 14.06.2018.

[66] Ibid., p. 2.

[67] UNHCR (2017), 'Desperate Journeys', *supra* note 10.

[68] EUROPEAN COMMISSION, 'EU-Turkey Statement, two years on', Factsheet, 14.03.2018, available at https://ec.europa.eu/home-affairs/sites/homeaffairs/files/what-we-do/policies/european-agenda-migration/20180314_eu-turkey-two-years-on_en.pdf, last accessed 12.06.2018.

[69] EUROPEAN COMMISSION (2017), 'Fifth Report on the Progress made in the implementation of the EU-Turkey Statement', *supra* note 65, p. 2.

[70] Ibid., p. 3.

The humanitarian situation in the Greek islands is deeply concerning with reception facilities being overcrowded and inadequate living conditions in the hotspots (lack of access to food, water, sanitation services, adequate clothing, shelter).[71] More legal officers also need to be deployed in the different hotspots to avoid delays in processing the asylum claims and asylum seekers being stranded in Greece in the meantime.

Thus, in 2017, more than a year after its implementation, the deal remained very much criticised by NGOs. The International Rescue Committee, the Norwegian Refugee Council and Oxfam jointly denounced the fact that 'Greece has become a testing ground for policies that erode protection for refugees'.[72] Several observers argued the situation had worsened with a displacement of the route towards the Central Mediterranean, which is far more dangerous. For Human Rights Watch, the main message sent by this deal is that 'protection for refugees could be commodified, outsourced and blocked'.[73] Debate also sparked among academic circles concerning the legality of the EU-Turkey statement, following the EU General Court decision from 28 February 2017.[74]

In March 2017, the Commission argued that 'one year on, the EU-Turkey is delivering on its main objectives of reducing the number of persons arriving irregularly to the EU and the loss of life in the Aegean whilst providing safe and legal routes to the EU for those in need'.[75] A year later, during the evaluation of the deal two years after its signing, the EU estimated that it has been successful as 'almost one million people have not taken dangerous

---

[71] AMNESTY INTERNATIONAL, 'The EU-Turkey deal: Europe's year of shame', 20.03.2017, available at www.amnesty.org/en/latest/news/2017/03/the-eu-turkey-deal-europes-year-of-shame, last accessed 12.06.2018.

[72] INTERNATIONAL RESCUE COMMITTEE, NORWEGIAN REFUGEE COUNCIL AND OXFAM INTERNATIONAL, 'The reality of the EU-Turkey statement', Joint Agency Briefing Note, 17.03.2017, available at www.oxfam.org/sites/www.oxfam.org/files/bn-eu-turkey-statement-migration-170317-en.pdf, last accessed 12.06.2018.

[73] HRW (2016), 'EU Policies put Refugees at Risk', *supra* note 48.

[74] In the cases *NF, NG and NM v European Council*, an Afghan and a Pakistani asylum seeker – who arrived in Greece by boat after the signing of the EU-Turkey Statement and were forced to lodge their asylum requests in Greece – tried to contest the legality of the EU-Turkey deal. These three cases were dismissed by the Court that considered that 'the deal cannot be challenged directly before EU courts, since it is not considered an act of an institution of the EU, but rather an act of Member States'. The General Court decisions were appealed, and the cases are still pending before the CJEU. See CJEU, *NF v European Council*, Case T-192/16, 28.02.2017, ECLI:EU:T:2017:128; *NG v European Council*, Case T-193/16, 28.02.2017, ECLI:EU:T:2017:129; and *NM v European Council*, Case T-257/16, 28.02.2017, ECLI:EU:T:2017:130. For a further analysis of these cases, see N. IDRIZ, 'The EU-Turkey statement or the 'refugee deal': the extra-legal deal of extraordinary times?', in D. SIEGEL and V. NAGY (eds.), *The Migration Crisis?: Criminalization, Security and Survival*, Eleven Publishing, The Hague 2018, pp. 61–84,.

[75] EUROPEAN COMMISSION (2017), 'EU Turkey-statement, one year on', *supra* note 64.

routes to get to the European Union, and more than 1,000 have not lost their lives trying'.[76]

Thus, despite the above-mentioned legal debate and criticism from civil society organisations, the statement remains perceived by Brussels as a core piece of the EU's comprehensive approach on migration and a model for future cooperation deals.

3.2. THE EUROPEAN BORDER AND COAST GUARD AGENCY (EBCG)

Another example of the EU's tendency towards focusing on border security is the creation of the EBCG Agency, established by Regulation (EU) 2016/1624[77] adopted on 14 September 2016 by the European Parliament and the Council. The EBCG was officially launched on 6 October 2016 at the Bulgarian external border with Turkey. According to Commissioner Avramopoulos, 'the European Border and Coast Guard is a symbol for the European Union. A symbol of a Europe that is able to deliver, united. We are now better equipped than before to face the migration and security challenges'.[78] The main mission of the new EBCG Agency is to ensure the border control of the Schengen area, along with the coordination of national border and coastguards of MS. The idea behind it was that 'the Schengen area without internal borders is only sustainable if the external borders are effectively secured and protected'.[79]

On 15 December 2015, the EU Commission proposed to better respond to the migration crisis by extending and strengthening the mandate of the previous Frontex agency, feeling there was a growing need to improve the security at the external borders of the Union in order to cope with massive influx of migrants and refugees. Weaknesses of the old agency were its unclear and limited mandate (its role was only to support MS' efforts), its insufficient budget and its lack of operational staff and equipment (Frontex was then only

---

[76] EUROPEAN COMMISSION (2018), 'EU-Turkey Statement, two years on', *supra* note 68.
[77] Regulation (EU) 2016/1624 of the European Parliament and of the Council of 14 September 2016 on the European Border and Coast Guard and amending Regulation (EU) 2016/399 of the European Parliament and of the Council and repealing Regulation (EC) No 863/2007 of the European Parliament and of the Council, Council Regulation (EC) No 2007/2004 and Council Decision 2005/267/EC, OJ L 251.
[78] EUROPEAN COMMISSION, 'Remarks by Commissioner Avramopoulos at the launch of the European Border and Coast Guard Agency', Press Release, 06.10.2016, available at http://europa.eu/rapid/press-release_SPEECH-16-3334_en.htm, last accessed 14.06.2018.
[79] EUROPEAN COMMISSION, 'Securing Europe's External Borders – A European Border and Coast Guard', Factsheet, June 2016, available at https://ec.europa.eu/home-affairs/sites/homeaffairs/files/what-we-do/policies/securing-eu-borders/fact-sheets/docs/20161006/a_european_border_and_coast_guard_en.pdf, last accessed 17.06.2018.

relying on voluntary contributions from MS). The need for a prior request of a Member State before the agency could undertake any action was seen as ineffective and as a lack of authority to effectively meet and address new challenges posed by the migration crisis.

Therefore, responsibilities for border control are from now on shared between the new Frontex and the MS: the day-to-day management of the external borders remains the responsibility of MS while the EBCG agency is in charge of supporting and coordinating controls at land, air and sea borders. It is also tasked with carrying out wider operational duties: processing personal data, return operations (notably in assisting MS in the return of migrants ineligible to stay in the EU), migration management, fighting against cross-border crimes, search and rescue operations and the training of coastguards from EU and non-EU countries. Frontex is now able to deploy its forces more rapidly and to step up in urgent situations when MS are overwhelmed or do not react, thanks to the rapid reaction pool of at least 1,500 border guards. Additionally, its permanent staff will be doubled by 2020 and the agency is henceforth able to buy its own equipment.

Operationalisation is currently underway: as of December 2017, 742 European Border and Coast Guard officers had been deployed in Greece, 322 in Italy, 78 in Spain, 91 in the Western Balkans and 137 in Bulgaria.[80] In total, over 1,400 border guards are currently deployed throughout the EU in addition to existing national capacities.[81] However, important gaps remain in terms of human resources and equipment[82] and the Commission called upon MS to quickly deliver on their commitments[83] so the agency is fully effective in the upcoming months.

Respect for fundamental rights is meant to be at the heart of the activities of the new Frontex. A written complaint mechanism has been created to serve any person whose human rights were violated whilst the agency was carrying out its activities.[84] Additionally, the development of a fundamental rights

---

[80] EUROPEAN COMMISSION, 'The European Border and Coast Guard Agency – The Commission's Contribution to the Leaders' Agenda', Factsheet, 07.12.2017, available at https://ec.europa.eu/home-affairs/sites/homeaffairs/files/what-we-do/policies/european-agenda-migration/20171207_the_european_border_and_coast_guard_agency_en.pdf, last accessed 14.06.2018.

[81] Ibid.

[82] As of January 2018, for the nomination of 206 officers for EBCG Rapid Reaction Pool is still pending. Additionally, officers still have to be deployed by Member States for the joint operations in frontline states (92 in Greece, 18 in Italy, 8 in Spain and 114 in Bulgaria). EUROPEAN COMMISSION, 'The European Border and Coast Guard Agency', *supra* note 80.

[83] EUROPEAN COMMISSION, Report from the Commission to the European Parliament, the European Council and the Council on the operationalisation of the European Border and Coast Guard, COM(2017) 42 final, 25.01.2017.

[84] For further details on the fundamental rights complaints mechanism, see H. ROSENFELDT, 'Establishing the European Border and Coast Guard: all-new or Frontex reloaded?',

strategy with a strong focus on children and unaccompanied minors should have taken effect since November 2017.[85] However, the overall ECBG approach concentrates very much on the training of border guards, investments in surveillance technology, the establishment of joint patrols and the increasing use of military assets.[86] As argued by Herbert Rosenfeldt, the wording of several articles of the EBCG Regulation – particularly its Articles 1, 4 and 15 – 'gives top priority to regaining and keeping control of the migration situation and to efficient border management'.[87]

A growing and permanent presence at sea to prevent further loss of life of migrants was one of the objectives set forward in the Juncker's Political Guidelines and the European Agenda on Migration. If the Frontex-trained border guards have to save lives at sea, the aim of this increased militarised border presence in the Mediterranean seems to be first and foremost to deter migration. These recent developments show that, although EBCG search and rescue operations contributed to save more than 33,000 lives in the Mediterranean in 2017,[88] priority is given to controlling and stopping migration flows, focusing once again on migration as a threat.

Yet Demetrios Papademetriou, president of the Migration Policy Institute, claims that:

> people feeling circumstances they consider intolerable will enter the [irregular] migration stream and test various receiving states' defences repeatedly. They will in fact do so regardless of whether they must risk their own lives, pay exorbitant fees, or subvert the asylum system or any other available means of entry.[89]

This argument is supported by François Gemenne, specialist researcher of international migration, who argued in an interview to the French radio broadcast *Un jour dans le Monde*[90] that the very reason why people are forced

---

EU Law Analysis, 16.10.2016, available at http://eulawanalysis.blogspot.com/2016/10/establishing-european-border-and-coast.html, last accessed 14.06.2018.

[85] EUROPEAN COMMISSION, 'Securing Europe's External Borders – A European Border and Coast Guard', Factsheet, June 2017, available at https://ec.europa.eu/home-affairs/sites/homeaffairs/files/what-we-do/policies/european-agenda-security/20170613_ebcg_en.pdf, last accessed 14.06.2018.

[86] FRONTEX, 'Risk Analysis for 2017', February 2017, available at http://frontex.europa.eu/assets/Publications/Risk_Analysis/Annual_Risk_Analysis_2017.pdf, last accessed 14.06.2018.

[87] H. ROSENFELDT (2016), 'Establishing the European Border and Coast Guard', *supra* note 84.

[88] F. LEGGERI, 'Foreword', FRONTEX, available at https://frontex.europa.eu/about-frontex/foreword, last accessed 13.06.2018.

[89] D. PAPADEMETRIOU, 'The Global Struggle with Illegal Migration: No End in Sight', Migration Policy Institute, 01.09.2005, available at www.migrationpolicy.org/article/global-struggle-illegal-migration-no-end-sight, last accessed 13.06.2018.

[90] FRANCE INTER, 'Crise migratoire: l'Europe menacée de dislocation', *Un jour dans le monde*, 27.12.2016 (author's translation from French).

to come to Europe by boats instead of by plane, is because the border is sealed and very well watched over.

3.3. REINVIGORATING COOPERATION WITH LIBYA?

The last example that will be examined in this section are the concerns raised by the increased cooperation between the EU and Libya to cope with the situation in the Central Mediterranean.

As previously mentioned, the EU-Turkey deal led to a displacement of the main migratory route towards the Central Mediterranean. UNHCR figures show that fewer people are using the Eastern Mediterranean Route while arrivals from North Africa to Italy have dramatically increased: from April 2016 onwards, Libya has become the main entry point to the EU. According to the UNHRC Bureau for Europe 'of the 181,436 refugees and migrants who reached Italy in 2016, 90% departed from Libya with most boats departing from the west of the country'.[91] The death toll along this route – longer and more dangerous due to violent tidal streams – raises to one death for every 40 crossings, so over 4,581 dead or gone missing for the whole year 2016, according to the IOM's Missing Migrants Project.[92]

During the spring of 2015, the series of shipwrecks triggered the need to step up and institutionalise EU naval operations in the Mediterranean waters. Although the Italian Navy had launched the humanitarian rescue operation Mare Nostrum in October 2013 – in reaction to the first Lampedusa sinking that caused the death of 368 migrants – it was phased out a year later, due to criticism accusing it of being a pull factor encouraging migrants to come to Europe. Mare Nostrum was replaced by the Frontex-led expanded Operation Triton which now operates in the territorial waters of Italy and some parts of the search and rescue zones of Italy and Malta. Triton supports the Italian navy with border control, surveillance and search and rescue tasks in the Central Mediterranean. Operation Poseidon provides Greece with the same kind of assistance.

A new surveillance operation was also introduced after the outbreak of the crisis: operation EUNAVFOR Med – interestingly renamed Operation Sophia after the name of the first baby born on board, so as to show the operation is positively aimed at assisting people, not only monitoring the European waters – was launched on 22 June 2015.[93] Operating outside the Libyan

---

[91] UNHCR (2017), 'Desperate Journeys', *supra* note 10, p. 6.
[92] IOM, 'Missing Migrants Project', *supra* note 8.
[93] EUROPEAN COUNCIL, 'Council launches EU naval operation to disrupt human smugglers and traffickers in the Mediterranean', Press Release, 22.06.2015, available at www.consilium. europa.eu/en/press/press-releases/2015/06/22-fac-naval-operation, last accessed 13.06.2018.

territorial waters, its mission is to identify, capture and dispose of vessels and enabling assets used or suspected of being used by migrant smugglers or traffickers. Along with this main mandate, Operation Sophia has two supporting tasks: training the Libyan coastguards and navy to enhance their capabilities and contributing to the implementation of the UN arms embargo on the high seas off the coast of Libya.

Although Operation Sophia indubitably contributed to saving lives at sea – over 33,296, along with the arrest of 101 traffickers[94] – it is important to stress that search and rescue activities are not its primary purpose and that its operational mandate does not provide its access to the Libyan territorial waters, where most of the incidents at sea take place: 'consequently, [its] assets were and continue to be deployed as required by [its] principal objectives.'[95]

The absence of 'assets patrolling the area of sea close to Libyan waters on a dedicated humanitarian mission'[96] is one of the reasons why an increasing number of NGOs stepped up to fill in the gaps left by states when it comes to rescue activities. In early 2017, the following non-governmental organisations were carrying out search and rescue operations at the limits of the Libyan territorial waters:[97] Médecins Sans Frontières, Sea Watch, Migrant Offshore Aid Station (MOAS), SOS Mediterranée, Pro-Activa, Sea-Eye, Jugend Rettet, Refugee Boat Foundation and Save the Children being the main players.[98] Their presence is somewhat controversial; the Frontex director, Fabrice Leggeri, has accused them of encouraging the business of human traffickers and criminal networks in early 2017[99] while other key stakeholders praised them for their contribution in saving lives.[100] According to the European Commission, these NGOs were responsible for 22% of the rescues in 2016.[101] This accusation of NGOs being pull factor for arrivals of migrants was reiterated in July 2017 by the Italian government who requested NGOs

---

[94] EUROACTIV, 'Operation Sofia has saved 33,296 migrants in the Mediterranean', 17.02.2017, available at www.euractiv.com/section/global-europe/news/operation-sofia-has-saved-33296-migrants-in-mediterranean, last accessed 14.06.2018.

[95] AMNESTY INTERNATIONAL (2017), 'A perfect storm', *supra* note 41, p. 15.

[96] Ibid., p. 14.

[97] P. Wintour, 'Italian plan to curb Mediterranean rescue boat charities "threatens lives"', *The Guardian*, 03.07.2017, available at www.theguardian.com/world/2017/jul/03/anger-at-rules-plan-for-migrant-charities-in-mediterranean, last accessed 12.06.2018.

[98] EUROPEAN COMMISSION, 'Irregular Migration via the Central Mediterranean – From Emergency Responses to Systematic Solutions', 02.02.2017, available at https://ec.europa.eu/epsc/publications/strategic-notes/irregular-migration-central-mediterranean_en, last accessed 14.06.2018, p. 2.

[99] P. Wintour, 'NGO rescues off Libya encourage traffickers, says EU borders chief', *The Guardian*, 27.02.2017, available at www.theguardian.com/world/2017/feb/27/ngo-rescues-off-libya-encourage-traffickers-eu-borders-chief, last accessed 12.06.2018.

[100] AMNESTY INTERNATIONAL (2017), 'A perfect storm', *supra* note 41, p. 17.

[101] EUROPEAN COMMISSION (2017), 'Irregular Migration via the Central Mediterranean', *supra* note 98, p. 4.

carrying search and rescue operations in the Central Mediterranean to sign a Code of Conduct[102] clearly asking them to operate within, and abide by a set of 11 rules. Despite insistence from the Italian government and the EU institutions, five humanitarian organisations refused to sign it, including Doctors without Borders, as they considered that several elements of the code could hinder their rescue activities, notably the presence of armed police officers on board.[103]

Regardless of this debate, what is certain is that the shifting of the route towards the Central Mediterranean and the increased naval presence in the European waters also induced a change in the *modus operandis* of smugglers, human trafficking having become a very lucrative business in the region. Amnesty International, in its report on the situation in the Central Mediterranean from July 2017, considers that increased surveillance of the European waters and enhanced border controls led to the deterioration of conditions for crossing, which for the NGO constitutes 'the immediate cause for the rising of the death toll'.[104] Nowadays, traffickers take even greater risks: since the journey between Libya and Italy requires more time (around three days as opposed to a few hours between Turkey and the Greek Islands), they want to make more profit and therefore put larger numbers of people on unseaworthy boats, without enough safety equipment[105] and sometimes only enough fuel to reach international waters.[106] To avoid detection from search and rescue vessels patrolling the Mediterranean, smugglers also started to use inflatable dinghies in place of wooden boats, which can fit up to 140 people but are also more prone to capsizing.

Fighting against these criminal networks is one of EU's main goals as demonstrated by the Commission, which states that 'controlling and reducing irregular flows is a political priority. The EU and Member States must demonstrate the ability to effectively protect their external borders against ruthless networks exploiting the aspiration and despair of irregular migrants and refugees'.[107] If this shift of techniques used for the smuggling of migrants can potentially be seen as a success of the EU policies over

---

[102] EURONEWS, 'Italy's code of conduct for NGOs involved in migrant rescue: text', 03.08.2017, available at http://www.euronews.com/2017/08/03/text-of-italys-code-of-conduct-for-ngos-involved-in-migrant-rescue, last accessed 14.06.2018.

[103] DOCTORS WITHOUT BORDERS, 'MSF Committed to Saving Lives on Mediterranean but Will Not Sign the Italian "Code of Conduct"', 01.08.2017, available at http://www.msf.org/en/article/msf-committed-saving-lives-mediterranean-will-not-sign-italian-code-conduct, last accessed 14.06.2018.

[104] AMNESTY INTERNATIONAL (2017), 'A perfect storm', *supra* note 41, p. 5.

[105] Ibid., p. 10.

[106] HRW, 'Letting People Drown is not an EU Value', 11.04.2017, available at https://www.hrw.org/news/2017/04/11/letting-people-drown-not-eu-value, last accessed 14.06.2018.

[107] EUROPEAN COMMISSION (2017), 'Irregular Migration via the Central Mediterranean', *supra* note 98, p. 1.

traffickers, its impact on the human rights and security of migrants is extremely harmful. Amnesty International reports that departures increasingly occur during the night or under uncertain weather conditions, and that most of the boats are no longer equipped with satellite phones which makes it harder to contact those vessels once they are in distress at sea, as well as to determine their location in the Mediterranean and to evaluate the number of persons on board. Furthermore, smugglers tend to make several boats leave at the same time which leads to rescue operations potentially taking place simultaneously[108] creating further complications. This has had dramatic consequences, making rescues attempts significantly more difficult and hazardous.

Before elaborating further on the cooperation between the EU and Libya, it is important to note that the country has remained in the grip of political instability since the 2011 revolution that led to the fall of Colonel Gaddafi who had ruled the country since the end of the 1960s. The security environment has deteriorated in recent years with the second Libyan civil war. The country is still divided between two governments, the Government of National Accord (GNA), backed by the EU and the UN, and the Libyan National Army (LNA) which controls a large part of the territory. Fighting is ongoing, state institutions are seriously hampered and terrorist groups have developed throughout the country. The situation is far from being stabilised.[109]

In February 2017 however, based on recommendations from the Commission,[110] the EU heads of states and governments decided to increase

---

[108] AMNESTY INTERNATIONAL (2017), 'A perfect storm', *supra* note 41, pp. 11–12.
[109] UNITED NATIONS, Report of the Secretary-General on the United Nations Support Mission in Libya, UN Doc. S/2017/726, 22.08.2017.
[110] The communication 'Migration on the Central Mediterranean route, managing flows, saving lives' was published on 25 January 2017 by the European Commission and the High-Representative of the Union for Foreign Affairs and Security Policy (HRVP) Federica Mogherini. In this document, the two EU institutions propose additional actions on how to better manage migration through the Central Mediterranean route. Cooperation with Libya plays a central part in this strategy since it is the point of departure for nine out of every ten migrants trying to make their way to Europe. The communication mainly focuses on short and medium-term goals, due to the volatile political and security situation in Libya, whose stability remains an objective for the EU foreign policy. When it comes to border management, the goals set up in this strategy are: reducing the number of crossings and saving lives at sea by stepping up support to the Libyan Coast Guard via the funding of training programmes or the delivery of patrolling assets; fighting smugglers of migrants and human traffickers by increasing the exchange of information with North African countries, EU Member States and the different EU institutions and agencies. EUROPEAN COMMISSION AND THE HIGH-REPRESENTATIVE OF THE UNION FOR FOREIGN AFFAIRS AND SECURITY POLICY (HRPV), Joint Communication to the European Parliament, the European Council and the Council on Migration on the Central Mediterranean route, managing flows, saving lives, JOIN(2017) 4 final, 25.01.2017.

cooperation with Libya to stem flows of migrants coming through this route. As a frontline state, Italy has played a crucial role in building up migration management cooperation with Libya, both at the diplomatic and operational level. Cooperation between the two countries is not a new policy trend, as several border control agreements had been signed in the 2000s. They were suspended in 2012, following the fall of the Gaddafi's regime and the European Court of Human Rights (ECtHR) landmark ruling in the case *Hirsi Jamaa and Others v Italy*[111] – in which the Strasbourg Court considered that collective expulsions from the high seas were not allowed in the Mediterranean and that Italy had violated its international obligations when its border guards returned migrants and refugees to Libya where there were insufficient guarantees they would not face persecution.[112]

On 2 February 2017, a Memorandum of Understanding (MoU) was signed between the then Italian Prime Minister Paolo Gentiloni and Fayez al-Serraj, Prime Minister of the GNA, in order to slow down the numbers of arrivals from North Africa. In this agreement, the Italian government resumed past cooperation and pledged to work the Libya coastguards to intercept boats and return irregular migrants to Libya. With the 'Malta Declaration on the external aspects of migration: addressing the Central Mediterranean route'[113] adopted by the European Council the following day, the EU embraced the Italian strategy. As directly signing a deal with Libya based on the EU-Turkey model was impossible for manifest diplomatic reasons, the EU decided instead to strongly endorse politically and support economically Italian cooperation efforts, resulting in a somehow similar outcome. In his 2017 State of the Union address, President Juncker paid tribute to Italy's 'tireless and noble work',[114] declaring that 'Italy is saving Europe's honour in the Mediterranean'.[115]

In the 2017 Malta Declaration, EU MS affirmed that 'a key element of a sustainable migration policy is to ensure effective control of our external border and stem illegal flows into the EU'.[116] In the same document, they

---

[111] ECtHR, *Hirsi Jamaa and Others v Italy*, no 27765/09, 23.02.2012.
[112] EUROPEAN AGENCY FOR FUNDAMENTAL RIGHTS, 'Handbook on European law relating to asylum, borders and immigration', June 2014, available at http://fra.europa.eu/en/publication/2013/handbook-european-law-relating-asylum-borders-and-immigration, last accessed 14.06.2018, pp. 38–39.
[113] EUROPEAN COUNCIL OF THE EUROPEAN UNION, 'Malta Declaration by the members of the European Council on the external aspects of migration: addressing the Central Mediterranean route', 03.02.2017, available at http://www.consilium.europa.eu/en/press/press-releases/2017/02/03/malta-declaration, last accessed 14.06.2018.
[114] EUROPEAN COMMISSION, 'President J.-C. Juncker's State of the Union Address 2017', 13.09.2017, available at http://europa.eu/rapid/press-release_SPEECH-17-3165_en.htm, last accessed 13.06.2018.
[115] Ibid.
[116] COUNCIL OF THE EUROPEAN UNION (2017), 'Malta Declaration', *supra* note 113, para. 2.

expressed their will to 'reduce migratory flows along the Central Mediterranean route and break the business model of smugglers'.[117] If once again enhancing partnership with a third country can be a legitimate part of the EU's comprehensive strategy, establishing such cooperation is not without concern, especially after leaders from the Visegrad group said the EU should establish a 'giant refugee city'[118] in Libya to process requests from African asylum seekers, whilst the United Nations recalled on several occasions in the last two years that the country was not a safe place.

First, throughout the Malta declaration, there is no mention of the human rights of migrants, except from a very vague introductory statement 'we reaffirm our determination to act in full respect of human rights, international law and European values'.[119] Priorities defined in the cooperation between the EU and Libya concern the training and equipment of the Libyan coastguards and efforts to disrupt the business model of smugglers. Little is said about ensuring better reception capacities and conditions for migrants in Libya, although these aspects were included in the Commission communication 'Migration in the Central Mediterranean route, managing flows, saving lives'[120] (which constituted the basis of the text of the Malta Declaration). The only reference is paragraph 6(d) of the Malta declaration stating that in cooperating with Libya, the EU will, as a matter of priority, seek to 'ensure adequate reception capacities and conditions in Libya for migrants together with the UNHCR and IOM'.[121] However, beforehand, the UNHCR and the IOM had warned MS that the UN being granted access to detention centres and being able to provide humanitarian aid was extremely limited due to 'security constraints'.[122] The UN agencies stressed their concern over this planned cooperation between the EU and Libya.[123]

A further issue outlined in the strategy is the protection of migrants, especially regarding the conditions in Libyan migration centres, through

---

[117] Ibid., para. 3.
[118] BBC, 'Hungary PM suggests giant migrant city in Libya', 24.09.2016, available at www.bbc.com/news/world-europe-37463386, last accessed 14.06.2018.
[119] COUNCIL OF THE EUROPEAN UNION (2017), 'Malta Declaration', *supra* note 113, para. 1.
[120] EUROPEAN COMMISSION and the HRPV (2017), 'Migration on the Central Mediterranean route', *supra* note 109.
[121] Ibid., para. 6 d.
[122] IOM, 'Joint UNHCR and IOM statement on addressing migration and refugee movements along the Central Mediterranean route', 02.02.2017, available at www.unhcr.org/afr/news/press/2017/2/58931ffb4/joint-unhcr-iom-statement-addressing-migration-refugee-movements-along.html, last accessed 14.06.2018.
[123] The IOM and UNHRC have since then become fully involved in the process of externalisation of migration controls, contributing to voluntary returns and resettlement from Libyan detention camps. They are also funded under the EU Trust Fund and the Italian African Fund to ensure their cooperation. IOM, 'Voluntary Humanitarian Returns from Libya Continue as Reintegration Efforts Step Up', 13.03.2018, available at https://www.iom.int/news/voluntary-humanitarian-returns-libya-continue-reintegration-efforts-step, last accessed on 14.06.2018.

increased cooperation with the Libyan authorities. This point is extremely important with regard to the human rights of migrants, but it is not without shortfalls. Indeed, as will be outlined at a later stage, UN representatives present on the ground alerted EU officials to the fact that Libya could not be considered as a safe third country at the moment, due to security constraints and the limited access given to humanitarian organisations.[124]

Secondly, in a joint report from December 2016 '"Detained and dehumanised" – Report on human rights abuses against migrants in Libya',[125] the United Nations Support Mission in Libya (UNSMIL) and the Office of the United Nations High Commissioner for Human Rights highlighted the tremendous human rights violations migrants suffer in the country. Arbitrary detention, torture, ill-treatment, sexual violence, forced labour and religious persecutions are some of the many abuses monitored by the international community's envoys. Situations in migrant detention centres – both official and unofficial – are particularly dramatic and fall well short of international standards. The UNSMIL's report describes detention conditions that are inhumane and amounting to torture.[126] The report also describes several cases of violations – including unlawful use of force – committed by alleged members of the Libyan coastguard forces when they intercepted migrants at sea. It should be noted that some militia groups – not controlled by the GNA – have been accused of exercising coastguard functions in some parts of the Libyan waters. Such claims were supported by the report of the UN Panel of Experts on Libya to the Security Council from June 2017, which details violations committed against migrants and refugees by the Libyan coastguards but also outlines allegations of their collaboration with smugglers.[127] Several incidents involving the Libyan Coast Guard – including attacks against migrants and against NGOs rescue boats – have been described by Amnesty International which maintains that:

> the intervention of Libyan coastguards units in the past year has repeatedly put in danger the safety and lives of both NGOs' crews engaged in rescue operations in international waters and also of refugees and migrants, both because they have resorted to firearms and violence, but also because of their operating at sea in plain disregard of basic security protocols and standards.[128]

---

[124] UNHCR (2017), 'Joint UNHCR and IOM statement', *supra* note 122.
[125] OHCHR, Report, '"Detained and dehumanised" – Report on human rights abuses against migrants in Libya', 13.12.2016, available at https://www.ohchr.org/Documents/Countries/LY/DetainedAndDehumanised_en.pdf, last accessed 13.06.2018.
[126] Ibid.
[127] UN SECURITY COUNCIL, Final report of the Panel of Experts on Libya established pursuant to resolution 1973(2011), UN Doc. S/2017/466, 29.06.2017, available at https://seenthis.net/sites/1209499, last accessed 14.06.2018.
[128] Amnesty International (2017), 'A perfect storm', *supra* note 41, p. 26.

So far, most of the perpetrators remain unpunished, due to the collapse of the Libyan justice system.[129]

Such findings are supported by evidence gathered in several reports from NGOs working in Libya or in the hotspots. At the end of February 2017, the International Federation for Human Rights alongside 27 other NGOs, warned the EU MS that 'the decision to transfer the responsibility for managing migratory movements along the central Mediterranean route to Libya will significantly increase harm and suffering'[130] and would have little to no effect on ending migrant smuggling, traffickers shifting their activities to other routes. In fact, the consequences of such a deal are likely to lead to greater numbers of arrests and detentions, that will therefore increase the likelihood of human rights violations, trapping migrants in a country torn by conflict and insecurity. In an open letter from May 2017 addressed to the Austrian Foreign Minister Sebastian Kurz – who during a visit to Libya said that 'migrants who are saved in the Mediterranean should not be guaranteed a ticket to Central Europe'[131] and praised the Australian model of offshore processing, based on practices notwithstanding denounced by the United Nations in 2016[132] – the HRW Libya researcher qualified detention facilities as places where 'authorities are holding detainees in abyssal, overcrowded conditions'.[133]

Fostering cooperation with Libyan border guards is presented as a capacity-building measure by the EU. Improving their capacities and providing them with better equipment so they can save lives at sea is indeed an important long-term goal but it cannot be used as a way for the EU to absolve itself of responsibility. Indeed, while the EU law and principles forbid sending back people to a third country where they could face persecution or torture, if migrants and refugees in distress at sea are rescued by Libyan border guards next to the Libyan coast, then the principle of *non-refoulement* is no longer applicable. As argued by HRW, 'people rescued in Libyan waters by Libyan authorities or intercepted and prevented from leaving those waters do not trigger an EU state responsibility and therefore no *non-refoulement* obligations'.[134]

---

[129] Ibid., pp. 19–21.

[130] FIDH, 'EU – Libya cooperation: serious risks of migrants' rights violations', 22.02.2017, available at www.fidh.org/en/issues/migrants-rights/eu-libya-cooperation-serious-risks-of-migrants-rights-violations, last accessed 14.06.2018.

[131] W. SCHNEIDER, 'Brauchen EU-Hilfe gegen Schlepper', *Die Presse*, 01.05.2017, available at http://diepresse.com/home/ausland/aussenpolitik/5209903/Kurz-in-Libyen_Brauchen-EUHilfe-gegen-Schlepper, last accessed 14.06.2018.

[132] UNITED NATIONS, 'Australia and Nauru must end offshore detention; investigate claims of abuse – UN rights office', 12.08.2016, available at www.un.org/apps/news/story.asp?NewsID=54669#.WWdidrZLfcs, last accessed 14.06.2018.

[133] HRW, 'Open Letter to Austrian Foreign Minister Sebastian Kurz on Libya', 03.05.2017, available at www.hrw.org/news/2017/05/03/open-letter-austrian-foreign-minister-sebastian-kurz-libya, last accessed 14.06.2018.

[134] HRW (2016), 'EU Policies put Refugees At Risk', *supra* note 48.

If this is deemed acceptable from a legal point of view, it remains problematic when it comes to the human security of migrants who will be disembarked in Libyan shores, despite the fact that it remains an unsafe place for returns.

Moreover, transferring responsibility to the Libyan authorities is also problematic because of the absence of legal protection regime in place in the country: Libya is not party to the 1951 Refugee Convention and has no effective migration governance framework in place at the national level according to the United Nations.[135] Ahead of the Malta Summit last February, the UN High Commissioner for Human Rights Zeid Ra'ad Al Hussein warned EU heads of states 'against supporting a system in which migrants are pushed back to places where they may be at risk of torture, and cruel, inhuman or degrading treatment'[136] in application of the principle of *non-refoulement*. He reminded them that 'any engagement with third countries needs to be in line with international human rights standards'.[137] When cooperating with third countries, the EU should encourage its partners to ratify and implement international human rights instruments, such as the Refugee Convention, in accordance with the Article 21 TEU.[138] Regarding the training activities undertaken by Frontex, effective vetting procedures must be put in place to ensure that border guards have not committed human rights abuses while carrying out their activities.

In the first six months of 2017, sea crossings from Libya to Europe increased by 14%[139] but fell by more than half during the summer.[140] Research from the IOM provides that 'the implementation of the new policies related to apprehensions on the sea and support provided to the Libya coast guard, from an average of more than 12,000 monthly arrivals recorded for the second quarter of 2017, to less than 6,000 arrivals per month in the second half of the year'.[141] Media observers argued that the crossing has been made more difficult due

---

[135] OHCHR (2016), 'Detained and dehumanised', *supra* note 125, p. 11.
[136] OHCHR, 'Malta Summit: "Is Libya the right disembarking point for migrants?" – UN rights expert', Press Release, 03.02.2017, available at www.ohchr.org/EN/NewsEvents/Pages/DisplayNews.aspx?NewsID=21140&LangID=E#sthash.XUEuwy5C.dpuf, last accessed 14.06.2018.
[137] Ibid.
[138] According to which the EU's action on the international scene is driven by the principles 'which have inspired its own creation', and shall seek 'to advance democracy, the rule of law, the universality and indivisibility of human rights and fundamental freedoms, respect for human dignity, the principles of equality and solidarity, and respect for the principles of the United Nations Charter and international law'.
[139] AMNESTY INTERNATIONAL (2017), 'A perfect storm', supra note 41, p. 5.
[140] According to Amnesty International, during the period from July to November 2017, 33 288 refugees and migrants arrived in Italy which represent 67% less than in 2016. AMNESTY INTERNATIONAL, 'Libya's dark web of collusion: abuses against Europe-bound refugees and migrants', 11.12.2017, p. 8, available at https://www.amnesty.org/en/documents/mde19/7561/2017/en/, last accessed 14.06.2018.
[141] IOM (2018), 'Migration flows to Europe – 2017 Overview', *supra* note 6.

to the *'aggressive turnaround policy'*[142] conducted by the Libyan coastguards with the support of the EU and Italy. More precisely, Amnesty International explains this decrease in numbers by the fact that 20,000 migrants and refugees have been intercepted by border guards in the Libyan territorial waters and sent back to Libyan detention centres.[143] This trend shows that the logic of deterrence has so far proven to be ineffective and that this EU focus on border security does not prevent people from attempting to make their way to Europe. Overall, if living conditions and security of migrants and refugees in Libya do improve, it will not stop people from undertaking desperate journeys.

Thus, as things stand, engagement with Libya remains at this stage clearly problematic. The EU is well aware of the tremendous violations migrants face in the country, as expressed in the Joint Statement on the Migrant Situation in Libya from the 5th EU-African Union Summit on 30 November 2017.[144] Nonetheless, its leaders decided to focus on keeping arrivals through the Central Mediterranean low, by making sure that border control is strengthened directly in the Libyan waters.

If it must be acknowledged that the EU is taking concrete steps towards the stabilisation of the country,[145] it is a political and diplomatic process that will require several years. For Matteo de Bellis, the 'current policy undermines any claim by the EU to be a standard bearer for human rights'.[146] Indeed the current migration cooperation with Libya does not reflect the values upon which the EU was founded, nor does it effectively protect the human rights of migrants and refugees who continue more each day to risk their lives at sea.

4. CONCLUSION

Article 2 of the Treaty on European Union asserts that 'the Union is founded on the values of respect for human dignity, freedom, democracy, equality,

---

[142] P. WINTOUR, 'Number of migrants arriving in Italy from Libya falls by half in July', *The Guardian*, 11.08.2017, available at https://www.theguardian.com/world/2017/aug/11/number-of-migrants-arriving-in-italy-from-libya-falls-by-half-in-july, last accessed 14.06.2018.

[143] AMNESTY INTERNATIONAL, 'A year after Italy-Libya migration deal, time to release thousands trapped in misery', Press Release, 01.02.2018, available at https://www.amnesty.org/en/latest/news/2018/02/a-year-after-italy-libya-migration-deal-time-to-release-thousands-trapped-in-misery, last accessed 14.06.2018.

[144] COUNCIL OF THE EUROPEAN UNION, 'African Union-European Union Summit – Joint Statement on the Migrant Situation in Libya' 01.12.2017, available at http://www.consilium.europa.eu/media/31871/33437-pr-libya20statement20283020nov2010.pdf, last accessed 14.06.2018.

[145] EUROPEAN EXTERNAL ACTION SERVICE, 'EU-Libya Relations', available at https://eeas.europa.eu/sites/eeas/files/eu-libya-relations._22-01-2018_.pdf, last accessed on 12.06.2018.

[146] AMNESTY INTERNATIONAL (2017), 'A radical change is needed to failing EU migration policy', *supra* note 49.

the rule of law and respect for human rights, including the rights of persons belonging to minorities'.[147] In 2012, the EU was awarded the Nobel Peace Prize for its role in 'advancing the causes of peace, reconciliation, democracy and human rights in Europe'.[148] Five years later, looking at the way in which the EU has handled and continues to handle the burgeoning migration crisis, it can be argued that these lofty promises have yet to be translated into reality.

Created as a community of values, the EU has a moral responsibility to uphold the principles upon which its very existence is based. It must respect its international legal obligations with regards to refugees and migrants, especially those recognised in the CFREU, legally binding since the adoption of the Lisbon treaty in 2007.

The period of study – from March 2016 to the end of 2017 – was characterised by an increased surveillance and control of the Mediterranean waters and the adoption of several measures aimed at restricting access to Europe. Developments analysed in this article show that in the field of border control, the main goal of the EU's migration policy remains the reduction of the migratory pressure at its borders by keeping the number of crossings and arrivals at its shores to the lowest level possible.

It can be argued that this increased tendency towards externalisation of border control and outsourcing responsibilities to third-countries impacts the human rights of migrants and may continue to have a human cost. One can maintain that the measures adopted by the EU since 2016 did not have a positive repercussion on migrants and refugees who find themselves trapped in countries where they might face grave violations of their human rights[149] and where their personal security is often at risk. Reports from NGOs[150] and international media outlets[151] continue to outline cases of automatic detention, forced expulsions or grave abuses of their most fundamental human rights, such as the right to life, freedom from torture or freedom from slavery. This combination of factors, along with the search of better life prospects, encourages irregular migrants to take greater risks to reach the southern shores of Europe. Despite the intentions of EU leaders, externalisation policies do not manage to have a deterrent effect.

---

[147] Article 2 TFEU.
[148] EUROPEAN UNION, 'European Union receives Nobel Peace Prize 2012', available at https://europa.eu/european-union/about-eu/history/2010-today/2012/eu-nobel_en, last accessed 14.06.2018.
[149] With the exception of Syrian refugees who benefit from special protection in Turkey since the implementation of the EU-Turkey deal.
[150] AMNESTY INTERNATIONAL (2017), 'Libya's dark web of collusion', *supra* note 140.
[151] N. ELBAGIR, R. RAZEK, A. PLATT AND B. JONES, 'People for sale – Where lives are auctioned for $400', *CNN*, 13.11.2017, available at https://www.cnn.com/2017/11/14/africa/libya-migrant-auctions/index.html, last accessed 14.06.2018.

The magnitude of the crisis shows the situation remains first and foremost a humanitarian issue which is putting European solidarity to the test. When implementing border management strategies, the human rights and human security of migrants and refugees are not sufficiently taken into consideration by the EU; even though they should be at the centre of EU's action, human dignity being the cornerstone of all human rights. Migration continues to be mostly apprehended as a threat to the security of Europe and its MS by a wide range of actors involved in the EU migration governance. The EU finds itself in a paradoxical situation in which it is legally committed to the international protection of the human rights of migrants and refugees who reach its territory, while at the same time dedicating a large part of its efforts to prevent them from reaching its territory via an increased externalisation of its border management activities.

The main policy recommendation advanced by different NGOs, international organisations and several EU politicians is the opening of legal and safe pathways to Europe, as the only effective way to prevent migrants and refugees from being victims of traffickers and from undertaking perilous journeys across the Mediterranean. The main problem is the lack of political consensus between MS over this issue. As a first step, EU countries could provide greater numbers of humanitarian visas to people eligible for refugee protection but currently unable to get access to European borders. More student visas or work permits could also be agreed upon.

Another recommendation addressed to the EU MS is to ensure that NGOs rescuing migrants in the Mediterranean are not criminalised for their activities, in accordance with the UN Guidelines on Human Rights at International Borders. The EU MS should dedicate resources to the establishment of operations having search and rescue activities close to the Libyan waters as their core mandate, based on the model of the former Mare Nostrum operation, to avoid naval operations aimed at securing the EU borders finding themselves responsible for the rescue of people drowning in the Mediterranean Sea.

As a conclusion, the very existence of the Union rests upon the principle of solidarity between its MS. This crisis shows that while trying to respond to transnational threats as one, the EU is not immune to national security thinking. If MS want to ensure burden-sharing and better protection to those arriving at European shores, they must overcome the political and ideological divide over the role of the Union in border management. The division is: those who favour returning to national borders, and those who tend toward strong common European control.

As expressed by the European Council on Foreign Relations, this EU tendency to externalise border control policies contributes to 'forge the image of a "fortress Europe" that has little interest in acknowledging or addressing the real causes of migration'.¹⁵² Therefore, to adequately answer to the plight of migrants, the EU must strike a balance between its moral and legal obligations and its duty to ensure safety of its citizens and the security of its borders. Otherwise, the legitimacy and the efficiency of the EU's action in the field of migration management will be deeply undermined. This will not happen overnight and there is certainly no easy solution to the very complex political situation which currently exists in Europe, 60 years after the adoption of the Rome Treaties that laid the foundations of the Union. One certainty is that this issue must be dealt with collectively if deemed to have long term and sustainable effects.

In his 2016 State of the Union, the president of the European Commission Jean-Claude Junker had declared: 'When it comes to managing the refugee crisis, we have started to see solidarity. I am convinced much more solidarity is needed. But I also know that solidarity must be given voluntarily. It must come from the heart. It cannot be forced.'¹⁵³ A year later, when renewing his annual address to the European Parliament, he proclaimed:

> it saddens me to see that solidarity is not yet equally shared across all our Member States [but] Europe as a whole has continued to show solidarity. Europe, contrary to what some say, is not a fortress and must never become one. Europe is and must remain the continent of solidarity where those fleeing persecution can find refuge.¹⁵⁴

To match this commitment, it is time EU MS truly implement holistic and comprehensive migration policies based on solidarity and human rights, revokes the 'fortress Europe' thinking and gives real life and meaning to their motto *in varietate concordia*: unity in diversity.

---

152   EUROPEAN COUNCIL ON FOREIGN RELATIONS, 'Migration through the Mediterranean: Mapping the EU Response', available at http://www.ecfr.eu/specials/mapping_migration, last accessed 14.06.2018.
153   EUROPEAN COMMISSION, 'The State of the Union 2016: Towards a Better Europe – A Europe that Protects, Empowers and Defends', 14.09.2016, available at http://europa.eu/rapid/press-release_IP-16-3042_en.htm, last accessed 14.06.2018.
154   EUROPEAN COMMISSION, State of the Union Address 2017, *supra* note 114.

DOES THE EU FRAMEWORK FOR ROMA INTEGRATION PROMOTE THE HUMAN RIGHTS OF ROMANI PERSONS IN THE UNION?

Gregor FISCHER*

1. Introduction: An Integration Framework, Why and for Whom? 168
   1.1. Who is the EU Targeting with its Policy, and How? 169
   1.2. Initiatives Aiming to Foster Equal Rights for Romani Persons in Europe before the Framework. 172
   1.3. The EU Framework for National Roma Integration Strategies up to 2020: Goals and Missed Chances. 175
2. The Implementation of the Framework. 177
   2.1. Evaluation of the Framework and Adjacent EU Law Pre-2017 178
   2.2. Preliminary Findings of the 2017 Public Consultation. 181
   2.3. Implementation of the Framework Until 2020 and Beyond 183
   2.4. Cases before the ECtHR and the CJEU: Lessons to be Learned 185
3. The National-Foreigner Divide in the Case of Austria 187
4. Conclusion. 191

ABSTRACT

The European Union (EU) Framework for National Roma Integration Strategies up to 2020 declaredly seeks to promote the integration/inclusion of Romani

---

* This article is one of the results of the research project 'Persistent Forms of Discrimination against Romani People in the Styrian-Burgenland Commemorative Culture and in the Access to Human Rights', implementing organisation: University of Graz, project leader: Ursula Mindler-Steiner, funded by the FEDERAL PROVINCE OF STEIERMARK, ABT. 8 (GZ ABT08-247132/2015-10), the FUTURE FUND OF THE REPUBLIC OF AUSTRIA (P16-2433) and the FEDERAL PROVINCE OF BURGENLAND ABT. 7 (7/KW.A134-10000-1-2015), available at https://romani-memory-human-rights.uni-graz.at, last accessed 18.06.2018.

communities in European societies. The European Commission's document urges Member State governments to improve Romani persons' access to employment, healthcare and housing and essential services. In this article, the author asks whether this approach has proven fruitful, or if legal and practical misconceptions inherent to the strategy and to the resulting national implementation plans have hampered the success of the – in principle – well-meant EU-attempt to formally engage in the struggle for Romani equality. To this end, the article takes into account the genesis of European Romani policy, inputs from Romani studies, the latest EU- and third-party evaluation reports of the Framework and qualitative interviews carried out with Romani representatives and experts in Austria.

1. INTRODUCTION: AN INTEGRATION FRAMEWORK, WHY AND FOR WHOM?

> A Roma middle class has to emerge alongside a culture of equality and diversity. […] [T]he European Union could be the catalyst for contesting the institutionalised forms of suppression Roma face in today's Europe.[1]

The inclusion of Roma in European societies has been discussed by scholars from various academic backgrounds, political decision-makers and within the respective societies at large for decades. Still, it took European Union (EU) institutions until 2011 to provide guidelines on Member State (MS) policies to integrate Romani communities in European societies. Have Márton Rövid's hopes come at least partly true in 2018? Are Romani communities moving from the margins to the centres of European societies, propelled by the EU Framework for National Roma Integration Strategies up to 2020 (hereinafter 'the Framework')?[2] Or do political centrifugal forces in Europe hinder the fulfilment of the promise of open societies and inclusiveness, protection of and respect for the human rights of Romani persons?

The aim of this article is to explore the impact and effectiveness of EU policies towards Romani persons, for their integration/inclusion in various areas of life and the approaches applied herein. The article analyses the effects of existing European Roma policies in the light of current evaluation reports, such as the European Commission's (EC's) mid-term review of the Framework issued in 2017, current (ongoing) legal proceedings and critical legal and Romani scholars' contributions. Together with the evaluation of the EU Framework for National Roma Integration Strategies up to 2020, whose preliminary results were

---

[1] M. RÖVID, 'One-Size-Fits-All Roma? – On the Normative Dilemmas of the Emerging European Roma Policy', (2011) 21(1) *Romani Studies*, p. 22. Rövid is a former research and policy officer at the Decade of Roma Inclusion.
[2] EUROPEAN COMMISSION, An EU Framework for National Roma Integration Strategies up to 2020, COM(2011) 173/4, 07.09.2010.

published in the beginning of 2018, qualitative information gathered in local case studies conducted in Austria in 2016 and 2017 is used to assess possible (legal and factual) shortcomings of the European and national strategies from the angle of the local level. In the mentioned case studies, opinions on how effective inclusion can flourish have been gathered in expert workshops and qualitative interviews with non-governmental organisation (NGO) representatives and activists partly identifying themselves as Roma. The conclusion of this article then seeks to show possible pathways towards more effective remedies to the devastating realities that Romani people still face in the EU.

1.1. WHO IS THE EU TARGETING WITH ITS POLICY, AND HOW?

A worthwhile look at the discourse on 'Roma' as a group provides much-needed context in the assessment of the present EU Roma policy. It is widely accepted and reiterated by Intergovernmental Organisations (IGOs) and academia alike that Roma are 'Europe's largest minority'.[3] With about 6–16 million Roma living in Council of Europe (CoE) Member States and 4–8 million in the EU area, respectively, it is indeed obvious that Romani persons make up a significant portion of the continent's population.[4] However, already the high fluctuation margins in these statistical numbers provided by the CoE show that there obviously is uncertainty even on who is considered 'Romani' in the first place. Moreover, Roma are recognised to be heavily disadvantaged and discriminated against throughout Europe, keeping individuals affiliated with the group from fully enjoying their (human and minority) rights.[5] It has been stressed therefore that '[Roma] have been framed as a European minority par excellence. Having no established connection with a kin state which will lobby and advocate on their behalf, it is claimed that Roma need to rely on European institutions and agreements to get their rights acknowledged'.[6] However, the generalisation of

---

[3] E.g. EUROPEAN COMMISSION, 'International Roma Day: Statement by First Vice-President Frans Timmermans and Commissioners Marianne Thyssen, Věra Jourová, Corina Crețu and Johannes Hahn', Press Release, available at http://europa.eu/rapid/press-release_STATEMENT-18-2868_en.htm, last accessed 20.06.2018.

[4] See COUNCIL OF EUROPE, 'Estimates and Official Numbers of Roma in Europe', 2012, available at http://rm.coe.int/CoERMPublicCommonSearchServices/DisplayDCTMContent?documentId=0900001680088ea9, last accessed 18.06.2018.

[5] See EUROPEAN UNION AGENCY FOR FUNDAMENTAL RIGHTS (FRA), 'Second European Union Minorities and Discrimination Survey (EU-MIDIS II) Roma – Selected Findings', p. 3, available at http://fra.europa.eu/en/publication/2017/eumidis-ii-main-results, last accessed 19.06.2018.

[6] C. DELCOUR and L. HUSTINX, 'Discourses of Roma Anti-Discrimination in Reports on Human Rights Violations', (2015) 3(5) *Social Inclusion*, p. 90; see also M. SURDU and M. KOVATS, 'Roma Identity as an Expert-Political Construction', (2015) 3(5) *Social Inclusion*, p. 6ff.

Roma as a (seemingly?) pan-European group in political rhetoric and official documents – while stimulated by the Romani national movement – seems to fail to adequately reflect the sociopolitical, economical and human rights realities that distinct Roma communities and individuals face in their specific national, regional and local contexts.[7] Romani communities are included in European societies in varying degrees, and whereas some Romani initiatives and individuals are outspoken actors on the political plane nowadays,[8] others remain as invisible as they were before the EU engagement for Romani rights. Due to these factors, assuming that there is one 'Romani cause' that is the same throughout Europe and has to be pursued on this level can be a dangerous fallacy when policies lack empirical foundations: 'We have seen how the political need for Roma data has outstripped the scientific ability to provide a standard definition of Roma and methods for comparative analysis between countries or over time.'[9] Policies that are unable to effectively address those who are highly in need of effective participation and political representation to have their rights respected, protected and fulfilled could leave exactly these persons (even further) behind: 'Roma who cannot identify with the new European Roma identity and its accompanying norms cannot, therefore, benefit from European-led inclusion. [...] Romani studies have warned that the Roma-focused inclusion policy can produce the opposite effect.'[10]

Fittingly, while the creation of political instruments promising support for Roma inclusion in European societies has flourished over the last years, the respective results vary greatly due to the fact that Romani communities themselves are as diverse as the very states and societies they ought to be included in. Translated to the language of international human rights law, there is a gaping gulf between the rights guaranteed by law and their implementation. Human rights have to be translated into national legal provisions, effectively

---

[7] As rightly pointed out by Doris Farget: 'For the most part, the Roma are citizens of the European Union and Council of Europe's Members States. Their situation and conditions of life vary from one country to another and within each of these States so much that it is difficult to draw a general portrait', D. FARGET, 'Defining Roma Identity in the European Court of Human Rights', (2012) 19(3) *International Journal on Minority and Group Rights*, p. 292.

[8] E.g. The Central Council of German Sinti and Roma publicly delivers its opinions on topical political issues, lately and prominently on the case of anti-Roma agitation in the aspiring EU-accessor states of the Western Balkans and in Turkey. See ZENTRALRAT DEUTSCHER SINTI UND ROMA, 'Ächtung von Antiziganismus in den Staaten des Westlichen Balkans und in der Türkei überfällig', 12.02.2018, available at http://zentralrat.sintiundroma.de/zentralrat-deutscher-sinti-und-roma-aechtung-von-antiziganismus-in-den-staaten-des-westlichen-balkans-und-in-der-tuerkei-ueberfaellig, last accessed 18.06.2018.

[9] I. LAW and M. KOVATS, *Rethinking Roma: Identities, Politicisation and New Agendas*, Palgrave Macmillan, London 2018, p. 156.

[10] C. DELCOUR and L. HUSTINX (2015), 'Discourses of Roma Anti-Discrimination', *supra* note 6, p. 91.

implemented by national authorities and judicially protected by national and international courts. The efficacy of human rights law and its implementation standards is therefore heavily reliant on the nation state. Conversely, this means that a centralised design of strategies for Romani inclusion depends heavily on the inputs of national, local and regional authorities: 'Though the Europeanisation of Roma policy is a contemporary phenomenon, it reproduces an historical structural problem of the centre's dependence on lower level authorities actually delivering *Roma* policy goals.'[11] What is more, in all of these steps from needs analysis to the effective implementation of human rights guarantees with all of the intermediate communication back and forth, there is a margin of error that must not be underestimated.

Despite concerns regarding the empirical basis of Roma policies, supra- and international coordination, if done diligently and precisely, could still fulfil an important role in gathering knowledge and best practices and in tailoring the national approaches throughout Europe to the needs of specific Romani populations. As the EU internal market and therefore the movement of goods and persons alike surpass the boundaries of national borders and policies,[12] effective impulses from Brussels could indeed facilitate addressing the political and social problematics that arise within the proclaimed ever closer Union.[13] Moreover, EU primary law itself states that the Union 'shall aim to combat discrimination based on sex, racial or ethnic origin, religion or belief, disability, age or sexual orientation.'[14] Roots for distinct actions to foster non-discrimination can therefore be found in the EU's contractual foundations themselves. Many Romani persons within the EU area are EU citizens, entitled to enjoy the fundamental freedoms of the Union and the fundamental rights enshrined in the Charter of Fundamental Rights of the European Union (CFR) in addition to the human rights *aquis*. In spite of the embeddedness of non-discrimination with regards to nationality, ethnicity and race in EU primary and secondary law and, moreover, the EU institutions' recognition of the problems Romani persons face, a Roma pilot study conducted by the EU Fundamental Rights Agency (FRA)

---

[11] I. LAW and M. KOVATS (2018), *Rethinking, supra* note 9, p. 156.

[12] The market-centred understanding of social matters laid down in EU primary law is blatantly visible, see Consolidated version of the Treaty on the Functioning of the European Union (TFEU) Article 151, OJ C 202 (2016): Article 151 lays down the need to maintain the competitiveness of the Union economy to ensure the 'functioning of the internal market, which will favour the harmonisation of social systems'. This programmatic orientation is mirrored in EU Roma policy, as shown throughout this article.

[13] Consolidated version of the Treaty on European Union (TEU) Article 1, OJ C 326 (2012): 'This Treaty marks a new stage in the process of creating an ever closer union among the peoples of Europe.'

[14] Article 10 TFEU. On the non-performativity of this provision due to the wording 'shall aim to', see A. WEISS, 'Whiteness as International Citizenship in European Union Law', *Völkerrechtsblog*, 02.03.2018, available at http://voelkerrechtsblog.org/whiteness-as-international-citizenship-in-european-union-law, last accessed 18.06.2018.

in 11 MS in 2011 found that 46% of the interviewed Romani persons had felt discriminated against in the 12-month timeframe before the study.[15] The need for an effective implementation was therefore obvious. Has the EU Framework for National Roma Integration Strategies up to 2020[16] been able to effectively supplement EU primary and secondary law since then?

1.2. INITIATIVES AIMING TO FOSTER EQUAL RIGHTS FOR ROMANI PERSONS IN EUROPE BEFORE THE FRAMEWORK

Engagement for the rights of Romani persons in Europe, obviously, has not begun with the EU Framework. Before the EU's present policy, several other international organisations played significant roles in the struggle for the effective realisation of human rights guarantees for the Romani populations all across Europe. To show the continuities of these developments, the most important actors in this field and their initiatives are described here briefly. This allows for an assessment of how policies have transformed over time, which will be used as a background for the discussion of relevant provisions of EU law and policy.

The need for action to improve the situation of Roma, albeit using the term 'Gypsies', was addressed early by CoE. Already in 1969, a recommendation of the CoE's Parliamentary Assembly (PACE) stated that: '[A]n integration of the Gypsy population into modern European society is called for and [...] such integration requires concerted action by the Council of Europe member governments.'[17] Since then, the CoE has passed several documents and renewed calls for action encouraging its Member States to include Romani people in their respective societies. Also, the Convention for the Protection of Human Rights and Fundamental Freedoms (ECHR)[18] has been and still is frequently used as a hard-law tool to legally combat discrimination against Roma. The European Court of Human Rights (ECtHR) plays a central role in the combat against ethnic discrimination against Romani persons in various areas of life.[19] The Court has been used as a forum for strategic

---

15   See FRA, 'Survey Data Explorer – Results from the 2011 Roma Survey, Discrimination and Participation', available at http://fra.europa.eu/en/publications-and-resources/data-and-maps/survey-data-explorer-results-2011-roma-survey, last accessed 18.06.2018.
16   EUROPEAN COMMISSION, COM(2011) 173/4, *supra* note 2.
17   CoE PACE, 'Situation of Gypsies and Travellers in Europe', 30.09.1969, Doc. 2629.
18   European Convention for the Protection of Human Rights and Fundamental Freedoms, 04.11.1950, ETS 5.
19   Focus areas were the right to private life (Article 8 ECHR), the right to education (Protocol 1 to the European Convention for the Protection of Human Rights and Fundamental Freedoms, Article 2, 20.03.1952, ETS 9, the right to effective remedy (Article 13 ECHR); all read together with the prohibition of discrimination (Article 14 ECHR).

litigation by NGOs and advocacy groups seeking to promote reforms for the benefit of Romani persons' equal enjoyment of their rights in a broader sense.[20] Cases of school segregation of Romani children have dominated the ECtHR's judgments in recent years.[21] However, the stance of the ECtHR has not remained unchallenged, its definition of the 'Gypsy way of life' being in the centre of scholars' criticism.[22]

The 2003 'Action Plan on Improving the Situation of Roma and Sinti within the OSCE Area' established the Contact Point for Roma and Sinti Issues (CPRSI) at the Organization for Security and Co-operation in Europe's (OSCE's) Office for Democratic Institutions and Human Rights (ODIHR) and called for national implementation measures to realise the goals set out in the plan.[23] The main issues addressed by the action plan are combating racism and discrimination, resolving socio-economic issues, improving the access to education, enhancing participation in public and political life, supporting Roma and Sinti in crisis/post-crisis situations and enhancing cooperation with international and non-governmental organisations. Romani rights are also taken into account by the OSCE when developing recommendations on the rights of minorities. The latest topical highlight in this context was the presentation of the 'Graz Recommendations on Access to Justice and National Minorities' in 2017.[24]

---

[20] 'Strategic litigation' is to be understood as 'legal action [...] taken with a focus on law and policy reform, with cases chosen and targeted for bringing to surface broader problems and issues', see D. ANAGNOSTOU, 'The Strasbourg Court, Democracy and the Protection of Marginalised Individuals and Minorities', in D. ANAGNOSTOU and E. PSYCHOGIOPOULOU (eds.), *The European Court of Human Rights and the Rights of Marginalised Individuals and Minorities in National Context*, Martinus Nijhoff Publishers, Leiden/Boston 2010, p. 14.

[21] E.g. ECtHR, *D.H. and Others v the Czech Republic*, no 57325/00, 13.11.2007; ECtHR, *Oršuš and Others v Croatia*, no 15766/03 [GC], 16.03.2010; ECtHR, *Horváth and Kiss v Hungary*, no 11146/11, 29.01.2013; ECtHR, *Sampanis and Others v Greece*, no 32526/05, 05.06.2008; ECtHR, *Sampani and Others v Greece*, no 59608/09, 11.12.2012.

[22] The main point of criticism is the non-consultation of Romani groups when defining this 'way of life' and applying the concept to a plethora of incongruent cases. For more details, see below section 2.4.

[23] OSCE, Action Plan on Improving the Situation of Roma and Sinti within the OSCE Area, MC.DEC/3/03, 01–02.12.2003, available at https://www.osce.org/odihr/17554, last accessed 19.06.2018.

[24] OSCE, 'The Graz Recommendations on Access to Justice and National Minorities', 14 November 2017, available at https://www.osce.org/hcnm/graz-recommendations, last accessed 19.06.2018. The minority rights approach in which the OSCE traditionally operates has not remained without criticism: 'To draw on the terminology of the European Court of Human Rights, international minorities [sic!] law appears too weak to play any effective part in the actual protection of people suffering from abuse by others in dominant position', G. FORTMAN, 'Minority Rights: A Major Misconception?', (2011) 33(2) *Human Rights Quarterly*, p. 273.

At the EU level, the European Parliament (EP) has shown awareness of the situation of Roma and the persistent discrimination against them 'in law and practice' already in 1984 and called

> [...] on the Commission to draw up, after consulting the gypsies' [sic!] representatives, programmes to be subsidized from Community funds aimed at improving the situation of gypsies without destroying their separate identity, particularly by making available adequate aid from the European Social Fund to develop areas designed for itinerant people.[25]

Ten years later, in 1994, the Parliament again stressed its concern about 'the growth of racism and xenophobia, and particularly [...] the acts of racist violence perpetrated against the minorities living in certain Member States of the Community[.]' and recommended unified efforts by the Council, the EC and Member States to eliminate *'gypsies'* [sic!] deprivation and poverty.[26] EU institutions also contributed to the Decade of Roma Inclusion (2005–2015) in which 12 states and international organisations such as the United Nations Development Programme (UNDP), CoE, OSCE and the World Bank participated in. Within the Roma Decade, the Hungarian government prominently supported a European Roma Policy.[27] In 2008, the EP again expressly urged 'the Commission to develop a European Framework Strategy on Roma Inclusion aimed at providing policy coherence at EU level as regards the social inclusion of Roma'.[28] Further policy proposals and recommendations, also informed by the conclusions drawn from Roma Decade efforts, were developed within the European Platform for Roma Inclusion and the European Council.[29] The Czech Republic's EU presidency linked the Roma Decade closer to the EU and enabled further focus on the topic of Romani inclusion.[30] Finally, in 2011, the Framework was proposed by the EC.

---

[25] EUROPEAN PARLIAMENT, Resolution on the situation of gypsies in the Community, OJ C 172/153, 02.07.1984.
[26] EUROPEAN PARLIAMENT, Resolution on the situation of gypsies in the Community, OJ C 128/372ff, 09.05.1994.
[27] I. Law and M. Kovats (2018), *Rethinking Roma, supra* note 9, p. 156.
[28] EUROPEAN PARLIAMENT, Resolution on a European strategy on the Roma, OJ C 68E, 21.03.2009.
[29] E.g. EUROPEAN COUNCIL, Council Conclusions on Inclusion of the Roma, 08.06.2009, available at http://www.consilium.europa.eu/uedocs/cms_data/docs/pressdata/en/lsa/108377.pdf, last accessed 19.06.2018; EUROPEAN COMMISSION, Common Basic Principles for Roma Inclusion, 12.04.2010, available at http://ec.europa.eu/social/BlobServlet?docId=2491&langId=en, last accessed 19.06.2018.
[30] Both EU-MS mentioned in this section as particularly active in the development of an EU policy framework for the integration of Roma, Hungary and the Czech Republic, are presently facing infringement proceedings due to the ever-persisting practice of segregating Romani children in their public school systems. For more details, see below section 2.3.

1.3. THE EU FRAMEWORK FOR NATIONAL ROMA INTEGRATION STRATEGIES UP TO 2020: GOALS AND MISSED CHANCES

As illustrated above, it took EU institutions almost three decades after recognising the need for action to present a policy approach seeking to foster the implementation of equal rights for Romani persons. While (hard) legal acts of the EU guaranteeing fundamental rights and prohibiting racial discrimination had entered into force in the meantime, discrimination against Romani persons persisted and continues to persist throughout the MS in varying degrees. The relevant Directive 2004/38/EC prohibiting racial discrimination[31] (hereinafter Racial Equality Directive) had not shown the desired results throughout the Union, especially not for Roma, and it would take until 2015 for the Court of Justice of the European Union (CJEU) to apply the Directive to a Romani-related case.[32] To finally tackle the ever-persistent issue of discrimination against Romani persons, the EC chose to apply a soft-law approach[33] paired with financial incentives for MS, sub-state levels of government and NGOs. When the Commission communicated the establishment of the Framework on 5 April 2011, it envisioned national policies aiming to improve the living conditions for Romani persons in 'four crucial areas: access to education, employment, healthcare and housing'.[34] This can be seen as a continuation of the approaches demanded and/or developed by the CoE, the OSCE, the EP and during the Roma Decade. As reasons for this new soft law approach 'reinforcing the EU's equality legislation', the EC mentions 'prejudice, intolerance, discrimination and social exclusion in their daily lives' Romani persons were (and are) still facing, and that these conditions were 'not acceptable in the [EU] at the beginning of the 21st century'.[35] It is especially noteworthy that the EC herein also explicitly refers to the Racial Equality Directive.[36]

---

[31] Council Directive No 2000/43/EC of 29 June 2000 implementing the principle of equal treatment between persons irrespective of racial or ethnic origin, OJ L 180, 19.07.2000 (hereinafter Racial Equality Directive).

[32] CJEU/GC, *CHEZ Razpredeleine Bulgaria AD v Komisia za zashtita ot discriminatsia*, Case C-83/14, 16.07.2015, ECLI:EU:C:2015:480; for more details, see below section 2.4.

[33] The legal nature of the EU's non-hard-law instruments does not seem to be carved in stone when taking into account CJEU rulings. It has been argued that 'it is legitimate to wonder whether soft does not transform into hard by the intervention of the European judicature'. See O.A. STEFAN, 'European Competition Soft Law in European Courts: A Matter of Hard Principles', (2008) 14(6) *European Law Journal*, p. 753; O.A. STEFAN, 'Helping Loose Ends Meet? The Judicial Acknowledgement of Soft Law as a Tool of Multi-Level Governance', (2014) 21(2) *Maastricht Journal of European and Comparative Law*, p. 359.

[34] EUROPEAN COMMISSION, COM(2011) 173/4, *supra* note 2, p. 4.

[35] Ibid., p. 2.

[36] Ibid.

The Framework does not contain specific guidelines on how its goals should be reached *in concreto*. Instead, the main contributions of the initial communication of the Framework are the programmatic goals set and the coordination measures prescribed. And indeed, the Framework has led to the setup, or, where such instruments had already been in place, the reform of the eponymous National Roma Integration Strategies (NRISs) containing specific national policy goals to be implemented by the respective MS within the first year after its inception. In addition, National Roma Contact Points (NRCPs) tasked with facilitating horizontal and vertical communication between Romani populations and activists, NGOs, political decision-makers, academia, EU and IGO representatives shall ensure an inclusive approach in the design of national policies. The initial Framework Communication also contains a request to MS to present their Roma strategies to the EC and to closely monitor the implementation of the NRISs. Acknowledging that affirmative action is compatible with EU and national non-discrimination law, the EC underlined the necessity of a targeted approach in national, regional and local integration policies to address the disadvantages Roma were and are still facing.[37] These national measures can rely on EU funding: mechanisms and projects can be implemented using the EU Structural Funds and the European Agricultural Fund for Rural Development. The EC explicitly stressed that the usage of these funds should be increased by MS to complement national funding of Roma initiatives.[38] However, the formal (legal) context the Framework operates in, especially whether it targets '[Roma] as an ethnic minority or as a socio-economic (vulnerable) group', remains nebulous.[39] Also, the Framework uses a plethora of legal keywords with a tendency towards economic integration rather than individual rights as such: 'Economic integration of the Roma will also contribute to social cohesion and improve respect for fundamental rights [...] and help eliminating discrimination.'[40] Moreover, the Framework does *not* refer to the common human rights (implementation) and non-discrimination *acquis* of the MS, such as fostering rights awareness among marginalised groups and the population as a whole and a possible role of national equality bodies therein as prescribed by the Racial Equality Directive.[41] Here, the EC missed a chance to give the Framework additional hard-law background and depth already at its inception. Instead, two years elapsed until the European Council issued a Recommendation

---

[37] Ibid., p. 4.
[38] Ibid., p. 9.
[39] OPEN SOCIETY EUROPEAN POLICY INSTITUTE, 'Revisiting the EU Roma Framework: Assessing the European Dimension for the Post-2020 Future', March 2017, p. 10, available at https://www.opensocietyfoundations.org/reports/revisiting-eu-roma-framework-assessing-european-dimension-post-2020-future, last accessed 19.06.2018.
[40] EUROPEAN COMMISSION, COM(2011) 173/4, 3, *supra* note 2.
[41] Racial Equality Directive, Article 13.

that finally named the ECtHR's case law as a yardstick for the conformity of national practices with the principle of non-discrimination and stressed the importance of international human rights norms and pro-active measures of MS to sensitise populations to anti-discrimination.[42] Moreover, political participation of Romani communities in general and in the implementation of the Framework, widely neglected in the initial Communication, was also addressed in more depth on this occasion.[43]

It is obvious that both, the Racial Equality Directive and the Framework require MS to ensure non-discrimination, and that the latter could benefit conformity with the former by offering MS additional incentives. However, when it comes to the implementation at the national level, it has been argued that:

> [t]he European Roma inclusion policy [...] is established as a political compromise on a transnational level. Thus its entanglements with domestic politics entail struggles and conflicts in the public sphere, or often the opposite: erasing the political content of the issue and turning it to technical mastering of policy programs.[44]

In other words: hardly remarkable, the slow progress in the formulation and concretisation of the EU instruments for Romani integration described above is mirrored by the respective implementation practices in MS that are dealt with in the subsequent section.

2. THE IMPLEMENTATION OF THE FRAMEWORK

This section gives an overview of the present implementation status of the Framework and the problematics at work herein. Márton Rövid and Angéla Kóczé wrote in 2017:

> [T]hese efforts [of the Roma Decade and the Framework] could not challenge deep-rooted anti-Roma racist prejudice and unjust redistributive systems. Even honest efforts with good intentions can preserve deep-seated anti-Roma discourses and exclusionary social, economic and political structures that racialise and relegate Roma to inferior status.[45]

---

[42] EUROPEAN COUNCIL, Recommendation on effective Roma integration measures in the Member States, C 378/01, 09.12.2013, paras. 2.1., 2.2.
[43] Ibid., paras. 2.8., 3.9., for the implications of active Romani participation in shaping the Framework's implementation, see below section 2.4.
[44] V. ZENTAI, 'National Roma Inclusion Policies in Central and Eastern Europe: Diverging Learning Paths with Residual Outcomes', in A. BATORY, A. CARTWRIGHT and D. STONE (eds.), *Policy Experiments, Failures and Innovations – Beyond Accession in Central and Eastern Europe*, Elgar, Cheltenham/Northampton 2018, pp. 88, 90.
[45] A. KÓCZÉ and M. RÖVID, 'Roma and the Politics of Double Discourse in Contemporary Europe', (2017) 24(6) *Global Studies in Culture and Power*, p. 684.

Is EU law, as the authors suggest, unable to effectively put an end to racial segregation and marginalisation of Romani persons, and may it even create new rifts in European societies rather than bridging divides? Has a major flaw in policy design been passed in a top-down process from the Union to the MS via the Framework? And what is the relationship between the Framework and EU hard law in the implementation process?

For the purpose of this article, one Framework evaluation report issued by the EP in 2015 and one EC report on the enforcement of non-discrimination law published in 2017 provide the background for the latest available public consultation whose preliminary findings were issued in the beginning of 2018. Besides official EU publications, comments and reports from other international and civil society organisations on the present EU Roma policy and the resulting NRISs provide further context. The subsequent section also takes the relevance of hard legal acts and judicial mechanisms for the Framework into account.

2.1. EVALUATION OF THE FRAMEWORK AND ADJACENT EU LAW PRE-2017

The EP-commissioned Framework progress report for select MS in 2015 found severe shortcomings imminent in the NRISs.[46] These deficiencies included lack of data, ill-developed targets linked to precise timeframes, failure in applying an integrated, holistic approach to the multi- and intersectional discrimination Romani persons face, unclear responsibilities of the respective levels of government, limited funding for Roma inclusion, lack of institutional knowledge to effectively attain EU funding, weak or non-existent monitoring and evaluation and poor communication between the levels of government. Reasons for the weak implementation of NRISs can, according to the study, be found in the 'dearth of political will at all levels of national and sub-national government' that was further nurtured by the 'insufficient "bite"' of the EU's soft-law instruments.[47] With regard to EU hard law, the report stresses that national equality bodies as prescribed by the Racial Equality Directive are equipped with varying degrees of competences throughout the MS and have failed to effectively protect victims of discrimination. A major factor hampering effective protection and pointing towards a lack of access to justice, according to the experts, is '[…] underreporting of incidents of

---

[46] See W. BARTLETT, C. GORDON and B. KAMPHUIS, 'Evaluation of the EU Framework for National Roma Integration Strategies', Study for the LIBE Committee of the, European Parliament, 2015, pp. 8f, available at http://www.europarl.europa.eu/thinktank/en/document.html?reference=IPOL_STU(2015)536485, last accessed 19.06.2018.
[47] See ibid., p. 57.

discrimination [...] compounded by a paucity of equality data and low levels of awareness among Roma populations of their existing protection under law'.[48]

Further, the evaluators substantiated shortcomings of the Framework itself: an unrealistic one-size-fits-all approach, failures in the development process, weak evaluation procedures, non-existence of sanctions in case of non-implementation and disregard for the needs of women and children.[49] This pessimistic assessment of the policy itself and its implementation is mirrored in the highly topical academic analysis which stresses an insufficient link to hard law in perpetuation of the Roma Decade approaches as one of the main reasons for the Framework's weak results on the ground: 'A lack of explicit anti-discrimination backing and legal force to social inclusion measures was a fundamental conceptual mistake stemming from the Decade National Action Plans and imported into the NRIS from 2011.'[50] Moreover, the shortcomings of the NRISs are characterised as already predetermined by the Framework: '[M]ember states were provided with faulty guidelines and manuals and felt comfortable by not being asked to do too much or anything too challenging. The result was a reasonably good policy transfer of a minimalist and skewed policy framing of EU norms.'[51] In other words, the supranational Framework as a top-down instrument reproduced its own deficiencies in the national strategies it demanded. Backing the findings of the EP report on the lack of efficacy of the Framework, the 2013 evaluation of the OSCE Action Plan for the improvement of Romani persons' living conditions identifies deepening gaps between Romani and non-Romani populations in EU MS exactly in the key focus areas of the Framework instead of progress towards effective equality.[52]

Strikingly, the EP evaluators, adopting the language of the EC, come to the conclusion that to remedy the situation, the EU should '[...] foster the economically led integration of Roma people while at the same time developing its crucial work in the area of anti-discrimination'. They also stress that 'Roma potentially represent a large pool of young and untapped labour'.[53] This wording

---

[48]   Ibid., p. 24.
[49]   Ibid., p. 58.
[50]   V. ZENTAI, 'National Roma Inclusion Policies', *supra* note 44, pp. 88, 98.
[51]   Ibid.
[52]   E.g. OSCE/ODIHR, 'Implementation of the Action Plan on Improving the Situation of Roma and Sinti Within the OSCE Area – Status Report 2013', 24.12.2013, 9: 'Despite this example of visible progress, the assessment also identifies negative trends that are deepening the gaps between the situation of Roma and Sinti and general populations, especially in the areas of housing, employment and access to social services. This overall context has been influenced most of all by the effects resulting from two significant events – EU enlargement and the global financial crisis – both of which have had a major impact on the situation of Roma and Sinti.'
[53]   W. BARTLETT, C. GORDON and B. KAMPHUIS (2015), 'Evaluation of the EU Framework', *supra* note 46, p. 61.

that yet again follows a market-centred rather than a human rights centred approach can be read as reducing the inclusion of Romani persons in European societies to a means to achieve higher competitiveness of European economies instead of establishing the implementation of human rights guarantees as an end defined within the Framework. Only after elaborating on further economic implications of Roma inclusion, the issues of human rights and non-discrimination resurface, when the report proposes a revamped EU Strategy for Roma Inclusion (as initially proposed by the EP in 2011) and a continuation of the EU's efforts in the area of non-discrimination on the basis of Article 19 TFEU, Article 21 CFR, the Racial Equality Directive and Framework Decision 2008/913/JHA. Further, more practically-oriented recommendations include fostering the MS' abidance to ECtHR rulings on Roma rights with additional acts of EU hard law, cooperation with national equality bodies and international organisations such as the CoE, but also NGOs such as the ERRC, e.g. by EU support for class actions before the ECtHR (!).[54]

Fittingly, in 2017, the EC analysed the functionality of EU equality law and issued a report on the enforcement of the Racial Equality Directive and the Employment Equality Directive with specific regard to Romani communities in 27 EU MS (except Malta).[55] To do so, official policy documents were used as well as monitoring and NGO reports. Herein, a positive effect of the Framework is only highlighted for four MS by the evaluating experts, while the transposition of hard law (relevant Directives) into national law is assessed as a firm basis for addressing discrimination of Romani persons in merely five states. According to the report, major challenges hindering effective implementation of non-discrimination for Romani persons in the MS are a lack of data, missing case law and underreporting, missing involvement of national equality bodies in Romani issues and the absence of political will and governmental perseverance and long-term prioritisation.[56] In Hungary, for example, even legal success did not seem to change the situation of Romani communities, as 'the negative political environment quietly tolerated situations where court decisions were not followed up by the necessary actors or when local authorities adopted measures and practices that aimed to drive away the Roma population'.[57] Also, infringement proceedings against the Czech Republic, Hungary and Slovakia do not seem to work as a means of external pressure.

---

[54] Ibid., p. 62f.
[55] I. CHOPIN, C. GERMAINE and J. TANCZOS, 'Roma and the Enforcement of Anti-discrimination Law', Study by the European Network of Legal Experts in Gender Equality and Non-discrimination for the EC DG for Justice and Consumers, Brussels 2017, p. 6, available at http://ec.europa.eu/newsroom/just/item-detail.cfm?item_id=605239, last accessed 19.06.2018.
[56] Ibid., pp. 7f.
[57] I. CHOPIN, C. GERMAINE and J. TANCZOS (2017), 'Roma and the Enforcement of Anti-discrimination Law', *supra* note 55, p. 12.

Legal amendments planned or enacted in Hungary and Slovakia, according to the EC experts, pose the danger of rather exacerbating school segregation than solving the problem.[58] Paradoxically, the experts then go on to mention 'external pressure', such as international monitoring and infringement proceedings, as a factor able to produce improvements for Romani communities. In this context, the question remains how these measures are really suited to improve the impact of the Framework, as exactly the MS against which infringement proceedings have already been initiated are the ones most criticised for their inability or unwillingness to effectively tackle discrimination against Romani persons.

All in all, the results of national policies for the inclusion/integration of Romani persons are mediocre at best according to both, the EP and the EC report. As already pointed out, lacking efficiency of national policies is not only due to a lack of political will or capacities in the MS, but lies embedded in the Framework and its imprecise or non-defined goals. Further data on the effectiveness of the Framework and its impact in law and practice in the EU MS was gathered until the end of 2017 in a public consultation, whose preliminary results are taken into account in the next sub-section.[59]

2.2. PRELIMINARY FINDINGS OF THE 2017 PUBLIC CONSULTATION

To enrich the existing evaluation data on Romani policies in Europe with the views of stakeholders, the EC designed an online questionnaire in the last quarter of 2017. Altogether, 240 organisations or individuals working in the field of Roma inclusion answered the survey (106 NGOs, 75 individuals, 44 public administrations), 202 of whom specified their ethnicity (91 Romani/111 non-Romani). It must be stressed that the final report on the public consultation is yet to be issued. However, including the highly topical opinions of those affected by the EU's Roma policy seems imperative in the context of this sub-section.

When answering the EC questionnaire, only 61% of respondents stated that they had knowledge on EU policies for Romani communities. While the high unawareness of EU policies in this field is by itself an important finding and points towards insufficient communication of the Framework's aims and goals, it does not impair the rest of the study's relevance, as the respondents' perception of progress/regress in the MS is the main empirical interest of the survey, whose

---

[58] Ibid., p. 15ff.
[59] EUROPEAN COMMISSION, 'Public Consultation on the Evaluation of the EU Framework for National Roma Integration Strategies up to 2020', available at https://ec.europa.eu/info/consultations/public-consultation-evaluation-eu-framework-national-roma-integration-strategies-2020_en, last accessed 18.06.2018.

findings yet again point towards – at best – mediocre progress in guaranteeing equal chances for Romani persons.

The only field in which a majority of respondents saw change for the better is education, with 49.6% answering that there had been (slight or strong) improvements. In three other focus areas of the Framework (employment, healthcare, housing/essential services), the survey results suggest that there has been no effective change. Significantly, in the area of discrimination as such, an issue overarching all the aforementioned target areas of the Framework, 37.6% indicated that the situation had worsened, while 45.5% opined that there had been no change.[60] Therefore, it can be stated that the most recent numbers gathered across EU MS support the findings of prior evaluations, namely that in spite of progress in specific policy areas, the Framework itself does not live up to its goals. In spite of the apparent but slow progress made since 2011, the majority of respondents (60%) indicated that EU institutions should further play a major role in supporting national, regional and local authorities, who are in their opinion unable to improve the situation of Romani persons on their own.[61] The participants rated putting Roma inclusion high on the European political agenda, direct EU funding for Romani projects and specific allocations under the ESIF as the main achievements of the Framework.[62] The top three challenges at the European level for the Framework 2011–2016 identified via the survey are insufficient mainstreaming of Roma inclusion in other policies and instruments, rising discrimination and antiziganism, and weak monitoring of the use of EU funds allocated for Roma inclusion.[63] With regards to the future of the Framework, respondents ranked access to education and employment and fighting discrimination as the top priorities.[64]

In addition to the abovementioned quantitative data, stakeholders contributed their expertise in 27 written submissions providing further details on their take on Roma inclusion in their line of work.[65] These ranged from

---

[60] Ibid., Section 'Figure 2: How do you see the direction of change in the situation of Roma when compared to 2011?'.
[61] EUROPEAN COMMISSION, 'Public Consultation', *supra* note 59, 'Figure 3: To which extent do you consider the following phenomena as a relevant cause of Roma exclusion?'.
[62] Ibid., 'Figure 4: What do you think, have been the main achievements (between 2011 and 2016) at European level?'.
[63] Ibid., 'Figure 5: What do you think have been the main challenges (between 2011 and 2016) at European level?'.
[64] Ibid, 'Which fields should in your opinion become key priorities to which extra effort in form of e.g. human capacities, policy discussions, funds, etc. should be attributed at European and national level?'.
[65] Written contributions were submitted by the European Public Health Alliance (EPHA), Eurocities, Eurochild, the ERRC, Equinet, Inter-Ethnic Initiative for Human Rights (IEI) Foundation, the Office of the United Nations High Commissioner for Human Rights (OHCHR), UNICEF, other IGOs and NGOs, public authorities and individual activists.

topical reports on certain phenomena impairing the effective inclusion of Romani persons⁶⁶ to detailed implementation assessments of action plans for Roma inclusion from public authorities.⁶⁷ Supporting this article's criticism of the reluctance of EU institutions to identify human rights guarantees as the key standards the Framework and national inclusion strategies must include, the Office of the United Nations High Commissioner for Human Rights (OHCHR) stressed in its statement that '[g]aps in achievement to date can be attributed to the at best partial extent to which the human rights framework has been deployed in the design and implementation of policies on Roma inclusion in Europe'.⁶⁸ Without question, the EC should include the substantive inputs delivered by the stakeholders in its final report and consider them as vital information for further developments in its policy.

2.3. IMPLEMENTATION OF THE FRAMEWORK UNTIL 2020 AND BEYOND

It can be deduced from the evaluations and reports above that while the Framework was (formally) widely accepted throughout the Union, political practices in MS heavily diverge from *prima facie* Roma-friendly political approaches (such as NRISs and NRCPs) and rhetoric at EU and national level. International (non-)governmental organisations and Romani advocacy groups alike have stressed that anti-Romani agitation, forced evictions and even violent assaults against Roma settlings occur in parallel to governments' pleas to effectively implement the Framework.⁶⁹ To give an example of the Doublethink at work in the political sphere, the Hungarian government, a driving

---

[66] See e.g. ERRC, 'Written Submission by the European Roma Rights Centre concerning Bulgaria to the Committee on the Elimination of Racial Discrimination, for consideration at its 92nd Session (24 April–12 May 2017)', available at http://www.errc.org/uploads/upload_en/file/bulgaria-cerd-submission-5-april-2017.pdf, last accessed 18.06.2018.

[67] For an impressive example of precise reporting and monitoring of inclusion measures, see SENAT VON BERLIN, 'Umsetzung des Berliner Aktionsplans zur Einbeziehung ausländischer Roma', 29.09.2017, available at https://www.parlament-berlin.de/ados/18/IntArbSoz/vorgang/ias18-0059-v.pdf, last accessed 20.06.2018.

[68] OHCHR, 'Lessons Learned: Views in the Context of Mid-Term Review of Implementation of the EU Framework for National Roma Integration Strategies 2012 – 2020', October 2017, p. 10, available at http://www.europe.ohchr.org/Documents/Press/Lessons%20Learnt%20EU%20Framework%20for%20National%20Roma%20Integration%20Strategies%202012%202020.pdf, last accessed 19.06.2018.

[69] For a very recent report on the 11,309 (!) Romani persons evicted in France from January to December 2017 in breach of recently reformed national equality legislation, see LIGUE DES DROITS DE L'HOMME/ERRC, 'Census of forced evictions in living areas occupied by Roma (or people designated as such) in France', 2018, available at http://www.errc.org/uploads/upload_en/file/france-census-of-forced-evictions-1st-quarter-11-april-2016.pdf, last accessed 19.06.2018.

force in the formalisation of the Framework before 2011, was not only harshly criticised by EC experts (see above, section 2.1) and presently faces infringement proceedings in the context of school segregation, but also seems to be unable to overcome anti-Romani agitation even within its own party ranks: '[A] [...] co-founder and member of the ruling Fidesz party, published an article in [a] newspaper in [...] 2013 in which he asserted that a significant portion of Roma are "animals" that "should not exist".'[70] This obvious lack of political will poses a hard challenge for EU institutions: not only are infringement proceedings against three MS not producing any results, but assessments of the latest reforms in these MS quoted above even point towards deterioration rather than improvements.

One measure proposed by NGOs to assure compliance with EU law is to include 'Roma conditionality' in (general) EU funding mechanisms.[71] While it seems unlikely that such drastic steps are going to be implemented in the next years, another approach could be more promising: since many projects for Romani inclusion are (co-) financed by EU financial instruments, conditionality could be introduced at least for the funds allocated in connection with the Framework and NRISs. Following the European Court of Justice's and the European Ombudsman's (EO's) confirmation of the CFR's applicability in all instances of EU funding in recent decisions on Regulation 1303/2013,[72] financial instruments provide a stable link between EU soft (Framework) and hard law (Racial Equality Directive, CFR, relevant provisions of the Treaties).[73] The EO herein explicitly urged the Commission to 'ensure that all Member State actions, which are funded under the EU cohesion policy, should respect fundamental rights' principles whether or not, strictly speaking, they are actions taken in the implementation of EU law'.[74] EU financial mechanisms also allow for close monitoring of the usage of the allocated funds. In case of non-conformity with EU cohesion policy, according to the EO, MS should also be sanctioned by the EC by initiating infringement proceedings, which would

---

[70] ECRI, 'Report on Hungary (fifth monitoring cycle)', CRI(2015)19, 09.06.2015, para. 31, available at https://www.coe.int/t/dghl/monitoring/ecri/Country-by-country/Hungary/HUN-CbC-V-2015-19-ENG.pdf, last accessed 20.06.2018.

[71] OPEN SOCIETY EUROPEAN POLICY INSTITUTE (2017), 'Assessing the European Dimension', *supra* note 39, p. 25.

[72] Regulation (EU) No 1303/2013 of the European Parliament and of the Council of 17 December 2013 laying down common provisions on the European Regional Development Fund, the European Social Fund [...] and the European Maritime and Fisheries Fund and repealing Council Regulation (EC) No 1083/2006, OJ L 347/320, 20.12.2013.

[73] See CJEU, *Liivimaa Lihaveis MTU*, Case C-562/12, 12.09.2014, ECLI:EU:C:2014:2229; Decision of the European Ombudsman closing her own-initiative inquiry OI/8/2014/AN concerning the European Commission, 11 May 2015; see also M. DAWSWON, *The Governance of EU Fundamental Rights*, Cambridge University Press, Cambridge 2017, p. 117ff.

[74] European Ombudsman, Decision of the European Ombudsman closing her own-initiative inquiry OI/8/2014/AN, *supra* note 73, para. 42.

additionally help victims of rights violations by providing them with strong arguments if they choose to seek compensation.[75] Just in October 2017, the European Parliament went a step further and directly urged the EC to reassess its own activities in the field of Roma integration, stating that

> whereas inadvertent anti-Gypsyism can even be observed in the workings of the EU institutions, as numerous EU programmes and funds that could have a positive impact on the living conditions and life prospects of Roma do not reach them, or they symbolically designate the Roma as one of their beneficiaries, but do not take into account their realities and the discrimination they face[.].[76]

On the same occasion, the EP stressed the importance of more suitable and effective ways of monitoring the usage of EU funds for Romani communities, including the feedback of programme addressees in these evaluations and taking effective action by suspending funds in the case of misuse.[77]

All in all, the quality of European law will have to be measured by its impact. And when the present methods of financial incentives and applying pressure by opening infringement proceedings continuously fail to deliver real change, the EC will have to take the cases at hand to the CJEU. To do so in an effective way, factors already established in front of the ECtHR must be taken into account.

2.4. CASES BEFORE THE ECtHR AND THE CJEU: LESSONS TO BE LEARNED

The umbrella term 'Roma', in court or in the context of policymaking, must be filled with meaning. In a strictly legal sense, such interpretation occurred when the ECtHR substantiated a state obligation to facilitate the *'gypsy [sic!] way of life'* in the context of cases relating to travellers. While indeed protecting a distinct way of life, this wording suggests that the ECtHR was equalising travelling and being Romani as such. This was rightly criticised by scholars:

> The presence of 'manipulated images' creates a distance between legally-protected rights and the social reality. Within a reluctant political and social context, it leads to the inefficiency of the Court's decisions. For instance, being restrictive and dealing with a specific situation – nomadic Roma – they cannot be applicable to the whole Roma minority living in Europe.[78]

---

[75] Ibid., para. 48 (vii).
[76] EUROPEAN PARLIAMENT, Resolution of 25 October 2017 on fundamental rights aspects in Roma integration in the EU: fighting anti-Gypsyism, 2017/2038(INI).
[77] Ibid.
[78] D. FARGET (2012), 'Defining Roma Identity', *supra* note 7, p. 314.

The ECtHR has rightly moved on towards applying a more nuanced approach in Romani cases since coining the 'gypsy way of life'.[79] It will be of paramount importance for the EU not to repeat the jurisdictional solidification of unsubstantiated and misleading outside perceptions of Romani communities in the first place.

Just like the ECtHR in its judgments, the Commission was working with an image of who it was targeting when establishing the Framework. Despite extensive fact-finding efforts, the evaluations quoted above agree that there is still a significant lack of data on the actual situation of Romani persons. There is a real danger of misinformed perceptions fed by stereotypes perpetuating the ineffectiveness of EU policies:

> [M]any Roma surveys have been based on the external identification of who is Roma, quantifying those who others see as Roma rather than those who consider themselves to be so (which would be an inherent characteristic), and so are dependent on social perceptions of Roma-ness (which, ironically, the politicisation of Roma identity seeks to change).[80]

In the future, the assessment of the situation of Romani communities and individuals, in order for policies to be suitable and effective and for judgments to be adequate, has to be sensitive to these persons' very own perceptions and definitions of their identity and life realities. This is true for the EC, but also for the CJEU.

In *CHEZ Razpredeleine Bulgaria AD v Komisia za zashtita ot discriminatsia*, the CJEU followed the ECtHR's assessment that Roma are indeed an ethnic group that requires special protection. An exact group definition was of no importance to the Court herein, and only the accused company's perception of a city district as 'Romani' sufficed to trigger the concept of ethnical/racial discrimination.[81] In further Romani-related cases, the EU judiciary could indeed play an active role in guaranteeing non-discrimination and equal enjoyment of rights for Romani persons. Still, it remains to be seen whether the objective stance taken in *CHEZ* widely dependent on the Court's own assessment will enable Romani representatives to actively define the role of their ethnicity in court. Also, as rightly stressed by Adam Weiss, head of the European Roma Rights Centre (ERRC),[82] the CJEU is not easily accessible for legal questions concerning Roma rights as cases have to be referred to the Court either by national courts

---

[79] Ibid., 314f.
[80] I. LAW and M. KOVATS (2018), *Rethinking Roma, supra* note 9, p. 156.
[81] See C. MCCRUDDEN, 'The New Architecture of EU Equality Law after CHEZ: Did the Court of Justice Reconceptualise Direct and Indirect Discrimination?', (2016) 3 *European Equality Law Review*, p. 5.
[82] A Roma-led international public interest law organisation.

or by the EC. Still, he concludes that strategic litigators had better prepare stable legal arguments for the 'Black Swan' case eventually blowing open the doors of the CJEU, may it be via an infringement proceeding or a preliminary ruling.[83] Lately, Weiss harshly criticised the efficacy of EU hard law in the elimination of racial discrimination:

> [T]he proposed project of eliminating racial inequality in Europe seems to be undermined by Article 18 TFEU's active role in enforcing the equality of European people regardless of their nationality. [...] [T]he struggle against race discrimination is ignored in EU law, in favour of a different anti-discrimination struggle (between national and European identities).[84]

When and if cases of discrimination against Romani persons reach the CJEU, it will be of paramount importance that the CJEU avoids ethnicised misconceptions of 'Romanity' altogether, a chance it should not leave unused. The CJEU's interpretation of EU law in relation to Romani persons and the further development of the Framework could mutually reinforce each other. The rights awareness and access to justice of Romani persons must herein be a core issue addressed within the Framework. Thereby, if and when ethnicised legal arguments appear in front of the Court, they will be the ones of the persons concerned, not of an uninformed majority, and existing initiatives such as the ERRC have the potential to be valuable sources informing CJEU judgments. The European Roma policy is already at risk to be seen as the embodiment of an ethnicisation of issues that are in fact social problems (as also indicated by scholars, see above, section 2).[85]

3. THE NATIONAL-FOREIGNER DIVIDE IN THE CASE OF AUSTRIA

> Why doesn't the EU develop a poverty strategy? Why is there a Roma strategy? Because it's cheaper![86]

Are Roma rights only a social issue as suggested in the quote above? Or is there more to the story? The following paragraphs take into account the opinions of

---

[83] A. WEISS, 'Can we litigate strategically in the Court of Justice of the European Union?', *ERRC Blog*, available at http://www.errc.org/blog/can-we-litigate-strategically-in-the-court-of-justice-of-the-european-union/75, last accessed 18.06.2018.
[84] See A. WEISS (2018), 'Whiteness as International Citizenship', *supra* note 14.
[85] Assessment of an expert in the field of Romani inclusion, Expert Workshop Working Group 4, 'Access to Justice – How Does Advocacy Work Specifically for Roma?', Morning Session Protocol, 14 September 2017, p. 4.
[86] Ibid.

experts that belong to the Austrian Romani minority and NGO representatives working for non-Austrian Romani individuals. These opinions were collected in the form of qualitative interviews and expert workshops that, among other topics, explicitly dealt with the impact of the European Roma policy, the Austrian NRIS targeting the key areas as defined by the Framework and the NRCP.

To begin with, the path to participation and inclusion in Austrian society was all but simple for Austrian Roma. Only about 15% of Austrian Roma survived the holocaust,[87] and in the years after World War II, they faced discrimination, school segregation and years of struggle to be recognised as a victim group of National Socialist terror.[88] Nowadays, however, 'autochthonous' Austrian Roma are a recognised national minority, are therefore politically represented and their activities are subsidised by the state.[89] Romani representatives see themselves in a lead role in (overall) Romani inclusion.[90] Austrian Romani initiatives, organised by minority members themselves, are playing an active role in public life. Their present programmes include afterschool mentoring for students, cultural activities, social work, facilitating the contact with public authorities, media programmes and courses in the minority language 'Romanes'. Representatives therefore claim that there has indeed been change for the better. School segregation against Romani children belonging to the recognised Austrian minority in the federal state Burgenland is not practised anymore, and more and more members of the minority are acquiring higher education, which is in large parts due to the community's own initiatives.[91]

The situation of non-Austrian Romani persons presents itself in a different way: even though many non-Austrian Roma live in cities and towns and are supported by different initiatives[92] to be able to access the education system

---

[87] See G. BAUMGARTNER and F. FREUND (eds.), *Die Burgenland Roma 1945–2000*, Amt der Burgenländischen Landesregierung, Eisenstadt 2004, pp. 54f, 297.

[88] See ibid., pp. 56ff. In the years after World War II, Austrian police authorities continued to report 'gypsy havoc' in the Eastern parts of the country, (former) Romani settlements were not recognised and it was difficult if not impossible for Romani persons to receive financial compensation for their persecution by the National Socialists.

[89] By amendment of para. 1 of the Decree on Minority Advisory Boards – original title: Verordnung über die Volksgruppenbeiräte, BGBl. Nr. 38/1977, last amended by BGBl. Nr. 895/1993.

[90] Expert interview transcript, 23 January 2017, p. 7f.: The interviewee states that he thinks that Austrian Romani initiatives have to persuade Austrian neighbouring countries to include Roma in their societies. Also, according to him, Austrian Romani representatives stand up for Romani persons, no matter where they come from.

[91] Ibid., p. 23f.

[92] E.g., the ecclesiastical organisations VinziWerke and Caritas serve as a contact point for victims of discrimination, offer empowerment workshops and language courses, but also provide emergency accommodation for persons in need. The network Bettellobby offers free legal counselling in cases of discrimination.

and the labour market, the issue of begging in public spaces has dominated the political and media rhetoric. The term 'Roma' is herein often equated with beggars.[93] These discourses have impacted and still impact local and regional policies that include bans on begging. In the past years, general bans on begging passed by local and municipal law- and decision-makers have been under the scrutiny of the Austrian Constitutional Court that held the right to freedom of speech violated by general bans on begging within city areas in a series of decisions.[94] Sectoral bans on begging, for example in highly frequented public spaces defined by municipality councils, however, are still prescribed by federal laws.[95] Furthermore, political confrontations at the local level show, to put it mildly, an alarming lack of awareness: after a series of arson attacks on tents of travelling non-Austrian Romani families in 2016, city politicians on the one hand condemned violence against minorities, but on the other hand, a statement issued by the local mayor indicated that the arson victims had exploited their children for begging. Other politicians denounced the assaulted persons as 'criminal gangs', even though no criminal proceedings had been lodged against them.[96]

Events at the Austrian NRCP in the form of 'Roma Dialogue Platforms' are a chance to provide counter-narratives and seek to engage Romani representatives in a dialogue with political and administrative decision-makers. Unlike national minority laws, Dialogue Platforms do not differentiate between 'autochthonous' Austrian and non-Austrian Roma. Experts positively emphasise that EU-funding schemes do not differentiate between recognised national minorities (Austrian Roma) and foreigners. They are therefore accessible for institutions working with non-Austrian Roma.[97] At the same time, the duration of EU-funding has been criticised as too short to be sustainable.[98] Recent meetings of the Dialogue Platform have, *inter alia*, dealt with EU-citizens migrating as Notreisende ('plight travellers').[99] However, the discussions at Dialogue Platform meetings and the measures combatting stereotypes and racism against Roma prescribed by the Austrian NRIS have not eradicated anti-Romani racism, as a recent

---

[93] For a well-founded overview of these discourses, see S. BENEDIK, B. TIEFENBACHER and H. ZETTELBAUER, *Die imaginierte „Bettlerflut"*, Drava, Klagenfurt 2013.
[94] E.g. in the Austrian Constitutional Court cases G155/10, 30.06.2012 and G64/11, 06.12.2012. For an anticipatory scientific analysis of the judgment and issue as such, see: C. BEZEMEK, 'Einen Schilling zum Telefonieren … – Bettelverbote im Lichte freier Meinungsäußerung', (2011) 19 *Journal für Rechtspolitik*, p. 279.
[95] E.g. Steiermärkisches Landes-Sicherheitsgesetz, LGBl. Nr. 24/2005, para. 3a; Salzburger Landessicherheitsgesetz, LGBl Nr 57/2009, para. 29.
[96] See ROMANO CENTRO, 'Antiziganismus in Österreich – Falldokumentation 2015–2017', December 2017, p. 10, available at http://www.romano-centro.org/downloads/Antiziganismus_in_Oesterreich_2015-2017_web.pdf, last accessed 19.06.2018.
[97] Expert interview transcript, 5 December 2016, p. 8.
[98] Ibid.
[99] 18th Roma Dialogue Platform held in Vienna, 25 November 2016.

report compiled by the Romano Centro shows: from 2015–2017, the NGO documented 55 cases throughout Austria.[100] Furthermore, NGO representatives reported cases of confiscation of begging persons' money without any legal grounds whatsoever,[101] transgression of competences by City Guards[102] and Romani families being sent to neighbouring states, pressured by authorities and without due process.[103] Moreover, legal advisers working pro-bono for begging persons and/or in anti-discrimination reported that there is a lack of access to justice for victims of discriminatory treatment and human rights violations due to complicated provisions in national antidiscrimination law and a lack of rights awareness.[104]

Summing up, there is a clear-cut differentiation in the real-life experiences of Austrian and non-Austrian Roma. With Romani EU citizens at risk of being expulsed from Austria without due process – just like from other EU MS – European citizenship has clearly failed to effectively grant freedom of movement, and the migrant-citizen dichotomy is ever more prevalent for those additionally affected by racial discrimination. A lack of efficacy of NRISs is obvious from the evaluations and statements cited in the prior sections in this article. Even in Austria with its well-established and legally recognised 'autochthonous' Romani minority, the integration of the very persons that ought to be targeted by the Framework, those at the margins of society coming from 'weak' economic backgrounds, fails. These individuals and groups are those without Austrian citizenship, and with the Framework aimed at the development of 'national' strategies, the (temporary) movement of persons across EU internal frontiers as Notreisende ('plight travellers') remains virtually unaddressed, even though the EU would be *the* forum to solve this trans-/supranational issue. As European integration will not lead to equal distribution of wealth throughout the MS any time soon (if at all) the movement of persons living in poverty to other MS is a reality that the EU has to effectively address. Lacking legitimacy of the Framework would indeed (further) hamper the effective implementation of equal rights for Roma, and such lack is palpable in scholars' statements: 'The overall persistence of the very problems that [European Roma] policy seeks to address means that this politicisation can be understood as effectively a form of racism.'[105]

Some positive developments in Austria, however, have been highlighted by Romano Centro: higher interest and sensitivity for the issue of antiziganism

---

[100] ROMANO CENTRO (2017), 'Antiziganismus 2015–2017', *supra* note 96.
[101] Expert interview transcript, 18 November 2016, p. 1.
[102] Ibid., p. 4.
[103] Expert Workshop Working Group 4 (2017), 'Access to Justice', *supra* note 85.
[104] Ibid., p. 6f.
[105] I. Law and M. Kovats (2018) *Rethinking Roma*, *supra* note 9, p. 161.

(the term used for anti-Romani racism by the NGO) is palpable in Austria according to the NGO.[106] This reflects the latest EC surveys' findings (see 2.2.). This sensitivity, just like at the EU level, has to be translated into further actions directed at the actual needs of Romani populations in Austria and equipped with sufficient national and EU funding.[107]

4. CONCLUSION

Taking into account the evaluations of the EU Roma policy, the local cases in Austria and the opinions expressed by local Romani representatives, it is obvious that EU Roma policies need further refinement. Lack of data, unclear goals in NRISs, ineffective use of national and EU funds and, in the end, missing political will are persistent issues to be solved by EU institutions and the MS. Márton Rövid's 2009 vision of an emerging Romani middle class and a self-empowered Romani movement able to trigger effective change effectively supported by EU institutions is still largely absent throughout Europe. Overall, as academia and experts in the field have stated, the problem of Romani inclusion is not primarily, as one could deduce from the formulation of the policy instruments, an ethnical, but a social problem. The EU's inability to remedy social inequalities is not only obvious in the case of Romani communities, but a problem closely linked with larger discrepancies of EU laws and national practice, as well as economic realities. The failure of the integration of Roma in the EU MS therefore represents overall failures in European integration: the legal guarantees provided by EU citizenship, the CFR and the Racial Equality Directive do not live up to the proclaimed 'ever closer Union'.

Ironically, discrimination against Roma is still overwhelmingly high in the very same countries whose governments have initially been supportive of the European Roma Policy: Hungary, Slovakia and the Czech Republic are still facing infringement proceedings. Exactly these MS receive a big portion of the funds allocated for Romani inclusion via EU mechanisms. A monitoring procedure on the spending of funds equipped with the possibility of infringement proceedings as proposed by the EO to ensure accountability might at first sight look promising. However, if not even the Racial Equality Directive's breach is referred to the CJEU by the EC, it is highly possible that juridical control of financing mechanisms would suffer the same fate. In the obvious absence of sufficient political will to bring about true change for Romani persons in the

---

[106] See ROMANO CENTRO (2017), 'Antiziganismus 2015–2017', supra note 96, p. 3.
[107] According to an expert currently working in an EU-funded project, the acquisition of EU funds for Romani projects itself can be difficult, but moreover, the administration of granted funds is very demanding for initiatives. See Expert interview transcript, 5 December 2016, p. 8.

EU, it is about time the EU judiciary was given the chance to clarify the MS' obligations in relation to racial equality.

Adam Weiss' assessment that nationality discrimination trumps racial discrimination in EU law must be complemented: non-Austrian Romani persons are often hindered to even bring up the legal argument of their EU citizenship. Therefore, both grounds of discrimination, racial and national, are mutually reinforcing in cases of migration of Romani persons within the EU. The issue of social equality for marginalised groups transcends the national borders of EU MS, and Romani inclusion can only truly flourish when EU institutions, together with the MS, arrive at a coherent strategy. Albeit having exchanged the term 'gypsies' for 'Roma', EU Roma policy still mirrors the language IGO efforts of the 20th century and needs to transform itself into an effectively usable and enforceable tool, incorporating the language of human rights rather than of economic growth and competitiveness of markets. By stressing the full range of human rights that must be guaranteed for Romani persons just like for everyone else in the EU and by fostering Romani empowerment rather than continuously referring to the historic and present economic marginalisation of Romani persons, general progress towards the effective equality of EU citizens can be achieved. Bottom-up movements, as shown in the case of Austria, can be crucial driving forces in this process. However, the persistent discrimination against non-Austrian Romani persons could be seen as a mere relocation of old prejudice to different victims who still lack even basic conditions to gain access to education, the labour market and justice. Support for Roma often comes from temporarily funded or even pro bono initiatives, which hampers sustainable strategies. When given sufficient funding and political support, these existing initiatives could become the crystallisation point of future Romani associations building agency and empowering minority members, not only in Austria, but throughout the Union. Taken seriously by EU and MS institutions, Romani associations could then also provide the solution to the problem of misinformed policies by passing on first hand insight to the difficulties Romani persons still face in Europe. To enable such development, EU Roma policy must be embedded in a common understanding of MS and EU institutions of a Union-wide social policy respecting, protecting and – in the end – fulfilling human rights.

THE EU GUIDELINES ON FREEDOM OF RELIGION OR BELIEF AT THEIR FIFTH ANNIVERSARY

Implementation Lagging Behind?

Adina PORTARU

1. Introduction 194
2. The EU Guidelines on FoRB 195
   2.1. What are the Goals of the EU Guidelines on FoRB? 201
   2.2. Review of Implementation 203
3. Recommendations 207
   3.1. Fostering Civic and Inter-Institutional Cooperation 207
   3.2. Consolidate and Strengthen the Role of the EU Special Envoy on FoRB Outside the EU in the Implementation of the EU Guidelines on FoRB 208
   3.3. Increase Transparency of Processes 209
   3.4. Increase and Intensify Training Programmes on the EU Guidelines on FoRB 209
4. Conclusion 209

ABSTRACT

When the European Union (EU) Guidelines on Freedom of Religion or Belief (FoRB) were adopted in 2013, they were applauded as an advancement of EU commitments to FoRB. The Guidelines sparked the hopes of both academics and practitioners in the field that FoRB would be placed higher on the EU agenda.

Although five years have passed since the adoption of the EU Guidelines on Freedom of Religion or Belief (EU Guidelines on FoRB), and despite the EU's commitment to evaluate implementation three years after their adoption, the Working Party on Human Rights in the Council (COHOM) has not produced any publicly available document to date. Such a situation lends itself to two hypotheses: either (a) reports on the implementation do exist institutionally, but are not made public (in which case, issues of transparency and weak inter-institutional and civic dialogue arise), or (b) no report on the implementation has been drawn up (in which case COHOM is in breach of its commitments set out by the EU Guidelines on FoRB).

This article will show that, in either case, the EU is not respecting its commitments in the area of FoRB. The research will also put forward recommendations on how the EU could make better and more efficient use of the EU Guidelines on FoRB.

1. INTRODUCTION

The Maastricht Treaty, adopted in 1992, enshrined human rights into treaty obligations of the Union and of Member States. Although the Maastricht Treaty does not bind the Union to a specific list of human rights, it sets the ground for subsequent treaties to articulate and crystallise the human rights obligations incumbent on the Union and on Member States.[1] More visibly, the Treaty of Lisbon enshrined the EU's commitment to promoting and securing human rights and fundamental freedoms in its external action, stating that the EU:

> Shall be guided by the principles which have inspired its own creation [...] and which it seeks to advance in the wider world: democracy, the rule of law, the universality and indivisibility of human rights and fundamental freedoms, respect for human dignity, the principles of equality and solidarity, and respect for the principles of the United Nations Charter and international law.[2]

It also commits the EU to a 'high degree of cooperation' intended to bring coherence and consistency between the internal and external actions of the EU.[3]

The EU adopted in 2012 the EU Strategic Framework and Action Plan on Human Rights and Democracy (2012 Strategic Framework and Action Plan on Human Rights and Democracy), which constitutes 'the backbone of the Union's external action on human rights'.[4] The 2012 Strategic Framework and Action Plan describes the ambition of the EU to become a global human

---

[1] E.F. DEFEIS, 'Human Rights, the European Union, and the Treaty Route: From Maastricht to Lisbon', (2017) 35(5) *Fordham International Law Journal*, pp. 1207–1230.
[2] Article 21.1 Treaty on European Union (TEU) 2016/C 202/1.
[3] Article 21.2 TEU.
[4] J. WOUTERS and M. HERMEZ, 'EU Guidelines on Human Rights as a Foreign Policy Instrument: An Assessment', Leuven Centre for Global Governance Studies, 2016, available at https://ghum.kuleuven.be/ggs/publications/working_papers/2016/170woutershermez, last accessed 29.05.2018, p. 4.

rights player on the international scene, in that it sets out principles, objectives and priorities in the area of human rights. The 2012 Strategic Framework and Action Plan, which ran from 2012–2015, was followed by the second Action Plan on Human Rights and Democracy (second Action Plan on Human Rights and Democracy) which is currently applicable and runs from 2015–2019. As is clear from its very title 'Keeping Human Rights at the Heart of the EU Agenda', the second Action Plan on Human Rights and Democracy seeks to strengthen the human rights dimension of EU external action. It specifically welcomes the Joint Communication 'Keeping human rights at the heart of the EU agenda', as presented by the High Representative of the European Union for Foreign Affairs and Security Policy and the European Commission, and it reaffirms 'the EU's commitment to promote and protect human rights and to support democracy worldwide'.[5]

Having set the larger context for human rights in the EU, the following sections will analyse EU commitments in the area of FoRB and will put forward recommendations on how the EU could make better and more efficient use of the EU Guidelines on FoRB.

2. THE EU GUIDELINES ON FoRB

The EU Guidelines on FoRB[6] complement prior EU commitments in this area, referring both to the internal and external actions of the EU, dating back to Declaration No. 11 on the status of churches and non-confessional organisations, which was annexed to the Treaty of Amsterdam.[7] This states:

> The European Union respects and does not prejudice the status under national law of churches and religious associations or communities in the Member States.
>
> The European Union equally respects the status of philosophical and non-confessional organisations.

Additionally, Article 17 of the Treaty on the Functioning of the EU provides for the first time a legal basis for the dialogue between EU institutions and

---

[5] Council of the European Union, Council Conclusions on the Action Plan on Human Rights and Democracy 2015–2019, 10897/15 of 20.07.2015, para. 1.
[6] Council of the European Union, EU Guidelines on the Promotion and Protection of Freedom of Religion or Belief, Foreign Affairs Council meeting, 24.06.2013.
[7] Treaty of Amsterdam amending the Treaty on European Union, the Treaties Establishing the European Communities and Certain Related Act [1997], Declaration No. 11 on the Status of Churches and Non-confessional Organisations, OJ C 340, 10.11.1997. For more, see R. GEIGER, D.E. KHAN and M. KOTZUR (eds.), *European Union Treaties: A Commentary*, C.H. Beck Hart, Oxford, 2015, pp. 234–236.

churches and religious associations or communities, and philosophical and non-confessional organisations. It reads as follows:

1. The Union respects and does not prejudice the status under national law of churches and religious associations or communities in the Member States.
2. The Union equally respects the status under national law of philosophical and non-confessional organisations.
3. Recognising their identity and their specific contribution, the Union shall maintain an open, transparent and regular dialogue with these churches and organisations.[8]

FoRB is also recognised and protected by the European Convention on Human Rights (ECHR), a Council of Europe (CoE) convention aimed at protecting human rights and fundamental freedoms within the Council of Europe Member States' jurisdictions. Article 9(1) states that 'everyone has the right to freedom of thought, conscience and religion', which also includes the right to manifest religion or belief 'in practice and observance'. The right to manifest one's religion or belief is not absolute, and is subject to certain limitations, set out by Article 9(2) ECHR.

Explicit protection for FoRB exists in the Charter of Fundamental Rights of the European Union (EU Charter), which became legally binding on all EU Member States when the Treaty of Lisbon entered into force in 2009. Article 10 repeats language from Article 9(1) of the ECHR, stating:

> Everyone has the right to freedom of thought, conscience and religion. This right includes freedom to change religion or belief and freedom, either alone or in community with others and in public or private, to manifest religion or belief, in worship, teaching, practice and observance.

Additionally, according to Article 6(3) of the Treaty on the European Union, the EU Charter shall be interpreted with 'due regard' to the Explanations related to the Charter. Regarding Article 10, the Explanations seek to clarify the relationship between the right to freedom of thought, conscience and religion enshrined in the EU Charter, on the one hand, and Article 9 of the European Convention on Human Rights, on the other hand: 'The right guaranteed in

---

[8] For an analysis of how Article 17 dialogue with churches and religious associations or communities, and philosophical and non-confessional organisations is carried out and to what extent the requirements of openness, transparency and regularity are respected, see A. PORTARU, 'Europe in Search of a Soul? Article 17 TFEU and Its Functioning', (2017) 37 *Nottingham Law Journal*, pp. 37–55.

para. 1 corresponds to the right guaranteed in Article 9 ECHR and, in accordance with Article 52 (3) of the Charter, has the same meaning and scope.'[9]

The EU more recently demonstrated its commitment to FoRB in its external action by creating a Special Envoy for the promotion of FoRB outside the EU. The creation of this position was announced on 6 May 2016 by the President of the European Commission, on the occasion of the awarding of the 'Charlemagne Prize' to Pope Francis, at the Vatican.[10] The EU Special Envoy currently operates as 'special advisor' to the Commissioner for International Cooperation and Development, Neven Mimica. The mandate, which runs for one year each term with the possibility of a renewal, is clearly more limited, weaker and narrower in scope than that of EU Special Representatives.[11] For example, the EU Special Envoy on FoRB only has two assistants, while each EU Special Representative since 2011 has had between 4 and 17 members of staff operating full time.[12]

The human rights commitments of the EU are not only enshrined in treaties, strategic frameworks and action plans, but also in a number of instruments bearing different legal force, such as Council Conclusions on different human rights-related matters, recommendations, European Parliament resolutions, reports, and guidelines.[13]

EU guidelines are non-binding documents on various substantive or procedural rights that the EU seeks to mainstream.[14] They are practical

---

[9] Explanations Relating to the Charter of Fundamental Rights, 2007/C 303/02, Explanation on Article 10.

[10] EUROPEAN COMMISSION, 'President Juncker Appoints the First Special Envoy for the Promotion of Freedom of Religion or Belief outside the European Union', Press Release, IP/16/1670, 06.05.2016, available at http://europa.eu/rapid/press-release_IP-16-1670_en.htm, last accessed 29.05.2018.

[11] For a critical perspective on the currently limited and weak mandate of the EU Special Envoy, see S. KUBY, 'The EU Special Envoy for the Promotion of Freedom of Religion or Belief outside the EU: Mandate, Mission, Perspective', in W. BENEDEK, M.C. KETTEMANN, R. KLAUSHOFER, K. LUKAS and M. NOWAK (eds.), *European Yearbook on Human Rights 2017*, NWV Neuer Wissenschaftlicher Verlag, Vienna 2017, pp. 91–102.

[12] For other data as a comparison between the EU Special Envoy on FoRB and other EU Special Representatives, see S. KUBY (2017), 'The EU Special Envoy for the Promotion of Freedom of Religion or Belief', *supra* note 11, and S. KUBY, 'The EU Needs a Special Representative for Freedom of Religion or Belief', *Euractiv*, 24.04.2017, available at https://www.euractiv.com/section/freedom-of-thought/video/the-eu-needs-a-special-representative-for-freedom-of-religion-or-belief, last accessed 29.05.2018.

[13] See, for example, Council of the European Union, Council Conclusions on Freedom of Religion or Belief, 2973rd General Affairs Council meeting of 16 November 2009, available at www.ceceurope.org/wp-content/uploads/2015/08/CofEU_111190.pdf, last accessed 29.05.2018 and Council of the European Union, Council Conclusions on Intolerance, Discrimination and Violence on the Basis of Religion or Belief, 3069th Foreign Affairs Council meeting of 21 February 2011, available at www.ceceurope.org/wp-content/uploads/2015/08/CofEU_119404.pdf, last accessed 29.05.2018.

[14] The EU Guidelines are complemented with the EU's human rights country strategies, which, in their preamble, always make reference to the relevant guidelines.

and rather detailed instructions on how to implement a larger policy in the various layers of the EU, including its representations around the world. While there is discretion regarding the issuing of guidelines, the reasonable expectation is that they are adopted depending on the urgency and relevance of the matter.

There are 11 guidelines dealing with human rights. Some were adopted before the Strategic Framework, and others were based on the first Action Plan on human rights and democracy, such was the case of the EU Guidelines on FoRB, which were adopted only in 2013. Five out of the 11 Guidelines were revised between 2008 and 2014 (see table). No new guidelines are foreseen in the new action plan 2015–2019.

Table 1. EU Human Rights Guidelines

Full Title	Date of Adoption	Date of Revision
Guidelines to EU policy towards third countries on the death penalty	29 June 1998	12 April 2013
Guidelines to EU policy towards third countries on torture and other cruel, inhuman or degrading treatment or punishment	9 April 2001	18 April 2008 20 March 2012
EU Guidelines on human rights dialogues with third countries	13 December 2001	19 January 2009
EU Guidelines on children and armed conflict	4 December 2003	5 June 2008
Ensuring protection – European Union Guidelines on human rights defenders	2 June 2004	8 December 2008
European Union Guidelines on promoting compliance with international humanitarian law (IHL)	5 December 2005	1 December 2009
EU Guidelines on the promotion and protection of the rights of the child	10 December 2007	NA
EU Guidelines on violence against women and girls and combating all forms of discrimination against them	8 December 2008	NA
EU Guidelines on the promotion and protection of freedom of religion or belief	24 June 2013	NA
Guidelines to promote and protect the enjoyment of all human rights by lesbian, gay, bisexual, transgender and intersex (LGBTI) persons	24 June 2013	NA
EU Human Rights Guidelines on freedom of expression online and offline	12 May 2014	NA
EU Guidelines on non-discrimination	Currently under debate in the Council	NA

Source: J. WOUTERS and M. HERMEZ, 'EU Guidelines on Human Rights as a Foreign Policy Instrument: An Assessment', Leuven Centre for Global Governance Studies, 2016, available at https://ghum.kuleuven.be/ggs/publications/working_papers/2016/170woutershermez, last accessed 09.08.2018.

The guidelines generally enshrine practical information on how EU officials, diplomats on the ground, Member States and non-EU countries should safeguard, protect and implement human rights more efficiently and coherently. They represent, as the name suggests, guidelines, toolkits and directions on how to achieve the standards of human rights protection contained in the guidelines by setting forth priority areas, instruments and timelines to protect and promote substantive and procedural human rights.

Although the main focus and sphere of application of the guidelines reside in the external action,[15] it would be inaccurate to present them as wholly external instruments on human rights matters. The guidelines have an internal dimension as well: they are not only addressed to EU officials dealing with non-EU Member States, but also target EU Member States by illustrating common grounds and standards to uphold, protect and secure human rights.[16] In doing so, EU guidelines seek to bring coherence, within EU competence, between the internal and external actions and to 'embody European unity as regards major principles'.[17]

Despite not having legally binding force, the guidelines are the EU's steering instruments to mainstream the external dimension. The manner in which the guidelines are adopted, following an intricate drafting and adoption process, also indicates that they do carry strong political value. They are initially negotiated within the Council at the working group level, usually in COHOM.[18] When the first draft is finalised, Member States can react in writing. Further discussions and negotiations are held within the responsible Council working group, until a compromise is found in the wording of the text. Subsequently, the final draft is sent to the Political and Security Committee for endorsement, and then to the Committee of the Permanent Representatives of the Governments of the Member States to the EU (COREPER), which is the Council's main preparatory body.[19] The final stage of approval is done by the Foreign Affairs

---

[15] The external dimension of the Guidelines is evidenced by the fact that all the Guidelines, except for the Guidelines on Promoting Compliance with international humanitarian law, have been developed by COHOM, which is the working party on human rights of the Foreign Affairs Council.

[16] J. WOUTERS and M. HERMEZ (2015), 'EU Guidelines on Human Rights', *supra* note 4, p. 7.

[17] F. FORET, 'How the European External Action Service Deals with Religion through Religious Freedom', EU Diplomacy Paper 2017, p. 12, available at https://www.coleurope.eu/system/files_force/research-paper/edp_7_2017_foret.pdf?download=1, last accessed 29.05.2018.

[18] The only exception to the Guidelines being negotiated in COHOM are the European Union Guidelines on promoting compliance with international humanitarian law, which were finalised in COJUR.

[19] COREPER is not an EU-decision making body. Its role and different settings are found in Article 240 (1) of the Treaty on the Functioning of the EU.

Council, a forum that brings together foreign affairs ministers of EU Member States.[20]

The incipient conceptual stages of the EU Guidelines on FoRB date back to the adoption of the 2012 EU Strategic Framework and Action Plan on Human Rights and Democracy. Adopting the Action Plan, the Council, the European External Action Service (EEAS) and Member States committed to promoting FoRB in their external action. A particular focus was put on participation within multilateral organisations, such as the UN, the Organization for Security and Cooperation in Europe (OSCE) and CoE, and in drafting and further developing the EU Guidelines on FoRB.[21] The goal was not only on spelling out FoRB commitments and engagements on the part of the EU, but also on having a practical toolkit on their implementation.

Shortly after the adoption of the 2012 EU Strategic Framework and Action Plan on Human Rights and Democracy, the EU started to draft guidelines on FoRB and engaging EU officials, the European Parliament, religious, philosophical and non-confessional organisations in the process.[22] The first draft of the guidelines was produced by the EEAS. On 13 June 2013, the European Parliament adopted a recommendation to the Council on Guidelines about the Promotion and Protection of Religion or Belief.[23]

The EU Foreign Affairs Council adopted the EU Guidelines on Freedom of Religion or Belief on 24 June 2013. Churches, religious associations and organisations, and humanists welcomed the adoption of the Guidelines, while expressing different viewpoints. The International Humanist and Ethical Union particularly appreciated how the Guidelines robustly protect free speech, by

---

[20] The fact that the Guidelines are adopted under the Common Foreign and Security Policy of the EU, means that the Court of Justice of the EU generally has no jurisdiction.

[21] For example, on 26 February 2018 the Council of the European Union adopted the Council Conclusions on EU Priorities in UN Human Rights Fora in 2018, stating that 'The EU will continue to promote freedom of religion or belief for all persons, strongly oppose religious intolerance, and strive for greater protection of persons belonging to religious and other minorities across the world against discrimination, persecution and violence. *It will pursue its initiatives on freedom of religion or belief at the Human Rights Council and UNGA with a particular focus on the implementation of the commitments previously undertaken.* The EU will continue to oppose worldwide all forms of racism, racial discrimination, xenophobia and related intolerance. It will continue to promote the principles of equality and nondiscrimination in UN fora and in its external action'. (emphasis added) The Council Conclusions on EU Priorities in UN Human Rights Fora in 2018, available at http://data.consilium.europa.eu/doc/document/ST-6346-2018-INIT/en/pdf, para. 23, last accessed 29.05.2018.

[22] European Parliament Working Group on Freedom of Religion or Belief, 'Annual Report. Conclusions and Recommendations regarding the Situation of Freedom of Religion or Belief in the World', 2013, available at www.religiousfreedom.eu/wp-content/uploads/2014/02/EPWG-2013-Report-Final-for-printing.pdf, p. 15, last accessed 29.05.2018.

[23] Recommendation 2013/2082(INI) of the European Parliament to the Council on the Draft EU Guidelines on the Promotion and Protection of Freedom of Religion or Belief, 13.06.2013.

putting forward checks and balances. They were nonetheless concerned with the EU's stance of not abolishing blasphemy laws.[24] The European Evangelical Alliance 'applauded EU major step' in adopting the EU Guidelines on FoRB by stating that 'promoting freedom of religion is not only a moral or legal obligation, but also a strategic political choice'.[25] The Catholic Church in the EU (COMECE) welcomed the adoption of the Guidelines, but identified three areas of improvement: adding a collective element to FoRB (replacing a focus on individualism), parental rights regarding institutional education, and a more balanced relationship between anti-discrimination and FoRB.[26]

2.1. WHAT ARE THE GOALS OF THE EU GUIDELINES ON FoRB?

The EU Guidelines on FoRB set out eight priority areas, in which the EU reaffirms its determination to promote – in its external human rights policy – freedom of religion or belief as a right to be exercised by everyone everywhere, based on the principles of equality, non-discrimination and universality. Through its external policy instruments, 'the EU intends to help prevent and address violations of this right in a timely, consistent and coherent manner'.[27]

The specific priority areas developed by the Guidelines are the following:

- Investigate and punish acts of violence;
- Freedom of expression;
- Promotion of respect for diversity and tolerance;
- Discrimination;
- Changing or leaving one's religion or belief;
- Manifestation of religion or belief;
- Support and protection for human rights defenders including individual cases;
- Support for – and engagement with – civil society.

---

[24] International Humanist and Ethical Union, 'Humanists in Europe Welcome New EU Guidelines on Freedom of Religion or Belief', 26.06.2013, available at http://iheu.org/humanists-europe-welcome-new-eu-guidelines-freedom-religion-or-belief, last accessed 29.05.2018.

[25] European Evangelical Alliance, 'EEA Applauds as EU Marks Major Step in Adopting Religious Freedom Guidelines', 14.06.2013, available at http://www.europeanea.org/index.php/eea-applauds-as-eu-marks-major-step-in-adopting-religious-freedom-guidelines, last accessed 29.05.2018.

[26] Catholic Voices Comment, 'EU's Religious Freedom Guidelines Need Improving in Key Areas', 25.06.2013, available at https://cvcomment.org/2013/06/25/eus-religious-freedom-guidelines-offer-room-for-improvement-in-key-areas, last accessed 29.05.2018.

[27] EU Guidelines on FoRB, para. 6.

As guidelines represent 'the basis for policy and action on the ground',[28] the EU Guidelines on FoRB provides a toolkit for action,[29] consisting of:

- Monitoring, assessing and reporting especially through EU local presence and capacities;
- Demarches and public diplomacy at the level of the HR/VP and EU special Representative for Human Rights and heads of delegation. The EU Guidelines on FoRB also make links with other Guidelines;[30]
- Political dialogues with non-EU Member States and regional organisations;
- EU and Member States visits;
- Use of external financial instruments, especially within the European Instrument for Democracy and Human Rights (EIDHR), and country-based support schemes;
- Training for staff in the field and at headquarters. Such trainings are made 'in coordination with Member States and in cooperation with civil society including churches and religious associations, philosophical and non-confessional organisations';[31]
- Promoting FoRB in multilateral fora. The EU Guidelines on FoRB commit to the promotion of initiatives at multilateral and international levels and contribute to the implementation of freedom of religion commitments at the UN through resolutions, the Universal Period Review of the UN Human Rights Council, recommendations and the monitoring of the implementation thereof as considered appropriate.[32]

Additionally, the EU Guidelines on FoRB provide that the EU will:

> [...] promote initiatives at the level of OSCE and the Council of Europe and contribute to better implementation of commitments in the area of freedom of religion or belief. Regular exchanges will be organized with these organisations. Particular attention shall be paid to engagement with OSCE and Council of Europe countries that are not EU Member States.[33]

The EU Guidelines on FoRB also target multilateral fora as frameworks for advancing FoRB. To this end, the EU commits to further strengthen its cooperation with the Office of the United Nations High Commissioner for

---

[28] J. WOUTERS and M. HERMEZ (2015), 'EU Guidelines on Human Rights', *supra* note 4, p. 18.
[29] For more information generally about the commitments contained by the EU, see E.M. LASSEN, 'EU Guidelines on the Promotion and Protection of Freedom of Religion or Belief', (2014) 14 *European Yearbook on Human Rights*, pp. 173–183.
[30] EU Guidelines on FoRB, para. 27.
[31] Ibid., para. 67.
[32] Ibid., paras. 58–66.
[33] Ibid., para. 65.

Human Rights and the UN Special Rapporteur on freedom of religion or belief, the Venice Commission, the Office for Democratic Institutions and Human Rights, and the OSCE.

2.2. REVIEW OF IMPLEMENTATION

While the commitments and human rights mainstreaming contained by the EU Guidelines represent a much-needed political tool to ensure internal and external coherence in human rights policies, they need to be implement efficiently, fully and consistently. In order to do so, regular implementation reports are essential, as are provided for by both the second Action Plan on Human Rights and Democracy and the EU Guidelines.

The Second Action Plan on Human Rights and Democracy specifically mentions that it seeks to strengthen the implementation of the relevant EU Guidelines.[34] In order to do so, it sets two specific milestones. First, it mentions that by 2017, it aims at 'intensify[ing] awareness raising and dissemination of EU Guidelines and related guidance documents as well as training of staff in EU Delegations and Member State Embassies, including at the level of Ambassadors'. Second, it states that by 2016, the European Commission, the EEAS and Member States:

> [...] systematise reporting on the Guidelines' implementation and introduce logbooks on EU action on specific thematic issues in partner countries, to ensure more systematic follow-up to individual cases and to promote regular exchange of best practice in Guidelines' implementation.[35]

The mid-term review of the second Action Plan, issued in 2017,[36] tackles the progress made in the area of FoRB since the adoption of the second action plan (two years). Regarding freedom of religion, one of the 'eight most pressing human rights issues to be addressed', the mid-term review states that:

> [...] the EU has continued its previous actions, including by issuing public statements and demarches, raising freedom of expression and FoRB during human rights dialogues whenever relevant, and engaging actively on individual cases. The EU's action in multilateral fora was also consistent: it supported HRC resolutions on the safety of journalists and the promotion, protection and enjoyment of human rights on the internet, as well as the UNGA resolution on 'the right to privacy in the digital age'. In March 2016, the EU presented a resolution extending the mandate of the

---

[34] Council of the European Union, Council Conclusions on the Action Plan on Human Rights and Democracy 2015–2019, 10897/15 of 20.07.2015, p. 10.
[35] Ibid., p. 28.
[36] Council of the European Union, EU Action Plan on Human Rights and Democracy (2015–2019): Mid-Term Review June 2017, 11138/17 of 07.07.2017.

Special Rapporteur on Freedom of Religion or Belief for three years [...] As concerns the promotion of interreligious dialogue, which was a specific priority of the Action Plan, in May 2016 the President of the European Commission created the new position of Special Envoy for the promotion of freedom of religion or belief outside the EU, which strongly supports the achievement of this objective.[37]

The mid-term review also restates the EU commitment 'to monitor continuously the implementation of its guidelines, also based on the input of civil society organisations, including social partners'.[38]

However, in addition, the Guidelines themselves have a special section that highlights their implementation in clear terms:

> COHOM and its Task Force on Freedom of religion or belief will support the implementation of the Guidelines while involving, when appropriate, geographic Council working groups. It will develop additional guidance for action for EU missions, in particular regarding systemic issues and individual cases. It will adopt 'lines to take' documents on key questions and topical issues when necessary.
>
> COHOM will evaluate the implementation of these guidelines *after a period of three years*, inter alia on the basis of the reports submitted by Heads of Mission and after consultation with civil society and relevant academic experts. Consultation of civil society should involve human rights defenders, NGOs including domestic and international human rights and women's organisations. This consultation will involve churches and religious associations, philosophical and non-confessional organisations in the context of the open, transparent and regular dialogue held under Article 17 of the Treaty on the Functioning of the European Union.[39]

In contrast to the other guidelines, the EU Guidelines on FoRB set out a clear obligation to produce a report on their implementation, unlike, for example, the EU Guidelines on Freedom of Expression Online and Offline, which provide only a mere possibility of a report on the implementation.[40] Additionally, the EU Guidelines on FoRB provide for a possibility of review.[41] Lastly, the EU Guidelines on FoRB are very precise about the time for the implementation

---

[37] Ibid., pp. 8–9.
[38] Council of the European Union, EU Action Plan on Human Rights and Democracy (2015–2019), p. 23.
[39] EU Guidelines on FoRB, paras. 69–71 (emphasis added).
[40] See Council of the European Union, EU Guidelines on Freedom of Expression Online and Offline, Foreign Affairs Council meeting, Brussels, 12.05.2014. In para. 71 it is only stated that 'COHOM will evaluate the implementation of these guidelines after a period of 3 years, *if appropriate*' (emphasis added).
[41] Council of the European Union, EU Guidelines to Promote and Protect the Enjoyment of all Human Rights by the Lesbian, Gay, Bisexual, Transgender and Intersex (LGBTI) Persons, Foreign Affairs Council meeting, Luxembourg, 24.06.2013.

of the Guidelines (three years), unlike the more general and vague wording employed in the EU Guidelines on the Promotion and Protection of the Rights of the Child, which state that COHOM will review the implementation of the Guidelines 'at regular intervals'.[42]

Despite these positive features of the EU Guidelines and the EU commitments to monitor implementation, 2018 marks the fifth anniversary of the EU Guidelines on FoRB, and there is no official and publicly available report on the implementation of the Guidelines, produced by the FoRB task force in COHOM. When the EU does speak about its FoRB commitments, it does so in a vague manner, which appears to be devoid of content:

> Many actions [...] addressing human rights challenges, such as freedom of expression and freedom of religion or belief, are regular, recurrent and ongoing. Furthermore the EU upgraded several policies and adopted a more systematic and holistic approach.[43]

There is only one analysis produced by Professor François Foret, which is not an institutional analysis, but a study from the series EU Diplomacy Papers. This reaches the conclusion that religion has a marginal importance in diplomatic practice:[44] '[w]hatever its salience as a problem needing to be dealt with, and its political visibility, it continues to meet indifference, mistrust or hostility among foreign affairs professionals whose ethos calls for issues.'[45] Rather limited sections regarding EU commitments to FoRB and the EU Guidelines on FoRB also exist in academic literature.[46] Similarly, civil society members have contributed to the public discourse on this matter, putting forward suggestions on the strengthening of the EU Guidelines on FoRB.[47]

---

[42] Council of the European Union, EU Guidelines on the Promotion and Protection of the Rights of the Child (2017): Leave No Child Behind, available at https://eeas.europa.eu/headquarters/headquarters-Homepage/22017/guidelines-promotion-and-protection-rights-child_en, last accessed 29.05.2018.

[43] Council of the European Union, EU Action Plan on Human Rights and Democracy (2015–2019): Mid-Term Review June 2017, 11138/17 of 07.07.2017, p. 22.

[44] F. Foret (2017), 'How the European External Action Service Deals with Religion', *supra* note 17.

[45] F. Foret, 'Freedom of Religion in EU Diplomacy: Defending a Cause or Promoting Divergent Interests?', *Euractiv*, 11.05.2017, available at https://www.euractiv.com/section/freedom-of-thought/opinion/freedom-of-religion-in-eu-diplomacy-defending-a-cause-or-promoting-divergent-interests, last accessed 29.05.2018.

[46] C.C. Muguruza, F. Gómez Isa et al., 'Mapping Legal and Policy Instruments of the EU for Human Rights and Democracy Support', FRAME Deliverable No. D12/1, 2014, available at www.fp7-frame.eu/wp-content/uploads/2017/03/Deliverable-12.1.pdf, last accessed 29.05.2018, pp. 86–87.

[47] A. Shepherd, 'Diplomacy and Determination: Five Years of the EU Guidelines on Freedom of Religion or Belief', *FoRB in Full*, 16.05.2018, available at www.forbinfull.org/2018/04/16/diplomacy-and-determination-five-years-of-the-eu-guidelines-on-freedom-of-religion-or-belief, last accessed 29.05.2018.

Nevertheless, in the absence of any official report on implementation, it is impossible to assess whether the two milestones set out by the Second Action Plan on Human Rights and Democracy were met and the extent to which the EU Guidelines are properly implemented.

Taking note of the lack of report on the implementation of the EU Guidelines on FoRB, there have been repeated calls for a report on the implementation of the Guidelines.

The European Parliament has already urged greater participation and input from civil society in the evaluation and revision of the Guidelines.[48] Specifically, the European Parliament Intergroup on Freedom of Religion or Belief and Religious Tolerance (EP Intergroup on FoRB and RT) has required the publication of the report on the implementation of the EU Guidelines on FoRB.[49]

The press release on the launch of the Interim Annual Report on FoRB also commented:

> The co-chairs of the Intergroup on Freedom of Religion or Belief (FoRB) are calling for a full report on the implementation of the EU Guidelines on FoRB by the European Commission and the EEAS, to make it possible to monitor the progress of the EU in ensuring that they are implemented.[50]

The European Peoples' Party Working Group on Interreligious Dialogue in the European Parliament held an event on 2 May 2017 on the topic of strengthening the EU Guidelines on Freedom of Religion or Belief. In this context, Members of the European Parliament, the UN Special Rapporteur on freedom of religion or belief, Ahmed Shaheed and the EU Special Envoy for the promotion of freedom of religion or belief outside the EU argued that the promotion of FoRB must be stepped up.[51]

Church leaders have also expressed dissatisfaction regarding the EU's failure implement the Guidelines on FoRB.[52]

---

[48] European Parliament Resolution of 12 March 2015 on the Annual Report on Human Rights and Democracy in the World 2013 and the European Union's Policy on the Matter (2015) 0076, para. 45.

[49] Interview in Brussels.

[50] European Parliament Intergroup on Freedom of Religion or Belief and Religious Tolerance, 'Human Rights Ought to Be a Fundamental Issue, Particularly for the EU', Press Release, available at www.religiousfreedom.eu/2017/07/05/intergroup-press-release-launch-of-freedom-of-religion-or-belief-interim-report, last accessed 29.05.2018.

[51] European People's Party Group in the European Parliament, 'Strengthen EU Guidelines on Freedom of Religion or Belief', Press release, 02.05.2017, available at www.eppgroup.eu/news/Strengthen-EU-Guidelines-on-Freedom-of-Religion-or-Belief, last accessed 29.05.2018.

[52] J. Luxmoore, 'Church Leaders Say EU Countries ignore Pledges on Religious Freedom', Crux, 05.05.2017, available at www.cruxnow.com/global-church/2017/05/05/church-leaders-say-eu-countries-ignore-pledges-religious-freedom, last accessed 29.05.2018.

On 19 February 2018, the EEAS convened a meeting of around 20 representatives of organisations advocating for FoRB, who were required to propose three ways in which the implementation of the EU Guidelines on FoRB could be improved. The conclusions of the meeting and the proposals were forwarded to COHOM. Nonetheless, given that the EEAS had not circulated any institutional report with concrete data regarding the five-year implementation of the EU Guidelines on FoRB, it is reasonable to believe that the recommendations advanced by civil society have not been tailored and are limited in their specificity and approach. Only by knowing what exactly the EU has done to keep to its FoRB commitments can one substantively recommend ways to improve, to continue or, perhaps, to adopt changes in EU policy on the matter. Only by knowing what has been done can one narrow down what needs to be done further. Ultimately, only by having a clear, transparent and accountable record on the implementation of EU Guidelines on FoRB can human rights lawyers and civil society assess whether a revision of the EU Guidelines on FoRB is needed.

3. RECOMMENDATIONS

3.1. FOSTERING CIVIC AND INTER-INSTITUTIONAL COOPERATION

Admittedly, in 2013, the EU made a step forward by taking on FoRB commitments and agreeing to set up regular exchanges of views on FoRB within different committees, subcommittees and working groups of the European Parliament. This should be read in conjunction with the Council Conclusions on the Action Plan on human rights and democracy (Foreign Affairs Council, 20 July 2015) which mentions that 'while respecting their distinct institutional roles, it is important that the European Parliament, the Council, the Member States, the European Commission and the EEAS commit themselves to working together ever more closely to realise their common goal of improving respect for human rights'.[53]

Albeit important and possibly impactful, this call has become devoid of substance, given that the reports on the implementation of the EU Guidelines on FoRB are either lacking, or are not made public. For example, the European Parliament Intergroup on Freedom of Religion of Belief or civil society cannot be expected to fully and substantially contribute to the exchanges

---

[53] Council of the European Union, Council Conclusions on the Action Plan on Human Rights and Democracy 2015–2019, 10897/15 of 20.07.2015, p. 13.

of views, as required by the EU Guidelines on FoRB, as long as they do not have access to the report on the implementation of the Guidelines, if such a report does exist within COHOM. On the other hand, if there is no report on the implementation of the EU Guidelines on FoRB, then the EEAS is in breach of the requirement set out by the Guidelines. In this case, COHOM should work towards drafting and shaping such a report. This can be done in partnership with civil society and academia, and also with the relevant actors dealing with FoRB at the EU level, such as the Special Envoy on Freedom of Religion or Belief outside the EU, the European Parliament Intergroup on FoRB, the responsible coordinators of the Article 17 dialogue within the European Commission and the European Parliament, as well as the EU Special Representative on Human Rights, and the Special Envoys on anti-Semitism and anti-Muslim hatred.

Additionally, the Commission, the European External Action Service, the EU Special Representative for Human Rights and Member States should systematically use the Council Guidelines to promote and protect the enjoyment of all human rights and maintain a unified position when responding to violations of these rights.

3.2. CONSOLIDATE AND STRENGTHEN THE ROLE OF THE EU SPECIAL ENVOY ON FoRB OUTSIDE THE EU IN THE IMPLEMENTATION OF THE EU GUIDELINES ON FoRB

To increase the efficiency of the implementation process and inter-institutional cooperation, the EU Special Envoy on FoRB outside the EU should play a more prominent role in monitoring and reporting on implementation, by steering political action. Currently, the EU Special Envoy on FoRB outside the EU is conducting ground visits in third countries, with a primary focus on FoRB and EU external action. With a much-needed strengthening of the position of the EU Special Envoy, by equipping the position further with staff and increased budget,[54] such visits and related reports would become regular. By building capacity, regularity and consistency in monitoring and reporting FoRB matters externally, the EU Special Envoy would feed and actively collaborate with COHOM on implementation reports of the EU Guidelines on FoRB. This would facilitate inter-institutional collaboration and would offer external representation of FoRB to partners world-wide.

---

[54] See *supra* section 2.1.

3.3. INCREASE TRANSPARENCY OF PROCESSES

The Guidelines mention that the consultation on their implementation, by COHOM, shall be done 'in the context of the open, transparent and regular dialogue held under Article 17 of TFEU'. This article has already raised issues regarding the lack of transparency within which it has been carried out,[55] and should hence not be further weakened by a lack of implementation of the Guidelines. In order to increase transparency, the EU should communicate the *concrete and specific manner* in which it has implemented and will further implement the EU Guidelines on FoRB. Simply repeating standard language, such as 'the EU has made considerable progress,'[56] 'the EU has improved mainstreaming',[57] 'the EU upgraded several policies and adopted a more systematic and holistic approach'[58] is not enough. In the absence of concrete data, the credibility of the EU's commitments in the area of FoRB will be undermined, as it will appear as only paying lip service to FoRB.

3.4. INCREASE AND INTENSIFY TRAINING PROGRAMMES ON THE EU GUIDELINES ON FoRB

The EU should invest further in building in-depth knowledge and awareness-raising of the EU Guidelines on FoRB. In line with the EU Guidelines on FoRB commitments, this should be done by concrete training programmes that should focus on the content, substance, and implementation of FoRB obligations. As with other guidelines, COHOM could compile a set of good practices, which come out of the EU experience in promoting, protecting and securing FoRB, and advance it in its external action. In so doing, the EU could secure coherence between its internal and external action in mainstreaming FoRB.

4. CONCLUSION

The fifth anniversary of the EU Guidelines on FoRB offers an opportunity for the EU to re-evaluate and to take its commitments in the area of FoRB more

---

[55] A. PORTARU (2017), 'Europe in Search of a Soul?', *supra* note 8.
[56] Council of the European Union, Council Conclusions on the Action Plan on Human Rights and Democracy 2015–2019, 10897/15 of 20.07.2015.
[57] Ibid.
[58] Council of the European Union, EU Action Plan on Human Rights and Democracy (2015–2019): Mid-Term Review June 2017, 11138/17 of 07.07.2017, p. 22.

seriously. If the EU seeks, as it publicly states, to become a leader in human rights promotion and protection, then it needs to be open and transparent about what progress, if at all, has been made on the topic of FoRB.

Only then can stakeholders (EU institutions, churches, confessional and non-confessional organisations) contribute, propose and work towards refining better protection and indeed a more efficient policy on FoRB. Ultimately, the end goal is not monitoring as a good in itself but monitoring for the sake of better protecting FoRB and all the victims around the world who suffer because of inadequate protection.

HUMAN RIGHTS COUNCIL IN TROUBLED WATERS

The EU as a Stabilising Factor

Theodor RATHGEBER

1. Introduction 212
2. HRC: Technical Constraints and Support 214
3. HRC Sessions in Brief 216
4. Syria in the Human Rights Council 221
5. Conclusion 224

ABSTRACT

The Human Rights Council (HRC) is considered one of the world's most authoritative human rights bodies at international level. While the HRC is facing a number of criticisms because of its insufficient impacts on the ground, at the same time, victims of human rights violations still count on the Council's visibility and accessibility. The Member States of the European Union (EU) and the EU as such are among those who uphold these expectations to a certain extent. This article provides an overview of selected discussions and decisions at the HRC in the year 2017, particularly considering the contribution by the EU and its Member States towards good practice. The section on Syria highlights the HRC's multi-year investigations, which have informed decision-makers at the highest level of the United Nations and will pave the way for holding the culprits accountable at a later stage under more conducive circumstances. Compared to a world which apparently suffers from a massive deconstruction of human values, the article addresses the HRC's good practice in sustaining a human rights centred discourse. In this context, the article further examines the contributions of EU in the HRC to keep human rights standards as well as the pertinent discourse alive.

1. INTRODUCTION

The United Nations (UN) HRC emerged in 2006[1] to become one of the world's most authoritative human rights bodies. Against all odds in the first four years of its existence, the HRC has set up new processes for scrutiny of human rights issues,[2] initiated vital investigations into new crises and severe human rights violations,[3] and consolidated the Universal Periodic Review (UPR). The UPR is meanwhile (2018), in its third cycle. The HRC has shown flexibility and has been alert to crises or fast-deteriorating situations.[4] Although the Council was less responsive to chronic or continuing human rights violations, the situation in Syria, for instance, has shown that the HRC has been able to maintain the flow of accurate and timely information. Irrespective of a certain exhaustion of the pertinent mechanisms and instruments, the HRC provided the data necessary to enable, in particular, the UN Security Council (UNSC) to adequately act upon the situation in Syria in accordance with human rights and international humanitarian law. However, unlike the HRC, the UNSC failed to act because one veto power, the Russian Federation, could obstruct those decisions. In the current world of turmoil, when a remarkable number of states still falter in their commitment to fundamental human rights norms, there is, nevertheless, no time for complacency regarding the HRC. Indeed, success should be measured by its impact on the ground.

The HRC will need to focus more on implementation within its own scope. As the UN High Commissioner for Human Rights (HCHR) Zeid Ra'ad Al Hussein stated in April 2016: 'For the Council's standing – and, more importantly, for the rights of millions of people across the world – it is crucial that its three annual sessions do not drift into becoming elaborate performances of ritualised, high-level theatre.' He warned of the widespread practice of what may be named human rights window-dressing and characterising an empty routine.[5]

---

[1] Resolution 60/251 (March 2006) of the UN General Assembly (UNGA).
[2] Such as the Commissions of Inquiry and fact-finding missions, and preserve, in addition, the system of the UN Special Procedures, their reports and recommendations.
[3] T. PICCONE, 'U.N. Human Rights Commissions of Inquiry: The Quest for Accountability', Foreign Policy at Brookings, Washington 2017, available at https://www.brookings.edu/wp-content/uploads/2017/12/fp_20171208_un_human_rights_commisions_inquiry.pdf, last accessed 13.06.2018; see also T. PICCONE and N. MCMILLEN, 'Country-Specific Scrutiny at the United Nations Human Rights Council. More than meets the eye', Project on International Order and Strategy, Brookings, Washington 2016, available at https://www.brookings.edu/wp-content/uploads/2016/07/UNHRC_Country_Specific_v1.pdf, last accessed 13.06.2018.
[4] By incremental and practical improvements such as urgent debates or informal briefings by the HCHR.
[5] ZEID RA'AD AL HUSSEIN, 'Strengthening the Human Rights Council's focus and impact on implementation and accountability', Written statement in view of the 10th anniversary of the HRC, UN Office of the High Commissioner for Human Rights, available at http://www.ohchr.org/EN/NewsEvents/Pages/DisplayNews.aspx?NewsID=19918&LangID=E, last accessed 13.06.2018.

Since its inception, the HRC has faced a number of shortfalls analysed in numerous articles. These can be summarised as issues such as erosion of credibility, lack of cooperation even by Member States of the HRC, attacks on mandate holders of the UN Special Procedures, selectivity, countries escaping from scrutiny and limited access of civil society to and participation in the work of the HRC. The intention by certain states to limit the access even included reprisals. These aspects are frequently listed to identify the downside of the HRC in failing to adequately address grave human rights violations for primarily political reasons.[6]

Among those who contributed to maintain and extend the Council's remaining credibility, visibility and accessibility, have been Member States of the EU as well as the EU representatives in Geneva. At the very beginning of the Council in 2006/2007, the EU was among the main players – with its then Presidency in the person of the German Ambassador[7] – who negotiated as counterpart to states such as Egypt or China, the structure of the HRC in terms of the Institution-Building Package, its basic regulation, and sustaining the vital role of Special Procedures and civil society. Since 2016, the HRC has been confronted with the next challenge which combines technical and procedural as well as substantive aspects.

Thus, this article provides in sections 2 and 3 an overview of the above-mentioned constraints as well as selected discussions and decisions at the HRC in the year 2017, particularly considering the contribution by the EU and its Member States towards good practice by the HRC. Section 4 explores the EU's attention on the disturbing situation in Syria within the scope of the mechanisms and instruments available to the HRC. The Syrian war and its casualties are highly controversial, and this article does not claim to present an overall clarification. For the purpose and the argument of the article it is sufficient to provide credible sources (see below).

---

[6] AMNESTY INTERNATIONAL, HUMAN RIGHTS WATCH, INTERNATIONAL SERVICE FOR HUMAN RIGHTS (eds.), 'Strengthening the Human Rights Council from the Ground Up, Report of a one-day dialogue', held on 22 February 2018, Geneva, available at http://www.ishr.ch/sites/default/files/documents/from_the_ground_up_report_final_web.pdf, last accessed 13.06.2018; GENEVA ACADEMY, *Universality in the Human rights Council: Challenges and Achievements*. Research Brief, December 2016; R. FREEDMAN, *Failing to protect: the UN and the politicisation of the human rights*, New York, Oxford University Press, 2015; T.G. WEISS, D.P. FORSYTHE, R.A. COATE, K.-K. PEASE (eds.), *The United Nations and Changing World Politics*, 7th edition, Westview Press, Boulder (Colorado) 2014, chapter 2; L. BLANCHFIELD, 'The United Nations Human Rights Council: Issues for Congress', *Congressional Research Service*, 2013, available at www.fas.org/sgp/crs/row/RL33608.pdf, last accessed 13.06.2018; T. RATHGEBER, 'Performance and Challenges of the Human Rights Council: An NGOs' View', *Friedrich-Ebert-Stiftung* Geneva Office, Berlin-Geneva 2013, available at http://library.fes.de/pdf-files/iez/global/09680.pdf, last accessed 13.06.2018.

[7] It is also worth mentioning the then Mexican Ambassador acting as first President of the emerging HRC.

Section 4 will thus highlight, on the one hand, the HRC's eminent role by the multi-year investigations of the Commission of Inquiry on Syria which have informed decision-makers at the highest level of the United Nations and beyond, despite difficult conditions. Though the question of accountability remains currently open, the reports will ground the examination of the culprits and their collaborators at a later stage under different circumstances. Altogether, the article will address the HRC's good practice in sustaining a human rights centred discourse and in examining its procedural instruments vis-à-vis a world, which apparently suffers from a deconstruction of human values at its worst. The article further aims to examine the less apparent contributions of EU in the HRC to counter such dishonour shown by states towards minimal human rights standards and to keep the discourse on human rights standards alive.

2. HRC: TECHNICAL CONSTRAINTS AND SUPPORT

The HRC is again situated at a critical juncture. Yet at the end of 2016, the HRC was informed by the Division of Conference Management at the United Nations Office at Geneva (UNOG), that due to financial constraints – and ordered by UNGA – the UNOG service to the Council meetings had to be restricted. Subsequently, the HRC was asked, among others, to decrease the number of its annual meetings from a total of 156 (in 2016) to 130 in 2018 and distributed among the three regular sessions. In 2017, the HRC reduced the number to 138 meetings in total. Despite these efforts, UNOG continued to emphasise that the Council needs to bring the number of meetings close to 130.[8]

What reads like a mere technical aspect, can be translated into risks for adequately addressing human rights situations on the ground and, thus, to the substance. The debates in 2017 and to date, May 2018, centred upon terms such as efficiency, rationalisation, technological facilities which also revealed their ambiguity. Efficiency should be developed into effective measures favouring rights-holders, victims, survivors but may also become measures which limit their access and participation in the HRC agenda and its mechanisms. Rationalisation may mean expanding the inclusion of all key stakeholders but may again turn into an undue disadvantage for civil society's participation.[9]

---

[8] Minutes of the Human Rights Council Bureau of 4th and 11th of May 2018, *HRC Extranet*, available at https://extranet.ohchr.org/sites/hrc/PresidencyBureau/BureauRegionalGroups Correspondence/Pages/Bureau-meetings.aspx, last accessed 13.06.2018.

[9] See AMNESTY INTERNATIONAL, HUMAN RIGHTS WATCH, INTERNATIONAL SERVICE FOR HUMAN RIGHTS (2018), 'Strengthening the Human Rights Council from the Ground Up', *supra* note 6.

In such circumstances, the EU and some of its Member States continued throughout the year 2017 to strengthen the work of the HRC and its institutional scope. The delegation of Ireland had already addressed in its concluding statement to the 32nd session of the HRC (July 2016) the question whether the Council is able to receive and consider information of a developing crisis. Ireland continued questioning whether the HRC would be able to react and take decisions quickly at an early stage with pertinent tools or mechanisms responding an emerging crisis.[10] The statement specified some guiding considerations on whether a situation or specific issue merits the attention of the HRC and if so, on how the Council should respond.

This initiative was followed-up by the delegation of the Netherlands one year later at the 35th session in June 2017. The concluding joint statement addressed the requirements for states who want to stand for candidacy as a member of the HRC and listed some principles in accordance with UNGA resolution 60/251.[11] In continuation, Norway and Switzerland issued a joint statement during the 36th session of HRC requesting the operationalisation of the tools of the HCHR. The statement stressed the need for an explicit and coherent policy framework for the HRC to turn prevention of human rights violations into reality and to make the Council responsive to human rights emergencies.[12]

These and further initiatives (see below) sustained a discourse to strengthen the mandate of HRC and its ability to promote and protect human rights on the ground. They did not gain much public attention but definitively contributed to enhance the HRC's work and strengthen a comprehensive approach in closer accordance with its normative mandate. This includes the role of civil society and its contributions in sustaining an independent verification of situations.

---

[10] 8 July 2016, on behalf of a cross-regional group of states including Austria, Belgium, Botswana, Canada, Chile, Croatia, Czech Republic, Denmark, Iceland, Ireland, Finland, France, Ghana, Hungary, Liechtenstein, Lithuania, Mexico, Netherlands, New Zealand, Norway, Republic of Korea, Romania, Rwanda, Slovakia, Slovenia, Spain, St Kitts and Nevis, Sweden, Switzerland, Ukraine, United Kingdom and Uruguay; accessible via HRC Extranet.

[11] 23 June of 2017, on behalf of a cross-regional group of 48 states including Albania, Algeria, Australia, Austria, Belgium, Bosnia and Hercegovina, Bulgaria, Canada, Chile, Croatia, Cyprus, Czech Republic, Denmark, Estonia, Fiji, Finland, France, Georgia, Germany, Haiti, Honduras, Iceland, Ireland, Italy, Japan, Republic of Korea, Latvia, Liechtenstein, Lithuania, Luxembourg, Malta, Mexico, Monaco, Montenegro, Netherlands, Norway, Paraguay, Poland, Romania, Slovenia, Spain, Sweden, Switzerland, Ukraine, United Kingdom of Great Britain and Northern Ireland, United States of America, Serbia, The former Yugoslav Republic of Macedonia; accessible via HRC Extranet.

[12] 12 September 2017, on behalf of 69 states: Norway, Switzerland, USA, Canada, Germany, Finland, Portugal, Australia, New Zealand, Lichtenstein, Cyprus, Italy, Luxembourg, Netherlands, Denmark, Ireland, United Kingdom, Spain, Austria, Sweden, Hungary, Malta, Bulgaria, Croatia, Belgium, Iceland, Czech Republic, Slovakia, Slovenia, Albania, Georgia, Estonia, Lithuania, Latvia, Romania, Montenegro, Poland, Serbia, Guatemala, Colombia, Haiti, Paraguay, Panama, Costa Rica, Chile, Uruguay, Sierra Leone, Ghana, Togo, Benin,

3. HRC SESSIONS IN BRIEF

In 2017 the HRC held three regular sessions (34–36) and one Special Session on human rights of the Rohingya and other minorities in Rakhine State in Myanmar (December 2017). Resolution S-27/1 requested the HCHR to provide oral updates to the Council for a period of three years. During the 34th regular session of HRC (March 2017) the decision was made to dispatch an independent fact-finding mission to Myanmar (34/22) to investigate the alleged human rights violations by military and security forces, in particular, in Rakhine State. The same resolution extended the mandate of the Special Rapporteur on the question of human rights in Myanmar for one year. Similarly, the HRC extended the mandate of the Special Rapporteur on Eritrea for a period of one year (35/35) and decided to hold an enhanced interactive dialogue on the human rights situation at its 37th session (March 2018). The resolution further requested the mandate holder to submit a written report to the 38th HRC session as well as to UNGA at its 72nd session. Thus, by the mere number of procedures, Myanmar and Eritrea were set on a permanent monitoring and reporting system.

A new mandate of the Special Procedures was established on the elimination of discrimination against persons affected by leprosy and their family members (Resolution [A/HRC/RES/]35/9). The mandate shall systematically collect information and look for best practice to overcome discrimination. In September, a new intergovernmental Working Group on accountability of private military and security companies was installed (36/11). By Presidential Statements, the HRC ended the monitoring on Haiti (PRST 34/1) and Ivory Coast (PRST 35/1). Thus, the HRC also has shown its capacity to adapt itself to new circumstances in favour of monitored countries, therefore countering the prejudice of a biased continuity on country mandates.

Throughout the year 2017 the normative standards of the Council's mandate were put in jeopardy by written amendments to draft resolutions which tended to dilute or even alter the common understanding of terms and norms. Though the Russian Federation has not been a HRC member since 2016, its delegation constantly presented amendments, in particular on civil society participation, cooperation with United Nations, women's rights, gender issues or other thematic issues such as the death penalty. Although not a Member State, the rules permit such initiatives. The status of membership is only required when

---

Burkina Faso, Thailand, Andorra, Fiji, Japan, Mexico, France, Ukraine, Israel, Zambia, Republic of Korea, Honduras, Greece, Bosnia and Herzegovina, Timor-Leste, Mozambique, Cote d'Ivoire, Rwanda, Indonesia; accessible via HRC Extranet. The further debate on adapted measures can be followed at HRC Extranet under 'Efficiency process', available at https://extranet.ohchr.org/sites/hrc/PresidencyBureau/BureauRegionalGroupsCorrespondence/Pages/Bureau-meetings.aspx, last accessed 13.06.2018.

such an initiative is subject to change by an oral amendment during the voting process, which has not been a problem so far.

For years, the contributions and involvement of civil society, in particular human rights defenders, has been a disputed area. As a result, the situation of the mandate holder on human rights defenders has become precarious, making the expert a preferred target for harsh criticism and categorical questioning of the mandate as such. During the 34th session, Norway presented a resolution on extending the mandate of the Special Rapporteur for human rights defenders for a further three years (34/5). Germany on behalf of the EU supported and co-sponsored the draft.[13] On the eve of the decision-making, almost 100 non-governmental organizations (NGOs) highlighted the need to renew this mandate. In the end, the mandate was extended without a vote though the Russian Federation, South Africa and China together presented six amendments. Their objections predominantly addressed the concept and term of human rights defenders. Amendment 34/L.42 (Russian Federation) emphasised the domestic law as the main framework for activities of human rights defenders. The amendments 34/L.44 and L.45 (Russian Federation) sought to omit the term human rights defenders completely, speaking instead of those engaged in the promotion and protection of universally recognised human rights and fundamental freedoms. Although the amendment L.46 by South Africa was withdrawn, it had listed the activities to be carried out by the mandate and, thus, sought to narrow its scope. China's amendment L.51 expressed political discontent by suggesting alternative language that simply 'takes note' of the work and report of the Special Rapporteur instead of 'welcoming' it. All amendments were rejected by majorities of 28 and 29 votes against the amendments.

A further obstacle course was the issue of cooperation with the United Nations, its representatives and mechanisms in the field of human rights. The report by the UN Secretary-General was presented to the 36th session (document A/HRC/36/31) and the subsequent resolution (36/21) faced 19 amendments (36/L.43-L.61) by China, Egypt, India, Russia and Venezuela. The report informed on intimidation and reprisals against those seeking to cooperate or having cooperated with the UN on human rights, including travel bans, harassment, threats, arbitrary arrests and detention, enforced disappearances, or economic measures such as frozen bank accounts. The report underscored that addressing such reprisals and intimidations are a core responsibility and priority of the UN system as a whole. The draft resolution was tabled by Ghana, Hungary, Ireland, Fiji and Uruguay and sponsored by 55 states from all regions.[14]

---

[13] Statement accessible at HRC Extranet to the 34th session.
[14] Andorra, Australia, Austria, Belgium, Bosnia and Herzegovina, Bulgaria, Chile, Croatia, Cyprus, Czech Republic, Denmark, Fiji, Finland, France, Georgia, Germany, Ghana, Greece,

During the voting process, Germany, on behalf of the EU, took the floor four times and presented the objections against various amendments.[15]

Many amendments objected to the concept and scope of cooperation with the UN, the legal grounds for cooperating or, conversely, aimed to reinforce the notion of the state as the primary source of information. For instance, amendment 36/L.46 highlighted that '[…] cooperation and genuine dialogue […] shall be aimed at strengthening the capacity of Member States to comply with their human rights obligations'. Far from denying the need to strengthen the state's capacity to comply with its human rights obligations, the problem is the language used that makes state capacity-building the reference for the responsibility on implementation. The German delegation on behalf of the EU frankly stressed that this amendment would diminish states' responsibilities and the lack of capacity would serve as an excuse for reprisals.[16] Unfortunately, L.46 was among the three amendments which were accepted, by 24:18.

Amendment L.56 was also accepted with a narrow majority (21:20) and inserted a new Operative Paragraph (OP) 8 into the resolution stating that '[…] information provided by all stakeholders, including civil society, to the United Nations and its representatives and mechanisms in the field of human rights should be credible and reliable, and must be thoroughly checked and corroborated'. Why is such seemingly inconspicuous and self-evident requirement on information a problem? Some of the states presenting amendments used this argument, in particular, to undermine the cases presented in the Secretary-General's report saying they are '[…] fabricated or politically motivated' (in L.53). Everybody is entitled to examine the substance and source of information, but matters become ambiguous when the examination never ends and becomes an instrument to prevent action. In the end, resolution 36/21 was adopted with a vote of 28 in favour, none against and 19 abstentions.[17]

A third thematic field of increasing controversies on the normative standards and its accurate implementation by the HRC relates to gender issues. There is a certain trend observed among some HRC Member States, which aim to

---

Guatemala, Haiti, Hungary, Iceland, Ireland, Israel, Italy, Japan, Latvia, Liechtenstein, Lithuania, Luxembourg, Malta, Mexico, Monaco, Montenegro, Netherlands, New Zealand, Norway, Panama, Paraguay, Peru, Poland, Portugal, Republic of Korea, Republic of Moldova, Romania, Slovakia, Slovenia, Spain, Sweden, Switzerland, the former Yugoslav Republic of Macedonia, Ukraine, United Kingdom of Great Britain and Northern Ireland, USA, Uruguay.

[15] The oral statements of Germany are accessible via HRC Extranet to the 36th session, available at https://extranet.ohchr.org/sites/hrc/PresidencyBureau/BureauRegionalGroupsCorrespondence/Pages/Bureau-meetings.aspx, last accessed 13.06.2018.

[16] Ibid.

[17] Voting and oral statements are accessible via HRC Extranet to the 36th session, available at https://extranet.ohchr.org/sites/hrc/PresidencyBureau/BureauRegionalGroupsCorrespondence/Pages/Bureau-meetings.aspx, last accessed 13.06.2018.

return to a traditional understanding of gender roles in society and family. Wherever possible, they show their reluctance to debates on equal rights by an explicit referral to gender terminology. As no Member State has so far dared to challenge women's rights and gender equality in a public statement, they use subtle means to undermine these rights. During the 35th session, resolution 35/18 on the elimination of discrimination against women and girls called upon states to repeal all laws that exclusively or disproportionately criminalise actions or behaviours of women and girls and discriminate them based on custom, tradition, culture or religion. Though the resolution was adopted without a vote, two amendments by Belarus, China, Egypt and Russian Federation sought to eliminate, in particular, the term 'women human rights defenders' (35/L.41) and to leave the term 'equality' for human rights' achievements in general (35/L.42). Germany on behalf of the EU, Albania and Switzerland[18] argued against the amendments, which were ultimately rejected.

Similarly, Belarus, China, Egypt and Russian Federation submitted two amendments against resolution 35/10 dealing with accelerating efforts to eliminate violence against women. The resolution asked for a review of efforts which challenge gender stereotypes and the negative social norms, attitudes and behaviours that underlie and perpetuate violence against women and girls. Both amendments were rejected. Conversely, resolution 35/13 on the protection of the family[19] nevertheless perpetuated the stereotype of family as a nuclear family composed of child, woman and man and found the support of 30 Member States.

Controversies on country situations have always existed and the terminology of double standards or politicisation are used to date by all sides. Nevertheless, some examples and statements presented to the HRC recently reveal an absolute dysfunctional approach to the situations. The EU traditionally addresses country situations in terms of draft resolutions, regularly supported by other Western states, countries from Latin America as well as some African countries. While not all these initiatives have been successful, they build a reference for a minimum standard in dealing with country situations under a human rights perspective.[20]

---

[18] Voting and oral statements are accessible via HRC Extranet to the 35th session, available at https://extranet.ohchr.org/sites/hrc/PresidencyBureau/BureauRegionalGroupsCorrespondence/Pages/Bureau-meetings.aspx, last accessed 13.06.2018.

[19] Sponsored by Bangladesh, Belarus, China, Côte d'Ivoire, Egypt (on behalf of the Group of Arab States), El Salvador, Mauritania, Morocco, Qatar, Russian Federation, Saudi Arabia, Tunisia.

[20] For an overview of voting patterns at the HRC see HUMAN RIGHTS WATCH, 'UN Rights Council: Voting Records Exposed, Analysis of Members That Protected Rights – or Didn't', 24.03.2015, available at www.hrw.org/news/2015/03/24/un-rights-council-voting-records-exposed, last accessed 13.06.2018.

During the 36th session, Belgium, Canada, Ireland, Luxembourg and the Netherlands presented draft resolution 36/L.4 on human rights in Yemen but were countered by Egypt on behalf of the Arab Group who proposed an optional text. Such a manoeuvre already happened in 2016 and in the end, the final resolution 33/16 failed to create an investigation mechanism. This time, the EU and others managed to insert into resolution 36/31 on technical assistance and capacity-building a request for an international investigative body to be established by the HCHR. This group of eminent international and regional experts shall monitor and report on the situation of human rights, and in particular, carry out a comprehensive examination of all alleged violations and abuses of international human rights and other appropriate and applicable international law since September 2014. If possible, the experts are asked to identify responsibilities, and to provide guidance on access to justice, accountability, reconciliation and healing. The written report shall be presented to the 39th session (September 2018).

In the framework of the 35th session (June 2017) the HRC was prompted to act on the human rights situation in the Democratic Republic of the Congo (DRC). Malta on behalf of the EU had submitted a draft text stressing impunity and accountability but withdrew when Tunisia on behalf of the African States' Group included in resolution 35/36 a team of international experts to be dispatched, in particular, to the DRC Kasaï region. One session later, in September 2017, Estonia on behalf of the EU submitted a further resolution due to human rights violations throughout the year 2017. Again, Tunisia on behalf of the African Group presented an optional text which (36/30) requested two oral reports by the OHCHR to the 37th and 38th HRC sessions and a comprehensive report to the 39th session. In a way, the human rights situation in DRC had come under continuous scrutiny although the US delegation criticised the insufficient efforts to investigate and hold accountable those who are responsible for the violations and the continued restrictions on political freedom. The US voted against resolution 36/30 and appealed to the DRC to postpone its candidacy to the HRC for the period 2018–2020. The resolution was adopted and UNGA voted in October 2017 the DRC into the HRC by a large majority of 151 countries.

The case of Burundi is one of the HRC Member States with a highly dubious human rights record. Elected in 2015 by a UNGA majority for the period 2016–2018, the human rights situation in Burundi was critically assessed even before the beginning of its membership. In December 2015, Burundi was the subject of the HRC Special Session 24 by which a number of states unsuccessfully sought to suspend Burundi's membership. Although this could not be achieved, resolution S-24/1 of the Special Session requested a thorough assessment by the HCHR. Subsequently, resolution 33/24 in March 2017 established a Commission of Inquiry (CoI) which later issued a number of press releases and public statements on serious human rights violations and presumed crimes against humanity.²¹ The assessments culminated in the CoI's report to the 36th session, which documented a horrific level of human rights violations and alleged crimes against humanity (A/HRC/36/54).²² Altogether there was enough evidence that should have led to a resolution, which would have recommended UNGA to suspend Burundi's membership in the HRC.

Such a draft resolution (36/L.9) was indeed submitted by Estonia on behalf of the EU, which even included a referral to the International Criminal Court. However, Tunisia on behalf of the African Group tabled an optional draft (36/L.33) which did not contain any call for investigation or suspension. The HRC dealt then with two draft resolutions. The EU revised its draft L.9 preserving the investigation mandate of 33/24 and turned the draft into a procedural resolution (36/19) which simply repeated CoI's mandate. The resolution presented by Tunisia and the African Group (36/2) limited the scope of activity to technical assistance. In addition, 36/2 requested the OHCHR to nominate another team of three experts to be dispatched to Burundi and to present oral briefings to the 37th and 38th session. Nominally, there are now six experts to follow the human rights situation in Burundi. While this might be considered a positive outcome at first glance, the work of the latter three experts is less favourable for a comprehensive fulfilment of the mandate. They are required to forward all the information collected to the judicial authorities of Burundi, which may jeopardise the willingness of witnesses to cooperate with the experts.

4. SYRIA IN THE HUMAN RIGHTS COUNCIL

The emerging protest in 2010 against several Arab regimes swept into Syria as well. A long-standing opposition demanded greater freedoms and justice against President Bashar al-Assad. Though at the beginning, the majority of opponents did not have complete regime change in mind, the tipping point came in March 2011, when a group of youths were arrested and tortured by the police for writing the anti-government graffiti 'The people want the regime to fall'. Assad's regime responded to further peaceful protests with brutal violence, and by the end of May 2011, estimations spoke of upwards of 1,000 civilians being killed, injured or detained. As people then turned against the government, armed opposition groups began to emerge, and the situation descended into civil war.²³

---

[21] See the documents available at http://www.ohchr.org/EN/HRBodies/HRC/CoIBurundi/Pages/CoIBurundi.aspx, last accessed 13.06.2018.

[22] The report listed among others extrajudicial executions, arbitrary arrests and detentions, enforced disappearances, torture, cruel treatment, sexual violence, restrictions to the right to freedom of association and suspensions of the work of human rights NGOs.

[23] See e.g., the reports and analysis from a viewpoint of human rights and rule of law by the INTERNATIONAL CRISIS GROUP, 'Syria', available at https://www.crisisgroup.org/

Since the very beginning of human rights violations in 2011 in Syria, the United Nations has been involved at various levels in seeking a peaceful resolution of the situation.[24] Besides the UNSC,[25] the HRC was particularly involved in the documentation process. Ironically, since the beginning of the HRC in 2006 (and even before in the time of the Human Rights Commission), Syria was the subject of resolutions addressing the human rights situations in the occupied Golan Heights and addressing the Israeli settlements and, thus, required a certain legitimacy for its governance. While those resolutions and the situation as such continued, the HRC has addressed since 2011 the facts of the inner-state violations, provided evidence on crimes against humanity as a matter of state policy and on war crimes such as murder, torture, rape, hostage taking, enforced disappearance and use of chemical weapons.

Special attention to the Syrian human rights situation was drawn by an investigation mission set up in April 2011 in the framework of the HRC's 16th Special Session. Resolution S-16/1 requested the OHCHR to dispatch such a mission and mandated the experts '[...] to investigate all alleged violations of international human rights law and to establish the facts and circumstances of such violations and of the crimes perpetrated, with a view to avoiding impunity and ensuring full accountability [...]'. The experts were requested to provide a preliminary report and oral update to the HRC at its 17th session (August 2011). As the situation deteriorated, a further (17th) Special Session was called in August 2011 which established by S-17/1 an independent international CoI of three experts with the same mandate mentioned before and which is in function today. In March 2017, the HRC extended the mandate of the CoI (34/26) and decided further to transmit all the reports and oral updates to all relevant bodies of the United Nations.[26] Given the constant deterioration of human rights in Syria, including the emergence of Islamic State of Iraq and Syria (ISIS), two more Specials Sessions followed consecutively in December 2011 and June 2012.

---

middle-east-north-africa/eastern-mediterranean/syria, last accessed 13.06.2018; HUMAN RIGHTS WATCH, 'Syria', available at https://www.hrw.org/middle-east/n-africa/syria, last accessed 13.06.2018; AMNESTY INTERNATIONAL, 'Syria', available at https://www.amnestyusa.org/countries/syria, last accessed 13.06.2018.

[24] For instance, the UN established a Supervision Mission in Syria in April 2012 aiming to monitor the armed violence and offer support for the Joint Special Envoy's six-point plan to help end the conflict. However, the Supervision Mission was terminated in August 2012. In December 2016, the UNGA established an international, impartial and independent mechanism (resolution 71/248) to assist in the investigation and prosecution of persons responsible for the most serious crimes under international law.

[25] See the documents issued by UNSC on Syria available at http://www.securitycouncilreport.org/un-documents/syria, last accessed 13.06.2018.

[26] All reports by the CoI on Syria are available at http://www.ohchr.org/EN/HRBodies/HRC/IICISyria/Pages/Documentation.aspx, last accessed 13.06.2018.

The ongoing crisis in Syria has significantly damaged the authority of the United Nations. In particular, the UNSC has failed in its responsibility of protection in Syria due to the fact that the Russian Federation and China used their power of veto to stop key resolutions.[27] While the UNSC has failed to act, Syria has been the subject of the HRC's agenda and mechanisms in nearly all three regular sessions to date. In addition, the HRC has held a total of six Special Sessions since 2011. Correspondingly, the HRC has issued since 2012 a significant number of resolutions in order to politically confront the human rights violations.[28] All reports by the HRC mechanisms assessed the responsibilities of both government and armed groups.[29] Meanwhile, the Commission of Inquiry is passing names of suspects to courts in Europe paving the way for accountability for the manifold crimes in Syria at a later stage. Yet by going through the documentation, the eminent role of the multi-year investigations of the Commission of Inquiry on Syria is evident. The HRC's actions on that country have been much more than mere paper exercise.[30]

The EU has been actively involved in trying to resolve the crisis from a humanitarian and human rights perspective as well as promoting accountability since 2011; at least at the level of HRC. Within the HRC, the EU constantly supported[31] or initiated resolutions on Syria[32] but also resorted to restrictive

---

[27] For an overview, see SECURITY COUNCIL REPORT, 'What's in Blue, Reports on Syria since 2011', available at http://www.securitycouncilreport.org/syria, last accessed 13.06.2018; OXFAM, 'Failing Syria'. Assessing the impact of UN Security Council resolutions in protecting and assisting civilians in Syria, 2015, available at https://www.oxfam.org/sites/www.oxfam.org/files/file_attachments/bp-failing-syria-unsc-resolution-120315-en1.pdf, last accessed 13.06.2018.

[28] See the resolutions of the HRC regular sessions starting with 19/1 in March 2012, followed by 13 more till March 2018; available at http://ap.ohchr.org/documents/sdpage_e.aspx?b=10&c=179&t=4, last accessed 13.06.2018 as well as at http://www.securitycouncilreport.org/un-documents/search.php?ctype=Syria&rtype=Human%20Rights%20Council%20Documents&cbtype=syria&search=%22Human%20Rights%20Council%20Documents%22%20AND%20%22Syria%22&__mode=tag&IncludeBlogs=10&limit=15&page=3, last accessed 13.06.2018.

[29] See reports by thematic mandate holders of the Specials Procedures such as UN Docs. A/HRC/16/49/Add.2, A/HRC/17/25/Add.3, A/HRC/24/58, A/HRC/32/35/Add.2 complemented by reports of the OHCHR and UN Secretary-General UN Docs. A/HRC/18/53, A/HRC/21/32, A/67/931, A/70/919, A/HRC/35/15 as well as special analysis such as the 'Updated Statistical Analysis of Documentation of Killings in the Syrian Arab Republic' by OHCHR in 2013 and 2014; all documents are available at http://www.ohchr.org/EN/Countries/MENARegion/Pages/SYIndex.aspx, last accessed 13.06.2018.

[30] See T. PICCONE, '5 Myths about the UN Human Rights Council', *Huffington Post Blog*, December 2016, available at https://www.huffingtonpost.com/ted-piccone/five-myths-about-the-un-h_b_8750184.html, last accessed 13.06.2018.

[31] See the oral statements by EU and Member States to the HRC regular sessions at HRC Extranet.

[32] The latest in 2017 was resolution 36/20 sponsored by France, Germany, Italy, Jordan, Kuwait, Morocco, Qatar, Saudi Arabia, Turkey, United Kingdom of Great Britain and Northern Ireland, United States of America.

measures and sanctions since May 2011 including an embargo on petrol and prohibition to enter European territory for 235 people and 67 entities. In addition, the EU has mobilised more than €10 billion for humanitarian support inside and outside Syria since the conflict started.[33]

With a certain regularity, the EU and its Member States undermine their commitment to human rights by geopolitical or national interests. On Syria, the EU adopted, however, in April 2017 a strategy that included justice for war crimes, the release of thousands of prisoners, clarification about enforced disappearances, lifting of sieges, and the end of unlawful attacks and the use of illegal weapons, irrespective of currently lacking effective action.[34]

Irrespective of the EU's role in the HRC, the EU would have had other additional capacities to address the human rights and rule of law situation before the war and even contain the war. Thus, the EU Commission was present in Damascus since the late 1990s in the framework of the Barcelona process.[35] It had and still has good connections with all major players. As events unfolded, everyone including the EU left the country silently. Thus, the EU could have been in a position to help manage the situation in a less violent way.

5. CONCLUSION

Given the nature of the HRC as a human rights body composed of both normative standards and political decision-making, the outcome in 2017 including EU's participation was a mixed success. The EU was part of the arduous struggle to strengthen the protection and enjoyment of international human rights around the world. The EU contributed to sustain the reporting and monitoring system, in particular the aspects of in-depth information, truth telling and accountability, critical for the HRC's mandate. Some of the compromises achieved in 2017 particularly on country situations may ensure

---

[33] See the overview by the EUROPEAN EXTERNAL ACTION SERVICE (EEAS), 'The EU and the crisis in Syria', 2017 and 2018, available at https://eeas.europa.eu/sites/eeas/files/eu-syria_fact_sheet.pdf, last accessed 13.06.2018; and https://eeas.europa.eu/headquarters/headquarters-homepage/22664/eu-and-crisis-syria_en; see also EEAS, 'Snapshot: Impact of EU response to Syria crisis', 2018, available at https://eeas.europa.eu/headquarters/headquarters-homepage/43037/snapshot-impact-eu-response-syria-crisis_en, last accessed 13.06.2018.

[34] See EEAS, 'Elements for an EU Strategy for Syria: joint communication', 2017, available at https://eeas.europa.eu/headquarters/headquarters-homepage_en/22659/Elements%20for%20an%20EU%20Strategy%20for%20Syria:%20joint%20communication, last accessed 13.06.2018.

[35] See A. GUPTA, R. REBELLO and A. GUPTA, 'Syria's Relations with the European Union under Barcelona Process: 1995–2010', Jawaharlal Nehru University, India 2016, available at https://www.researchgate.net/publication/307856579, last accessed 13.06.2018.

that a given situation will at least remain on the HRC agenda and thus constantly be monitored. This may increase the chance that at a later stage accountability will be achieved.

This is particularly true for the example of Syria, which provides in-depth documentation conducive for bringing suspects to court and paving the way for accountability at a later stage. The instruments of the HRC and its working methodology have been increasingly used and extended for the purpose of accountability. Irrespective of additional options and capacities of the EU in other frameworks to address the situation in Syria more adequately, the EU played a substantial role in the achievements at the level of HRC.

The HRC remains an ambiguous human rights institution. The membership of Burundi and of DRC (since 2018) is deplorable, and majorities are fragile. Nevertheless, the HRC's membership is mostly composed of states that meet the free and partly free standards of Freedom House (between 74% and 85%). In addition, since 2006, 20 new mandates of independent experts have been established,[36] and these mandates are generating reports and documents on abuses of international (human rights) law. Currently, the HRC is among those international institutions which can claim with certain legitimacy to protect and promote human rights and address most situations of severe human rights violations. The HRC does not entirely live up to its mandate but compared to other international and United Nations' institution, it does make a difference.

---

[36] See T. PICCONE (2016), '5 Myths about the UN Human Rights Council', *supra* note 30.

PART III
CoE

THE JURISPRUDENCE OF THE EUROPEAN COURT OF HUMAN RIGHTS IN 2017

Stefan KIEBER*

1. Introduction 230
2. Grand Chamber and Other Leading Judgments 232
   2.1. Admissibility: Matter Already Examined by the Court
        (Article 35 Para. 2 (b) ECHR) 232
   2.2. Right to Life (Article 2 ECHR)............................. 233
   2.3. Prohibition of Inhuman and Degrading Treatment
        (Article 3 ECHR) 235
   2.4. Prohibition of Forced Labour (Article 4 ECHR) 236
   2.5. Right to Liberty (Article 5 ECHR).......................... 237
   2.6. Right to a Fair Trial (Article 6 ECHR)..................... 237
        2.6.1. Civil Proceedings 237
               2.6.1.1. Application of Article 6 ECHR............. 237
               2.6.1.2. Fairness of Proceedings................... 239
        2.6.2. Criminal Proceedings................................ 240
               2.6.2.1. Applicability 240
               2.6.2.2. Fairness of Proceedings................... 240
               2.6.2.3. Defence Rights 242
   2.7. No Punishment without Law (Article 7 ECHR) 243
   2.8. Right to Respect for Private and Family Life (Article 8 ECHR) 243
        2.8.1. Private Life.. 243
        2.8.2. Private and Family Life............................. 244
        2.8.3. Private Life and Correspondence 245
        2.8.4. Private Life and Freedom of Religion................ 246
   2.9. Freedom of Thought, Conscience and Religion (Article 9 ECHR)...247
   2.10. Freedom of Expression, Freedom of the Press and Freedom
         to Receive and Impart Information (Article 10 ECHR).......... 248
         2.10.1. Freedom of Expression............................. 248

---

* The author would like to thank Sara Grumbach for her support with regard to research and Sabrina Lipp for proofreading.

2.10.2. Freedom of the Press 250
  2.10.3. Freedom to Receive and Impart Information 250
 2.11. Prohibition of Discrimination (Article 14 ECHR) 251
 2.12. Protection of Property (Article 1 of Protocol No 1 to the ECHR) ... 255
 2.13. Right to Free Elections (Article 3 of Protocol No 1 to the ECHR)... 255
 2.14. Freedom of Movement (Article 2 of Protocol No 4 to the ECHR)...256
 2.15. Prohibition of Collective Expulsion of Aliens (Article 4 of Protocol
        No 4 to the ECHR).. 258
 2.16. Right Not to be Tried or Punished Twice (Article 4 of Protocol
        No 7 to the ECHR).. 258
 2.17. Other Issues.. 258
  2.17.1. Limitation on Use of Restrictions on Rights
           (Article 18 ECHR)...................................... 258
  2.17.2. Just Satisfaction (Article 41 ECHR) 259
  2.17.3. Execution of Judgments (Article 46 ECHR) 260
3. Conclusion.. 262

ABSTRACT

The article will give an overview of the European Court of Human Rights' (ECtHR) most important judgments and decisions in 2017, that is to say judgments and decisions that contributed to the development or the clarification of the Court's case law in a considerable way. Those judgments covered a broad range of issues such as private and family life, data protection, the detention of asylum seekers, discrimination, the responsibility of a politician for his conduct during the financial crisis, the integration of Muslims in western society, the proportionality of measures envisaging the improvement of the social mix in certain underprivileged areas in order to avoid social problems or the applicability and violation of the right to a fair trial. The ECtHR also clarified the scope and interpretation of some provisions of the European Convention on Human Rights (ECHR) which have not been dealt with often so far in its case law, for example Article 18 ECHR or Article 2 of Protocol No 4 to the ECHR. Although the year 2017 brought a reduction of the number of pending applications to the lowest level since 2004, it must be kept in mind that the Court still faces big challenges regarding its workload. The observance of the subsidiarity principle will remain the key to the Convention system's success.

1. INTRODUCTION[1]

In 2017, a significantly higher number of applications (63,350) was allocated to a judicial formation than in the years before.[2] Some 49,400 of these were identified

---

[1] For the statistical facts of 2017 see ECtHR, 'Analysis of statistics 2017', 2018, available at https://www.echr.coe.int/Documents/Stats_analysis_2017_ENG.pdf, last accessed 07.06.2018, and

as single-judge cases likely to be declared inadmissible, 13,950 applications were identified as probable Chamber or Committee cases. That general increase of applications can mainly be explained by a huge number of complaints (especially by journalists and judges taken into custody) coming from Turkey following the attempted military coup in 2016.

Nevertheless, the Court was able to reduce the number of applications pending before a judicial formation to 56,250[3] in 2017, as a very high number of applications (85,951) could be disposed of judicially.[4] This was also because many of the above-mentioned Turkish applications could be decided very quickly by the Court. Since the beginning it declared 27,000 of such applications inadmissible for failure to exhaust domestic remedies. It argued that the applicants had not made use of – according to the ECtHR – effective appeals to the Constitutional Court or to an ad hoc commission set up in January 2017.[5] In addition, in its Grand Chamber Judgment of *Burmych and others*,[6] the Court struck out thousands of applications concerning a problem already dealt with in a pilot judgment. As regards the applications pending by the end of 2017, more than two-thirds of them concerned only six Member States: Romania (17.6%), Russia (13.8%), Turkey (13.3%), Ukraine (12.6%), Italy (8.3%) and Hungary (6.3%).[7]

Of the 85,951 applications disposed of judicially in 2017, 70,356 applications were declared inadmissible or struck out of the list of cases by decision of a single judge, Committee, Chamber or Grand Chamber, which amounts to an increase of 92% compared to 2016.[8] Around 66,150 of them were decided by a single judge (an increase of 113% compared to 2016), 3,500 by Committees of three judges, 700 by Chambers and one by the Grand Chamber (*Harkins v the United Kingdom*).[9]

In 2017, the Court delivered 1,068 judgments regarding 15,595 applications.[10] That high number of applications disposed of by judgment

---

ECtHR, 'Annual Report 2017', pp. 155 et seq. The Annual Reports are also available on the Court's website, available at https://echr.coe.int/Pages/home.aspx?p=court/annualreports&c, last accessed 07.06.2018.

2   2016: 53,400 see ECtHR, 'Annual Report 2016', p. 4; 2015: 40,650 see ECtHR, 'Annual Report 2015', pp. 187 both available at https://echr.coe.int/Pages/home.aspx?p=court/annualreports&c, last accessed 12.06.2018.
3   By the end of 2016 there were 79,750, by the end of 2015 64,850.
4   Compare 2016: 38,505, see ECtHR, 'Annual Report 2016' p. 191; and 2015: 45,576, see ECtHR, 'Annual Report 2015', p. 187, both *supra* note 2.
5   ECtHR, 'Annual Report 2017', *supra* note 1, p. 8.
6   See below 2.17.3.
7   ECtHR, 'Analysis of statistics 2017', *supra* note 1, p. 8.
8   Ibid., p. 4.
9   See below 2.1.
10 2016: 993 judgments in respect of 1,926 applications see ECtHR, 'Annual Report 2016', pp. 181–182; and 2015: 823 judgments concerning 2,441 applications see ECtHR, 'Annual Report 2015', p. 187, p. 65 and p. 187, both *supra* note 2.

is notably due to the fact that the Grand Chamber struck out more than 12,000 applications in *Burmych and others*.[11] Nineteen judgments were delivered by the Grand Chamber, 526 by Chambers and 523 by Committees of three judges.[12] Most of the violations found concerned the right to a fair trial (28.03%), the prohibition of torture and inhuman and degrading treatment (18.29%), the right to liberty and security (14.51%), the right to an effective remedy (11.63%) and the right to property (8.34%).

The following section shall give an overview of the most important judgments and decisions in 2017, that is, judgments and decisions that contributed to the development or the clarification of the Court's case law in a considerable way. It focuses on Grand Chamber judgments but also includes other judgments and decisions that are of special interest in this regard.

2. GRAND CHAMBER AND OTHER LEADING JUDGMENTS

2.1. ADMISSIBILITY: MATTER ALREADY EXAMINED BY THE COURT (ARTICLE 35 PARA. 2 (B) ECHR)

Harkins v the United Kingdom, no 71537/14, Grand Chamber Decision of 15 June 2017

In its only decision on admissibility in 2017 the Grand Chamber was involved with the extradition of a British national to the United States of America (USA). He complained that his extradition would lead to a violation of Articles 3 and 6 ECHR because he would face a life sentence without possibility of parole in the USA if convicted. As the Court had already ruled on a complaint by the applicant concerning his extradition in 2012[13] and the present application concerned 'substantially the same' questions within the meaning of Article 35 para. 2 (b) ECHR, it held that the new complaint had to be declared inadmissible. In this connection, the Grand Chamber discussed in detail the first admissibility criterion contained in Article 35 para. 2 (b) ECHR. It notably elaborated on the notion of 'relevant new information' and denied that the development of its own case law after its first decision with regard to the applicant could constitute such new information. According to the ECtHR, to hold otherwise would undermine the strict grounds permitting revision of its judgments as set out in Article 80 of its Rules of Procedure.[14] The decision of

---

[11] See below 2.17.3.
[12] ECtHR, 'Annual Report 2017', *supra* note 1, p. 156.
[13] ECtHR, *Harkins and Edwards v the United Kingdom*, nos 9146/07 and 32650/07, 17.01.2012.
[14] ECtHR, *Harkins v the United Kingdom*, no 71537/14 [GC] 15.06.2017, Decision, para. 56.

Harkins is of special importance because the above-mentioned admissibility criterion has not yet been dealt with very often by the Court.

2.2. RIGHT TO LIFE (ARTICLE 2 ECHR)

Lopes de Sousa Fernandes v Portugal, no 56080/13, Grand Chamber Judgment of 19 December 2017

The case of *Lopes de Sousa Fernandes* concerned the death of a patient after a series of medical problems in connection with an operation for the removal of nasal polyps. The patient's wife complained to the ECtHR that the death had been due to negligence on the part of the medical staff during the post-operation period. She further alleged that the authorities had failed to elucidate the reasons for the deterioration of her husband's health. With regard to the substantive aspect of Article 2 ECHR the Court seized the opportunity to clarify its case law on the positive obligations of Member States in the context of cases of alleged medical negligence.[15] It first reaffirmed that their obligations were limited to a duty to regulate. That meant that they had to provide for an effective regulatory framework compelling (private or public) hospitals to adopt appropriate measures for the protection of patients' lives and for securing high professional standards among health professionals. Where a state had complied with that obligation, an error of judgment on the part of a health professional or negligent coordination among health professionals in the treatment of a particular patient could not be regarded as sufficient in themselves to call the state to account from the standpoint of its positive obligations under Article 2 of the Convention. However, states also had a duty to ensure the effective functioning of such a regulatory framework. Thus, the positive obligations included the necessary measures to guarantee implementation, especially supervision and enforcement. The Grand Chamber accepted that state responsibility under the Convention is engaged in two very exceptional circumstances with regard to acts or omissions of healthcare providers: (1) where an individual patient's life is knowingly put in danger by denial of access to life-saving emergency treatment and (2) where 'a systemic or structural dysfunction in hospital services results in a patient being deprived of access to life-saving emergency treatment and the authorities knew about or ought to have known about that risk and failed to undertake the necessary measures to prevent that risk from materialising, thus putting the patients' lives, including the life of the particular patient concerned, in danger'.[16] In order to decide whether, in a given case, there was a denial of access to life-saving emergency

---

[15] ECtHR, *Lopes de Sousa Fernandes v Portugal*, no 56080/13 [GC] 19.12.2017, paras. 185 et seq.
[16] Ibid., para. 192.

treatment, the Court then established a number of cumulative factors which had to be met. In the present case the Court concluded that the regulatory framework did not disclose any shortcomings and found no violation with regard to the substantive aspect of Article 2 ECHR (15 votes to 2).[17] Concerning the procedural aspect of Article 2 ECHR, the Court held that the domestic system had failed to provide an adequate and timely response regarding the circumstances of the patient's death and unanimously found a violation of the aforementioned provision.[18]

The approach taken by the Court concerning the responsibility of the state for medical negligence under the Convention is rather strict. Unlike the Chamber,[19] which had also found a violation of the substantive aspect of Article 2 ECHR because there had been no adequate intervention by the medical staff in the days after the operation due to a lack of coordination between different departments of the hospital, the Grand Chamber noticeably limited the states' obligations. Although it may be understandable that the Court did not want to extend its level of scrutiny with regard to cases of medical malpractice too far,[20] it is deplorable from a human rights perspective that the Grand Chamber took a step backwards and reduced protection for those suffering such malpractice. What is all the more unsatisfactory is the fact that the Grand Chamber's intention obviously was to clarify its case law but that its approach is somewhat confusing as the Court introduced two different types of cases on the one hand and then a criteria catalogue which seems to be applicable to both of them without making a difference.[21] One will be interested to see how the Court will apply those standards to similar cases in the future.

Other judgments and decisions

The Chamber judgment *Tagayeva and others v Russia*[22] concerned mainly alleged violations of Article 2 ECHR in connection with the hostage-taking at a school in Beslan in 2004 which resulted in hundreds of dead and injured people. The Court found that the authorities had failed to protect the victims against a foreseeable threat to life, that there had been serious shortcomings in

---

[17] Ibid., paras. 197 et seq. See also the partly dissenting opinions of Judges Pinto de Albuquerque and Serghides.
[18] Ibid., paras. 222 et seq.
[19] ECtHR, *Lopes de Sousa Fernandes v Portugal*, no 56080/13, 15.12.2015.
[20] See in this regard the dissenting opinion of Judges Sajó and Tsotsoria to the Chamber Judgment and L. LAVRYSEN, 'Medical negligence after Lopes de Sousa Fernandes: a blank check to the Member States with respect to the substance of the right to life?', *Strasbourg Observers*, available at https://strasbourgobservers.com/category/lopes-de-sousa-fernandes-v-portugal, last accessed 07.06.2018.
[21] For a further discussion of the judgment see L. LAVRYSEN, 'Medical negligence after Lopes de Sousa Fernandes'.
[22] ECtHR, *Tagayeva and others v Russia*, no 26562/07 and six others, 13.04.2017.

the planning and control of the security operation as well as an excessive use of lethal force and that the investigation into the incident had not been appropriate. Other cases worth mentioning concerned the failure to protect a mentally ill person against suicide (*Fernandes de Oliveira v Portugal*[23] – violation of Article 2 ECHR; referred to the Grand Chamber), the judicial order to terminate artificial ventilation with regard to a baby suffering from a rare and fatal genetic disease (*Gard and others v the United Kingdom*[24] – complaint was manifestly ill-founded and therefore inadmissible), the death of a mentally ill prisoner following the use of force by prison officers (*Tekin and Arslan v Belgium*[25] – violation of Article 2 ECHR) and the death of a migrant during immigration detention (*Ceesay v Austria*[26] – no violation of Articles 2 or 3 ECHR).

2.3. PROHIBITION OF INHUMAN AND DEGRADING TREATMENT (ARTICLE 3 ECHR)

Hutchinson v United Kingdom, no 57592/08, Grand Chamber Judgment of 17 January 2017[27]

The case of *Hutchinson* pertained to a complaint by a prisoner serving a whole life sentence who alleged that he had no prospect of release.[28] The Court summed up its principles concerning the compatibility of life sentences with Article 3 ECHR and underlined the importance of the reducibility of such sentences. It concluded (14 votes to 3) that the system for life sentences in the United Kingdom could be regarded as compatible with the Convention after domestic case law had evolved following a previous ECHR judgment.[29]

Other judgments and decisions

In a couple of noteworthy judgments, the Chamber was involved with the detention of migrants. *S.F. and others v Bulgaria*[30] (violation of Article 3

---

[23] ECtHR, *Fernandes de Oliveira v Portugal*, no 78103/14, 28.03.2017.
[24] ECtHR, *Gard and others v the United Kingdom* no 39793/17, Decision, 27.06.2017.
[25] ECtHR, *Tekin and Arslan v Belgium*, no 37795/13, 05.09.2017.
[26] ECtHR, *Ceesay v Austria*, no 72126/14, 16.11.2017.
[27] The Grand Chamber case *Khamtokhu and Aksenchik v Russia* also concerned life sentencing but mainly dealt with an alleged violation of the prohibition of discrimination under Article 14 ECHR in combination with Article 5 ECHR, see below 2.11.
[28] For a further discussion of the judgment see K. DZEHTSIAROU, 'Is there Hope for the Right to Hope?', *Verfassungsblog*, available at https://verfassungsblog.de/is-there-hope-for-the-right-to-hope, last accessed 07.06.2018; M. PETTIGREW, 'A Vinter Retreat in Europe. Returning to the Issue of whole Life Sentences in Strasbourg', (2017) 8(2) *New Journal of European Criminal Law*, pp. 128 et seq. See also the dissenting opinion of Judge Pinto de Albuquerque.
[29] ECtHR, *Vinter and Others v the United Kingdom*, no 66069/09 and others [GC] 09.07.2013.
[30] ECtHR, *S. F. and others v Bulgaria*, no 8138/16, 07.12.2017.

ECHR) concerned the conditions of detention of accompanied minor migrants during the refugee crises 2015 on the Bulgarian-Serbian border. It is of special interest because it gives a comprehensive overview of the Court's case law with regard to the immigration detention of accompanied minors. The case of *Ilias and Ahmed v Hungary*[31] (violation of Article 3 ECHR; referred to the Grand Chamber)[32] pertained to the removal of asylum seekers from Hungary to Serbia, which exposed them to the risk of inhuman and degrading reception conditions in Greece, the case of *Z.A. and others v Russia*[33] (violation of Article 3 ECHR; referred to the Grand Chamber)[34] pertained to the detention conditions of asylum seekers at an airport. Other interesting cases under Article 3 ECHR concerned the insufficient treatment of a mentally ill offender due to language problems (*Rooman v Belgium*[35] – violation of Article 3 ECHR; referred to the Grand Chamber) and a police operation in connection with a football game where the police officers did not wear individually identifying signs, so that the identities of the persons responsible for the alleged ill-treatment of the applicants were difficult to establish (*Hentschel and Stark v Germany*[36] – no violation of the substantive limb of Article 3 ECHR, but violation of its procedural limb).

2.4. PROHIBITION OF FORCED LABOUR (ARTICLE 4 ECHR)

In 2017 the Chamber issued two important judgments concerning human trafficking and forced labour. The case of *J. and others v Austria*[37] mainly pertained to the procedural obligation under Article 4 ECHR to investigate alleged offences of human trafficking committed in a state not party to the Convention. The applicants had allegedly been exploited in the United Arab Emirates but escaped from their employers' control during a three day trip to Austria where they also lodged a criminal complaint on account of human trafficking. The Court found no violation of Article 4 ECHR by Austria. The case of *Chowdury and others v Greece*[38] concerned the exploitation of illegal migrants through work in a strawberry field. The Court specified that exploitation through labour was one aspect of trafficking in human beings and that the state had failed in its positive and procedural obligations to prevent situations of human trafficking, to protect the victims, to properly investigate the offences committed and to punish those responsible.

---

[31] ECtHR, *Ilias and Ahmed v Hungary*, no 47287/15, 14.03. 2017.
[32] See also below 2.5.
[33] ECtHR, *Z.A. and others v Russia*, no 61411/15 and three others, 28.03.2017.
[34] See also below 2.5.
[35] ECtHR, *Rooman v Belgium*, no 18052/11, 18.07.2017.
[36] ECtHR, *Hentschel and Stark v Germany*, no 47274/15, 09.11.2017.
[37] ECtHR, *J. and others v Austria*, no 58216/12, 17.01.2017.
[38] ECtHR, *Chowdury and others v Greece*, no 21884/15, 30.03.2017.

2.5. RIGHT TO LIBERTY (ARTICLE 5 ECHR)

Three Chamber judgments concerning Article 5 ECHR deserve special mention. The first is *Oravec v Croatia*[39] (violation of Article 5 para. 4 ECHR) where the Court confirmed the applicability of Article 5 para. 4 ECHR – which normally provides a remedy for persons deprived of their liberty – to an individual who was still at liberty after his detention had been ordered in his absence. The second is *Ilias and Ahmed v Hungary*[40] (violation of Article 5 para. 1 and para. 4 ECHR; referred to the Grand Chamber)[41] where the Court found that the detention of migrants had been ordered without any formal or reasoned decision and was not subjected to appropriate judicial review. The third case, *Z.A. and others v Russia*[42] (violation of Article 5 para. 1 ECHR; referred to the Grand Chamber), concerned the detention of asylum seekers at an airport.[43] In the two latter cases the Court discussed the existence of a 'deprivation of liberty' with regard to the specific situation of immigration detention.

2.6. RIGHT TO A FAIR TRIAL (ARTICLE 6 ECHR)

2.6.1. Civil Proceedings

2.6.1.1. Application of Article 6 ECHR

De Tommaso v Italy, no 43395/09, Grand Chamber Judgment of 23 February 2017

While that judgment mainly concerned questions under Article 2 of Protocol No 4 to the ECHR[44] the Court also confirmed that the civil limb of Article 6 ECHR can be applicable to proceedings imposing preventive police supervision measures on an individual. In the present case it held that the restrictions complained of by the applicant (such as the prohibition on going out at night, leaving the district where he lived, attending public meetings or using mobile phones or radio communication devices) fell within the sphere of personal rights and were therefore civil in nature.[45]

---

[39] ECtHR, *Oravec v Croatia*, no 51249/11, 11.07.2017.
[40] ECtHR, *Ilias and Ahmed v Hungary*, no 47287/15, 14.03.2017.
[41] See also above 2.3.
[42] ECtHR, *Z.A. and others v Russia*, no 61411/15 and three others, 28.03.2017.
[43] See also above 2.3.
[44] See below 2.14.
[45] ECtHR, *De Tommaso v Italy*, no 43395/09 [GC] 23.02.2017, para. 154.

Károly Nagy v Hungary, no 56665/09, Grand Chamber Judgment
of 14 September 2017

The judgment of *Károly Nagy* is related to a compensation claim lodged by a pastor after his dismissal by the Hungarian Reformed Church. The applicant alleged a violation of his right of access to court after the domestic courts had rejected his claim on the ground that the latter could not be enforced under civil law as he was employed under ecclesiastic law. Considering the Hungarian legal framework, the Court held that the applicant had no right which was recognised under domestic law and that therefore Article 6 ECHR could not apply to his case. Therefore, the application had to be declared inadmissible (10 votes to 7).[46]

Regner v the Czech Republic, no 35289/11, Grand Chamber Judgment
of 19 September 2017[47]

In *Regner* the Court found that Article 6 ECHR applied to proceedings challenging the revocation of a security clearance of an employee of the Ministry of Defence. Although the case did not concern the latter's dismissal, the security clearance was a prerequisite for carrying out his functions and its revocation thus had a decisive effect on the applicant's personal and professional situation, preventing him from further carrying out certain duties at the Ministry of Defence and adversely affecting his ability to obtain a new post in the civil service.[48] The applicant could therefore rely on a 'right' within the meaning of Article 6 ECHR to challenge the lawfulness of the revocation before the courts. As that right could also be regarded as civil in nature (employment within state administration was based on the Labour Code and access to court was not expressly excluded for the post or category of staff in question) the Grand Chamber found Article 6 ECHR to be applicable.

Other judgments and decisions

The issue of applicability of Article 6 ECHR was also discussed in the Chamber Judgment *Selmani and others v the former Yugoslav Republic of Macedonia*[49] which concerned proceedings initiated in order to challenge the forcible removal of the applicants (who were journalists) from the press gallery of the Parliament. The Court pointed out that domestic law recognised the right of

---

[46] See also the dissenting opinions to the judgment.
[47] For questions raised by the judgment with regard to the fairness of proceedings see below 2.6.1.2.
[48] ECtHR, *Regner v the Czech Republic*, no 35289/11 [GC] 19.09.2017, paras. 115 et seq.
[49] ECtHR, *Selmani and others v the former Yugoslav Republic of Macedonia*, no 67259/14, 09.02.2017.

accredited journalists to report from the Parliament and that such reporting was necessary for the applicants to exercise their profession and inform the public. Therefore, that right fell within the applicants' freedom of expression and was a 'civil right' for the purposes of Article 6 para. 1 ECHR.[50]

2.6.1.2. Fairness of Proceedings

Regner v the Czech Republic, no 35289/11, Grand Chamber Judgment of 19 September 2017

The applicant complained of his lack of access to classified evidence in proceedings challenging the withdrawal of his security clearance.[51] The decision to revoke the latter had mainly been based on that confidential material. As the Ministry of Defence had had access to the relevant documents, the case concerned restrictions on the adversarial and equality-of-arms principles. Bearing in mind the proceedings as a whole, the Court decided to examine whether those restrictions had been sufficiently counterbalanced by other procedural safeguards. As the national courts had had unlimited access to the classified documents and had been able to review them – as well as the decisions reached on the basis of that information – in an adequate manner, the Court concluded that there had been sufficient compensation for the limitations suffered by the applicant and found no violation of Article 6 para. 1 ECHR (10 votes to 7). The approach taken by the Grand Chamber has been criticised harshly because of the priority given to security considerations over the applicant's individual interests.[52] Indeed the impression cannot be avoided that it would have been possible to partially disclose the evidence relied on by the authorities, e.g. in the form of a summary, without prejudicing national security interests and thus to inform the applicant of the accusations against him at least in principle.[53] Somewhat surprisingly, the Court accepted as well – also referring to security considerations – that the national courts did not give sufficiently reasoned judgments allowing the applicant to understand their decision on the substance of his request. A more differentiated approach would be welcome in future cases.

---

[50] Ibid., para. 27.
[51] See already above 2.6.1.1.
[52] See e.g. A. Preziosi, 'Regner v. Czech Republic: has the European Court of Human Rights forgotten the fair trial rights when national security is at stake?', *Strasbourg Observers*, available at https://strasbourgobservers.com/2017/10/23/regner-v-czech-republic-has-the-european-court-of-human-rights-forgotten-the-fair-trial-rights-when-national-security-is-at-stake, last accessed 07.06.2018. See also the joint partly dissenting opinion of Judges Raimondi, Sicilianos, Spano, Ravarani and Pastor Vilanova, the partly dissenting opinion of Judge Serghides and the dissenting opinion of Judge Sajó.
[53] See the partly dissenting opinion of Judge Serghides, paras. 87 et seq. and A. Preziosi, 'Regner v. Czech Republic'.

2.6.2. Criminal Proceedings

2.6.2.1. Applicability

Moreira Ferreira v Portugal (no. 2), no 19867/12, Grand Chamber Judgment of 11 July 2017

The case of *Moreira Ferreira* concerned the refusal of the Portuguese Supreme Court to reopen criminal proceedings against the applicant after the ECtHR had found a violation of Article 6 ECHR in an earlier judgment[54] because the applicant had not been heard in person during those proceedings. The ECtHR had to decide whether Article 6 ECHR applied to the reopened proceedings.[55] It first held that Article 6 ECHR applied under its criminal aspect to extraordinary remedies in domestic law where the domestic court is called upon to determine the charge.[56] With regard to the scope of the Supreme Court's review it then pointed out that the retrial could be regarded as an extension of the proceedings concluded earlier and that the domestic court had in fact to determine the criminal charge against the applicant once again.[57] According to a majority of the judges Article 6 ECHR was therefore applicable to the reopened proceedings.[58]

2.6.2.2. Fairness of Proceedings

Moreira Ferreira v Portugal (no. 2), no 19867/12, Grand Chamber Judgment of 11 July 2017

In the above-mentioned case of *Moreira Ferreira* the applicant also complained about a 'denial of justice' because the Supreme Court had refused to reopen the criminal proceedings against her after the finding of a violation of Article 6 ECHR by the ECtHR.[59] The Grand Chamber held that the Chamber had found in its earlier judgment that the reopening of the case represented in principle an appropriate way of redressing the violation.[60] However, it had not held that solution to be the only way to comply with its judgment, therefore

---

[54] ECtHR, *Moreira Ferreira v Portugal*, no 19808/08, 05.07.2011.
[55] For questions concerning the competence of the Court under Article 46 ECHR to examine the complaint and the fairness of the retrial see below 2.17.3. and 2.6.2.2.
[56] ECtHR, *Moreira Ferreira v Portugal (no. 2)*, no 19867/12 [GC] 11.07.2017, para. 65.
[57] Ibid., para. 72.
[58] See in this regard also the joint dissenting opinion of Judges Raimondi, Nußberger, De Gaetano, Keller, Mahoney, Kjølbro and O'Leary who denied applicability of Article 6 ECHR to the present case.
[59] For questions concerning the applicability of Article 6 ECHR and the competence of the Court to examine the complaint under Article 46 ECHR see above 2.6.2.1 and below 2.17.3.
[60] ECtHR, *Moreira Ferreira (no. 2)*, *supra* note 56, paras. 96 et seq.

giving discretion to the domestic courts on how to execute it.[61] The Grand Chamber limited itself to pointing out that the Supreme Court's decision on the refusal to reopen proceedings had not been arbitrary but well within its margin of appreciation as it did not distort or misrepresent the earlier judgment delivered by the ECtHR. That meant that no manifest factual or legal error leading to a 'denial of justice' could be found and that on this ground there had been no violation of Article 6 para. 1 of the ECHR (9 votes to 8).[62]

Other judgments and decisions

The Chamber judgment of *Cerovšek and Božičnik v Slovenia*[63] concerned the applicants' trial and conviction by a single judge who later retired before giving written reasons for his judgment. Two judges who had not participated in the trial later composed written judgments on the basis of the case files. The ECtHR found a violation of Article 6 ECHR. The judgment is worth mentioning as it confirms the importance of the principle of the immediacy in criminal proceedings. In the case of *Grba v Croatia*[64] (violation of Article 6 para. 1 ECHR) the Court summed up the guiding principles from its case law regarding conformity of police entrapment with the Convention. In *Haarde v Iceland*[65] the Court discussed the fairness of impeachment proceedings against the former Prime Minister of Iceland. The latter was accused of unlawful omissions previous to the financial crisis the country suffered from 2008 onwards. The Court held that when addressing questions of responsibility of members of government, it was necessary to balance their political and criminal responsibility. However, regardless of the special character of such cases the states had to comply with the guarantees flowing from Article 6 ECHR in an adequate manner. With regard to the application at hand, the Court found that the participation of the Parliament in deciding on the introduction of criminal proceedings against members of government or in appointing the majority of the judges of the special court competent to determine the case could not make the proceedings unfair. The case of *Ramda v France*[66] (no violation of Article 6 para. 1 ECHR) concerned the principle that reasons should be given by judges for their decisions in criminal cases.[67] For the first time the

---

[61] Ibid., para. 94.
[62] See also the dissenting opinion of Judge Pinto de Albuquerque joined by Judges Karakaş, Sajó, Lazarova Trajkovska, Tsotsoria, Vehabović and Kūris; the dissenting opinion of Judge Kūris, joined by Judges Sajó, Tsotsoria and Vehabović, and the dissenting opinion of Judge Bošnjak.
[63] ECtHR, *Cerovšek and Božičnik v Slovenia*, nos 68939/12 and 68949/12, 07.03.2017.
[64] ECtHR, *Grba v Croatia*, no 47074/12, 23.11.2017.
[65] ECtHR, *Haarde v Iceland*, no 66847/12, 23.11.2017.
[66] ECtHR, *Ramda v France*, no 78477/11, 19.12.2017.
[67] See also under Article 4 of Protocol No 7 to the ECHR below 2.16.

Court applied exceptions from that principle granted to lay judges in earlier judgments also to professional judges.

2.6.2.3. Defence Rights

Simeonovi v Bulgaria, no 21980/04, Grand Chamber Judgment of 12 May 2017

The case of *Simeonovi* concerned a restriction on the applicant's right to legal assistance for the first three days of his police custody during which he had allegedly been questioned. The Court applied the guidelines developed in its Grand Chamber Judgment *Ibrahim and others v the United Kingdom*[68] and found no violation of Article 6 paras. 1 and 3(c) ECHR (12 votes to 5) because that limitation had not irremediably infringed the criminal proceedings as a whole. In particular, no evidence against the applicant had been obtained and included in the case file during that period; the applicant had later – then assisted by a lawyer – confessed after having been informed about his procedural rights; he had been able to actively participate in all stages of the proceedings; his conviction had not been solely based on his confession but also on a lot of other evidence; and the case and the issue of compliance with his procedural rights had been reviewed at three judicial stages and the courts had provided sufficient reasons for their decisions. The dissenting judges underlined the vulnerable situation of persons during the first days of their custody and criticised the approach taken by the majority which would, according to them, leave the individuals concerned without any defence at all throughout that period.[69] Indeed it can be difficult for those individuals to secure proper conduct from the part of the authorities in such situations without the assistance of a lawyer. The majority's approach thus could enable shortcomings which are not easy to correct and might therefore irreversibly influence later stages of the proceedings. In the light of these considerations, the Court should be careful when following that approach in future cases.

Other judgments and decisions

The case of *M. v the Netherlands*[70] related to restrictions on the communication between the applicant (a former member of the secret service) and his defence team in proceedings concerning divulgence of confidential information. The applicant was – on pain of further prosecution – not allowed to disclose classified information (like e.g. the name of witnesses) to his lawyers in order

---

[68] ECtHR, *Ibrahim and others v the United Kingdom*, no 50541/08 and 3 others [GC] 13.09.2016.
[69] See the partly dissenting opinions of Judges Sajó, Lazarova-Trajkovska and Vučinić, joined by Judge Turković, on the one hand and of Judge Serghides on the other hand.
[70] ECtHR, *M. v the Netherlands*, no 2156/10, 25.07.2017.

to prepare his defence. The Court accepted the necessity of also protecting secrecy during criminal proceedings but criticised that the applicant had to decide himself and without legal advice whether to disclose secret information and to take the risk of further criminal prosecution or to abstain from presenting exonerating facts. It concluded that there had been a violation of Article 6 paras. 1 and 3(c) ECHR.

2.7. NO PUNISHMENT WITHOUT LAW (ARTICLE 7 ECHR)

The Chamber judgment *Koprivnikar v Slovenia*[71] is noteworthy as it was the first time that the Court applied Article 7 ECHR to a procedure for the calculation of an overall sentence to replace multiple sentences.[72]

2.8. RIGHT TO RESPECT FOR PRIVATE AND FAMILY LIFE (ARTICLE 8 ECHR)

2.8.1. Private Life

The Chamber judgment *A.-M. V. v Finland*[73] afforded an opportunity for the Court to deal with the right to self-determination of disabled persons. The applicant, who was intellectually disabled, wanted to move from his place of residence to a different area in Finland against the will of his mentor because the latter was of the opinion that it was best for him to stay in his home town. After the domestic courts had confirmed the mentor's assessment, the applicant complained to the ECtHR who found no violation of Article 8 ECHR as a fair balance had been struck between the competing interests. The national courts had reached their decisions on the basis of a concrete and careful consideration of all the relevant aspects of the particular case and not merely on the ground that the applicant was a person with a disability.[74] In *A.P., Garçon and Nicot v France*,[75] an important judgment on transgender rights, the Court found a violation of Article 8 ECHR in a case where the applicants (who were transgenders) were required to undergo sterilisation or treatment involving a very high probability of sterility in order to have the entries on their birth certificates changed. Another noteworthy case, *Aycaguer v France*,[76] pertained

---

[71] ECtHR, *Koprivnikar v Slovenia*, no 67503/13, 24.01.2017.
[72] ECtHR, 'Annual Report 2017', *supra* note 1, p. 72.
[73] ECtHR, *A.-M. V. v Finland*, no 53251/13, 23.03.2017.
[74] Ibid., para. 89.
[75] *A.P., Garçon and Nicot v France*, no 79885/12 and 2 others, 06.04.2017.
[76] *Aycaguer v France*, no 8806/12, 22.06.2017.

to a conviction for refusing to be included in a computerised DNA database. The Court found a violation of Article 8 ECHR, especially because the regulations on the storage of DNA profiles did not provide the persons concerned with sufficient protection.

2.8.2. Private and Family Life

Paradiso and Campanelli v Italy, no 25358/12, Grand Chamber Judgment of 24 January 2017

The case concerned the separation of a nine-month-old child from the applicants and its placement for adoption. The child had been born in Russia to a Russian woman following a surrogacy contract. After the child had been brought to Italy by the first applicant, the Italian courts ordered the child's removal from the applicants because their conduct had been contrary to Italian assisted-reproduction and adoption laws. The Grand Chamber first held that – regardless of the existence of a parental project and close emotional bonds with the child – there had been no de facto 'family life' in terms of Article 8 ECHR, especially because there were no biological ties between the child and the intended parents, the duration of the relationship between them had been short and the ties had been uncertain from a legal perspective.[77] However, the case concerned the right to respect for the applicants' decision to become parents and the applicants' personal development through the taking of that role and therefore fell within the scope of the applicants' private life.[78] Finally, the Court found no violation of Article 8 ECHR (11 votes to 6) because the Italian courts had – having regard to their wide margin of appreciation in the case at hand – struck a fair balance between the different interests at stake.[79] It underlined in particular that prevailing importance had to be given to the public interests in putting an end to an illegal situation created by the applicants themselves. Moreover, the child did not suffer grave harm from the separation, notably because the Italian authorities had reacted quickly.[80]

---

[77] ECtHR, *Paradiso and Campanelli v Italy*, no 25358/12 [GC] 24.01.2017, para. 157.
[78] Ibid., paras. 163–164.
[79] Ibid., paras. 215–216.
[80] For a further discussion of the judgment see E. IGNOVSKA, 'Paradiso and Campanelli v. Italy: Lost in Recognition. Filiation of an Adopted Embryo born by Surrogate Woman in a Foreign Country', *Strasbourg Observers*, available at https://strasbourgobservers.com/2017/04/04/paradiso-and-campanelli-v-italy-lost-in-recognition-filiation-of-an-adopted-embryo-born-by-surrogate-woman-in-a-foreign-country, last accessed 07.06.2018; G. PUPPINCK and C. DE LA HOUGUE, 'Surrogacy: general interest can prevail upon the desire to become parents – about the Paradiso and Campanelli v. Italy Grand Chamber judgment of 24th January 2017', (2017) 146 *Revue Lamy de Droit Civil* (RLDC). See also the joint dissenting opinion of Judges Lazarova Trajkovska, Bianku, Laffranque, Lemmens and Grozev.

Other judgments and decisions

In its decision *K2 v United Kingdom*[81] the Court had to deal with the deprivation of the applicant's citizenship and his exclusion from the United Kingdom because of terroristic activities. With regard to the revocation of citizenship the Court applied an arbitrariness test (which according to it was a stricter standard than that of proportionality) and concluded that the withdrawal had not been arbitrary. Therefore, the application was manifestly ill-founded and had to be declared inadmissible. The case of *Orlandi and others v Italy*[82] concerned the fact that the domestic authorities did not recognise marriages of homosexual couples which had been concluded abroad. The Court found a violation of Article 8 ECHR.

2.8.3. Private Life and Correspondence

Bărbulescu v Romania, no 61496/08, Grand Chamber Judgment of 5 September 2017

In the case of *Bărbulescu* the Court had to deal with the monitoring of an employee's electronic communication in the workplace which led to the latter's dismissal because he had used company resources for private Internet messages even though internal regulations prohibited such use. The applicant complained about a breach of his right to respect for private life and correspondence to the ECtHR. The latter found a violation of Article 8 ECHR (11 votes to 6).[83] *Bărbulescu* is a landmark judgment with regard to the private use of electronic communication in the workplace and the options for employers to prevent it. First, the Court held that Article 8 ECHR was applicable because employees had a right to respect for their private life and for the privacy of their correspondence irrespective of a reasonable expectation of privacy (such an expectation was open to doubt in the present case because of the interdiction to use company resources for personal purposes).[84] With regard to the issue whether Romania had complied with its positive obligations under that provision, the Court accepted that Member States should 'be granted a wide margin of appreciation in assessing the need to establish a legal framework governing the conditions in which an employer may regulate electronic or other communications of a non-professional nature by its

---

[81] ECtHR, *K2 v United Kingdom*, no 42387/13, Decision, 07.02.2017.
[82] ECtHR, *Orlandi and others v Italy*, no 26431/12 and others, 14.12.2017.
[83] See also the joint dissenting opinion of Judges Raimondi, Dedov, Kjølbro, Mits, Mourou-Vikström and Eicke.
[84] See ECtHR, *Bărbulescu v Romania*, no 61496/08 [GC] 05.09.2017, paras. 69 et seq.

employees in the workplace'.[85] However, measures of an employer to monitor communications by his employees had to be accompanied by adequate and sufficient safeguards against abuse and arbitrariness and had to comply with the requirement of proportionality.[86] The Court listed several criteria which it found to be relevant in this context.[87] Moreover, it underlined that an employee should be granted access to a remedy before a judicial body in order to have a monitoring measure reviewed with regard to the above-mentioned criteria.[88] Concerning the case at hand the Court found that the domestic courts had not offered sufficient protection to the applicant as they had not taken into account the criteria mentioned above.[89]

First, it should be welcomed that the Grand Chamber overturned the Chamber judgment which had found no violation of Article 8 ECHR in the present case because the Chamber had been of the opinion that the interference with the applicant's right to privacy had been reasonable under the given circumstances. Secondly, it should be appreciated that the Court established a criteria catalogue to be used by domestic authorities when assessing if the monitoring of an employee's correspondence and other communications was reasonable and accompanied by adequate safeguards. In sum, the ECtHR's decision therefore strengthens employees' rights to protection of their privacy and private data. However, the Court also emphasised the broad margin of appreciation afforded to Member States when regulating the monitoring of employees in the workplace. It therefore may be possible for those states to significantly reduce the protection offered to those concerned by such measure in a particular case.

2.8.4. Private Life and Freedom of Religion

The Chamber judgment of *Belcacemi and Oussar v Belgium*[90] concerned the ban on wearing a face covering in public. It is noteworthy because it confirmed the guidelines established in the famous Grand Chamber Judgment of *S.A.S. v France*.[91] While in the latter the wearing was sanctioned by a

---

[85] Ibid., para. 119.
[86] Ibid., paras. 120–121.
[87] Ibid., para. 121.
[88] Ibid., para. 122.
[89] For a further discussion of the judgment see A. CHATZINIKOLAOU, 'Bărbulescu v Romania and workplace privacy: is the Grand Chamber's judgment a reason to celebrate?', *Strasbourg Observers*, available at https://strasbourgobservers.com/2017/10/19/barbulescu-v-romania-and-workplace-privacy-is-the-grand-chambers-judgment-a-reason-to-celebrate, last accessed 07.06.2018; C. JERVIS, 'Barbulescu v Romania: Why There is no Room for Complacency When it Comes to Privacy Rights in the Workplace', *Strasbourg Observers*, available at https://www.ejiltalk.org/barbulescu-v-romania-why-there-is-no-room-for-complacency-when-it-comes-to-privacy-rights-in-the-workplace, last accessed 07.06.2018.
[90] ECtHR, *Belcacemi and Oussar v Belgium*, no 37798/13, 11.07.2017.
[91] ECtHR, *S.A.S. v France*, no 43835/11 [GC] 01.07.2014.

fine only, in the former it was sanctioned by a prison sentence. The Court nevertheless found no violation of Articles 8 or 9 ECHR alone or together with Article 14 ECHR.

2.9. FREEDOM OF THOUGHT, CONSCIENCE AND RELIGION (ARTICLE 9 ECHR)

Besides the above-mentioned judgment of *Belcacemi and Oussar* the Court delivered some more important judgments with regard to the freedoms guaranteed under Article 9 ECHR. The case of *Osmanoğlu and Kocabaş v Switzerland*[92] also touched topical questions with regard to the tension between freedom of religion and integration. It concerned the imposition of a fine on the applicants, who are Muslims, because they refused to allow their daughters to attend compulsory mixed swimming lessons in school.[93] The parents complained that their right to freedom of religion had been violated. Having regard to the principles from its case law on Article 2 of Protocol No 1 to the ECHR (which has not been ratified by Switzerland) the Chamber held that the domestic authorities had not exceeded their margin of appreciation and found no violation of Article 9 ECHR. It especially noted the importance of school for the children's social integration and also pointed to the concessions made to the applicants by the school in order to balance the interests at stake and that the fine (which had also been proportionate) had been imposed only after the applicants had been warned. Moreover, the parents had had an effective remedy to challenge the fine inflicted on them. The case of *Adyan and others v Armenia*[94] concerned the conviction of Jehovah's Witnesses because of their refusal to perform civilian service (which was an alternative to military service to which they also objected) on grounds of conscience and religion. The Chamber found a violation of Article 9 ECHR notably because the civilian service was not sufficiently separated from the military system and therefore constituted no adequate alternative for the applicants. In addition, the alternative service lasted 42 months whereas the military service lasted 24 months only, a situation which created a deterrent effect for those preferring the first one. Finally, the judgment of the Chamber in *Hamidović v Bosnia and Herzegovina*[95] pertained to the conviction of the applicant because of his refusal to remove his skullcap in court when being

---

[92] ECtHR, *Osmanoğlu and Kocabaş v Switzerland*, no 29086/12, 10.01.2017.
[93] For a further discussion of the judgment see S. TROTTER, "Living Together', 'Learning Together', and 'Swimming Together': Osmanoğlu and Kocabaş v Switzerland (2017) and the Construction of Collective Life', (2018) 18(1) *Human Rights Law Review*, pp. 157 et seq.
[94] ECtHR, *Adyan and others v Armenia*, no 75604/11, 12.10.2017.
[95] ECtHR, *Hamidović v Bosnia and Herzegovina*, no 57792/15, 05.12.2017.

questioned as a witness. The ECtHR saw a violation of Article 9 ECHR. It held that the state had exceeded its margin of appreciation especially as the applicant was a private individual and not a public official with a duty of neutrality and impartiality, had been inspired by his sincere religious beliefs, had not been unwilling to testify and had shown sufficient respect towards the domestic laws and courts.[96]

2.10. FREEDOM OF EXPRESSION, FREEDOM OF THE PRESS AND FREEDOM TO RECEIVE AND IMPART INFORMATION (ARTICLE 10 ECHR)

2.10.1. Freedom of Expression

Medžlis Islamske Zajednice Brčko and others v Bosnia and Herzegovina, no 17224/11, Grand Chamber Judgment of 27 June 2017

The case concerned the conviction of the applicant non-governmental organisations (NGOs) for defamation after they had written a letter to the district authorities in which they criticised a candidate for the post of director of a local multi-ethnic public radio station for her disrespectful and contemptuous attitude towards Muslims and ethnic Bosniacs.[97] The letter was published later but it could not be established that the NGOs were responsible for that publication. Thus, only the private correspondence to the authorities could be attributed to the applicant NGOs. The Grand Chamber nevertheless did not find their conviction to be in violation of Article 10 ECHR (11 votes to 6)[98] as the domestic court had based their decisions on relevant and sufficient reasons and had struck a fair balance between the applicants' interest in free speech and the candidate's right to protection of her reputation.[99] Notably it held

---

[96] On religious dress see also P. CUMPER and T. LEWIS, 'Empathy and Human Rights: The Case of Religious Dress', (2018) 18(1) *Human Rights Law Review*, pp. 61 et seq.

[97] For further discussion of the judgment see S. SMET, 'Medžlis Islamske Zajednice Brčko v Bosnia and Herzegovina: A Simple Speech Case Made Unbelievably Complex?', *Strasbourg Observers*, available at https://strasbourgobservers.com/2017/08/09/medzlis-islamske-zajednice-brcko-v-bosnia-and-herzegovina-a-simple-speech-case-made-unbelievably-complex, last accessed 07.06.2018; A. BAILIN and J. JONES, 'Case Law, Strasbourg: Medžlis Islamske Zajednice Brčko v. Bosnia and Herzegovina, "Political defamation" and public servants' reputational rights', *The International Forum for Responsible Media Blog*, available at https://inforrm.org/2017/07/11/case-law-strasbourg-medzlis-islamske-zajednice-brcko-v-bosnia-and-herzegovina-political-defamation-and-public-servants-reputational-rights-alex-bailin-qc-and-jessica-jones, last accessed 07.06.2018.

[98] See also the joint dissenting opinion of Judges Sajó, Karakaş, Motoc and Mits, the dissenting opinion of Judge Vehabović as well as the dissenting opinion of Judge Kūris.

[99] ECtHR, *Medžlis Islamske Zajednice Brčko and others v Bosnia and Herzegovina*, no 17224/11 [GC] 27.06.2017, para. 121.

that the applicant NGOs had had no sufficient factual basis for their allegations and had failed to properly verify them. It also criticised the wording of the letter which did not make clear that they partly relied on external information and that the letter was intended to request the authorities to investigate or verify their allegations.[100] The judgment is of special interest because it clarified the liability of NGOs when assuming a role as public watchdogs similar to that of the media. Due to that similarity, the Grand Chamber[101] decided to take into account the criteria that generally apply to the dissemination of defamatory statements by the media in the exercise of its public watchdog function as established in the cases of *Von Hannover v Germany (no. 2)*,[102] *Axel Springer AG v Germany*[103] and *Couderc and Hachette Filipacchi Associés v France*.[104] Somewhat surprisingly, it did not matter that the case concerned the private correspondence between the applicant NGOs and the authorities only and not the publication of that correspondence. It is also worth mentioning that the Court expressly distinguished the applicants' reporting from cases of whistle-blowing.[105]

Other judgments and decisions

In *Bayev and others v Russia*[106] the Chamber found a violation of Article 10 ECHR alone and in combination with Article 14 ECHR in a case concerning the conviction of the applicants (gay rights activists) in administrative proceedings because they had contravened a legislative prohibition on the promotion of homosexuality. The judgment is of special interest because the Court discussed in detail the arguments the government advanced in order to justify that prohibition in the interest of moral and public health as well as on grounds relating to the protection of minors. It found clear words for condemning laws like those adopted in Russia because it was of the opinion that they reinforce stigma, prejudice and homophobia. The Chamber Judgment of *Döner and others v Turkey*[107] (violation of Article 10 ECHR) is important because the Court discussed the relationship between the right to freedom of expression and the fight against terrorism. The case concerned a request by the applicants to educate their children in the Kurdish language in a public elementary school. Following that request they were arrested and charged on suspicion of aiding and abetting an illegal armed organisation. The Court confirmed that the fight against terrorism could not absolve the state from

---

[100] Ibid., paras. 100 et seq.
[101] ECtHR, *Medžlis Islamske Zajednice Brčko and others*, para. 88.
[102] ECtHR, *Von Hannover v Germany (no. 2)*, nos 40660/08 and 60641/08 [GC] 07.02.2012.
[103] ECtHR, *Axel Springer AG v Germany*, no 39954/08 [GC] 07.02.2012.
[104] ECtHR, *Couderc and Hachette Filipacchi Associés v France*, no 40454/07 [GC] 10.11.2015.
[105] ECtHR, *Medžlis Islamske Zajednice Brčko and others*, para. 80.
[106] ECtHR, *Bayev and others v Russia*, nos 67667/09, 44092/12 and 56717/12, 20.06.2017.
[107] ECtHR, *Döner and others v Turkey*, no 29994/02, 07.03.2017.

its obligation under Article 10 ECHR and that restrictions of the freedom of expression nevertheless had to be justified by relevant and sufficient reasons.[108]

2.10.2. Freedom of the Press

In connection with the freedom of the press, two judgments shall be highlighted. In its Chamber Judgment *Selmani and others*,[109] which concerned the forcible removal of journalists from the press gallery of the Parliament, the Court found a violation of Article 10 ECHR because the government failed to substantiate convincingly that the removal had been necessary in a democratic society. The case of *Becker v Norway*[110] pertained to the protection of journalistic sources. The applicant journalist was fined for refusing to testify in proceedings against the person who had provided her with incorrect information she had used for an article and had already admitted that he had been the applicant's source. The Court thus had to discuss (and affirmed) the question if the applicant could rely on the protection of Article 10 ECHR regardless of the fact that her source had already disclosed its identity.

2.10.3. Freedom to Receive and Impart Information

Satakunnan Markkinapörssi Oy and Satamedia Oy v Finland, no 931/13, Grand Chamber Judgment of 27 June 2017

The case pertained to the ban of the publication of personal tax data of 1.2 million people by a newspaper. The data were also disseminated by means of an SMS service. Albeit the data was already accessible to the public under domestic law, the national courts held that its mass publication was contrary to the national data protection law. The applicant organisations – who published the newspaper – complained of a violation of Article 10 ECHR to the ECtHR because they were of the opinion that the restrictions on their activities constituted a violation of their right to impart information. Transferring the criteria established in earlier judgments concerning the balancing of press freedom against the right to private life (*Von Hannover v Germany (no. 2)*, *Axel Springer AG v Germany* and *Couderc and Hachette Filipacchi Associés v France*)[111] to the case at hand, the Court found no violation of Article 10 ECHR (15 votes to 2) as the domestic authorities had duly considered the principles flowing from its case law.[112] It notably pointed out that the finding of the Supreme Administrative Court

---

[108] Ibid., para. 102.
[109] See already above 2.6.1.1 under Article 6 ECHR.
[110] ECtHR, *Becker v Norway*, no 21272/12, 05.10.2017.
[111] See the quotations above under 2.10.1.
[112] ECtHR, *Satakunnan Markkinapörssi Oy and Satamedia Oy v Finland*, no 931/13 [GC] 27.06.2017, paras. 162 et seq. See also the dissenting opinion of Judges Sajó and Karakaş.

whereupon the publication of the taxation data in the manner and to the extent given did not contribute to a debate of public interest and had not been carried out solely for a journalistic purpose, was completely acceptable. Thus, it was not necessary for the Grand Chamber to substitute its view for that of the domestic courts. The present case is of specific interest because the ECtHR discussed in detail the protection offered by Article 8 ECHR with regard to personal data which are accessible to the public under certain conditions.[113] The Court found that because of the systematic publication of the data there was an additional legitimate interest in protecting them as compared to the situation before where accessing them had been a lot more difficult. That conclusion must be welcomed from a data protection perspective. However, the approach taken by the Court is remarkable in a way, as it could not be taken for granted from the outset, bearing in mind the importance the Court usually attaches to the imparting of information by the press in its case law (see e.g. *Von Hannover v Germany (no. 2), Bladet Tromsø and Stensaas v Norway*[114] or *Couderc and Hachette Filipacchi Associés v France*).

Other judgments and decisions

In the judgment of *Jankovskis v Lithuania*[115] the Chamber dealt with the topical issue of the access of prisoners to the Internet. The applicant (who was a prison inmate) was refused Internet access to a website indicated to him by the Ministry of Education and Science which offered information about distance learning possibilities and programmes in Lithuania. The Court found that there had been an unjustified interference with the applicant's right to receive information.

2.11. PROHIBITION OF DISCRIMINATION (ARTICLE 14 ECHR)

Khamtokhu and Aksenchik v Russia, nos 60367/08 and 961/11, Grand Chamber Judgment of 24 January 2017

In that case the applicants – who were serving life sentences – complained under Article 14 ECHR in connection with Article 5 ECHR that they had

---

[113] For a further discussion of the judgment see D. VOORHOOF, 'No journalism exception for massive exposure of personal taxation data', *Strasbourg Observers*, available at https://strasbourgobservers.com/2017/07/05/no-journalism-exception-for-massive-exposure-of-personal-taxation-data/#more-3801, last accessed 07.06.2018; for a discussion of the Chamber Judgment see S. MIHAIL, 'Does Privacy Overpower Journalistic Freedom', (2016) 1 *European Data Protection Law Review*, pp. 130 et seq.
[114] ECtHR, *Bladet Tromsø and Stensaas v Norway*, no 21980/93 [GC] 20.05.1999.
[115] ECtHR, *Jankovskis v Lithuania*, no 21575/08, 17.01.2017.

been discriminated against because life sentences could be given to adult men only and not to women or persons below the age of 18 or over 65. The Government had held that the difference in treatment served the purpose of promoting justice and humanity which required taking account of the age and physiological characteristics of various categories of offenders.[116] The Grand Chamber first noted that Article 14 in connection with Article 5 para. 1 ECHR applied to exemptions of certain categories of persons from life imprisonment by national legislation even though Article 5 of the Convention did not preclude the imposition of life imprisonment. Then it concluded that there had been no violation of the Convention (16 votes to 1 as regards the difference in treatment on account of age and 10 votes to 7 as regards the difference in treatment on account of sex)[117] because there had been a reasonable and proportionate justification for the difference in treatment. The Court took into account the wide margin of appreciation given to the Member States in that matter – especially because a consensus between states existed only with regard to not imposing life imprisonment on juvenile offenders and providing for a subsequent review of life sentences.[118]

Fábián v Hungary, no 78117/13, Grand Chamber Judgment of 5 September 2017

The case of *Fábián* concerned the suspension of the applicant's (a civil servant) old-age pension, after he had continued to be employed in the public sector. That measure aimed at reducing public expenditure. The applicant complained about a violation of his right to protection of property under Article 1 of Protocol No 1 to the ECHR.[119] He also saw himself discriminated against under Article 1 of Protocol No 1 to the ECHR in combination with Article 14 ECHR because he had allegedly been subjected to an unjustified difference in treatment compared with persons who received pensions and continued to work in the private sector. With regard to the latter complaint the Court had to determine whether public and private-sector employees were in a 'relevantly similar situation' for the purposes of Article 14 ECHR. It found that the applicant had not sufficiently demonstrated that that was the case.[120] It based its conclusion on

---

[116] ECtHR, *Khamtokhu and Aksenchik v Russia*, nos 60367/08 and 961/11 [GC] 24.01.2017, para. 70.
[117] See also the joint partly dissenting opinion of Judges Sicilianos, Møse, Lubarda, Mourou-Vikström, and Kucsko-Stadlmayer and the dissenting opinion of Judge Pinto de Albuquerque.
[118] ECtHR, *Khamtokhu and Aksenchik*, supra note 116, paras. 83 et seq. For further discussion of the judgment see C. HERI, 'Between a Rock and a Hard Place: The Court's Difficult Choice in Khamtokhu and Aksenchik v. Russia', *Strasbourg Observers*, available at https://strasbourgobservers.com/2017/03/17/between-a-rock-and-a-hard-place-the-courts-difficult-choice-in-khamtokhu-and-aksenchik-v-russia, last accessed 07.06.2018.
[119] See below 2.12.
[120] ECtHR, *Fábián v Hungary*, no 78117/13 [GC] 05.09.2017, paras. 130 et seq.

four relevant factors:[121] (1) the wide latitude enjoyed by the states in organising their functions and public services; (2) the substantial legal and factual differences between employment in the public sector and in the private sector for institutional and functional reasons; (3) the difference of the terms and conditions of employment, including the financial ones, and the eligibility for social benefits linked to employment between the two sectors; and (4) the difference in the role of the state when acting in its capacity as employer compared to private-sector entities as regards the institutional framework they operate under or the financial and economic fundamentals of their activities. In conclusion the Court found no violation of Article 14 in combination with Article 1 of Protocol No 1 to the ECHR (11 votes to 6).

It is doubtful if the majority was right in taking the view that public and private-sector employees were not in an 'analogous or relevantly similar situation'. As the dissenting judges rightly pointed out, there actually were no structural differences between private and public-sector employees in the national pension system, the latter applied to both categories of persons and the entitlement of the applicant to an old-age pension was based on the same rules and contributions to the system.[122] Accordingly, the Court should have accepted that there was a difference in treatment between those two categories of employees whereas differences between the public and the private sector should have been taken into account on the level of justification of that unequal treatment only. In that case, however, the finding of a violation of Article 14 ECHR would not have been improbable, as has convincingly been shown by the minority's dissenting opinion.[123]

Other judgments and decisions

The Chamber delivered a couple of more judgments with regard to the right not to be discriminated against in 2017. *Škorjanec v Croatia*[124] concerned a racially motivated attack on the applicant and her partner because the latter was of Roma origin. The aggressors were convicted on account of the attack on the applicant's partner and the courts had taken into consideration the racist dimension of the crime. However, the applicant herself was treated as a witness only and not as a victim. She complained to the ECtHR because there had been no effective investigation of the racially motivated act of violence against her. The judgment is of special interest because the Court held that a person may also be victim of a hate crime if he or she has not been attacked because of

---

[121] Ibid., paras. 121 et seq.
[122] See the joint dissenting opinion of Judges Sajó, Vehabović, Turković, Lubarda, Grozev and Mourou-Vikström, para 9.
[123] See paras. 10 et seq.
[124] ECtHR, *Škorjanec v Croatia*, no 25536/14, 28.03.2017.

his or her own characteristics but because of his or her 'actual or presumed association or affiliation with another person who actually or presumably possesses a particular status or protected characteristic'.[125] Therefore, states have an obligation to recognise and investigate both types of hate crimes. In the case at hand the ECtHR found a violation of Article 14 ECHR in connection with Article 3 ECHR because the authorities had failed to comply with that obligation with regard to the applicant. The case of *Carvalho Pinto de Sousa Morais v Portugal*[126] concerned the reduction of the compensation awarded to the applicant because a surgery had caused problems for her in having sexual relations. The Court found a discrimination on the ground of age and sex as the domestic courts had based that reduction, *inter alia*, on the ground that sex was not as important for the applicant as a 50-year-old woman and mother of two children as it was in younger years. Thus, there had been a violation of Article 14 in connection with Article 8 ECHR (private life). In the case of *Alexandru Enache v Romania*[127] the Court found no violation of Article 14 in connection with Article 8 ECHR (right to family life) in a case concerning the difference in treatment of female and male offenders with regard to the possibility of suspending their prison sentence until their child had reached the age of one. It notably pointed out that the provisions challenged by the applicant intended taking into account the particular bond between the mother and her child during the first year of the latter's life and that they therefore could not be said to be discriminatory. The judgment of *Ratzenböck and Seydl v Austria*[128] is also worth mentioning as it concerned a rather unusual complaint, namely that of a different-sex couple with regard to the impossibility of entering into a registered partnership which was open to same-sex couples only. In the past, the ECtHR had to deal with applications by different-sex couples complaining about a difference in treatment, especially on account of exclusion from legal recognition. The Court found no violation of Article 14 ECHR in combination with Article 8 ECHR (family life) in the case at hand, as it concluded that the applicants were not in a relevantly similar or comparable position to same-sex couples with regard to their need for legal recognition because they had access to the institution of marriage. The case of *Saumier v France*[129] concerned a complaint about different legal rules for compensation as regards accidents at work and job-related diseases on the one hand and as regards damage suffered in a different context on the other. The Court, however, found that the two situations were not analogous or comparable and that consequently there had been no discrimination in breach of the Convention.

---

[125] Ibid., paras. 56 and 66.
[126] ECtHR, *Carvalho Pinto de Sousa Morais v Portugal*, no 17484/15, 25.07.2017.
[127] ECtHR, *Alexandru Enache v Romania*, no 16986/12, 03.10.2017.
[128] ECtHR, *Ratzenböck and Seydl v Austria*, no 28475/12, 26.10.2017.
[129] ECtHR, *Saumier v France*, no 74734/14, 12.01.2017.

2.12. PROTECTION OF PROPERTY (ARTICLE 1 OF PROTOCOL NO 1 TO THE ECHR)

Fábián v Hungary, no 78117/13, Grand Chamber Judgment of 5 September 2017

The case of *Fábián*, which pertained to the suspension of the applicant's pension because he had continued to work after having reached retirement age, also concerned a complaint under Article 1 of Protocol No 1 to the ECHR alone.[130] In this regard, the Court held that the state – bearing in mind its wide margin of appreciation in that matter – had struck a fair balance between the general interest in protecting the public purse and ensuring the long-term sustainability of the Hungarian pension system on the one hand and the rights of the applicant under the Convention on the other. As the applicant had not been made to bear an excessive individual burden (his pension was only suspended for the time of his employment and did not get lost, he was free to choose to end his employment in order to receive his pension, he was not left devoid of all means of subsistence), the ECtHR found no violation of Article 1 of Protocol No 1 to the ECHR alone (unanimously).[131]

Other judgments and decisions

The admissibility decision of *P. Plaisier B.V. and others v the Netherlands*[132] concerned the compatibility of austerity measures (additional tax on high salaries) with Article 1 of Protocol No 1 to the ECHR. The Court found the complaint to be manifestly ill-founded as the state had not exceeded its margin of appreciation. The case is of special interest as it pertains to the proportionality of state measures in response to the worldwide economic crisis and sums up the Court's case law on austerity measures.

2.13. RIGHT TO FREE ELECTIONS (ARTICLE 3 OF PROTOCOL NO 1 TO THE ECHR)

The Chamber judgment *Davydov and others v Russia*[133] concerned allegations of irregularities during the counting of votes in St Petersburg for the city and federal elections of December 2011, as well as a lack of effective review of those allegations. In that case the Court first confirmed that only

---

[130] For the complaint under Article 1 of Protocol No 1 to the ECHR in combination with Article 14 ECHR see above 2.11.
[131] See ECtHR, *Fábián*, *supra* note 120, paras. 69 et seq.
[132] ECtHR, *P. Plaisier B.V. and others v the Netherlands*, no 46184/16 and others, Decision, 14.11.2017.
[133] ECtHR, *Davydov and others v Russia*, no 75947/11, 30.05.2017.

serious breaches in the process of counting and tabulation of votes could constitute a breach of the individual right to free elections. It then held that the domestic authorities had a duty to effectively examine complaints about such irregularities that could lead to gross distortion of the voters' intent. As the applicants, however, had been denied effective examination of their complaints, the Court found a violation of Article 3 of Protocol No 1 to the ECHR. Also of special interest is the admissibility decision of *Moohan and Gillon v the United Kingdom*[134] where the Court held that Article 3 of Protocol No 1 to the ECHR was not applicable to referenda (in the case at hand the referendum on independence for Scotland).

2.14. FREEDOM OF MOVEMENT (ARTICLE 2 OF PROTOCOL NO 4 TO THE ECHR)

De Tommaso v Italy, no 43395/09, Grand Chamber Judgment of 23 February 2017

The Grand Chamber Judgment of *De Tommaso*, which pertained to preventive police supervision measures, mainly concerned questions of freedom of movement.[135] Those measures included, *inter alia*, the duty to report once a week to the police authority responsible for his supervision; not to change his place of residence; to lead an honest and law-abiding life and not give cause for suspicion; not to associate with persons who had a criminal record and who were subject to preventive or security measures; not to return home later than 10 p.m. or to leave home before 6 a.m., except in case of necessity and only after giving notice to the authorities in good time; not to go to bars, nightclubs, amusement arcades or brothels and not to attend public meetings; and not to use mobile phones or radio communication devices. The Court seized the opportunity to elaborate on the relationship between Article 5 ECHR and Article 2 of Protocol No 4 to the ECHR and held that the obligations imposed on the applicant had not amounted to a deprivation of liberty but merely to a restriction on his freedom of movement. It then found a violation of Article 2 of Protocol No 4 to the ECHR (unanimously) due to the fact that the pertinent legislation lacked foreseeability as the legal basis for the supervision measures had been couched in vague and excessively broad terms and did not identify with sufficient precision and clarity the individuals to whom preventive

---

[134] ECtHR, *Moohan and Gillon v the United Kingdom*, nos 22962/15 and 23345/15, Decision, 13.06.2017.
[135] For questions regarding Article 6 para. 1 ECHR see above 2.6.1.1. For a detailed discussion of the judgment see S. SEBASTIAN, 'Inhaltliche Anforderungen an Präventivmaßnahmen gegen potentiell gefährliche Personen', (2017) 11/12 *Informationsbrief Ausländerrecht*, pp. 413 et seq.

measures were applicable or the content of certain of those measures.[136] With 12 to 5 votes the Court held that there had been no violation of Article 13 in combination with Article 2 of Protocol No 4 to the ECHR because the applicant had had an effective remedy under Italian law affording him the opportunity to raise his complaints.

Garib v the Netherlands, no 43494/09, Grand Chamber Judgment of 6 November 2017

The case of *Garib* pertained to a restriction on choosing residence in the inner-city of Rotterdam. According to the impugned legislation the taking up of residence in certain areas was subject to the granting of a housing permit, which was only issued to persons who had been living for six years in the Rotterdam Metropolitan Area before or who generated an income from work. The goal of that measure was to secure a better socio-economic mixing, thereby avoiding further impoverishment of the designated areas and, as a result, social problems. The applicant, however, did not fulfil those conditions as she was dependent on social welfare and had not been a resident of the Rotterdam Metropolitan Area for six years immediately preceding her request. The Court found no violation of Article 2 of Protocol No 4 to the ECHR (12 votes to 5)[137] because the state's policy choices – in the light of the situation at the material time – had not exceeded the broad margin of appreciation afforded to it in social and economic matters. Notably, the applicant had not suffered disproportionate hardship and the legislation in question included a number of safeguards (an obligation of the authorities to ensure that sufficient housing remained available locally for those who did not qualify for a housing permit, a periodic review by the Minister and the Parliament, adequate legal remedies as well as an individual hardship clause). The judgment is of special interest because it is the first to discuss interpretative and dogmatic questions connected with Article 2 of Protocol No 4 to the ECHR in detail. In particular, it differentiated between the restrictions under the third and the fourth paragraph of Article 2 of Protocol No 4 to the ECHR and distinguished the protection offered by Article 8 from that guaranteed by Article 2 of Protocol No 4 to the ECHR.[138] However, the Court has been criticised for not

---

[136] ECtHR, *De Tommaso, supra* note 45, paras. 125–126.
[137] See the joint dissenting opinion of Judges Tsotsoria and De Gaetano, the dissenting opinion of Judge Pinto de Albuquerque, joined by Judge Vehabović, and the dissenting opinion of Judge Kūris.
[138] For a further discussion of the judgment see V. DAVID and S. GANTY, 'Strasbourg fails to protect the rights of people living in or at risk of poverty: the disappointing Grand Chamber judgment in Garib v the Netherlands', *Strasbourg Observers*, available at https://strasbourgobservers.com/2017/11/16/strasbourg-fails-to-protect-the-rights-of-people-living-in-or-at-risk-of-poverty-the-disappointing-grand-chamber-judgment-in-garib-v-the-netherlands/#more-4046, last accessed 07.06.2018.

dealing with fundamental questions concerning discrimination on poverty-related grounds. The judgment has therefore been considered as a missed opportunity for strengthening the rights of those struggling with poverty and social exclusion.[139]

2.15. PROHIBITION OF COLLECTIVE EXPULSION OF ALIENS (ARTICLE 4 OF PROTOCOL NO 4 TO THE ECHR)

N.D. and N.T v Spain[140] (referred to the Grand Chamber) was one of the rare cases where the Court had to deal with a collective expulsion of aliens (here: of migrants from a Spanish enclave on the North-African coast).

2.16. RIGHT NOT TO BE TRIED OR PUNISHED TWICE (ARTICLE 4 OF PROTOCOL NO 7 TO THE ECHR)

In *Ramda v France*[141] the Chamber had to deal with the complaint of a terrorist with regard to his convictions because of his participation in a terrorist organisation on the one hand and because of murder and attempted murder in specific cases, committed within the framework of a terrorist conspiracy, on the other. In applying the guidelines from its Grand Chamber Judgments *Sergey Zolotukhin v Russia*[142] and *A and B v Norway*[143] the Court concluded that there had been no violation of Article 4 of Protocol No 7 to the ECHR.

2.17. OTHER ISSUES

2.17.1. Limitation on Use of Restrictions on Rights (Article 18 ECHR)

Merabishvili v Georgia, no 72508/13, Grand Chamber Judgment of 28 November 2017

In the case of *Merabishvili* the Court elaborated for the first time in detail on the interpretation and application of Article 18 ECHR, a provision rarely considered in its previous case law. The case concerned the pre-trial detention

---

[139] See for example dissenting opinion of Judge Pinto de Albuquerque, joined by Judge Vehabović, and V. DAVID and S. GANTY, 'Strasbourg fails to protect the rights of people living in or at risk of poverty'.
[140] ECtHR, *N.D. and N.T v Spain*, nos 8675/15 and 8697/15, 03.10.2017.
[141] ECtHR, *Ramda v France*, no 78477/11, 19.12.2017. See also under Article 6 ECHR 2.6.2.2.
[142] ECtHR, *Sergey Zolotukhin v Russia*, no 14939/03 [GC] 10.02.2009.
[143] ECtHR, *A and B v Norway*, nos 24130/11 and 29758/11 [GC] 15.11.2016.

of the former Prime Minister of Georgia who was the leader of the main opposition party at that time. The ECtHR found that the detention had been justified at the beginning, but then had been used as a means to exert pressure on him in order to obtain information. Thus, there had been a violation of Article 18 ECHR in combination with Article 5 para. 1 ECHR (9 votes to 8).[144] First, the judgment at hand brought a comprehensive overview of the application of Article 18 of the Convention in the former Commission's and the Court's case law and identified some areas which required clarification.[145] Secondly, the ECtHR held that Article 18 ECHR had no independent existence but could only be applied in combination with another provision of the Convention. It nevertheless found that Article 18 ECHR had an autonomous role because it expressly prohibited the restriction of the rights guaranteed by the Convention for purposes not prescribed by the Convention itself. Hence – and similar to Article 14 ECHR – there could be a breach of Article 18 ECHR even if there was no breach of the Article in combination with which it applied.[146] Thirdly, the Grand Chamber explained the approach to be followed where the applicant alleged that a right was restricted both for an ulterior purpose and a purpose prescribed by the Convention.[147] It held that in such cases it was necessary to decide which purpose was predominant. That depended on all the circumstances of the case, particularly bearing in mind the 'nature and degree of reprehensibility of the alleged ulterior purpose'.[148] The Court finally clarified how it could be proven that an ulterior purpose existed and that it was predominant.[149]

2.17.2. Just Satisfaction (Article 41 ECHR)

Nagmetov v Russia, no 35589/08, Grand Chamber Judgment of 30 March 2017

In the judgment of *Nagmetov v Russia* the Court discussed the question whether just satisfaction could be awarded in the absence of a properly made

---

[144] See the joint partly dissenting opinion of Judges Raimondi, Spano, Kjølbro, Grozev, Ravarani, Pastor Vilanova, Poláčková and Hüseynov.
[145] ECtHR, *Merabishvili v Georgia*, no 72508/13 [GC] 28.11.2017, paras. 282 et seq.
[146] Ibid., paras. 287 et seq.
[147] Ibid., paras. 292 et seq.
[148] Ibid., para. 307.
[149] Ibid., paras. 309 et seq. For a further discussion of the judgment see C. HERI, 'Merabishvili, Mammadov and Targeted Criminal Proceedings: Recent Developments under Article 18 ECHR', *Strasbourg Observers*, available at https://strasbourgobservers.com/2017/12/15/merabishvili-mammadov-and-targeted-criminal-proceedings-recent-developments-under-article-18-echr/#more-4073, last accessed 07.06.2018 and B. ÇALI, 'Merabishvili v. Georgia: Has the Mountain Given Birth to a Mouse?', *Verfassungsblog*, available at https://verfassungsblog.de/merabishvili-v-georgia-has-the-mountain-given-birth-to-a-mouse, last accessed 07.06.2018.

claim (according to the Rules of the Court the applicants who want to obtain just satisfaction in the event of a finding of a violation of the Convention by the Court normally have to make a specific claim to that effect, see Article 60 para. 1). The ECtHR held by 14 votes to 3 that it was possible under exceptional circumstances, at least for non-pecuniary damage. An award of compensation especially depended on the gravity and impact of the violation, the overall context of the case as well as the (un)availability of adequate reparation at domestic level.[150]

Chiragov and others v Armenia, no 13216/05, and *Sargsyan v Azerbaijan*, no 40167/06, Grand Chamber Judgments (just satisfaction) of 12 December 2017

In the cases of *Chiragov* and *Sargsyan* the Grand Chamber – after it had found violations of Articles 8 and 13 ECHR and Article 1 of Protocol No 1 to the ECHR in two judgments on the merits in 2015[151] – awarded the applicants just satisfaction for damage suffered on account of the denial of access to their property during the conflict over Nagorno-Karabakh. The judgments are of particular interest with regard to the award of compensation for the violation of Convention rights in conflicts. They also discussed questions in connection with the awarding of just satisfaction in the case of the death of the original applicants.

2.17.3. *Execution of Judgments (Article 46 ECHR)*

Burmych and others v Ukraine, no 46852/13, Grand Chamber Judgment (striking out) of 12 October 2017

The judgment of *Burmych and others* concerned complaints regarding the prolonged non-enforcement of final judicial decisions. It is of special interest because it dealt with the distribution of roles between the ECtHR and the Committee of Ministers with regard to Articles 19 and 46 ECHR and therefore affected the structures of the protection system under the Convention. The cases dealt with in *Burmych and others* raised similar questions to those

---

[150] ECtHR, *Nagmetov v Russia*, no 35589/08 [GC] 30.03.2017, paras. 80 et seq. See also the joint dissenting opinion of Judges Raimondi, O'Leary and Ranzoni and the discussion of the judgment by E. LAMBERT ABDELGAWAD, 'Nagmetov v. Russia: opening up Pandora's Box on Article 41?', *Strasbourg Observers*, available at https://strasbourgobservers.com/2017/05/02/nagmetov-v-russia-opening-up-pandoras-box-on-article-41, last accessed 07.06.2018.

[151] ECtHR, *Chiragov and Others v Armenia*, no 13216/05 [GC] 16.06.2015 and *Sargsyan v Azerbaijan*, no 40167/06 [GC] 16.06.2015. See in this regard B. OHMS and E. HANDL-PETZ, 'The Jurisprudence of the European Court of Human Rights in 2015: A Year of Transition', in W. BENEDEK, F. BENOÎT-ROHMER, M.C. KETTEMANN et al. (eds.), *European Yearbook on Human Rights 2015*, Neuer Wissenschaftlicher Verlag, Vienna-Graz 2015, pp. 265 et seq. (pp. 273 et seq.).

already examined by the Court in its pilot judgment in *Yuriy Nikolayevich Ivanov v Ukraine*.[152] In that judgment the Chamber had found a violation of Article 6 para. 1 ECHR and Article 1 of Protocol No 1 to the ECHR and had held that the respondent state should set up an effective domestic remedy within one year at the latest that could provide adequate and sufficient redress for the non-enforcement or delayed enforcement of domestic decisions. The Court decided to adjourn the proceedings in all similar pending and future cases in the meantime. However, as Ukraine had not yet complied with the pilot judgment and had not adopted the general measures required thereby, by the time of the Grand Chamber judgment more than 12,000 such cases were pending before the Court. The latter therefore had to decide whether it was appropriate for it to examine all similar applications lodged after the *Ivanov*-judgment in similar cases or whether it was for the Committee of Ministers in its capacity as supervisor of the execution of the pilot judgment to ensure that all persons affected by the systemic problem found in that judgment obtained justice and compensation. The Court pointed out that it had already resolved the legal issues under the Convention concerning prolonged non-enforcement of domestic decisions in Ukraine in the pilot judgment and had thus discharged its function under Article 19 of the Convention.[153] Referring to the principle of subsidiarity, the Grand Chamber then held that the matter treated by *Ivanov* was a question of execution of judgments under Article 46 ECHR which fell in the Committee of Minister's competence. In the end, the Court decided, pursuant to Article 37 para. 1 (c) ECHR, to strike out of its list of cases all *Ivanov*-type cases and to transmit them to the Committee of Ministers in order for them to be dealt with in the framework of the general measures of execution of the pilot judgment (10 to 7 votes).[154] It also stated that it could strike out similar future applications and transmit them directly to the Committee of Ministers.[155]

Moreira Ferreira v Portugal (no. 2), no 19867/12, Grand Chamber Judgment of 11 July 2017

The case of *Moreira Ferreira v Portugal* also touched important questions with regard to the definition of the competence of the Court as distinguished from

---

[152] ECtHR, *Yuriy Nikolayevich Ivanov v Ukraine*, no 40450/04, 15.10.2009.
[153] ECtHR, *Burmych and others v Ukraine*, no 46852/13 (GC) 12.10.2017, paras. 197–198.
[154] The approach taken by the majority was heavily criticised by the joint dissenting opinion of Judges Yudkivska, Sajó, Bianku, Karakaş, De Gaetano, Laffranque and Motoc.
[155] ECtHR, *Burmych and others, supra* note 153, para. 221. For a further discussion of the judgment see E. KINDT, 'Non-execution of a pilot judgment: ECtHR passes the buck to the Committee of Ministers in Burmych and others v. Ukraine', *Strasbourg Observers*, available at https://strasbourgobservers.com/2017/10/26/non-execution-of-a-pilot-judgment-ecthr-passes-the-buck-to-the-committee-of-ministers-in-burmych-and-others-v-ukraine/#more-3972, last accessed 07.06.2018.

the competence of the Committee of Ministers concerning the supervision of the execution of judgments.[156] The Grand Chamber found that the Supreme Court's refusal to reopen criminal proceedings after the ECtHR's Chamber Judgment in the case concerned a new issue and that therefore Article 46 ECHR could not preclude it from reviewing the present complaint.[157] Moreover, the present case raised questions as to the ordering of individual measures by the Court in connection with the execution of the judgment.[158]

3. CONCLUSION

As can be seen, the Grand Chamber and other leading judgments covered a broad range of topics in 2017. For example, the Court had to deal with some interesting cases concerning the right to privacy and data protection (notably *Bărbulescu* and *Satakunnan*). Those judgments show that the Court is perfectly aware of the danger for human rights associated with new technologies and that it truly seeks to adapt its case law to new developments in this area. In 2017, the Court especially strengthened the rights of employees, which are subjected to monitoring by their employer. Furthermore, the ECtHR decided on human rights violations (particularly Articles 3 and 5 ECHR) in connection with the detention of asylum seekers – also during the refugee crisis in 2015 (*S.F. and others, Ilias and Ahmed, Z.A. and others*). A number of decisions pertained to discrimination issues. In this regard, the Court also had to judge on the extent of the prosecution of racially motivated crimes (*Škorjanec*). In addition, the Court for the first time had to deal with the responsibility of a politician for his conduct during the financial crisis (*Haarde*). Other cases in 2017 dealt with highly topical issue in connection with the integration of Muslims in western society (see *Osmanoğlu and Kocabaş* and also *Belcacemi and Oussar*) and the proportionality of measures envisaging the improvement of the social mix in certain underprivileged areas in order to avoid social problems *(Garib)* – some European cities face big challenges in this regard. Other important cases pertained to the applicability of Article 6 and the violation of the right to a fair trial as well as to the right to respect for private and family life.

---

[156] For questions concerning the applicability of Article 6 ECHR and a violation of the principle of fair trial see above 2.6.2.1 and 2.6.2.2.
[157] See ECtHR, *Moreira Ferreira (no. 2), supra* note 56, paras. 52 et seq.
[158] For further discussion see the dissenting opinion of Judge Pinto de Albuquerque joined by Judges Karakaş, Sajó, Lazarova Trajkovska, Tsotsoria, Vehabović and Kūris and A. DONALD, 'Judges at odds over Court's authority to order remedies', *Strasbourg Observers*, 28 July 2017, available at https://strasbourgobservers.com/2017/07/28/judges-at-odds-over-courts-authority-to-order-remedies/#more-3854, last accessed 07.06.2018.

In general, 2017 brought a couple of important clarifications and systematisations of the Court's case law. Thus, in *Lopes de Sousa Fernandes* the ECtHR explained in detail the states' positive obligations with regard to medical negligence and established a criteria catalogue to be used when deciding whether state responsibility under the Convention was engaged in a given case. Likewise, in *Bărbulescu* it developed a set of factors which should be considered by domestic courts when ruling on the reasonableness of the monitoring of an employee's communications. In *Simeonovi*, the Court systematised the guiding principles for restricting the right to legal assistance during the investigation stage. Further, in *P. Plaisier B.V. and others* the Court summed up its case law on austerity measures. The case of *De Tommaso* gave the possibility to the Court to discuss and confirm its previous case law on the applicability of Article 5 ECHR to special police supervision measures as well as to elaborate on the interplay between Article 5 ECHR and Article 2 of Protocol No 4 to the ECHR. In *N.D. and N.T v Spain* it summed up its case law on collective expulsions. Finally, the ECtHR generally had to discuss some provisions of the ECHR in 2017 which had not been dealt with very often so far in its case law, such as Article 35 para. 2 (b) ECHR (*Harkins*), Article 18 ECHR (*Merabishvili*) or Article 2 of Protocol No 4 to the ECHR (*De Tommaso* and *Garib*). It took this opportunity to clarify their scope and interpretation.

Remarkably, the year of 2017 brought a reduction of the number of pending applications to the lowest level since 2004. However, it remains to be seen if that is the start of a positive trend that will continue throughout the next years. It must be kept in mind that the Court still faces big challenges with regard to its workload.[159] One deserving special mention is the backlog of more than 26,000 Chamber cases which require detailed examination. Another one results from the Court's decision from the middle of 2017 to provide reasons for single-judge decisions.[160] Before, applicants received a decision letter rejecting their complaints in a global manner only. Although that development is to be welcomed in the interest of the applicants who are now better able to understand the reasons for the rejection of their complaint, it implies greater effort on the part of the Court, especially when bearing in mind the high number of single-judge decisions issued per year (66,156 in 2017). In addition, Protocol No 16 to the ECHR (which has entered into force on 1 August 2018 for those states that have ratified it) may lead to extra workload for the ECHR. It offers a new possibility for national high courts and tribunals of a Member State to request the ECtHR to give an advisory opinion on questions of principle relating

---

[159] See ECtHR, 'Annual Report 2017', *supra* note 1, p. 8.
[160] See ECtHR, 'Launch of new system for single judge decisions with more detailed reasoning', Press Release, 01.06.2017, available at http://hudoc.echr.coe.int/eng-press?i=003-5735020-7285664, last accessed 12.06.2018.

to the interpretation or application of the rights or freedoms defined in the Convention and the Protocols thereto. However, it must be seen to what extent the states will make use of that instrument in the future, how it will work and what exactly will be its implications for the Court's workload. Furthermore, it seems not sure how the changes envisaged by Protocol No 15 to the ECHR (which has not entered into force yet)[161] will have an impact on that workload. The change of Article 30 ECHR (relinquishment of a case by a Chamber to the Grand Chamber will become easier) is, *inter alia*, intended to accelerate proceedings before the Court in cases which raise serious questions affecting the interpretation of the Convention or its Protocols or the resolution of a question that might have a result inconsistent with the Court's previous case law.[162] Nevertheless it might at the same time lead to a certain increase of cases transferred to the Grand Chamber, thus considerably tying up the Court's resources. The changes made to Article 35 para. 2 (b) ECHR (the admissibility criterion of no significant disadvantage shall also be applicable to cases which have not been duly considered by a domestic tribunal – the Court will be less involved with insignificant cases) and Article 35 para. 1 ECHR (reduction of the time limit for submitting applications from six months to four months – some cases might not manage to reach the Court due to that amendment) might lead to a reduction of the Court's workload.

In any case, as President Raimondi put it,[163] observance of the subsidiarity principle remains the key to the system's success. Convention violations should above all be remedied at the national level. Consequently, the Court even found that principle to be applicable to the many Turkish complaints in the aftermath of the attempted military coup in 2016, although in those cases the applicants feared being arrested by the regime on political grounds. Of utmost importance with regard to the subsidiarity principle was the above-mentioned Grand Chamber Judgment of *Burmych and others* where the Court refused to deal with new similar applications after the non-enforcement of a pilot judgment and found that it was for the Committee of Ministers and the Member States in connection with the execution of the pilot judgment to deal with those cases. Protocol No 15 to the ECHR will add a new paragraph to the Preamble to the Convention explicitly confirming the principle of subsidiarity as well as the margin of appreciation enjoyed by states according to the Court's case law when applying and implementing the Convention. That addendum is intended to 'enhance the transparency and accessibility of these

---

[161] As for June 2018.
[162] COUNCIL OF EUROPE, 'Explanatory Report to Protocol No. 15 amending the Convention for the Protection of Human Rights and Fundamental Freedoms', para. 17, available at https://rm.coe.int/CoERMPublicCommonSearchServices/DisplayDCTMContent?documentId=09000016800d383d, last accessed 07.06.2018.
[163] ECtHR, 'Annual Report 2017', *supra* note 1, p. 7.

characteristics of the Conventions system'.[164] Protocol No 16 to the ECHR may also contribute to a reinforcement of the subsidiarity principle. Its Preamble points out that the extension of the Court's competence to give advisory opinions will further enhance the interaction between the court and national authorities and thereby improve implementation of the Convention at the national level.

---

[164] COUNCIL OF EUROPE, 'Explanatory Report to Protocol No. 15', *supra* note 162, para. 7.

A DECADE OF VIOLATIONS OF THE EUROPEAN CONVENTION ON HUMAN RIGHTS

Exploring Patterns of Repetitive Violations

David Reichel and Jonas Grimheden*

1. Introduction 268
2. Methodology... 270
3. ECtHR Cases Finding Violations between 2007 and 2017.............. 271
4. Leading Cases Cited by the ECtHR 275
5. Violations of Articles and Their Connections....................... 279
6. Conclusion: What Can Be Learnt from Data Analysis? 284

ABSTRACT

This article examines human rights violations of the European Convention on Human Rights (ECHR) between 2007 and 2017 from a statistical perspective. For many years, the European Court of Human Rights (ECtHR) has had to deal with large numbers of repetitive cases, dealing with issues that the Court has previously ruled in other cases from the same country. After a general descriptive analysis of numbers of violations of the ECHR, the article provides an exploration of patterns of repetitive cases and general connections between leading cases and provisions of the treaty (articles) – using network analysis. The role leading cases play in repetitive cases differs across countries. In some countries several leading cases are cited in repetitive cases at the same time. This means that there are more complex structural issues that need to be addressed. The variety of leading cases mentioned in repetitive cases in Romania, but also Russia, Bulgaria and Ukraine, is higher compared to other countries, with strong connections between leading cases.

---

* The views expressed in this article are solely those of the authors and do not necessarily reflect the views or position of the European Union Agency for Fundamental Rights. The authors are grateful for critical comments from Matylda Pogorzelska and the two anonymous reviewers.

1. INTRODUCTION

The European Convention on Human Rights (ECHR) is arguably the most important human rights law instrument in Europe. Together with its monitoring body, the European Court of Human Rights (ECtHR), they constitute a global role model for protection of human rights. Opened for signature in 1950, with all 47 Member States of the Council of Europe (CoE) being parties, the ECHR serves as the foundation of Europe's human rights framework – in particular for civil and political rights.[1] Cases concerning violations of the ECHR can be brought to the ECtHR in Strasbourg. In the past decades, the Court has dealt with thousands of cases, which also has led to the Court struggling with its caseload. The majority of cases are so-called repetitive cases from a few states.

Long evident but explicitly expressed in the Interlaken Declaration of 2010 of the High Level Conference on the Future of the ECtHR, too large a share of the Court's resources are devoted to repetitive applications – dealing with types of situations that have already been settled and which could be dealt with more effectively at national level.[2] The Declaration also called for more attention to the follow-up on implementation of judgments through supervision of execution of judgments. Resolving these issues, in different ways, has also been an important aspect of the more recent Optional Protocols to the ECHR, in particular Protocols 14,[3] 15[4] and 16.[5] After several further High Level Conferences and yet again in April 2018 in Copenhagen at the initiative of the Danish Chairmanship of the Committee of Ministers of the CoE, a High Level Conference pointed to the problem of repetitive cases. The conference's 'Copenhagen Declaration' invited the Committee of Ministers, in consultation with other stakeholders and the ECtHR, to explore ways to facilitate effective handling of repetitive cases.[6]

---

[1] Economic and social rights are monitored by the less known European Committee on Social Rights.

[2] High Level Conference on the Future of the European Court of Human Rights, 'Interlaken Declaration', 19.02.2010, available at https://www.echr.coe.int/Documents/2010_Interlaken_FinalDeclaration_ENG.pdf, last accessed 06.06.2018.

[3] Protocol No 14 to the Convention for the Protection of Human Rights and Fundamental Freedoms, amending the control system of the Convention (ETS 194), adopted 2004, into force 2009; the Protocol addresses admissibility, repetitive and inadmissible cases.

[4] Protocol No 15 amending the Convention for the Protection of Human Rights and Fundamental Freedoms (ETS 213), adopted in 2013, not yet in force – all 47 states have signed but four ratifications are still missing to reach 47 and trigger the entry into force; the Protocol addresses subsidiarity, margin of appreciation, court efficiency, etc.

[5] Protocol No 16 to the Convention for the Protection of Human Rights and Fundamental Freedoms (ETS 214), adopted in 2013, into force on 1 August 2018; the Protocol provides for the possibility of the highest national courts to request advisory opinions from the ECtHR.

[6] High Level Conference meeting in Copenhagen on 12 and 13 April 2018 at the initiative of the Danish Chairmanship of the Committee of Ministers of the Council of Europe, 'Copenhagen Declaration', available at https://rm.coe.int/copenhagen-declaration/16807b915c, last accessed 06.06.2018.

Indeed, at the beginning of 2018, there were over 57,000 cases pending before the ECtHR, many of which are repetitive cases, deriving from common problems at national level. The Court developed a technique addressing structural problems through so-called pilot judgments in order to identify structural problems underlying the many repetitive cases of countries – addressing its root cause.[7]

Practically, if a case before the Court is deemed to be a repetitive case, meaning that the case raises an issue on which the Court has already ruled in a number of cases concerning the country before, it will be handled by a Committee of three judges. Contrary to that, if not deemed a repetitive case, a Chamber of seven judges examines the case.

The number and types of cases brought before the ECtHR tells a story about human rights problems in a country. While it is true that this type of 'complaints-based' data is not the complete picture, such data can still provide a lot of insight. A larger number of cases is not necessarily indicating that there are more violations, it could be that there is greater awareness of human rights or that there are incentives to make use of legal avenues like the ECtHR. Still, if one looks at the cases where violations are found, the data reveals much of relevance when assessing human rights – and can indicate structural issues. This article presents an analysis of cases finding violations of the ECHR over ten years. The aim is to show general patterns of violations determined by the ECtHR in order to explore what can be learnt from such data. We address specifically repetitive cases and its relation to leading cases. In which countries are most repetitive cases and how do they link to each other via leading cases? The results show that several countries show particularly high numbers of repetitive cases, linked to the same interconnected leading cases. This analysis can support identifying patterns of violations in countries, which contributes to understanding main human rights issues in countries from a quantitative perspective. Since the ECtHR is struggling with a quantitative problem, quantitative analysis is required to further understand structural issues related to repetitive cases, complementing qualitative legal analysis. Contrary to other research, this analysis is not deemed at predicting any outcomes of cases but at contributing to understand where most repetitive cases come from, which articles are concerned and what patterns can we find about linkages between leading cases in different countries.

Based on CoE's Department of Executions (HUDOC-EXEC), this article explores what can be learnt from data on human rights violations in Europe. More explicitly, the article analyses the following questions based on the HUDOC-EXEC database: Which countries violate most often, which rights are most often violated and when? The relationship between provisions of

---

[7] ECtHR, 'Factsheet – Pilot judgements', February 2018, available at https://www.echr.coe.int/Documents/FS_Pilot_judgments_ENG.pdf, last accessed 08.06.2018.

the ECHR is explored in order to better understand which articles are applied most often together to define areas of application of the ECHR. The analysis investigates the differences between repetitive and leading cases.[8] We analyse connections of leading cases which are cited in repetitive cases, where several cases are cited together repeatedly in judgments.

The article proceeds as follows: after outlining the methodology applied, we describe the number of cases per country, year and type of cases and supervision. We continue by looking into the ECHR articles most often found to be violated by a country and explore connections between articles. Then, leading cases are analysed as to how they relate to other repetitive cases and the relationships between leading articles themselves. The last section analyses linkages of articles in violations, pointing to topics of violations. The conclusions point to what can be learned from such data analysis and what it could lead to.

2. METHODOLOGY

All data used in the article were downloaded from the HUDOC-EXEC database covering the time period from 2007–2017.[9] ECtHR cases have been available in a public database called HUDOC for many years. In 2017, the HUDOC database was expanded to include work of the HUDOC-EXEC, which monitors and follows up the implementation of ECtHR judgments where a violation is found to ensure that states take action. This database provides a very useful source for exploring human rights compliance in Europe.

This article answers the questions raised above by carrying out basic descriptive statistical analysis complemented by network analysis.

Network analysis is often used in social science to establish links between social actors – for example friendships between people.[10] Basically, a network (graph)

---

[8] Leading cases, according to the glossary of the ECtHR, is a '[c]ase which has been identified as revealing new structural and / or systemic problems, either by the Court directly in its judgment, or by the Committee of Ministers in the course of its supervision of execution. Such a case requires the adoption of new general measures to prevent similar violations in the future.' This is distinct from a pilot judgment, which, according to the same source is '[w]hen the Court identifies a violation which originates in a structural and / or systemic problem which has given rise or may give rise to similar applications against the respondent State [...]'. Here, 'the Court will identify the nature of the structural or systemic problem established, and provide guidance as to the remedial measures which the respondent State should take'. See CoE, 'Glossary' available at https://www.coe.int/en/web/execution/glossary, last accessed 06.06.2018.

[9] The database is available at http://hudoc.exec.coe.int, last accessed 06.06.2018. Data were downloaded on 28.05.2018. The statistics presented required the data to be reorganised and partly recoded. The authors are responsible for any presentation of the results in this article.

[10] For an accessible introduction see D. Knoke and Y. Song, *Social Network Analysis*, 2nd edition, SAGE Publications, Los Angeles et al. 2008 or T. Arnold and L. Tilton, *Humanities Data in R.*, Springer, Cham 2015.

consists of a set of objects (vertices) and links between the objects (edges). Whenever there is a set of relationships connecting objects, network analysis can reveal the patters of relationships, through exploratory visualisation and description. The method is not usually used to formally prove statistical relationships, however, it is an important starting point to better understand connections between objects. It is increasingly used in legal analysis, most notably to analyse connections between cases through analysing citation networks of cases cited within cases. For example, Olsen and Kücüksu (2017) used information on citation networks to find hidden patterns in ECtHR's case law with respect to cases concerning Article 14 read together with Article 2. Their analysis shows that the patterns of citation networks can support case law selection by revealing hidden patterns, which can otherwise not be seen.[11] Similarly, Lupu and Voeten (2010) analyse precedents through looking into ECtHR's case citations and reveal the way the Court uses legal justifications.[12] To give another example of the method using ECtHR case law data, Christensen, Olsen and Tarissan (2017), recently published their work on identifying case content with network analysis. They use network analysis to investigate the article citations of ECtHR cases to determine which articles are related to the content of the case.[13]

We are interested to learn to what extent leading cases, which are cited in repetitive cases, link to each other – hence being cited alongside each other in the same case several times. In this way we can indicate if there are potential structural issues in a country, raised in several leading cases, that need further attention. This analysis is one of the few attempts to use statistical analysis for contributing to better understanding of judgments concerning violations of the ECHR.

3. ECtHR CASES FINDING VIOLATIONS BETWEEN 2007 AND 2017

The ECtHR deals with a large number of cases every year, out of which a significant proportion ends with a violation being concluded. We downloaded data on violations found in the ten years from 2007–2017, including violations

---

[11] O.H. PALMER and A. KÜCÜKSU, 'Finding Hidden Patterns in ECtHR's Case Law: On how Citation Network Analysis can Improve our Knowledge of ECtHR's Article 14 Practice', (2017) 17(1) *International Journal of Discrimination and the Law*, pp. 4–22.
[12] Y. LUPU and E. VOETEN, 'Precedent on International Courts: A Network Analysis of Case Citations by the European Court of Human Rights', (2011) 42 *British Journal of Political Science*, pp. 413–439.
[13] C.M. LOLLE, O.H. PALMER and F. TARISSAN, 'Identification of Case Content with Quantitative Network Analysis: an Example from the ECtHR', 29th International Conference on Legal Knowledge and Information Systems (JURIX'16), 2017, available at https://hal.archives-ouvertes.fr/hal-01386810/document, last accessed 08.06.2018.

in 15,265 cases.[14] The dates are based on judgment dates. The annual number of judgments is relatively stable and ranged from 1,270 in 2015 to 1,545 in 2011 with an average of 1,388 per year. The average number of cases per country in the period of observation is 325. Most cases concerned Turkey (2,401), Russia (2,110), Romania (1,341) and Poland (1,272). The lowest number of cases concern the smaller CoE Member States, Andorra, Monaco, Liechtenstein and San Marino with six or fewer cases.

As for the European Union (EU) Member States, the countries with the fewest cases in the period are Ireland (14) and Denmark (16) and most cases are in Romania and Poland. The CoE monitors the implementation of the Court decisions to ensure that they are properly 'executed'. At the beginning of 2018, 61% of the cases from the decade covered were closed. This means that changes have been implemented to address the causes of the violation found in the judgment. The remaining cases are mainly open cases. These either follow a standard procedure or an enhanced procedure, the latter meaning that they are related to a particularly important aspect, such as structural and systemic issues. A total of 18% of all cases follow a standard procedure and 20% an enhanced procedure. Just 1% are new cases, not yet classified or closed.

Figure 1 shows the total number of cases per year by type of supervision (standard and enhanced as well as new and closed). Of the cases stemming from the years 2007–2015, approximately 60–70% are closed, whereas the share of closed cases logically decreases in the remaining years from 43% in 2016 to 18% in 2017. The share of closed cases is much higher in EU Member States as opposed to the other 19 of the 47 CoE Member States.

Part of the implementation monitoring is based on the state in question adopting an action plan. This is still pending for 235 cases of the approximately 15,000 in the database as per May 2018. This amounts to 1.5%, (including 31 cases under enhanced procedures), and again logically, most of them are from 2017. It is important to keep in mind that the year of a judgment is not the year when the case was brought to Court and also not necessarily the year when the alleged violation took place. The judgments in the database covered between 2007 and 2017 include cases that were brought to Court as early as 1990. In fact, almost 50% of the cases were brought to the ECtHR before 2007.

With respect to the main question of interest of this article, the CoE classifies cases as leading or repetitive. Irrespective of a case being leading or not (repetitive), ECtHR cases pending implementation can be settled.[15] Figure 2 shows the number of cases by country and type of case, including leading, repetitive and settled ('friendly settlement')[16] cases. Overall, about 17%

---

[14] Including 15,257 unique case numbers.
[15] Article 39 ECHR (ETS 005).
[16] Very few are considered as a mix of leading and repetitive or friendly settlements as well as leading and repetitive cases.

Figure 1. Number of cases of the ECtHR finding violations in CoE Member States by supervision and date of judgment, 2007–2017

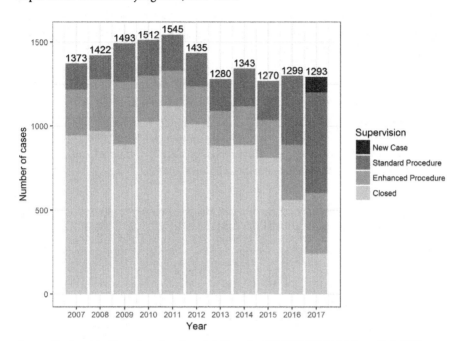

Source: Produced by the authors based on data from the HUDOC-EXEC database, CoE, 2018.

of all cases from 2007–2017 are leading cases, about 25% of the cases are resolved through friendly settlements and 62% of the cases are repetitive cases.[17] Most friendly settlements are cases concerning Poland, with half of all cases during the decade in Poland (50%, amounting to 636 cases). Turkey has the second most friendly settlements (523 cases), which represent 22% of all cases that found a violation in that country. Hungary, Romania, Greece and Serbia also have significant numbers of friendly settlements ranging from 267 to 355 – all other countries have fewer than 200 friendly settlements. The country with the highest share of friendly settlements in the total number of violations is Serbia (63%) and the former Yugoslav Republic of Macedonia (59%).[18]

Of the total number of leading cases in the time period covered (2,609), most leading cases are recorded for Turkey (207), Russia (200), Romania (196), Bulgaria (169), Ukraine (146), and France (119). When looking at the proportion of leading cases among all cases, it should be considered that this proportion is related to the overall number of cases. Countries with very few

---

[17] This takes into account that there are some cases filed as leading and repetitive or friendly settlements as well as leading and repetitive cases, so the percentages add up to over 100%.
[18] The highest percentage is actually San Marino with four out of the five cases, but the number of cases is too low to speak about percentages.

violations also tend to show higher percentages of leading cases as the bulk of violations concerns repetitive cases. Hence, a country with many repetitive cases consequently has a lower share of leading cases. Poland, Turkey, Russia, Hungary and Greece have the lowest percentage of leading cases, which means that these countries either often repeat violations (such as Russia, Turkey and Greece) or are able to settle cases more often (such as Poland and Hungary).

Finally, let us have a look at the numbers and percentages of repetitive cases in a country. By far the highest share of repetitive cases is found in Russia, where 84% of cases are repetitive (a total of 1,776 repetitive cases). Other countries with high shares of repetitive cases are Azerbaijan, Ukraine, Slovenia, Turkey and Italy with 70% or more. The overview of cases by type of case with the percentage of repetitive cases is shown in Figure 2 below.[19]

Figure 2. Number of cases per country in CoE Member States from 2007–2017 by type of case (and percentage of repetitive cases in brackets)

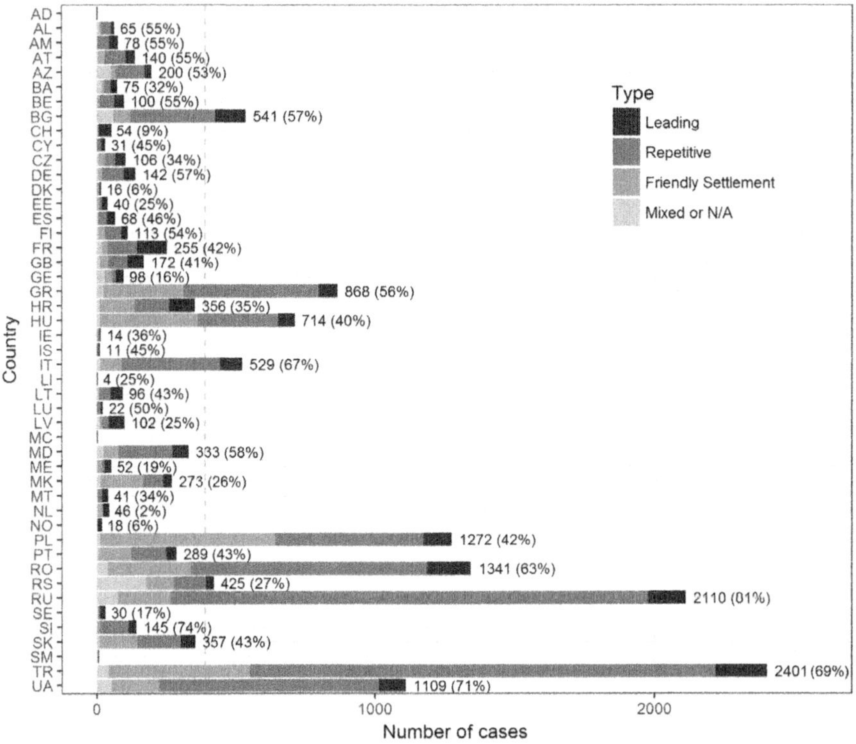

Note: The vertical dashed line gives the average number of cases across all countries.

Source: Produced by the authors based on data from the HUDOC-EXEC database, CoE, 2018.

---

[19] There is a slight deviation of the percentages between the text and the graph, because the graph only includes the percentages of repetitive cases that are not mixed.

4. LEADING CASES CITED BY THE ECtHR

Leading cases with many repetitive ones are particularly important to implement, given the likely ripple-effect when a resolution is found resolving the leading case as well as the many repetitive ones. In this section, we consider questions of which leading cases are more important in the sense of being cited in most repetitive cases and in the sense of being connected to a greater number of other leading cases, through being cited together in the same repetitive cases. In the dataset, there are up to eight leading cases cited in one repetitive case.

The case *Klyakhin v Russia*,[20] about an unreasonably long pre-trial detention (Article 5(3)), is most often cited in repetitive cases – 332 times. Other important leading cases cited in many repetitive cases from 2007–2017 are *Ormanci and Others v Turkey*,[21] about the length of proceedings (related to compensation), cited in 274 repetitive cases, *Khashiyev and Akayeva v Russia*[22] concerning violations of Articles 2, 3 and 13 with respect to the right to life and the prohibition of torture (failure to investigate), cited in 245 repetitive cases, and *Zhovner v Ukraine*,[23] which found violations of Articles 6 and P1-1 (i.e. 1st Additional Protocol, fair trial and the right to property), cited in 239 cases. The two cases *Timar v Hungary* (36186/97)[24] and *Manios v Greece*[25] are the most important leading cases cited in repetitive cases in EU Member States (in 213 and 206 repetitive cases, respectively). Both concern violations of Article 6(1) about the length of proceedings. Leading cases are only cited in repetitive cases within the same country, since they are only leading in relation to that one state. Still, in very few instances a case can concern more than one country. Altogether, there are 1,153 unique leading cases cited in the 9,406 repetitive cases. However, there are some 11,400 leading case citations since one repetitive case can refer to more than one leading case. Of the 1,153 leading cases, 642 have only been cited without any other leading case, while the other 511 cases were cited at least once alongside another leading case. This means that the repetition of topics in a repetitive case, do not concern one single aspect, but often several issues, as already ruled about in other leading cases. If there are many leading cases connected through repetitive ones, this points to more complex issues of rights violations in countries. A network analysis of leading cases – as being cited alongside each other in repetitive case citations – has been carried out. Figure 3 shows the connections of leading cases as determined by being cited in the same repetitive case.

Figure 3 thus shows that there are larger clusters with several leading cases jointly cited, indicating that it is likely that several repetitive issues are dealt

---

20   ECtHR, *Klyakhin v Russia*, no 46082/99, 30.11.2004.
21   ECtHR, *Ormanci and Others v Turkey*, no 43647/98, 21.12.2004.
22   ECtHR, *Khashiyev and Akayeva v Russia*, no 57942/00, 24.02.2005.
23   ECtHR, *Zhovner v Ukraine*, no 56848/00, 29.06.2018.
24   ECtHR, *Timar v Hungary*, no 36186/97, 25.02.2003.
25   ECtHR, *Manios v Greece*, no 70626/01, 11.03.2018.

Figure 3. Network of leading cases cited together in repetitive cases, 2007–2017

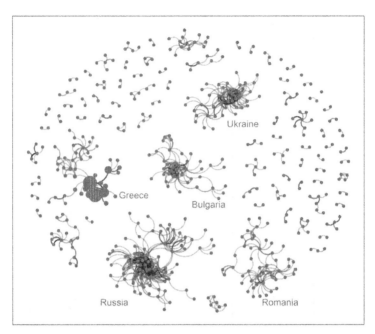

Note: Each dot represents a leading case cited in a repetitive case. Leading cases cited together in the same repetitive case are linked with lines. The size of the dots reflects how central a case is in being cited with other leading cases.

Source: Produced by the authors based on data from the HUDOC-EXEC database, CoE, 2018.

with in one case. The main clusters include five countries: Russia, Ukraine, Bulgaria, Romania and Greece. These clusters indicate that repetitive cases are similar in the sense that there are connected to many leading cases. For example, a repetitive case cites two leading cases A and B. Another leading case cites B and C, which makes A and C be connected indirectly. Such connections create a network of leading cases as being cited in repetitive cases. Contrary to that, several other countries do not often have leading cases mentioned together in repetitive cases – rather only two leading cases mentioned together, but none of these mentioned together with another case in another repetitive case (instances in Figure 3, where there are only two connected dots, cases with only one leading case cited are not shown). However, while the leading cases in four of these countries, Russia, Ukraine, Bulgaria and Romania, are more interconnected compared to other countries – hence building clusters – the leading cases cited in these countries are still more loosely linked compared to Greece. In Greece, there are a few leading cases, which are very often cited together in repetitive cases – therefore a lot of repetition of the same problems. The clusters of leading cases in repetitive cases can point to potential structural issues of similar problems in the same countries that occur repeatedly.

For zooming into the connection of leading and repetitive cases, we selected two countries that appear to have clusters of leading cases often cited in repetitive cases.

In this sense, the network of leading cases among repetitive cases is denser compared to other countries. In Greece there are 545 repetitive cases and over 760 connections between cases. The case of *Manios v Greece*[26] is the most central case, followed by the case of *Vassilios Athanasiou and Others v Greece*.[27] Both cases concern the length of administrative procedures. In Manios the proceedings took more than eight years and in Vassilios, which also concerned Article 13 (access to remedy), the proceedings lasted over 13 years. Different from the other cases mentioned in relation to Figure 4, Vassilios is also considered a pilot judgment by the Court, meaning that the Court deemed that the case refers to structural problems in the countries. However, in terms of appearing in other repetitive cases, the other cases highlighted in Figure 4 apparently point towards structural issues as well.

Yet, while these cases are central in terms of being cited most often, the cases *S.D. v Greece*[28] and *Vasilakis v Greece*[29] are those that are most interconnected to other cases (i.e. have the highest 'betweenness score' in network analysis terminology). Both cases refer to Article 3 (detention conditions) but also, respectively, Article 5 (liberty and security) and Article 6 (fair trial).

In the case of Romania, there are 955 cases with just over 1,000 connections. Here, the case of *Bragadireanu v Romania* (22088/04) is the most central and most interconnected case, which concerned conditions of detention (Article 3) and length of the procedure (Article 6). In more detail, the detention conditions for Mr Bragadireanu, given particular medical conditions, were not adequate and court proceedings in his case had lasted more than eight years. Detention conditions is a frequent issue before the ECtHR in relation to Romania, due mainly to overcrowding but also other conditions – in this case access to sanitary facilities.[30] Another central case in Romania is *Stoianova and Nedelcu v Romania*,[31] concerning length of criminal proceedings (and thus the link to Bragadirenau in relation to Article 6), followed by several other cases, even though, as mentioned, the network of cases is not as dense as the one in Greece.

---

[26] ECtHR, *Manios v Greece*, no 70626/01, 11.03.2004.
[27] ECtHR, *Vassilios Athanasiou and Others v Greece*, no 50973/08, 21.12.2010.
[28] ECtHR, *S.D. v Greece*, no 53541/07, 11.06.2009.
[29] ECtHR, *Vasilakis v Greece*, no 25145/05, 17.01.2008.
[30] Detention conditions in Romania has also been an issue before the Court of Justice of the European Union, see, prominently, C-404/15 Aranyosi and Căldăraru, Grand Chamber Judgment, 5 April 2016.
[31] ECtHR, *Stoianova and Nedelcu v Romania*, no 77517/01, 04.08.2005.

Figure 4. Network of leading case citations in repetitive cases in Greece (upper panel) and Romania (lower panel), 2007–2017

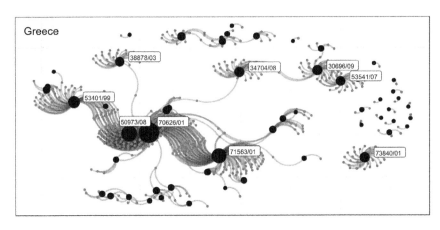

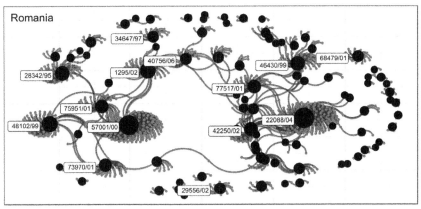

Note: Small grey dots indicate repetitive cases and large black dots are the leading cases cited. The size of the black dots reflects the importance of the cases in terms of being cited most often in repetitive cases.

Source: Produced by the authors based on data from the HUDOC-EXEC database, CoE, 2018.

Apart from the important case of *Bragadireanu v Romania*,[32] the case of *Calmanovici v Romania*[33] is also strongly interlinked to other cases, as it also concerns many articles, including Articles 5 (liberty and security), 6 (fair trial, thus the link to Bragadirenau in relation length of proceedings), 8 (private and family life) and Article 3 of Protocol 1 (P1-3, free elections). The case of *Barbu Anghelescu v Romania*,[34] has strong links to Bragadireanu and Calmanovici due to a violation of Article 3 in terms of degrading

---

32   ECtHR, *Bragadireanu v Romania*, no 22088/04, 06.12.2007.
33   ECtHR, *Calmanovici v Romania*, no 42250/02, 01.07.2008.
34   ECtHR, *Barbu Anghelescu v Romania*, no 46430/99, 05.10.2004.

treatment. These are the frequently cited leading cases with many links to other leading cases. Interesting is also to observe the two significant leading cases that are more isolated. In *Driha v Romania*[35] Article 1 of Protocol 1 (property) was violated, together with Article 14 (discrimination), in relation to salaries paid to a state employee. In *Radovici and Stănescu v Romania*,[36] the case concerned property and an emergency ordinance which put such a heavy burden on landlords so as to amount to a violation. The network graphs in Figure 4 visualise how repetitive cases (small dots) are linked to leading cases.

5. VIOLATIONS OF ARTICLES AND THEIR CONNECTIONS

While the overall number of cases and their connections to each other via repetitive cases is interesting concerning the (quantitative) importance of leading cases, the question of which articles were violated is of high relevance for understanding which areas of rights are mainly affected in the cases. It is interesting to examine which rights were violated by which country and how the articles of the ECHR are linked to each other, not the least since more than one provision can be violated in one case.

It is important to note that the 'scope' of different provisions of the ECHR varies considerably. Not only is the actual text of some articles varying significantly in length but they also deal with different and quite distinct issues, that makes them more or less likely to end up before court. For these reasons, the frequency of violations of a particular right needs to be understood and interpreted with the scope of the right in mind.

The detailed ECHR articles violated are not recorded for many cases (approximately 4,000 cases) in the quantitative database (i.e. in the column giving the exact article number). The cases where the exact article is missing, most often refer to 'Peaceful enjoyment of possessions' (which is Article P1-1, but this is not noted in the database). Therefore, the following analysis is limited to those cases, where the exact ECHR provision is recorded in the HUDOC-EXEC database, which concerns 10,887 cases across the 47 CoE Member States in the period from 2007–2017. However, the cases include 15,297 violations, showing that one case often concludes violations of several provisions.[37]

The most often violated provision is Article 6 (right to a fair trial), with 5,867 cases (38%). Other articles frequently violated are Article 3 (prohibition of torture, 2018 times, 13%), Article 5 (right to liberty and security, 1,805, 12%),

---

[35] ECtHR, *Driha v Romania*, no 29556/02, 21.02.2008.
[36] ECtHR, *Radovici and Stănescu v Romania*, no 68479/01, 02.11.2006.
[37] In fact, the database shows the detailed articles including the paragraph. However, we limit the analysis only to the general article.

Article 13 (right to an effective remedy, 1,558, 10%) and Article 1 of the first Additional Protocol to the Convention (right to property, 1,316 times, 9%). Table 1 below shows the number of violations by article for the ten articles with most violations recorded. Violations of Articles 6 and 3 present over 50% of all violations and all these five articles just over 80% of violations. What is interesting to observe is that for all these five articles, the clear majority of over 85% concerns repetitive cases. The percentage is even close to 90% concerning violations of Article 13. For the other article violations shown in Table 1, only Article 2 also concerns over 80% of repetitive cases. The rest has a much lower percentage of repetitive cases, yet still 50% or more.

Again, it is important to recall that articles are often rather different in scope and likelihood to be litigated, so comparisons of this sort must be read with that in mind. There are arguably also violations that are very severe in terms of human suffering and violations that are of different nature – this importance of cases in terms of severity is not accounted for in this quantitative analysis. An additional aspect to highlight is in relation to Article 3 (prohibition of torture), which in quite some cases deals with extradition to countries where there is a risk of torture, rather than torture happening in the country in question.

Table 1. ECHR articles with most violations recorded in the HUDOC-EXEC database from 2007–2017

Article	Number violations	% of total	Cum. %[38]	Repetitive	% repetitive of number violations	Name
6	5,867	38.4	38.4	5,023	85.6	Right to a fair trial
3	2,018	13.2	51.5	1,750	86.7	Prohibition of torture
5	1,805	11.8	63.3	1,545	85.6	Right to liberty and security
13	1,558	10.2	73.5	1,395	89.5	Right to an effective remedy
P1-1	1,316	8.6	82.1	1,155	87.8	Protection of property
8	903	5.9	88.0	495	54.8	Right to respect for private and family life
2	639	4.2	92.2	533	83.4	Right to life
10	452	3.0	95.2	292	64.6	Freedom of expression
14	187	1.2	96.4	93	49.7	Prohibition of discrimination
11	177	1.2	97.5	121	68.4	Freedom of assembly and association

Source: Produced by the authors based on data from the HUDOC-EXEC database, CoE, 2018.

---

[38] Cumulative percentage. Minor differences in the two columns are due to rounding.

The trend over time for the six articles most often violated is shown in Figure 5 and a map showing which countries most violated the top four articles is shown in Figure 6. Most of the Article 6 violations took place in the years 2007–2010 and decreased afterwards until 2015. In the past two years an increase can be observed again. Most article violations have been recorded for Turkey, Russia and Ukraine (together 40% of all violations). The increase in the past two years is mainly due to the increase in violations in these three countries – accounting for 52% of all Article 6 violations in 2017.

Russia, Turkey and Romania are the top violators of Article 3 (prohibition of torture) – together 60% of all violations in the years 2007–2017. Overall the number of violations is rather stable over the years since 2009. However, there was a decrease in violations of Article 3 in most countries in 2017, in Russia the number of Article 3 violations has increased considerably in 2017, from 60 in 2016 to 116 in 2017.

Article 5 – the right to liberty and security – is most often violated by Russia (603 or one-third of all Article 5 violations), followed by Turkey and Poland. Violations were steadily decreasing from 2009–2015 but increased strongly in 2016 – mainly due to the increase of violations in Russia – however, decreased again in 2017.

Figure 5. Trend in article violations 2007–2017 for the six most often violated articles

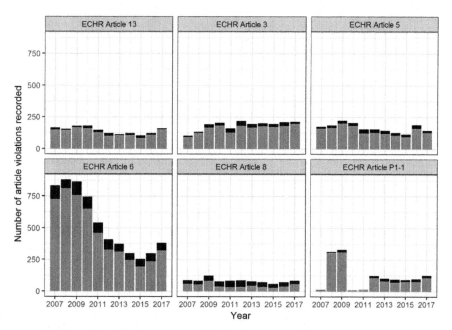

Note: Grey bars indicate repetitive cases and black bars other cases.

Source: Produced by the authors based on data from the HUDOC-EXEC database, CoE, 2018.

Figure 6. Article violations by country of the four most often violated articles

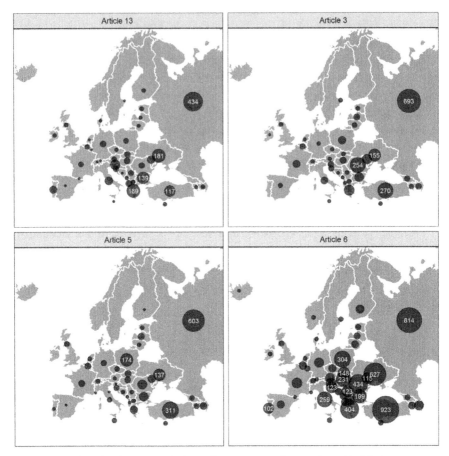

Note: The number of violations is only shown for countries with more than 100 violations.
Source: Produced by the authors based on data from the HUDOC-EXEC database, CoE, 2018.

For Articles 13 (remedy), P1-1 (property) and 8 (privacy and family) and the other top articles in Table 1, Russia always has most violations. Apart from Russia, Article 13 is most often violated by Greece, Article P1-1 by Romania and Article 8 by Italy. Violations of these three articles increased slightly in 2017.

Altogether, there are 27 different articles violated in the period of observation. Often articles are violated together in the same cases, which presents a connection between two or more articles. For example, when the freedom of expression in Article 10 and the right to a fair trial in Article 6 are violated in the same case, the articles are linked together – hence article violations can be analysed as a network of relations in cases. The density of the network of all articles would be 100%, if each article were violated with all other articles at least once. In the dataset of violations from 2007–2017, there are 137 different connections of articles, which means that the network of articles has a density of 38.5%. In general, there are clusters of articles that are more often violated together and some articles are more central than others. Article 6 as well as Articles 13, 5, 3 and 8 are the most central articles in terms of being violated most often together with many other articles. Article 6 is the most central article in this sense, because it is violated together with 24 other articles at least once (not at the same time, but in different cases), hence the most connected article. The other articles mentioned before are linked to 19 to 22 other articles at least once.

The network graph of articles being violated together is shown in Figure 7. It shows the central role of Article 6 not only in the sense of being connected to most other articles, but also with the very strong and obvious connection to Article 13 (remedy) but also to Article 1 of Protocol 1 (P1-1, property).

Based on the linkages to other articles, there are three central – though not exclusive – groups that can be identified.[39] One group (group A) consists mainly of Articles 9, 8, 14, P1-2, P7-1, 12, P1-3, P12-1 and 46. This group includes rights

Figure 7. Network of ECHR article violations in CoE countries from 2007–2017

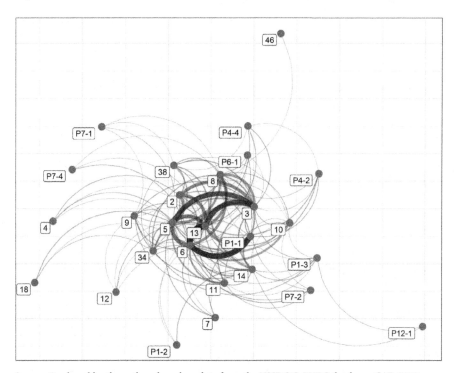

Source: Produced by the authors based on data from the HUDOC-EXEC database, CoE, 2018.

---

[39] The groups are general patterns according to relations between articles, based on group identification algorithms in network analysis.

related to family life or anti-discrimination. Another group (group B) includes Articles 3, 5, 2, 11, 38, 34, 18, P7-2, 7, 4, P4-4 and P6-1, which relates to security related aspects, such as prohibition of torture, right to life, slavery and death penalty. The third group (group C) consists of Articles 6, 10, 13, P1-1, P4-2 and P7-4; with the greatest number of violations, compared to the other two groups. This group includes issues related to access to justice, such as the right to a fair trial and the right to an effective remedy.

Taking all violations together within the groups of articles, there are no specific countries that are top violators in one or the other group. This means that while there are differences in which rights are complied with by countries, there is no strong structural difference across countries in terms of which types or groups of rights are mainly violated. So, countries with many human rights violations, violate in all different areas. However, some countries show a relatively greater number of violations in one group rather than another. Looking at countries with at least 100 article violations in the ten-year period, the United Kingdom, Austria, Italy and Croatia, relatively often violate in group A (equality), although, not so often articles of the other groups. Group B-violations (security) is predominant in Russia, while violations in group C (access to justice) are comparatively more frequent in Albania, Portugal, Serbia, Slovenia and Montenegro.

6. CONCLUSION: WHAT CAN BE LEARNT FROM DATA ANALYSIS?

Examining human rights violations from a statistical perspective contributes to the understanding of the occurrence of violations. Systematic analysis of where, which and when most violations take place is important, as is looking at connections between cases, countries and articles and if certain 'trends' or patterns of violations are discernible. This article provides an exploration of patterns of repetitive cases and general connections between leading cases and articles, highlighting connections, which otherwise would not have been so apparent.

The number of violations found by the ECtHR in Strasbourg was relatively stable in the years from 2007–2017 between about 1,280 and 1,550 per year. Most violations were found in Turkey (2,401), Russia (2,110), Romania (1,341) and Poland (1,272). Almost two-thirds (62%) of these violations are repetitive cases, dealing with issues that have already been dealt with by the Court. The highest share of repetitive cases is found in Russia, where 84% of cases are repetitive. Azerbaijan, Ukraine, Slovenia, Turkey and Italy also show large shares of repetitive cases with 70% or more.

The role leading cases play in repetitive cases differs across countries. In some countries several leading cases are cited in repetitive cases at the same time. This means that there are more complex (interlinked) structural issues that need to be addressed. The variety of leading cases mentioned in repetitive cases in Romania, but also Russia, Bulgaria and Ukraine, is higher compared to other countries, with strong connections between leading cases, pointing to interconnected problems. In Greece, also, several leading cases are cited together in repetitive cases, but there are a few cases which are cited very often in repetitive cases.

Finally, there are clusters of ECHR articles that are often violated together in the same case, most notably, Article 6 with Article 13 (the typical access to justice combination) or Article 6 with Article 1 of Protocol 1 (P1-1) as well as Article 3 with Article 5 or Article 3 with Article 13. Further exploring the linkages between articles points to three indicative groups of articles often being violated together referring to issues of equality, security and access to justice.

The ECHR is shaping the legal systems in Europe, not only through the ECtHR's jurisprudential value but also through the CoE's systematic monitoring of implementation. Quantitative analysis of Court data can reveal patterns that are otherwise not visible, which adds value by informing scholars and practitioners. What is more, the Court has a quantitative problem with too many repetitive cases, which requires – among other things – a quantitative analysis of structural issues underlying the many repetitive cases.

This article is one of the few attempts to explore patterns of repetitive violations and its linkages to leading cases. In order to find national level solutions to structural problems, the examples of leading cases, cited in several repetitive cases, can support the search for solutions to reduce the number of repetitive cases and persisting human rights issues. More work of this type can contribute to more automated analyses and information dashboards including quantitative indicators, which highlight potential structural issues. For example, the number of leading cases cited in repetitive cases could be monitored over time, where an increase in certain leading cases could point to persisting structural problems. Quantitative analysis needs to be employed to complement and reinforce the qualitative legal analysis of cases to understand the contextual and structural issues of human rights violations and to effectively address the issues underlying human rights violations.

THE BOUNDARIES TO DIALOGUE WITH THE EUROPEAN COURT OF HUMAN RIGHTS

Lize R. Glas

1. Introduction 288
2. The International Perspective 291
    2.1. VCLT 291
    2.2. ECHR: The Respondent State 292
    2.3. ECHR: The Other States Parties 294
        2.3.1. The Interpretive Authority of the ECtHR Judgments 294
        2.3.2. The Obligation to Take into Account 297
    2.4. Sub-Conclusion 299
3. The Domestic Perspectives 300
    3.1. Austria 300
    3.2. Belgium 301
    3.3. Germany 303
    3.4. Iceland 304
    3.5. Italy 305
    3.6. Latvia 307
    3.7. The Netherlands 308
    3.8. Russia 308
    3.9. Spain 310
    3.10. The UK 311
    3.11. Ukraine 312
    3.12. Sub-Conclusion 312
4. Conclusion 315

ABSTRACT

This article aims to answer the question which legal boundaries are applicable when domestic courts engage in a dialogue with the European Court of Human Rights (ECtHR) about a Strasbourg judgment. This question is answered from an international legal perspective, i.e. the perspective of the ECtHR, and the perspective of eleven domestic legal orders. Where possible, this article will comment on the practical significance of the legal boundaries found, so as to put their significance into perspective.

1. INTRODUCTION

The States Parties to the European Convention on Human Rights (ECHR) have invited the European Court of Human Rights (ECtHR) to 'deepen' its dialogue with the highest national courts 'further'.[1] For the ECtHR, dialogue is a 'high priority' as well.[2] Dialogue has been on the agenda of the ECtHR and the States for some years[3] and, therefore, has turned out to be more than just a fashionable buzzword; it is here to stay. The States Parties have even drafted a 'Protocol of Dialogue'[4] to the ECHR. This optional protocol will enable the highest domestic judges to request the ECtHR to give an advisory opinion on questions of principle relating to the ECHR.[5] The requesting court should present, *inter alia*, a 'statement of its own views on the question'[6] and decide itself 'on the effects of the advisory opinion in the domestic proceedings'.[7] The Protocol thus makes it possible for the domestic and European judges to respond to each other. The appeal of engaging in a dialogue with the ECtHR is clear: it facilitates that domestic judges can explain to the ECtHR how their legal system works and why they make certain choices within their specific domestic context. Dialogue can, thus, contribute to the smooth cooperation between the ECtHR and the domestic judges.[8] Nevertheless, not every instance of dialogue has been equally eagerly applauded. When the Supreme Court of the United Kingdom (UK) declined to follow the Chamber judgment in the case of *Al-Khawaja and Tahery v the UK* 'so that there takes place what

---

[1] Brussels Declaration (2015), para. A(1)(b); See also Brighton Declaration (2012), para. 12(c); Copenhagen Declaration (2018), para. 33.
[2] ECtHR, 'Annual Report 2017', p. 9; See also ECtHR, 'Annual Report 2016', p. 16, both available at www.echr.coe.int/Pages/home.aspx?p=court/annualreports&c, last accessed 29.05.2018.
[3] See for examples L.R. GLAS, *The Theory, Potential and Practice of Procedural Dialogue in the European Convention on Human Rights System*, Intersentia, Antwerp 2016, pp. 129–133.
[4] D. SPIELMANN, 'Opening Speech', Strasbourg, 31.01.2014, available at www.echr.coe.int/Documents/Dialogue_2014_ENG.pdf, last accessed 29.05.2018.
[5] Articles 1(1) and 5 Protocol 16 ECHR.
[6] Explanatory Report to Protocol 16 ECHR, para. 12 (provided this is 'possible and appropriate'); Article 1(1) Protocol 16 ECHR.
[7] Ibid., para. 25. This is possible because the advisory opinions are not binding see Article 5 Protocol 16 ECHR.
[8] See more elaborately L.R. GLAS, 'Dialogue in the European Convention on Human Rights System: Inspiration, Added-value and Means', (2015) 3 *European Journal of Human Rights*, pp. 258–260.

may prove to be a valuable dialogue',⁹ the Strasbourg judges welcomed that decision in the Grand Chamber judgment in the same case.¹⁰ The Russian Constitutional Court, referring to, *inter alia*, its British counterpart, has also objected to Strasbourg judgments, 'proceeding form the need of constructive interaction and mutually respectful dialogue'.¹¹ When the right to object to a Strasbourg judgment was subsequently laid down in a law,¹² Russia did not receive applause. On the contrary, the Venice Commission concluded that the law 'prevents dialogue' and that Russia 'should have recourse to dialogue, instead of resorting to unilateral measures'.¹³ Apparently, the British judges have not crossed a boundary, while the Russians have, even though they both say they want to engage in a dialogue.

Against the background just sketched, this article aims to answer the question which legal boundaries are applicable when domestic courts engage in a dialogue with the ECtHR about a Strasbourg judgment. The answer depends on one's perspective, as is illustrated by the contrasting views of the Russian Constitutional Court and the Venice Commission. More specifically, the answer depends on whether it is approached from the ECtHR's perspective or that of the State Parties, because the former looks through the lens of international law, including the ECHR, whilst the relations of the latter 'to the ECtHR are primarily determined by their national constitutions and national laws'.¹⁴ Therefore, the question that this article sets out to answer is answered from different perspectives: the international legal perspective (in section 2), i.e. the perspective of the ECtHR, and the perspective of eleven domestic legal orders (in section 3). These domestic legal orders have been selected to include both predominantly monist¹⁵ and dualist systems;¹⁶ and systems in which the ECHR has a different status.¹⁷ Additionally, domestic legal orders in which the

---

[9] UK Supreme Court, *R v Horncastle & Others* [2009] UKSC 14, para. 11.
[10] ECtHR, *Al-Khawaja and Tahery v UK*, nos 26766/05 and 22228/06 [GC], 15.12.2001, Concurring opinion of Judge Bratza, para. 2 and joint partly dissenting and partly concurring opinion of Judges Sajó and Karakaş.
[11] VENICE COMMISSION, 'Final Opinion on the Amendments to the Federal Constitutional Law of the Constitutional Court', No. 832/2015, CDL-AD(2016)016, 13.06.2016, Appendix, para. 72, referring to judgment No. 21-П/2015, 14.07.2015.
[12] See also section 3.8.
[13] VENICE COMMISSION (2016), 'Final Opinion', *supra* note 11, Appendix, paras. 136, 146.
[14] B. PETERS, 'The Rule of Law Effects of Dialogues between National Courts and Strasbourg: An Outline', in A. NOLLKAEMPER and M. KANETAKE (eds.), *The Rule of Law at the National and International Levels: Contestations and Deference*, Hart Publishing, Oxford and Portland 2016, p. 206.
[15] E.g. Germany, the Netherlands and Spain, see W. CZAPLINSKI, 'International Law and Polish Municipal Law. A Case Study', (1995) 8 *Hague Yearbook of International Law*, p. 35.
[16] E.g. Italy, UK and Iceland, see ibid.
[17] Constitutional status (e.g. Austria and the Netherlands), 'super-legislative ranking' (e.g. Belgium and Spain), 'legislative ranking' (e.g. Italy and Germany), see G. MARTINICO, 'Is the European Convention Going to Be 'Supreme'? A Comparative-Constitutional

judges have elaborated on the boundaries to dialogue with the ECtHR have been included.[18] Where possible, this article will comment on the practical significance of the legal boundaries found, so as to put their significance into perspective. This article, in sum, engages in doctrinal research, as it sets out to describe and analyse the applicable legal rules.[19] Additionally, it undertakes a comparative exercise, both horizontally, by comparing the domestic rules with each other (in section 3.12), and, vertically, by comparing the domestic rules with the international rules (in section 4).

Answering the question from different perspectives will, as just described, make it possible to compare the domestic perspectives with each other and to compare the domestic perspectives with the international legal perspective. The latter comparison helps gain insight into whether the ECtHR and the domestic judges agree on the legal boundaries that apply to the dialogue between them. If this were not the case, they arguably would not speak the 'same language', something that may prove to be a bar to a fruitful dialogue. Considering the widespread agreement about the desirability of dialogue, it is important to conduct research into potential bars to a dialogue. Research into the boundaries to dialogue with the ECtHR is also important, because, in practice, this court, like other courts, can only encourage domestic authorities 'to listen, but not [force them] to act'.[20] Moreover, unlike some other courts, the ECtHR does not have the power to reverse judgments of the courts that it reviews, to invalidate legislation or to impose punitive sanctions. Therefore, room for disagreement with Strasbourg and inaction after it has adopted a judgment is particularly broad. Considering this reality, it is important to clarify that there indeed exist legal boundaries to the dialogue.

The limitations of this article are fourfold. First, the article addresses dialogue between the ECtHR and the domestic courts, i.e. judicial dialogue, and, therefore, does not focus on other domestic actors. This choice has been made because most abstractly defined boundaries that originate from the domestic legal systems have been formulated by domestic judges, for domestic judges[21] and because these judges are the 'main interlocutors' of the ECtHR.[22] Nevertheless, section 2 mainly uses the term States, because this is the terminology of the ECtHR. The boundaries that apply to the States also apply to domestic judges,

---

Overview of ECHR and EU Law before National Courts', (2012) 23(2) *The European Journal of International Law (TEJoIL)*, 404.

[18] See section 3.

[19] P. CHYNOWETH, 'Legal Research', in A. KNIGHT and L. RUDDOCK (eds.), *Advanced Research in the Built Environment*, Wiley-Blackwell, Oxford 2008, p. 29.

[20] R. AHDIEH, 'Between Dialogue and Decree. International Review of National Courts', (2004) 79(6) *New York University Law Review*, p. 2035.

[21] See section 3.

[22] N. BRATZA, 'Future of the ECtHR – Role of National Parliaments', Speech, Strasbourg, 20.09.2012, available at http://website-pace.net/documents/10643/2356226/EntireProceedings-EN.pdf/01becec8-67e7-4cfc-b6f5-26516f0d58b8, last accessed 20.05.2018.

since the 'duty in international law to comply with the requirements of the Convention may require action to be taken by any State authority'.[23] Second, the 'sample' of the research is limited: the domestic perspectives are researched based on eleven domestic legal systems, while there are 47 States Parties to the ECHR. Third, the article considers only legal boundaries. Language and resource barriers, for example, can form practical boundaries to dialogue, but go beyond the scope of this research. Finally, the article analyses only one part of the dialogue that can take place between the domestic judges and the ECtHR and defines this dialogue as the possibility for a domestic court to 'reverse, modify or avoid' an ECtHR judgment or part thereof.[24] This is only one part of the dialogue, since the domestic court's decision is a response to an ECtHR judgment, a response to which the ECtHR may reply in a subsequent judgment, which is possible if a comparable case is brought before it.

2. THE INTERNATIONAL PERSPECTIVE

This section explains which boundaries exist for the dialogue between the ECtHR and domestic judges from the international legal perspective. Section 2.1 describes the boundaries that can be derived from the Vienna Convention on the Law of Treaties (VCLT). The VCLT is considered, because the ECHR 'is an international treaty to be interpreted in accordance with the relevant norms and principles of public international law, and, *in particular*, in light of the [VCLT]'.[25] The boundaries based directly on the ECHR are discussed in two sections: the boundaries that apply with regard to dialogue with the States that are party to a case (section 2.2) and the boundaries that apply with regard to other ECHR States Parties that were not parties to the case (section 2.3).

2.1. VCLT

A provision in the VCLT on which the ECtHR has relied is Article 26 VCLT. This provision embodies the principle of *pacta sunt servanda* and stipulates that '[e]very treaty in force is binding upon the parties to it and must be performed in good faith'.[26] The States Parties to the ECHR, therefore, must perform the

---

[23] ECtHR, *Aslakhanova and Others v Russia*, no 2944/06 et al., 18.12.2012, para. 210.
[24] P.W. HOGG and A.A. BUSHELL, 'The Charter Dialogue between Courts and Legislatures (or Perhaps the Charter of Rights Isn't Such a Bad Thing after All)', (1997) 35 *Osgoode Hall Law Journal*, p. 80.
[25] ECtHR, *Naït-Liman v Switzerland*, no 51357/07 [GC], 15.03.2018, para. 174 (emphasis added).
[26] The ECtHR sometimes relies on this provision in its judgments see e.g. *Janowiec and Others v Russia*, nos 55508/07 and 29520/09 [GC], 21.10.2013, para. 211.

obligation to 'secure to everyone within their jurisdiction' the ECHR rights in good faith.[27] Consequently, any dialogue with the ECtHR that influences a State's performance of the ECHR should take place in good faith. The ECtHR has also relied on Article 27 VCLT, to emphasise that a State 'may not invoke the provisions of its internal law as justification for its failure to perform a treaty'.[28] Article 27 VCLT codifies the 'fundamental principle of international law that international law prevails over domestic law'.[29] This means that, in a dialogue, the States Parties cannot use their domestic laws as an argument to justify a failure to abide by the ECHR. The ECtHR, however, does not oblige the States Parties to incorporate the Convention into domestic law; they must secure the Convention rights 'in some form or another'.[30]

2.2. ECHR: THE RESPONDENT STATE

This section focuses on the boundaries to dialogue that can be derived from the ECHR and that apply to the respondent State. The bottom line is that this State must abide by the operative provisions of the final Strasbourg judgment that establishes a breach of the ECHR.[31] A failure to perform the 'unconditional'[32] obligation to execute a judgment can engage a State's international responsibility.[33] Therefore, no dialogue, however eloquent, can justify a failure to execute a judgment.

Executing a judgment means that the respondent State ends the breach, makes reparation for the consequences of the breach and guarantees non-repetition.[34] These are obligations of result, meaning that the ECtHR does

---

[27] Article 1 ECHR.
[28] E.g. ECtHR, *Janowiec and Others, supra* note 26, para. 211.
[29] ICJ, *Applicability of the Obligation to Arbitrate under Section 21 of the United Nations Headquarters Agreement of 26 June 1947* (Advisory Opinion), ICJ Reports 1988, p. 12, para. 57; See also Article 3 Draft articles on Responsibility of States for Internationally Wrongful Acts ('DARSIWA').
[30] ECtHR, *James and Others v UK*, no 8793/79, 21.02.1986, para. 84.
[31] Article 46(1) ECHR.
[32] Ministers' Deputies, 'Decision: *Yukos v Russia*', CM/Del/Dec(2017)1280/H46-26, 10.03.2017, para. 3.
[33] ECtHR, *VgT v Switzerland (no. 2)*, no 32772/02 [GC], 30.06.2009, para. 85.
[34] ECtHR, *Papamichalopoulos and Others v Greece* (just satisfaction), no 14556/89, 31.10.1995, para. 34; The ECtHR does not often mention the third obligation, but this obligation can be derived from, e.g., its statement that execution measures 'must also be taken in respect of other persons in the applicant's position, notably by solving the problems that have led to the Court's findings', see ECtHR, *Savriddin Dzhurayev v Russia*, no 71386/10, 25.04.2013, para. 247; PCJ, *Case Concerning the Factory at Chorzów (Germany v Poland)* (Merits), PCIJ Reports Series A No. 17, p. 47 (which is a 'precious source of inspiration' for the ECtHR, see ECtHR, *Papamichalopoulos and Others*, para. 36); Articles 28, 30–31 DARSIWA; Rules of the CoM for the supervision of the execution of judgments and of the terms of friendly settlements, Rule 6(2).

not prescribe how the obligation should be fulfilled.[35] The respondent State is, therefore, in principle free to choose the means by which it will execute a judgment,[36] provided the means are 'compatible with the conclusions set out in the Court's judgment'.[37] Consequently, the respondent State can engage in a dialogue about which execution measures it will take. This dialogue normally takes place with the Committee of Ministers (CoM) and its Execution Department.[38] The CoM assesses 'in light of [relevant] principles of international law and the information provided by the respondent State, whether the latter has complied in good faith' with the obligation to execute a judgment.[39]

The ECtHR occasionally circumscribes the respondent State's freedom as to the choice of means and, thereby, the extent to which the State can engage in a dialogue with the CoM about the required execution measures. Most commonly, the ECtHR obliges the respondent State to pay a sum of money by way of just satisfaction to the applicant.[40] This obligation is unconditional.[41] Much more exceptionally, the ECtHR describes which other execution measures the respondent State must take.[42] The degree of specificity of the descriptions varies: the descriptions of individual measures are usually relatively precise,[43] whereas, for general measures, the ECtHR 'may propose various options and leave the choice of measure and its implementation to the discretion of the State concerned'.[44] Strictly legally speaking, the descriptions also vary in the sense that they can be an 'indication' that does not appear in the operative provisions or an 'order' that the ECtHR repeats in the operative provisions.[45] In the latter case, States are not permitted to engage in a dialogue about the described execution measure.[46]

The respondent State does not have the right to appeal a judgment and to engage in a dialogue with the ECtHR in this manner. The parties to a case, however, can ask a Panel of five Grand Chamber judges to consider referring

---

[35] ECtHR, *Tagayeva and Others v Russia*, no 26562/07, 13.04.2017, para. 638.
[36] Ibid.
[37] Ibid.
[38] Article 46(2) ECHR; L.R. GLAS (2016), *The Theory, Potential and Practice of Procedural Dialogue*, supra note 3, pp. 376–378.
[39] ECtHR, *Savriddin Dzhurayev*, supra note 34, para. 249.
[40] Article 41 ECHR.
[41] J. POLAKIEWICZ, 'Between 'Res Judicata' and 'Orientierungswirkung – ECHR Judgments Before National Courts', Speech, Brno, 19–21.06.2017, available at www.coe.int/en/web/dlapil/-/between-res-judicata-and-orientierungswirkung-, last accessed 29.05.2018.
[42] L.R. GLAS (2016), *The Theory, Potential and Practice of Procedural Dialogue*, supra note 3, pp. 383–386.
[43] Ibid., p. 389.
[44] *Oleksandr Volkov v Ukraine*, no 21722/11, 09.01.2013, para. 195.
[45] L.R. GLAS (2016), *The Theory, Potential and Practice of Procedural Dialogue*, supra note 3, pp. 391–392.
[46] Ibid., p. 392.

a Chamber case to the Grand Chamber.[47] The Panel will do so only if the case raises a serious question affecting the interpretation or application of the ECHR or a serious issue of general importance.[48] If the Panel accepts the request, it is possible to engage in a dialogue about the Chamber judgment.

2.3. ECHR: THE OTHER STATES PARTIES

The boundaries of dialogue applying to the respondent State, as described the previous section, do not apply to the States that are not a party to a case. Still, one can wonder whether these other States should 'take into account' the ECtHR's interpretation of the ECHR in a judgment to which they were not a party,[49] because a judgment has *res interpretata* or interpretive authority.[50] Although the ECHR does not regulate such authority 'precisely',[51] the interpretive authority may be derived from the ECHR, the ECtHR's judgments and the ECtHR's comments on Protocol 16 ECHR, as is explained below. Additionally, this section specifies what the phrase 'take into account' can mean from the ECHR's perspective.

2.3.1. The Interpretive Authority of the ECtHR Judgments

Articles 1, 19 and 32 ECHR point to the interpretive authority of the ECtHR judgments.[52] Article 19 establishes the ECtHR so it can ensure the observance of the engagements undertaken by the States, including the engagement to

---

[47] Article 43(1) ECHR.
[48] Article 43(2) ECHR; In practice, the panel refers only few cases for reconsideration to the Grand Chamber: in 2017, about 6%, see ECtHR, 'Annual Report 2017', *supra* note 2, p. 156.
[49] Interlaken Declaration (2010), para. B(4)(c); O.M. ARNARDÓTTIR, '*Res Interpretata, Erga Omnes* Effect and the Role of the Margin of Appreciation in Giving Domestic Effect to the Judgments of the European Court of Human Rights', (2017) 28(3) *TEJoIL*, p. 826.
[50] O.M. ARNARDÓTTIR (2017), '*Res Interpretata, Erga Omnes* Effect', *supra* note 49, pp. 825–826; See about this term S. BESSON, 'The Erga Omnes Effect of Judgments of the European Court of Human Rights – What's in a Name?', in S. BESSON (ed.), *The European Court of Human Rights after Protocol 14*, Schulthess, Geneva 2011.
[51] A. BODNAR, '*Res Interpretata*: Legal Effects of the European Court of Human Rights' Judgments for other States Than Those which Were Party to the Proceedings', in Y. HAECK and E. BREMS, *Human Rights and Civil Liberties in the 21st Century*, Springer, Dordrecht 2014, p. 224.
[52] A. DRZEMCZEWSKI, 'Quelques réflexions sur l'autorité de la chose interprétée par la Cour de Strasbourg', (2011)58 *Revista da Faculdade de Direito da UFMG*, p. 87; A. BODNAR (2014), '*Res Interpretata*', *supra* note 51, pp. 224, 226–227; O.M. ARNARDÓTTIR (2017), '*Res Interpretata, Erga Omnes* Effect', *supra* note 49, pp. 824–825; PACE, 'The Future of the European Court of Human Rights and the Brighton Declaration', AS/Jur (2012) 42, 03.12.2012, para. 18; Cf. D.T. BJÖRGVINSSON, 'The Effect of the Judgments of the ECtHR before the National Courts – A Nordic Approach?', (2016) 85(4) *Nordic Journal of International Law*, p. 305.

secure the ECHR rights by virtue of Article 1 ECHR. The establishment of a mechanism for reviewing compliance is, according to the ECtHR, 'one of the most significant features of the Convention system'.[53] Article 32 ECHR stipulates that the ECtHR's jurisdiction extends to 'all matters concerning the interpretation and application of the Convention' that are referred to it in conformity with the ECHR. Since it is the ECtHR's task to interpret the ECHR – as the court of last instance[54] – and to ensure the engagements of the States Parties to secure the ECHR rights, the States should take into consideration the ECtHR's interpretation of the ECHR in judgments against other States Parties. Considering the content of Article 19 and 32 ECHR, a failure to do so arguably amounts to a violation of Article 1 ECHR and Article 26 VCLT.[55]

The ECtHR has acknowledged that its judgments 'establish precedents albeit to a greater or lesser extent'.[56] Furthermore, its judgments serve 'to elucidate, safeguard and develop the rules instituted by the Convention, thereby contributing to the observance by the States of the engagements undertaken by them'.[57] These quotes already indicate that the ECtHR attaches interpretive authority to its judgments.[58] The structure of the judgments confirms this: they usually first outline the 'general principles' applicable to the relevant provision and then apply the principles to the case at hand.[59] The ECtHR's acceptance of the interpretive authority can also be seen in its autonomous interpretation of certain terms in the ECHR,[60] since an autonomous interpretation is 'transversally applicable to all the states'.[61] Moreover, the ECtHR draws consequences from the interpretive authority of its judgments: it expects that the domestic authorities

---

[53] ECtHR, *VgT v Switzerland (no. 2)*, supra note 33, para. 84.
[54] Article 35(1) ECHR.
[55] A. BODNAR (2014), '*Res Interpretata*', supra note 51, 227; O.M. ARNARDÓTTIR (2017), '*Res Interpretata, Erga Omnes* Effect', supra note 49, p. 825.
[56] ECtHR, *Pretty v UK*, no 2346/02, 29.04.2002, para. 75.
[57] ECtHR, *Rantsev v Cyprus and Turkey*, no 25965/04, 07.01.2010, para. 197; See also ECtHR, *Ireland v UK*, no 5310/71, 18.01.1978, para. 154.
[58] M. O'BOYLE, 'The Convention as a Subsidiarity Source of Law', Speech, Skopje, 01–02.10.2010, partially available at www.assembly.coe.int/CommitteeDocs/2010/20101125_skopje.pdf, last accessed 30.05.2018.; A. DRZEMCZEWSKI (2011), 'Quelques réflexions sur l'autorité', supra note 51, p. 90; A. BODNAR (2014), '*Res Interpretata*', supra note 51, p. 227; Venice Commission, 'Report on the Implementation of International Human Rights Treaties in Domestic Law and the Role of Courts', No. 690/2012, CDL-AD(2014)036, 08.12.2014, para. 52; VENICE COMMISSION (2016), 'Final Opinion', supra note 11, para. 96.
[59] J.H. GERARDS, 'The European Court of Human Rights and the National Courts – Giving Shape to the Notion of 'Shared Responsibility'', in J.W.A. FLEUREN and J.H. GERARDS (eds.), *Implementatie van het EVRM en de uitspraken van het EHRM in de nationale rechtspraak. Een rechtsvergelijkend onderzoek*, Radboud Universiteit, Nijmegen 2013, p. 78; e.g. ECtHR, *Merabishvili v Georgia*, no 72508/13 [GC], 28.11.2017, paras. 181–208.
[60] E.g. ECtHR, *Pellegrin v France*, no 28541/95, 08.12.1999, para. 63.
[61] J.H. GERARDS (2013), 'The European Court of Human Rights and the National Courts', supra note 59, p. 78.

act in accordance with the autonomous ECHR terms[62] and that they apply the ECHR 'in the manner that most closely corresponds [...] to the Convention *as interpreted in the Court's case-law*'.[63] Comparably, the ECtHR can verify whether a State has 'sufficiently taken into account the principles flowing from its judgments on similar issues, *even when they concern other States*'.[64]

In its reflection paper on the proposal for Protocol 16 ECHR, the ECtHR noted that, '[d]espite the fact that the advisory opinions would not have the binding character of a judgment [...], they would [...] have "undeniable legal effects"'.[65] The ECtHR added that it would consider the advisory opinions as 'valid case-law which it would follow when ruling on potential subsequent individual applications'.[66] As in an advisory opinion, the ECtHR can decide on questions of principle in a judgment.[67] When the ECtHR does so, a judgment is no different from an advisory opinion and therefore also has 'undeniable legal effects'[68] and will be relied upon by the ECtHR as 'valid case-law'.[69] Therefore, the States Parties must consider such judgments.

The above leads to the conclusion that the Strasbourg judgments have interpretive authority.[70] Indeed, the ECtHR's judges have acknowledged this authority[71] and the States Parties have too.[72] The States Parties must, therefore,

---

[62] Ibid.
[63] ECtHR, *Pla and Puncernau v Andorra*, no 69498/01, 13.07.2004, para. 62 (emphasis added); See also ECtHR, *Kolevi v Bulgaria*, no 1108/02, 05.12.2009, para. 214; ECtHR, *Nunez v Norway*, no 55597/09, 28.06.2011, para. 36; S. BESSON (2011), 'The Erga Omnes Effect', *supra* note 49, p. 141.
[64] ECtHR, *Opuz v Turkey*, No. 33401/02, 09.06.2009, para. 163; See also S. BESSON (2011), 'The Erga Omnes Effect', *supra* note 51, p. 138; ECtHR, *Yıldırım v Turkey*, no 3111/10, 18.12.2012, para. 66; ECtHR, *Fabris v France*, no 16574/08 [GC], 07.02.2013, para. 75.
[65] ECtHR, 'Reflection Paper on the Proposal to Extend the Court's Advisory Jurisdiction', available at www.echr.coe.int/Documents/2013_Courts_advisory_jurisdiction_ENG.pdf, last accessed 25.05.2018, para. 44. The ECtHR cites the Inter-American Court of Human Rights see: footnote 46 of the Reflection Paper.
[66] Ibid., see also Explanatory Memorandum to Protocol 16 ECHR, para. 27.
[67] This is in particular the task of the Grand Chamber, see Articles 30 and 43(2) ECHR.
[68] See ECtHR, 'Reflection Paper', *supra* note 65.
[69] See Explanatory Memorandum to Protocol 16 ECHR, *supra* note 66.
[70] See also J. POLAKIEWICZ (2017), 'Between 'Res Judicata' and 'Orientierungswirkung', *supra* note 41. It can also be regarded as 'sound judicial policy', see D.T. BJÖRGVINSSON (2016), 'The Effect of the Judgments of the ECtHR', *supra* note 52, p. 305.
[71] ECtHR, 'Memorandum of the President to the European Court of Human Rights to the States with a View to Preparing the Interlaken Conference', 03.07.2009, available at www.echr.coe.int/Documents/Speech_20090703_Costa_Interlaken_ENG.pdf, last accessed 25.05.2018, p. 6. M. LAZAROVA TRAJKOVSKA, 'Ways and means to recognise the interpretative authority of judgments against other States', Speech, Skopje, 01–02.10.2010; ECtHR, *Fabris v France*, *supra* note 64, Concurring opinion of Judge Pinto de Albuquerque; ECtHR, *Al-Dulimi and Montana Management Inc. v Switzerland*, no 5809/08, 21.06.2016, Concurring opinion of Judge Pinto de Albuquerque, joined by Judges Hajiyev, Pejchal and Dedov, para. 60.
[72] Interlaken Declaration (2011), para. B(4)(c); Brighton Declaration (2012), paras. 7, 9(iv); Brussels Declaration (2015), para. B(I)d.

in the words of the ECtHR, take the Strasbourg judgments with such authority 'sufficiently [...] into account'.[73] Although it is clear that the ECtHR's judgments cannot be ignored, 'taking into account' is hardly a clear requirement and, therefore, does not help to delineate clearly the extent to which the States Parties can enter into a dialogue with the ECtHR. The next section aims to clarify this matter.

2.3.2. The Obligation to Take into Account

The dictionary definition of to 'take into account' is 'to consider or remember something when judging a situation'.[74] 'To consider' can be defined as 'to give attention to a particular subject or fact when judging something else'.[75] Indeed, the domestic judges must consider the ECtHR judgments when adjudicating something else: the case before them with its specific factual and legal context.[76] Since the domestic judges unavoidably adjudicate something else than the ECtHR and because the ECtHR delivers judgments in individual cases, which establish principles to 'a greater or larger extent',[77] the domestic judges cannot blindly follow Strasbourg. Therefore, the more the ECtHR's reasoning is intertwined with the facts of the individual case, the harder it becomes to simply copy its reasoning. The obligation to take into account, in short, cannot be an obligation to follow the ECtHR. Instead, the obligation requires that the domestic judges decide on the relevance of a Strasbourg judgment to the case before them and distinguish relevant differences.[78] When making this decision, the judges cannot rely on domestic law to justify not taking into account an ECtHR judgment.[79] These judges must also demonstrate good faith,[80] which can be interpreted to mean, in the current context, that they give reasons for the course they have taken. In the absence of any reasoning, it will be hard for the ECtHR to respond and thus to engage in dialogue.[81]

Since the domestic judges should take into account the Strasbourg judgments because these judgments have interpretive authority, the question arises how it can be established to what extent a judgment has such authority. I propose

---

[73] ECtHR, *Opuz v Turkey*, supra note 64, para. 163.
[74] Cambridge Dictionary (English), available at https://dictionary.cambridge.org, last accessed 25.05.2018.
[75] Ibid.
[76] O.M. ARNARDÓTTIR (2017), 'Res Interpretata, Erga Omnes Effect', supra note 49, p. 831; See also A. BODNAR (2014), '*Res Interpretata*', supra note 51, p. 238.
[77] ECtHR, *Pretty v UK*, supra note 56, para. 75.
[78] As the ECtHR does, see e.g. ECtHR, *O'Halloran and Francis v UK*, nos 15809/02 and 25624/02, 29.06.2007, para. 43.
[79] See sections 2.1. and 2.2.
[80] Ibid.
[81] See also L.R. GLAS (2016), *The Theory, Potential and Practice of Procedural Dialogue*, supra note 3, pp. 162–165.

that the judgments are neither authoritative nor lacking all authority, but authoritative to a greater or lesser extent.[82] The authoritativeness of a judgment can be assessed based on different factors, as is discussed below. These factors offer viewpoints that do not necessarily point in the same direction; they are, therefore, not prerequisites that must all be fulfilled before a judgment should be taken into account. The factors are derived from features of the ECHR system and are based on a practical consideration.

One factor is the formation that has delivered the judgment.[83] The Grand Chamber of seventeen judges is the ECtHR's largest and, therefore, most 'inclusive' formation whose 'reasoning has benefited from enhanced deliberation'.[84] This formation decides cases raising 'a serious question affecting the interpretation or application of the Convention [...] or a serious issue of general importance'.[85] These features make a Grand Chamber judgment, in principle, more authoritative than a judgment of a Chamber of seven judges or a judgment of a Committee of three judges.[86] Additionally, one could check the size of the majority that has adopted the judgment and the content of any concurring opinions.[87] When a nine-to-eight majority adopts a Grand Chamber judgment and when some judges explain in their concurring opinions that they have reached the same conclusion as the majority, but for different reasons than the majority, that judgment inevitably is less authoritative than a Grand Chamber with a larger majority and without concurring opinions.

In addition to the formation, the domestic judges can also check 'the degree of entrenchment of a precedent'.[88] If the ECtHR has applied a certain interpretation repeatedly, without overruling it, the authoritativeness of that interpretation increases.[89] However, when a precedent, even when it is well established, is rather old,[90] this may undermine its authoritativeness, especially

---

[82] See also E. LAMBERT, *Les effets des arrêts de la Cour européenne des droits de l'homme*, Bruylant, Brussels 1999, pp. 304–305.
[83] S. BESSON (2011), 'The Erga Omnes Effect', *supra* note 50, p. 169.
[84] Ibid.
[85] Article 43 ECHR; See also Article 30 ECHR.
[86] See also A. CALIGIURI and N. NAPOLETANO, 'The Application of the ECHR in Domestic Proceedings', (2010) 20 *Italian Yearbook of International Law*, p. 158; A. BODNAR (2014), 'Res Interpretata', *supra* note 51, p. 237; CDDH, 'Report on the longer-term future of the system of the European Convention on Human Rights', CM(2015)176-add1final, 03.02.2016, para. 131; O.M. ARNARDÓTTIR (2017), 'Res Interpretata, Erga Omnes Effect', *supra* note 49, p. 841.
[87] See also A. BODNAR (2014), 'Res Interpretata', *supra* note 51, p. 241.
[88] S. BESSON (2011), 'The Erga Omnes Effect', *supra* note 50, pp. 161, 169.
[89] Ibid., p. 169; See also: LAMBERT, *supra* note 82, p. 305; CALIGIURI and NAPOLETANO, *supra* note 86, p. 158; CDDH, *supra* note 86, para. 131; O.M. ARNARDÓTTIR (2017), 'Res Interpretata, Erga Omnes Effect', *supra* note 49, p. 841.
[90] See also A. CALIGIURI and N. NAPOLETANO (2010), 'The Application of the ECHR', *supra* note 86, p. 158.

when the consensus in the States Parties about a certain matter has evolved.[91] A changed consensus is relevant, because the ECHR is a 'living instrument' that 'must be interpreted in the light of present-day conditions'.[92]

From a practical perspective, the clarity of a judgment is relevant. The clearer an ECtHR judgment is, the easier it becomes to take it into account.[93] A clear statement is, for example, that 'a general, automatic and indiscriminate restriction'[94] on prisoner voting violates Article 3 Protocol 1 ECHR.[95]

The result of taking into account the same branch of case-law, can lead to different results in different States.[96] Different results are not only unavoidable since the factual and legal circumstances differ in each case, but also because a matter may fall within the margin of appreciation of the domestic authorities. A margin of appreciation applies in particular if ECHR rights are restricted, i.e. are 'balanced' against another ECHR right or against a public interest, such as public safety.[97] Furthermore, different results are possible, because the States may go beyond the protection that the ECHR, as interpreted by the ECtHR, offers.[98]

2.4. SUB-CONCLUSION

Irrespective of whether a State is a respondent State, it must engage in a dialogue in good faith and cannot rely on domestic laws to justify a failure to follow the ECtHR. The boundaries to dialogue that apply to the respondent State are rather strict. Its room for dialogue is limited by the unconditional requirement to execute a judgment by ending a breach, providing reparation and guaranteeing non-repetition. The respondent State, therefore, cannot engage in dialogue about the result it must achieve,[99] but it can engage in dialogue about the means that it chooses. When the ECtHR spells out part of the result to be achieved,

---

[91] See also S. BESSON (2011), 'The Erga Omnes Effect', *supra* note 50, p. 167.
[92] ECtHR, *Tyrer v UK*, no 5856/72, 25.04.1978, para. 31.
[93] E. LAMBERT (1999), *Les effets des arrêts*, *supra* note 82, p. 305; Brighton Declaration (2012), para. 23; S. BESSON (2011), 'The Erga Omnes Effect', *supra* note 50, p. 163; A. BODNAR (2014), '*Res Interpretata*', *supra* note 51, pp. 239–240; O.M. ARNARDÓTTIR (2017), '*Res Interpretata*, Erga Omnes Effect', *supra* note 49, 841.
[94] ECtHR, *Hirst v UK (no. 2)*, no 74025/01 [GC], 06.10.2005, para. 82.
[95] O.M. ARNARDÓTTIR (2017), '*Res Interpretata, Erga Omnes* Effect', *supra* note 49, 841.
[96] J. POLAKIEWICZ (2017), 'Between 'Res Judicata' and 'Orientierungswirkung', *supra* note 41.
[97] S. GREER, *The Margin of Appreciation: Interpretation and Direction under the European Convention on Human Rights*, Council of Europe Publishing, Strasbourg 2000, pp. 24–26.
[98] Article 53 ECHR; S. BESSON (2011), 'The Erga Omnes Effect', *supra* note 50, p. 167; ECtHR, *Hutchinson v UK*, no 57592/08, 17.01.2017, Dissenting opinion of Judge Pinto de Albuquerque, para. 41.
[99] Provided the result to be achieved is clear. If the result to be achieved is not very clear, this opens up some room for domestic judges to make different choices.

tighter boundaries apply. The respondent State does not have the right to engage in dialogue by way of appealing a judgment.

The other States Parties have more room to engage in dialogue than the respondent State, although they must take certain judgments into account. Therefore, these States cannot simply ignore what Strasbourg has said. They are, however, not obliged to blindly follow Strasbourg or to follow the same course of action as another State. The extent to which a judgment must be followed depends on its authoritativeness, which can be determined with the help of these factors: the size of the majority, the content of concurring opinions and the entrenchment and clarity of the judgment. If the State does not follow Strasbourg, the requirement of good faith necessitates motivating that decision.

3. THE DOMESTIC PERSPECTIVES

The previous section concerned the international legal boundaries that apply to domestic courts' dialogue with the ECtHR. This section will discuss these boundaries from the perspective of eleven domestic legal systems (sections 3.1–3.11) and ends with a section (3.12) that includes some general observations about the domestic approaches and that compares these approaches.

3.1. AUSTRIA

The Austrian judges seek to interpret the Convention, which is part of the Constitution, in accordance with the ECtHR's case law;[100] that body of case law is 'the relevant point of reference of [the Constitutional Court's] own interpretation'.[101] The Constitutional Court has, moreover, emphasised that it '"abides" by the ECtHR's case law, even where this requires it to "depart" from its own, previous case law'.[102] Nevertheless, the Constitutional Court decided in the *Miltner* judgment[103] that it could not follow the ECtHR's increasingly broad interpretation of 'civil rights' under Article 6 ECHR.[104] It refused to

---

[100] K. PABEL, 'The implementation of judgments of the European Court of Human Rights in Austria', Speech, Saint-Petersburg, 22–23.10.2015, available at https://rm.coe.int/16806fe1a5, last accessed 30.05.2018; A. GAMPER, 'Austria: Endorsing the Convention System, Endorsing the Constitution', in P. POPELIER, S. LAMBRECHT and K. LEMMENS (eds.), *Criticism of the European Court of Human Rights*, Intersentia, Cambridge 2016, p. 95.
[101] A. GAMPER (2016), 'Austria: Endorsing the Convention System', *supra* note 100, pp. 94–95.
[102] Ibid., referring to VfSlg 15.129/1998, 19.166/2010.
[103] VfSlg 11.500/1987.
[104] A. GAMPER (2016), 'Austria: Endorsing the Convention System', *supra* note 100, p. 79.

follow, because following would require amending the Constitution, something that only parliament can do, although the Constitutional Court can call on parliament to do so.[105] The Constitutional Court additionally noted that the ECHR 'had developed in a way that led to new obligations for the State Parties that they had never been willing to accept',[106] thus criticising the ECtHR's dynamic interpretation of the ECHR.[107] Only one year after the *Miltner* judgment, the Constitutional Court furthermore remarked that it could not interpret the ECHR in line with the Strasbourg case law at all times, because 'it was necessary to interpret the ECHR in a systemic context with all other parts of the' Constitution.[108] The Constitutional Court thus points out that it must also consider other Constitutional provisions than the ECHR (as interpreted by the ECtHR). The approach of the Constitutional Court has led it to not only interpret Article 6 ECHR differently from the ECtHR; it also adopted a less broad definition of the scope of Article 1 of Protocol 1 ECHR than the ECtHR[109] and it approaches the question of the 'same offence' under Article 4 of Protocol 7 ECHR slightly differently from the ECtHR.[110] Still, the number of cases in which the Constitutional Court does not follow the ECtHR completely, remains 'relatively small'.[111]

3.2. BELGIUM

From a formal, legal point of view, 'the ECtHR's judgments are not part of the national legal system and they only have declaratory force'.[112] These judgments are, therefore, only binding 'regarding the concrete disputes resolved'.[113]

---

[105] M. STELZER, *The Constitution of the Republic of Austria: A Contextual Analysis*, Hart Publishing, Oxford 2011, p. 183; K. PABEL (2015), 'The implementation of judgments of the European Court of Human Rights in Austria', *supra* note 100.

[106] D. THURNHERR, 'Austria and Switzerland', in H. KELLER and A. STONE SWEET (eds.), *A Europe of Rights: The Impact of the ECHR on National Legal Systems*, OUP, Oxford 2008, p. 361.

[107] A. GAMPER (2016), 'Austria: Endorsing the Convention System', *supra* note 100, p. 79.

[108] Ibid., p. 95, referring to VfSlg 11.937/1988.

[109] D. THURNHERR (2008), 'Austria and Switzerland', *supra* note 106, pp. 362-363; The author refers to VfSlg 4879/1964, 6648/1972, 6733/1972, 11198/1986; More recently, the Constitutional Court has shown also 'an inclination to follow the ECtHR's case law' at this point, see A. GAMPER (2016), 'Austria: Endorsing the Convention System, *supra* note 100, p. 96, referring to VfSlg 18.069/2007, 19.341/2011.

[110] See the judgment of 02.07.2009, B 559/08, summarised in English by CODICES, available at www.codices.coe.int/NXT/gateway.dll/Codices/Precis/ENG/EUR/AUT/AUT-2009-3-002? f=templates$fn=document-frameset.htm$q=$uq=$x=$up=1, last accessed 25.05.2018; See also A. GAMPER (2016), 'Austria: Endorsing the Convention System', *supra* note 100, p. 97.

[111] A. GAMPER (2016), 'Austria: Endorsing the Convention System', *supra* note 100, p. 95.

[112] P. POPELIER and K. LEMMENS, *The Constitution of Belgium. A Contextual Analysis*, Hart Publishing, Oxford 2015, p. 229.

[113] Oxford Pro Bono Publico, 'Reconciling domestic superior courts with the ECHR and the ECtHR: A Comparative Perspective (Submission to the Commission on a Bill of Rights)',

Nevertheless, the Constitutional Court is described as 'Strasbourg-friendly'[114] and takes into account the Strasbourg judgments, including those against other States, 'as if they were binding'.[115] Yet, the Constitutional Court may be reluctant to 'fully follow' the ECtHR at all times,[116] although its 'deviances [...] remain rare'.[117] The main course of contention seems to be that the Constitutional Court is more willing than the European judges to 'accept the legislature's assumptions and to appeal to the general interest to justify interferences with fundamental rights', whereas the ECtHR seems to attach more importance to 'evidence-based substantiation' in this regard.[118] According to some authors, the Constitutional Court will 'provide extensive reasoning' for its deviances;[119] according to another author, its deviances are 'implicit'.[120] The Council of State, for its part, follows Strasbourg judgments, regardless of whether Belgium was a party to a case, seemingly without limiting 'their effects in the Belgian legal order'.[121] The Court of Cassation is also regarded as 'Strasbourg-friendly' and accepts the interpretative authority of the ECtHR's judgments.[122] Nevertheless, this court, due to its lack of a tradition of 'source referencing', seems to ignore Strasbourg case law or refers to it implicitly or *in abstracto*.[123] Furthermore, this court may interpret Strasbourg judgments against other States restrictively and seems to be more reluctant than the Constitutional Court to follow.[124] The Court of Cassation interpreted, for example, the *Salduz v Turkey*[125] judgment restrictively in the period before the legislature took action with respect to the judgment.[126] This was, however, not a sign of hostility, as the Court of Cassation aimed at

---

24.11.2011, available at https://issuu.com/opbp/docs/2011_-_echr_and_domestic_courts, last accessed 25.05.2018, p. 20.

[114] P. POPELIER, 'Belgium: Faithful, Obedient, and Just a Little Irritated', in P. POPELIER, S. LAMBRECHT and K. LEMMENS (eds.), *Criticism of the European Court of Human Rights*, Intersentia, Cambridge 2016, p. 119.

[115] G. SCHAIKO, P. LEMMENS and K. LEMMENS, 'Belgium', in J.W.A. FLEUREN and J.H. GERARDS (2013), *Implementatie van het EVRM en de uitspraken van het EHRM in de nationale rechtspraak*, supra note 59, p. 159. See also P. POPELIER and K. LEMMENS (2015), *The Constitution of Belgium*, supra note 112, p. 229.

[116] G. SCHAIKO, P. LEMMENS and K. LEMMENS (2013), 'Belgium', supra note 115, p. 154.

[117] P. POPELIER (2016), 'Belgium', supra note 114, p. 125.

[118] Ibid.

[119] G. SCHAIKO, P. LEMMENS and K. LEMMENS (2013), 'Belgium', supra note 115, p. 154, referring to this example Const. Ct., No. 153/2007.

[120] P. POPELIER (2016), 'Belgium', supra note 114, p. 125.

[121] G. SCHAIKO, P. LEMMENS and K. LEMMENS (2013), 'Belgium', supra note 115, p. 159.

[122] P. POPELIER (2016), 'Belgium', supra note 114, p. 121, referring to Cass. C.08.0384N, 10.06.2009.

[123] Ibid., p. 122.

[124] G. SCHAIKO, P. LEMMENS and K. LEMMENS (2013), 'Belgium', supra note 115, p. 159; P. POPELIER (2016), 'Belgium', supra note 114, p. 125.

[125] ECtHR, *Salduz v Turkey*, no 36391/02 [GC], 27.11.2008.

[126] G. SCHAIKO, P. LEMMENS and K. LEMMENS (2013), 'Belgium', supra note 115, p. 159, referring to Cass. No. P.12.0106.N, 24.01.2012.

compliance 'in good faith', 'while at the same time, for pragmatic reasons, it did not want to complicate criminal proceedings to such an extent that, until further action by the legislature, investigators would be faced with practical difficulties of considerable importance'.[127] Also more in general, if a Strasbourg judgment goes against its own practice, the Court of Cassation does not 'openly contest' the judgment, but instead 'tries to find a pragmatic solution'.[128]

3.3. GERMANY

In *Görgülü*, the Federal Constitutional Court explained 'the relevance of the judgments of the [ECtHR] in German law'.[129] These judgments, including judgments rendered against Germany, are not binding,[130] but the domestic judges must 'duly consider'[131] the ECHR as interpreted by the ECtHR.[132] Failing to do so, 'may pave the way for an individual constitutional complaint alleging that the corresponding constitutional right [...] and the Rechtsstaat principle have been violated'.[133] The domestic judges may disagree with the ECtHR, considering that the former may need to decide in 'multipolar' fundamental rights situations,[134] for example in civil law, where 'conflicting fundamental rights' need to be balanced.[135] The ECtHR, more narrowly, decides on the dispute between an individual and the State[136] and, therefore, may not consider all 'the legal positions and interests involved'.[137] Furthermore, the 'actual or legal circumstances'[138] before the domestic judge may be different from the circumstances as presented before the ECtHR, which also justifies a departure from a Strasbourg judgment.[139] The Constitutional Court has also formulated the rule that reliance on the ECtHR's case law may not decrease the protection that an individual enjoys under the Basic Law[140] or violate 'prior-ranking law,

---

[127] Ibid., referring to Cass. No. P.12.0106.N, 24.01.2012.
[128] P. POPELIER (2016), 'Belgium', *supra* note 114, p. 125.
[129] K. PABEL, 'Germany: The Long Way of Integrating the Strasbourg Perspective into the Protection of Fundamental Rights', in P. POPELIER, S. LAMBRECHT and K. LEMMENS (eds.), *Criticism of the European Court of Human Rights*, Intersentia, Cambridge 2016, p. 165.
[130] E. KLEIN, 'Germany' in J.W.A. FLEUREN and J.H. GERARDS (2013), *Implementatie van het EVRM en de uitspraken van het EHRM in de nationale rechtspraak, supra* note 59, pp. 211–212; BVerfG, 2 BvR 1481/04 of 14.10.2004 ('*Görgülü*'), para. 48.
[131] BverfG, *Görgülü, supra* note 130, para. 62.
[132] Ibid., para. 48.
[133] E. KLEIN (2013), 'Germany', *supra* note 130, 212.
[134] BverfG, *Görgülü, supra* note 130, para. 50.
[135] Ibid., para. 58.
[136] Ibid.
[137] Ibid., para. 59.
[138] Ibid., para. 50.
[139] Ibid., para. 50.
[140] Ibid., para. 32.

in particular constitutional law'.[141] The domestic judges must justify a departure from the ECtHR 'understandably'.[142]

In *Preventive Detention II*,[143] the Constitutional Court explained more specifically that the ECHR obligations should be 'translated'[144] 'to the specificities of the German legal system'.[145] Thus, the domestic judges have 'some leeway' when they cannot follow Strasbourg precisely.[146] Nevertheless, they tried to avoid going against the ECtHR,[147] aiming for dialogue rather than hostility,[148] and they regarded the ECHR and the ECtHR's case law as interpretative 'aids'.[149] Therefore, when German and ECHR law are incompatible, the domestic judges will try to remove the compatibility.[150] In the aforementioned judgment, the Constitutional Court was confronted with the incompatibility between its own previous judgment that declared certain domestic legal provisions constitutional and a European judgment.[151] The Constitutional Court removed this incompatibility by qualifying the latter judgment as a 'legally relevant change', which meant it could set aside its own judgment.[152]

3.4. ICELAND

The Icelandic ECtHR Act stipulates in Article 2 that the ECtHR judgments, including those against Iceland, 'are not binding in Icelandic domestic law'.[153] The explanatory report to this provision clarifies that domestic judges must

---

[141] Ibid., para. 62.
[142] Ibid., para. 48.
[143] BVerfGE 128, 04.05.2011, 326; Welcomed by the ECtHR in *Schmitz v Germany*, no 30493/04, 09.06.2011, para. 41.
[144] B. Bjorge, *Domestic Application of the ECHR: Courts as Faithful Trustees*, OUP, Oxford 2015, p. 77.
[145] A. Nussberger, 'The European Court of Human Rights and the German Federal Constitutional Court', available at www.cak.cz/assets/pro-advokaty/mezinarodni-vztahy/the-echr-and-the-german-constitutional-court_angelika-nussberger.pdf, last accessed 25.05.2018, p. 10.
[146] B. Bjorge (2015), *Domestic Application of the ECHR*, supra note 144, p. 77.
[147] Ibid., p. 91.
[148] K. Pabel (2016), 'Germany', *supra* note 129, p. 170.
[149] Ibid., p. 167.
[150] B. Bjorge (2015), *Domestic Application of the ECHR*, supra note 144, p. 92; See e.g. also *Von Hannover No. 2 v Germany*, No. 40660/08 and 60641/08, paras. 114–123, in which the ECtHR approves the new approach of the German Federal Constitutional Court, which it adopted in No. 1 BvR 1606/07, 26.02.2008. See for a description of these cases K. Pabel (2016), 'Germany', *supra* note 129, pp. 169–170.
[151] K. Pabel (2016), 'Germany', *supra* note 129, p. 168.
[152] Ibid.
[153] D.T. Björgvinsson, 'The Effect of the Judgments of the ECtHR before the National Courts – A Nordic Approach?', in A. Kjeldgaard-Pedersen (ed.), *Nordic Approaches to International Law*, Nijhoff, Leiden 2018, p. 105.

interpret the ECHR '*independently*'¹⁵⁴ and, therefore, 'regardless of' the Strasbourg case-law.¹⁵⁵ The same report assumes nevertheless that the domestic judges will turn to the ECtHR's case-law for guidance when interpreting the ECHR.¹⁵⁶ Comparably, the Icelandic Supreme Court has noted that the ECtHR's interpretation should be 'considered' and interprets domestic law whilst taking into consideration the ECHR and the ECtHR's case law.¹⁵⁷ More generally, that court has 'sought to interpret Icelandic law in conformity with Iceland's international obligations'.¹⁵⁸

3.5. ITALY

According to the Italian Constitutional Court in 2007, the domestic judges should take the ECtHR judgments into consideration when interpreting the ECHR,¹⁵⁹ which amounted to an 'unconditional obligation [...] to give to the Convention only the meaning given to it by the ECtHR'.¹⁶⁰ Moreover, in 2009, the Constitutional Court ruled that the ECtHR's interpretation of the ECHR had 'binding effect',¹⁶¹ considering that it is the ECtHR's task to interpret the ECHR under Article 32 ECHR.¹⁶² Consequently, domestic judges cannot interpret the ECHR differently from the ECtHR¹⁶³ and they can only influence the ECHR's interpretation where the ECtHR has not yet ruled on a

---

[154] Ibid., p. 106 (emphasis in original).

[155] Ibid., p. 107.

[156] G. GAUKSDOTTIR and T. INGADOTTIR, 'Compliance with the Views of the UN Human Rights Committee and the Judgments of the European Court Of Human Rights in Iceland', in A. EIDE, J.TH. MÖLLER and I. ZIEMELE, *Making Peoples Heard: Essays on Human Rights in Honour of Gudmundur Alfredsson*, Nijhoff, Leiden 2011, p. 513.

[157] R. HELGADOTTIR, 'Nonproblematic Judicial Review: A Case Study', (2011) 9 *International Journal of Constitutional Law*, 538; The case the author refers to is from 2005.

[158] G. GAUKSDOTTIR and T. INGADOTTIR (2011), 'Compliance with the Views', *supra* note 156, p. 514; The authors give the following judgment as an example: H 2000, 4480 (section IV, para. 2).

[159] G. MARTINICO, 'National courts and judicial disobedience to the ECHR: a comparative overview', in O.M. ARNARDÓTTIR and A. BUYSE (eds.), *Shifting Centres of Gravity in Human Rights Protection: Rethinking Relations Between the ECHR, EU, and National Legal Orders*, Routledge, New York 2017, p. 69.

[160] O. POLLICINO, 'The European Court of Human Rights and the Italian Constitutional Court: No 'Groovy Kind of Love'', in K. SIEGLER (ed.), *The UK and of European Court of Human Rights – A Strained Relationship?*, Hart Publishing, Oxford and Portland 2015, p. 371.

[161] A. CALIGIURI and N. NAPOLETANO (2010), 'The Application of the ECHR', *supra* note 86, 157, referring to judgment No. 317 of 2009.

[162] Ibid.; See also A. BODNAR (2014), '*Res Interpretata*', *supra* note 51, p. 234.

[163] A. CALIGIURI and N. NAPOLETANO (2010), 'The Application of the ECHR', *supra* note 86, p. 157, referring to judgment No. 317 of 2009.

certain matter.¹⁶⁴ The court added, however, that 'only *the essence* of the case of the ECtHR should be binding'.¹⁶⁵ Thus, the Constitutional Court created some room for divergence from Strasbourg and could, thus, prevent a 'direct clash' when not following Strasbourg entirely.¹⁶⁶ The Constitutional Court probably came up with this technique, because the constraints that it had imposed upon itself gave it 'too little room for manoeuvre with regards to the ECtHR case law'.¹⁶⁷ Subsequently, the Constitutional Court has invented other techniques that provide room for manoeuvre.¹⁶⁸ One such technique is that of distinguishing between a relevant Strasbourg judgment and the case before it.¹⁶⁹ Additionally, whilst noting that the Italian judges should not be 'passive recipients' of the ECtHR, the Constitutional Court explained that these judges should take into account the conditions giving rise to the ECtHR's interpretations.¹⁷⁰ More specifically, the judges should only follow pilot judgments,¹⁷¹ judgments concerning 'a specific individual dispute remitted to the national court'¹⁷² and well-established case-law.¹⁷³ A judgment does not count as well-established when 'some' of these indicators apply:¹⁷⁴ the judgment is innovative, the judgment conflicts with other judgments, 'robust' dissents have been written, the Grand Chamber has not endorsed the judgment or the domestic judges doubt if the ECtHR 'had correctly considered the peculiar characteristics of the domestic legal system at stake'.¹⁷⁵ Yet another technique that creates room for manoeuvre, is to emphasise 'the differences existing in terms of contexts'¹⁷⁶ between the Constitutional Court and the ECtHR:¹⁷⁷ whilst the latter performs an 'isolated' evaluation, the former performs a 'systemic' evaluation 'of the

---

164 Ibid., p. 158.
165 O. POLLICINO (2015), 'The European Court of Human Rights', *supra* note 160, p. 372 (emphasis added).
166 Ibid., pp. 372–373.
167 Ibid., p. 371.
168 G. MARTINICO, 'Italy: Between Constitutional Openness and Resistance', in P. POPELIER, S. LAMBRECHT and K. LEMMENS (eds.), *Criticism of the European Court of Human Rights*, Intersentia, Cambridge 2016, p. 193.
169 O. POLLICINO (2015), 'The European Court of Human Rights', *supra* note 160, pp. 372–373.
170 MARTINICO, *supra* note 159, p. 77, referring to decision No. 49/2015.
171 G. NESSI, 'Constitutionality of Legislation Imposing Confiscation without Conviction', *Oxford Reports on International Law*, 2016, para. H12.
172 D. TEGA, 'A National Narrative: The Constitution's Axiological Prevalence on the ECHR – A Comment on the Italian Constitutional Court Judgment No. 49/2015', *International Journal of Constitutional Law Blog*, 01.05.2015.
173 G. NESSI (2016), 'Constitutionality of Legislation, *supra* note 171, para. H6.
174 Ibid., para. H12.
175 Ibid., para. H11.
176 MARTINICO, *supra* note 168, p. 191.
177 Ibid., p.187, referring to and citing judgment No. 230 of 2012.

values involved by the norm under analysis, and it is therefore obliged to [perform a] balancing exercise'.[178]

3.6. LATVIA

The Latvian Constitutional Court has ruled that the domestic judges are bound to the ECtHR's case-law, also in respect of judgments not issued against Latvia. Additionally, the Latvian judges must rely on the Strasbourg judgments when interpreting the Constitution;[179] these judgments serve as 'means of interpretation'.[180] Still, the Constitutional Court 'has elaborated its own understanding of the content and scope of' the Constitutional rights.[181] A case in point is the reaction of the Constitutional Court to the judgment *Andrejeva v Latvia*,[182] in which the ECtHR found a violation of Article 14 ECHR in conjunction with Article 1 of Protocol No 1 ECHR, because the applicant was denied a retirement pension for the years employed in the USSR, because she did not have Latvian citizenship.[183] In response, the Constitutional Court maintained 'Latvia's principled position that Latvia was not the successor to the obligations of the USSR, and that such rights that may have been acquired during the times of the USSR could not be binding upon Latvia in calculating pensions'.[184] The Latvian judges justified their refusal to follow Strasbourg[185] by explaining that the ECtHR had 'assessed only particular facts rather than compliance of the contested norm with legal norms of a higher legal force' and by pointing out that the facts in the case before it were 'considerably' different from the facts in *Andrejeva*.[186] Additionally, the Constitutional Court

---

[178] Ibid., referring to and judgment No. 230 of 2012.
[179] I. Jarukaitis, 'Report on Estonia, Latvia and Lithuania', in G. Martinico and O. Pollicino (eds.), *The National Judicial Treatment of the ECHR and EU Laws*, Europa Law Publishing, Groningen, 2010, p. 178; M. Mits, 'Latvia', in I. Motoc and I. Ziemele (eds.), *The Impact of the ECHR on Democratic Change in Central and Eastern Europe*, CUP, Cambridge 2016, p. 216; A. Cozzi et al., *Comparative Study on the Implementation of the ECHR at the National Level*, Council of Europe, Belgrade 2015, p. 20.
[180] I. Ziemele, 'The Significance of the European Convention for the Protection of Human Rights and Fundamental Freedoms in the Case-Law of the Constitutional Court of the Republic of Latvia', Speech, 02.10.2017, Ljubljana, referring to the judgment of 13.05.2005 in the case no. 2004-18-0106 and the judgment of 18.10.2007 in the case no. 2007-03-01.
[181] Ibid.
[182] ECtHR, *Andrejeva v Latvia*, no 55707/00 [GC], 18.02.2009.
[183] ECtHR, 'Press release issued by the Registrar. Grand Chamber Judgment Andrejeva v Latvia', 18.02.2009, available at http://hudoc.echr.coe.int/eng-press?i=003-2638285-2882154, last accessed 30.05.2018.
[184] I. Ziemele (2017), 'The Significance of the European Convention', *supra* note 180.
[185] Ibid.
[186] Judgment of the Latvian Constitutional Court, No. 2010-20-0106, 17.02.2011, para. 9 (English translation).

emphasised the wide margin of appreciation that States have in relation to socioeconomic policies.[187]

3.7. THE NETHERLANDS

With reference to the 'incorporation doctrine', the Dutch judges interpret the ECHR as the ECtHR has interpreted that document, regardless of whether a specific judgment was rendered against the Netherlands.[188] Although this approach means that the judges follow the ECtHR 'loyally', they do not follow 'slavishly'.[189] The Supreme Court interpreted the *Salduz v Turkey* judgment, for example, in a 'narrow' manner,[190] not so much because it was critical of the ECtHR, but due to 'the limitations of its role within the Dutch constitutional system';[191] it was 'beyond its judicial task to change the relevant legislation'.[192] Reluctance to follow Strasbourg, may, however, also be 'more substantially driven'.[193] In these circumstances, the domestic judges do not follow Strasbourg precisely or only minimally, without making this very explicit,[194] because they disagree with a European judgment or because they '"translate" the Convention standards into standards which are more easily applicable in domestic law'.[195] So the domestic judges 'often appear to use the Court's case law to supplement, build and refine their own sets of standards, rather than applying them exactly as they have been formulated by the ECtHR'.[196]

3.8. RUSSIA

As was noted in in the introduction (section 1), the Russian Constitutional Court is now permitted by law to establish that a judgment of an international

---

[187] Ibid., para. 10.
[188] M. KUJIER, 'Mechanisms for effective implementation of the European Convention on Human Rights in the Netherlands', Speech, 22–23.10.2015, Saint-Petersburg.
[189] G. CORSTENS, 'De veranderende constitutionele rol van de rechter', in M. DIAMANT and OTHERS (eds.), *The Powers that Be. Op zoek naar nieuwe checks and balances in de verhouding tussen wetgever, bestuur, rechter en media in de veellagige rechtsorde*, Wolf Legal Publishers, Oisterwijk 2013, p. 88.
[190] J.H. GERARDS, 'The Netherlands: Political Dynamics, Institutional Robustness', in P. POPELIER, S. LAMBRECHT and K. LEMMENS (eds.), *Criticism of the European Court of Human Rights*, Intersentia, Cambridge 2016, p. 353, referring to Supreme Court Judgment of 20.06.2009, ECLI:NL:HR:2009:BH3079; (GK), No. 36391/02, 27.11.2008.
[191] Ibid., p. 353.
[192] Ibid., p. 354.
[193] Ibid.
[194] Ibid., p. 355.
[195] Ibid.
[196] Ibid.

court, including the compensation orders, is not enforceable.[197] The Constitutional Court renders such a ruling in response to a petition of the executive.[198]

Before the relevant law entered into force, parliamentarians requested the Constitutional Court to declare unconstitutional laws requiring compliance with the Strasbourg judgments.[199] This request was brought against the background of several new ECtHR judgments that met with criticism in Russia (*Konstantin Markin v Russia*[200] and the two judgments discussed in the following two paragraphs).[201] In response, the Constitutional Court clarified that Russia does not have to enforce a Strasbourg judgment if this is the only way to avoid violating 'principles and norms of the Constitution'.[202] The said violation can take place, *inter alia*, if Strasbourg interprets the ECHR differently from what the States Parties agreed to at the time of ratification or if the judgment would violate *jus cogens*.[203] Although the Constitutional Court rejected the request, it allowed for the development of a law establishing a mechanism to block the execution of international judgments violating the Constitution.[204]

Upon the creation of the law, the Constitutional Court was asked whether the judgment *Anchugov and Gladkov v Russia*, on the disenfranchisement of persons serving a prison sentence,[205] was enforceable. The Constitutional Court explained that it would reconcile the 'letter and spirit' of the Strasbourg judgment with the Constitution.[206] It furthermore noted that, because Russia can only ratify treaties that are in conformity with the Constitution, Russia ratified the ECHR in 1998 assuming that the Constitution complied with the ECHR.[207] Therefore, if the ECtHR adopts an interpretation to which Russia did not consent in 1998 and which would require amending the Constitution, Russia may stick to the ECtHR's interpretation of the Convention from 1998.[208]

---

[197] VENICE COMMISSION (2016), 'Final Opinion', *supra* note 11, Appendix, para. 74.
[198] Ibid., Appendix, paras. 74–75.
[199] M. AKSENOVA, 'Anchugov and Gladkov is not Enforceable: the Russian Constitutional Court Opines in its First ECtHR Implementation Case', *Opinio Juris*, 25.04.2016.
[200] ECtHR, *Konstantin Markin v Russia*, no 30078/06 [GC], 22.03.2012.
[201] L. MÄLKSOO, 'Russia's Constitutional Court Defies the European Court of Human Rights: Constitutional Court of the Russian Federation Judgment of 14 July 2015, No. 21-П/2015', (2016) 12 *European Constitutional Law Review*, p. 378–380.
R. HELGADOTTIR, 'Nonproblematic judicial review: A case study', (2011) 9 *International Journal of Constitutional Law*, 538, referring to judgment No. 21-П/2015, 14.07.2015.
[202] L. MÄLKSOO (2016), 'Russia's Constitutional Court', *supra* note 201, 381.
[203] Ibid.
[204] M. AKSENOVA (2016), 'Anchugov and Gladkov', *supra* note 199.
[205] ECtHR, *Anchugov and Gladkov v Russia*, nos 11157/04 and 15162/05, 04.07.2013.
[206] VENICE COMMISSION (2016), 'Final Opinion', *supra* note 11, Appendix, para. 12, referring to the judgment of 19.04.2016, No. 12-П/2016.
[207] Ibid., referring to referring to judgment No. 21-П/2015, 14.07.2015.
[208] Ibid.

Because the ECtHR adopted such an interpretation, Russia could not execute the judgment.[209]

The second ruling on the enforceability of an ECtHR judgment concerned the judgment *Yukos v Russia*, in which the ECtHR ordered Russia to pay €1.866 billion as just satisfaction.[210] The Constitutional Court clarified that Russia will only refuse to execute in exceptional circumstances. Such circumstances exist when the ECtHR interprets the ECHR in violation of a general rule of treaty interpretation, 'such as a wholly novel and unsustainable interpretation [...], which departed from the *"jus cogens"* principles of treaty interpretation, or was inconsistent with the Convention's object and purpose'.[211] The court concluded that Russia did not have to pay the just satisfaction, because this would go against certain constitutional principles.[212]

3.9. SPAIN

Article 10(2) of the Spanish Constitution requires that the fundamental rights provisions in the Constitution are construed in conformity with the international treaties ratified by Spain. The Constitutional Court has, in connection to this provision, 'underlined the interpretative value of [ECHR] and the [ECtHR] judgments'[213] and has taken the judgments of the ECtHR into account.[214] Nevertheless, the Constitutional Court has interpreted this provision as not requiring 'a literal translation' of the ECtHR judgments against Spain, considering that there may be 'normative differences' between the ECHR and the Constitution.[215] The Constitutional Court, for example, upheld a higher threshold for finding a violation of Article 8 ECHR than the ECtHR in its *Lopez Ostra v Spain* judgment.[216] The Spanish judge therefore retains 'flexibility as to the weight it accords to Strasbourg judgments'.[217]

---

[209] Ibid.
[210] ECtHR, *Yukos v Russia*, no 4902/04, 20.09.2011.
[211] J. POLAKIEWICZ (2017), 'Between 'Res Judicata' and 'Orientierungswirkung', *supra* note 41, referring to judgment of 19.01.2017, No. 1-П/2017.
[212] I. MARCHUK, 'The Tale of Yukos and of the Russian Constitutional Court's Rebellion against the European Court of Human Rights', *Osservatoris Costituzionale*, Fasc. 1/2017, 16.04.2017, p. 10.
[213] P.J. TENORIO SÁNCHEZ, 'Convergence of the Protection of Fundamental Rights Between the Spanish Constitutional Court and the European Court of Human Rights', in A. RAINER (ed.), *The Convergence of the Fundamental Rights Protection in Europe*, Springer, Dordrecht 2016, p. 15, referring to judgment 91/2000 as an example.
[214] Ibid., p. 18.
[215] N. KRISCH, 'The Open Architecture of European Human Rights Law', (2008) 71 *The Modern Law Review*, 190. The Constitutional Court 'does not make a difference between Convention and jurisprudence', see ibid., p. 188.
[216] Ibid., pp. 190–191.
[217] Ibid., p. 189; See also Oxford Pro Bono Publico, *supra* note 113, p. 66.

3.10. THE UK

The Strasbourg case law is 'not strictly binding',[218] but the UK Human Rights Act imposes a duty on the domestic judges to 'take into account' relevant Strasbourg judgments against the UK and other States.[219] This duty was interpreted as a requirement to 'mirror' the Strasbourg approach,[220] by keeping 'pace with the Strasbourg jurisprudence as it evolves over times: no more, but certainly no less'.[221] Over time, however, the domestic judges moved from the so-called mirror approach, which 'implied unquestioning acceptance of applicable Strasbourg authority' to accepting 'variance of, and deviation from, the European Court's jurisprudence'.[222] Nevertheless, the domestic judges rarely disagree with the ECtHR[223] and they should have convincing reasons for not following it.[224] A unanimous Grand Chamber judgment is 'in itself, a formidable reason for' following Strasbourg.[225] The UK judges should also follow 'any clear and constant jurisprudence of the Strasbourg court'.[226] The judges, therefore, should wonder whether the ECtHR has followed an interpretation 'repeatedly in subsequent cases' and thus 'firmly established [the interpretation] in its jurisprudence'.[227] Special reasons warranting departing from the ECtHR are,[228] for example, that a judgment lacks 'clarity', is not 'entirely convincing' or does not speak with 'one voice'.[229] Other such reasons are that 'the ECtHR has misunderstood or been misinformed about some aspect of English law'[230]

---

[218] UK House of Lords, *R v Special Adjudicator, ex parte Ullah* [2004] UKHL 26, para. 20.
[219] R. MASTERMAN, 'United Kingdom', in J.W.A. FLEUREN and J.H. GERARDS (2013), *Implementatie van het EVRM en de uitspraken van het EHRM in de nationale rechtspraak, supra* note 59, p. 285.
[220] Ibid., p. 287; C.C. MURPHY, 'Human Rights Law and the Challenges of Explicit Judicial Dialogue', *Jean Monnet Working Paper* 10/12, 18, p. 23.
[221] UK House of Lords, *R v Special Adjudicator, supra* note 218, para. 20; See also UK Supreme Court, *Ambrose v Harris, Procurator Fiscal, Oban (Scotland)* [2011] UKSC 43, para. 19.
[222] R. MASTERMAN, 'The United Kingdom: From Strasbourg Surrogacy Towards a British Bill of Rights?', in P. POPELIER, S. LAMBRECHT and K. LEMMENS (eds.), *Criticism of the European Court of Human Rights*, Intersentia, Cambridge 2016, p. 476.
[223] A. DONALD, J. GORDON and P. LEACH, *The UK and the European Court of Human Rights*, Equality and Human Rights Commission, Research Report 83, p. 141; N. KRISCH (2008), 'The Open Architecture' *supra* note 215, p. 203.
[224] UK House of Lords, *R v Special Adjudicator, supra* note 218, para. 20.
[225] UK Supreme Court, *Cadder v Her Majesty's Advocate (Scotland)* [2010] UKSC 43, para. 46 (emphasis added).
[226] UK House of Lords, *R v Special Adjudicator, supra* note 218, para. 20.
[227] UK Supreme Court, *Cadder v Her Majesty's Advocate, supra* note 225, paras. 47–48.
[228] UK House of Lords, *R v Special Adjudicator, supra* note 218, para. 20.
[229] M. AMOS, 'The Dialogue between the United Kingdom Courts and the European Court of Human Rights', (2012) 61 *International and Comparative Law Quarterly*, 568; See e.g.: *N. v Secretary of State for the Home Department* [2005] UKHL 31, para. 14.
[230] UK Appeal Court, *R. v Lyons* [2003] 1 AC 979, 997, para. 46; The ECtHR accepted this reason in *Cooper v UK*, no 48843/99, 16.12.2003, paras. 107, 122–126, thus, departing from *Morris v UK*, no 38784/97, 26.02.2002.

or that the judges 'have concerns as to whether [an ECtHR judgment] sufficiently appreciates or accommodates particular aspects of [their] domestic process'.[231] If the judges do not follow Strasbourg, they must give reasons for their decision.[232]

3.11. UKRAINE

In 2006, Ukraine adopted the law 'on the Enforcement of Judgments and the Application of the Case-Law of the [ECtHR]'. This law stipulates that final judgments of the ECtHR that establish a violation in a case against Ukraine are 'binding and subject to enforcement throughout the whole territory of Ukraine pursuant to Article 46 [ECHR]'.[233] Additionally, the law provides that domestic courts 'shall apply the Convention and the case-law of the [ECtHR] as a source of law'.[234] There is some uncertainty as to whether domestic judges must also rely on judgments against other States.[235]

3.12. SUB-CONCLUSION

The legal boundaries applicable to dialogue with the ECtHR about judgments against one's own State vary widely in the eleven domestic legal systems. In only some States, domestic legislation or case-law spells out that these judgments are binding (Belgium,[236] Ukraine and Latvia). Therefore, there seems to be little room for dialogue about the judgments. Despite this requirement, the Latvian Constitutional Court has refused to follow a Strasbourg judgment against Latvia and the Belgian Court of Cassation a judgment against Belgium.[237] Therefore, the legal requirement to follow judgments adopted against one's own State does, in practice, not imply that there is no room to engage in dialogue with the ECtHR at all. In this connection, it is interesting to recall that the Italian Constitutional Court and the UK Supreme Court first demanded quite a lot of themselves and other domestic judges in terms of following Strasbourg, but then modified their position in order to allow for more room manoeuvre. Apparently,

---

[231] UK Supreme Court, *R v Horncastle & Others*, supra note 9, para. 11.
[232] Ibid.
[233] Article 2(1) of the said law. An unofficial English translation of the law can be found in PACE, 'Implementation of judgments of the European Court of Human Rights', Doc. 11020, 18 September 2006, Appendix III.
[234] Article 17(1) of the said law.
[235] M. GNATOVSKYY, 'Twenty Years of the ECHR in Ukraine', *EJIL: Talk!*, 18.09.2017, available at www.ejiltalk.org/twenty-years-of-the-echr-in-ukraine/, last accessed 29.05.2018.
[236] Regarding the concrete dispute.
[237] As described in ECtHR, *Vermeire v Belgium*, no 12849/87, 29.11.1991, para. 25.

therefore, domestic judges consider it to be important to be able to engage in dialogue, to some extent irrespective of their previous position or more abstract proclamations as to the binding nature of the ECtHR judgments.

In some other States, the highest domestic judges do not consider themselves to be bound to the Strasbourg judgments (Germany and the UK) or this is laid down in law (Iceland). In these States, it is, from a legal perspective at least, possible to fully engage in dialogue about the judgments against one's own State. Russia goes some steps further, thereby stretching the boundaries to dialogue the most, to the extent that the Constitutional Court is no longer engaging in dialogue according to the Venice Commission.[238] In Russia, the executive can ask the judiciary to declare that a Strasbourg judgment, including the award of just satisfaction, cannot be executed. In the other States, such a procedure does not exist and the award of just satisfaction does not seem to be the subject of dialogue. Nevertheless, the domestic judges, including the Russian, have expressed their willingness to consider Strasbourg judgments and follow these judgments in principle, while still permitting for some exceptions. Moreover, in practice, they usually follow the ECtHR and even try to solve incompatibilities between domestic law and the ECHR as interpreted by the ECtHR, even when they are, legally speaking, not obliged to do so (Germany and Iceland).

The variation in boundaries can also be observed, although comparably less, when looking at the boundaries that apply to engaging in a dialogue about the judgments against other States. Some domestic judges are bound to these judgments (Latvia and previously Italy) or these judgments are probably a source of law (Ukraine). Other domestic judges may take into account the Strasbourg judgments, usually regardless of whether they were issued against their own State[239] (Austria, Germany, Iceland, Netherlands, Russia and the UK).[240]

More generally it must be observed that, although the legal boundaries indeed vary widely, the practical differences between what the highest domestic judges do with relevant Strasbourg precedents seem to vary less: they generally follow the ECtHR. Additionally, the domestic judges who are legally bound to Strasbourg, still create room for manoeuvre, and domestic judges who are legally *not* bound to Strasbourg, still usually follow. This finding points to the importance of both dialogue, as many domestic judges want to be able to engage in it, irrespective of domestic prescripts, and of complying with Strasbourg, as

---

[238] As was already noted in the introduction (section 1), see VENICE COMMISSION (2016), 'Final Opinion', *supra* note 11, Appendix, para. 136, para. 146.
[239] See also A. BODNAR (2014), '*Res Interpretata*', *supra* note 51, p. 252. 'In most countries, ECtHR jurisprudence is treated as a whole body of case-law, without distinguishing between judgments having *res judicata* and *res interpretata* status.'
[240] See also A. CALIGIURI and N. NAPOLETANO (2010), 'The Application of the ECHR', *supra* note 86, p. 156: 'The majority of courts in the Contracting States do not take the view that they are effectively bound by Strasbourg jurisprudence.'

it is something many domestic judges want, irrespective of whether they are legally obliged to do so.

When considering more specifically the reasons to not only take a European judgment into account, but also to follow it, this may happen, because interpretation is constant, well-established or clear (Italy and the UK) or that a judgment is a pilot (Italy) or Grand Chamber judgment (UK).

The most common and general reason *not* to follow is that the Strasbourg case-law is incompatible with constitutional fundamental rights or other norms (Germany, Italy, Russia and Spain). More specifically, the domestic judges may find that the ECtHR 'has gone too far'. Going too far includes going beyond what the States accepted when ratifying the ECHR (Austria[241] and Russia), issuing a judgment that is innovative and/or in conflict with previous judgments (Italy) or defying the general rules of treaty interpretation (Russia). Alternatively, the domestic judges are not convinced by Strasbourg, because of dissenting opinions or because the Grand Chamber has not endorsed an interpretation (Italy). Other reasons to see a judgment as unconvincing is that the ECtHR did not understand (the UK and Italy) or insufficiently accommodated (UK) the domestic system. Furthermore, the domestic judges may invoke the margin of appreciation to diverge from Strasbourg (Latvia) or point to normative differences between themselves and Strasbourg (Spain). Additionally, the domestic judges may consider that they cannot follow Strasbourg, because they are confronted with another context than the ECtHR. The Austrian Constitutional Court, unlike the ECtHR does not just consider the ECHR, but also other constitutional provisions, and the German Federal Constitutional Court has explained that it may have to decide in multipolar situations, whereas the ECtHR looks at a case between the applicant and the respondent State. The Italian Constitutional Court reasoned along comparable lines. Also, with reference to the different contexts, the domestic judges may not follow Strasbourg precisely, because they engage in a process adapting the European standards to the specificities of their domestic legal system (Germany and the Netherlands).

A refusal to follow with reference to the constitution, may, however, also be less 'substantially driven'[242] and may instead have to do with distribution of powers in the domestic setting. Following Strasbourg may imply amending the constitution or another type of domestic law, which is something that only parliament may be entitled to do, not the judiciary (Austria, Belgium[243] and the

---

[241] The Austrian Court only mentioned this reason once however, see the *Miltner* judgment discussed in section 3.1.

[242] J.H. GERARDS (2016), 'The Netherlands: Political Dynamics, Institutional Robustness', *supra* note 190, p. 354.

[243] As to execution of *Marckx v Belgium*, no 6833/74, 13.07.1979, the ECtHR 'took the view that it was for the legislature to execute the *Marckx* judgment', see E. LAMBERT, *The Execution of Judgments of the European Court of Human Rights*, Council of Europe Publishing, Strasbourg 2002, p. 8.

Netherlands). In these circumstances, the hands of domestic courts are tied and they have to wait until the legislature enters the dialogue and takes legislative action.

Regardless of the reason that applies for not following Strasbourg, some judges have clarified that they will motivate a departure from the Strasbourg case-law (Germany and the UK). Not all judges are so vocal however. The Dutch judges may silently apply Strasbourg case-law in a minimal manner, without pointing out the fact that they engage in dialogue.

4. CONCLUSION

The answers to the questions which boundaries apply to dialogue with the ECtHR from the international legal perspective and from 11 domestic perspectives have already been given in the sub-conclusions in sections 2.4 and 3.12. Therefore, this conclusion will focus on comparing these answers. As was noted in section 1, this comparison makes it possible to see if the ECtHR and the domestic judges speak the same 'language' when engaging in dialogue.

As for the differences between the two perspectives: the requirement of good faith that features in the international legal system does not feature as such in the domestic systems or the judgments of the domestic judges. Nevertheless, the requirement can be read into the requirement that some domestic judges impose on themselves to reason any disagreement with Strasbourg. An important difference between the international system and several domestic systems is the possibility to rely on domestic law as a justification for failing to follow the ECtHR. The domestic judges are prepared to or allowed to follow the ECtHR, provided they stay within what is permissible under the constitution, whereas the international perspective does not permit invoking domestic law to justify a failure to implement the ECHR. Furthermore, from the international perspective, the State Party that is not a party to a case has comparably more room to engage in dialogue than the respondent State. This distinction is not relevant to each domestic system: the duty that applies when the State is a respondent State may be the same as when it is a non-respondent State. In short, the boundaries that apply from the international legal perspective and a domestic perspective may differ. This can imply that the domestic systems set boundaries that are more or less strict than the international perspective, as is explained below.

In some domestic systems, the judges seem to have less room for dialogue than the international perspective would permit. This is the case when the judges are bound to the Strasbourg judgments to which their State was not a party, whereas they 'only' need to take into account such judgments from the international perspective. For these judges, Protocol 16 ECHR will be of particular benefit, because the Protocol enables them to request an advisory opinion, about which they can engage in dialogue, since the advisory opinion is not binding.[244] Nevertheless, even when, from a legal perspective, there seems to be no or hardly any room for dialogue, the domestic judges may still engage in dialogue with the ECtHR under very exceptional circumstances, meaning that the domestic and international perspectives differ less in practice than in theory.

In other domestic systems, the judges have more room to engage in dialogue than the international perspective envisages. These domestic judges do not consider themselves bound to the Strasbourg judgments against their own State, whilst the international perspective requires that these judgments are executed, including by the judiciary if necessary. This domestic stance implies that the domestic judges may not change their case-law to prevent new violations, not that they obstruct the implementation of individual execution measures. This is only different in Russia, where the domestic judges can even halt the payment of just satisfaction. However, even these domestic judges aim to follow Strasbourg as a rule, meaning that the difference in approach between these domestic judges and the ECtHR will, in practice, not lead to many clashes and has indeed not led to many clashes.

A striking similarity between the international perspective and some domestic perspectives is the existence of the duty to take into account the ECtHR's case-law, which depends on the interpretive authoritativeness of an ECtHR judgment from the international perspective. Moreover, some of the factors that can help establish whether a judgment has interpretive authority, can also be found in the case law of domestic judges.[245] However, not all the factors that the domestic judges rely on to determine whether they need to take into account the Strasbourg case-law have something to do with the interpretive authority of a judgment, because some factors depart from the logic of the domestic system. These factors include that the Strasbourg case-law is incompatible with the domestic system, that the ECtHR has gone too far, that the ECtHR did not understand the domestic system or insufficiently accommodated that system and that the domestic judges' hands are tied due to the distribution of powers.

Considering the above, it must be concluded that the domestic judges and the ECtHR hardly speak the same language when it comes to defining the boundaries to dialogue. Both perspectives set different boundaries and may define the scope of what is permissible differently. Moreover, even when the two perspectives seem to speak 'the same language', because they both refer to 'taking into account' this does not necessarily mean that they rely on the same factors to determine whether a judgment must be considered. Therefore, clashes are an ever-present possibility. However, it has also already been concluded that the clashes do not often happen in practice, due to the willingness of the domestic judges to follow their European counterparts.

---

[244] Article 5 Protocol 16 ECHR.
[245] Formation, size of the majority, separate opinions, entrenchment and clarity.

Returning to the example in the introduction, the question arises if the difference in how the Russian and British judges' attempts to engage in dialogue have been received, can be explained with reference to the boundaries of the international legal system. Interestingly, the British judges stayed within these boundaries, because they refused to follow the Chamber judgment, before the Grand Chamber adopted its judgment. Due to the referral procedure, the Chamber judgment never became final.[246] Consequently, the obligation to execute the final judgment never materialised and the British judges could not fail to fulfil this obligation.[247] The Russian judges, on the contrary, have obstructed fulfilling this obligation. Nevertheless, I do not think that this legal technicality fully explains the difference in reception, since the ECtHR has also accepted that the British judges departed from a judgment that had become final. The ECtHR accepted this, based on the arguments of the domestic judges and the government's clarification of domestic laws.[248] The ECtHR, therefore, like some domestic judges (as explained in section 3.12) permits room for dialogue, irrespective of the precise legal obligation that the ECHR imposes on the State. Rather, the difference in reception may be explained by the fact that the Russians have created a procedure for not executing individual and general measures on the request of the executive, whereas the UK does not have such a procedure and its judges engage in dialogue about the general measures only. It is relatively hard to know which general measures are required, because their scope is broad and because the ECtHR normally only stipulates individual measures rather precisely.[249] Therefore, there is more room to engage in dialogue about general rather than individual measures. The requirement of good faith can also help explain the difference.[250] The ECtHR seems convinced that the UK judges engaged in a 'bona fide dialogue'.[251] Therefore, the ECtHR welcomes the dialogue – even when the UK judges would not strictly stay within the international legal boundaries. The involvement of the executive in the case of Russia probably makes it harder to believe that the dialogue is performed in good faith and, therefore, the dialogue is received with little enthusiasm.[252]

---

[246] Article 44 ECHR.
[247] Article 46(1) ECHR.
[248] See *supra* note 230.
[249] See section 2.2.
[250] See on the importance of the concept of good faith and dialogue: B. Bjorge (2015), *Domestic Application of the ECHR*, *supra* note 144, p. 241.
[251] ECtHR, *Al-Khawaja and Tahery v UK*, *supra* note 10, Joint partly dissenting and partly concurring opinion of Judges Sajó and Karakaş.
[252] In a different context, the ECtHR described the Russian Government's argument as 'disingenuous', thus implying that the Government is not acting in good faith, see *Berkovich v Russia*, no 5871/07, 27.04.2018, para. 94.

UNPRINCIPLED DISOBEDIENCE TO INTERNATIONAL DECISIONS

A Primer from the Russian Constitutional Court

Kanstantsin Dzehtsiarou and Filippo Fontanelli[*]

1. Introduction 320
2. The Core Elements of the Reasoning of the RCC 322
   2.1. The Background: ECtHR and Arbitral Proceedings 322
   2.2. The Decision 324
3. The Issues with the RCC's Decision 327
   3.1. The Irrelevance of Domestic Law............................. 328
   3.2. Constitutionally Allowed is Not Constitutionally Required 333
4. Questionable Legitimacy of the RCC Decision 338
5. Conclusion.. 341

ABSTRACT

This article uses the opportunity of a decision by the Russian Constitutional Court (RCC) to test whether unprincipled disobedience can be detected. Disobedience indicates the refusal, by domestic authorities, to implement the binding decisions of international courts and tribunals. Unprincipled disobedience is dictated by convenience rather than principled reasons. In *Yukos*, the Russian Court declared the eponymous judgment of the European Court of Human Rights (ECtHR) impossible to execute, for incompatibility with the Russian Constitution. The reasons put forward by the Russian judges are deeply problematic from the perspective of constitutional and international law. The fragility of this decision's arguments reveals the real motives of the RCC and qualifies its decision as a glaring instance of unprincipled disobedience.

---

[*] We are grateful to anonymous reviewers for their helpful comments. Usual disclaimers apply. The article is the result of a joint effort of the authors. Sections 2.2, 4 and 5 were written by Dzehtsiarou. Sections 1, 2.1 and 3 were written by Fontanelli.

1. INTRODUCTION

On 19 January 2017, the Russian Constitutional Court (RCC) delivered a decision[1] concerning the execution of the European Court of Human Rights (ECtHR)'s judgment against Russia in the *Yukos* case.[2] In this decision, the RCC answered the Ministry of Justice's official request to consider whether Russia could, under its Constitution, comply with the ECtHR's order to pay just satisfaction to the applicant.

The RCC found that Russia's compliance with the ECtHR's decision would breach its Constitution and the judgment was, therefore, 'impossible to execute'. This decision forms part of an increasing trend of States – prominent among them the Russian Federation – expressing disobedience[3] towards the ECtHR's judgments. The decision of the RCC is legally unwarranted as it subordinated international obligation to ordinary Russian legislation and prior decisions of the RCC. It is also argued that the RCC's disagreement with the principles of the *Yukos* judgment by the ECtHR is a cover-up. What prompted the RCC's decision was the government's unwillingness to pay major monetary compensation to the shareholders of *Yukos*.

Any failure to enforce a judgment of the ECtHR is a violation of international law. Although the reasons for non-enforcement do not matter from the legal point of view, they may add some legitimacy to the State's resistance. De Londras and Dzehtsiarou elaborated the theoretical distinction between principled disobedience and dilatoriness.[4] The former is based on a reasonable disagreement about human rights,[5] in which the objections of the respondent State reflect its constitutional identity; the latter is mere unwillingness to transfer the necessary authority to the ECtHR, expressed through attitudinal and/or organisational resistance. Disobedience unsupported by a reason (or supported by preposterous reasons that disguise mere unwillingness) frustrates all attempts

---

[1] RCC, *Judgment of 19.01.2017 No. 1-Π/2017 in the case concerning the resolution of the question of the possibility to execute in accordance with the Constitution of the Russian Federation the Judgment of the European Court of Human Rights of 31 July 2014 in the case of OAO Neftyanaya Kompaniya Yukos v Russia in connection with the request of the Ministry of Justice of the Russian Federation*. A courtesy translation is available on the website of the Russian Constitutional Court, and all quotations will be drawn from it, unless otherwise noted, available at http://www.ksrf.ru/en/Decision/Judgments/Documents/2017__January_19_1-P.pdf, last accessed 08.05.2018.

[2] ECtHR, *OAO Neftyanaya Kompaniya Yukos v Russia*, no 14902/04, 20.09.2011.

[3] See generally, P. POPELIER, S. LAMBRECHT and K. LEMMENS (eds.), *Criticism of the European Court of Human Rights*, Intersentia, Antwerp 2017.

[4] F. DE LONDRAS and K. DZEHTSIAROU, 'Mission Impossible? Addressing Non-execution through Infringement Proceedings in the European Court of Human Rights' (2017) 66 *ICLQ*, p. 467.

[5] On reasonable disagreement, see for example J. WALDRON, 'The Core of the Case against Judicial Review' (2006) 115 *Yale Law Journal*, p. 1346.

at dialogue, as is known very well by those who remember the story of Bartleby, who declined all assignments on the workplace with a simple 'I would prefer not to'.[6] We apply this theory to the reasoning of the RCC in *Yukos* case and argue that its reasoning is a manifestation of unprincipled disobedience.

This article makes three interrelated claims.

First, national constitutions cannot be used to stay the enforcement of international judgments, irrespective of the domestic legality or legitimacy of such practice. Pursuant to Article 46 of the ECHR, every judgment of the ECtHR creates an enforceable international legal obligation that national law cannot displace. Moreover, no such constitutional conflict arose in the case at hand, as the ECtHR judgment did not contradict the Russian constitution, much less the tenets of the Russian constitutional order. The ECtHR did not test the compatibility of any provisions of the Russian constitution with the ECHR; it only declared some provisions of Russian law, as applied by the Russian authorities, to be in violation of the Convention. The only relevance of the Russian Constitution to the case was that the same domestic measures reviewed by the ECtHR had been previously scrutinised by the RCC, which considered their application by the authorities to be in line with the Constitution. However, such declaration of constitutionality only determined that the Constitution allowed – not required – these State measures.

Second, the RCC effectively declared the ECtHR judgment unenforceable for contradicting Russian statutory law, as interpreted by the RCC. This approach undermines not just the legality of the RCC's decision from an international law perspective, but also its domestic legality. Under Russian law, the RCC can declare unenforceable only those judgments of human rights tribunals which contradict the Russian Constitution.[7]

Third, the legal reasons offered by the RCC in the *Yukos* decision raise doubts about the genuine motivations of the RCC. The RCC framed the decision as if it disagreed with the principles stated in the ECtHR judgment. Throughout its judgment, the RCC discussed the fairness and proportionality of the sanctions imposed on *Yukos*. The RCC seemed to disagree with the ECtHR as to how these principles should apply. However, the Russian government had not objected to the principles enshrined in the ECtHR's *Yukos* judgment on liability, and only took issue with the decision whereby the Strasbourg judges ordered Russia to pay the shareholders of Yukos almost €2 billion. The difference over the interpretation of ECHR law is not the real reason behind the RCC's judgment. Tellingly, after the *Yukos* judgments by the ECtHR, Russia took positive steps to bring its law and practice in line with the judgment on

---

[6] See H. MELVILLE, 'Bartleby, the Scrivener' in *The Piazza Tales*, Dix & Edwards, United States 1856.

[7] Article 104.1 of the Federal Constitutional Law of the Constitutional Court of the Russian Federation.

liability but did not honour the compensation order. In a nutshell, Russia proved through conclusive behaviour that the *Yukos* judgment was, in fact, possible to implement, and that it would adhere with the principles of law established therein. There was no hint of principled disagreement. For these reasons, more fully elaborated below, it is argued that Russia, through its RCC, disguised a choice of convenience and dilatoriness as principled disobedience.

2. THE CORE ELEMENTS OF THE REASONING OF THE RCC

2.1. THE BACKGROUND: ECtHR AND ARBITRAL PROCEEDINGS

The proceedings before the Strasbourg Court had been brought by the company Yukos[8] in the wake of the State-driven process of tax assessment, auctioning and liquidation which resulted, ultimately, in the dissolution of the company and the nationalisation of its assets. In 2011, the Chamber of the ECtHR concluded[9] that Russia breached the applicant's right to property, protected under Article 1 of Protocol 1 to the Convention, in two respects. First, Russia lifted retroactively the statutory three-year time bar, which would have otherwise protected Yukos from the tax audit relating to the year 2000.[10] Second, the tax authorities imposed on Yukos a 7% enforcement fee, calculated on the total tax debt. Russia's refusal to reduce its amount or grant Yukos's requests to postpone its payment accelerated the company's demise.[11]

Russia did not request that the case be referred to the Grand Chamber. It is difficult to divine the reason of Russia's yielding stance.[12] Perhaps, it considered the judgment a partial success (most of the applicants' claims were rejected by the Court) and it chose to devote its efforts to the parallel arbitral proceedings

---

[8] The original company was liquidated in November 2007, but the Court admitted the application (submitted in 2004) even if the applicant had since ceased to exist as a legal person. See ECtHR, *OAO Neftyanaya Kompaniya Yukos v Russia*, no 14902/04, Decision on Admissibility, para. 443: 'Striking the application out of the list under such circumstances would undermine the very essence of the right of individual applications by legal persons, as it would encourage governments to deprive such entities of the possibility to pursue an application lodged at a time when they enjoyed legal personality.'
[9] ECtHR, *OAO Neftyanaya Kompaniya YUKOS v Russia*, supra note 2.
[10] Liability relating to that year resulted in the company being considered a repeat offender for the following year's assessment, a finding causing the penalties to double.
[11] ECtHR, *OAO Neftyanaya Kompaniya YUKOS v Russia*, supra note 2, para. 655.
[12] RCC judge Yaroslavtsev, in his dissenting opinion to the RCC decision on the execution of the *Yukos* judgment, also questioned the motives of the Russian authorities in failing to request the referral of the Chamber judgment. RCC, *Judgment of 19.01.2017 No. 1-П/2017*, supra note 1, Dissenting Opinion of Judge Yaroslavtsev, p. 40.

hinging on the same facts, which had by then proceeded to the merits stage of the arbitration proceedings, and in which Yukos's majority shareholders were claiming more than US $114 billion.[13] On 18 July 2014, the arbitral tribunal, constituted at the Permanent Court of Arbitration in The Hague, found Russia in breach of the Energy Charter Treaty and ordered it to pay more than US $50 billion to the claimants.[14] The claimants tried to pre-empt any Russian objection of double recovery, and pledged to deduct from said amount 'any pecuniary damages [...] [subsequently] awarded to Yukos in the ECtHR proceedings' that they would actually receive.[15] The arbitral tribunal expressly chose not to address this risk in the award.[16] The award was set aside by a Dutch court in 2016,[17] with a decision that is currently under appeal.[18]

A couple of weeks after the arbitral award, the ECtHR considered the question of just satisfaction and ordered Russia to pay to the applicants more than €1.8 billion, the highest amount ever awarded in Strasbourg.[19] Also, the ECtHR rejected Russia's arguments regarding the risk of double recovery.[20] This time, the Russian authorities requested the referral of the judgment to the Grand Chamber, perhaps surprised by the magnitude of the award and concerned about the lack of any safeguard against double recovery.[21] The request was declined, and the government publicly criticised the decision.[22]

---

[13] *Yukos Universal Limited (Isle of Man) v The Russian Federation*, UNCITRAL, PCA Case No. AA 227 (claims brought under the Energy Charter Treaty), see Final Award of 18.07.2014, para. 110.

[14] Ibid., para. 1823. For a comparison between the arbitral award and the decisions of the ECtHR, see E. DE BRABANDERE, '*Yukos Universal Limited (Isle of Man) v The Russian Federation*: Complementarity or Conflict? Contrasting the Yukos Case before the European Court of Human Rights and Investment Tribunals', (2015) 30 *ICSID Review*, pp. 345–355.

[15] *Yukos Universal Limited (Isle of Man) v The Russian Federation*, supra note 13, para. 1266.

[16] Ibid., paras. 1828–1829.

[17] *The Russian Federation v Veteran Petroleum Limited, Yukos Universal Limited and Hulley Enterprises Limited*, 20.04.2016, the District Court of The Hague (C/09/477160/HA ZA 15-1, 15-2, and 15-112).

[18] In the meanwhile, recognition and enforcement proceedings are pending in several jurisdictions, see for instance *Hulley Enterprises ltd. et al v The Russian Federation*, Memorandum Opinion of the US District Court for the District of Columbia, Civil Action No. 14-1996 (BAH), 30.09.2016.

[19] ECtHR, *OAO Neftyanaya Kompaniya Yukos v Russia* (just satisfaction), no 14902/04, 31.07.2014.

[20] Ibid., see paras. 43–44. Para. 43 belies the close chronological succession of the two decisions, noting mistakenly that in the PCA proceedings 'no final award has been adopted so far'.

[21] Which, had it been included in either decision, would have essentially absorbed the amount of the ECtHR-ordered satisfaction into the far bigger liability arising from the arbitration, rendering the ECtHR decision largely irrelevant.

[22] The Minister of Justice of Russia pointed out that the *Yukos* judgment is based on systemic legal errors, and these errors cast doubts on the prospect of acceptance of this judgment in Russia. See 'The ECtHR Judgment on Compensation to Yukos Shareholders Was Deemed Groundless by the Ministry of Justice', Interfax news, 15.06.2015 (Решения ЕСПЧ о компенсациях акционерам ЮКОСа Минюст счел безосновательным), available at http://www.interfax.ru/russia/447571 (in Russian, translated by the authors), last accessed 08.05.2018.

The Ministry of Justice of Russia subsequently questioned the constitutionality of such payment. It noted that the findings of the ECtHR, and the attending obligation to compensate a large cohort of Yukos's shareholders who had not partaken in the Strasbourg proceedings, would contravene the Russian Constitution, as interpreted by the RCC. The question was presented to the RCC and occasioned the decision annotated here.

2.2. THE DECISION

At the outset, the RCC noted that the Convention forms part of the Russian legal system[23] and that Russia is obliged to execute the ECtHR's judgments. This duty operates even when the ECtHR uses evolutive or teleological interpretation and deviates from its own case law.[24]

Thereupon, the Russian judges qualified that premise. They opined that the relationship between the Russian legal order and the ECHR's could not be one of 'subordination': some degree of dialogue must inform it to preserve the 'appropriate balance'.[25] The RCC stated that the effectiveness of the Convention 'depends' on the ECtHR's respect for national constitutional identity.[26] Ultimately, the RCC 'reserv[es]' for itself the right to determine Russia's 'degree of readiness'[27] for the judgments coming from Strasbourg. This reservation is essential to preserve the 'compromise'[28] between the two legal orders, on which the Convention's system is built.

The RCC explored the scenario in which the compatibility between constitutional law and international obligations, assured at the time of accession to a treaty regime, is subsequently undermined through the interpretive activity of an international body.[29] In this scenario, the principle of Article 26 Vienna Convention on the Law of Treaties (VCLT) (*pacta sunt servanda*) would not suffice to elicit unconditional compliance with international decisions. In particular, Russia would be 'entitled as an exception'[30] to non-compliance when the ECtHR's interpretation of the Convention contradicts the Constitution

---

[23] Article 15(4) of the Constitution of the Russian Federation states that the universally-recognised norms of international law and international treaties and agreements of the Russian Federation shall be a component part of its legal system. If an international treaty or agreement of the Russian Federation fixes other rules than those envisaged by law, the rules of the international agreement shall be applied.
[24] RCC, *Judgment of 19.01.2017 No. 1-П/2017, supra* note 1, p. 5.
[25] Ibid., p. 6.
[26] Ibid.
[27] Ibid.
[28] Ibid.
[29] Ibid., p. 7.
[30] Ibid., p. 9.

and, at the same time, does not follow the canons of treaty interpretation (because it is '[un]usual' or runs contrary to the Convention's object and purpose).

The Court identified one such exceptional scenario in the situation at hand. It took notice of a conflict between the Constitution and the Convention resulting not so much from the Convention's text but from the ECtHR's interpretation thereof. The RCC added that the Russian measures deemed unlawful by the ECtHR had been legitimately passed by the legislator and their constitutionality had been previously confirmed by the RCC.

Indeed, in 2005[31] the RCC upheld the constitutionality of a 'differentiated approach' to the application of the statutory period of limitation for tax crimes.[32] Namely, it approved the imposition of sanctions over crimes for which the period of limitation had expired, if the taxpayer had obstructed tax inspections. In so doing, the RCC found that the practice conformed to a constitutionally-oriented reading of the Tax Code, which did not contravene the principle of non-retroactivity of tax law.[33]

As a result, the RCC held that payment of the monetary award to the shareholders of a large-scale tax evader would contradict the 'constitutional principles of equality and justice in tax relations'.[34] The unfairness would stem from the fact that the majority shareholders, who were responsible for the company's wrongdoing, would be the main beneficiaries of the ECtHR's order of just satisfaction.[35] In essence, the RCC noted that the shareholders' losses brought before the ECtHR were the result of the shareholders' negligence or bad faith, and that compensation would be inappropriate.

Similar arguments applied to the breach of Article 1 of Protocol 1 caused by the modalities of the enforcement process, including the 7% enforcement fee. The RCC had already reviewed the constitutionality of the enforcement fee in 2001.[36] On that occasion, the RCC acknowledged the punitive character of the said fee and that its application should be flexible: 7% was in fact a maximum rate, applicable only in the most serious cases. The use of the highest fee and the refusal to delay its payment were, however, justifiable in the specific procedure

---

[31] RCC, *Judgment of 14.07.2005 No. 9-П in the case concerning the review of the constitutionality of the provisions of Article 113 of the Tax Code of the Russian Federation, in connection with a complaint of G.A. Polyakova and upon a request of the Federal Arbitration Court of the Moscow Circuit*.

[32] Article 113 of the Tax Code of the Russian Federation.

[33] Article 57 of the Constitution of the Russian Federation.

[34] RCC, *Judgment of 19.01.2017 No. 1-П/2017*, supra note 1, p. 20, referring to Article 17, Section 3; Article 19, Sections 1 and 2; Article 55, Sections 2 and 3; Article 57 of the Constitution of the Russian Federation.

[35] Ibid., 21.

[36] RCC, *Judgment of 30.07.2001 No. 13-П in the case concerning the review of the constitutionality of the provisions of subsection 7 of section 1 of article 4, section 1 of article 77 and section 1 of article 81 of the Federal Law on 'Enforcement Proceedings', in connection with requests of the Arbitration Court of Voronezh region, the Arbitration Court of Saratov region and complaint by Joint Stock Company 'Razrez Izyhskiy'*.

against Yukos, since the company's evasion scheme 'directly threatened the principles of the law-governed democratic social State'.[37]

Therefore, the RCC concluded that enforcement of the ECtHR would infringe on the constitutional principle of equality in fiscal matters.[38]

The RCC, after declaring the unconstitutionality of paying the compensation ordered by the ECtHR, declared that it would explore the possibility of a 'lawful compromise' in order to preserve the system.[39] Namely, it did not rule out the possibility of the Government showing goodwill in providing some relief to the shareholders who suffered from unlawful actions of the company and its management.[40] Such payment, however, would not be drawn from the Russian budget but, for instance, from the assets which Yukos might still conceal abroad.[41]

Two noticeable opinions were attached to the judgment of the RCC.[42] In his dissenting opinion, Judge Yaroslavtsev argued that the request of the Ministry of Justice should have been deemed inadmissible. Essentially, he observed that the RCC should not be a 'judge in its own case'. According to Judge Yaroslavtsev, the RCC had already expressed its position on the matter when it declared that the sanctions applied to Yukos were constitutionally lawful. To some extent, the review of the ECtHR judgment was therefore akin to the RCC reviewing its own previous judgment.[43] In his rather confusing opinion, Judge Aranovskiy noted that the Russian government was only partially dissatisfied with the *Yukos* judgment on liability.[44] For Judge Aranovskiy, the Russian authorities did not in fact question the constitutionality of the ECtHR judgment.[45] Moreover, the RCC overstepped its competence, assuming an unwarranted right to review and reconsider the judgments of the ECtHR. Since the validity,

---

[37]   RCC, *Judgment of 19.01.2017 No. 1-П/2017*, supra note 1, p. 28.
[38]   It declined to entertain the Ministry's claims regarding Yukos's alleged failure to exhaust local remedies and the ECtHR's lack of precision regarding the identity of the shareholders to whom satisfaction was owed, see ibid., p. 29.
[39]   RCC, *Judgment of 19.01.2017 No. 1-П/2017*, supra note 1, pp. 30–31.
[40]   Ibid., p. 30.
[41]   Ibid., p. 31.
[42]   A short commentary on these individual decisions is provided also in M. GÓRSKI, 'Quo vadis, Russia? On the Country's Recent Approach towards Implementing Judgments of European Court of Human Rights' (2017) 23 *Comparative Law Review*, pp. 147–148.
[43]   RCC, *Judgment of 19.01.2017 No. 1-П/2017*, supra note 1, Dissenting Opinion of Judge Yaroslavtsev, p. 43.
[44]   This is another sign that the government is not concerned with the principles put forward in the judgment of the ECtHR but rather the amount of compensation awarded to the shareholders of Yukos.
[45]   Yaroslavtsev made a similar remark in his opinion. He referred to the general measures that the Russian government submitted to the Committee of Ministers of the Council of Europe to prove the implementation of the judgment. He called this approach of the Russian authorities 'inconsistent and highly contradictory,' pointing out that the request to the RCC was a 'simplified solution' to the situation. RCC, *Judgment of 19.01.2017 No. 1-П/2017*, supra note 1, Dissenting Opinion of Judge Yaroslavtsev, pp. 40–42.

conformity to the Convention and binding nature of these judgments cannot be changed, the RCC should have refrained from handing down the *Yukos* decision. Judge Aranovskiy also opined that, by failing to execute the judgment of the ECtHR, national authorities commit a violation of international and constitutional law.[46] However, the judge also observed that the *Yukos* judgment of the ECtHR was invalid, since the shareholders had not taken part in the proceedings and, therefore, the decision was a non-judgment for serious violation of their procedural rights.

3. THE ISSUES WITH THE RCC'S DECISION

Ultimately, the RCC found a contradiction between Russia's obligation to honour the ECtHR's 2014 judgment and its own mandate to protect the values of the Constitution. In essence, the contradiction arose because the measures found to breach the Convention had been previously found to be constitutional. On the surface, the conflict is characterised as one between the Convention and the Constitution, and so it is presented in the *dispositif*. However, if one strips the RCC's reasoning to the bone, the only conflict at hand is between the Convention (as interpreted in Strasbourg) and Russian *statutory* law (as interpreted in Saint Petersburg, where the RCC sits). This conflict is more difficult to accept as the sufficient reason for the RCC's decision of non-compliance: Article 15(4) of the Russian Constitution unambiguously establishes the priority of international law over conflicting domestic statutory laws.[47] Whether those statutory laws are compatible with the domestic constitution is irrelevant; a statutory measure that does not breach the Constitution remains, in the hierarchy of sources, statutory law.

---

[46] RCC, *Judgment of 19.01.2017 No. 1-П/2017*, supra note 1, Dissenting Opinion of Judge Aranovskiy, p. 55.

[47] If an international treaty or agreement of the Russian Federation fixes other rules than those envisaged by law, the rules of the international agreement shall be applied. Although the Russian Constitution does not clearly state the priority of the Constitution over international law it has been interpreted that way by the RCC. See, for example RCC, *Judgment of 14.07.2015 N 21-П Verification of Constitutionality of Art. 1 of the Federal Law 'On Ratification of the Convention for the Protection of Human Rights and Fundamental Freedoms and Its Protocols', Sections 1 and 2 of Art. 32 of the Federal Law 'On International Treaties of the Russian Federation', Sections 1 and 4 of Art. 11, Subsection 4 of Section 4 of Art. 392 of the Civil Procedural Code of the Russian Federation', Sections 1 and 4 of Art. 13, Subsection 4 of Section 3 of Art. 311 of the Arbitration Procedural Code of the Russian Federation, Sections 1 and 4 of Art. 15, Subsection 4 of Section 1 of Art. 350 of the Administrative Court Proceedings Code of the Russian Federation, and Subsection 2 of Section 4 of Art. 413 of the Criminal Procedural Code of the Russian Federation in Relation to the request of the Group of the Members of State Duma (Parliament)*, available at rg.ru/2015/07/27/ks-dok.html, last accessed 08.05.2018. All this notwithstanding, the Russian Constitution is unambiguous as to the point that the statutory laws are subordinate to the rules of international law.

The RCC's determination of constitutionality of a statute only spares that act from annulment, but it certainly does not confer to it a constitutional status, above international obligations. Constitutionality and constitutional rank are distinct notions: the former does not imply the latter.[48] What is permitted and what is required are not the same: it is hard to envisage a genuine conflict of obligations between the ECtHR's judgment and the Russian Constitution, if no textual constitutional requirement is breached.

The RCC presented its own constitutional review of the challenged measures – resulting in a positive finding of constitutionality – as a decisive argument. Throughout the decision, there seems to be a constant juxtaposition of the reasoning of the RCC (which found the Russian measures to be constitutional) and that of the ECtHR (which found the same measures to violate the Convention). The RCC seemingly insisted on this comparison to contrast the arguments of the two courts. It indicated the ECtHR's mistakes in application of the Convention's right to property, and the better course that its reasoning should have taken, using the RCC's application of the Constitution's right to property as a template.[49]

This approach is objectionable for at least two reasons. First, any argument invoking domestic law to justify a breach of international law runs counter Article 27 of the VCLT. The following section chronicles the development of Russian law that resulted in the RCC assuming the role of the final arbiter, deciding which judgments of the ECtHR cannot be executed. Second, the simple fact that a constitutional court has not found fault with a measure's constitutionality cannot *per se* rule out the possibility that such a measure breaches the Convention. In this light, we analyse the specific reasoning of the RCC in the case, and its repercussions on the interplay between the Convention and Russian law.

3.1. THE IRRELEVANCE OF DOMESTIC LAW

The first major problem with the RCC's judgment is the failure to mention Article 27 VCLT, which is all the more revealing since the RCC discussed the application of Article 26 VCLT. Whereas Article 26 VCLT simply postulates that

---

[48] T. Khramova, 'To Pay or Not to Pay – Russia's Next Step Away from the European Convention', *IACL BLOG*, 18.05.2017: '[the RCC] wrongly suggests that acting against legislative provisions which had been previously declared constitutional leads to violation of the Constitution itself', available at https://iacl-aidc-blog.org/2017/05/18/analysis-to-pay-or-not-to-pay-russias-next-step-away-from-the-european-convention, last accessed 18.05.2018.

[49] Dissenting Judge Aranovskiy pointed out that the RCC does not have a competence to review judgments of the ECtHR and cannot act as an arbiter in the cases between the Russian government and the ECtHR. RCC, *Judgment of 19.01.2017 No. 1-П/2017*, *supra* note 1, Dissenting Opinion of Judge Yaroslavtsev, p. 48.

international obligations must be honoured, Article 27 VCLT is more specific: it expressly rules out the possibility of using domestic law as an excuse to avoid international obligations.[50]

The RCC tried to read an exception into Article 26 VCLT – or, more to the point, Article 46 of the Convention.[51] The arguments used, however, contradicts the principle of Article 27 VCLT. This is not a novel scenario. In fact, there have been several developments in the Russian legal system, even before the 2017 judgment, which paved the way for an outright rejection of selected ECtHR's judgments.[52] In 2010, the president of the RCC had declared that 'ECtHR's decisions should be executed unconditionally – whether we are talking about payment of compensation or restoration of the violated rights of the applicant in a particular case'.[53]

Still in 2013, the Supreme Court of the Russian Federation had issued a ruling[54] reminding all Russian courts of the task to implement all ECtHR's decisions.[55] Things have changed thereafter.

The process commenced in 2015 with the RCC decision[56] that was prompted by a request made by 93 members of the Duma.[57] They essentially questioned the constitutionality of the 1998 law requiring the enforceability of Strasbourg decisions in Russia,[58] in case of contradiction with the Constitution.

---

[50] Article 27 VCLT provides 'A party may not invoke the provisions of its internal law as justification for its failure to perform a treaty […]'.

[51] Article 46(1) ECHR states 'The High Contracting Parties undertake to abide by the final judgment of the Court in any case to which they are parties'.

[52] For an overview of this process, see P. PUSTORINO, 'Russian Constitutional Court and the execution "à la carte" of ECtHR judgments' (2016) *Questions of International Law*, p. 5. Another comprehensive and impeccable account is provided in B. BOWRING, 'Russia's cases in the ECtHR and the question of implementation' in L. MÄLKSOO and W. BENEDEK (eds.), *Russia and the European Court of Human Rights, The Strasbourg Effect*, Cambridge University Press, Cambridge 2017, p. 188.

[53] The quote is reported (and translated from the original) in M. GÓRSKI (2017), 'Quo vadis, Russia?', *supra* note 42, p. 148, and is excerpted from a presentation made by the President of the RCC Valeryy Zorkin at a conference in 2010, available at http://www.ksrf.ru/ru/News/Speech/Pages/ViewItem.aspx?ParamId=39, last accessed 17.05.2018.

[54] Ruling of the Plenary session of the Supreme Court of the Russian Federation No. 21, 'On Application by Courts of General Jurisdiction the Convention for the Protection of Human Rights and Fundamental Freedoms and Protocols,' 27.06.2013, (Постановление Пленума Верховного Суда Российской Федерации от 27 июня 2013 г. N 21 г. Москва "О применении судами общей юрисдикции Конвенции о защите прав человека и основных свобод от 4 ноября 1950 года и Протоколов к ней"), available at https://rg.ru/2013/07/05/konvencia-dok.html, last accessed 08.05.2018.

[55] Already in 2003, the Supreme Court had issued a ruling confirming the binding nature of ECtHR's rulings upon Russian courts. See the relevant excerpt in B. BOWRING (2017), 'Russia's cases in the ECtHR', *supra* note 52, pp. 203–204.

[56] RCC, *Judgment of 14.07.2015 N 21-П*, *supra* note 47.

[57] The lower chamber of the Russian Parliament.

[58] Federal Law of 30.03.1998 N 54-ФЗ 'On Ratification of the Convention on protection of human rights and fundamental freedoms and the Protocols', available at http://base.garant.ru/12111157, last accessed 08.05.2018.

Whereas the question was made in the abstract, it was widely believed that the request was motivated by the recent judgments of the ECtHR in the *Anchugov* and *Yukos* cases.[59] In its judgment, the RCC confirmed Russia's sovereignty and its right to avoid unconstitutional judgments by the ECtHR, pointing out that the matter of unconstitutionality might be the result of an unusual interpretation of the Convention carried out by the Strasbourg judges. The RCC declined to declare the 1998 law unconstitutional but authorised the legislator to pass a law empowering the RCC to 'declare impossible to implement' certain ECtHR's judgments breaching the Constitution's core values.

The legislator obliged,[60] and in April 2016 the RCC could already exercise its powers under the new law in the *Anchugov* case. In *Anchugov*, the ECtHR had found Russia in breach of the Convention for its blanket ban on prisoner voting,[61] enshrined in a provision of the Constitution.[62] In its judgment,

---

[59] See L. MÄLKSOO, 'Russia's Constitutional Court Defies the European Court of Human Rights. Constitutional Court of the Russian Federation Judgment of 14 July 2015, No 21-П/2015', (2016) 12 *European Constitutional Law Review*, pp. 377, 379 for a careful reconstruction drawing also on the declarations of Russian authorities and public officials. A few hours after the RCC, *Judgment of 14.07.2015*, supra note 47, was delivered, for instance, the Ministry of Justice of Russia released a statement that 'further actions of the Ministry of Justice in relation to the judgments of the European Court of Human Rights in cases *Anchugov and Gladkov v Russia* and *Yukos v Russia*, will be conducted in accordance with the legally binding position of the Constitutional Court of the priority of the Convention of the Russian Federation over the decisions of international tribunals'. V. NEHEZIN, Ministry of Justice: the right not to enforce judgments of the ECtHR will be taken into account in the Yukos case, BBC Russia, 14.07.2015, in Russian, translated by the authors, available at http://www.bbc.com/russian/international/2015/07/150714_constitutional_court_echr, last accessed 08.05.2018. Suggestions that the new law would be applied to prevent the execution of the Yukos judgment on just satisfaction also appeared immediately in the press, see B. BOWRING (2017), 'Russia's cases in the ECtHR', supra note 52, p. 210.

[60] Federal Law of the Russian Federation no. 7-ФКЗ, introducing amendments to the Federal Constitutional Law no. 1-ФКЗ of 21.07.1994 on the Constitutional Court of the Russian Federation, available at http://pravo.gov.ru/proxy/ips/?docbody=&nd=102384035&rdk=&backlink=1, last accessed 08.05.2018. The Venice Commission produced a critical assessment of these amendments, see VENICE COMMISSION, 'Final Opinion on the Amendments to the Federal Constitutional Law on the Constitutional Court', Venice, 10–11.06.2016, available at http://www.venice.coe.int/webforms/documents/default.aspx?pdffile=CDL-AD(2016)016-e, last accessed 16.05.2018.

[61] ECtHR, *Anchugov and Gladkov v Russia*, no 11157/04, 04.07.2013, finding a violation of Article 3 of Protocol 1. See P. PUSTORINO (2016), 'Russian Constitutional Court', supra note 52, pp. 10–13; K. DZEHTSIAROU, S. GOLUBOK and M. TIMOFEYEV, 'The Russian Response to the Prisoner Voting Judgment', available at http://echrblog.blogspot.co.uk/2016/04/the-russian-response-to-prisoner-voting.html, last accessed 08.05.2018, M. AKSENOVA, 'Anchugov and Gladkov is not Enforceable: the Russian Constitutional Court Opines in its First ECtHR Implementation Case', available at http://opiniojuris.org/2016/04/25/anchugov-and-gladkov-is-not-enforceable-the-russian-constitutional-court-opines-in-its-first-ecthr-implementation-case, last accessed 08.05.2018.

[62] Article 32(3) of the Constitution of the Russian Federation: Deprived of the right to elect and be elected shall be citizens recognised by court as legally unfit, as well as citizens kept in places of confinement by a court sentence.

the ECtHR had invited Russia to explore the available ways to bring its law into compliance with the Convention, without enjoining a specific process:

> It is open to the respondent Government to explore all possible ways in that respect and to decide whether their compliance with Article 3 of Protocol No. 1 can be achieved through some form of political process or by interpreting the Russian Constitution by the competent authorities – the Russian Constitutional Court in the first place – in harmony with the Convention in such a way as to coordinate their effects and avoid any conflict between them.[63]

In other words, the ECtHR had suggested that an effort of consistent interpretation might be sufficient to bring Russian law into compliance with the Convention, without amending the Constitution. However, the Russian Ministry of Justice doubted whether compliance with this judgment was possible, given that the Russian Constitution expressly stated that prisoners cannot vote. Noting the clear provision of the Constitution and the impossibility of a conventional interpretation, the RCC declared the *Anchugov* judgment impossible to enforce insofar as the change of the Russian Constitution is necessary. The RCC also suggested that some modifications to the Russian legislation would be enough to enforce this judgment.[64]

In a somewhat unnecessary specification (the conflict emerged from the literal interpretation of the Constitution), the RCC also envisaged the possibility that a decision from Strasbourg could be unenforceable when it collides not with the letter of the Constitution, but with its interpretation given by the RCC.[65] This hermeneutic collision occurred in *Yukos*.

If the RCC's interpretation of the Constitution operates as filter for international judgments' enforceability, it is easy to anticipate incidents of inter-system collision.[66] The RCC, effectively, arrogated to itself a power to shelter any statutory provision from effective review by the Strasbourg Court, by sanctioning its status as constitutionally required. This power ranges widely

---

[63] ECtHR, *Anchugov and Gladkov v Russia*, supra note 61, para. 111.

[64] BOWRING (2017), 'Russia's cases in the ECtHR', *supra* note 522, p. 213. The possibility that compliance be achieved through a change of ordinary legislation has been explored in the literature, but not yet seized by the Russian authorities.

[65] RCC, *Judgment of 19.04.2016 No. 12-П/2016 in the case concerning the resolution of the question of the possibility to execute in accordance with the Constitution of the Russian Federation the Judgment of the European Court of Human Rights of 04.07.2013 in the case of Anchugov and Gladkov v Russia in connection with the request of the Ministry of Justice of the Russian Federation*, available at http://www.ksrf.ru/en/Decision/Judgments/Documents/2016_April_19_12-P.pdf, last accessed 08.05.2018.

[66] As noted by Mälksoo: 'Here everything depends on how Russia's constitutional identity will be constructed and which constitutional values will be emphasised by the Court.' See L. MÄLKSOO (2016), 'Russia's Constitutional Court Defies the European Court of Human Rights', *supra* note 59, p. 388.

especially if the principle of 'state sovereignty' is deemed a core value of the Constitution. This principle might be used to immunise any statutory law at odds with the Convention, in a self-serving circle. Namely, the measure would breach international law, but there would be a constitutional principle allowing Russia to preserve its sovereignty in the face of international obligations; as a result this measure would be safe (and so would be any other that the RCC cares to rescue).

Another 'core value' that the RCC has mentioned systematically (in 2015, in *Anchugov*, and in *Yukos*) is the protection of fundamental rights. In essence, a Strasbourg judgment would be impossible to enforce if it encroached on the protection of fundamental rights granted under the Constitution. This scenario is reminiscent of the various 'untouchable core' doctrines developed by national courts against the effects of the Court of Justice of the EU.[67] In that scenario, domestic courts wanted to reserve the right to contain the human-right impact of EU law – a faculty they have virtually never exercised. However, the doctrine appears to be ill-equipped to justify resistance against the decision of a human rights court. By definition, the ECtHR's judgments against a State sanction that State's *failure* to uphold a fundamental right: it is hard to see how they could undermine the protection of fundamental rights. If several rights are in tension, and the ECtHR indicates a balance (through proportionality) different from what the State measure entailed, one of the rights involved could lose out as a result of the international judgment, in favour of other fundamental rights. Relative detriment to a fundamental right, however, would be incidental to the better reconciliation between rights identified by the ECtHR judges. The ECtHR's task is precisely to review the balancing performed by national authorities and, when they unnecessarily sacrifice one right to pursue another public interest, to point out a better balancing option.

In essence, recourse to the concepts of 'state sovereignty' and fundamental rights protection causes the RCC to second-guess the overall desirability of ECtHR's judgments. Mention of these principles might suggest that such scrutiny is triggered only past a high threshold of gravity. However, their construction might give rise to conflicts that are not mandated by the Constitution,[68]

---

[67] See M. CLAES, 'The Validity and Primacy of EU Law and the 'Cooperative Relationship' between National Constitutional Courts and the European Court of Justice' (2016) 23(1) *Maastricht Journal of European and Comparative Law*, p. 151; M. CLAES, 'The Primacy of EU Law in European and in National Law' in A. ARNULL and D. CHALMERS (eds.), *The Oxford Handbook of European Law*, OUP, Oxford 2015, pp. 178–211; J. KOMÁREK, 'The Place of Constitutional Courts in the EU', (2013) 9 *European Constitutional Law Review*, p. 420.

[68] L. MÄLKSOO (2016), 'Russia's Constitutional Court Defies the European Court of Human Rights', *supra* note 59, p. 389: 'This situation is no longer about open conflict with the text of the Russian Constitution like arguably was in *Anchugov and Gladkov*, but about further weighing, interpretation and value judgments.'

but occasion from the RCC's interpretation of what the Constitution requires. This scenario, which emerged in *Yukos*, does not apply only in cases of high-level constitutional conflicts.[69] The puzzling repercussion of this loose standard of disobedience are analysed in the next section.

3.2. CONSTITUTIONALLY ALLOWED IS NOT CONSTITUTIONALLY REQUIRED

The second major problem of the *Yukos* judgment is that it seems to assume mistakenly that the constitutionality of a measure and its conformity with the ECHR go hand in hand.

To illustrate the problems of this approach, the saga regarding the Italian regime of compensation in case of unlawful expropriation for public purposes[70] can assist the analysis as a control case.[71] In certain circumstances, Italian law granted the dispossessed owners compensation lower than full market value. Moreover, the compensation formula, codified in statutory law, applied in compensation proceedings already pending before the law's entry into force (i.e., retroactively). The Italian Constitutional Court confirmed until 2002 the constitutionality of such regime, noting that full compensation is not always necessary (as the ECtHR often declares in cases on the right to property) and that retroactivity can be justified in non-criminal matters.[72] However, the ECtHR

---

[69] See T. KHRAMOVA (2016), 'To Pay or Not to Pay', *supra* note 48. The author noted that in *Yukos* the RCC refused to enforce the ECtHR decision even if there was no evidence of a 'evident contradiction between the Convention and the text of the Russian Constitution'.

[70] More precisely, the issues concerned the phenomenon of acquisition by right of occupancy *(occupazione acquisitiva)*, whereby the State acquires the property of an expropriated land by building public facilities on it, rather than by virtue of a formal expropriation order. For a fuller analysis, see F. BIONDI DAL MONTE and F. FONTANELLI, 'The Decisions No. 348 and 349/2007 of the Italian Constitutional Court: The Efficacy of the European Convention in the Italian Legal System' (2008) 9 *German LJ*, p. 889.

[71] Other examples could be brought, see for instance the *revirement* of the German Federal Constitutional Court in the *Von Hanover* case. Compare the judgment of the Constitutional Court BVerfGE 120, 180 (210) with the ECtHR's judgment in *Von Hannover v Germany*, no 59320/00, 24.06.2004. Another example concerns the constitutionality of preventive detention, which had been confirmed in 2004 (see BVerfGE 109, 133) and then rejected in 2011 (BVerfGE 128, 326), in the wake of the ECtHR's decision in *M. v Germany*, no 19359/04, 17.12.2009.

[72] See Italian Constitutional Court, Judgment No. 148 of 1999 of 30 April 1999, available at http://www.giurcost.org/decisioni/1999/0148s-99.html, last accessed 18.05.2018; Order No. 396 of 1999 of 22 October 1999, available at http://www.giurcost.org/decisioni/1999/0396o-99.html, last accessed 18.05.2018; Judgment No. 24 of 2000 of 4 February 2000, available at http://www.giurcost.org/decisioni/2000/0024s-00.html, last accessed 18.05.2018; and Judgment No. 251 of 2000 of 17 July 2001, available at http://www.giurcost.org/decisioni/2001/0251s-01.html, last accessed 18.05.2018.

declared in 2006 that the Italian law breached Article 1 of Protocol No 1 to the Convention.[73] Thereupon, the same Italian measures were impugned again before the Italian Constitutional Court, for breach of the Constitution.[74]

The Italian Constitutional Court acknowledged the supra-statutory ranking of the Convention, as interpreted by the ECtHR. It contrasted its own previous conclusions with the ruling of the Strasbourg Court, and held that the balance struck in the past needed re-thinking, in line with Italy's international obligations. Even if potentially lawful under the Constitution, less-than-market value compensation contravened the Convention. This conflict alone, emerging from the ECtHR's formulation of a new and more precise standard of review, rendered the Italian measures also unconstitutional.[75] The Italian legislator, less than a month after the *revirement* of the Italian Constitutional Court, changed the law[76] to comply with the ECtHR's judgment, and the Supreme Court applied the new calculation criteria shortly thereafter.[77]

In essence, the critical elements of the Italian saga case are the same as those that emerged in the *Yukos* one. In Russia, the Convention has quasi-constitutional status, as it does in Italy: it displaces domestic statutes but not the Constitution itself. As in Italy, the Russian statutory measures' constitutionality had been challenged unsuccessfully, and the Constitutional Court's decision had used a test comparable to the ECtHR's own – a scrutiny of the proportionality of the restriction of property rights. As in the Italian case, the ECtHR had essentially struck a different balance and found that the Russian restrictions were, in ultimate analysis, disproportionate. Here the similarities stop. The Italian Constitutional Court, mindful that ECHR law 'lives in the interpretation given by the ECtHR on it',[78] adopted the ECtHR's views on proportionality as good law. Instead, the Russian Court rejected them and stuck to its own proportionality analysis, essentially challenging the legal authority of the ECtHR's judgment.[79]

Yukos was not the first case in which the ECtHR found fault with Russian statutory measures that the RCC had previously ruled to be constitutional.

---

[73] ECtHR, *Scordino v Italy*, no 36813/97 [GC] 29.03.2006, para. 1.
[74] Article 117 of the Italian Constitution provides that legislative powers be exercised in compliance with Italy's international obligations, including those deriving from the Convention.
[75] Italian Constitutional Court, Joint Judgments Nos. 348 and 349/2007 of 24 October 2007, available at http://www.giurcost.org/decisioni/2007/0348s-07.html, last accessed 18.05.2018 and http://www.giurcost.org/decisioni/2007/0349s-07.html, last accessed 18.05.2018.
[76] Italian Law no. 244 of 24 December 2007, article 2, para. 89.
[77] Italian Supreme Court, Decision No. 8384 of 30.03.2008.
[78] Italian Constitutional Court, Judgments 348/2007, *supra* note 75, para. 4.7: 'le norme della CEDU vivono nell'interpretazione che delle stesse viene data dalla Corte europea.'
[79] Likewise, the RCC seemingly disputed the merits ECtHR's decision in *Anchugov*, see P. PUSTORINO (2016), 'Russian Constitutional Court', *supra* note 52, p. 14.

The RCC declared that inability to get paternity leave for a military serviceman was compatible with the Constitution,[80] but the ECtHR subsequently found in *Konstantin Markin v Russia* that this measure breaches the Convention.[81] In *Khoroshenko v Russia*, the ECtHR found Russia in violation of the Convention for not allowing long-term family visits to life-long prisoners during the first decade of their imprisonment.[82] The RCC had beforehand declared inadmissible a challenge of constitutionality aimed at the measure.[83] In neither case did the RCC question the enforceability of the ECtHR's judgments.[84] It did so in the *Yukos* judgment.

This element of *Yukos* sets it apart from other instances of disobedience to international decisions. Occasionally, domestic courts invoke the right to disobey international decisions when, irrespective of their legal tenability, their implementation would undermine some core values of the domestic legal order. In the case at hand, instead, most of the Russian Court's reasoning focused rather on the specific proportionality test carried out by the two courts, respectively, on the same measures: the constitutionality of the Russian laws should have entailed, by extension or by analogy, their conventionality too.[85] This argument is one that – through *de novo* review – challenges the *correctness* of the ECtHR's decision, not one that simply recommends disobedience to avert the risk of a constitutional crisis.[86] The RCC's apparent concern is not so much the gravity of the consequences of complying with the ECtHR's judgment, but the alleged mistakes in its reasoning.

This impression, however, might flow from the RCC's disguising of its real preoccupation, which did in fact lie with the judgment's practical consequences rather than its reasoning. It can be argued that the RCC, in line with

---

[80] RCC, *Ruling of 15.01.2009 about the rejection to consider the complaint by Markin Konstantin Aleksandrovich of violation of his constitutional rights*, available at http://doc.ksrf.ru/decision/KSRFDecision18793.pdf, last accessed 08.05.2018.
[81] ECtHR, *Konstantin Markin v Russia*, no 30078/06 [GC] 22.03.2012.
[82] ECtHR, *Khoroshenko v Russia*, no 41418/04 [GC] 30.06.2015.
[83] RCC, *Ruling of 21.12.2006 about the rejection to consider the complaint by Khoroshenko Andrey Anatolievich of violation of his constitutional rights*, available at http://doc.ksrf.ru/decision/KSRFDecision15613.pdf, 08.05.2018.
[84] To enforce the ECtHR judgment in *Khoroshenko* the Constitutional Court, on 15.11.2016, issued a ruling, in which it declared as unconstitutional the provisions which violated the Convention. The Constitutional Court also ordered that, until the necessary changes are made to the domestic legislation, all persons in the position similar to Khoroshenko should enjoy less restrictive regime of imprisonment as demanded by the ECtHR.
[85] While discussing a similar aspect of the RCC decision in the case of *Anchugov and Gladkov*, Mälksoo points out that 'this seems to be in the first place a warning of the Constitutional Court to the Strasbourg Court to be careful when critically dismissing judgments of the former'. L. MÄLKSOO (2016), 'Russia's Constitutional Court Defies the European Court of Human Rights', *supra* note 59, p. 389.
[86] We do not expand here on the second-order critique raised by the RCC against the interpretive canon used by the ECtHR to interpret the Convention, chastised as being 'unusual'.

the Ministry's request of constitutionality review, was more concerned with the massive order of compensation than with any matter of principle raised by the judgment's implementation. Some circumstantial evidence would support this reading.

First, it does not transpire from the judgment of the RCC that the Russian constitutional system is actually threatened by the ECtHR's *Yukos* judgments to the extent necessary to clear the 'impossible to execute' line. The RCC mentioned a flurry of constitutional provisions variously relating to Russia's sovereignty,[87] to illustrate the high stakes of the collision. Yet, the key legal ground of constitutional review used in this case was Article 57 of the Constitution, which simply sets the duty to pay taxes and the non-retroactivity of tax law.[88] Article 57, taken alone, could hardly codify a core constitutional principle (the Constitution itself identifies only its first 16 articles as the core provisions). To justify its resorting to putatively extreme measures the RCC engineered a connection between Article 57 and all these other provisions. More importantly, the mere fact of paying Strasbourg-ordered compensation, relating to an act of over-charging in tax assessment, cannot possibly undermine such hypothetically core value.[89]

Second, while the challenge concerned the judgment of just satisfaction, the RCC's decision spent an inordinate amount of reasoning criticising the ECtHR judgment on the merits.[90] This lack of alignment is understandable: the order of just satisfaction is a routine consequence of ECtHR proceedings, one that every Contracting Party to the Convention is used to facing. It is not easy to mount a principled challenge against a judgment on just satisfaction as such,[91]

---

[87] Reference is made to the norms that confirm Russia's sovereignty over its territory and the supremacy of Russian law thereupon (Article 4, Sections 1 and 2); the higher rank of the Constitution over other domestic laws (Article 15, Section 1); the automatic priority of international law over domestic law (Article 15, Section 4); the priority of the core Constitutional principles – among which all the above – over the rest of the Constitution (Article 16, Section 2); and the possibility for Russia to delegate powers through international treaty-making, if that exercise does not restrict fundamental rights or contradicts 'the principles of the constitutional system' (Article 79).

[88] Article 57 in conjunction with Articles 15 (Sections 1, 2 and 4), 17 (Section 3), 19 (Sections 1 and 2), 55 (Sections 2 and 3) and 79.

[89] Dissenting Judge Aranovskiy was also not sure that a breach of the Russian Constitution can arise simply through the payment of just satisfaction. He pointed out that the Ministry of Justice in its request in fact focused on 'a collision between the decision of the ECtHR with ordinary laws and decisions of the Constitutional Court'. He concluded that such conflict does not necessarily render a particular judgment constitutionally impossible to implement. RCC, *Judgment of 19.01.2017 No. 1-П/2017*, supra note 1, Dissenting Opinion of Judge Aranovskiy, 49.

[90] Of course, the possibility to declare enforcement impossible only arose with the 2015 law, after the judgment on liability. Therefore, the liability decision – and the reasoning thereof – should have been immune from the RCC's scrutiny.

[91] Consider, in a different field of law, the remarks of a US judge called upon to declare whether an arbitral award ordering a State to pay compensation should be denied enforcement for

and the mere inconvenience of this specific judgment – given its magnitude – cannot be characterised as a legal threat to Russian constitutional order.[92] It is therefore understandable that the Ministry – and the RCC – concentrated their efforts on the precursor of just satisfaction (the proportionality test leading to a finding of breach), rather than its consequences (Russia's duty to make the payment).

In other words, whilst apparently dealing with the remedy the RCC, in fact, re-assessed the ECtHR's judgment on the merits. This disconnect might be revealing. The RCC framed its decision as one of dualism: being fully cognisant of the immunity of ECtHR's judgments from domestic review, the RCC must nevertheless sanction the unconstitutionality of the domestic acts required to implement them. However, its reasoning is, in several passages, one that betrays the monist ambitions of RCC: the Russian judges ultimately explained why the Court of Strasbourg was wrong *as a matter of Convention law* and, therefore, why this ruling is essentially invalid or at least ineffective *ab origine*.

Perhaps, the most revelatory aspect of the RCC's decision is that it failed to mention a damning contradiction.[93] Russian authorities have, in fact, complied diligently with the ECtHR's decision on liability, making several plausible efforts to bring their acts in line with the principles established therein. In May 2013, the Russian Federation liaised with the Committee of Ministers of the Council of Europe, communicating an action plan of all the measures taken and planned to ensure compliance with the ECtHR judgment on liability.[94] As explained above, the ECtHR found Russia in breach of Articles 6(1) and 6(3)(b), as well as Article 1 of Protocol 1, for not granting a sufficient time for Yukos to prepare its defence in the tax assessment proceedings, for applying new provisions retroactively, for imposing a disproportionate collection fee, and for refusing to accept deferred payments.

---

contravening public policy: 'enforcing this award does not risk violating public policy. The award does not interfere with Venezuela's environmental rules or regulations, but only requires Venezuela to compensate Crystallex for the results of its inequitable actions and expropriation. Venezuela fails to meet the demanding threshold by demonstrating that holding it to the terms of its own treaty would violate our basic notions of morality or justice'. United States District Court for the District of Columbia, 25.03.2017, p. 28, available at https://ecf.dcd.uscourts.gov/cgi-bin/show_public_doc?2016cv0661-32, last accessed 08.05.2018.

[92] The Venice Commission opined prior to the *Yukos* judgment that '[i]t is very difficult to conceive that an order for payment of a sum of money may be found to be unconstitutional in the light of Chapters 1 and 2 of the Constitution'. See VENICE COMMISSION (2016), 'Final Opinion', *supra* note 60, para. 30.

[93] Which was highlighted only in the dissenting opinion of judge Yaroslavtsev. RCC, *Judgment of 19.01.2017 No. 1-П/2017* (n 1), Dissenting Opinion of Judge Yaroslavtsev.

[94] Council of Europe, Secretariat of the Committee of Ministers, Communication from the Russian Federation concerning the case of *OAO Neftyanaya Kompaniya Yukos against Russian Federation*, no 14902/04, Document DH-DD(2013)565, 22.05.2013.

Russia informed the Committee of Ministers that the *Yukos* 2011 judgment was circulated widely and used in training sessions for judges and bailiffs. The specific purpose of this dissemination plan was 'for implementation into the practice and for taking general measures to eliminate and prevent further violations of the Convention found by the European Court'.[95] Moreover, enforcement measures included amendments to the Russian Commercial Procedure Code to extend the procedural time-limits. The action plan remarked on the precise function of such legislative reform: '[t]he adopted measures correspond to the European Court's conclusions and serve as additional guarantee for ensuring the rights of parties in the proceedings.'[96] Finally, new legislative provisions entered into force, providing for the possibility to reduce the enforcement fees, or to authorise their collection in instalments.[97]

Russia, far from detecting any threat to its own constitutional values, embraced the principles of the *Yukos* judgment on liability. It put its administration in motion and effected all necessary changes in the domestic law and practice to prevent the breaches found by the ECtHR to arise in the future. The Committee of Ministers validated Russia's efforts to implement the judgment on liability and stressed that 'the main outstanding issue' remained the execution of the subsequent order of just satisfaction.[98]

4. QUESTIONABLE LEGITIMACY OF THE RCC DECISION

The RCC is not the only domestic authority refusing compliance with international decisions. Several other instances can be given. For the purposes of this article, we isolate some other instances of possible or actual disobedience to ECtHR's judgments.

Dzehtsiarou and de Londras have divided disobedience to ECtHR judgments into principled disobedience and dilatoriness.[99] Of course, disobedience is usually presented by States as principled disobedience. The true intentions can be fathomed by reference to the State actions that undermine the authority and the legitimacy of the Strasbourg Court. In other words, in cases of unprincipled disobedience, the State is not concerned about the principles but

---

[95] Ibid., point 1.1.
[96] Ibid., point 2.
[97] Ibid., point 4.1.
[98] Committee of Ministers, 1,302nd meeting (05–07.12.2017), Notes: 'It is recalled that the more general problems underlying the violations have been addressed by the authorities and that the main outstanding issue relates to the payment of the just satisfaction as ordered in the European Court's judgment under Article 41 of the Convention.'
[99] F. DE LONDRAS and K. DZEHTSIAROU (2017), 'Mission Impossible?', *supra* note 4.

about the consequences of the Strasbourg judgments, such as the amount of compensation, the power-sharing arrangements required to comply, or other practical repercussions at the national level. In Germany, the Constitutional Court reserved some space for principled disagreement in its *Görgülü* decision.[100] In the UK, the mirror principle of application of the ECtHR law also leaves the national judges with some discretion on how to implement controversial judgments.[101]

From an international law point of view, there is hardly any difference between principled disagreement and dilatoriness: irrespective of the justification, non-implementation of the judgments of the ECtHR is a violation of Article 46 of the Convention. The purported inability of implement the judgment in *Hirst (no. 2) v United Kingdom*[102] is just as illegal as Russia's failure to enforce *Yukos*.

Nevertheless, there is a difference on the level of legitimacy of the State actions. Even if the constitutional structure leaves some space for principled disagreement, this space is often filled by the willingness to find a solution to the constitutional confrontation between the national law and the ECtHR. In Italy, for instance, the Convention has quasi-constitutional status: it can be used to invalidate statutory law (as part of the *bloc de constitutionnalité*)[103] but cannot trump the norms of the Constitution. Hence, the system suggests that there can be a principled disagreement between the ECHR and the Italian Constitution. This particular setup, however, concerns the respective position of the sources in the domestic system and does not imply that ECtHR's decisions can be reviewed for constitutionality, or rejected. First, the possibility that there is a conflict between the Constitution and the Convention that cannot be moderated through consistent interpretation is remote. Second, a potential conflict would

---

[100] *Görgülü* 2 BvR 1481/04 (14.10.2004) BVerfGE 111, 307 (Ger). See also K. DZEHTSIAROU and N. MAVRONICOLA, 'Relation of Constitutional Courts / Supreme Courts to ECtHR' (2017) *Max Planck Encyclopedia of Comparative Constitutional Law*, available at http://oxcon.ouplaw.com/view/10.1093/law-mpeccol/law-mpeccol-e572, last accessed 08.05.2018.

[101] UK House of Lords, *R (Ullah) v Special Adjudicator* [2004] UKHL 26 (UK).

[102] In 2005, the ECtHR declared that total disenfranchisement of prisoners in the UK is a violation of Article 3 of Protocol 1. See ECtHR, *Hirst (no. 2) v the United Kingdom*, no 74025/01 [GC] 06.10.2005. From this judgment the whole line of prisoner voting case law originated, *Anchugov* was one of the follow-ups. The UK disagreed with this judgment using vocabulary of principled disagreement.

[103] L. FAVOREU, 'Bloc de constitutionnalité', in O. DUHAMEL and Y. MÉNY (eds.), *Dictionnaire Constitutionnel*, Presses Univ. de France, Paris 1992, p. 87. The same mechanism is in place in France, with the difference that the review of compatibility of domestic law with the Convention, instead of being the prerogative of the Conseil Constitutionnel, is carried out also by the ordinary judges, who can set domestic statutes aside without voiding them, see O. DUTHEILLET DE LAMOTHE, 'Contrôle de constitutionnalité et contrôle de conventionnalité', in *Juger l'administration, administrer la justice. Mélanges en l'honneur de Daniel Labetoulle*, Dalloz, Paris 2007, p. 315.

more likely trigger constitutional reform than a deliberate disregard of the ECtHR's decision.[104]

Of course, some judgments of the ECtHR could hypothetically impose such obliteration of a constitutional value or fundamental right that the Italian or German authorities would be forced to question the constitutionality of the required measures. In principle, the scenario is comparable to that of the execution of *Yukos*. What is lost in the comparison is the actual import of this safety-valve scenario. In *Yukos* the RCC did not point to an ECtHR-made doctrine that would frustrate an essential component of its constitutional identity, but only to an (allegedly) wrong decision. The post-2011 diligent actions of the Russian authorities, that changed the law and reformed their practice to implement the ECtHR's judgment, demonstrate that implementation was indeed harmless for the Russian constitutional identity, and perhaps not so wrong after all. The RCC merely reflected the considerations of dilatoriness that do not call for dialogue but halt it.

The RCC's judgment in *Anchugov*, taken alone and not as a strategic precursor for the subsequent *Yukos* judgment, can be considered as an episode of principled disagreement. After *Anchugov*, Russia should have modified its laws on prisoners' voting, possibly also Article 32 of its Constitution. This kind of systemic change is harder to implement and is politically harder to digest – the post-*Hirst* scenario in the UK is similar in this respect.[105] Complexity of the law reform required to enforce the judgments also distinguishes *Yukos* from *Sejdić and Finci v Bosnia and Herzegovina*.[106] In the latter judgment, the ECtHR ruled that the provisions of the Constitution of Bosnia (Dayton agreement), stating that three presidents of the country should be representatives of ethnic communities of Bosniacs, Serbs and Croats, discriminate against the members of other ethnic groups.[107] This judgment was not implemented effectively, and its execution still pends before the Committee of Ministers.[108] However, implementing this judgment would entail amending the Constitution of a very

---

[104] There are many examples when incompatibility with the ECHR triggered constitutional reforms, for example in Turkey, Slovenia, etc.
[105] See generally, K. DZEHTSIAROU, 'Prisoner voting saga', in H. HARDMAN and B. DICKSON (eds.), *Electoral rights in Europe: Advances and Challenges*, Routledge, London and New York 2017.
[106] ECtHR, *Sejdić and Finci v Bosnia and Herzegovina*, nos 27996/06 and 34836/06 [GC] 22.12.2009, ECHR 2009.
[107] The applicants in this case were of Roma and Jewish origin respectively.
[108] In 2017, the Committee of Ministers expressed 'its deepest concern in respect of the lack of tangible progress in the adoption of measures envisaged to ensure that the Constitution of Bosnia and Herzegovina and its electoral legislation are aligned with Convention requirements', see http://hudoc.exec.coe.int/eng?i=004-3141, last accessed 08.05.2018. See also, ECHR BLOG, 'Sejdic and Finci – Lack of Bosnian Progress', 16.05.2012, available at http://echrblog.blogspot.co.uk/2012/05/sejdic-and-finci-lack-of-bosnian.html, last accessed 08.05.2018.

unstable country. The implementation measures are not only complex from the legal point of view but might lead to unpredictable negative consequences.

Conversely, compliance with the *Yukos* decision would only entail a one-off financial disbursement, which is huge only because it is measured upon the value of the possessions taken.[109] The systemic effects on Russian law are minor: after *Yukos*, Russian authorities are simply reminded to avoid retroactive tax assessments (but the legislator is free to readjust the application of the time-bar, for the future) and to avoid the rigid application of steep enforcement fees that unnecessarily harm the taxpayer. In other words, enforcing the *Yukos* judgment would not do violence to the Constitution: even if retroactive assessments of recalcitrant taxpayers were effectively allowed under the Constitution, they would hardly be mandated by it.

The RCC essentially refused to carry out its duty to find a consistent interpretation of its Constitution that would also align with the interpretation of the Convention given by the ECtHR. In *Yukos*, the RCC tried to cover up its dilatoriness through a flood of references to the constitutional principles. However, the gulf between the Constitution's terse text, Russia's own acts and the involved reasoning of the *Yukos* judgment tries so hard to disguise the true intentions of the RCC that they surface all too clearly.

5. CONCLUSION

The RCC declared the ECtHR judgment in *Yukos v Russia* impossible to implement because it contradicted the founding norms of the Russian Constitution. Moreover, its decision was drafted in terms that suggest sincere disagreement with the key principles of the ECtHR judgment. The RCC's decision is questionable for at least two legal reasons. First, the RCC cannot alter the international obligation of Russia to enforce the judgment in *Yukos*. Second, this article has demonstrated that although the RCC in its reasoning tried to establish a link between the founding norms of the Russian Constitution and the unenforceability of *Yukos*, there was in fact no such link.

In fact, the ECtHR judgment contradicts only ordinary Russian law and some previous decisions of the RCC that concerned it. Ultimately, the RCC acted *ultra vires*, as Russian law does not allow it to declare a judgment of the ECtHR unenforceable because of a clash with ordinary law. Finally, this article has proved that the putative disagreement of the RCC with the principles of the ECtHR *Yukos* judgments was merely a cover-up for dilatoriness and unwillingness to pay substantive compensation to the shareholders of *Yukos*.

---

[109] For reference, consider the US $50 billion evaluation of Yukos's possession carried out by the PCA arbitral tribunal, after a 25% deduction for contributory fault.

THE IMPACT OF ECtHR AND CJEU JUDGMENTS ON THE RIGHTS OF ASYLUM SEEKERS IN THE EUROPEAN UNION

Adversaries or Allies in Asylum?

Joyce DE CONINCK

1. Introduction 344
2. Judicial Dialogue: A Tale of Apprehension and Compromise 346
   2.1. Pre-Lisbon Intricacies between the CJEU and the ECtHR......... 346
   2.2. Judicial Coherence in Fundamental Rights: The Status Quo 349
        2.2.1. The Lisbon Innovations 349
        2.2.2. The *Opinion 2/13* Upheaval 351
        2.2.3. The Current State of Affairs 353
3. Dysfunctional Dialogue in Asylum and Migration? 354
   3.1. Entry..354
        3.1.1. CJEU: *X and X v Belgium*............................. 354
        3.1.2. An ECtHR Perspective 356
        3.1.3. Analysis 359
   3.2. Detention..360
        3.2.1. CJEU: *J.N. v Staatssecretaris van Veiligheid en Justitie* 360
        3.2.2. An ECtHR Perspective 364
        3.2.3. Analysis 366
   3.3. Return and *Non-Refoulement* 368
        3.3.1. CJEU: *N.F. v European Council* 368
        3.3.2. An ECtHR Perspective 369
        3.3.3. Analysis 370
4. Conclusion...370

ABSTRACT

Article 52(3) of the Charter of Fundamental Rights of the European Union (CFR) holds that the Court of Justice of the European Union (CJEU) is bound by the interpretation of case law by the European Court of Human Rights (ECtHR) for corresponding rights in the ECtHR. As such, the ECtHR – for corresponding rights – functions as the absolute minimum level of protection that is to be afforded by the CJEU. This provision ensures the necessary consistency and coherence between the ECtHR and the CJEU in matters that concern identical rights. However, in the assessment of case law in the field of asylum and migration – a highly politicised and topical area of law – it appears that this consistency and coherence is at times lost. Seemingly, the CJEU sometimes follows the line of reasoning by the ECtHR for corresponding asylum and migration related rights, sometimes explicitly rules against the line of reasoning by the ECtHR and sometimes simply does not pronounce itself on the standard of protection to be applied to corresponding rights. Bearing this in mind, legitimate expectations, legal certainty and the effectiveness of fundamental rights protection may be detrimentally affected vis-à-vis the right-holders, not to mention the institutional legitimacy of both Courts.

1. INTRODUCTION

Past decades have been indicative of the tumultuous relationship shared between CJEU and the European Court of Human Rights (ECtHR). Whereas in certain fields of fundamental rights protection, both Courts appear to apply a similar – if not equivalent – standard of protection,[1] this cooperative approach is seemingly absent in the field of asylum and migration. Rather, it appears that both Courts, in protecting the fundamental rights of migrants and asylum seekers, apply an ad hoc approach in their reasoning, as a result of which their judgments often explicitly contradict each other, at other times converge, or alternatively are inconclusive as to the standard of protection to be afforded. This is particularly troubling in view of Article 52(3) of the Charter of Fundamental Rights of the European Union (CFR/Charter)[2] and the Explanations[3] thereto – brought about by the Treaty of Lisbon – which binds the CJEU to the interpretation of the European Convention on Human Rights (ECHR)[4] and its case law, as being the lowest common denominator in terms of protection concerning corresponding rights.[5] In other words, as concerns rights and freedoms found in the CFR

---

[1] F. FABBRINI and J. LARIK, 'The Past, Present and Future of the Relation between the European Court of Justice and the European Court of Human Rights', (2016) 35(1) *Yearbook of European Law*, pp. 171–172.
[2] Charter of Fundamental Rights of the European Union [2012] OJ C-326/39.
[3] Explanations Relating to the Charter of Fundamental Rights, OJ C-303/17, 14.12.2007.
[4] European Convention for the Protection of Human Rights and Fundamental Freedoms, as amended by Protocols Nos. 11 and 14 [1950] Council of Europe, ETS 5.
[5] There are three sources of EU (European Union) human rights law as indicated by Article 6 TEU: CFR (1); ECHR (2); general principles of EU law. By virtue of all three sources of EU human rights law, the EU binds itself directly and indirectly to the interpretations given to corresponding rights in the ECHR. See for a more detailed discussion P. CRAIG and G. DE BÚRCA, *EU Law: Text, Cases, and Materials*, OUP, Oxford 2015, pp. 362–363, p. 366

which correspond to rights and freedoms in the ECHR, the CFR holds that the ECHR and resulting case law, function as a 'floor' in terms of human rights protection, which the Union and Member States cannot – by any means – fall below (see below section 2.2.1).[6] Hence, the ambiguity and lacking coherence in the judgments by the CJEU, which sometimes seem to conflict with consistent case law by the ECtHR for corresponding rights in asylum and migration, in turn could detrimentally affect the principles of legal certainty and legitimate expectations of those seeking relief before either one of the Courts, as well as the effectiveness of said protection and ultimately, the institutional legitimacy of both Courts.

In demonstrating the potentially detrimental affects vis-à-vis right-holders and Member States as a result of these unpredictable approaches in the case law of both Courts, this article will focus on three areas of aslyum and migration, which have proved to be politically sensitive and have generated the most case law in both Courts.[7] In particular, judgments in the field of entry (visas), reception (detention), as well as return (*non-refoulement*) will be addressed, as these areas have resulted in a number of controversial judgments delivered by both Courts in recent years. In addition, each of these judgments provided the CJEU with a novel and first-time opportunity to assess the compliance of Union legislation and action in these aforementioned fields with corresponding human rights provisions in the ECHR.[8] This is particularly relevant again, in view of Article 52(3) CFR following the Treaty of Lisbon, as a result of which *de iure* the

---

as well as, CJEU, *J. Nold, Kohlen- und Baustoffgroßhandlung v Commission of the European Communities*, Case C-4/73, 14.05.1974, ECLI:EU:C:1974:51, para. 13.

[6] Conversely, the EU and its Member States retain the discretion, in accordance with Article 52(3) CFR to provide more extensive protection than the ECHR and resulting case law, for corresponding rights. See P. CRAIG and G. DE BÚRCA (2015), *EU Law, supra* note 5, p. 367; S. PEERS and S. PRECHAL, 'Art. 52', in S. PEERS, T. HERVEY, J. KENNER and A. WARD (eds.), *The EU Charter of Fundamental Rights – A Commentary*, Hart Publishing, Oxford 2014, pp. 1490–1503.

[7] COUNCIL OF EUROPE AND EUROPEAN AGENCY FOR FUNDAMENTAL RIGHTS, *Handbook on European Law Relating to Asylum, Borders and Immigration*, Publications Office of the European Union, Luxembourg 2014, p. 16. Family reunification also generates a large number of cases, albeit that this is less controversial, as the Union framework provides more extensive protection than the ECHR framework. Whereas Article 8 ECHR does not explicitly recognise family reunification as a right, this right is embedded in the Union framework. As a result thereof, the ECHR does function as the lowest common denominator in terms of protection, which is surpassed by the Union by virtue of its case law and legislative measures. See Council Directive 2003/86/EC of 22 September 2003 on the right to family reunification [2003] OJ L 251, 03.10.2003, pp. 12–18, and P. VAN ELSUWEGE and D. KOCHENOV, 'On the Limits of Judicial Intervention: EU Citizenship and Family Reunification Rights', (2011) 13(4) *European Journal of Migration and Law*, p. 462.

[8] The three selected judgments are selected based upon the fact that they respectively provided the CJEU with a first-time opportunity to assess the compliance of the respective aspects of secondary Union legislation in the three aforementioned fields of asylum and migration with its corresponding counterparts in the ECHR.

Union legislator has bound itself directly and indirectly to the interpretation of ECHR rights that correspond to rights in the CFR. In elaborating thereupon, the article will first provide some insight into the relationship between both courts prior to and following the Lisbon Treaty (section 2). Subsequently, an analysis will be made of the level of protection provided by both Courts in the three aforementioned fields based on recent judgments, focusing in particular on, and mindful of Article 52(3) CFR, whether the Courts provide for a comparable[9] or contradictory level of protection, or, alternatively, whether they take no stance whatsoever (section 3). Finally some concluding remarks and an analysis of the impact on legal certainty, legitimate expectations and the institutional legitimacy of both organisations will be provided (section 4).

2. JUDICIAL DIALOGUE: A TALE OF APPREHENSION AND COMPROMISE

There was a clear divide in the jurisprudential relationship between the CJEU and the ECtHR prior to and following the entry into force of the Treaty of Lisbon.[10] Prior to the entry into force thereof, the relationship between both Courts underwent a number of different phases, whereby at times the Courts seemed to cooperate – albeit not always directly – and at other times the Courts seemed to take a rather non-cooperative stance vis-à-vis each other.[11] Bearing in mind the objectives pursued by the Council of Europe (CoE) in the enactment of the ECHR and the very different constitutional objectives that are at the heart of the establishment of the European Union (EU), which by its very nature was not human rights oriented,[12] it need not surprise that the relationship between both Courts was tumultuous at best.

2.1. PRE-LISBON INTRICACIES BETWEEN THE CJEU AND THE ECtHR

As held by Fabbrini and Larik, the interaction between the CJEU and the ECtHR prior to the enactment of the Lisbon Treaty can be subdivided in

---

[9] The term comparable is used, as opposed to an *identical* level of protection. This because by virtue of Article 52(3) CFR, more extensive protection is permitted from an EU perspective, insofar this does not detrimentally affect the autonomy of the EU legal order. See also S. PEERS and S. PRECHAL (2014), 'Art. 52', *supra* note 6, pp. 1498–1503.
[10] P. CRAIG and G. DE BÚRCA (2015), *EU Law, supra* note 5, pp. 363–364.
[11] F. FABBRINI and J. LARIK (2016), 'Relation Between the ECtHR and the CJEU', *supra* note 1, pp. 171–172.
[12] D. SPIELMANN, 'The Judicial Dialogue between the European Court of Justice and the European Court of Human Rights – or how to remain good neighbours after Opinion 2/13',

three distinct phases.¹³ The first phase, dating from the 1950s to the 1990s, saw both Courts develop case law independently of each other and was demonstrative of a rather weak jurisprudential relationship.¹⁴ It quickly became clear that the safeguarding of fundamental rights would not be one of the priorities pursued by the Community at that time.¹⁵ This does not entail, however, that fundamental rights were entirely absent in the workings of the CJEU. As commonly known, the CJEU affirmed the status of fundamental rights as being general principles of EU law in the *Stauder*¹⁶ and *Handelsgesellschaft*¹⁷ judgments in the 1960s and subsequently confirmed in the *Nold* judgment of 1974 that the substantive understanding of such rights was to be drawn from common constitutional traditions of the Member States in conjunction with the understanding thereof stemming from international human rights treaties.¹⁸ The *Rutili* decision of 1975 went even further, as the CJEU acknowledged therein the fundamental importance of the ECHR in the development and understanding of fundamental rights as general principles of EU law.¹⁹ Conversely, despite the fact that the CJEU was thus to a limited extent incorporating references to the international human rights treaties and the ECHR in particular, the ECtHR refrained at this point from engaging in any legal assessment of the acts by Member States stemming from Community legislation.²⁰

The onset of the 1990s marked the start of a second phase in the judicial relationship between both Courts.²¹ This phase, which lasted until 2000, drastically altered the dynamic between the two Courts.²² Whilst European

---

Frame Project, Brussels, 27.03.2017, available at http://www.fp7-frame.eu/wp-content/uploads/2017/03/ECHRCJUEdialog.BRUSSELS.final_.pdf, last accessed 15.06.2018; P. CRAIG and G. DE BÚRCA (2015), *EU Law, supra* note 5, p. 364.

[13] F. FABBRINI and J. LARIK (2016), 'Relation Between the European Court of Justice and the European Court of Human Rights', *supra* note 1, pp. 149–151.

[14] Ibid.

[15] Ibid.

[16] CJEU, *Erich Stauder v City of Ulm, Sozialamt 2*, Case C-29/69, 12.11.1969, ECLI:EU:C:1969:57; see also P. CRAIG and G. DE BÚRCA (2015), *EU Law, supra* note 5, p. 365.

[17] CJEU, *Internationale Handelsgesellschaft mbH v Einfuhr- und Vorratsstelle für Getreide und Futtermittel*, Case C-11/70, 17.12.1970, ECLI:EU:C:1970:114. See also P. CRAIG and G. DE BÚRCA (2015), *EU Law, supra* note 5, pp. 365–366.

[18] CJEU, *J. Nold, Kohlen- und Baustoffgroßhandlung v Commission of the European Communities*, *supra* note 5, para. 13. See also P. CRAIG and G. DE BÚRCA (2015), *EU Law, supra* note 5, p. 366.

[19] CJEU, *Roland Rutili v Ministre de l'intérieur* Case C-36/75, 28.10.1975, [1975] EU:C:1975:124. See also F. FABBRINI and J. LARIK (2016), 'Relation between the ECtHR and the CJEU', *supra* note 1, p. 150.

[20] Typically, at this point the ECtHR ruled such cases as inadmissible on account of the fact that the Community was not a party to the ECHR. For a more in-depth discussion see: F. FABBRINI and J. LARIK (2016), 'Relation Between the CJEU and the ECtHR', *supra* note 1, pp. 149–159.

[21] Ibid., pp. 151–155.

[22] Ibid.

integration in the Union was deepening and references to fundamental rights became more prevalent in not only the case law of the CJEU, but also in the constituent treaties of the Union, the territorial application of the ECHR grew significantly as a result of the democratisation of a number of European States.[23] In light of these developments, both Courts sought to take on the role of the main human rights guarantor, leading from time to time to confrontations in the case law by the Courts.[24] A prime example of this tension can be found in *Opinion 2/94*[25] in which the CJEU explicitly held that for accession of the Union to the ECHR to occur, treaty amendments would be requisite.[26] This resulted in a counter reaction by the ECtHR, whereby in the *Cantoni*[27] case as well as the *Matthews*[28] case the ECtHR engaged in a limited review – contrary to the first phase – of EU acts implemented by EU Member States.[29] It need be noted, however, that the review in both cases was limited to situations where the Member States retained a certain level of discretion in the implementation of EU legislation.[30] In following judgments, however, the ECtHR refrained from further elaborating upon its findings in *Matthews*, rendering it unclear when the ECtHR would refuse to engage in any form of review of acts by the Union.[31]

In the third phase of the judicial dialogue prior to the Treaty of Lisbon it appears that both Courts seem to acknowledge the importance of not directly antagonising each other. The focus by the Union in this third phase was predominantly on the constitutional reform of the Union, which ultimately resulted in the entry into force of the Treaty of Lisbon, which brought about the Charter. In line with this increased focus on the incorporation of fundamental rights in the Union-*acquis*, the CJEU similarly took on the role of an active fundamental rights protector.[32] During this same phase, the ECtHR in turn, delivered the infamous *Bosphorus* judgment, in which it acknowledged that the Union provides for a system of equivalent protection.[33] Consequently, the

---

[23] F. FABBRINI and J. LARIK (2016), 'Relation between the CJEU and the ECtHR', *supra* note 1.
[24] Ibid.
[25] CJEU, *Opinion 2/94 – Accession by the Community to the European Convention for the Protection of Human Rights and Fundamental Freedoms*, Case C-2/94, 28.03.1996, ECLI:EU:C:1996:140.
[26] Ibid.
[27] ECtHR, *Cantoni v France*, no 17862/91 [GC] 15.11.1996.
[28] ECtHR, *Matthews v the United Kingdom*, no 24833/94, 18.02.1999.
[29] F. FABBRINI and J. LARIK (2016), 'Relation between the CJEU and the ECtHR', *supra* note 1, p. 155.
[30] P. CRAIG and G. DE BÚRCA (2015), *EU Law*, *supra* note 5, p. 403; L. LAVRYSEN, 'European Asylum Law and the ECHR', (2012) 4(1) *GoJIL*, pp. 226–227.
[31] F. FABBRINI and J. LARIK (2016), 'Relation between the CJEU and the ECtHR', *supra* note 1, p. 155.
[32] D. SPIELMANN (2017), 'Judicial Dialogue', *supra* note 12.
[33] ECtHR, *Bosphorus Hava Yollari Turizm Ve Ticaret Anonim Sirketi v Ireland*, no 45036/98 [GC] 30.06.2005. See also L. LAVRYSEN (2012), 'European Asylum Law and the ECHR', *supra* note 30, pp. 226–227.

ECtHR held that it would not engage in judicial review of acts by States stemming from Union measures as long as no manifest deficiencies could be established. As a result of these developments, both Courts appeared thus to have engaged in a *détente* and thus refrained from engaging in direct confrontation with each other via the means of their respective rulings.

2.2. JUDICIAL COHERENCE IN FUNDAMENTAL RIGHTS: THE STATUS QUO

Two events were pivotal to the jurisprudential relationship between the Courts and created a schism in this jurisprudential dialogue, of which the effects are still felt today. On the one hand there was the aforementioned Lisbon Treaty, which brought with it the entry into force of the much heralded Charter (section 2.2.1), and on the other hand there was the highly controversial *Opinion 2/13* concerning the accession of the EU to the ECHR, delivered by the CJEU on 18 December 2014 (section 2.2.2).

2.2.1. *The Lisbon Innovations*

The Treaty of Lisbon brought an end to the wavering uncertainty concerning the legal personality of the Union within the international community. Article 47 TEU holds that the EU has legal personality as a result of which it can, amongst others, participate in the international community by concluding agreements with third parties and become a party to other international organisations.[34] In line with this trend, the Lisbon Treaty further clarified the position of the EU as an international actor vis-à-vis the international community generally and its position in a system of multi-layered human rights governance.

Under international law, the Union as an international organisation does not solely acquire competences. Rather, as confirmed by the International Court of Justice (ICJ) '[…] International organisations are subjects of international law and, as such, are bound by any obligations incumbent upon them under general rules of international law, under their constitutions or under international agreements to which they are parties […]'.[35]

As concerns international human rights law specifically, the EU as an international organisation is thus bound by customary international law, general

---

[34] Article 47 – Consolidated Version of the Treaty on European Union [2007] OJ C 326, 26.10.2012 (TEU).
[35] ICJ, *Interpretation of the Agreement of 25 March 1951 Between the WHO and Egypt – Advisory Opinion of 20 December 1980*, ICJ Reports 1980, para. 37; see also ICJ, *Reparation for Injuries Suffered in the Service of the United Nations – Advisory Opinion of 11 April 1949*, ICJ Reports 1949, para. 179.

principles relating to fundamental rights and the human rights provisions enshrined in its own constitution (see above) – *in casu* the Charter, the Treaty on the Functioning of the European Union (TFEU) and the Treaty on European Union (TEU). The Charter functions as the fundamental rights catalogue of the Union, by which Union institutions and Member States are bound and which, by virtue of Article 6(1) TEU, has the same legal value as the Treaties.[36] Innovative for the jurisprudential relationship between the ECtHR and the CJEU is the clarification that '[…] fundamental rights, as guaranteed by the European Convention for the Protection of Human Rights and Fundamental Freedoms and as they result from the constitutional traditions common to the Member States, shall constitute general principles of the Union's law […]',[37] which seemingly seeks to ensure that no obstacles are imposed upon the Member States in the adherence of their obligations to ECHR – a clear conciliatory step towards the ECtHR by the Union legislator.

Adding to this direct reference of the ECHR in the TEU, the aforementioned Article 52(3) CFR elaborates upon the interpretation of the fundamental rights enshrined in the Charter, noting in particular that the rights therein, corresponding to the rights enshrined in the ECHR, shall be accorded the same meaning as accorded under the ECHR and by the ECtHR.[38] As a result of the foregoing, the Union thus indirectly binds itself to the interpretation accorded to rights in the Charter to ensure a '[…] necessary level of consistency between the Charter and the ECHR […]',[39] albeit subject to the caveat that this cannot adversely affect the autonomy of the Union, nor that of the CJEU.[40] Crucial in this respect however, is the subsequent premise enunciated in the Explanations Relating to the Charter of Fundamental Rights,[41] whereby the level of protection granted to corresponding Charter rights should never fall below the level of

---

[36] Article 6 TEU: '1. The Union recognises the rights, freedoms and principles set out in the Charter of Fundamental Rights of the European Union of 7 December 2000, as adapted at Strasbourg, on 12 December 2007, which shall have the same legal value as the Treaties. The provisions of the Charter shall not extend in any way the competences of the Union as defined in the Treaties. The rights, freedoms and principles in the Charter shall be interpreted in accordance with the general provisions in Title VII of the Charter governing its interpretation and application and with due regard to the explanations referred to in the Charter, that set out the sources of those provisions. 2. The Union shall accede to the European Convention for the Protection of Human Rights and Fundamental Freedoms. Such accession shall not affect the Union's competences as defined in the Treaties. 3. Fundamental rights, as guaranteed by the European Convention for the Protection of Human Rights and Fundamental Freedoms and as they result from the constitutional traditions common to the Member States, shall constitute general principles of the Union's law.'
[37] Ibid.
[38] Article 52 (3) Explanations Relating to the Charter of Fundamental Rights, *supra* note 3.
[39] Ibid.
[40] Ibid.
[41] The value of the Explanations is confirmed by Article 6(1) and in CJEU, *J.N. v Staatssecretaris van Veiligheid en Justitie*, Case C-601/15 PPU, 15.02.2016, ECLI:EU:C:2016:84, para. 21.

protection afforded by the ECHR.[42] In view of the precarious and changeable relationship between both Courts, it appears yet again, that this is a clear step by the Union to ensure the necessary level of consistency and cooperation between both institutions in furtherance of legal certainty, legitimate expectations and the effectiveness of fundamental rights protection in the Union. This cooperative approach however – according to some – stands in stark contrast to the subsequent approach taken by the CJEU in the infamous *Opinion 2/13* delivered several years later.

The Lisbon Treaty also dramatically altered the playing field and governance of asylum and migration in the Union. Early cooperation in asylum and migration between the EU Member States was limited and happened predominantly outside of the Community framework. The CJEU lacked jurisdiction in the realm of asylum and migration and measures taken within this field were of a soft law nature.[43] The Tampere Programme – a work programme adopted by the European Council in 1999 – jumpstarted the legislative reform within the field of asylum and migration and facilitated the establishment of a Common European Asylum System.[44] However, this initial legislative reform was solely aimed at establishing minimum standards. With the entry into force of the Treaty of Lisbon, the EU was accorded new competences that went beyond the adoption of minimum standards in asylum and migration. In addition, institutional reform was facilitated in the Union by according more competences to the European Parliament and the CJEU and the adoption of the Charter reinforced applicable rights to rights-holders within an asylum and migratory context.[45] The increase in judicial control was achieved by incorporating Area, Freedom, Security and Justice (AFSJ) matters into the scope of the preliminary jurisdiction of the CJEU, which inevitably provided the CJEU with a significant opportunity to help shape EU migration and asylum policy, as exemplified below.

2.2.2. *The* Opinion 2/13 *Upheaval*

Opinion 2/13 has been the object of much discourse and discussion and this article does not seek to further delve into an analysis thereof.[46] However, amidst

---

[42] Article 52 (3) Explanations Relating to the Charter of Fundamental Rights, *supra* note 3.
[43] C. KAUNERT and S. LEONARD, 'The European Union Asylum Policy After the Treaty of Lisbon and the Stockholm Programme: Towards Supranational Governance in a Common Area of Protection', (2012) 31(4), *Refugee Survey Quarterly*, p. 8.
[44] Ibid.
[45] Ibid.
[46] For detailed discussions, see amongst others: P. EECKHOUT, 'Opinion 2/13 on EU accession to the ECHR and judicial dialogue: Autonomy or autarky', (2015) 38 (4) *Fordham Int'l L.J.*, p. 955; D. HALBERSTAM, 'It's the Autonomy, Stupid: A Modest Defense of Opinion 2/13 on EU Accession to the ECHR, and the Way Forward', (2015) 16(1) *German L.J.*, p. 105; E. SPAVENTA, 'A very fearful court? The protection of fundamental rights in the European

the various perspectives, one conclusion remains clear – the Opinion as such is a step away from the previously discussed conciliatory approach taken by the Union legislator in the strengthening of the relations between the ECtHR and CJEU pursuant to the Treaty of Lisbon. This new schism in the relationship of the Courts, reverberated – and continues to do so – clearly in the case law by the CJEU (see below).

Generally, the CJEU held that the draft accession agreement concerning the accession of the Union to the ECHR was incompatible with Article 6(2) TEU and Protocol No 8 EU owing to four general contentions.[47] First, it held that the draft accession agreement was incompatible with the specific characteristics of the autonomous EU legal order, as it failed to limit the potential of EU Member States to provide for more extensive human rights protection in fields of EU law that were already subject to full EU harmonisation.[48] In other words, the fact that the Member States would be permitted via the draft accession agreement to provide for more extensive human rights protection, would – according to the CJEU – upset the autonomy of the EU legal order alongside the primacy, effectiveness and unity of Union measures.[49] Secondly, the incompatibility was alleged on account of the fact that it did not explicitly exclude the possibility for the ECtHR to rule on disputes of EU law between Member States violated its own prerogative as provided for by Article 344 TFEU.[50] This is yet again a clear assertion that the CJEU would thus not tolerate any form of external control concerning interstate disputes that fall within the scope of fundamental rights in combination with any area of EU law. Thirdly, the CJEU held that the envisaged co-respondent mechanism whereby a procedure could be started before the ECtHR with both Member States and the EU as parties, similarly would permit the ECtHR to rule on EU law – a prerogative reserved exclusively for the CJEU

Union after opinion 2/13', (2015) 22(1) *Maastricht Journal of European and Comparative Law*, pp. 35–56; J. ODERMATT, 'A Giant Step Backwards – Opinion 2/13 on the EU's Accession to the European Convention on Human Rights', (2015) 47(4) *N.Y.U. J. Int'l L. & Pol.* pp. 783–798; A. LAZOWSKI, and R.A. WESSEL, 'When caveats turn into locks: Opinion 2/13 on accession of the European Union to the ECHR', (2015) 16(1) *German L.J.*, pp. 179–212; C. KRENN, 'Autonomy and effectiveness as common concerns: a path to ECHR accession after Opinion 2/13', (2015) 16(1) *German L.J.*, pp. 147–168.

[47] CJEU, *Opinion 2/13 – Accession of the European Union to the European Convention for the Protection of Human Rights and Fundamental Freedoms – Compatibility of the draft agreement with the EU and FEU Treaties*, Case 2/13, 18.12.2014, ECLI:EU:C:2014:2454, para. 258.

[48] Ibid., paras. 179–200; S. PEERS, 'The CJEU and the EU's accession to the ECHR: a clear and present danger to human rights protection', *EU Law Analysis*, 18.12.2014, available at http://eulawanalysis.blogspot.com/2014/12/the-cjeu-and-eus-accession-to-echr.html, last accessed 15.06.2018.

[49] Ibid.

[50] CJEU, *Opinion 2/13, supra* note 47, paras. 201–214; S. PEERS, 'The CJEU and the EU's accession to the ECHR: a clear and present danger to human rights protection', *EU Law Analysis*, 18.12.2014, available at http://eulawanalysis.blogspot.com/2014/12/the-cjeu-and-eus-accession-to-echr.html, last accessed 15.06.2018.

by the Treaties.⁵¹ Finally, concerning the provisions of the Union's Common Foreign and Security Policy in which the CJEU has only limited jurisdiction, the CJEU recalls '[…] that jurisdiction to carry out a judicial review of acts, actions or omissions on the part of the EU, including in the light of fundamental rights, cannot be conferred exclusively on an international court which is outside the institutional and judicial framework of the EU'.⁵² Here too, the CJEU thus rejects any form of external review of its acts.

The attitude adopted by the CJEU in *Opinion 2/13* did not go unnoticed by the ECtHR, which up until that point – in line with the *Bosphorus* ruling – had shied away from engaging in indirect review of acts by States stemming from Union measures.⁵³ However, post-*Opinion 2/13* saw several judgments by the ECtHR which in principle did reaffirm the *Bosphorus* equivalent protection doctrine, albeit to a much lesser degree.⁵⁴ In fact, Dean Spielmann – former president of the ECtHR and current judge in the General Court of the EU – contends that the *Avotiņš* judgment by the ECtHR⁵⁵ indicates that the latter Court is no longer steadfast in applying the *Bosphorus* presumption in an automated manner and that this should no longer be taken for granted.⁵⁶ Rather, he holds that the ECtHR, following *Opinion 2/13*, seems more inclined to strictly scrutinise acts by States stemming from EU measures, as opposed to the cooperative stance it had previously adopted.⁵⁷

2.2.3. The Current State of Affairs

In view of the foregoing, two clear trends can be distilled from Union action vis-à-vis the ECtHR and the incorporation of the ECHR in its own legal order. On the one hand, it appears the Union legislator pursues a relationship of cooperation and coherence with the ECtHR, as attested to by the insertion of Article 52(3) in the CFR, which explicitly identifies the ECHR as the absolute minimum norm that must be respected for corresponding rights in the Charter.⁵⁸ Moreover, it holds that more extensive human rights protection may be provided than envisaged by the ECtHR in matters pertaining to Union law insofar as this does not upset the autonomy of the EU legal order, along with the primacy, effectiveness and unity of Union law.⁵⁹ Here the emphasis thus seems to rest on the fact that the ECHR is the absolute point of reference for corresponding

---

51   CJEU, *Opinion 2/13*, *supra* note 47, paras. 215–235.
52   Ibid., para. 256.
53   D. SPIELMANN (2017), 'Judicial Dialogue', *supra* note 12.
54   Ibid.
55   ECtHR, *Avotiņš v Latvia*, no 17502/07 [GC] 23.05.2016.
56   D. SPIELMANN (2017), 'Judicial Dialogue', *supra* note 12.
57   Ibid.
58   S. PEERS and S. PRECHAL (2014), 'Art. 52', *supra* note 6, pp. 1498–1503.
59   Ibid.

rights, and that the reference to autonomy is solely of relevance in cases where more extensive protection would be provided than envisaged by the ECHR.[60] Yet on the other hand, the CJEU seems to shift this emphasis as demonstrated by its *Opinion 2/13*, and places much more emphasis on the notions of autonomy of the EU legal order and its special characteristics, which must not – according to the CJEU – be undermined by judicial review – direct or indirect – by the ECtHR. Whilst this stance may be defendable from a Union vantage point, it does risk reopening old wounds in the already volatile relationship it shares with the ECtHR.

The shifts in attitudes by both Courts, as witnessed in the pre-Lisbon phases and particularly in the post-Lisbon phase, undoubtedly affect the right-holders, as legal certainty, legitimate expectations and the effectiveness of fundamental rights protection of those seeking redress in the Union are at stake. This is particularly noticeable in the case law discussed below. Similarly, the legitimacy of the Union as a law-abiding international actor may be detrimentally affected as well as the duty of loyal cooperation within the Union, between the institutions and its Member States. Some hold that thus far open conflict has been avoided by both Courts.[61] However, a closer look at case law within the field of asylum and migration of both Courts does seem to indicate that this is only partially true. Rather, the changing attitudes of both Courts generally, taken in conjunction with politically charged topics both Courts are confronted with in regard to asylum and migration, seem only to aggravate the dangers posed to the rights of individuals in the Union.

3. DYSFUNCTIONAL DIALOGUE IN ASYLUM AND MIGRATION?

3.1. ENTRY

3.1.1. *CJEU:* X and X v Belgium

In the recent *X and X*[62] preliminary ruling, the CJEU was asked, for the first time, to interpret Article 25(1)(a) of the Visa Code, which concerns the

---

[60] Ibid.
[61] D. Spielmann (2017), 'Judicial Dialogue', *supra* note 12; P. Craig and G. De Búrca (2015), *EU Law*, *supra* note 5, p. 405; G. De Búrca, 'The Road Not Taken: the European Union as a Global Human Rights Actor', (2011) 105(4) *American Journal of International Law*, pp. 678–680.
[62] CJEU, *X and X v Belgium*, Case C-638/16 PPU, 07.03.2017, ECLI:EU:C:2017:173. For a further analysis of *X and X* see also the article by L. Heschl and A. Stankovic, 'Beyond the Crisis: The Decline of Fundamental Rights in CJEU Jurisprudence after the 2015 "Refugee Crisis"', in this volume.

exceptional issuance of a visa with limited territorial validity for humanitarian reasons.[63] The case concerned a Syrian family of five, of which the father had seemingly already been subjected to torture, and three children under the age of ten. The father travelled to Lebanon to request a short-term territorial visa for Belgium on humanitarian grounds for him and his family members in line with Article 25 Visa Code. The Visa Code harmonises the procedure and conditions for the acquisition of short-term visas for third country nationals entering the Schengen zone. Article 32 of the Visa Code subsequently identifies the grounds upon which a short-term visa can be denied, albeit that Article 25(1) of that same code holds that – as an exception thereto – a Member State can nevertheless provide third country nationals with limited territorial visas when it '[…] considers it necessary on humanitarian grounds, for reasons of national interest or because of international obligations […]'.[64] In this respect the CJEU was asked three questions in a preliminary reference: (1) to what extent can the request made by the Syrian family be considered as falling within the scope of Union law; (2) what is the scope of application of the humanitarian grounds and international obligations referenced in Article 25 of the Visa Code; and to what extent do Member States retain discretion in applying Article 25 of the Visa Code and granting short-term territorial visas for humanitarian purposes or as the result of international obligations.

In casu, the CJEU held that the Visa Code regulates short-term visas not exceeding the time span of three months. Hence, the fact that the applicants requested a short-term territorial visa for the purpose of subsequently applying for asylum for humanitarian reasons in Belgium, according to the CJEU, essentially entailed a request for a long-term visa, as opposed to a short-term visa regulated by the Visa Code.[65] The CJEU drawing on this line of reasoning, consequently held that requests for long-term visas in accordance with Article 79(2)(a) TFEU have yet to be regulated on a Union level, and thus do not fall within the scope of Union law – thereby evading any substantive analysis of the matter concerned. In solidifying this approach, the CJEU held that ruling in the alternative would have the effect of detrimentally affecting the effectiveness of the Dublin Regulation[66] and the

---

[63] Regulation (EC) No 810/2009 of the European Parliament and of the Council of 13 July 2009 establishing a Community Code on Visas (Visa Code), OJ L 243, 15.9.2009.
[64] A simple reading of Article 25 Visa Code already demonstrates a first point of contention. By referencing the margin of discretion Member States and offsetting this by reference to international obligations that may be incumbent upon them, the question is inevitably raised as to whether Member States can indeed be obligated to grant short-term territorial visas in the event that humanitarian grounds and/or international obligations, require them to do so, and the extent to which Member States retain discretion in this respect.
[65] CJEU, *X and X v Belgium*, *supra* note 62, paras. 41–43.
[66] Regulation (EU) No 604/2013 of the European Parliament and of the Council of 26 June 2013 establishing the criteria and mechanisms for determining the Member State responsible for

Asylum Procedures Directive.[67] As a result of the foregoing conclusion, the matter was thus to be decided upon nationally and could allegedly not fall within the ambit of Union law, nor was the Charter deemed applicable.[68] This seemingly runs counter to the approach taken in the *N.S. v Secretary of State for the Home Department* judgment, where it is held that even when Member States retain a certain level of discretion in the implementation of EU law – as is the case in the application of Articles 25 and 32 of the Visa Code – it is nevertheless considered to still be implementing EU law thus rendering the Charter applicable on account of Article 52 CFR.[69] This approach by the CJEU is furthermore striking in view of the fact that in the later *El Hassani* judgment of 13 December 2017,[70] which also concerned Article 32 of the Visa Code, the CJEU did not even consider that Union law and subsequently the Charter would not apply. Rather, contrary to the *X and X* ruling, the CJEU confirms in the *El Hassani* ruling that the Charter is indeed applicable, even where national authorities refuse to provide the applicants with a visa based on Article 32 of the Visa Code. In both cases there is thus a very clear application of the Visa Code based upon Article 32 thereof, yet the Court – via a factual reinterpretation – chose to negate the applicability of the Charter, thereby not having to rule on the substance of the matter and its compliance with the corresponding *non-refoulement* provision in the ECHR.

3.1.2. An ECtHR Perspective

In addition to this internal inconsistency in CJEU case law, the refusal by the CJEU to rule on the substance of the matter creates ambiguity as to

---

examining an application for international protection lodged in one of the Member States by a third-country national or a stateless person OJ L 180, 29.6.2013.

[67] Directive 2013/32/EU of the European Parliament and of the Council of 26 June 2013 on common procedures for granting and withdrawing international protection, OJ L 180, 29.06.2013; CJEU, *X and X v Belgium*, *supra* note 62, paras. 48–49.

[68] This approach stands in stark contrast with the fact that Article 51 of the Charter opts for a broad scope of application. There must be a direct link between national action and Union measures for the Charter to be applicable. *In casu* it was clear that the national proceedings had happened in accordance with the provisions enshrined in the Visa Code – an EU measure. The CJEU failed to convince as to why Union law thus would not apply and why in turn the Charter was not applicable to the proceedings at hand. See for a detailed discussion on the matter S. Peers, T. Hervey, J. Kenner and A. Ward (2014), 'The EU Charter of Fundamental Rights', *supra* note 6, p. 1436.

[69] CJEU, *N. S. v Secretary of State for the Home Department* Case C-411/10, 21.12.2011, ECLI:EU:C:2011:865, paras. 68–69. This was also confirmed in Advocate General Mengozzi's opinion in the *X and X* judgment see CJEU, *Opinion of Paolo Mengozzi in X and X v Belgium*, Case C-638/16 PPU, 07.02.2017, ECLI:EU:C:2017:93, paras. 80 and 84. See also A. Ward (2014), 'Art. 51', *supra* note 6, p. 1432.

[70] CJEU, *Soufiane El Hassani v Minister Spraw Zagraniznych*, Case C-403/16, 13.12.2017, ECLI:EU:C:2017:960.

whether the CJEU would otherwise have followed the standard of protection afforded in similar cases before the ECtHR. *In casu* it appears that the lack of substantive review by the CJEU resulted in a situation where the applicants did not enjoy the minimum level of protection they would have been entitled to according to the ECHR. Member States issuing visas according to the Visa Code are held to respect the CFR, by virtue of preambular clause 29 thereof and as confirmed by Advocate General Mengozzi in his Opinion concerning the *X and X* case.[71] This entails that when Member States are determining whether a visa should be granted or rejected, this should be done in accordance with the CFR provisions pertaining to asylum and migration, and the *non-refoulement* principle in particular. *In casu*, the *X and X* case concerned the application of the Visa Code and the refusal of entry of the applicants to the Belgian territory. The refusal of entry, in and of itself, amounts to a measure preventing access to asylum procedures and thus the interpretation and application of the *non-refoulement* principle enshrined in Article 4 CFR, Article 18 CFR and Article 3 ECHR had to be respected.

As this concerns the application of EU law and mindful of Article 52(3) CFR, the CJEU should have applied ECtHR practice concerning *non-refoulement*. The ECtHR has consistently held in its case law concerning Article 3 ECHR, that extra-territorial jurisdiction arises in situations where effective and exclusive control is exercised over a person, as an exception to the territoriality princple.[72] In other words, the ECHR provisions will apply and may result in Member State responsibility for acts by its authorities which 'produce effects outside its own territry'.[73] Within this vein, the ECtHR has held consistently that acts and measures by diplomatic and consular agents when exercising authority over the individuals concerned, may render the ECHR applicable – including the *non-refoulement* principle – and place the individuals concerned under its jurisdiction.[74] This will additionally be the case, if the acts or omissions by the diplomatic or consular agents are of direct concern to the individual concerned,

---

[71] E. BROUWER, 'AG Mengozzi's conclusion in *X. and X. v. Belgium* on the positive obligation to issue humanitarian visas: A legitimate plea to ensure safe journeys for refugees', *CEPS Policy Insights*, 01.03.2017, available at https://www.ceps.eu/publications/ag-mengozzi%E2%80%99s-conclusion-x-and-x-v-belgium-positive-obligation-issue-humanitarian-visas, last accessed 15.06.2018; CJEU, *Opinion of Paolo Mengozzi in X. and X. v Belgium*, *supra* note 69, para. 84.

[72] ECtHR, 'Guide on Article 1 of the European Convention on Human Rights – Obligation to respect human rights – Concepts of "jurisdiction" and imputability', 2018, *Case-Law Guides*, Council of Europe, p. 8 and references therein, available at https://www.echr.coe.int/Documents/Guide_Art_1_ENG.pdf, last accessed 15.06.2018.

[73] Ibid. See also ECtHR, *Al Skeini and others v United Kingdom*, no 55721/07 [GC] 07.07.2011, para. 133 and references therein.

[74] Ibid. See also ECtHR, *Banković and others v Belgium and 16 contracting States*, no 52207/99 [GC] 12.12.2001, para. 73.

despite the individual remaining in his or her own State.[75] Similarly, the *Bankovic* ruling does not limit the scope of this reasoning to certain acts by diplomatic or consular agents – it merely stipulates that:

> recognised instances of the extra-territorial exercise of jurisdiction by a State include cases involving the activities of its diplomatic or consular agents abroad [...] In these specific situations, customary international law and treaty provisions have recognised the extra-territorial exercise of jurisdiction by the relevant State.[76]

As held by Moreno-Lax, visa issuance forms a core task of diplomatic and consular agents and the *non-refoulement* principle becomes theoretical and illusory if visa authorities can simply refuse the issuing of a visa without taking any positive measures, despite ample evidence attesting to a potential violation of this principle and the risk of ill-treatment upon return to the country of origin.[77]

This positive obligation was elaborated upon in *Hirsi Jamaa*[78] as well as *Sharifi*[79] by the ECtHR. The *Hirsi Jamaa* judgment concerned the application by 11 Somalian and 13 Eritrean nationals against Italy for their return to Libya following an interception on high seas as the individuals concerned and others were trying to reach the European territory. *In casu* the ECtHR held that it was irrelevant that the interception had occurred on high seas as the applicants had been taken onboard an Italian military vessel, entailing that they had been under continuous and exclusive control of the Italian authorities and thus fell within its jurisdiction thereby rendering the ECHR rights applicable.[80] The ECtHR furthermore held that it was irrelevant that the applicants had not requested international protection on the vessel, as the *non-refoulement* obligation nevertheless places the positive obligation upon the Italian authorities to verify whether the applicants would be subjected to ill-treatment upon return to Libya. These positive obligations to assess whether individuals would face ill-treatment following an expulsion order were confirmed in the *Sharifi* judgment later that year. In this case, complaints were lodged against Italy and Greece

---

[75] ECtHR (2018), 'Guide on Article 1 of the European Convention on Human', *supra* note 72, p. 8.

[76] ECtHR, *Banković*, *supra* note 74, para. 73; T. Spijkerboer, E. Brouwer and Y. Al Tamimi, 'Advice in Case C-638/16 PPU on prejudicial questions concerning humanitarian visa', 05.01.2017, available at http://thomasspijkerboer.eu/wp-content/uploads/2017/01/Advies-VU-English1.pdf, last accessed 15.06.2018; V. Moreno-Lax, 'Asylum Visas as an Obligation under EU Law: Case PPU C-638/16 X, X v Etat belge (Part I)', *EU Migration Law Blog*, 16.02.2017, available at http://eumigrationlawblog.eu/asylum-visas-as-an-obligation-under-eu-law-case-ppu-c-63816-x-x-v-etat-belge, last accessed 15.06.2018.

[77] V. Moreno-Lax (2017), 'Asylum Visas as an Obligation under EU Law', *supra* note 76.

[78] ECtHR, *Hirsi Jamaa and others v Italy*, no 27765/09 [GC] 23.02.2012, para. 180.

[79] ECtHR, *Sharifi and others v Italy and Greece*, no 16643/09, 21.10.2014, paras. 112–114.

[80] ECtHR *Hirsi Jamaa*, *supra* note 78, para. 180.

for the return by Italy of Afghan nationals to Greece, where they subsequently were subject to the risk of being sent back to Afghanistan without due regard for their situation. The ECtHR reiterated in this case that the positive obligation incumbent upon the receiving State entails that a proper assesment must be made to ensure that asylum seekers are not indirectly refouled to a State where they face the risk of being subject to ill-treatment.

Both cases clarify that responsibility may arise under the ECHR when a measure whereby third country nationals are prevented from reaching the border of a State, could result in a violation of the *non-refoulement* principle. Advocate General Mengozzi in *X and X* rightly recalls said case law, noting in particular that the prohibition of *refoulement* would be deprived of any effectiveness, if positive measures are not taken to ensure the entry into a State for applicants who could otherwise be subjected to ill-treatment, as there would otherwise be no means by which they can effectively and legally apply for asylum.[81] Hence, ECtHR case law indicates, as confirmed by Advocate General Mengozzi, that the *non-refoulement* principle encompasses a positive obligation to potentially provide for entry via the means of visa issuance, to be determined according to a case-by-case assessment.

3.1.3. Analysis

Seemingly, by denying the application of the Visa Code – despite the fact that the parties did not dispute its applicability – the CJEU managed to circumvent the obligations incumbent upon it in accordance with Article 52(3) CFR to the detriment of the rights of the third country nationals that were deprived of any effective protection of the *non-refoulement* principle.[82] The CJEU thus reassessed the facts in the *X and X* to rule that Union law did not apply, as a result of which there would allegedly be no application of the Charter and in particular the corresponding *non-refoulement* obligation also found in the ECHR. This in turn, allowed for a standard of protection vis-à-vis the individuals concerned that appears to be in direct contravention of the principles established by the ECtHR concerning *non-refoulement* and results in a level of protection which

---

[81] CJEU, *Opinion of Paolo Mengozzi in X and X v Belgium*, supra note 69, para. 158.
[82] In the preliminary reference, it is perplexing that the CJEU appears to re-qualify the facts of the case as presented by the national courts. This is especially so in view of Article 267 TFEU, which merely allows the CJEU to provide interpretations concerning the Treaties and guidance on '[...] on the validity and interpretation of acts of the institutions, bodies, offices or agencies of the Union [...]'. This provision does not, however, allow the CJEU to apply said interpretations to the facts of the case, assess the validity of national measures, much less re-qualify the facts of the case. Whilst the line between interpretation and application of EU law in preliminary references is not always an easy distinction to make, it is clear that it is not for the CJEU to re-qualify the facts of a case.

falls below the standards established in its own case law[83] and that of the ECHR – contrary to the very coherence envisaged by Article 52(3) CFR.[84]

In view of the foregoing, it is unclear how the CJEU would have ruled had the Visa Code been considered applicable, which has potentially detrimental ramifications for legal certainty and legitimate expectations, as there is no certainty as to whether the CJEU would have ruled in line with the minimum standards provided by the ECtHR concerning *refoulement*. *In casu*, legal certainty and legitimate expectations are affected, because the CJEU does not seem to contradict the ECtHR, nor does it agree with the ECtHR. It does not take a stance, notwithstanding the in-depth analysis and application of fundamental rights by Advocate-General Mengozzi in his Opinion. This ambiguity is clearly problematic and furthermore exemplified by the recent lodging of the same complaints in this particular case before the ECtHR – thus opening up a path of potential judicial conflict.[85]

3.2. DETENTION

3.2.1. *CJEU*: J.N. v Staatssecretaris van Veiligheid en Justitie

On 15 February 2016 the CJEU pronounced itself on the reference for a preliminary ruling in *J.N. v Staatssecretaris voor Veiligheid en Justitie*.[86] This marked the first time that the CJEU interpreted the recast Reception Conditions Directive (RCD) concerning the detention of asylum seekers pending the asylum application and its compliance with its corresponding ECHR provision on the right to liberty.

Mr. J.N. – a Tunisian national – entered the Netherlands in September 1995, whereupon he submitted an application for asylum immediately.[87] This application was rejected, as was the appeal against the refusal in June 1997.[88] A subsequent application was then again filed by Mr. J.N. in December 2012 but

---

[83] In its judgments, *N. S. and Others*, Case C-411/10 and C-493/10, 21.12.2011, ECLI:EU:C:2011:865, para. 94, 106 and 113, and of *Aranyosi and Căldăraru*, Case C-404/15 and C-659/15 PPU, 05.04.2016, ECLI:EU:C:2016:198, paras. 90 and 94, the Court already held that, like Article 3 of the ECHR, Article 4 of the Charter imposes a positive obligation on the Member States under certain circumstances.

[84] It is interesting that the CJEU applies this factual maneuver in order not to pronounce itself on the matter, whereas in *Elgafaji* (Case C-465/07, 17.02.2009, ECLI:EU:C:2009:94), the CJEU went beyond the standard of protection provided for by the ECtHR in *Sufi and Elmi* (ECtHR, *Sufi and Elmi v the United Kingdom*, nos 8319/07 and 11449/07, 28.11.2011) by ruling that individuals are not required to furnish proof of an individual threat of ill-treatment.

[85] ECtHR, *Mohamad Nahhas and others v Belgium*, no 3599/18 (pending).

[86] CJEU, *J.N. v Staatssecretaris van Veiligheid en Justitie*, supra note 41.

[87] Ibid., para. 21.

[88] CJEU, *J.N. v Staatssecretaris van Veiligheid en Justitie*, supra note 41, para 21.

withdrawn later that month.[89] A third application was submitted in July 2013, albeit rejected on 8 January 2014 and complemented with a return decision, whereby Mr. J.N. was ordered to leave the Netherlands and subjected to a ten-year entry ban to the EU as a result of recurring instances of theft and failure to comply with the return decision.[90] The return order and entry ban were confirmed on appeal in April 2014.[91] However, Mr. J.N. submitted a fourth asylum application on 27 February 2015. At the time of the preliminary reference in this case, a decision had yet to be taken with respect to this fourth application.

Mr. J.N. was held, upon order of the State Secretary, to undergo administrative detention based upon the Dutch legislative provisions that transpose Article 8(3)(e) of the RCD and hold that asylum seekers may exceptionally be placed in detention insofar as they constitute a threat to national security and/or public order of the host Member State.[92] The decision ordering the administrative detention made reference to previous criminal offences – for which he had already been held accountable – as well as the suspicion that Mr. J.N. had committed additional crimes.[93] The decision placing Mr. J.N. in administrative detention was contested by the latter on 28 September 2015 where it was dismissed.[94] The appeal to that dismissal is the basis for the preliminary request brought before the CJEU and seeks to contest the validity of Article 8(3)(e) of the RCD against the background of Article 6 CFR and Article 5 ECHR pertaining to the right to liberty.

The main contention brought forward by Mr. J.N. *in casu* is thus the alleged non-conformity of Article 8(3)(e) of the RCD with the standards and safeguards against violations to the right to liberty as encompassed in Article 6 CFR and Article 5 ECHR. The RCD exceptionally permits detention of asylum seekers for the aforementioned reasons of public order and national security. Under Article 8 of the RCD, asylum seekers cannot be held in detention solely on account of having submitted an application for asylum.[95] However, the third paragraph of this provision does allow detention in six defined set of circumstances, subject to the conditions of proportionality, encompassing a test of necessity and the requirement of a legal basis.[96] The administrative detention of Mr. J.N. is founded upon the fifth ground of these exceptions, which holds that detention may be possible 'when protection of national security or public

---

[89] Ibid., para. 23.
[90] Ibid., para. 24.
[91] CJEU, *J.N. v Staatssecretaris van Veiligheid en Justitie*, supra note 41, para 24.
[92] Ibid., para. 30.
[93] Ibid.
[94] Ibid., para. 31, *in juncto* 34.
[95] Article 8 Directive 2013/33/EU of the European Parliament and of the Council of 26 June 2013 laying down standards for the reception of applicants for international protection (recast), OJ L 180, 29.06.2013.
[96] Ibid., Article 8(3).

order so requires'.⁹⁷ This limitation to the right to liberty must, however, be in accordance with the right to liberty in Article 6 CFR and its corresponding provision, Article 5 ECHR. Again, this entails that the minimum level of protection to be afforded under the right to liberty by the Union must be in conformity with the meaning accorded thereto by the ECtHR.⁹⁸ This is in fact confirmed by the current judgment.⁹⁹ Whereas more extensive protection is tolerated in accordance with Article 53 CFR, the ECHR and the relevant case law by the ECtHR set the minimum level of required protection, which the Union must uphold when safeguarding the Charter rights.¹⁰⁰

The right to liberty in the ECHR explicitly and exhaustively notes six situations in which limitations to the right to liberty may be deemed permissible, subject also to notions of proportionality, necessity and a legal basis.¹⁰¹ As a result, limitations to the right to liberty under EU law must, albeit indirectly, fall under one of these grounds listed by the ECHR to be deemed legitimate under Article 52(3) CFR.¹⁰² This is precisely the issue that was brought forward by the referring Court – to what extent can the generalised ground of concerns pertaining to national security or public order warrant the detention of an asylum seeker, in line with the permissible exceptions listed exhaustively in Article 5 ECHR?¹⁰³ Subsidiarily, this also raises the question of the relationship between Article 5 ECHR and Article 6 CFR as well as the compliance of Dutch legislation and practice with the interpretation given to Article 8(3)(e) of the RCD by the CJEU.

The CJEU, in this particular case, addresses the crux of the preliminary reference – whether Article 8(3)(e) of the RCD and the permitted detention on account of national security and public order can be deemed compliant with the right to liberty protected by Article 6 CFR and the general limitations clause of Article 52 CFR – in much detail.¹⁰⁴ Having indicated that the RCD indeed serves as the required legal basis to warrant the detention, the Court subsequently explains that indeed, it seeks to pursue an objective that is of a general interest – namely the protection of national security and public order – and that this objective, by its very nature, renders detention of asylum seekers appropriate.¹⁰⁵ The CJEU embarks upon an extensive analysis whereby the necessity and the proportionality of the order are assessed, which in essence entails an assessment of the facts.¹⁰⁶ In doing so, the Court takes into account the exceptional nature

---

⁹⁷ Ibid.
⁹⁸ Ibid.
⁹⁹ Ibid., para. 77.
¹⁰⁰ S. PEERS and S. PRECHAL (2014), 'Art. 52', *supra* note 6, pp. 1455–1521, para. 52.121.
¹⁰¹ Article 5 ECHR.
¹⁰² Article 52 (3) Explanations Relating to the Charter of Fundamental Rights, *supra* note 3.
¹⁰³ CJEU, *J.N. v Staatssecretaris van Veiligheid en Justitie*, *supra* note 41, para. 35.
¹⁰⁴ Ibid., paras. 49–73.
¹⁰⁵ CJEU, *J.N. v Staatssecretaris van Veiligheid en Justitie*, *supra* note 41, paras. 51–55.
¹⁰⁶ Ibid., paras. 56–73.

of the detention measure, the strict circumscription of national security and public order, the individualised assessment, and the ten-year entry ban that had previously been imposed upon the applicant, allowing the CJEU to come to the conclusion that neither *de iure* nor *de facto* incompatibility issues arise between the detention measure based upon Article 8(3)(e) of the RCD and the Charter pertaining to the right to liberty.[107]

Finally, the CJEU proceeds by elaborating, albeit in a limited manner, on the relationship and conformity of Article 8(3)(e) of the RCD with Article 5 ECHR.[108] Here the Court's reasoning fails to convince as it finds that – contrary to the applicable practice in the Netherlands whereby all return proceedings lapse upon the submission of a new asylum claim – the return proceedings to which Mr. J.N. was subject, did not, notwithstanding his pending asylum application.[109] In other words, consistent practice in the Netherlands holds that upon the submission of a new asylum claim any and all return proceedings are definitively discontinued and cease to exist, thus entailing that the person concerned is yet again to be deemed an asylum seeker. However, the CJEU refutes said practice of higher protection, by holding that this endangers the effectiveness of the Return Directive, thus concluding that in fact the return proceedings do not lapse upon the submission of a new asylum claim but rather are solely temporarily halted.[110] This entails that the return proceedings are, under this construct by the CJEU, still pending. The relevance of this factual construction by the CJEU lies in the qualification of the person concerned. Insofar as an asylum application is pending, the person concerned will be deemed an asylum seeker. However, insofar as return proceedings are pending, the person concerned will no longer be deemed an asylum seeker. It is precisely this distinction that the ECHR makes in the corresponding provision on the right to liberty enshrined in Article 5 ECHR, where a difference in the standard of human rights protection is made depending on whether the individual concerned is an asylum seeker or not. As a result of this legal construction, the measure can subsequently be considered to fall within the scope of Article 5(1)(f) ECHR – the second limb – concerning deportation and extradition, as opposed to the first limb, which essentially deals with asylum applications submitted for the purpose of acquiring a legal right to remain.[111] This is relevant again, as the scope of protection differs depending on whether an individual is detained under the first limb as opposed to the second limb of Article 5(1)(f) ECHR.[112]

---

[107] Ibid., para. 82.
[108] Ibid., paras. 74–81.
[109] Ibid., para. 75.
[110] Ibid., para. 75.
[111] Ibid., para. 77.
[112] ECtHR, *Suso Musa v Malta*, no 42337/12, 23.07.2013, paras. 90–91, 97.

What is striking is the fact that the CJEU thus disregards national Dutch practice of higher protection[113] whereby return proceedings are discontinued in the event of a (new) application for asylum as this would otherwise hamper the autonomy of the Union and the effectiveness of EU legislation.[114] The CJEU then holds that the proceedings fall within the ambit of Article 5(1)(f) ECHR and that no issues arise concerning the compatibility of Article 8(3)(e) RCD with Article 5 ECHR. However, the question needs to be raised as to whether this approach is not faulty at best, given that the level of protection differs based on Article 5(1)(f) ECHR. Depending on whether the applicant falls within the scope of Article 5(1)(f) first limb as an asylum seeker or, alternatively, the second limb of that same provision – applicable in return proceedings – will determine whether the individual concerned will be less or more readily placed in detention respectively. This then raises the question as to whether the CJEU went too far in reassessing the facts, in order to create a legal construct (similar to the previously discussed X and X judgment), which facilitates a situation where the individual concerned is receiving less protection than provided by the corresponding right in the ECHR.

3.2.2. An ECtHR Perspective

For detention to be lawful under the ECHR, it must occur in compliance with one or more of the grounds for detention exhaustively enunciated in Article 5(1) ECHR.[115] If and when detention occurs outside of the framework of these grounds enshrined in Article 5(1)(a)–(f) ECHR, it will automatically be deemed unlawful.[116] Within this vein, Article 5(1)(f) ECHR specifically provides for the possibility to detain within an asylum and immigration context and provides two grounds upon which to do so.[117] First, detention is permitted to prevent the unauthorised entry by an individual into a signatory State, as encompassed in the first limb of Article 5(1)(f) ECHR. Secondly, detention will be authorised for the purpose of facilitating deportation or extradition, as encompassed in the second limb of that same provision.[118] This distinction is relevant as the standard of protection differs depending on the ground invoked upon which the detention is based.

---

[113] The CJEU held that the Dutch practice whereby a return procedure is to be deemed terminated upon the submission of a new application for asylum, is not in line with EU law. CJEU, *J.N. v Staatssecretaris van Veiligheid en Justitie, supra* note 41, para. 75.
[114] Ibid.
[115] N. MOLE and C. MEREDITH, 'Asylum and the European Convention on Human Rights 2010 – Human Rights Files 09', *Council of Europe Publishing*, Strasbourg 2010, p. 143.
[116] Ibid.
[117] ECtHR, *Saadi v United Kingdom*, no 13229/03 [GC] 29.01.2008, para. 65.
[118] Ibid. See also COUNCIL OF EUROPE AND EUROPEAN AGENCY FOR FUNDAMENTAL RIGHTS, *Handbook on European Law Relating to Asylum, Borders and Immigration, supra* note 7, p. 153.

The *Saadi* judgment by the ECtHR provided a first opportunity to clarify detention of asylum seekers based upon the first limb of Article 5(1)(f) ECHR. The *Saadi* case concerned an Iraqi Kurd who had fled Iraq and availed himself to the UK authorities upon arrival and was granted temporary admission into the country. Shortly thereafter however, he was subsequently detained. *In casu* the ECtHR held that merely availing oneself to the immigration authorities does not suffice as authorisation to enter and remain in the country, so as to circumvent the detention ground in Article 5(1)(f) first limb ECHR.[119] However, in *Suso Muso v Malta*, the ECtHR clarified the foregoing by holding that insofar as a State has enacted legislation irrespective of whether its origin is in EU law or not, which explicitly authorises the entry or stay of the individual into the State concerning pending the asylum procedure, any detention subsequent thereto could be deemed unlawful and thus a violation of the right to liberty in Article 5 ECHR.[120] In addition, in *A and others v the United Kingdom* the ECtHR has found 'internment and preventive detention without charge to be incompatible with the fundamental right to liberty under Article 5 para. 1'[121] entailing that purely preventive detention for the purpose of public order and/or national security will deprive the detention of its lawfulness. For detention under the first limb to thus be in compliance with the right to liberty, the detention must be founded in national law, should be executed in good faith, must be closely connected to the ground upon which the detention is founded, the detention conditions need be appropriate and the length of the detention should not go beyond what is necessary.[122]

In the case of *J.N.* indeed, legislation has been enacted on a Union level, whereby it is held in the Asylum Procedures Directive that pending an asylum application, an applicant has the right to remain in the territory (Article 9) and cannot be held in detention on account of his or her asylum application only (Article 26) – immediately rendering detention under the first limb difficult to justify.[123] Furthermore, it appears that Article 8(3)(e) RCD, which condones detention for reasons of national security and public order, may run afoul of the principles enunciated in *A and others v United Kingdom*, which clarifies that purely preventive detention of individuals is not permitted.[124]

Conversely, for detention to occur under the second limb of Article 5(1)(f) ECHR, the conditions to be met are slightly less stringent.[125] It suffices that

---

[119] ECtHR, *Saadi v United Kingdom, supra* note 117, para. 65.
[120] ECtHR, *Suso Musa, supra* note 112, para. 97.
[121] ECtHR, *A and others v the United Kingdom*, no 3455/05 [GC] 19.02.2009, para. 172.
[122] Ibid., para. 164.
[123] Directive 2013/32/EU of the European Parliament and of the Council of 26 June 2013 on common procedures for granting and withdrawing international protection OJ L 180, 29.06.2013.
[124] ECtHR, *A and others v the United Kingdom, supra* note 121, paras. 171–172 and references therein.
[125] ECtHR (2018), 'Guide on Article 1 of the European Convention on Human', *supra* note 72, pp. 25–26.

action is being taken to facilitate the deportation or extradition and that these proceedings are in progress. There is no need for the detention to be deemed necessary and the underlying cause for the detention is also irrelevant, as long as the return proceedings are effectively underway.[126]

Clearly, in complying with the ECtHR case law on the right to liberty in an asylum and migratory context, the applicant could not have legitimately been detained in compliance with the first limb of Article 5(1)(f) ECHR, as there is effectively legislation in place which provides asylum seekers with a right to remain. Hence, in line with *Suso Musa*, this enhanced protection founded in EU law would have prevented any detention of an asylum seeker.

The CJEU in its judgment, however, did not seem inclined to make this finding, as in paragraph 75 it applies a creative manoeuvre in order to circumvent the stricter bounds of the first limb of Article 5(1)(f) ECHR.[127] Specifically, it held that due to the principle of effectiveness and the duty of sincere cooperation inherent to the Return Directive,[128] the return procedure vis-à-vis Mr. J.N., instigated before the pending asylum procedure, should be deemed as being on-going, as opposed to ceased and could thus be resumed once a final decision concerning the asylum application had been made.[129] This despite the fact that Dutch law holds that all return decisions lapse upon the introduction of a new asylum application.[130] In other words, according to the finding of the CJEU, the termination of the return procedure in accordance with Dutch law should thus be negated and the return procedure should consequently be deemed as merely suspended instead.[131] Following this reasoning the CJEU held that in fact, the particular situation of Mr. J.N. should be deemed as falling within the second limb of Article 5(1)(f) ECHR, as opposed to the first limb, given that the detention in its view should be seen as being with a view to deportation.[132]

3.2.3. Analysis

De facto the CJEU is thus impeding and preventing the higher protection offered by the Dutch authorities via the means of the cessation of the return procedure in case of a newly submitted asylum application, in the interest

---

[126] Ibid.
[127] CJEU, *J.N. v Staatssecretaris van Veiligheid en Justitie*, supra note 41, paras. 75–76.
[128] Directive 2008/115/EC of the European Parliament and of the Council of 16 December 2008 on common standards and procedures in Member States for returning illegally staying third-country nationals OJ L 348, 24.12.2008.
[129] CJEU, *J.N. v Staatssecretaris van Veiligheid en Justitie*, supra note 41, para. 76.
[130] Article 3 Vreemdelingenwet 2000; CJEU, *J.N. v Staatssecretaris van Veiligheid en Justitie*, supra note 41, para. 75; CJEU, *View of Eleanor Sharpston in J.N. v Staatssecretaris*, Case C-601/15 PPU, 26.01.2016, ECLI:EU:C:2016:85, para. 123.
[131] CJEU, *J.N. v Staatssecretaris van Veiligheid en Justitie*, supra note 41, paras. 75–76.
[132] Ibid., paras. 75–76.

of ensuring the effectiveness of the Return Directive. In line with *Melloni*, a reading of Article 52(3) CFR and the Explanations thereto, this does not seem too problematic from a purely legal perspective as the limitation of higher protection provided than the CFR is deemed permissible.[133] However, whilst this finding may be in line with the increasing political will in favour of securitisation and externalisation of EU asylum and migration policy, it may raise significant concerns from an effectiveness and coherency perspective.

First, by applying the aforementioned manoeuvre whereby the higher protection offered by the Dutch authorities is negated, the Court has managed to circumvent the stricter standards and conditions to detain under the first limb concerning asylum seekers, and applied instead the more lenient ground to detain under the second limb applicable to individuals who are subject to return proceedings and are thus no longer deemed as asylum seekers. Recall for instance that the notion of vulnerability is stressed significantly under the first limb, whilst (not inconceivably) this is not the case for individuals subject to detention under the second limb, or that higher protection standards under the first limb of Article 5(1)(f) ECHR may very well rule out the possibility to detain thereunder.

More importantly, by discarding Dutch practice on the matter and artificially qualifying the detention under the second limb of Article 5(1)(f) ECHR, the Court has managed to evade the prohibition of preventive detention for national security and public order reasons as explicitly stated in *A and Others v the United Kingdom* before the ECtHR[134] and applicable to the first limb. Remember in this respect that detention under the second limb must not be deemed necessary – it suffices that the individual is detained pending a return proceeding irrespective of the underlying reason. Hence, whether he or she is being held for security reasons under the second limb is irrelevant so long as the return proceeding is being executed with due diligence. *In casu* this entails that Mr. J.N. – an asylum-seeker – is thus being held on account of security reasons without charge, seemingly contrary to the interpretation of Article 5(1)(f) ECHR given in *A and Others v the United Kingdom*.

Thirdly, though not obliged to do so, the Court has yet to address how this reasoning is to be applied vis-à-vis asylum seekers who have not yet been subjected to return proceedings in a given Member State. Does the reasoning in this judgment entail that these individuals would indeed fall within the scope of the first limb, and if so, does Article 8(3)(e) of the RCD thus permit preventive detention for security reasons? In the affirmative, this would entail that Article 8(3)(e) RCD is indeed not in compliance with the first limb of Article 5(1)(f) ECHR and the case law concerning this provision.[135] What is

---

[133] S. Peers and S. Prechal, 'Art. 52', *supra* note 6, pp. 1455–1521, para. 52.121.
[134] ECtHR, *A and Others v the United Kingdom*, paras. 171–172.
[135] Ibid.

more, this would be contradictory to the provision in the Asylum Procedures Directive,[136] which authorises entry and stay into a Member State pending an asylum application, entailing that detention under the first limb of Article 5(1)(f) ECHR would in any event not be possible. This all of course remains to be seen, albeit that the Court explicitly states in paragraph 55 of the judgment, that the detention of an asylum seeker on grounds of national security and public order is 'by its very nature, an appropriate measure for protecting the public from the threat which conduct [...]' – without any regard for this distinction between asylum seekers who have already been served with a return order vis-à-vis those who have not been served with a return order of any sort.

On a final note, for the detention under the second limb of Article 5(1)(f) ECHR not to be deemed arbitrary, a close link must be established between the ground for detention – namely deportation – and the detention itself. Regrettably, in this particular case, the Court does not elaborate upon the requirement of this close link. The question may thus very well be raised as to how, if at all, there is effectively a close link between detention for security reasons pending an asylum application, and the objective of deportation, the latter which by its very nature is to be situated at the conclusion of the asylum application.

In view of the foregoing, it appears that this judgment, which seems to have passed under the radar despite its potentially far-reaching consequences, directly contravenes the practice and application of the right to liberty in the ECHR and as explained in *inter alia* the *Suso Musa v Malta* ruling and the *A and Others v United Kingdom* ruling by the ECtHR. This yet again places both Courts in a somewhat tense stand-off vis-à-vis each other, potentially to the detriment of the rights-holders seeking refuge in the European Union. In particular, this results in a situation where yet again, legal certainty and legitimate expectations are affected, as there is no certainty as to the standard of protection that prevails. Furthermore, the effectiveness of the right to liberty is in murky waters due to the different standards that are applied by the Courts, thereby also endangering the institutional legitimacy of both Courts.

3.3. RETURN AND *NON-REFOULEMENT*

3.3.1. *CJEU:* N.F. v European Council

Deriving from the foregoing analysis that both Courts are in a consistent judicial conflict with each other is simply not true. Rather, it appears that as concerns the EU-Turkey Statement of 18 March 2016, the Courts – albeit

---

[136] Articles 9 and 26 Directive 2013/32/EU of the European Parliament and of the Council of 26 June 2013 on common procedures for granting and withdrawing international protection OJ L 180, 29.06.2013.

implicitly – seem to reinforce each other's rulings. In the judgment *N.F. v European Council*[137] by the CJEU, it was held that the EU-Turkey Statement was not a legally binding agreement and as such the provisions enshrined therein could not be contested. This despite the clear concerns that were raised pertaining to the *non-refoulement* principle, due to the automated return of Syrian asylum seekers back to Turkey.[138]

The Statement in particular – albeit in the form of a political agreement – appears to facilitate the qualification of Turkey as a safe third country.[139] However, the indiscriminate violence vis-à-vis Syrian individuals and violence instigated by Turkish border guards vis-à-vis said individuals seeking refuge in the Union indicate that the qualification of Turkey as a safe third country is, at the very least, highly questionable.[140] In addition thereto, the reception and detention conditions of irregular migrants in Turkey seemingly do not comply with the standards enshrined in the *non-refoulement* principle as found in the Charter and the ECHR.[141]

Notwithstanding the widespread consternation concerning the enactment and application of the EU-Turkey Statement, the General Court refused to engage in a substantive analysis thereof, which on its face is demonstrative of its implicit consent with this political agreement and the consequences as a result thereof.

3.3.2. An ECtHR Perspective

Interestingly, on 25 January 2018, the ECtHR delivered its ruling in the case of *J.R. and Others v Greece* concerning the detention of three Afghan nationals – Mr. J.R., Ms. N.R. and Mr. A.R. – who had fled Afghanistan and arrived on Chios island on 21 March 2016 – a day after the entry into force of the EU-Turkey Statement. Upon their arrival on the Chios island, the individuals concerned were brought to the Vial Hotspot migrant reception facility, where they remained. In view of the deplorable detention conditions of the Vial Hotspot the

---

[137] CJEU, *N.F. v European Council*, T-192/16, 28.02.2017, ECLI:EU:T:2017:128.
[138] EUROPEAN COUNCIL, 'EU-Turkey statement, 18 March 2016', Press Release, 18.03.2016, available at http://www.consilium.europa.eu/en/press/press-releases/2016/03/18-eu-turkey-statement, last accessed 15.06.2018.
[139] J. DE CONINCK, 'Incongruity in Accountability – Contesting EU *De Facto* Impunity for International Human Rights Violations in the Field of Asylum and Migration: The EU-Turkey Statement', *Jean Monnet Working Paper Series*, March 2017, p. 7, available at https://www.city.ac.uk/__data/assets/pdf_file/0007/357856/Joyce-De-Coninck.pdf, last accessed 15.06.2018.
[140] HUMAN RIGHTS WATCH, 'Turkey: Border Guards Kill and Injure Asylum Seekers. Border Lock-down Puts Syrian Lives at Risk', 2016, available at https://www.hrw.org/news/2016/05/10/turkey-border-guards-kill-and-injure-asylum-seekers, last accessed 15.06.2018.
[141] Z. WEISE, 'Turkish refugee camp hailed as success by Merkel hit by child sex abuse scandal', *The Telegraph*, 12.05.2016, available at http://www.telegraph.co.uk/news/2016/05/12/turkish-refugee-camp-hailed-as-success-by-merkel-hit-by-child-se, last accessed 15.06.2018.

applicants submitted a complaint to the ECtHR on account of alleged violations of Article 3 ECHR and Article 5 ECHR. The ECtHR held that these conditions were, however, not severe enough to trigger a violation of either provision. However, what is truly interesting *in casu*, is the fact that the ECtHR had an excellent opportunity to pronounce itself on the implementation of an act by the Union – albeit in the form of a political agreement – and refrained from doing so. This seems to yet again indicate a shift back towards the *Bosphoros* doctrine previously discussed[142] (see above) although in this particular case it is clearly based on the General Court's ruling in *N.F. v Council* that the General Court did not deem the EU-Turkey Statement a legally binding agreement and thus could not engage in any substantive legal review of its consequences. The question could thus be legitimately raised to what extent there is an equivalent standard of protection given that in this particular case the General Court refused to engage in substantive review of the Statement.

3.3.3. Analysis

It appears thus that *in casu* the ECtHR preferenced not engaging in any form of (in-)direct critique of the Statement, despite the inherent risk of *non-refoulement* violations as a result thereof. This in turn seems to indicate that on this particular point in asylum and migration related matters, the ECtHR – albeit implicitly – affirms the stance taken by both the Union and more specifically the General Court of the CJEU. Whilst this may be in line with Article 52(3) CFR, when placed in the larger context of judgments in asylum and migration by both Courts in asylum and migration generally, one can only question why the ECtHR seemingly takes a step away from its own consistent practice in the interest of safeguarding judicial coherence with the CJEU.

4. CONCLUSION

Despite the laudable efforts taken by the CJEU towards the ECtHR in ensuring sufficient substantive symbiosis between these two fundamental rights catalogues – whilst safeguarding the structural autonomy of the Union – it appears that this constructive dialogue is under increasing pressure. This tension permeates the discussed judgments and could – insofar as this approach is maintained – detrimentally affect the attempts that have been made and the potential for coherent co-existence of these two frameworks.

---

[142] Despite the margin of discretion retained by the Member States in the implementation of the EU-Turkey Statement.

As such, the CJEU has placed itself in a sensitive position vis-à-vis the ECtHR, whereby seemingly contradictory signals are sent to not only the Member States concerning the standard of protection to be granted, but more importantly, to the individual applicants as to the level of protection they are entitled to. Where the CJEU sometimes deviates from ECtHR case law concerning corresponding rights (*J.N. v Staatssecretaris van Veiligheid en Justitie*), does not pronounce itself on corresponding asylum and migration provisions (*X and X v Belgium*) and where both Courts (implicitly) agree on the standard of protection to be granted (*N.F. v European Council*), there exists the danger that applicants are left in a haze of legal ambiguity concerning the standards of protection they are entitled to, despite the CJEU being bound by the ECtHR case law on corresponding rights as the minimal permissable protection. In addition thereto, the existing judicial dialogue between the two Courts may be adversely affected, not to mention the legitimacy and authority emanating from both institutions. Furthermore, this trajectory upon which both Courts have embarked, places Member States in an increasingly difficult position, as they are bound by two instruments that are sending different signals concerning the level of protection to be provided in the case of asylum seekers and applications. As this is not an isolated instance, Member States are facing increasing pressure to be compliant with possibly diverging, yet binding instruments, placing them at the centre of a potentially growing dysfunctional dialogue between the ECtHR and the CJEU.

More importantly however, the question needs to be raised as to how said tumultuous judicial dialogue affects the rights of those who see their rights violated within an asylum-related context. As is the case for the Member States, this lacking coherency in certain areas relating to asylum, is liable to affect the very principles of legal certainty, legitimate expectations and the effectiveness of fundamental rights protection concerning rights that are found in both the CFR and the ECHR. This in turn runs counter to the very essence of the judicial coherence that was envisaged by Article 6(3) TEU and Article 52(3) of the Charter. As aforementioned, it appears that the Courts theoretically agree on the standard of protection to be provided. In practice, however, it appears that said coherence is not always maintained due to diverging obligations stemming from case law of both institutions. It is not surprising that it is not only Member States who see legal certainty, legitimate expectations and the effectiveness of fundamental rights in asylum detrimentally affected by these, often, ambiguous and diverging legal standards. This confusion also holds true for individual right-holders, for whom the protection and enforecement of their fundamental rights is no longer a certainty upon which they can rely, particularly when the two courts attach different significance to the obligations enshrined therein.

THE HUMAN RIGHT TO LEAVE ANY COUNTRY

A Right to be Delivered

Elspeth GUILD and Vladislava STOYANOVA

1. Introduction 374
2. Measures that Affect the Right to Leave 375
3. The Jurisdictional Challenge 377
4. The Definitional Scope 381
5. Permissible Limitations 386
   5.1. Legality 387
   5.2. The Objectives Pursued 388
   5.3. The Suitability, the Necessity of the Measures and the Existence of Alternatives 390
   5.4. Balancing 391
6. Conclusion 393

ABSTRACT

The right to leave a country is enshrined in both international human rights law and its European counterpart. It is a right which is independent and does not require the individual exercising it to show that he or she is admissible in some other country. It is exercisable even in the absence of evidence of possible admission to a destination country. However, in Europe (and some other parts of the world) some states are seeking to encourage their neighbours to interfere with people's right to leave a country on the grounds that these European states fear that people want to come to their borders. This article examines the right to leave a state from the perspective of international and European human rights law and questions the legality of various efforts to make it dependent on a right of entry to another country.

1. INTRODUCTION

Human rights law instruments enshrine the right to leave any country, including one's own. Article 13(2) of the Universal Declaration of Human Rights contains the first expression of the right. Article 12(2) of the International Covenant on Civil and Political Rights (ICCPR) is the global legally binding instrument enshrining the right to leave. At European level, Article 2(2) of Protocol 4 to the European Convention on Human Rights (ECHR) also expresses this right.[1] The right to leave any country has not gained much attention; neither has it been an object of frequent invocations.[2] However, in light of the current situation where in practice many people are contained in countries of origin and transit,[3] the importance of this right needs to be explained and the challenges to its application clarified.

Historically, the right to leave was included in the catalogue of rights for the purpose of targeting and critiquing the countries on the east side of the Berlin Wall and their restrictions on external mobility.[4] In this context, the right to leave was considered a key indicator of the democratic foundations of states.[5] Reflective of this historical background, the Human Rights Committee General Comment No. 27 on Freedom of Movement, issued ten years after the fall of the Berlin Wall, is framed predominantly from the perspective of countries of departure. The existing communications and judgments delivered respectively by the UN Human Rights Committee and the European Court of Human Rights (ECtHR) are against countries of departure. Currently, it is however countries of destination that develop policies and measures to contain people in countries of origin and transit. The latter countries are enrolled in the destination countries' migration control policies to act as gate-keepers.

To examine these policies, we will undertake four steps in this article. After the Introduction, section 2 gives an overview of the measures that affect

---

[1] See also Article 5(2) International Covenant on the Elimination of all Forms of Racial Discrimination; Article 10(2) Convention on the Rights of the Child.
[2] The existing literature has rather focused on preventing arrivals and on pushbacks. For rare exceptions see N. MARKARD, 'The Right to Leave by Sea: Legal Limits on the EU Migration Control by Third Parties', (2016) 27(3) *European Journal of International Law*, p. 591; CoE Commissioner for Human Rights, *The Right to Leave a Country* (2013); M. DEN HEIJER, *Europe and Extraterritorial Asylum*, Hart Publishing, Oxford 2011, p. 153.
[3] Libya: European Governments Complicit in Horrific Abuse of Refugees and Migrations (Amnesty International, 12 December 2017), available at https://www.amnesty.org/en/latest/news/2017/12/libya-european-governments-complicit-in-horrific-abuse-of-refugees-and-migrants, last accessed 17.05.2018.
[4] See B. RUDOLF, 'Streletz, Kessler and Krenz v. Germany and K.H.W. v. Germany', (2001) 95(4) *American Journal of International Law*, p. 904.
[5] '[…] for the individual who finds his society intolerable, and who has made the difficult decision to extradite himself, denial of this right may be tantamount to a total deprivation of [personal] liberty.' S. JAGERSKIOLD, 'The Freedom of Movement' in L. HENKIN (ed.) *The International Bill of Rights*, Columbia University Press, New York 1981, pp. 166, 167.

the right to leave. Section 3 addresses the issue of jurisdiction in human rights law and the related challenges in making the argument that the affected individuals are within the jurisdiction of countries of destination for the purpose of triggering these countries' human rights obligations. Section 4 is engaged with the definitional scope of the right to leave and, more specifically with the question as to how the Human Rights Committee and the ECtHR have interpreted the circumstances when the right is breached. Not every breach of the right, however, is impermissible under human rights law. For this reason, section 5 examines the scope of permissible limitations and the conditions that need to be fulfilled so that any limitation of the right to leave is in compliance with human rights law.

2. MEASURES THAT AFFECT THE RIGHT TO LEAVE

Greater clarity is necessary as to the type of measures that affect the right to leave. Pre-entry controls like visas, refusals of boarding airplanes by private carriers on their own initiative or on the advice of immigration liaison officers (because of carrier sanctions) and maritime interdictions, have been examined and their compatibility with human rights law challenged from the perspective of the *non-refoulement* principle.[6] These controls can also negatively affect the right to leave. In fact, the Human Rights Committee in it General Comment No. 27 has been quite clear to the effect that 'State parties should also include information in their reports on measures that impose sanctions on international carriers which bring to their territories persons without required documents, where those measures affect the right to leave another country'.[7] In this way, the Human Rights Committee has indicated that carrier sanctions can actually implicate the right to leave. What is specific about the above-indicated measures, including the enforcement of carrier sanctions, is that they presuppose some form of physical contact between the affected migrants and agents. In this way, the causal relationship between these measures and any harm sustained by migrants (not being allowed to leave or being pushed back to a place where there might be a real risk of ill-treatment) is tangible.[8]

---

[6] G.S. GOODWIN-GILL, 'The Right to Seek Asylum: Interception at Sea and the Principle of Non-Refoulement', (2011) 23 *International Journal of Refugee Law*, p. 447; V. MORENO-LAX, *Accessing Asylum in Europe: Extraterritorial Border Controls and Refugee Rights under EU Law*, Oxford University Press, Oxford 2017.

[7] HUMAN RIGHTS COMMITTEE, General Comment No. 27, UN Doc. CCPR/C/21/Rev.1/Add.9, 02.11.1999, para. 10.

[8] V. MORENO-LAX, 'Seeking Asylum in the Mediterranean: Against a Fragmentary Reading of EU Member States' Obligations Accruing at Sea', (2011) 23(2) *International Journal of Refugee Law*, p. 174, p. 204; V. MORENO-LAX (2017), *Accessing Asylum*, supra note 6, p. 323; ECtHR, *Hirsi Jamaa and Others v Italy*, no 27765/09 [GC], 23.02.2012, para. 81.

Since 2016, European countries have started to apply new and more sophisticated forms of migration control that are based on strengthening of contacts with third countries that are countries of origin or transit and enlisting them to apply exit/departure controls.[9] This has been part of the external dimension of the European Union (EU) migration policy,[10] which has taken various forms. Example are: supporting the Libyan coastguard so that Libya can 'take ownership' of the security in its own territorial waters;[11] enhanced engagement with countries in West Africa so that they can better control their own borders; assisting Mali to exercise stronger control over border areas with neighbouring countries like Niger and Burkina Faso.[12] A similar objective has been formulated in relation to Egypt.[13] Another example is the training of the Libyan coastguard and navy.[14] Another shape that the external dimension of the EU migration policy has taken is providing third countries with border control equipment[15] and intelligence.[16] In this way, countries of destination demand countries of departure and transit to control their own borders to contain movement. This demand usually comes as part of a larger package of financial forms of assistance and other incentives.[17]

The causal link between these measures aggressively pursued by European states and any damage to interests protected by human rights law is more subtle. These measures have been thus framed as 'contactless' controls.[18] Despite the absence of a direct contact, their practical effect is containment of people within certain countries and prevention of their movement, which certainly raises an issue as to the compliance of these measures with the right to leave.

---

[9] Establishing a New Partnership Framework with Third Countries under the European Agenda on Migration, COM(2016) 385 final, 07.06.2016.
[10] Malta Declaration by the members of the European Council on the external aspects of migration: addressing the Central Mediterranean route, 3 February 2017.
[11] Progress Report on the European Agenda on Migration, COM(2017) 669, 15.11.2017, p. 8.
[12] Fifth Progress Report on the Partnership Framework with third countries under the European Agenda on Migration, COM(2017) 471, p. 6.
[13] Ibid., p. 9.
[14] Communication on establishing a new Partnership Framework with third countries under the European Agenda on Migration, COM(2016) 385, 15.
[15] See Art. 1, Italy-Libya Memorandum Agreement: 'the Italian party commits to provide technical and technological support to the Libyan institutions in charge of the fight against illegal immigration.'
[16] See Council Decision (CFSP) 2017/1385 of 25.07.2017 where it was also added that within its area of operation, EUNAVFOR MED operation Sophia shall conduct surveillance activities and the information gathered '*may* be released to the legitimate Libyan authorities' (emphasis added).
[17] For example, within the EU-Turley Deal, Turkey was promised visa liberalisation.
[18] M. GIUFFRÉ and V. MORENO-LAX, 'The Rise of Consensual Containment: From "Contactless Control" to "Contactless Responsibility" for Forced Migration Flows', in S. JUSS (ed.), *Research Handbook on International Refugee Law*, Edward Elgar, Cheltenham 2018 (forthcoming).

The assessment of this compliance requires an engagement with the following questions. First, which countries can the right to leave be claimed against? Countries of origin and transit (referred to as countries of departure) that are bound by Article 12 of the ICCPR or countries of destination that are also bound the ECHR? If the right is claimed against countries of destination, how can the jurisdiction threshold under human rights law be overcome? Second, what challenges arise in terms of triggering the application of the right to leave (the definitional threshold)? Finally, once the right is triggered, what limitations can be legitimately imposed upon the right to leave?

3. THE JURISDICTIONAL CHALLENGE

The panoply of measures undertaken by countries of destination to prevent leaving affects individuals who are not physically within their territories. This raises the issue as to whether the affected individuals are within the destination countries' jurisdiction in the sense of Article 1 of the ECHR.[19] The ECtHR itself has not yet engaged with the question in this specific context of 'contactless' control. In the existing literature, two broad approaches can be identified for addressing the issue. The first one is relying on the complicity framework to the effect that European states assist other countries in the commission of acts contrary to human rights law.[20] Even if complicity could be established,[21] human rights law still demands surpassing the jurisdictional threshold.[22] Accordingly, further analysis of complicity under international law is not undertaken here. The second approach is arguing for an expansive interpretation of jurisdiction.[23] The latter approach is attempted below.

---

[19] This section does not engage with the meaning of jurisdiction under Article 2(1) of the ICCPR. The European states that take measures to limit departures from countries of origin and transit are certainly bound by the ICCPR. However, the ECHR offers a much stronger enforcement mechanism and the engagement by the ECtHR with the issue of jurisdiction under human rights law has been more sophisticated, which warrants a specific attention.

[20] T. GAMMELTOFT-HANSEN and J. HATHAWAY, 'Non-refoulement in a World of Cooperative Deterrence', (2015) 53(1) *Columbia Journal of Transnational Law*, p. 235.

[21] A. SKORDAS, 'A "Blind Spot" in the Migration Debate? International Responsibility of the EU and its Member States for Cooperating with the Libyan Coastguard and Militias', EU Migration Law Blog, 30.01.2018; N. MARKARD (2016), 'The Right to Leave by Sea', *supra* note 2, pp. 591, 615.

[22] '[...] the test for establishing the existence of "jurisdiction" under Article 1 of the Convention has never been equated with the test for establishing a State's responsibility for an international wrongful act under international law.' ECtHR, *Catan and Others v Moldova and Russia*, no 43370/04 [GC], 19.10.2012, para. 115. For further clarification as to the distinction between attribution and jurisdiction see S. BESSON, 'The Extraterritoriality of the European Convention on Human Rights: Why Human Rights Depend on Jurisdiction and What Jurisdiction Amounts to', (2012) 25 *Leiden Journal of International Law*, p. 857, p. 860.

[23] See, for example, M. JACKSON, 'Freeing *Soering*: The ECHR, State Complicity in Torture and Jurisdiction', (2016) 27(3) *European Journal of International Law*, p. 817.

This necessitates a short foray into how the ECtHR has interpreted the notion of jurisdiction under Article 1 of the ECHR. The judgment in *Al Skeini* offers a starting point since therein the Court outlined a catalogue of jurisdiction grounds that have been followed in the subsequent cases.[24] In particular, the Court introduced the distinction between territorial and personal models of jurisdiction. As already suggested, the territorial model can be ruled out.[25] As to the personal model, *Al Skeini* has introduced the following alternative possibilities within this model: 'acts of diplomatic and consular agents', exercise of 'public powers' and 'physical power and control over the person in question'.

As to the first possibility, the refusal to issue a visa is certainly an 'act of diplomatic and consular agents'; therefore, this refusal by itself seems to engage the jurisdiction of the state whose agents refuse the visa. It is a separate question whether this refusal engages the right to leave since, depending on the circumstances, it might be possible to argue that the affected person can leave for other countries. However, this argument needs to be addressed at the definitional level of the analysis that will be undertaken below.

As to the 'physical power and control over the person in question' option, its invocation might be possible in circumstances where state agents of the extraterritorially acting state prevent departures at, for example, foreign airports. This scenario transpired in the case of *Regina v Immigration Officer at Prague Airport*.[26] A brief outline of the factual circumstances underlying the case is appropriate here. British immigration officers were stationed at the Prague airport to pre-clear passengers boarding flights to the United Kingdom. If the officers concluded that the passenger would claim asylum upon arrival, they would be refused boarding the airplane. Some of the affected passengers initiated legal proceedings in the United Kingdom and argued that the measures of preventing departures were in breach of Article 33(1) of the Convention Relating to the Status of Refugees that enshrines the prohibition on *refoulement*.

---

[24] ECtHR, *Al-Skeini and Others v United Kingdom*, no 55721/07 [GC] 07.07.2011.
[25] Within this territorial model, I also include 'effective control over an area'. See ECtHR, *Al-Skeini*, supra note 24, paras. 138–140. The EU has plans to enhance its presence in Libya: 'The EU Border Assistance Mission in Libya will establish a light presence in Tripoli before the end of November. This will be followed by a gradual and phased built-up of staff by spring 2018, allowing greater routine engagement with the Libyan authorities responsible for border management, law enforcement and criminal justice, including the civilian and coastal police.' Progress Report on the European Agenda on Migration, COM(2017) 669, 15.11.2017, p. 910. In this report, the Commission identifies the '[e]stablishment of permanent EU presence in Libya as soon as security conditions allow' as a key future action. Even if this ever happens, it is doubtful whether the presence in Libya could amount to 'effective control over an area'. However, such a presence might trigger the physical control over individuals model of jurisdiction.
[26] UK House of Lords, *Regina v Immigration Officer at Prague Airport* [2004] UKHL 55, 09.12.2004.

This argument failed: the passengers did not fall within the personal scope of the latter convention since they were not outside the country of their nationality.[27] They also invoked the prohibition on discrimination, in which respect they succeeded since individuals of Roma origin were profiled and refused boarding. The right to leave was not invoked in the case.

A scenario where 'physical power and control' is exercised over a person could transpire in circumstances where state agents of the extraterritorially acting state intercept boats before they have departed or while they are still in, for example, Libyan territorial waters.[28] It would be difficult, however, to invoke this option in relation to measures such as sharing of intelligence, equipment, etc. that do not imply any physical contact between agents of countries of destination and the individuals whose departure is prevented. It should also be added that even if the measures preventing departures imply physical contact, there is still uncertainty as to the level of control that the extraterritorially acting state has to exercise.[29]

Could the exercise of 'public powers' as a basis for establishing jurisdiction be helpful then? In *Al Skeini*, the Court recognised that:

> [...] the exercise of extraterritorial jurisdiction by a Contracting State when, *through the consent, invitation or acquiescence of the Government of that territory*, it exercises all or *some of the public powers* normally to be exercised by that Government. Thus, where, in accordance with custom, treaty or other agreement, authorities of the Contracting State carry out *executive* or judicial function on the territory of another State, the Contracting State may be responsible for breaches of the Convention thereby incurred, *as long as the acts in question are attributable to it rather than to the territorial State*. [references omitted and emphasis added][30]

The 'public powers' model of jurisdiction is an uncharted territory in the area of migration control. However, a reasonable argument can be made that, first,

---

[27] Being outside the country of one's nationality or of former habitual residence is one of the necessary elements for the application of the protection regime under the 1951 Refugee Convention.

[28] See ECtHR, *Xhavara and Others v Italy and Albania*, no 39473/98, 11.01.2001 (inadmissible due to non-exhaustion of domestic remedies). The case was about the interception of an Albanian ship carrying Albanians wishing to enter Italy illegally. The Italian intercepting ship collided with the Albanian ship as a result of which many people perished. This collision happened 35 nautical miles from the Italian coast, i.e. on high seas. The ECtHR noted that 'the measures challenged by the applicants were not intended to deprive them of the right to leave Albania, but to prevent them from entering Italian territory' and concluded that the right to leave was not engaged.

[29] It seems to be questionable whether the personal model of jurisdiction applies to circumstances where merely a cause-effect relationship exists between state action and extraterritorial harm. M. MILANOVIC, 'Human Rights Treaties and Foreign Surveillance: Privacy in the Digital Age', (2015) 56(1) *Harvard International Law Journal*, p. 81.

[30] ECtHR, *Al-Skeini, supra* note 24, para. 135.

measures aimed at controlling migration constitute an exercise of 'public powers'[31] and that, second, countries of departure consent with, invite and acquiesce to these measures, including by signing agreements (e.g. memoranda of understanding) with countries of destination.[32] The final requirement indicated in the above quoted paragraphs refers to attribution: 'as long as the acts in question are attributable to it rather than to the territorial State.' The act of preventing departures by boats from the African coast can be taken as an example. Admittedly, each circumstance has to be assessed individually; however, it is questionable whether the mere provision of equipment, training, money or intelligence suffices for exclusively attributing the above-described act to the state providing these forms of assistance.[33] An argument could be attempted that the Libyan border guards are under the 'effective control' of European states.[34] Importantly, the attribution of the Libyan border guards' acts to the territorial state has to be also excluded, a requirement that is not likely to be fulfilled.

Finally, what could have purchase in the Libyan context is that practically the Libyan coastguards would not operate in the first place if it were not for the support that Libya receives from European states. This support has a 'decisive influence', a test invoked by the Court in *Illascu* and *Catan* and used for establishing the jurisdiction of Moldova and Russia (imposing ECHR obligations on states exercising 'decisive influence' over foreign governments).[35]

In sum, there are some serious challenges for triggering the jurisdictional threshold under human rights law, which might prevent the examination as to whether the measures undertaken by countries of destination are in violation of the right to leave. Still, as suggested above, some possibilities are open and remain to be tested. These challenges in no way affect the assessment as to how countries of departure comply with their obligations corresponding to the right to leave.

---

[31] The administration of migration is generally considered an act of 'governmental authority'. See generally G.S. GOODWIN-GILL, *International Law and the Movement of Persons between States*, Clarendon Press, Oxford 1978.

[32] See the Italy-Libya Memorandum available at https://www.asgi.it/wp-content/uploads/2017/02/ITALY-LIBYA-MEMORANDUM-02.02.2017.pdf, last accessed 17.05.2018.

[33] The rules on attribution connect agents and entities to the state. Conduct is attributable to the state when committed by its actual organs (Articles 4–7 of the ILC Draft Articles) and *de facto* organs (Article 4(2), ILC Draft Articles) or by entities directed and controlled by the state (Article 8, ILC Draft Articles). As to the latter the ICJ has applied the 'effective control' test. Contrast *Military and Paramilitary Activities in against Nicaragua* (*Nicaragua v US*) (Merits) [1986] ICJ Rep 14, paras. 109–115.

[34] Additional complication arises here in light of the fact that the assistance of the Libyan border guards is provided by the EU and/or various EU MS, which raises also the question as to the division of their responsibility. This question is not addressed in this article.

[35] This argument has been made by M. GIUFFRÉ and V. MORENO-LAX (2018), 'The Rise of Consensual Containment', *supra* note 18.

4. THE DEFINITIONAL SCOPE

In this section, we will examine the definitional scope of the right to leave through the opinions of the Human Rights Committee and the ECtHR. The first step in determining the scope of the right is to identify the state which actually takes the measure which obstructs the exercise of the right. Generally, this will be the state where the individual is present. As discussed above, Article 13(2) Universal Declaration of Human Rights (UDHR) contains the first post WWII expression of the right to leave a country.[36]

The ICCPR has been ratified by 169 states and signed by another six. Only 22 states have taken no action in respect of this convention.[37] It is important to bear this in mind particularly in the European context as non-European Mediterranean countries are parties to the ICCPR but not to the ECHR. Thus, the duty to protect the right to leave for these countries arises from the ICCPR only. As noted in the introduction, in the European regional setting, Article 2(2) Protocol 4 ECHR states that 'everyone shall be free to leave any country, including his own'. Article 2(3) permits restrictions only where they are in accordance with the law, necessary in a democratic society in the interests of national security or public safety, for the maintenance of *ordre public*, for the prevention of crime, for the protection of health or morals, or for the protection of the rights and freedoms of others. Of the 47 Member States of the Council of Europe only four have not ratified this Protocol.[38] Most European states which are not members of the EU but which share borders with EU states have ratified the ECHR and its 4th Protocol but with the important exception of Turkey. Turkey is a transit country for people fleeing Afghanistan, Iraq and Syria and seeking refuge in EU states. In 2015–2016 approximately two million people entered the EU mainly via Turkey to seek asylum.[39]

In both instruments, the ICCPR and the ECHR, the right to leave is independent of any right to enter another country. While the absence of a right to enter another country is frequently commented upon in the literature as a weakness of the right to leave, in fact it may be one of its most important strengths.[40] The right to leave as contained in both instruments is not dependent on any right to enter a specific country of destination or indeed any

---

[36] '[…] everyone has the right to leave any country, including his own, and to return to his country.'
[37] Most of these are small states, often islands, see http://indicators.ohchr.org, last accessed 17.05.2018.
[38] Greece, Switzerland, Turkey and the UK.
[39] Eurostat, 'Asylum statistics', available at http://ec.europa.eu/eurostat/statistics-explained/index.php/Asylum_statistics, last accessed 17.05.2018.
[40] C. HARVEY and R.P. BARNIDGE JR., 'Human rights, free movement, and the right to leave in international law', (2007) 19.1 *International Journal of Refugee Law*, pp. 1–21.

country at all.⁴¹ It is a right in itself. Logically this must be the case for the right to leave to include departure by sea onto the high seas rather than into the territory of another state. Both conventions have a Treaty Body (ICCPR) or a Court (ECtHR) charged with the duty to provide definitive interpretation of the rights contained in them. These instances have considered the right to leave, discussed below, and consistently confirmed that this is an independent right which is not dependent on the willingness of any specific state to admit or not the person who is exercising it.

As mentioned above, the UN Treaty Body responsible for the ICCPR, the Human Rights Committee issued a General Comment on Article 12 ICCPR on 1 November 1999 clarifying the issues around the right to freedom of movement.⁴² The opening salvo of this General Comment states that 'Liberty of movement is an indispensable condition for the free development of a person'. The Human Rights Committee determined that the right to leave a country may not be made dependent on any specific purpose or on the period of time the person chooses to stay outside the country. Travelling abroad as well as permanent departure are covered. The choice of where to go is that of the individual protected by Article 12 and is not dependent on the person being lawfully present in the country from which he or she wishes to leave. According to the Committee, even an alien who is being expelled is entitled to choose his or her state of destination. The right to leave also includes the right to a passport or other necessary travel documents which is normally a duty on the state of nationality. However, the Committee notes that state practices often adversely affect the right to leave. In order to assess the compatibility of such practices with the Article 12(2) right, the Committee called on all states' parties to report on their legal and practical restrictions on the right to leave including all information on measures that impose sanctions on international carriers which bring to their territory persons without required documents where those measures affect the right to leave another country.

The Optional Protocol to the ICCPR provides for a dispute resolution mechanism (a Treaty Body) to which individuals who consider that their rights as set out in the ICCPR have been violated may present their complaints against states for adjudication (communications). Ratification of the Optional Protocol is not mandatory but 116 states parties to the ICCPR have ratified it, three have signed but not yet ratified and only 78 have taken no action (of which only two in the Council of Europe – Switzerland and the United Kingdom (UK)). The Human Rights Committee is designated as the body competent to receive complaints from individuals regarding the protection of their human

---

41   M. DEN HEIJER (2011), *Europe and Extraterritorial Asylum*, *supra* note 2, p. 153: 'the right to enter and to leave are firmly set apart in human rights law and subject to different principles of international law.'
42   HUMAN RIGHTS COMMITTEE, General Comment No. 27, *supra* note 2.

rights contained in the ICCPR. There is an obligation for individuals to exhaust domestic remedies before making a complaint to the Committee.

So far, there have been only four communications from the Human Rights Committee regarding complaints of breaches of Article 12(2) ICCPR which are of relevance here.[43] The first against Libya involved a Libyan student resident in Morocco who sought a passport.[44] The Libyan authorities offered her only a laissez-passer to travel to Libya but she insisted that she wanted a passport as her objective was not to travel to Libya. The Committee found a violation of Article 12(2) as the student had been refused a passport (a document necessary for travel elsewhere than to Libya) without valid justification and subject to an unreasonable delay. This had prevented the student from travelling abroad to continue her studies. She was also entitled to compensation. In the second case published on 31 August 2007, the claim was once again against Libya.[45] The applicant was a Libyan national who had fled the country because of his political beliefs for which he was persecuted there. He was granted asylum in Switzerland. His wife and children sought to join him there, but they were stopped at the Libyan Tunisian border and their passport was confiscated. The wife had sought on numerous occasions to retrieve her passport unsuccessfully. Once again, the Committee found a violation of Article 12(2) and required the state to return the wife's passport (which included the children on it) so she could join her husband in Switzerland and to pay her compensation.

In the third case, Canada was the defendant state in a communication published on 28 April 2009.[46] The applicant claimed a breach of Article 12(2) because the Canadian authorities, following a rejection of his asylum application, refused to return his passport to him for the purpose of leaving the country. The Committee found this part of his claim inadmissible as he had failed to substantiate his claim in light of the state party's explanation that his passport was seized pursuant to national law for the purpose of executing the applicant's lawful removal.

The final communication regarding Article 12(2) was published on 21 August 2009 and the defendant country was Uzbekistan.[47] The applicant claimed that her father had been convicted illegally for travelling abroad on business in circumstances which were not a threat to any of the interests protected by Article 12(3). The Committee found a violation of Article 12(2) making reference to General Comment No. 27 that it is not sufficient that restrictions on leaving a country serve permissible purposes; the restrictions

---

[43] These are substantive opinions about the right to leave a country (not internal movement) and are not related to pending criminal proceedings or convictions.
[44] CCPR/C/82/D/1107/2002 published 15.11.2004, Communication No. 1107/2002.
[45] CCPR/C/90/D/1143/2002 published 31.08.2007, Communication No. 1143/2002.
[46] CCPR/C/95/D/1551/2007 published 28.04.2009, Communication No. 1551/2007.
[47] CCPR/C/96/D/2007 published 21.08.2009, Communication No. 1585/2007.

must also be necessary to achieve these purposes. The state had provided no information about the necessity of the restriction on the applicant's father's travel, nor any justification of its proportionality.

From these communications of the Human Rights Committee, it is clear that the right to leave a country in Article 12(2) includes the right to leave a country of which one is not a citizen. It also requires states to provide travel documents so that a person can travel, even if that is for the purpose of family reunification with a refugee who is a national of that state enjoying asylum elsewhere. States are entitled to hold the passport of someone who wants to leave the state where this is for the purpose of expulsion. The proportionality requirement which is referred to in the most recent communication probably also applies to this reason for preventing a person from leaving the state. It is likely that if the state does not pursue the expulsion of the person in an expeditious manner the time will come when the retention of the passport is no longer consistent with Article 12(2). Finally, if states seek to prevent a person from leaving the country then should they do so, the legality of any criminal prosecution of the individual for unlawfully leaving the state will be dependent on the consistency of the restriction on leaving the state with Articles 12(2) and (3). If the state cannot justify the restriction on leaving the country in accordance with Article 12(3) then the criminal prosecution will also be inconsistent with that provision. Further any restriction on leaving a country must be proportionate to a legitimate aim (as contained in Article 12(3)) which is discussed further in the next section.

The right to leave a country contained in Article 2(2) Protocol 4 ECtHR has been the subject of substantial challenge before the ECtHR. Since 1994, the jurisdiction of this Court has been mandatory for the 47 Council of Europe states parties to the Convention. So far 18 cases have considered, on the merits, the right to leave a country. The first case was determined in 2002[48] and the most recent in 2016.[49] The country with the most substantial number of cases brought against it for a violation of Article 2 Protocol 4 is Russia (six cases and violations found in five of the six). Next comes Bulgaria with five cases, and violations found in respect of all of them. Romania has had two cases, but no violation found. All the other countries; Azerbaijan, Croatia, Italy, Hungary and Ukraine had one violation found against them by the Court. The majority of the cases involve questions about the legal basis for preventing a person from leaving the country on the basis of national law and the justification of the measures. The most notorious of the judgments is that of *Stamose v Bulgaria* (no 29713/05, 27 November 2012) where the state authorities' refusal to provide the applicant with a passport was at the request of a foreign government (the USA) from whence the person had been expelled. The Court found

---

[48] ECtHR, *Lindner and Hammermayer v Romania*, no 35671/9, 03.12.2002.
[49] ECtHR, *Shioshvili and others v Russia*, no 19356/07, 20.12.2016.

a violation of Article 2 Protocol 4 not least as the denial of passport facilities prevented the applicant from going anywhere, not just to the USA. This case will be considered in further detail in the next section.

The ECtHR's jurisprudence on Article 2 Protocol 4 is primarily in respect of former Soviet block countries where restrictions on travel were the norm before 1989. However, the former Soviet style legislation placing restrictions on travel outside the country have been mainly dismantled in the decades since the fall of the Berlin Wall. Yet, many of the cases which have come before the Court have been decided after 2012. Even bearing in mind the fairly long gestation of cases before the Court, this is a matter for concern.

The right to leave a country whether one's own or any other country is a fundamental right both in international and European law. It is independent of any right to enter another country. An individual always has the right to leave the country where he or she is irrespective of where he or she may be planning to go. The only exceptions which apply to the right to leave are those set out in the two conventions and these do not include the fact that the individual is planning to go somewhere where state officials in the country of departure have doubts whether the individual will be admitted. A restriction on the right to leave on the basis of concerns by officials that the individual might not be admitted in a possible destination state is tantamount to extraterritorial application of the border and immigration laws of another state carried out by officials of a third state (the state where the individual is present) who are not qualified to carry out such an examination. As indicated in the Prague airport case (only a decision by a UK court and not on the basis of the ECHR or ICCPR) the advice given by officials of a proposed destination state on the possibly admissibility of an individual planning to exercise his or her right to leave can be inaccurate. If the Czech Roma travellers were permitted to travel to the UK they would have had the right to seek asylum and the entitlement to remain on the UK's territory while the consideration of their cases was carried out. Thus, the advice given by the UK officials to the airline to refuse boarding to these individuals was erroneous. Not only was it erroneous but the objective was to frustrate the application of another UK international obligation this time under the Refugee Convention[50] to refrain from *refoulement* where an individual claims to be a refugee.

Careful examination of the circumstances of a breach of the right to leave and the search for remedies by individuals who claim their right has been violated is a matter of international concern. Returning to the issue raised in the previous section – at what point can a state other than the one from which the individual is seeking to leave be complicit in the breach of the right – as yet there is no clear jurisprudence from either the Human Rights Committee or the ECtHR on the subject. In the next section, we consider the permitted limitations which can be

---

[50] Convention relating to the Status of Refugees, 189 UNTS 150, entered into force 22.04.1954.

placed on the right as determined by the Treaty Body and the ECtHR. We will also address the question of the extent to which a limitation which is placed on an individual's departure by one state at the instigation of another may give rise to liability on the instigating state for a breach of the right to leave by the state of departure.

5. PERMISSIBLE LIMITATIONS

The right to leave any country can be an object of limitations. The enquiry as to the permissibility of the limitations implies an engagement with the following questions: Are these limitations provided by law? For what purpose/objective has the right been limited and are these purposes legitimate? Is there a rational connection between the purpose and the measures that restrict the right? Are these measures necessary? Is there a proportionate relation between the restrictive measures and the objectives pursued?[51] Article 12(2) of the ICCPR also adds that any restrictions must be 'consistent with the other rights recognized in the present Covenant'.

Before looking at each question separately, it is important to highlight the Human Rights Committee's position that 'States should always be guided by the principle that the restrictions must not impair the essence of the right; the relation between right and restriction, between norm and exception, must not be reversed'.[52] Such a reversal might have transpired in the light of the sweeping measures of preventing departures from countries of origin and transit. Measures that have the effect of general and indiscriminate prevention of departure cannot be compatible with the right to leave and, in fact, render the right meaningless.

The forthcoming analysis is framed from the perspective of assessing the permissibility of the limitations of the right and, in this sense, it implicates the negative obligations corresponding to the right to leave owned by countries of departure and countries of destination. Both groups of countries can also own positive obligations so that the right to leave can be ensured.[53] Given the instability of the distinction between positive and negative obligations[54] and the

---

[51] These questions are the expression of the classic proportionality analysis as generally applied in human rights law. They are reflected in the practice of the ECtHR and in the text of the HUMAN RIGHTS COMMITTEE, General Comment No. 27.
[52] HUMAN RIGHTS COMMITTEE, General Comment No. 27, *supra* note 2, para. 13.
[53] HUMAN RIGHTS COMMITTEE, General Comment No. 31, Nature of the General Legal Obligation on States Parties to the Covenant, U.N. Doc. CCPR/C/21/Rev.1/Add.13 (2004), paras. 6 and 8; L. Lavrysen, *Human Rights in a Positive State. Rethinking the Relationship between Positive and Negative Duties under the European Convention on Human Rights*, Intersentia, Cambridge 2016.
[54] For example, in cases under Article 8 implicating states' immigration control interests, the ECtHR sometimes refuses to explicitly frame the case as one implicating negative or positive obligations. See, for example, *Arvelo Aponte v the Netherlands*, no 28770/05, 03.11.2011, para. 35.

high intrusiveness of the measures affecting the right that are jointly adopted by both groups of countries (see section 2 above), in what follows we focus on negative obligations.

5.1. LEGALITY

Any restriction has to be 'in accordance with the law', which means that the impugned measures have to have a legal basis.[55] The Human Rights Committee has clarified that '[t]he laws authorizing the application of restrictions should use precise criteria and may not confer unfettered discretion on those charged with their execution.'[56] It is fair to say that, for example, Libya lacks any national framework regulating migrants' rights, which amounts to arbitrariness.[57] As to the Memorandums of Understanding concluded between countries that agree to limit departures, these memorandums are not legally binding. In addition, it is questionable whether they can meet the quality of the law requirement.[58] From the perspective of countries of destination, the fulfilment of the legality requirement implies that the assistance measures that European states provide that limit departures must have a legal basis. If operation European Union Naval Force Mediterranean (EUNAVFOR MED) Sophia is taken as an example,[59] its legal basis is clearly established.[60] However, the law must be also accessible, foreseeable and an object of adversarial proceedings; it is questionable whether

---

[55] For an outline of the meaning of legality specifically in relation to the right to leave see ECtHR, *Dzhaksybergenov v Ukraine*, no 12343/10, 10.02.2011, paras. 59–60. HUMAN RIGHTS COMMITTEE GENERAL, Comment No. 16, para. 3: 'Interference authorized by States can only take place on the basis of law, which itself must comply with the provisions, aims and objectives of the Covenant.'

[56] HUMAN RIGHTS COMMITTEE, General Comment No. 27, *supra* note 2, para. 13.

[57] UN HIGH COMMISSIONER FOR HUMAN RIGHTS, 'Detained and Dehumanised. Report on Human Rights Abuses against Migrants in Libya', 13.12.2016, p. 11, available at http://www.ohchr.org/Documents/Countries/LY/DetainedAndDehumanised_en.pdf, last accessed 22.05.2018.

[58] See, for example, the Memorandum of Understanding between Italy and Libya signed 2 February 2017, available at http://itra.esteri.it/vwPdf/wfrmRenderPdf.aspx?ID=50975, last accessed 17.05.2018.

[59] The core mandate of the operation has been framed as the undertaking of 'systemic efforts to identify, capture and dispose of vessels and enabling assets used or suspected of being used by migrant smugglers or traffickers, in order to contribute to wider EU efforts to disrupt the business model of human smuggling and trafficking networks in the Southern Central Mediterranean and prevent the further loss of life at sea', available at https://eeas.europa.eu/csdp-missions-operations/eunavfor-med-operation-sophia/36/about-eunavfor-med-operation-sophia_en, last accessed 17.05.2018.

[60] Council Decision (CFSP) 2015/778 of 18 May 2015 on an EU military operation in the Southern Central Mediterranean (EUNAVFOR MED); see also Council Decision (CFSP) 2016/993 that added two supporting tasks to EUNAVOFOR MED and Council Decision (CFSP) 2017/1385 of 25 July 2017 where it was also added that within its area of operation, EUNAVFOR MED operation SOPHIA shall conduct surveillance activities.

the last two of these requirements that pertain to the quality of the law will be met.[61] If the legality test is not fulfilled, the measures can be declared contrary to the right to leave.

5.2. THE OBJECTIVES PURSUED

Article 12(3) ICCPR allows limitations only for specific purposes: national security, public order, public health or morals or for the protection of the rights and freedoms of others. Article 2(3) Protocol 4 ECHR refers to two additional purposes: public safety and prevention of crime. In light of the EU legal and policy documents, the objectives pursued with the measures that limit departures seem to be saving lives and avoiding migrants' embarkation on hazardous journeys.[62] Another objective is framed as combating human trafficking and smuggling. Both of these objectives are part of a broader agenda of imposing restrictions in furtherance of destination states' immigration control interests. All these objectives could fit within those explicitly provided in the text of the relevant human rights law provisions and thus be assessed as legitimate. 'Public order' and 'public safety' could provide the best fit.[63] Here it needs to be clarified that the ECtHR is very cautious in finding illegitimate aims.[64] Admittedly, the objectives of the measures of departure prevention are not purely humanitarian in their nature (from the perspective of the individual migrants affected) since they are clearly driven by the destination states' immigration control interests. Yet, it is doubtful that the ECtHR will assess the measures as illegitimate for this reason.[65]

---

[61] '[...] the requirement of legal certainty, inherent in all Convention provisions.' ECtHR, *M. and Others v Bulgaria*, no 41416/08, 26.07.2011, para. 69.

[62] EUROPEAN COMMISSION, Addressing the Refugee Crisis in Europe: the Role of EU External Action JOIN(2015) 40, 09.09.2015, p. 3; EUROPEAN COMMISSION, Migration on the Central Mediterranean Route. Managing Flows, Saving Lives JOIN(2017) 4, 25.01.2017, p. 2.

[63] M. DEN HEIJER (2011), *Europe and Extraterritorial Asylum*, supra note 2, p. 163: 'Pre-border control, [...] have been described as primary aiming at reducing the potential burden posed by 'failed' migrants altogether: by preventing persons who are unlikely to have right to entry from presenting themselves at the border, the risk of having to incur administrative, financial and social costs as a result of processing asylum-seekers and not being able to enforce the removal of failed asylum-seekers or other categories of migrants is minimized.' All of these can be deemed to be for the benefit of 'public order'.

[64] The relevance of Article 18 of the ECHR should be also assessed here. This article is intended to prevent 'hidden agendas' and improper reasons for restricting rights when the state's real aim might be different from the one that has been proclaimed. See W. SCHABAS, *The European Convention on Human Rights. A Commentary*, Oxford University Press, Oxford 2015, p. 635.

[65] On the ECtHR's reluctance to challenge the legitimacy of the states' objectives in the context of migration control see V. STOYANOVA, 'Populism, Exceptionality, and the Right to Family Life of Migrants under the European Convention on Human Rights', (2018) 10.2 *European Journal of Legal Studies*, p. 106.

An important nuance however must be added in relation to countries of departure in relation to the objective of protecting other states' immigration interests. This specific issue was addressed by the ECtHR in *Stamose v Bulgaria*.[66] The applicant was banned from leaving Bulgaria for a period of two years on account of having breached the USA immigration laws. The prohibition was prompted by the USA embassy. The measure of interference, i.e. the ban on leaving, was 'designed to discourage and prevent breaches of the immigration laws of other States, and thus reduce the likelihood of those States refusing other Bulgarian nationals entry to their territory, or roughening or refusing to relax visa regime in respect of Bulgarian nationals'.[67]

The ECtHR observed that:

> Even if the Court were prepared to accept that the interference pursued the legitimate aim of maintenance of order public or the protection of the rights of others, in the instant case it is not necessary to pursue further this point, since in any case, as explained below, the travel restriction failed the 'necessary in a democratic society' test and the implicit proportionality test.[68]

The Court did not outright say that this objective is not legitimate, but it did clarify that:

> Although the Court might be prepared to accept that a prohibition to leave one's own country in relation to breaches of the immigration laws of other State may in certain *compelling situations* be regarded as justified, it does not consider that the automatic imposition of such a measure without any regard to the individual circumstances of the person concerned may be characterized as necessary in a democratic society [emphasis added].[69]

The standard of 'compelling situation' appears to be a very high one. Therefore, it is questionable whether human rights law permits restrictions to prevent breaches of other states' immigration laws. In the case, the instigating country, the USA, was not a party to the ECHR so there was no question of allocating legal responsibility to it for the breach. Only Bulgaria as a party to the ECHR 4th Protocol was responsible for the breach. However, if the instigating country had been another Council of Europe country the situation might have been different. The fact that a specific individual was the object of both countries' actions to prevent his departure – the requesting state (the USA) and the state carrying out the request (Bulgaria) must be borne in mind when considering

---

[66] ECtHR, *Stamose v Bulgaria*, no 29713/05, 27.11.2012.
[67] Ibid., para. 32.
[68] Ibid.
[69] ECtHR, *Stamose*, supra note 66, para. 36.

the possible extension of this jurisprudence to the legality of measures adopted generally to prevent departure of classes of persons with only limited definition.

5.3. THE SUITABILITY, THE NECESSITY OF THE MEASURES AND THE EXISTENCE OF ALTERNATIVES

The suitability test implies that there is some empirical relationship between the measures and the objective pursued. The test requires that the measures of preventing departures actually save lives and prevent human trafficking and human smuggling. The empirical evidence and studies raise serious questions as to whether this is achieved; rather, the smuggling networks choose to use more dangerous routes in this way making the crossings more dangerous.[70] As to the objective of preventing of human trafficking, it is important to clarify that there is little empirical evidence that those who actually organise the departures and the journey do so 'for the purpose of exploitation'. For human trafficking to be constituted, a requisite element is the specific intention of exploitation.[71] Migrants might be deceived about many aspects related to the journeys and their vulnerabilities abused; however, an elementary consideration of the international law definition of human trafficking does require that the recruitment or the transportation by deception or abuse of vulnerability is done 'for the purpose of exploitation'.[72]

Even if the suitability test is somehow passed, human rights law imposes an additional test of necessity. It requires that when there is a variety of means to achieve the objectives, the least restrictive/intrusive one from the perspective of the right must be chosen.[73] The necessity test prompts an enquiry into possible alternative measures for achieving the objectives. These alternatives might be more protective for the individual.[74] If there are such more protective alternatives,

---

[70] UK HOUSE OF LORDS EU COMMITTEE, 'Operation Sophia: A Failed Mission' 2nd Report of Session 2017-19, p. 8, available at https://publications.parliament.uk/pa/ld201719/ldselect/ldeucom/5/5.pdf, last accessed 17.05.2018.

[71] V. STOYANOVA, *Human Trafficking and Slavery Reconsidered. Conceptual Limits and States' Positive Obligations in European Law*, Cambridge University Press, Cambridge 2017, p. 43.

[72] Migrants might be subjected to exploitation amounting to slavery, servitude or forced labour in countries of destination; however, this is a separate problem that relates to the conditions that they are exposed to once in countries of destination.

[73] In General Comment No. 27, the Human Rights Committee has noted that state have to use the 'least intrusive instrument amongst those which might achieve the desired result.' See HUMAN RIGHTS COMMITTEE, General Comment No. 27, *supra* note 2, para. 14. The *Michigan Guidelines on Refugee Freedom of Movement* invoke the same standard: 'A limitation is only necessary if shown to be the least intrusive means to safeguard the protected interest.'

[74] For a very useful discussion of the necessity test in the context of the ECHR see J. GERARDS, 'How to Improve the Necessity Test of the European Court of Human Rights', (2013) 11(2) *International Journal of Constitutional Law*, p. 466 and E. BREMS and L. LAVRYSEN '"Don't Use a Sledgehammer to Crack a Nut": Less Restrictive Means in the Case Law of the European Court of Human Rights', (2015) 15 *Human Rights Law Review*, p. 139.

the measures of preventing departure are not necessary and thus contrary to human rights law. Alternatives do exist: safe passages can be offered[75] and for those who have already departed from the shore, enhancement of research and rescue operations will be useful.[76] Therefore, in relation to the objectives of saving lives and preventing human smuggling, it is doubtful whether the necessity test is met.

Are there any alternatives for achieving the objective of preventing arrivals? Can destination countries' migration control interests be preserved through other alternative means? These are the difficult questions since ultimately European states have engaged with third countries with the objective of preventing departures precisely to avoid physical contacts with asylum seekers of the *Hirsi Jamaa and Others v Italy* type of scenario. *Hirsi* could be interpreted to the effect that after the interception of the migrants at high sea the European states have to grant access to territory where an assessment can be made as to the asylum claims.[77] The difficulties involved can be considered at the balancing stage which is the last step in the analysis as to the permissibility of any limitations upon the right to leave.

5.4. BALANCING

The actual balancing exercise presupposes the assignment of values to the competing interests and relating the values.[78] Let us look at both sides of

---

[75] C. COSTELLO, 'It need not be like this', (2016) 51 *Forced Migration Review*, p. 12.
[76] UN Special Rapporteur of the Human Rights Council on Extrajudicial, Summary or Arbitrary Execution, Unlawful Death of Refugees and Migrants, UN Doc. A/72/335, 15.08.2017, p. 16.
[77] M. GIUFFRÉ, 'Access to Asylum at Sea? *Non-refoulement* and a Comprehensive Approach to Extraterritorial Human Rights Obligations' in V. MORENO-LAX and E. PAPASTAVRIDIS (eds.), *Boat Refugees and Migrants at Sea*, Brill Nijhoff, Leiden 2017, p. 248; V. MORENO-LAX (2011), 'Seeking Asylum in the Mediterranean', *supra* note 8, p. 174.
[78] It could be objected that when the right to leave interacts with other rights that are not subject to inherent limitations (e.g. *non-refoulement* or the right not to be subjected to slavery or servitude), balancing of competing interests should not be undertaken. In principle, human rights that are framed in absolute terms are not subject to limitations and thus to balancing between the interests that they protect and any competing state interests. Admittedly, the importance of the interests that these absolute rights protect weighs heavily in the balancing exercise under Article 12(2) ICCPR and Article 2(2) Protocol 4 ECHR (the right to leave). However, these important interests cannot displace the balancing itself in the context of the right to leave. After all, the right to leave is an independent right (one of the major arguments advanced in this article) and the assessment whether it has been violated inevitably implies a balancing of competing interests. In addition, it should also be acknowledged that when the rights that are not subject to limitations trigger positive obligations (e.g. the obligations upon the state not to *refoule*, to prevent slavery or to prevent loss of life could be also framed as positive obligations), the latter are subject to the test of reasonableness that presupposes balancing of competing interests. For elaboration see V. STOYANOVA 'How Exceptional Must "Very Exceptional" Be? Non-refoulement, Socio-Economic Deprivation and *Paposhvili v Belgium*', (2017) 29(4) *International Journal of Refugee Law*, p. 580.

the scale. The detriment to the individuals' interests is on one side. Here, where the right to leave is related to the right to seek asylum an issue of the right to enter arises.[79] This is the result of the application of the Refugee Convention. Although the convention does not address the issue of how refugees leave their countries of origin and come within the jurisdiction of countries of protection, Article 31(1) clearly acknowledges that refugees can resort to illegal entry. The latter provision stipulates that:

> The Contracting States shall not impose penalties, *on account of their illegal entry* or presence, on refugees who, coming directly from a territory where their life or freedom was threatened in the sense of article 1, *enter* or are present *in their territory without authorization*, provided they present themselves without delay to the authorities and show good cause for their illegal entry or presence [emphasis added].

As the plain wording of Article 31(1) of the Refugee Convention suggests, it targets countries of destination. This must have an impact in the proportionality assessment to the effect of weakening the importance of satisfying states interests. True, if controls operate prior to departure from countries of origin, Article 31(1) of the Refugee Convention cannot be invoked. This provision is of relevance only if the individuals have left their countries of origin. It can certainly be invoked in relation to measures impeding departures from transit countries. However, the right to leave may provide a more robust ground on which to attack pre-departure obstacles.

Further importance to the individual interests is added by the fact that these individuals try to leave circumstances of arbitrary detention, slavery, torture and inhuman and degrading treatment that are pervasive in the countries where they are contained.[80] In *M.S.S. v Belgium and Greece*, the ECtHR held that '[t]he fact that [...] the applicant had been trying to leave Greece cannot be held against him [...] when the applicant was attempting to find a solution to a situation the Court considers contrary to Article 3 [inhuman and degrading treatment]'.[81]

---

[79] V. MORENO-LAX (2017), *Accessing Asylum*, supra note 6, p. 341; M. DEN HEIJER (2011), *Europe and Extraterritorial Asylum*, supra note 2, p. 165. Despite the relationship between the right to leave and the right to seek asylum, Martin den Heijer correctly observes that '[a]lthough the *materials* scope of the right to leave is limited on account of its qualified nature, the *personal* scope is wider than that of the duties inherent to the prohibition of refoulement [...]' (emphasis in the original).

[80] UN HIGH COMMISSIONER FOR HUMAN RIGHTS, 'Detained and Dehumanised', supra note 57; BBC, 'Migrant Slavery in Libya: Nigerians Tell of Being Used as Slavery', 02.01.2018, available at http://www.bbc.co.uk/news/world-africa-42492687, last accessed 17.05.2018; Aljazeera, 'Slavery in Libya: Life Inside a Container', 26.01.2018, available at http://www.aljazeera.com/news/2018/01/slavery-libya-life-container-180121084314393.html, last accessed 17.05.2018.

[81] ECtHR, *M.S.S. v Belgium and Greece*, no 30696/09 [GC] 21.01.2011, para. 315. For a similar argument see V. MORENO-LAX (2017), *Accessing Asylum*, supra note 6, p. 364.

The intrusion into the integrity of persons has a heavy weight in the balancing exercise. The intrusion is of an immense magnitude when it comes to the individuals whose departure from, for example Libya, is prevented.

The importance of the European states' migration control interests is on the other side of the scale. Here one cannot fail to acknowledge that 'the effectiveness of the state as a guarantor of rights and freedoms presuppose the idea of a bounded community'.[82] Immigration control is thus a tool for securing the human rights of citizens and denizens. The quantification of the intrusion is difficult to specify, and heterogeneous factors need to be taken into account, which renders the whole exercise complex and indeterminate. Still, on this general level of abstraction, one should not fail to notice the failure of the EU states to forge a common resolution to the challenge, which could lead to sharing of the burden in the spirit of solidarity.[83]

6. CONCLUSION

In this article, we have shown the discrete analytical issues that arise when making the determination as to whether the right to leave is engaged in terms of definitional scope and whether the right to leave is violated in terms of fulfilment of the conditions that permit its limitations. In terms of definitional scope, it is of paramount importance to highlight that the right to leave is a freestanding right. When someone claims a need for international protection, the right may be coupled with a right of entry arising from other sources of international law such as the Refugee Convention or Article 3 ECHR. But this right of entry is not a condition precedent on the right to leave a country. In other words, the exercise of the right to leave is not dependent on any precondition concerning allowing of entry into a country. As to its personal scope, the right to leave applies to everyone whether nationals of the country or not.

Measures of general nature that limit leaving on a massive scale, cannot be compatible with the right to leave since no assessment has been made as to their proportionality in relation to the specific individuals affected (many of whom are asylum seekers and/or subjected to severe forms of ill-treatment in the countries that they are prevented from leaving). Human rights law requires that any limitation measures must pursue legitimate objectives and that there is

---

[82] G. NOLL, *Negotiating Asylum. The EU Acquis, Extraterritorial Protection and the Common Market of Deflection*, Brill, The Hague 2000, p. 489.

[83] G. NOLL, 'Why the EU Gets in the Way of Refugee Solidarity' *Open Democracy*, 22 September 2015, available at https://www.opendemocracy.net/can-europe-make-it/gregor-noll/why-eu-gets-in-way-of-refugee-solidarity, last accessed 17.05.2018. See also V. MORENO-LAX, 'Solidarity's reach: Meaning, dimensions and implication for EU (external) asylum policy', (2017) 24(5) *Maastricht Journal of European and Comparative Law*, p. 740.

a rational connection between the objectives and the measures. We expressed doubts as to the existence of such a connection. Human rights law imposes an additional requirement of necessity, which demands that the EU states actually use measures that are less intrusive to the right to leave and more effective for saving lives and combatting human smuggling and human trafficking. Even if the European states migration control interests are assigned a heavy weight in the proportionality analysis, we explained that given the circumstances in countries of origin and transit, heavy weight needs to be also assigned to the individual interests.

The EU's policy of externalisation of its border controls (examples of which are set out in section 1 above), raises questions about state responsibility for breaches of the right to leave. Where the EU policy is designed and implemented to enable states outside the European Union to breach the right of people to leave their territories, the possibility of liability on those EU states participating in this policy (probably all 28) for the actions of the implementing state becomes possible. The concern expressed by the Human Rights Committee in General Comment No. 27 regarding the compatibility of carrier sanctions with the right to leave indicates that measures of a general nature which apply to all persons leaving a state may be inconsistent with the ICCPR right to leave. The apparent effort of the EU and its Member States in designing measures which externalise border controls to prevent people from coming to the EU so that the role of the EU is shielded from liability under Article 12(2) ICCPR and Article 2(4) ECHR may even indicate liability. In any event, the independent nature of the right to leave must be respected by all states. As we have demonstrated here, this right cannot be made subject to any condition not expressed in the ICCPR and ECHR. Demonstrating that an individual has the possibility or right to enter another country is not a ground on the basis of which states are permitted to interfere with the free-standing right of that person to leave their territory.

SOME REFLECTIONS ON THE PRINCIPLE OF THE BEST INTERESTS OF THE CHILD IN EUROPEAN EXPULSION CASE LAW

Mathieu Leloup

1. Introduction 395
2. The Court's Use of the Best Interests Principle in Expulsion Cases....... 400
   2.1. The Expulsion of a Parent and the Right to Family Life........... 401
   2.2. The Prohibition of Torture or Inhuman or Degrading Treatment....405
3. A More Principled Use of the Principle............................ 409
   3.1. A Constant Use of the Best Interests Principle.................. 410
   3.2. A Consistent Use of the Best Interests Principle 413
4. Conclusion... 417

ABSTRACT

According to Article 3 of the United Nations (UN) Convention on the Rights of the Child, the child's best interests shall be a primary consideration in any decision concerning this child. Expulsion measures, where either the child itself or the parent of a child get expelled, are such decisions concerning children. This article aims to discuss how the European Court of Human Rights uses the best interests principle in its expulsion case law. It examines the case law concerning the right to family life and the prohibition of torture or inhuman or degrading treatment. This case law shows that in the sphere of expulsion cases the Court's use of this principle is inconsistent or even non-existent. It is argued that the Court should adopt a more principled approach towards the best interests principle, which implies a constant and a consistent use of this principle.

1. INTRODUCTION

It is not exactly ground-breaking news to state that for several years Europe has been dealing with a migration crisis. Countless pages of scholarly work from a multitude of scientific fields have been written on the issue and it was even one of the 'topics of the year' of this yearbook two years ago.[1] From the most recent available European Union statistics, the number of third country nationals who were returned to their home country following an order to leave increased to over 250,000 in 2016.[2] Unfortunately, there are no official statistics on the age of these expelled persons. It stands to reasons however, that several tens of thousands of them were minors.[3] Such an expulsion has a big psychological impact on these children and will possibly return them to a country where their mental or physical well-being is guaranteed less or perhaps even not at all.[4]

One of the most important principles in international law[5] is the principle of the best interests of the child, enshrined in Article 3 of the UN Convention on the Rights of the Child (CRC).[6] According to this principle, in all decisions concerning a child his or her best interests shall be a primary consideration. It can safely be assumed that a decision to expel either a child or the parent of a child is a decision concerning this child.[7] According to Article 3 CRC then, the best interests of this child will have to be a primary consideration when taking this decision.

---

[1]   See M. NOWAK and A.E. WALTER, 'The Crisis of the European Refugee Policy', in W. BENEDEK, F. BENOÎT-ROHMER, M.C. KETTEMANN, R. KLAUSHOFFER and M. NOWAK (eds.), *European Yearbook on Human Rights*, Intersentia, Antwerp 2016, pp. 31–56. See also the article by Theodor Rathgeber in T. RATHGEBER, 'EU Migration Policy: The Ongoing Challenge – Views from the UN Human Rights Council in 2015', ibid., pp. 79–82.

[2]   EUROSTAT, 'Third country nationals returned following an order to leave – annual data (rounded)', 23.05.2018, available at http://appsso.eurostat.ec.europa.eu/nui/show.do?dataset=migr_eirtn&lang=en, last accessed 06.06.2018.

[3]   To get an idea of how many minors are among these illegal immigrants, one can look at the number of people that were found to be illegally present in the EU. In 2016, 983,860 third country nationals were found to be illegally present in the EU; 161,455 of them were minors. This amounts to 16.41%, available at http://appsso.eurostat.ec.europa.eu/nui/submitViewTableAction.do, last accessed 28.05.2018.

[4]   For recent studies on the impact of (the threat of) expulsion or the expulsion of a parent on the child see B. ALLEN, E.M. CISNEROS and A. TELLEZ, 'The Children Left Behind: the Impact of Parental Deportation on Mental Health', (2015) 24(2) *Journal of Child and Family Studies*, pp. 386–392; K.M. BRABECK, M.B. LYKES and C. HUNTER, 'The Psychosocial Impact of Detention and Deportation on U.S. Migrant Children and Families', (2014) 84(5) *American Journal of Orthopsychiatry*, pp. 496–505; J. DREBY, 'The Burden of Deportation on Children in Mexican Immigrant Families', (2012) 74(4) *Journal of Marriage and Family*, pp. 829–845.

[5]   McAdam referred to it as an absolute principle of international law. J. MCADAM, 'Seeking Asylum under the Convention for the Rights of the Child: A case for Complementary Protection', (2006) 14(3) *International Journal of Children's Rights*, p. 251.

[6]   Adopted and opened for signature, ratification and accession by General Assembly Resolution 44/25 of 20 November 1989. Even though Article 3 CRC is now the most commonly used point of reference for the best interest principle, it was already mentioned in earlier documents. For example see Article 2 CRC or Article 16(d) of the Convention on the Elimination of All Forms of Discrimination against Women (CEDAW).

[7]   Similarly M. KLAASSEN and P. RODRIGUES, 'The Best Interests of the Child in EU Family Reunification Law: A Plea for More Guidance on the Role of Article 24(2) Charter', (2017) 19(2) *International Journal of migration and law*, p. 196; J. POBJOY, 'The Best Interests of the Child Principle as an Independent Source of International Protection', (2015) 64(2) *International and Comparative Law Quarterly*, p. 330; See also the draft articles on the

The Committee on the Rights of the Child considers the best interests principle as one of the four fundamental values that underlie the entire CRC, together with the right to life, survival and development of the child, the prohibition of discrimination and the right of the child to express his or her views.[8] The Committee has issued several general comments in which it has advised on how the best interests principle should be interpreted and applied. The best interests principle is a general principle that aims to ensure both the full and effective enjoyment of all the rights recognised in the Convention and the holistic development of the child[9] and that therefore should be considered when implementing these other Convention rights.[10]

According to the Committee, the principle is a threefold concept which can be used as a substantive right, an interpretative legal principle or a rule of procedure.[11] In case the principle is used as a substantive right, the child has the right to have his or her interests assessed and taken as a primary consideration when different interests are being considered.[12] In this way a decision should be made that is beneficial for the child(ren) concerned. The fact that these interests should be a 'primary consideration' implies that there is a hierarchical primacy, where a larger weight must at least be attributed to them.[13] However, this does not mean that it is impossible for other interests to outweigh these interests of the child. In this sense, the child's best interests cannot be used as a trump card that automatically overrides any conflicting interest.[14] When dealing with expulsion cases, the Court ordinarily uses the best interests principle as a substantive right.[15] In case the principle is used as an interpretative legal principle, the domestic authorities are held to choose the interpretation that most effectively serves the

---

    expulsion of aliens, adopted by the International Law Commission. Article 15 reiterates that in all actions concerning children who are subject to expulsion, their best interests shall be a primary consideration, available at http://legal.un.org/ilc/texts/instruments/english/commentaries/9_12_2014.pdf, last accessed 28.05.2018.

[8] COMMITTEE ON THE RIGHTS OF THE CHILD (ComRC), General Comment No. 5 General measures of implementation of the Convention on the Rights of the Child, UN Doc. CRC/GC/2003/5, para. 12.

[9] COMMITTEE ON THE PROTECTION OF THE RIGHTS OF ALL MIGRANT WORKERS AND MEMBERS OF THEIR FAMILIES and ComRC, Joint General Comment No. 4 on State obligations regarding the human rights of children in the context of international migration in countries of origin, transit, destination and return, UN Doc. CMW/C/GW/4-CRC/C/GC/23, para. 12; ComRC, General Comment No. 14 on the right of the child to have his or her best interests taken as a primary consideration, UN Doc. CRC/C/GC/14, para. 4.

[10] ComRC, Concluding observation to Jordan in 2006, CRC/C/JOR/CO/3, para. 37.

[11] ComRC, General Comment No. 14, *supra* note 9, para. 6.

[12] Ibid.

[13] Ibid., para. 39; C. SMYTH, 'The Best Interests of the Child in the Expulsion and First Entry Jurisprudence of the European Court of Human Rights: How Principled Is the Court's Use of the Principle?', (2015) 17(1) *European Journal of Migration and Law*, pp. 100–101.

[14] See also ECtHR, *El Ghatet v Switzerland*, no 56971/10, 08.11.2016, para. 46; ECtHR, *I.A.A. v UK*, no 25960/13, 08.03.2016, para. 46.

[15] See below 2.1, footnotes 54–56 and the accompanying text.

child's interests when a legal provision is open to multiple interpretations.[16] The Court only occasionally applies the principle in this way.[17] The principle can also be used as a rule of procedure. Interpreted in this sense, the principle demands that whenever a decision is made that will affect a child, the decision-making process must include an evaluation of the possible impact – negative as well as positive – of this decision on the child concerned.[18] In the past, the Court has sometimes used the principle in this sense.[19] However, in expulsion cases, such practice is only noticeable in the most recent cases.[20]

This article aims to discuss how the European Court of Human Rights (hereafter: the Court) uses the best interests principle in its case law concerning the expulsion of aliens. Despite the volume of scholarly work analysing the place of this principle in the Court's case law,[21] its use in expulsion cases has so far

---

[16] ComRC, General Comment No. 14, *supra* note 9, para. 6.
[17] K. TURKOVIC and A. GRGIC, 'Best Interests of the Child in the Context of Article 8 of the ECHR', in J. CASADEVALL e.a. (eds.), *Liber Amicorum Dean Spielmann*, Wolf Legal Publishers, Oisterwijk 2015, p. 633. See for example ECtHR, *Mennesson v France*, no 65192/11, 26.06.2014; ECtHR, *Wagner and J.M.W.L. v Luxemburg*, no 76240/01, 28.06.2007. No examples in expulsion cases can be found.
[18] ComRC, General Comment No. 14, *supra* note 9, para. 6.
[19] See for example, below note 117.
[20] See below note 118.
[21] See by way of recent examples: P. LEMMENS and I. DE CONINCK, 'International Child Abduction and the Assessment of the Best Interests of the Child, in the Light of the Hague Convention and the European Convention on Human Rights', in I. BOONE, J. PUT, F. SWENNEN and G. VERSCHELDEN (eds.), *Liber Amicorum Patrick Senaeve*, Kluwer, Mechelen 2017, pp. 639–662; L. BRACKEN, 'Assessing the Best Interests of the Child in Cases of Cross-border Surrogacy: Inconsistency in the Strasbourg Approach?', (2017) 39(3) *Journal of Social Welfare and Family Law*, pp. 368–379; S. MUSTASAARI and S. KOULU, 'State Curriculum and Parents' Convictions under the European Convention on Human Rights', in M. JANTERA-JAREBORG (ed.), *The Child's Interests in Conflict*, Intersentia, Antwerp 2016, pp. 55–72; J. TIGCHELAAR and M. JONKER, 'How is a Judicial Decision Made in Parental Religious Disputes? An Analysis of Determining Factors in Dutch and European Court of Human Rights Case Law', (2016) 12(2) *Utrecht Law Review*, pp. 24–40; S. SAROLEA, 'L'intérêt Supérieur de l'enfant dans les Affaires de Droit International Privé devant la Cour Européenne des Droits De L'homme', in L. BARNICH, A. NUYTS, S. PFEIFF and P. WAUTELET (eds.), *Le Droit des Relations Familiales Internationales à la Croisée des Chemins*, Bruylant, Brussels 2016, pp. 107–147; P. MCELEAVY, 'The European Court of Human Rights and the Hague Child Abduction Convention: Prioritising Return or Reflection?', (2015) 62(3) *Netherlands International Law Review*, pp. 356–405; A. YOUNG, 'Advances in Children's Rights over the Past Decade: The Inter-American Court of Human Rights and the European Court of Human Rights' Progressive Incorporation of the Convention on the Rights of Children', (2015) 28 *Journal of the American Academy of Matrimonial Lawyers*, pp. 285–307; H. KELLER and C. HERI, 'Protecting the Best Interests of the Child: International Child Abduction and the European Court of Human Rights', (2015) 84(2) *Nordic Journal of International Law*, pp. 270–296; P. BEAUMONT, K. TRIMMINGS, L. WALKER and J. HOLLIDAY, 'Child Abduction: Recent Jurisprudence on the European Court of Human Rights', (2015) 64(1) *International and Comparative Law Quarterly*, pp. 39–63; G. ALVES DE FARIA, 'Sexual Orientation and the ECtHR: What Relevance is given to the Best Interests of the Child? An Analysis of the European Court of Human Rights' Approach to the Best Interests of the Child in LGBT Parenting Cases' (2015), *Family and Law*, available at http://www.familyandlaw.eu/tijdschrift/fenr/2015/04/FENR-D-15-00002.pdf, last accessed

been only scarcely examined.²² This article begins with the observation that, even though the Court's use of the best interests principle in its case law has been steadily increasing,²³ such use is either inconsistent or completely absent when the Court is dealing with expulsion cases. To demonstrate this, a brief overview will be given of the Court's use of this principle in expulsion cases regarding the right to family life and regarding the prohibition of torture or inhuman or degrading treatment, as these are the two fundamental rights that are invoked most often in expulsion cases.²⁴ Both strands of case law provide a valuable insight. First, the case law on Article 3 demonstrates that the Court does not involve the best interests principle in all expulsion cases where children are involved. This is somewhat of an anomaly in the Court's jurisprudence and no compelling arguments for this omission can be discerned from the Court's judgments.²⁵ Secondly, the case law regarding Article 8 shows that the current, substantive use of the principle in the Court's expulsion cases leads to inconsistency in its case law.

It could be argued that these two strands of case law are hard to compare. Whereas the prohibition of torture or inhuman or degrading treatment is absolute, the right to family life is a relative right. Consequently, whereas the child's interests can be incorporated in the balancing exercise flowing from Article 8 of the Convention, such a weighing of interests is absent in cases

---

28.05.2018; K. BALL, 'The Rights-bearing Child's Best Interests: Implications of the European Court's Rejection of a Child-return Order in X. v Latvia', (2015) 1 *Journal of Global Justice and Public Policy*, pp. 163–198.

[22] The articles that do describe the use of the best interests principle in expulsion cases often only examine the situation in one or more specific countries rather than in general. For example see (France) F. LANGROGNET, 'De l'Incantation à la Norme: L'Incidence Statistique croissante de l'Intérêt Supérieur de l'Enfant dans le Contentieux de l'Éloignement des Étrangers', (2015) 8(1) *La Revue des Droits de l'Homme*, pp. 1–11; (Norway and Russia) T. HAUGLI and E. SHINKAREVA, 'The Best Interests of the Child versus Public Safety Interests: State Interference into Family Life and Separation of Parents and Children in Connection with Expulsion/deportation in Norwegian and Russian Law', (2012) 26(3) *International Journal of Law, Policy and the Family*, pp. 351–377; (Sweden) A. LUNDBERG, 'The Best Interests of the Child Principle in Swedish Asylum Cases: The Marginalization of Children's Rights', (2011) 3(1) *Journal of Human Rights Practice*, pp. 49–70. For an exception see C. SMYTH (2015), 'The Best Interests of the Child', *supra* note 13, pp. 71–103.

[23] This has recently been demonstrated by Jacobsen. See A.F. JACOBSEN, 'Children's Rights in the European Court of Human Rights – An Emerging Power Structure', (2016) 24(3) *International Journal of Children's Right*, pp. 548–574. Kilkelly noticed that the European Court has been increasingly referring to the UN Convention on the Rights of the Child in general. U. KILKELLY, 'The Best of Both Worlds for Children's Rights? Interpreting the European Convention on Human Rights in the Light of the UN Convention on the Rights of the Child', (2001) 23(2) *Human Rights Quarterly*, p. 309.

[24] It should be noted, however, that other Convention rights could also be breached by an expulsion. For example, an expulsion to a country where a child runs a real risk of being subjected to forced labour is prohibited under Article 4 ECHR (see the dissenting opinion by Judge Pinto De Albuquerque, joined by Judge Tsotsoria on ECtHR, *J. and others v Austria*, no 58216/12, 17.01.2017).

[25] See below 2.2.

pertaining to Article 3 European Convention on Human Rights (ECHR). Indeed, the different nature of these two provisions makes it difficult for the best interests principle to be applied in a similar manner in both strands of case law. However, this remark cannot detract from the fact that the best interests principle should be taken into account in all expulsion measures concerning a child.[26] To overcome these issues, the article argues that the Court should adopt a more principled approach towards the principle, which implies a constant and a consistent use of the principle in its case law. This new approach would allow the Court to involve the best interests principle in all expulsion cases, while retaining consistency in its case law.

2. THE COURT'S USE OF THE BEST INTERESTS PRINCIPLE IN EXPULSION CASES

In general, the Court has a good relationship with children's rights. Despite the low number of rights in the ECHR that are specifically tailored to minors,[27] the Court has significantly contributed to the protection of children's rights with its case law.[28] In the Court's jurisprudence multiple examples can be found of landmark cases in which it relies on the best interests principle to come to its conclusion. Themes like international child abduction,[29] parental access restrictions[30] and juvenile justice[31] are all marked by reasoning grounded on the best interests of the child. In the sphere of migration law as well, significant improvements to the human rights situation of migrants have developed because of reasoning that attached importance to the child's interests. Examples of this can be found in the case law on the detention of families with children,[32] on the quality of detention facilities[33] and on the means of

---

[26] M. KLAASSEN and P. RODRIGUES (2017), 'The Best Interests of the Child', J. POBJOY (2015), 'The Best Interests of the Child Principle' and the ILC 'Draft articles on the expulsion of aliens', all *supra* note 7.

[27] The only provisions in the Convention that explicitly mention children are Article 5(1)(d) and Article 6(1). The only right in the Convention that is of special relevance to children is the right to education, enshrined in Article 2 of the First Protocol.

[28] A. YOUNG, 'Advances in Children's Rights over the Past Decade', p. 306; U. KILKELLY, 'The CRC in Litigation Under the ECHR', in T. LIEFAARD and J. DOEK (eds.), *Litigating the Rights of the Child*, Springer, Dordrecht 2014, p. 194.

[29] See ECtHR, *X. v Latvia*, no 27853/09 [GC], 26.11.2013; ECtHR, *Neulinger and Shuruk v Switzerland*, no 41615/07 [GC], 06.07.2010.

[30] ECtHR, *Mohamed Hasan v Norway*, no 27496/15, 26.04.2018, paras. 142–163; ECtHR, *Jovanovic v Sweden*, no 10592/12, 22.10.2015, para. 77; ECtHR, *Sahin v Germany*, no 30943/96 [GC], 08.07.2003; ECtHR, *Gnahoré v France*, no 40031/98, 19.09.2000, para. 59.

[31] ECtHR, *Blokhin v Russia*, no 47152/06 [GC], 23.03.2016; ECtHR, *T. v UK*, no 24724/94 [GC], 16.12.1999.

[32] ECtHR, *A.B. v France*, no 11593/12, 12.07.2016, paras. 110–115.

[33] ECtHR, *Popov v France*, nos 39472/07 and 39474/07, 19.01.2012, paras. 132–148.

subsistence for immigrant families with children.³⁴ What these cases have in common, is that the best interests principle was the crucial argument in the Court's reasoning. In expulsion cases however, such a consistent approach, where genuine significance is attached to the principle, is absent. In what follows, the case law of the Court on two specific subjects will be discussed. First, the use of the best interests principle in cases where the expulsion of a parent might entail a violation of the right to family life is highlighted.³⁵ Secondly, the case law on a possible violation of the prohibition of torture or inhuman or degrading treatment by an expulsion measure is examined. These different strands of case law will demonstrate that the Court's use of the best interests principle in expulsion cases is sometimes inconsistent and sometimes even non-existent.

2.1. THE EXPULSION OF A PARENT AND THE RIGHT TO FAMILY LIFE

As regards the expulsion of a parent and a possible violation of the right to family life, the first judgment of interest is *Üner*. In this case the Grand Chamber held for the first time that when a parent is expelled because of criminal offences, the best interests of his or her child(ren) are one of the criteria that should be taken into account when ascertaining whether the expulsion measure was necessary in a democratic society.³⁶ More specifically, regard should be had to the difficulties these children will encounter if they were to follow the expelled parent. In subsequent case law, the principle was also introduced as a criterion in cases where the parent is expelled for non-criminal offences, like administrative breaches of immigration law.³⁷ Even though it can only be encouraged that such express reference is made to the principle in the case law, in practice the child's best interests are dealt with very briefly. From the existing cases it becomes clear that the Court evaluates the children's interests based on three factors: their age, their ties to the host as well as to the receiving country and the effective family bonds. This article by no means intends to give an exhaustive overview of this case law,³⁸ but aims to draw attention to some of the inconsistencies that exist in the Court's application of these three factors.

---

34   ECtHR, *V.M. v Belgium*, no 60125/11, 07.07.2015, paras. 139–163.
35   The question how the best interest principle is used in cases where the child itself is the subject of an expulsion decision falls outside the scope of this article. The landmark case in this connection is ECtHR, *Maslov v Austria*, no 1638/03 [GC], 23.06.2008.
36   ECtHR, *Üner v Belgium*, no 46410/99 [GC] 18.10.2006, para. 58.
37   For example ECtHR, *Nunez v Norway*, no 55597/09, 28.06.2011, para. 78.
38   For a more in-depth overview see M. LELOUP, 'The principle of the best interests of the child in the expulsion case law of the European Court of Human Rights: Procedural rationality as a remedy for inconsistency' (2019) 37(1) *Netherlands Quarterly of Human Rights*; C. SMYTH (2015), 'The Best Interests of the Child', *supra* note 13, pp. 71–103.

With regard to the child's age, the Court is of the opinion that younger children will have less developed ties to their host country and will therefore have less trouble growing accustomed to a new environment. Because of this, their best interests will less intensely oppose the expulsion. In this connection the Court has often referred to the young and adaptable age of the parent's child(ren).[39] Some critical remarks on the use of this criterion could be made. It should first of all be pointed out that the Court is inconsistent at which point it counts this age.[40] In its case law, examples can be found when it counts the child's age at the final domestic proceedings,[41] when the parent is actually expelled[42] or exceptionally when the case comes before the Court.[43] Moreover, in some judgments the Court neglects to consider the child's age in its reasoning altogether.[44] This is surprising because the outcome of these cases might have been different if the Court had incorporated this aspect into its considerations.[45] Finally, it should be noted that when the Court does take the child's age into account, it does not always do so in a consistent manner. Ordinarily, the Court considers very young children adaptable.[46] Conversely, children that are close

---

[39] For example ECtHR, *Salija v Switzerland*, no 55470/10, 10.01.2017, para. 50; ECtHR, *Adeishvili v Russia*, no 43553/10, 16.10.2014, para. 83; ECtHR, *Palanci v Switzerland*, no 2607/08, 25.03.2014, para. 61; ECtHR, *S.J. v Belgium*, no 70055/10, 27.02.2014, para. 142; ECtHR, *Kissiwa Koffi v Switzerland*, no 38005/07, 15.11.2012, para. 68; ECtHR, *Bajsultanov v Austria*, no 54131/10, 12.06.2012, para. 27; ECtHR, *Arvelo Aponte v the Netherlands*, no 28770/05, 03.11.2011, para. 60; ECtHR, *Omojudi v UK*, no 1820/08, 24.11.2009, para. 46; ECtHR, *Onur v UK*, no 27391/07, 17.02.2009, para. 60; ECtHR, *Darren Omoregie and others v Norway*, no 265/07, 31.07.2008, para. 66; ECtHR, *Üner v Belgium*, no 46410/99 [GC] 18.10.2006, para. 64; ECtHR (dec.), *Amara v the Netherlands*, no 6914/02, 05.10.2004.

[40] T. SPIJKERBOER, 'Structural Instability: Strasbourg Case Law on Children's Family Reunion', (2009) 11(3) *European Journal of Migration and Law*, p. 289.

[41] ECtHR, *Palanci v Switzerland*, no 2607/08, 25.03.2014, para. 61; ECtHR, *Kaya v Germany*, no 31753/02, 28.06.2007, para. 57; ECtHR, *Yildiz v Austria*, no 37295/97, 31.10.2002, para. 44.

[42] ECtHR, *Maslov v Austria*, no 1638/03 [GC] 23.06.2008, para. 93; ECtHR (dec.), *Akbulut v UK*, no 53586/08, 10.04.2012, para. 23.

[43] For example ECtHR, *Neulinger and Shuruk v Switzerland*, no 41615/07 [GC] 06.07.2010, para. 145; See also the dissenting opinion Judge Sajo in ECtHR, *Berisha v Switzerland*, no 948/12, 30.07.2013.

[44] For example ECtHR, *Zakayev and Safanova v Russia*, no 11870/03, 11.02.2010.

[45] See for example ECtHR, *Paposhvili v Belgium*, no 41615/07, 17.04.2014. Here, no reference was made to the age of the children, who were six and 14 years old. In particular, the latter is too old to still be considered of an adaptable age. His age would therefore object to the parent's expulsion. However, the Court did not find a violation of Article 8 ECHR in this case. Another example is ECtHR, *Sezen v the Netherlands*, no 50252/99, 31.01.2006. Here the children were two and eight years old, which ordinarily would be considered adaptable and would not object to an expulsion. However, the Court – without making a reference to the children's age – found a violation of Article 8 ECHR. This was brought to the attention by the dissenting Judges Thomassen and Jungswiert.

[46] For example a one-year-old child, see ECtHR, *Arvelo Aponte v the Netherlands*, no 28770/05, 03.11.2011. or a two-year-old child, see ECtHR, *Adeishvili v Russia*, no 43553/10, 16.10.2014.

to maturity are found to be no longer of an adaptable age.[47] However, whereas the Court has on multiple occasions found children of six years old[48] or even older[49] to be adaptable, it seems to have come to the opposite conclusion in a recent case. In *Kolonja* the Court had to rule on the expulsion of the father of a six-year-old boy who had been living in Greece his entire life and went to school there. According to the Court, the father's expulsion would therefore mean that he would grow up without a father and found a violation of Article 8 ECHR.[50] It is apparent that the Court in this connection does not refer to the adaptable age of the child and even seems to consider that the six-year-old boy could not adapt to life in Albania.

The second factor the Court takes into account are the child's ties to both the host and the receiving country. When a child has very strong social and cultural ties to his or her host country, but has virtually no ties to the receiving country, his or her best interests will more strongly oppose the expulsion. Conversely, when a child already has some ties to the receiving state, the expulsion will less likely be considered against his or her best interests.[51] Yet again, however, the Court is inconsistent in its application of this factor and sometimes neglects to consider this aspect.[52]

From these examples,[53] it becomes clear that the Court is not consistent in its application of the criteria to assess whether it is in the child's best interests to follow the expelled parent. However, even when it comes to the conclusion that the expulsion is not in the best interests of the child(ren), it will not automatically find a violation of Article 8 ECHR. The child's interests are namely

---

[47] See for example ECtHR, *Omojudi v UK*, no 1820/08, 24.11.2009, para. 46. Where three children, respectively 16, 17 and 20 years old were found not to be adaptable.
[48] See among others ECtHR, *S.J. v Belgium*, no 70055/10, 27.02.2014, para. 142; ECtHR, *Bajsultanov v Austria*, no 54131/10, 12.06.2012, para. 27; ECtHR, *Üner v Belgium*, no 46410/99 [GC] 18.10.2006, para. 64.
[49] See ECtHR, *Salija v Switzerland*, no 55470/10, 10.01.2017, para. 50. In this case two children of nine and five years old were considered adaptable.
[50] ECtHR, *Kolonja v Greece*, no 49441/12, 19.05.2016, para. 56.
[51] In this connection the Court has taken into account that the child already knows the language, see ECtHR, *Palanci v Switzerland*, no 2607/08, 25.03.2014, para. 61 or the culture, see ECtHR, *Salija v Switzerland*, no 55470/10, 10.01.2017, para. 50 or has the nationality, see ECtHR, *Paposhvili v Belgium*, no 41615/07, 17.04.2014, para. 152 of the receiving country.
[52] ECtHR, *Bajsultanov v Austria*, no 54131/10, 12.06.2012; ECtHR, *Darren Omoregie and others v Norway*, no 265/07, 31.07.2008; ECtHR, *Üner v Belgium*, no 46410/99 [GC] 18.10.2006.
[53] One other example that can be mentioned here is the Court's views on the impact an expulsion has on a child's education. The Court held that the fact that the educational opportunities are better in the host country than in the receiving state should not be taken into account. See: ECtHR, *S.J. v Belgium*, no 70055/10, 27.02.2014, para. 142. However, in *Palanci* the Court stated that the receiving country had a well-established education system and interpreted this as a factor in favour of expulsion. See ECtHR, *Palanci v Switzerland*, no 2607/08, 25.03.2014, para. 61. It should be noted that it is inconsistent to state that bad education in the receiving country is irrelevant, while simultaneously interpreting good education as a positive factor for expulsion.

only one of the criteria that the Court takes into account when deciding on the proportionality of an expulsion decision and can be outweighed by the state's interests in migration control.[54] The threshold set out by the Court is very high. It will only find a violation of Article 8 ECHR when there are 'insurmountable obstacles' for the child to follow the expelled parent.[55] The Court sometimes even expressly states that following the expelled parent would not be in the child's best interests but raises no insurmountable obstacles.[56]

Some serious questions could be raised by the use of this threshold. It appears that the prerequisite of insurmountable obstacles is fundamentally at odds with the principle of best interests of the child as a primary consideration. Even though there is no consensus on the precise scope of the best interests principle and the weight that has to be prescribed to it, it is generally accepted that the interests of the child should receive some hierarchical primacy.[57]

---

[54] C. SMYTH (2015), 'The Best Interests of the Child', *supra* note 13, p. 72.

[55] See among many others ECtHR, *Bajsultanov v Austria*, no 54131/10, 12.06.2012, para. 90; ECtHR, *Nacic and others v Sweden*, no 16567/10, 15.05.2012, para. 85; ECtHR, *Antwi v Norway*, no 26940/10, 14.02.2012, para. 98; ECtHR (dec.), *Zuluaga v UK*, no 20443/08, 18.01.2011, para. 31; ECtHR, *Darren Omoregie and others v Norway*, no 265/07, 31.07.2008, para. 66; ECtHR, *Konstatinov v the Netherlands*, no 16351/03, 26.04.2007, para. 52; ECtHR (dec.), *Useinov v the Netherlands*, no 61292/00, 11.04.2006; ECtHR (dec.), *Amara v the Netherlands*, no 6914/02, 05.12.2004. Note that in some cases the Court does not verify if there were insurmountable obstacles, but rather if there were 'obstacles' see ECtHR (dec.), *Priya v Denmark*, no 13594/03, 06.07.2006, 'major obstacles', see ECtHR, *Palanci v Switzerland*, no 2607/08, 25.03.2014, para. 61; ECtHR (dec.), *Ramos Andrade v the Netherlands*, no 53675/00, 06.07.2004 or if 'it could realistically be expected from the spouse and children to move to the other country', see ECtHR, *Sezen v the Netherlands*, no 50252/99, 31.01.2006, para. 47.

[56] ECtHR, *Antwi v Norway*, no 26940/10, 14.02.2012, paras. 97–98. See also ECtHR, *S.J. v Belgium*, no 70055/10, 27.02.2014, para. 142.

[57] For example H. STALFORD, 'The Broader Relevance of Features of Children's Rights Law: The 'Best Interests of the Child' Pinciple', in E. BREMS, E. DESMET and W. VANDENHOLE (eds.), *Children's Rights Law in the Global Human Rights Landscape. Isolation, Inspiration, Integration?*, Routledge, London 2017, p. 39; A.-C. RASSON, 'L'Intérêt de l'Enfant, Valeur Fondamentale?', in A. HOC, S. WATTIER and G. WILLEMS (eds.), *Human Rights as a Basis for Reevaluating and Reconstructing the Law*, Bruylant, Brussels 2016, p. 352; J. POBJOY, 'The Best Interests of the Child Principle as an Independent Source of International Protection', pp. 357–358; C. SMYTH (2015), 'The Best Interests of the Child, *supra* note 13, pp. 100–101; M. FREEMAN, 'Article 3: the Best Interests of the Child', in A. ALEN, J. VANDE LANOTTE, E. VERHELLEN, F. ANG, E. BERGHMANS, M. VERHEYDE and B. ABRAMSOM (eds.), *Commentary on the United Nations Convention on the Rights of the Child*, Brill Nijhoff, Leiden 2007, p. 61; S. DETRICK, *A Commentary on the United Nations Convention on the Rights of the Child*, Martinus Nijhoff, Leiden 1999, p. 91. The ComRC took a similar point of view in its General Comment on Article 3 CRC, see ComRC, General Comment No. 14 *supra* note 9, para. 37. This approach is furthermore in accordance with the *travaux préparatoires* of the CRC, see Report of the Working Group on a Draft Convention on the Rights of the Child, UN Doc. E/CN.4/L.1575, para. 24. Finally it should be noted that the ECtHR itself has stated that there is 'a broad consensus – including in international law – in support of the idea that in all decisions concerning children, their best interests are of *paramount importance*' (emphasis added), see ECtHR, *Neulinger and Shuruk v Switzerland*, no 41615/07 [GC], 06.07.2010, para. 135. Most recently ECtHR, *Mohamed Hasan v Norway*, no 27496/15, 26.04.2018, para. 149.

It can hardly be asserted that the children's interests receive such a prominent position when it has to be demonstrated that it would be insurmountable for them to relocate to another country. Rather, it appears that the balancing exercise is set in favour of the state's interests, while the best interests principle is often merely paid lip service to.[58]

2.2. THE PROHIBITION OF TORTURE OR INHUMAN OR DEGRADING TREATMENT

Whereas the principle of the best interests of the child is used – albeit inconsistently – in expulsion cases infringing on the right to family life, such practice is absent in cases where the expulsion might raise an issue under the prohibition of torture or inhuman or degrading treatment. Not a single case can be found in which the Court includes the principle in its reasoning concerning an application based on Article 3 ECHR. A telling example can be found in *S.J.*, where a single mother with three children claimed that their expulsion to Nigeria entailed a violation of Articles 3 and 8 of the Convention. In its judgment, the Court did not mention the best interests principle once in its considerations regarding Article 3 of the Convention but referred to it several times in its balancing exercise of Article 8.[59] Several other examples can be found as well of cases where the Court did not invoke the best interests principle in cases where a child's expulsion might violate Article 3 ECHR, even though the applicant expressly mentioned these interests in his or her application.[60]

---

[58] C. DRAGHICI, *Legitimacy of Family Rights in Strasbourg Case Law 'Living Instrument' or Extinguished Sovereignty?*, Hart Publishing, Oxford 2017, pp. 378–379. See also the dissenting opinion of Judge Sicilianos, joined by Judge Lazarova Trajkovska in ECtHR, *Antwi v Norway*, no 26940/10, 14.02.2012. They held that 'Admit[ting] that the impugned measure was "clearly not" in – i.e. against – the best interests of the third applicant, while at the same time affirming that such interests have been duly taken into account seems to pay lip service to a guiding human rights principle'.

[59] ECtHR, *S.J. v Belgium*, no 70055/10, 27.02.2014. The Court stated that the interests of the children were not 'not capable of altering its assessment of the threshold of severity required by Article 3, but fall within the scope of the assessment of the situation from the standpoint of Article 8'. Ibid., para. 125.

[60] The clearest example is ECtHR (dec.), *Ovdienko Iryna and Ivan v Finland*, no 1383/04, 31.05.2005. Here the first applicant, a mother, explicitly claimed that the expulsion of her and her son, the second applicant, to Ukraine would be against the child's best interests and would entail a violation of Article 3 ECHR. The Court however declared the application inadmissible because it was manifestly ill-founded. It did not refer to the best interests principle once in its reasoning. Other examples are ECtHR, *X. v Switzerland*, no 16744/14, 26.01.2017; ECtHR (dec.), *Giusto, Bornacin and V. v Italy*, no 38972/06, 15.05.2007; ECtHR, *Nsona v the Netherlands*, no 23366/94, 28.11.1996. This final case was criticised in scholarly work because the Court's judgment did not attach sufficient weight to the best interests of the child: E. NYKANEN, 'Protecting Children? The European Convention on Human Rights and Child Asylum Seekers', (2001) 3(3) *European Journal of Migration and Law*, pp. 337–338;

Another case that should be mentioned in this regard is *Tarakhel*.[61] In this case, a family with six children – all between two and fourteen years old – left Iran for Turkey, after which they went to Italy. From there they travelled to Switzerland, where they applied for asylum. According to the rules laid out in the Dublin Regulation[62] the country where the asylum seekers first enter the European Union is responsible for handling the asylum application.[63] The Swiss authorities, relying on this regulation, rejected the asylum claim and made an order for the family's removal to Italy. The family, however, stated that the reception facilities in Italy were overcrowded and unsafe for small children and held that their referral would expose them to inhuman or degrading treatment. The case was eventually brought before the Grand Chamber of the European Court of Human Rights.

The Court started off its reasoning by reiterating its well-established case law that the expulsion of an asylum seeker may give rise to a violation of Article 3 ECHR if substantial grounds have been shown that the person concerned faces a real risk of being subjected to torture or inhuman or degrading treatment in the receiving country.[64] In *M.S.S.* the Court had decided that such a situation might be present if asylum seekers, who are completely dependent on the receiving state, find themselves in a situation of extreme want and poverty.[65] In this connection the Court also attaches considerable importance to the vulnerability of asylum seekers.[66] For minors, this vulnerability is even stronger and it is important to note that their extreme vulnerability takes precedence over their status of illegal immigrant.[67]

When the Court applied these principles to the case of *Tarakhel*, it came to the conclusion that the situation in the Italian reception arrangements were

---

U. KILKELLY, 'Nsona v. the Netherlands. The Treatment of Minors and the European Convention on Human Rights', (1996) 8(4) *International Journal of Refugee Law*, p. 648.

61   ECtHR, *Tarakhel v Switzerland*, no 29217/12 [GC], 04.11.2014.
62   Regulation (EU) No 604/2013 of the European Parliament and the Council of 26 June 2013 establishing the criteria and mechanisms for determining the Member State responsible for examining an application for international protection lodged in one of the Member States by a third-country national or a stateless person [2013] OJ L180/31.
63   It should be noted that the ECJ made an important exception to this rule based on Article 24 of the Charter and the best interests of the child. In *Ma and others* the Court ruled that the best interests of the child oppose the referral to the first country when an unaccompanied minor already asked for asylum in a second one. According to the Court it is in the child's best interests to conclude the asylum proceedings as quickly as possible and the referral would needlessly take more time. CJEU, *MA and others/Secretary of State for the Home Department*, Case C-648/11, 06.06.2013, ECLI:EU:C:2013:367, paras. 57–66.
64   For example ECtHR, *M.S.S. v Belgium and Greece*, no 30696/09 [GC], 21.01.2011, para. 365; ECtHR, *Saadi v UK*, no 37201/06 [GC], 28.02.2008, para. 152; ECtHR, *Soering v UK*, no 14038/88 [GC] 07.07.1989, paras. 90–91.
65   ECtHR, *M.S.S. v Belgium and Greece*, supra note 64, paras. 252–253.
66   Ibid., para. 251.
67   ECtHR, *Tarakhel v Switzerland*, no 29217/12 [GC] 04.11.2014, para. 99; ECtHR, *Popov v France*, nos 39472/07 and 39474/07, 19.01.2012, para. 91.

not as bad as the ones in Greece during the *M.S.S.* case.⁶⁸ A referral to Italy in compliance with the Dublin Regulation would therefore not automatically entail a violation of Article 3 ECHR.⁶⁹ However, the Court also noted that there was a distinct possibility that the family on arrival may be left without accommodation or would be accommodated in overcrowded facilities without any privacy, or even in insalubrious or violent conditions. Having regard to the extreme vulnerability of the children, the Court ruled that a referral to Italy would be in breach of Article 3 ECHR if the Swiss authorities did not first obtain individual guarantees from the Italian authorities that the family would be taken charge of in a manner adapted to the age of the children and that the family would be kept together.⁷⁰ The Court has confirmed this approach in its subsequent case law.⁷¹

It is clear that the entire ruling is based on concerns about the children's protection and well-being.⁷² At the core of the *Tarakhel* case lies the concern that in case of referral, the children would be subjected to treatment that was against their best interests: separation from their family and possibly reception facilities that were not adapted to their age.⁷³ In this connection it is peculiar to note that the Court has not once referred to the best interests principle in its reasoning, even more so seeing as the third party interveners expressly mentioned this principle in their observations.⁷⁴ Rather, the Court repeatedly mentioned the notion of vulnerability, a concept that more recently has gained prevalence in the Court's case law.⁷⁵ This vulnerability provides the basis for stronger protection⁷⁶ and for the special rights they enjoy under the CRC.⁷⁷

---

68   See ECtHR, *M.S.S. v Belgium and Greece*, supra note 64, paras. 249–263.
69   ECtHR, *Tarakhel v Switzerland*, supra note 67, paras. 114–115.
70   Ibid., para. 122.
71   See for example ECtHR (dec.), *S.M.H. v the Netherlands*, no 5868/13, 17.05.2016). In this case a mother with three minor children was going to be referred to Italy. However, because the Dutch government had contacted the Italian authorities to make sure there was space for her and her children in the reception facilities, the claim was manifestly ill-founded. See for two very similar cases ECtHR (dec.), *N.A. v Denmark*, no 15636/16, 28.06.2016 and ECtHR (dec.), *J.A. v the Netherlands*, no 21459/14, 03.11.2015.
72   Proof of this can be found in the decision ECtHR, *A.M.E. v the Netherlands*, no 51428/10, 13.01.2015. In this case, the Court found a claim based on Article 3 ECHR of an asylum seeker who was going to be referred from the Netherlands to Italy manifestly ill-founded. The Court stated that 'unlike the applicants in the case of Tarakhel, who were a family with six minor children, the applicant is an able young man with no dependents'.
73   ECtHR *Tarakhel v Switzerland*, supra note 67, para. 120.
74   Ibid., paras. 83–86.
75   F. IPPOLITO and S. I. SANCHEZ, 'Introduction', in F. IPPOLITO and S. I. SANCHEZ (eds.), *Protecting Vulnerable Groups*, Hart Publishing, Oxford 2015, p. 2; C. RUET, 'La vulnérabilité dans la jurisprudence de la Cour européenne des droits de l'homme', (2015) 6(5) *Revue Trimestrielle des Droits de l'Homme*, p. 318.
76   ECtHR, *Khlaifia v Italy*, no 16483/12 [GC] 15.12.2016, para. 161; ECtHR, *Tarakhel v Switzerland*, supra note 67, para. 119.
77   J. TOBIN, 'Understanding Children's Rights: A Vision beyond Vulnerability', (2015) 84(2) *Nordic Journal of International Law*, p. 164.

According to the Committee of the Rights of the Child, a child's vulnerability is an important factor to take into account when determining his or her best interests.[78]

These above-mentioned cases demonstrate that the Court refrains from considering the best interests of the child in expulsion cases where a breach of the prohibition of torture is raised. In one case it even outright refused to consider the best interests of the children.[79] This is remarkable seeing as it does incorporate this principle in its reasoning in expulsion cases involving Article 8 ECHR and in virtually all other cases where children are involved.[80] The reasons for this reluctance are unclear and cannot be inferred from the Court's judgments. One possible explanation is that the Court thinks such incorporation would lower the threshold of Article 3 ECHR too much, trivialising its fundamental nature.[81] Another reason could be that the Court is of the opinion that the relative threshold of Article 3 ECHR allows adequate protection of the child's interests, making a reference to the best interests principle superfluous.[82] A third possibility is that the Court believes that the best interests principle implies a weighing of interests, which is incompatible with the absolute nature of the prohibition of torture or inhuman or degrading treatment.

Whether or not it is one of these reasons is uncertain. The negative consequences of this practice on the children, however, are not difficult to imagine. If their best interests are overlooked or not given due weight in cases regarding inhuman or degrading treatment, the expulsion can have detrimental consequences for their physical or psychological well-being. The case of *S.J.* provides a poignant example of this. In this case the asylum application of a mother with three small children – all under seven years old – was rejected and she was subsequently ordered to return to her home country, Nigeria. In the meantime, the mother had been diagnosed with HIV and tried to be granted leave to remain in Belgium on medical grounds. Her request was ultimately

---

[78]   ComRC, General Comment No. 14 *supra* note 9, para. 6.
[79]   ECtHR (dec.), *Hussein Diirshi and others v the Netherlands and Italy*, nos 2314/10, 18324/10, 47851/10 and 51377/10, 10.09.2013, para. 152. In this case the applicant had alleged a violation of his rights under Article 3 CRC. The Court stated that according to Article 19 of the Convention it is only competent to find violations of the ECHR and found the complaint inadmissible. Even though this is of course not incorrect, it is strange that the Court dismisses this argument so rapidly, instead of using the best interests of the child as a guiding principle like it does in other case law.
[80]   See the case law mentioned in *supra* notes 29–34.
[81]   See similarly U. KILKELLY (1996), 'Nsona v. the Netherlands', *supra* note 60, p. 648.
[82]   According to well-established case law, the assessment of the minimum level of severity depends on all the circumstances of the case, such as the duration of the treatment, its physical and mental effects and, in some cases, the sex, age and state of health of the victim. ECtHR, *Saadi v UK*, no 37201/06 [GC], 28.02.2008, para. 134. It is possible that the Court incorporates the child's best interests in this relative threshold, when it considers the age of the victim.

denied, after which she lodged a complaint at the European Court of Human Rights. She held that her expulsion would give rise to a violation of Article 3 of the Convention on account of her illness. The Court, however, ruled that her expulsion did not entail a violation.[83]

Even though the decision that the mother's expulsion did not amount to a violation of Article 3 ECHR was in accordance with the case law of the Court at that time,[84] it is argued here that a violation should have been found in respect of the children. As was pointed out by dissenting Judge Power-Forde, the children in this case would be forced to follow their mother to Nigeria, where they would see her slowly deteriorate and die on account of her illness, after which they would be left as orphans in a country where they knew no one.[85] Given their young age, the vulnerable position they were in and the stress which all of this undoubtedly caused, their expulsion should have been qualified as degrading treatment.[86] By finding no violation in respect of the three children, one can hardly claim that their best interests have been duly taken into account.[87]

It is important to note that in the near future the Court will be forced to take a clear stance on the significance of the best interests principle in expulsion cases regarding Article 3 ECHR. In the communicated case of *M.S. v Slovakia and Ukraine* the applicant – a minor – complained that 'in ordering his expulsion to Afghanistan, the Ukrainian authorities did not consider his best interests as a child and did not make sure that appropriate arrangements were in place in Afghanistan to accept him'.[88] Barring any reason to find this application inadmissible, it will be very interesting to see how the Court rules in this case.

3. A MORE PRINCIPLED USE OF THE PRINCIPLE

The previous section gave an overview of the Court's use of the best interests principle in expulsion cases regarding the right to family life and the prohibition

---

[83] ECtHR, *S.J. v Belgium*, no 70055/10, 27.02.2014, paras. 117–127.
[84] The relevant criteria were set out in the cases, ECtHR, *D v UK*, no 30240/96, 02.05.1997 and ECtHR, *N v UK*, no 26565/05 [GC], 27.05.2008. These criteria made the threshold very high and were strongly criticised in doctrine, see for example F. JULIEN-LAFERRIERE, 'L'Éloignement des Étrangers Malades: Faut-il Préférer les Réalités Budgétaires aux Préoccupations Humanitaires?', (2009) 18(1) *Revue Trimestrielle des Droits de l'Homme*, pp. 261–277. Recently however, this threshold was considerably lowered by the Grand Chamber. See ECtHR, *Paposhvili v Belgium*, no 41615/07 [GC], 13.12.2016.
[85] See dissenting opinion by Judge A. Power-Forde in ECtHR, *S.J. v Belgium*, no 70055/10, 27.02.2014.
[86] Compare U. KILKELLY, *The Child and the European Convention on Human Rights*, Ashgate, Aldershot 1999, p. 231; U. KILKELLY (1996), 'Nsona v. the Netherlands', *supra* note 60, p. 648.
[87] See in a similar sense, J.-P. MARGUENAUD, 'L'Éloignement des Etrangers Malades du Sida: la Cour Européenne des Droits de l'Homme sur "Les Sentiers de la Gloire"', (2014) 23(4) *Revue Trimestrielle des Droits de l'Homme*, pp. 987–988.
[88] ECtHR (communicated), *M.S. v Slovakia and Ukraine*, no 17189/11, 15.01.2016.

of torture or inhuman or degrading treatment. It aimed to demonstrate that in the sphere of expulsion cases the Court refrains from using the principle in its judgments or – when it does use it – does so inconsistently. The judges themselves also seem to disagree on its use, with dissenting opinions stating that either too much[89] or too little importance[90] was attached to the principle in a certain case. Consequently, the interests of the children are sometimes overlooked, which can lead to distressing results like in the *S.J.* case. Nevertheless, there are convincing arguments for the Court to take a more principled approach on the matter. It is argued here that a principled approach implies a constant use of the principle, where the Court always includes the best interests principle in its judgments, while also doing this in a more consistent way. This section will first provide arguments for a constant use of the best interests principle in all expulsion cases. To do this, the question as to why the European Court should incorporate the UN Convention on the Rights of the Child in its case law should first be answered.

3.1. A CONSTANT USE OF THE BEST INTERESTS PRINCIPLE

The Court is of the opinion that the Convention cannot be interpreted and applied in a vacuum, but that it must rather also take into account any relevant rules of international law.[91] It often reiterates that the Convention is a living instrument that should be read in the light of present-day conditions and should be influenced by the developments and commonly accepted standards of the Council of Europe.[92] Furthermore, in accordance with Article 31(3)(c) of the

---

[89] See for example dissenting opinion of Judges Villiger, Mahoney and Silvis. ECtHR, *Jeunesse v the Netherlands*, no 12738/10 [GC], 03.10.2014; dissenting opinion of Judges Mijovic and De Gaetano. ECtHR, *Nunez v Norway*, no 55597/09, 28.06.2011.

[90] In cases regarding the right to family life, see dissenting opinion by Judges Jociene and Karakas in ECtHR, *Berisha v Switzerland*, no 948/12, 30.07.2013. Dissenting opinion by Judges Sicilianos and Lazarova Trajkovska in ECtHR, *Antwi v Norway*, no 26940/10, 14.02.2012. Dissenting opinion by Judge Steiner in ECtHR, *Chair and J.B. v Germany*, no 69735/01, 06.12.2007. See similarly the dissenting opinion by Judge Turkovic in ECtHR, *Ndidi v UK*, no 41215/14, 14.09.2017. In cases regarding the prohibition of torture or inhuman or degrading treatment, see dissenting opinion by Judge A. Power-Forde in ECtHR, *S.J. v Belgium*, no 70055/10, 27.02.2014.

[91] See among many authorities ECtHR, *Nada v Switzerland*, no 10593/08 [GC] 12.09.2012, para. 169; ECtHR, *Neulinger and Shuruk v Switzerland*, no 41615/07 [GC], 06.07.2010, para. 131; ECtHR, *Demir and Baykara v Turkey*, no 34503/97 [GC], 12.11.2008, para. 67; ECtHR, *Fogarty v UK*, no 37112/97 [GC], 21.11.2001, para. 33; ECtHR, *Loizidou v Turkey*, no 15318/89 [GC], 18.12.1996, para. 43.

[92] The Court stated this for the first time in ECtHR, *Tyrer v UK*, no 5856/72, 25.04.1978, para. 31. See for more recent authorities ECtHR, *Vallianatos and others v Greece*, nos 29381/09 and 32684/09 [GC], 07.11.2013, para. 84; ECtHR, *Chirstine Goodwin v UK*, no 28957/95 [GC] 11.07.2002, para. 75.

Vienna Convention on the Law of Treaties (VCLT) it should take into account all relevant rules and principles of international law applicable in relations between the Contracting Parties.[93] Therefore, it holds the opinion that in defining the meaning of terms and notions in the text of the Convention it can and must[94] take into account elements of international law other than the Convention.[95] In general, this method of interpretation allows the Court to include sources external to the Convention into its reasoning and take into account the broader normative environment.[96]

One of these relevant elements of international law is the UN Convention on the Rights of the Child. It is the most generally ratified human rights treaty in the world[97] and has been ratified by all members of the Council of Europe.[98] This unanimous approval of the UN Convention sends an important signal to the Court with regard to the approval of the standards contained therein.[99] The Court has not been blind to this signal. In many cases it has iterated that the Convention articles must be interpreted in light of the requirements of the CRC.[100]

It is thus not disputed that the European Convention should be read in the light of the UN Convention on the Rights of the Child when children are

---

[93]   See for example ECtHR, *Bosphorus Hava Yollari Turizm Ve Ticaret Anonim Sirketi v Ireland*, no 45036/98 [GC], 30.06.2005, para. 150.

[94]   One scholar has raised attention to the fact that the words 'can and must' are one of the most important dicta by the Court in this case. I. ZIEMELE, 'Customary International Law in the Case Law of the European Court of Human Rights – The Method', (2013) 12(2) *The Law & Practice of International Courts and Tribunals*, p. 246.

[95]   ECtHR, *Demir and Baykara v Turkey*, no 34503/97 [GC] 12.11.2008, para. 85.

[96]   V. TZEVELEKOS, 'The Use of Article 31(3)(c) of the VCLT in the Case Law of the ECtHR: An Effective Anti-Fragmentation Tool or a Selective Loophole for the Reinforcement of Human Rights Teleology? Between Evolution and Systemic Integration', (2010) 31(3) *Michigan Journal of International Law*, p. 631. The way in which the Court does this has not been exempt from criticism however. See C. PITEA, 'Interpretation and Application of the European Convention on Human Rights in the Broader Context of International Law: Myth or Reality?' in Y. HAECK and E. BREMS (eds.), *Human Rights and Civil Liberties in the 21st Century*, Springer, Dordrecht 2014, pp. 1–14.

[97]   U. KILKELLY, *The Child and the European Convention on Human Rights*, supra note 86, p. 259.

[98]   The CRC has been signed by every country in the world and has been ratified by all countries except the United States of America, available at http://indicators.ohchr.org, last accessed 28.05.2018.

[99]   M. FOROWICZ, *The Reception of International Law in the European Court of Human Rights*, Oxford University Press, Oxford 2010, p. 123. See for an identical conclusion: C. DRAGHICI (2017), *Legitimacy of Family Rights*, supra note 58, p. 374.

[100] For example, in the sphere of the expulsion of a minor see ECtHR, *Maslov v Austria*, no 1638/03 [GC] 23.06.2008, para. 82. In the sphere of international child abduction, see ECtHR, *X. v Latvia*, no 27853/09 [GC] 26.11.2013, para. 93; ECtHR, *Neulinger and Shuruk v Switzerland*, no 41615/07 [GC] 06.07.2010, para. 132; ECtHR, *Maumousseau and Washington v France*, no 39388/05 [GC] 06.12.2007, para. 60. In the sphere of intercountry adoption: ECtHR, *Harroudj v France*, no 43631/09, 04.10.2012, para. 42; ECtHR, *Wagner and J.M.W.L. v Luxembourg*, no 76240/01, 28.06.2007, para. 120. In the sphere of detention facilities: ECtHR, *Popov v France*, nos 39472/07 and 39474/07, 19.01.2012, para. 139.

involved. In this connection, the best interests principle is especially relevant. The Committee on the Rights of the Child has namely stated that this principle is one of the four fundamental values underlying the Convention[101] and is aimed at the full and effective enjoyment of all the rights in the CRC.[102] It is a general principle of relevance to the implementation of the whole Convention.[103] This means that the best interests principle is important for the interpretation of all the rights in the CRC. When the European Court holds that it should read the European Convention in light of the UN Convention on the Rights of the Child, it should therefore always take the best interests principle into account. Recently, the Court expressly confirmed this idea by stating that 'where children are involved, their best interests must be taken into account'.[104] However, as was clearly demonstrated above, the Court fails to do this consistently in its expulsion case law. It is therefore advisable for the Court to start adopting a more constant use of this principle, where the best interests of all children concerned are verified in each expulsion case involving one or more children. This would have three main advantages.

First of all, it would make sure that the children's interests are always taken into account, even when they are not an applicant before the Court. Currently, the Court is not obliged to examine the impact of an expulsion on such a non-party to the proceedings. In the past, this has led the Court to refuse to consider the child's interests.[105] If the Court consistently uses the best interests principle in expulsion cases, it will be held to consider the impact of the expulsion measure on all children involved, even when they are not an applicant to the proceedings. The consequences of such an approach should not be underestimated. Arguably, the case of *S.J.* might have been decided differently if the Court had expressly taken the interests of the three children into account.

Secondly, such an approach would make the case law of the Court a more coherent whole. As was mentioned above, in other fields the best interests principle is consistently relied on by the Court to ground its reasoning.[106]

---

[101] ComRC, General Comment No. 5 on the General measures of implementation of the Convention on the Rights of the Child, UN Doc., CRC/GC/2003/5, para. 12.
[102] ComRC, General Comment No. 14, *supra* note 9, para. 4.
[103] ComRC, Concluding observation to Jordan in 2006, *supra* note 10, para. 37.
[104] ECtHR, *Strand Lobben v Norway*, no 37283/13, 30.11.2017, para. 108. For a similar statement, see ECtHR, *Neulinger and Shuruk v Switzerland*, no 41615/07 [GC] 06.07.2010, para. 135.
[105] See C. SMYTH (2015), 'The Best Interests of the Child, *supra* note 13, p. 91, references in note 77. With references to ECtHR, *Paposhvili v Belgium*, no 41615/07, 17.04.2014, para. 153; ECtHR (dec.), *I.M. v the Netherlands*, no 41226/98, 25.03.2003. For a very recent example, see ECtHR, *M.A. v France*, no 9373/15, 01.02.2018, paras. 74–76.
[106] Ziemele held that the best interests principle forms part of the scope of Article 8 ECHR. I. ZIEMELE, 'Other Rules of International Law and the European Court of Human Rights: A Question of a Simple Collateral Benefit?', in D. SPIELMANN, M. TSIRLI and P. VOYATZIS (eds.), *The European Convention on Human Rights, a Living Instrument. Essays in Honour of Christos L. Rozakis*, Bruylant, Brussels 2011, p. 745.

Even though there are no convincing arguments for it, this is currently not the case in expulsion cases. By involving the principle in expulsion cases as well, the Court would remedy this inconsistency and increases the protection of child migrants.[107]

Finally, this approach fits best with the idea behind Article 31(3)(c) VCLT and the reason why the Court looks at other international texts and instruments in the first place. This provision of the VCLT namely leads to a 'systemic integration', which improves the coherence in international law.[108] As was mentioned earlier, international law is imbued with the idea that children should be protected.[109] Furthermore, the Committee on the Rights of the Child, together with several other international instruments have stated that the best interests of the child should be taken into account during expulsion proceedings.[110] By consistently applying the best interests principle in expulsion cases, the Court acknowledges that this principle is part of a European 'common ground'[111] that must be taken into account when defining the meaning of the Convention. In this way, the Court searches for common values in various sources of international law and looks how each part of it can be made coherent with each other.[112]

3.2. A CONSISTENT USE OF THE BEST INTERESTS PRINCIPLE

The previous section 3.1 gave arguments for the Court to take the best interests of children involved into account in all its expulsion cases. However, as the

---

[107] Compare U. KILKELLY (2001), 'The Best of Both Worlds for Children's Rights?', *supra* note 23, p. 326.
[108] C. MCLACHLAN, 'The Principle of Systemic Integration and Article 31(3)(c) of the Vienna Convention', (2005) 54(2) *International and Comparative Law Quarterly*, p. 318.
[109] Compare with the speech of T. Hammarberg, Commissioner for Human Rights. He states that 'the idea that society should act in a way as to optimally benefit children is seen as fundamental in all cultures'. T. HAMMARBERG, 'The principle of the best interests of the child – what it means and what it demands from adults', available at https://rm.coe.int/16806da95d, last accessed 28.05.2018.
[110] ComRC, General Comment No. 6 on the treatment of unaccompanied and separated children outside their country of origin, UN Doc. CRC/GC/2005/6, para. 84; Recommendation of the Committee of Ministers to member states on the legal status of persons admitted for family reunification, Rec(2002)4; Article 5 of Directive 2008/115/EC of the European Parliament and of the Council of 16 December 2008 on common standards and procedures in Member States for returning illegally staying third-country nationals; Article 28 of the Directive 2004/58/EC of the European Parliament and of the Council of 29 April 2004 on the right of citizens of the Union and their family members to move and reside freely within the territory of the Member States; Article 15 of the Draft articles on the expulsion of aliens, adopted by the International Law Commission.
[111] ECtHR, *Demir and Baykara v Turkey*, no 34503/97 [GC] 12.11.2008, para. 86.
[112] In this sense G. LETSAS, 'Strasbourg's Interpretive Ethic: Lessons for the International Lawyer', (2010) 21(3) *European Journal of International Law*, p. 523.

above-mentioned case law on the right to family life has made clear, this is no guarantee for a consistent application of this principle. The argument could nonetheless be raised that the Court cannot shoulder all the blame for this. As an international court with a virtually exclusively written procedure, it is inherently in an ill-equipped position to assess a child's best interests in a given situation. As the Court has regularly noticed itself, the national authorities have the benefit of having direct contact with the persons concerned.[113] The task of assessing the best interests of the child in a given case should therefore primarily fall to these domestic authorities.[114]

The question then arises how the Court can sufficiently safeguard the child's best interests in its judgments while retaining consistency in its case law. A possible answer may lie in the procedural turn the Court has been taking for the last couple of years.[115] During a procedural review the Court looks at the decision-making process of the national authorities, rather than conducting a substantive proportionality review itself.[116] A similar approach could be introduced with regard to the best interests principle. Rather than making its own assessment of what would be in the best interests of the child in each given case, the Court leaves this to the national authorities and subsequently verifies whether due attention was given to these interests.

In the past, the Court has sometimes applied the best interests principle in such a manner.[117] However, in expulsion cases such a procedural approach has

---

[113] ECtHR, *El Ghatet v Switzerland*, no 56971/10, 08.11.2016, para. 47; ECtHR, *Neulinger and Shuruk v Switzerland*, no 41615/07 [GC], 06.07.2010, para. 138.

[114] Recently Kalverboer, Beltman, Van Os and Zijlstra have designed a model to assess the best interests of a child in a migration context. M. KALVERBOER, D. BELTMAN, C. VAN OS and E. ZIJLSTRA, 'The Best Interests of the Child in Cases of Migration', (2017) 25(1) *International Journal of Children's Rights*, pp. 114–139. More generally, regard could be had to UNCHR, 'Guidelines on determining the best interests of the child', 2008, available at http://www.unhcr.org/4566b16b2.pdf, last accessed 28.05.2018.

[115] See for a more thorough description of this procedural turn: P. POPELIER and C. VAN DE HEYNING, 'Subsidiarity Post-Brighton: Procedural Rationality as an Answer?', (2017) 30(1) *Leiden Journal of International Law*, pp. 5–23; O.M. ARNARDOTTIR, 'The "Procedural Turn" under the European Convention on Human Rights and Presumptions of Convention Compliance', (2017) 15(1) *International Journal of Constitutional Law*, pp. 9–35; E. BREMS, 'The "Logics" of Procedural-type Review by the European Court of Human Rights', in J. GERARDS and E. BREMS (eds.), *Procedural Review in European Human Rights Cases*, Cambridge University Press, Cambridge 2017, pp. 17–39; A. NUSSBERGER, 'Procedural Review by the ECHR: View from the Court', in J. GERARDS and E. BREMS (eds.), *Procedural Review in European Human Rights Cases*, Cambridge University Press, Cambridge 2017, pp. 161–176.

[116] J. GERARDS, 'The European Court of Human Rights and the National Courts: Giving Shape to the Notion of "Shared Responsibility"', in J. GERARDS and J. FLEUREN (eds.), *Implementation of the European Convention on Human Rights and of the Judgments of the ECtHR in National Case-law*, Intersentia, Cambridge 2014, pp. 13–94.

[117] See for example ECtHR, *X. v Latvia*, no 27853/09 [GC] 26.11.2013. See for recent examples, ECtHR, *Mohamed Hasan v Switzerland*, no 27496/15, 26.04.2018, paras. 158–136; ECtHR, *Lazoriva v Ukraine*, no 6878/14, 17.04.2018, para. 69; ECtHR, *Magomadova v Russia*,

so far been absent, since the Court applied the principle as a substantive right. Only in some of the most recent cases pertaining to migration, does the Court seem to apply a procedural review towards the principle.[118] Such an approach can be encouraged as it provides several considerable advantages.

Most importantly it allows for a more consistent use of the best interests principle. The inconsistency in the Court's current case law namely stems from its practice of assessing the child's interests itself, based on the child's age, country ties and family bonds.[119] In a procedural review towards the best interests principle, this assessment would fall to the national authorities. The Court then only has to verify whether the decision taken by these authorities took due account of the interests of the child(ren) involved.[120] If no such assessment was made on the national level, or if it was insufficient, the Court can find a violation of the fundamental right that was invoked. Conversely, when the Court concludes that this assessment was diligently performed, no violation can be found on account of the child(ren)'s interests.[121] In this way, the Court can indirectly and consistently enforce adherence to the best interests principle.

A second advantage of this approach is that it can be applied in all expulsion cases, irrespective of the fundamental right at issue.[122] As was demonstrated above, both the national authorities and the Court are in principle required to incorporate the child's interests as a factor in their decisions. However, the

---

no 77546/14, 10.04.2018, para. 69; ECtHR, *Leonov v Russia*, no 77180/11, 10.04.2018, para. 72; ECtHR, *Malinin v Russia*, no 70135/14, para. 71

[118] For example ECtHR, *Guliyev and Sheina v Russia*, no 29790/14, 17.04.2018, para. 58; ECtHR (dec.), *A.L. v UK*, no 32207/16, 13.03.2018, para. 46; ECtHR, *Ejimson v Germany*, no 58681/12, 01.03.2018, para. 62; ECtHR, *Ndidi v UK*, no 41215/14, 14.09.2017, para. 80; ECtHR (dec.), *Alam v Denmark*, no 33809/15, 06.06.2017, paras. 33–37; ECtHR, *El Ghatet v Switzerland*, no 56971/10, 08.11.2016, para. 53.

[119] See above 2.1.

[120] This means that the Court will sometimes still have to assess what the interests of the child demand in a certain case. Indeed, one of the dangers inherent in the procedural review in general is that an acceptable decision-making process does not irrefutably lead to an outcome that is acceptable under human rights law, making a substantive assessment inevitable in some cases. E. BREMS, 'Procedural Protection: An Examination of Procedural Safeguards Read into Substantive Convention Rights', in J. GERARDS and E. BREMS (eds.), *Shaping Rights in the ECHR: The Role of the European Court of Human Rights in Determining the Scope of Human Rights*, Cambridge University Press, Cambridge 2013, 159. However, in most of the cases the procedural approach described here will yield clear results. It will therefore still lead to a more consistent case law.

[121] Of course, this does not mean that no violation can be found for another reason pertaining to the case at hand.

[122] It is possible – albeit quite rare – that an expulsion case concerning children raises an issue under a fundamental right other than the right to family life or the prohibition of torture or inhuman or degrading treatment. One could think of an expulsion to a country where the child is likely to be subjected to child labour (Article 4 ECHR). A procedural review of the child's best interests allows for the Court to safeguard these interests in this kind of cases in the same way as in an expulsion case concerning Article 3 ECHR or Article 8 ECHR. See *supra* note 24.

absolute nature of the prohibition of torture or inhuman or degrading treatment and the relative nature of the right to family life make it difficult to make this assessment in a comparable manner. In a procedural approach however, this difficulty disappears. Because the Court only has to verify whether due consideration was afforded to the interests of the child in a given case, it no longer has to balance them to the other interests at hand. This way, the best interests principle can also be incorporated in cases concerning Article 3 ECHR, without lowering the threshold of the minimum level of severity.

These advantages notwithstanding, the Court will have to make sure that this procedural review does not become a formality, where a mere mention of the child's best interests in the domestic decision will be enough to persuade the Court. It is important that the national authorities do not merely pay lip service to the best interests principle without giving proper weight to the interests of the child(ren) concerned. From the available case law, it appears the Court retains some form of review, by finding a violation of Article 8 ECHR when the national authorities neglected to provide proper reasoning concerning the best interests of the child.[123] This stance can be commended, and the Court should continue to do this. Similarly, it should beware not to make its procedural review too brief.[124] The decision of *Alam v Denmark* gives an example of a sufficient procedural review by the Court. In this decision it held that '[the City Court] noted the children's age, which had significant importance when compared with the sentence imposed [...], and found that considerations for the applicant's children could not lead to another decision. It made an overall assessment, taking into account especially that the applicant had had all her upbringing, schooling and education in Denmark, that she had maintained a real attachment to Pakistan and Pakistani culture, that she had two children in Denmark, and that she had been convicted of very serious crimes'.[125] By providing extensive reasoning in its judgments, the Court can authoritatively guide the national authorities on what constitutes an adequate assessment of the child's interests. Thus it sets out guidelines for the protection of human rights and encourages the strengthening of human rights protection at the national level.[126]

---

[123] See ECtHR, *El Ghatet v Switzerland*, no 56971/10, 08.11.2016, para. 53. See similarly: ECtHR, *Jeunesse v the Netherlands*, no 12738/10 [GC] 03.10.2014, para. 120. However, see the dissenting opinion of Judge Turkovic in ECtHR, *Ndidi v UK*, no 41215/14, 14.09.2017.

[124] See for example ECtHR (dec.), *A.L. v UK*, no 32207/16, 13.03.2018, para. 46. Here the Court merely stated that 'it was considered that the best interests of her minor children (including the applicant) were to live with and be brought up by their parents [in Nigeria]'. In this case, the Court ruled that the complaint was manifestly ill-founded and declared it inadmissible. Even though this decision appears to be correct, because the judgment of the national court was in conformity with the Court's case law, it would be advisable to give a more thorough reasoning regarding the best interests of the child.

[125] ECtHR (dec.), *Alam v Denmark*, no 33809/15, 06.06.2017, para. 33. (citation omitted).

[126] See more comprehensively F. KRENC, '"Dire le Droit", "Rendre la Justice". Quelle Cour européenne des Droits de l'Domme?', (2018) 27(2) *Revue Trimestrielle des Droits de l'Homme*,

4. CONCLUSION

Decisions concerning migration law always imply a difficult balancing exercise on a tightrope between policy and protection. When the measure involves children, this exercise becomes all the more difficult. In this kind of cases it is easy to 'let oneself be guided by what is humane rather than what is right'.[127]

This article in no way means to contend that it should be impossible to expel children or their parents. In cases concerning the right to family life exceptional circumstances can indeed cause the interests of the state in immigration control to outweigh the interests of the child. Similarly, it is possible that the consequences of the expulsion do not reach the minimum level of severity required by Article 3 ECHR, even though the expulsion itself is not in the best interests of the child. The child's interests can therefore not be used as a trump card to overrule any conflicting interests.[128] Rather, this article started from the observation that the Court does not systematically verify the best interests of the child when it is dealing with expulsion cases and that even when it does examine them, it does so inconsistently and without attaching significant importance to them. Considering the importance of this principle in international law and the interest the entire world has in protecting children, this article is a call to the Court to start doing this.[129]

In this article, it is argued that the Court should adopt a more principled approach towards the best interests principle. This principled approach consists of both a constant and a consistent use of the principle. A constant use implies that the Court verifies the child's best interests in every expulsion case where children are involved. It was demonstrated that thus far the Court neglects to do this in expulsion cases concerning Article 3 ECHR. In this article several arguments were brought forward for the Court to take the child's interests into account in all its cases. A consistent use of the best interests principle implies that it is used in a similar way in all expulsion cases. The case law that was discussed in this article demonstrates that the current use of the best interests principle by the Court is inconsistent on several aspects. A possible solution to mitigate this problem is for the Court to adopt a procedural approach towards the best interests principle. In such an approach, the Court would not assess the child's best interests in each case itself but would rather verify whether the

---

pp. 311–346; R. SPANO, 'Universality or Diversity of Human Rights? Strasbourg in the Age of Subsidiarity', (2014) 14(3) *Human Rights Law Review*, pp. 487–502.

[127] Dissenting opinion of Judges Villiger, Mahoney and Silvis in ECtHR, *Jeunesse v the Netherlands*, no 12738/10 [GC] 03.10.2014.

[128] See the cases mentioned in *supra* note 14.

[129] For an identical conclusion concerning the Family Reunification case law by the European Court of Justice see M. KLAASSEN and P. RODRIGUES (2017), 'The Best Interests of the Child in EU Family Reunification Law', *supra* note 7, pp. 191–218.

national authorities have afforded due attention to these interests when making their decision. This procedural review towards the principle would enable the Court to safeguard the best interests of all children concerned in all expulsion cases, while keeping its case law clear and consistent.

From this article it becomes clear that the Court's case law can be improved on several key aspects. It can only be hoped that the Court uses opportunities like the one provided in *M.S. v Slovakia and Ukraine* to take steps in the right direction. After all, as the most senior human rights court in the world, a more principled, grown up case law may be expected from it.

SALAFISM IN EUROPE

A Legal and Political Analysis of Human Rights and Security

Claudia V. Elion

1. Introduction 420
2. Shari'a as the Legal Theory Behind Salafism 421
   2.1. United but Divided 422
   2.2. Salafism and Other Islamic Beliefs. 424
3. The ECtHR's Approach Towards (Violent) Religious Extremism 425
   3.1. Ban of a Religious Association after Advocating
        the Use of Violence. 428
   3.2. Anti-Democratic Ideals in the Pursuit of Religious Beliefs 429
   3.3. The ECtHR's Assessment of Shari'a and Legal Pluralism 431
4. Potential Human Rights Issues Arising Out of Contemporary
   Counter-Terrorism Measures 434
   4.1. Belgium 435
   4.2. France. 436
   4.3. The United Kingdom 438
5. Conclusion. 441

ABSTRACT

This article introduces the topic of Salafism, an Islamic fundamentalist ideology, which it puts within the existing framework of European values as enshrined in the European Convention on Human Rights (ECHR). By first discussing the legal theory behind Salafism, being Shari'a, and illustrating some of the many differences within the Salafist movement, this article demonstrates the non-generalisability of both Shari'a and Salafism. It then analyses relevant case law of the European Court of Human Rights (ECtHR) on (violent) religious extremism. It signals that there is need for clarification of the Court's perspective on the institution of Shari'a without political pretensions, as well as on the justifiable State interference on freedoms of religion, expression and association and assembly when it comes to (non-)violent support for Shari'a and Salafism. The article further exposes the dilemma which Western societies face between guaranteeing individual rights and safeguarding national security in the fight against terrorism. It concludes that the European values of democracy, rule of law and human rights are put under pressure by the theocratic, universalist pretensions of Salafists, but also by States potentially undermining human rights in the fight against terrorism.

1. INTRODUCTION

When between 2014 and 2017 the Western world was hit by several terrorist attacks, the general public for the first time heard of the notion 'jihadi-Salafism'. The attacks were claimed by Islamic State (IS), fighting to establish a so-called Islamic caliphate in Syria and North Iraq, inspired by the Islamic fundamentalist theology of Salafism. The terrorist attacks in Paris, Brussels, Nice, Berlin and other places increased the demand of strict security and counter-terrorism measures. Those States which are Party to the ECHR are required to take measures within the framework of human rights and rule of law. This article will examine the following three subjects: the notion of Salafism in Europe; the response of the ECtHR on the issue of Islamic fundamentalism; and the recently taken counter-terrorism measures in the light of Salafism and human rights.

The ECHR aims to avoid unlawful State interference through the established rights to freedom of religion (Article 9 ECHR), freedom of expression (Article 10 ECHR) and freedom of association (Article 11 ECHR), whereas at the same time the general principle not to abuse such rights under the Convention (Article 17 ECHR) applies. The freedoms undoubtedly protect all those on European soil, including those with extremist views, such as adherents of Salafism. However, as many European citizens and policy-makers increasingly believe that Salafism poses a threat to a democratic society, a tension between politics and law might appear unavoidable.[1] On the one hand, the current, real terrorist threat asks for a firm approach in countering extremism, but, on the other hand, all individuals in European societies are protected against the sovereign State through the ECHR.

This contribution to the Yearbook sheds light on the dilemma between, on the one hand, individual freedoms and rights in the modern society and, on the other hand, national security in the context of the threat of Salafist-inspired violence against European values of human rights, democracy and rule of law. This article therefore researches the legal tradition behind Salafism, after which

---

[1] PEW RESEARCH CENTER, 'Europeans Face the World Divided', 13.06.2016, available at http://assets.pewresearch.org/wp-content/uploads/sites/2/2016/06/14095145/Pew-Research-Center-EPW-Report-FINAL-June-13-2016.pdf, last accessed 07.06.2018.

it continues by analysing relevant case law of the ECtHR on (violent) extremism. Some practical examples to illustrate the dilemma between individual rights and public safety are provided by recent counter-terrorism measures of Belgium, France and the United Kingdom, which all are States Parties to the ECHR. It appears that the democratic society and rule of law principles as established in the European Convention on Human Rights are under pressure from both the universalistic, theocratic pretensions of Salafists and the counter-terrorism measures taken by countries as a result of the threat of Salafist-inspired terrorism.

2. SHARI'A AS THE LEGAL THEORY BEHIND SALAFISM

Islam is the youngest of the major world religions. The religion won followers, only from the 7th century CE, starting in today's Saudi Arabic cities of Mecca and Medina. Shari'a is the religious law of the Islamic creed – although it is noteworthy that this 'law' only partly overlaps with the Western notion of law as it also partly corresponds to God's will. Moreover, Shari'a contains a system of religious norms that can create a normative framework for social, economic, moral, educational, intellectual and cultural practices.[2] It is applied in almost every Muslim-majority country, on the basis of the Quran and the habits, sayings and teachings of Prophet Muhammad ('Sunna').[3] Although Shari'a emphasises unity among all Muslims, the majority of rules varies strongly among the jurisdictions as a result of 14 centuries of juristic interpretations, scholarly work and pronouncements by authorities.[4] Due to the great variety of Shari'a interpretation among Muslim societies, it remains important to distinguish between progressive, moderate or conservative approaches to Shari'a. By way of example, the Moroccan legal system differs fundamentally in terms of punishments from the Saudi Arabic system;[5] and the testimony of a woman in

---

[2] A. BLACK, H. ESMAEILI and N. HOSEN, *Modern Perspectives on Islamic Law*, Edward Elgar Publishing Ltd, Cheltenham, 2013; Council on Foreign Relations, 'Sharia and Militancy', 30.11.2010, available at https://www.cfr.org/backgrounder/sharia-and-militancy, last accessed 07.06.2018. There are progressive, moderate or conservative Islamic understandings of Shari'a. Progressive Shari'a interpretations do not necessarily contain anti-democratic principles. Likewise, many Muslims believe Shari'a can exist within a democratic and inclusive framework.
[3] S.S. ALI and J. REHMAN, 'The Concept of Jihad in Islamic International Law', (2005) 10 *Journal of Conflict and Security Law*, pp. 321–343.
[4] R. MEIJER, *Global Salafism: Islam's New Religious Movement*, Columbia University Press, New York 2009.
[5] Since 2011, when a new constitution was adopted, Morocco banned corporal punishment for criminal offences whereas Saudi Arabia still applies such sanctioning.

Egypt in the Family Court is only worth half of that of a man whereas in Oman such unequal treatment generally has been dismissed.[6]

2.1. UNITED BUT DIVIDED

Salafists rely on a distinct interpretation of Shari'a rules. They are united in their common religious creed, which revolves around the obedience to God and a fervent rejection of human reasoning, personal desires and logic. Only their religious interpretation is accepted; other Muslim or 'non-believer' religious views are disregarded. Therefore, religious pluralism according to Salafists is non-existent, not accepted.[7] However, the Salafist movement is not centrally organised and thus no common rules are applied among the Salafist believers. Internal and informal collaboration takes place between religious leaders and organisations as the religious authority is diffuse and subject to change among communities.[8] Paradoxically, the Salafists are united in their beliefs, but divided when it comes to manifestation and practice.

With regard to the manifestation, one can distinguish three factions of contemporary Salafists, which are the so-called 'quietists', 'politicos' and 'jihadists'.[9] In general, quietists reject any political or communal involvement, but instead propagate non-violent methods of purification and education on an individual level. Politicos regard politics as a necessity to attain social justice according to God's ultimate legislation but reject violence. Jihadists transcend politics by adhering to a militant stance to fulfil purification.[10] Their reliance on violence is based on the belief that the current context of Islam in contemporary society is degenerated to such an extent that non-violent measures would not suffice for a return to Islamic sources. A common explanation reads that

---

[6] UNICEF, 'Egypt', 2011, available at https://www.unicef.org/gender/files/Egypt-Gender-Eqaulity-Profile-2011.pdf, last accessed 07.06.2018; The Freedom House, 'Oman', available at https://freedomhouse.org/sites/default/files/inline_images/Oman.pdf, last accessed 07.06.2018.

[7] See for an extensive analysis of Salafism: Q. WIKTOROWICZ, 'Anatomy of the Salafi Movement', (2006) 29(1) *Studies in Conflict & Terrorism*, pp. 207–239.

[8] K.M.H.D. ROEX, *Leven als de Profeet in Nederland: Over de Salafi-beweging en Democratie*, Universiteit van Amsterdam (UvA-DARE), Amsterdam 2013.

[9] Other applicable terms are predicative/purist; political/pietistic; or revolutionary/radical Salafists. S. AMGHAR, 'Salafism and Radicalisation of Young European Muslims', in S. AMGHAR, A. BOUBEKEUR and M. EMERSON (eds.), *European Islam: Challenges for Public Policy and Society*, Centre for European Policy Studies, Brussels 2007; M.I. LAZAR, 'The Salafism in Europe: between Hijra and Jihad', (2009) 9(4) *Studia Politica: Romanian Political Science Review*, pp. 691–707; Q. WIKTOROWICZ (2006), 'Anatomy of the Salafi Movement', *supra* note 7, pp. 207–239.

[10] F. EGERTON, *Jihad in the West: the Rise of Militant Salafism*, Cambridge University Press, Cambridge 2011. The author adopts the term 'militant Salafism' for what is, in this article, called 'jihadi-Salafism'.

jihadi-Salafists 'are part of a faction within a faction, which in turn is marked by deep divisions, especially over the question of violence'.[11]

The notion of jihad is known not only to those jihadi-Salafists, but also to the quietists, politicos and even non-Salafist Muslims. Again, its notion is contested for both its legal and linguistic meaning, as well as its way of implementation and practice.[12] A jihad could take place on an individual level, through which one liberates him-/herself from sins; but also on a communal or societal level, in which a family or community is benefiting from one's ability to help others within its closer circle of company. A last form of jihad, which today is most commonly known in Western European countries, is the struggle against oppression and injustice perpetrated against individuals and the community. Hereby individuals pursuing a jihad can potentially engage in violent activities to liberate the Muslim people as a struggle for the sake of God.[13] Those individuals using the Quran to propagate, perpetrate and justify terrorist violence are also known as jihadi-Salafists.

Jihadi-Salafism as we encounter today, is a recent term for the use of defensive measures to protect the Muslims against outside aggressions and crimes against Islam. The Islamic community, in the view of jihadi-Salafists, is and was threatened at various moments in recent history: during the Israeli-Palestinian conflict; the Serbian genocide against Bosnian Muslims; the US invasion in Afghanistan; by the international interference in Libya; by the Philippine aggression against Muslims in the South-Philippines; etc.[14] One of the most 'famous' contemporary jihadi-Salafists was Osama bin Laden, the leading figure of Al-Qaeda. He and leaders of other groups distinguish sharply between adherents of (jihadi-)Salafism and those who reject its doctrines – hence non-Salafism Muslims can be victim of its militancy as well.[15] Although Al-Qaeda and IS share the Islamic vision of establishing a global caliphate, the execution strategies differ: IS has distinguished itself from Al-Qaeda by focusing on establishing an Islamic State rather than toppling the United States of America.[16]

---

[11] S. COTTEE, 'Mind Slaughter: The Neutralizations of Jihadi Salafism', (2010) 33 *Studies in Conflict & Terrorism*, pp. 330–352.
[12] S. MAHER, *The History of an Idea*, Hurst & Company, London 2016.
[13] A. SAEED, 'Jihad and Violence: Changing Understandings of Jihad among Muslims', in T. COADY and M. O'KEEFE (eds.), *Terrorism and Justice. Moral Argument in a Threatened World*, Melbourne University Press, Melbourne 2002, pp. 72–86.
[14] Q. WIKTOROWICZ and J. KALTNER, 'Killing in the Name of Islam: Al-Qaeda's Justification for September 11', (2003) 10(2) *Middle East Policy Council*, pp. 76–92.
[15] A. MOGHADAM, 'The Salafi-Jihad as a Religious Ideology', (2008) 1(3) *Combating Terrorism Center Sentinel*, pp. 14–16.
[16] COUNTER EXTREMISM PROJECT, 'The Muslim Brotherhood' Ties to ISIS and Al-Qaeda', available at https://www.counterextremism.com/content/muslim-brotherhood%E2%80%99s-ties-isis-and-al-qaeda, last accessed 07.06.2018.

2.2. SALAFISM AND OTHER ISLAMIC BELIEFS

Salafism is only one of countless interpretations of Quran and Sunna. Differentiating between all various creeds is not a simple matter; however, for the sake of clarity the movements closest to Salafism will be explained. The number of interpretations can be brought back to four 'schools' in Sunni Islam, which are the Hanafi, Maliki, Shari'a and Hanbali school – all named after four master-jurists, or teachers, who attracted many followers with their compelling ideas and views of their interpretation and application of Shari'a.[17] They were born in different eras and their ideas have different levels of influence among societies, but the schools are still highly relevant for today's Islam. The supporters compromised to 'agree to disagree', as the interpretations can vary substantially on a certain topic. Salafism developed from the Hanbali school, which adheres to orthodoxy and tradition, minimalising the role of analogical reasoning as a method to solve legal issues.[18] Another stream springing from the Hanbali school is Wahhabism: its leader Muhammad ibn 'Abd al-Wahhab gained influence and support among Muslims by advocating a very strict adherence to traditionalism. Its adherents generally condemn innovations or any deviation from the Quranic rulings.[19]

The modernist Salafists Muhammad 'Abduh, Jamal al-Din al-Afghani and Rashid Rida were arguably most influential for contemporary Salafism. They believed it necessary for Muslims to break with the 'present manifestation of Islam' and the state of the world, and to return to the glorious past of the beginning of Islam to contest and oppose the Western powers in the (Arab) world. They sought general principles for such return in authoritative texts that would permit flexibility and adaptation to novel forms of governance, law and education, while simultaneously adhering to the traditions of the past.[20] Modern Wahhabists, by contrast, focused on fidelity on their view of the creed and cult of the Pious Fathers, who are the Prophet and his most direct successors.[21] Arguably, Wahhabism forms part of Salafism, whereas not all

---

[17] R. MEIJER (2009), *Global Salafism*, supra note 4.
[18] S. HASAN, 'Islamic Jurisprudence: Sources and Traditions Creating Diversity in Human Relationships', in S. HASAN (ed.), *The Muslims World in the 21st Century. Spance, Power and Human Development*, Springer, Dordrecht, 2012, pp. 23–42; International Network to Promote the Rule of Law, 'Islamic Law: Practitioner's Guide', 2013, available at https://namati.org/resources/practitioners-guide-to-islamic-law, last accessed 07.06.2018.
[19] S. HASAN (2012), *Islamic Jurisprudence*, supra note 18, pp. 23–42; R. MEIJER (2009), *Global Salafism*, supra note 4, pp. 1–33.
[20] H. LAUZIERE, *The Making of Salafism: Islamic Reform in the Twentieth Century*, Columbia University Press, New York 2016.
[21] D. COMMINS, 'From Wahhabi to Salafi', in B. HAYKEL, T. HEGGHAMMER and S. LACROIX (eds.), *Saudi Arabia in Transition: insights on Social, Political, Economic and Religious Change*, Cambridge University Press, New York 2015, pp. 151–166.

Salafists are Wahhabists.[22] Furthermore, Wahhabism is the fundamental creed of Saudi Arabia and practised almost solely in Saudi Arabia and, to a certain, less rigid extent, in Qatar, whereas Salafist interpretations of Islam appeal to a large number of Muslims worldwide.[23]

Countless scholarly contributions are written and developed to acquire a complete understanding of the development and practices of Shari'a, modern religious practices and Salafism as both a theocratic ideology and a lifestyle. However, within the scope of this article, it becomes most evident that neither Islam, nor Shari'a or Salafism can be generalised. Interpretation varies substantially among adherents of the Islamic thought including all its sub-movements like Salafism. Seemingly, Salafism is a disparate interpretation of Shari'a with an apparent lack of consensus on the explanation of the Quran and Sunna. Hence, paradoxically, even within the singular approach towards Islam and Shari'a as practiced by Salafists, a wide range of interpretations and applications of the religious-legal rules and traditions occurs; one faction does not prevail over the others.

Some questions can be posed about the basic understanding of Western policy-makers and public officials of the difficulties and tensions within the Islamic creed in the context of the contemporary counter-terrorism dilemma. In this regard, an examination of Western political and legal authorities' acknowledgment of the variability of Islam will be made.

3. THE ECtHR'S APPROACH TOWARDS (VIOLENT) RELIGIOUS EXTREMISM

While the legal framework regarding Salafism and the ECtHR is not (yet) extensive, there is existing jurisprudence on religious fundamentalism.[24] The ECtHR generally has taken complaints under a combination of the articles on freedom of religion (Article 9); freedom of expression (Article 10) and freedom of assembly and association (Article 11). By doing so, it has established that religions *per se* should not be subjected to the protection of the ECHR, but

---

[22] A. MOUSSALI, 'Wahhabism, Salafism and Islamism: Who is the Enemy?', 2009, available at http://conflictsforum.org/briefings/Wahhabism-Salafism-and-Islamism.pdf, last accessed 07.06.2018.

[23] C.M. BLANCHARD, 'The Islamic Traditions of Wahhabism and Salafiyya', CRS Report for Congress, 2005, available at https://www.everycrsreport.com/files/20050210_RS21695_ 4afb647996229fc3304a6f872f8c369d4e3bc605.pdf, last accessed 07.06.2018.

[24] Freedom of religion as enshrined in Article 9 ECHR might appear most accurate for the topic of religious extremism and Salafism. Indeed, freedom of religion has been discussed ever since the *Kokkinakis* case, which granted freedom of religion to Greek Jehovah's Witnesses who were previously restricted for proselytism, see ECtHR, *Kokkinakis v Greece*, no 14307/99, 25.05.1993.

instead practices of the religions can be subject thereto – e.g. political parties,[25] religious associations[26] or religious clothing.[27] Moreover relevant in this regard is the Court's jurisprudence on Article 17, prohibition of the abuse of rights, which could provide a basis for the (il)legitimacy of manifesting publicly or individually an extremist ideology. The general purpose of Article 17 is to prevent individuals or groups with totalitarian aims from exploiting in their own interests the principles enunciated by the Convention.[28] To understand the ECtHR's approach towards the topic of religious fundamentalism and to apply this knowledge on the issue of Salafism in Europe, hereafter four cases will be discussed. But, to start with, the general principles of the ECHR and ECtHR regarding religious fundamentalism and manifestation thereof are outlined.

The ECtHR has further delineated the ECHR's values of constitutionalism, political pluralism and non-discrimination through its 60 years of establishing jurisprudence. It has clearly stated that democracy is the only political system acceptable within the sphere of the ECHR.[29] Democratic and political pluralism are therefore key to European democracies. Moreover, freedom of expression is crucial as a means for the people to oppose the government. In a democracy, not only such ideas favourable to the government can be formulated, but also those which are considered as offending, shocking or disturbing to the State or any sector of the population.[30] Under Article 11, the ECtHR considered that the risk of violence can form sufficient reason for interference by the State. A (political) party proposing change in a seemingly non-violent manner can still form justifiable ground for interference in case the authorities have identified the risk of violence, even when such is not real, current or imminent.[31] The three freedoms are subject to a wide margin of appreciation of the State for a justifiable intervention in its citizens' rights and freedoms. Limitations must be prescribed by law and are necessary in a democratic society. Hence invocation of any legitimate purpose must fulfil the 'rule of law test' and the 'democratic necessity test', although the latter can be flexible as a result of the margin of appreciation.[32]

---

[25] See, for example, ECtHR, *Refah Partisi (the Welfare Party) and Others v Turkey*, nos 41340/98 and 3 others [GC], 13.02.2003.

[26] E.g. ECtHR, *Jehovah's Witnesses of Moscow and Others v Russia*, no 302/02, 10.06.2010.

[27] E.g. ECtHR, *S.A.S. v France*, no 43835/11 [GC], 01.07.014; ECtHR, *Leyla Sahin v Turkey*, no 44774/98 [GC], 10.11.2005.

[28] ECtHR, *Norwood v The United Kingdom*, no 23131/03, 16.11.2004.

[29] E.g. ECtHR, *United Communist Party v Turkey and Others v Turkey*, no 1939/292 [GC] 30.01.1998, para. 45. The ECtHR stated that 'democracy appears to be the only political model contemplated by the Convention and, accordingly, the only one compatible with it'.

[30] ECtHR, *Informationsverein Lentia and Others v Austria*, nos 13914/88 and three others, 24.11.1993, para. 38; ECtHR, *Handyside v The United Kingdom*, no 5493/72, 07.12.1976.

[31] E.g. ECtHR, *United Communist Party of Turkey v Turkey*, supra note 29, para. 49.

[32] S. GREER, *The Exceptions to Articles 8 to 11 of the European Convention on Human Rights*, Human rights files No. 15, Council of Europe Publishing, Strasbourg 1997; C.A. GEARTY,

Article 17 ECHR on the prohibition of the abuse of rights can provide support for the rightfulness of interference against comments amounting to hate speech or undermining the fundamental values of the Convention.[33] Concretely, 'any remark directed against the Convention's underlying values would be removed from the protection of Article 10 (freedom of expression) by Article 17'.[34]

Two preliminary remarks on the topic of Islamic fundamentalism should be made. First, the ECtHR has previously considered that 'the mere fact of defending sharia, without calling for violence to establish it, cannot be regarded as "hate speech"'.[35] The ECtHR stated that, in the context of religious opinions and beliefs, there is an 'obligation to avoid as far as possible expressions that are gratuitously offensive to others and thus an infringement of their rights, and which therefore do not contribute to any form of public debate capable of furthering progress in human affairs'.[36] Offending statements, in the respective case on Shari'a, were not regarded as a call to violence or as 'hate speech' based on religious intolerance. Secondly, on the contrary, there is a limit to freedom of expression regarding Shari'a. In *Belkacem v Belgium* the ECtHR found that remarks with a considerable hateful content had constituted a general and vehement attack on others, which was incompatible with the values of tolerance, social peace and non-discrimination underlying the ECHR.[37]

It appears that remarks on Shari'a can be regarded as protected by freedom of expression, however ambiguity continues to exist between those comments protected under Article 10 and similar remarks amounting to hate speech falling under Article 17. But any State interference, notwithstanding the States' wide margin of appreciation, must be proportionate, serving a legitimate aim and necessary in a democratic society.

These issues have been discussed in-depth by the ECtHR in four recent cases. To start with, the ECtHR found in *Kalifatstaat v Germany*[38] that banning a religious association advocating the use of violence in the pursuit of its religious ideals was legitimised. Consequently, the ECtHR indicated that radical ideas,

---

'The European Convention on Human Rights and the Protection of Civil Liberties. An Overview', (1993) 52(1) *Cambridge Law Journal*, pp. 89, 98–99, 116.

[33] It has often been applied in cases of anti-Semitism, racial hate and (aiming for) totalitarianism. See e.g. ECtHR, *W.P. and Others v Poland*, no 42264/98, 02.09.2004; ECtHR, *Pavel Ivanov v Russia*, no 35222/04, 20.02.2007; ECtHR, *Glimmerveen and Hagenbeek v The Netherlands*, nos 8348/78 and 8506/78, 11.10.1979; ECtHR, *Communist Party of Germany v The Federal Republic of Germany*, no 250/57, 20.07.1957; ECtHR, *B.H., M.W., H.P. and G.K. v Austria*, no 12774/87, 12.10.1989; ECtHR, *Norwood v the United Kingdom*, supra note 28.

[34] ECtHR, *Seurot v France*, no 57383/00, 18.05.2004.

[35] ECtHR, *Gündüz v Turkey*, no 35071/97, 04.12.2003, para. 37.

[36] Ibid.; mutatis mutandis, ECtHR, *Otto-Preminger-Institut v Austria*, no 13470/87, 20.09.1994, para. 49; ECtHR, *Wingrove v the United Kingdom*, no 17419/90, 25.11.1996, para. 52.

[37] ECtHR, *Belkacem v Belgium*, no 34367/14, 17.06.2017.

[38] ECtHR, *Kalifatstaat v Germany*, no 13828/04, 11.12.2006.

even when they do not contain a call for violence, might be sufficient reason for State interference through the application of Article 17, as becomes clear from *Hizb Ut-Tahrir v Germany*[39] and *Kasymakhunov and Saybatalov v Russia*.[40] Finally, the ECtHR discussed the existence and practice of Shari'a and legal pluralism in Europe in *Refah Partisi (the Welfare Party) and Others v Turkey*.[41] First, *Kalifatstaat v Germany* will be analysed due to its close ties with Islamic fundamentalism, as Kalifatstaat was an organisation close to Salafist values. Subsequently, the two cases concerning Hizb Ut-Tahrir are explained, to be followed by Refah Partisi. The latter remains of interest for the general remarks the ECtHR made on the topics of Shari'a and legal pluralism, which are relevant for all European Muslims.

3.1. BAN OF A RELIGIOUS ASSOCIATION AFTER ADVOCATING THE USE OF VIOLENCE

It is generally known that (violent) extremism poses major challenges to a democratic society. However, within the framework of the law, individuals adhering to religious extremism have an equal right to assemble and associate as all other individuals protected under Article 11 ECHR. The ECtHR considered this right limited for 'Kalifatstaat' ['Caliphate State', non-official translation], a German fundamentalist Islamic organisation whose members strived for the instalment of a worldwide Islamic caliphate based on (their interpretation of) Shari'a. The German authorities banned the association on the grounds that the motives of the association were contrary to the constitutional order and to the idea of international understanding, and that they posed a threat to national security and other interests of Germany.

The ECtHR, in a decision on the admissibility of *Kalifatstaat v Germany*, decided that the ban imposed on the association had been proportionate to the legitimate aims pursued. Moreover, the ECtHR stated that 'the pursuit of a worldwide Islamic regime based on Shari'a law was incompatible with the fundamental democratic principles articulated in the Convention'.[42] Less stringent measures would not have sufficed to counter the real and imminent threat the association posed to the State and its political system.[43] Following the provisions of Article 11, the ECtHR decided the association was founded on beliefs contrary to the idea of a 'democratic society', and therefore decided to not take the application any further.

---

[39] ECtHR, *Hizb Ut-Tahrir v Germany*, no 31098/08, 12.06.2012.
[40] ECtHR, *Kasymakhunov and Saybatalov v Russia*, nos 26261/05 and 26377/06, 14.03.2013.
[41] ECtHR, *Refah Partisi v Turkey*, supra note 25.
[42] ECtHR, *Kalifatstaat v Germany*, supra note 38, para. 3.
[43] Ibid., para. 1.

The ECtHR's decision reveals a strong dedication to protection of the democratic society, as well as a wide margin of appreciation attributed to the State, both within the framework of the ECHR. However, it also disguises a slightly limited consideration of the various interpretations of Shari'a while establishing jurisprudence applicable to all future cases regarding Islam. Indeed, the ECtHR in *Kalifatstaat v Germany* confirmed that the use of violence to establish a worldwide Islamic regime based on Shari'a might justify interference, proportionate to the legitimate aim pursued. However, as established in previous case law, particularly in *Gündüz v Turkey*, a wide margin of appreciation is attributed to the State also to examine the threat of the use of violence – not all risks of violence need to be real, current or imminent. This article will discuss the consequences of such conclusions.

3.2. ANTI-DEMOCRATIC IDEALS IN THE PURSUIT OF RELIGIOUS BELIEFS

Anti-democratic ideals pursued by any association can provide sufficient ground for State interference, often under Article 17. Such is also established in two cases concerning Hizb Ut-Tahrir, an international Islamic fundamentalist organisation which is prohibited in several Council of Europe Member States (including the Russian Federation and Germany) due to suspicions and allegations of involvement in terror and/or the use of violence. Its aim is to liberate the Palestinian territories, but politically it has been involved in the overthrowing of governments in Muslim-majority states while advocating for a pan-Islamic State in the form of a caliphate.[44] But information on the nature and activities of Hizb Ut-Tahrir is scarce and contradictory, and the group's reliance on violence is disputed.[45]

Although the ECtHR has not yet decided on the prohibition of national branches of Hizb Ut-Tahrir in its jurisdictions, it has considered two cases regarding members of the group. First, in *Hizb Ut-Tahrir v Germany*, the activities of the German branch of the association were banned after a multitude of public statements attributable to the group. Such comments included calls for the violent elimination of the State of Israel and for the killing of its inhabitants, and were based on the claim of a jihad. The German Ministry of Interior ordered the ban of the group as its activities were directed against the principle of international understanding, and because the group had advocated violence to achieve its goals. After the ban, some of Hizb Ut-Tahrir Germany's members

---

[44] The ECtHR applied the conclusion of the research conducted by the Counter Extremism Project, 'Hizb Ut-Tahrir', 2017, available at https://www.counterextremism.com/threat/hizb-ut-tahrir, last accessed 07.06.2018.

[45] ECtHR, *Kasymakhunov and Saybatalov v Russia*, supra note 40.

lodged an application against the prohibition order with the ECtHR. The ECtHR declared the application inadmissible under Article 17. The branches' goals were considered incompatible with the ECHR's values. The jihad, as propagated by Hizb Ut-Tahrir Germany, was considered to 'constitute a call to take violent action with the intention of causing physical destruction and banishment'.[46] The ECtHR did not analyse the beliefs and values of the group but relied on the German courts and its own previous case law with regard to totalitarianism and anti-democratic values. Although the ECtHR did not elaborate on the group's outlook with regard to the Islamic creed, the case can be exemplary for future cases in which certain religious extremist ideas perceivable as contrary to the Convention can be examined under Article 17. This idea has been elaborated upon in the case concerning members of the Russian branch of Hizb Ut-Tahrir.

In the case *Kasymakhunov and Saybatlov v The Russian Federation*, two members of the Russian branch of Hizb Ut-Tahrir complained before the ECtHR. The latter examined the case also under Article 17. The Russian authorities had prohibited the activities of Hizb Ut-Tahrir on Russian territories as it was considered a terrorist organisation. Consequently, the two members of the branch were arrested and convicted for offences related to terrorism. In their defence before the Russian court, the members individually denied any involvement in violence or terrorism, but instead insisted that they resorted to a peaceful manifestation of their so-called 'political ideology', and that the main purpose of the group was Islamic proselytism.[47] They repeated such arguments before the ECtHR. For this case, the ECtHR took into account the Russian court's and other experts' analyses on Hizb Ut-Tahrir.

The ECtHR subsequently concluded that Hizb Ut-Tahrir's proposals to change the legal and constitutional structures of the State were incompatible with the ECHR, because 'Hizb Ut-Tahrir proposed to establish a regime which rejects political freedoms, such as, in particular, freedoms of religion, expression and association, declaring that they are contrary to Islam'. Key issues regarding legal pluralism and introduction of Shari'a were also found contrary to the Convention's values.[48] The ECtHR declared the complaints inadmissible under Article 17, on the anti-democratic ideals the applicants were pursuing. Among other arguments, it reiterated its own decision in *Hizb Ut-Tahrir v Germany* about the intention of destruction of Israel and killing of its inhabitants. It is noteworthy that the ECtHR did not consider the complaints on the basis of the (potential) willingness of the organisation's members to use violence, but instead on constitutional changes threatening the underlying values of the ECHR.

---

[46] ECtHR, *Hizb Ut-Tahrir v Germany, supra* note 39, para. 16.
[47] ECtHR, *Kasymakhunov and Saybatalov v Russia, supra* note 40, para. 21.
[48] See ECtHR, *Refah Partisi v Turkey, supra* note 25.

Again, the ECtHR has missed its chance to clarify the existing grey area between protection of a democratic society and individual freedoms in the light of Islamic fundamentalism. It appears that anti-democratic ideals and Article 17 are prioritised over the freedom of religion, expression and association under Articles 9–11, which is based particularly on political ideals pursued rather than on the basis of the threat of religious claims. This line of reasoning was first applied in *Refah Partisi v Turkey*, which had been discussed several years before the Hizb Ut-Tahrir cases.

3.3. THE ECtHR'S ASSESSMENT OF SHARI'A AND LEGAL PLURALISM

Already in 2003, the ECtHR has set a precedent regarding the (non-)justifiability of the application of Shari'a in Council of Europe Member States in the case of *Refah Partisi (the Welfare Party) and Others v Turkey*. The ideals pursued by the Turkish political party Refah Partisi, being the introduction of legal pluralism and Shari'a in the State of Turkey, were both regarded contrary to the Convention. As a consequence of the judgment, the party remained banned; the ECtHR had justified a limitation of a principle of one of Europe's largest religions, and considerable criticism was directed at the ECtHR. Although the case does not question the issue of Salafism in Europe, it is regarded as highly relevant in the context of this article as the ECtHR has expressed and exposed concerns over Islamic fundamentalist thought.

The Turkish political party Refah Partisi had won local elections in 1995 and 1996 and had thus become the largest political party in Turkey. It formed part of the coalition and had delivered the Prime Minister. However, according to the Turkish Constitutional Court, which ordered the party's dissolution in 1997, the party had become a 'centre of activities contrary to the principle of secularism'.[49] In this regard, Refah indeed had pursued the introduction of a legal pluralist system in Turkey under which adherents to a certain religion could opt for their religion's legal system to be applied in legal cases. The Constitutional Court also held that Refah intended to replace the Turkish democratic order with a Shari'a-based political-religious state system. The leaders of Refah, after its dissolution, complained to the ECtHR of a breach of their freedom of association. The ECtHR in a Grand Chamber setting found that the measure to dissolve the party was justified as it was prescribed by law and had pursued a legitimate aim. The ECtHR applied a threefold legitimation of the ban, namely: the party had pursued the implementation of a plurality of legal systems; had sought to introduce Shari'a; and had suggested the use of jihad and political violence.

---

49   ECtHR, *Refah Partisi v Turkey*, supra note 25, para. 23.

First, the plurality of legal systems:

> would do away with the State's role as the guarantor of individual rights and freedoms and the impartial organiser of the practice of the various beliefs and religions in a democratic society, since it would oblige individuals to obey, not rules laid down by the State in the exercise of its above-mentioned functions, but static rules of law imposed by the religion concerned.

Moreover, such a plurality of legal systems 'would undeniably infringe the principle of non-discrimination between individuals with regard their enjoyment of public freedoms, which is one of the fundamental principles of democracy'.[50]

Secondly, the Shari'a was found incompatible with the fundamental principles of democracy:

> the Court considers that sharia, which faithfully reflects the dogmas and divine rules laid down by religion, is *stable and invariable* [emphasis added]. Principles such as pluralism in the political sphere or the constant evolution of public freedoms have no place in it. [...] It is difficult to declare one's respect for democracy and human rights while at the same time supporting a regime based on sharia, which clearly diverges from Convention values, particularly with regard to its criminal law and criminal procedure, its rules on the legal status of women and the way it intervenes in all spheres of private and public life in accordance with religious precepts.[51]

Thirdly, the possibility of recourse to violence had been raised by several speeches of Refah members, some of which included references to 'jihad'. According to the ECtHR, the primary meaning of jihad is 'holy war and the struggle to be waged until the total domination of Islam in society is achieved'.[52]

The outcomes of the case are generally considered controversial by legal experts and scholars, for a variety of reasons.[53] First of all, Refah was a well-established political party, and therefore 'the fact that a political programme is considered incompatible with the current principles and structures of a State does not make it incompatible with the rules of democracy [...]'.[54]

---

[50] Ibid., para. 119.
[51] Ibid., para. 123.
[52] Ibid., paras. 129–131.
[53] See, besides the sources mentioned below, also e.g. D. Schilling, 'European Islamophobia and Turkey – Refah Partisi (The Welfare Party) v Turkey', (2004) 26 *Loy. L.A. Int'l & Comp. L. Rev.*, p. 501; S. Langlaude, 'Indoctrination, Secularism, Religious Liberty and the ECHR', (2006) 55(4) *International and Comparative Law Quarterly*, pp. 929–944; C. Moe, 'Refah Partisi (The Welfare Party) and Others v. Turkey', (2003) 6(1) *The International Journal of Not-for-Profit Law*, available at http://www.icnl.org/research/journal/vol6iss1/special_5.htm, last accessed 07.06.2018.
[54] Joint dissenting opinion of Judges Fuhrmann, Loucaides, and Sir Nicolas Bratza, ECtHR, *Refah Partisi v Turkey*, supra note 25, p. 38.

This provision ultimately was not incorporated in the *Refah* judgments. Besides, 'at no point had Refah proposed legislation or taken other palpable initiatives, including the use of violence, that bring about the "theocratic order" that the ECtHR concludes they envisioned', instead the judgment would be based solely on statements and symbolic public acts by party members of various standing over a six-year period.[55]

Secondly, the ECtHR is criticised because it ignored the diverse interpretation of key Islamic concepts, such as Shari'a and jihad. The assumptions made by the ECtHR are couched in problematic language, even called 'provocative to all those Muslims who do not identify with the fundamentalist project', and neglect the possible rapprochement between Islamic law and human rights.[56] The language used disseminates 'a wholly unnecessary and inappropriate critique of [Islam], which has over 100 million followers in the European legal space [...]'.[57] This impact, as well as the 'unmodulated' findings, 'especially as regards the extremely sensitive issues raised by religion and its values', raised concerns among academics and an ECtHR judge.[58]

Thirdly, Judge Kovler in a concurring opinion regrets the direct connection the ECtHR makes between legal pluralism and Shari'a. The judge regards legal pluralism as an ancient notion which should not be plainly rejected, and the ECtHR's characterisation of Shari'a does not do justice to the variability of Shari'a.[59] The judge considers that the ECtHR has followed the Turkish line of reasoning on limiting the individual manifestation of religious identify in the public sphere, whereas the ECtHR normally respects a certain legal autonomy for religious groups. Indeed, most Western countries have long traditions of respecting the self-governance of religious groups in certain matters of faith and doctrine, e.g. Catholic, Protestant and Jewish traditions enjoy certain autonomy when it comes to marriage and divorce, or churches and other faith communities enjoy a certain independence with regard to employment policies.[60]

Whatever the judgment and the criticisms, the conclusions on Shari'a and legal pluralism bring far-reaching consequences to (Islamic) religious groups acting in today's European societies. First, the ECtHR has excluded legal pluralism as a possibility within States' national legal frameworks.

---

[55] C. MOE, 'Refah Revisited: Strasbourg's Construction of Islam', in W. COLE DURHAM JR., R. TORFS, D.M. KIRKHAM et al (eds.), *Islam, Europe and Emerging Legal Issues*, Ashgate, Surrey 2012, p. 237.
[56] Ibid., p. 29.
[57] K. BOYLE, 'Human Rights, Religion and Democracy: The Refah Party Case', (2004) 1(1) *Essex Human Rights Review*, pp. 1–16.
[58] Concurring opinion by Judge Kovler, ECtHR, *Refah Partisi v Turkey*, supra note 25, p. 48.
[59] ECtHR, *Refah Partisi v Turkey*, supra note 25, para. 48.
[60] I.T. PLESNER, 'The European Court of Human Rights: Between Fundamentalist and Liberal Secularism', in W.C. DURHAM, JR., R. TORFS, D.M. KIRKHAM et al (eds.), *Islam, Europe and Emerging Legal Issues*, Ashgate, London 2012, p. 237.

Second, following the judgment it appears that any advocacy for the implementation of Shari'a in Council of Europe Member States is strongly prohibited, no matter the non-violent character of such a call. Even more general, support for a Shari'a based regime yet appears critical – although it must be noted that 'defending' Shari'a seems permitted.[61] Future case law is needed to clarify the grey area of defending, supporting and advocating for Shari'a. It remains uncertain how the ECtHR approaches dilemmas concerning Salafists, their individual freedoms and threats to the public safety. The future may clarify the ECtHR's approach towards the topics of Islam and Islamic fundamentalism.[62]

As for the Salafist movement, by applying the ECtHR's case law, it might be concluded that, depending on the circumstances, any public advocacy for the implementation of Shari'a (with political pretensions) in Council of Europe Member States is prohibited. However, defending the religious law might be acceptable, within the borders of the freedom of expression and depending on the context in which the defending comments or remarks are made. Overall, the ECtHR has adopted a firm stance against Shari'a, which would be 'stable and invariable', especially in cases in which supporters are driven by political pretensions. This could be a critical development, as Shari'a is an issue that requires deeper knowledge and understanding, or at least acknowledgement of the variability in interpretation among Muslim communities, for a fair and legitimate argument to be valid in today's multicultural European societies.

4. POTENTIAL HUMAN RIGHTS ISSUES ARISING OUT OF CONTEMPORARY COUNTER-TERRORISM MEASURES

The ECtHR and the Council of Europe offer a broad response to countering terrorism while adhering to its values of human rights and rule of law, through both the ECHR and specific counter-terrorism conventions and recommendations. A set of measures was introduced over a period of 30 years, ranging from recommendations on promoting co-operation between Council of Europe Member States to declarations and guidelines on human rights in the fight against terrorism, which prohibit arbitrariness in the States' counter-terrorism measures and require States to guarantee legal protection for suspects of terrorist offences following the right to a fair trial (Article 6 ECHR).

---

61 See the ECtHR's conclusions in ECtHR, *Gündüz v Turkey*, supra note 35.
62 Such opportunity rises in the currently pending case before the ECtHR Grand Chamber of *Molla Sali v Greece* [no 20452/14], in which the ECtHR will decide over the application of Shari'a for a family conflict on inheritage in a region in Western Greece. See ECtHR, *Molla Sali v Greece*, no 20452/14 [GC], GC hearing 06.12.2017.

Moreover, the ECtHR has developed case law on counter-terrorism measures related to, *inter alia*, personal data access in the fight against terrorism;[63] the monitoring and interception of communications without preliminary provision of notice to the individuals concerned;[64] and the dissolution of political parties in the light of a state's history.[65] But with the current threat jihadi-Salafists pose on the democratic society and public safety, as well as the trend of Europeans viewing the scourge of IS as the greatest threat to democracies, there is a general demand for strict counter-terrorism measures.[66] Consequently, the risk arises that such measures raise tensions with human rights.

Recent counter-terrorism measures against Salafism-inspired violence in Western European States are generally divided between measures enacted against foreign terrorist fighters (FTFs), e.g. nationals who have joined IS at location, and measures against (groups of) fundamentalists which do not necessarily have to have demonstrated ties with IS. The former are directed also against children of FTFs who were born in war territories, and concentrate mostly on legal and de-radicalisation measures, e.g. amendments to the law to cover fully the definition of FTF, obtaining a returned FTF's passport and de-radicalisation, reintegration programmes. A legitimate basis for such measures is relatively easily found, e.g. support/financing/participation in terrorist activities should be criminalised in all jurisdictions.[67] Measures of a more general nature with regard to non-FTFs are not as obviously justifiable, but the more interesting for the topic of Salafism and counter-terrorism. This article will examine recent counter-terrorism measures taken against Salafism and/or Jihadi-Salafism specifically.

4.1. BELGIUM

Belgium has been struck by multiple jihadist terrorist attacks over the course of years. Belgium also rates highest in the number of foreign fighters per capita: recent numbers estimate that 451 individuals travelled to Syria or Iraq for terrorist purposes. Moreover, the suspect of the *Stade de France/Bataclan* terrorist attacks in Paris on 13 November 2015 was a Belgian-born French national of Moroccan descent, who had grown up in the Brussels borough of Molenbeek. This area recently came into news as Belgian police in the district

---

[63] ECtHR, *Segerstedt-Wiberg and Others v Sweden*, no 62332/00, 06.06.2006.
[64] ECtHR, *Klass and Others v Germany*, no 5029/71, 06.09.1978.
[65] ECtHR, *Herri Batasuna and Batasuna v Spain*, nos 25803/04 and 25817/04, 11.06.2009.
[66] PEW RESEARCH CENTER, 'Europeans Face the World Divided', Global Attitudes Survey, Spring 2016, available at http://www.pewglobal.org/2016/06/13/europeans-see-isis-climate-change-as-most-serious-threats, last accessed 07.06.2018.
[67] Belgium, France and the United Kingdom are all Member States of the Financial Action Task Force and the Council of Europe Counter-Terrorism Committee.

uncovered 51 organisations with suspected ties to terrorism.[68] In an effort to counter the threat of terrorism, the Belgian government has adopted a 'holistic and coordinated' strategy containing, *inter alia*, the provisional removal of identity cards of foreign terrorist fighters; the establishment of data banks on terrorism and foreign terrorist fighters; a thorough screening and possible arrest or extradition of all imams present in Belgium after November 2015; and the dissolution of all unofficial or not (yet) officially recognised associations and houses of worship.[69]

Depending on the final execution within the context and circumstances on the ground, the measures above may pose tension with the ECHR, as they are not necessarily justifiable in the light of the State's duty to protect its citizens and public safety. In particular the screening of imams present in Belgium, and arresting or extraditing those that spread hate or advocate violence, may raise problems with counter-terrorism from a human rights perspective. The Belgian authorities embrace surveillance measures to execute this approach. Depending on the scope, nature and duration of the surveillance measures, as well as the grounds provided for the order of such measures, a State might justify interference of the right to privacy enshrined in Article 8 ECHR. However, the ECtHR has clearly asserted that any 'exploratory' or 'general surveillance' would be contrary to the provisions established in Article 8.[70] Notably the apparent absence of differentiation between imams, e.g. concerning the specific legal schools or the ideology they adhere to, and the general nature of the screening measures could indicate a potential conflict with the ECHR.

4.2. FRANCE

In France, a comparable approach to Belgium was taken after the January 2015 Charly Hebdo attacks in which 12 people were killed. The French government announced that it would give greater prominence to the intelligence services and the generation of intelligence to counter terrorism.[71] These included increasing the human resources of the counter-terrorism operations; strengthening the surveillance of air travel by preparing the ground for the implementation of

---

[68] C. KROET, 'Belgiums Molenbeek home to 51 groups with terror links', *Politico Europe*, 20.03.2017, available at https://www.politico.eu/article/belgiums-molenbeek-home-to-51-groups-with-terror-links-report, last accessed 07.06.2018.

[69] BELGIAN GOVERNMENT, 'Fight against terrorism', 2016, available at https://diplomatie.belgium.be/en/policy/policy_areas/peace_and_security/terrorism/fight_against_terrorism, last accessed 07.06.2018.

[70] A. DE FRÍAS, *Counter-terrorism and Human Rights in the Case Law of the European Court of Human Right*, Council of Europe Publications, Strasbourg 2012.

[71] V. CHALKIADAKI, 'The French "War on Terror" in the post-Charlie Hebdo Era', 2015, *eucrim* no 1/26, available at https://eucrim.mpicc.de/archiv/eucrim_15-01.pdf, last accessed 07.06.2018.

the proposed European Union (EU) Directive on the exchange of passengers' data (PNR); and paying increasing attention to early warnings and weak signals detection, which were tagged under the 'radicalisation' banner.[72] Those measures did not prove their efficiency as only few months later, in November 2015, the *Stade de France/Bataclan* attacks were carried out by perpetrators of which some were known to law enforcement officials prior to the attacks. French President Hollande declared a state of emergency, which allowed derogation of the ECHR under Article 15 ('derogation in times of emergency', particularly in states of war) to attribute special competences to the police to carry out house searches without a warrant, put anyone under house arrest without trial and block websites that encouraged acts of terrorism. The number of preventive actions skyrocketed after the declaration. The state of emergency also allowed for a ban of public demonstrations.[73]

However, several concerns must be raised on the emergency counter-terrorism measures. In its first six months of application, nearly 3,500 house searches and 400 house arrests had taken place. A dozen mosques had been closed. Controversially, nearly 600 legal proceedings had started, but only as few as five individuals were charged with terrorism.[74] Moreover, the government could lay down restrictions on public activities and impose (partial) house arrest. Amnesty International critically assessed the government's capability of doing so and found that restrictions were imposed pursuing a doubtful legitimate aim with unnecessary or disproportionate measures. They were adopted to maintain the public order over the course of two weeks following the November 2015 attacks. At this exact same period of time, many demonstrations were planned ahead of the World Climate Conference (COP 2015) to be held in Paris, and over 600 individual measures were imposed, thus preventing the participation of citizens in public assemblies against governmental policies, although these individuals did not have ties or liaisons to acts of terrorism.[75] The provisions would have been used not just against suspected terrorists, but also to ban suspected radical leftists from demonstrations. In short, the freedom of assembly and association appears increasingly limited for activities not (necessarily) linked to terrorism.

A state derogation from the ECHR has both the duty to protect its citizens against threats to public safety, democratic state and national security, but it must also ensure that the state of emergency is applied only in exceptions so

---

[72] M. HECKER and E. TENENBAUM, 'France vs. Jihadism', 2017, available at https://www.ifri.org/sites/default/files/atoms/files/hecker_tenenbaum_france_vs_jihadism_2017.pdf, last accessed 07.06.2018.
[73] The state of emergency is replaced by a sweeping counter-terrorism law since November 2017.
[74] Ibid.
[75] Amnesty International, *France: a Right not a Threat. Disproportionate Restrictions on Demonstrations under the State of Emergency in France*, Amnesty International, London 2017.

that it does not become a norm. Restrictions on fundamental freedoms should therefore not be applied in cases where it appears avoidable and should be lifted as soon as possible. Even a derogatory policy must refrain from unnecessary restrictions on an individual's rights and freedoms, because measures holding a wide interpretation of Article 15 ECHR might inflict on human rights. This article does not intend to sketch a possible court-scenario on the measures taken, but instead seeks to demonstrate the tension between human rights and counter-terrorism. It would nonetheless be interesting to follow a case as to whether the government has adopted a wider mandate than necessary during the state of emergency.

4.3. THE UNITED KINGDOM

The United Kingdom has adopted a rather different strategy. Between 2003 and 2015, the UK applied a four-way approach to understand and combat terrorism. Central to the UK 'anti-terror' policy-making was CONTEST, introduced in 2003 and replaced in 2015, a strategy 'to reduce the risk to the UK and its interests overseas from terrorism'.[76] CONTEST set outs a series of measures and approaches on policy and programme level, divided into 'Pursue', 'Prevent', 'Protect' and 'Prepare'. Perhaps the most contentious of these four strands is Prevent, which has led the UK government to develop a preventive strand to 'stop people becoming terrorists or supporting terrorism'.[77] Notwithstanding the expiration of CONTEST, Prevent remains applicable today as it was placed on a statutory footing by the *Counter-terrorism and Security Act 2015*.[78] The main aim of the Prevent approach is to prevent radicalisation. There are, however, considerable questions regarding this approach in the light of counter-terrorism and human rights. Notably the lack of a common definition of radicalisation and the risk of disproportional use of the measures on certain ethnic groups raise concerns.

First, adopting the idea of radicalisation comes with a distinct lack of clarity as to what it actually means.[79] The terms of extremism, radicalism,

---

[76] HM GOVERNMENT, 'Counter-terrorism Strategy (CONTEST)', 2011a, p. 40; V. COPPOCK and M. MCGOVERN, 'Dangerous Minds'? Deconstructing Counter-Terrorism Discourse, Radicalisation and the 'Psychological Vulnerability' of Muslim Children and Young People in Britain', (2014) 28(3) *Children & Society*, pp. 242–256.

[77] HM GOVERNMENT, 'Prevent Strategy', 2011, available at https://assets.publishing.service.gov.uk/government/uploads/system/uploads/attachment_data/file/97976/prevent-strategy-review.pdf, last accessed 08.06.2018.

[78] C. MASTROE, 'Evaluating CVE: Understanding the Recent Changes to the United Kingdom's Implementation of Prevent', (2016) 10 *Perspectives on Terrorism*, p. 50.

[79] D.R. MANDEL, 'Radicalization: What does it mean?', in T.M. PICK, A. SPECKHARD and B. JARUCH (eds.), *Home-grown terrorism: Understanding and addressing the root causes of radicalisation among groups with an immigrant heritage in Europe*, IOS Press,

fundamentalism, Salafism, Islamism, etc., are subject to interchangeable application, whereas this lack of precision does not advance a constructive public debate.[80] In the UK it has not has been outlined in the Prevent strategy what is meant and understood by 'radicalised', who are subject to it, what its parameters are, and, as a result, who is targeted by 'counter-radicalisation' in the context of counter-terrorism. Moreover, although the UK knows a long history of terrorism and radicalisation, such as in Northern Ireland in the late 1960s and early 1970s, the term 'radicalisation' emerged only in academic literature on terrorism and political violence from the early 2000s – particularly the 9/11 attacks.[81] Radicalisation in the Prevent strategy thus concentrates on ideology. It has been explained as 'a process whereby "extremist ideas" are propagated and disseminated by key activists and thinkers who therefore "radicalise" others because of their "vulnerabilities" to such a message'.[82] The understanding of 'vulnerabilities' also lacks further detail. Part of the Prevent strategy is the *Channel* programme, in which individuals in England and Wales deemed vulnerable to recruitment to extremism should be identified, relying upon the vigilance and co-operation of workers in the social, youth and health sector as well as teachers and the local police. Most critically, although Channel, Prevent and CONTEST are supposed to be directed at tackling all forms of 'radicalisation' and 'extremism', including political, religious and social radicalism, it emerges that those identified as vulnerable to extremism are over 90% Muslim.[83] Moreover in 2018, it appears Prevent has targeted Muslims in general, and in many cases where there is no suspicion or evidence of criminal activity.[84]

The CONTEST Strategy as a whole expired in 2015 and was replaced by various bills. First, a new Extremism Bill was introduced, aimed at addressing non-violent forms of extremism, but the proposal proved controversial and shortly after a new Counter-Extremism Strategy was published.[85] It did not

---

Amsterdam 2009, pp. 101–113; A. RICHARDS, 'The Problem with 'Radicalization', the Remit of 'Prevent', and the Need to Refocus on *Terrorism* in the UK', (2009) 86(4) *International Affairs*.

[80] A. SCHMID, 'Violent and Non-Violent Extremism: Two Sides of the Same Coin?' ICCT Research Paper, 2014, available at https://www.icct.nl/download/file/ICCT-Schmid-Violent-Non-Violent-Extremism-May-2014.pdf last accessed, 07.06.2018.

[81] P. NEUMANN, 'Perspectives on Radicalisation and Political Violence', 2008, available at http://icsr.info/wp-content/uploads/2012/10/1234516938ICSRPerspectivesonRadicalisation.pdf, last accessed 07.06.2018.

[82] V. COPPOCK and M. MCGOVERN (2014), 'Dangerous Minds?', *supra* note 76, pp. 242–256.

[83] Association of Chief Police Officers (ACPO), 'National Channel Referral Figures', 2011, available at http://www.acpo.police.uk/ACPOBusinessAreas/PREVENT/NationalChannelRef, last accessed 07.06.2018.

[84] B. COHEN and W. TUFAIL, 'Prevent and the Normalization of Islamophobia', in F. ELAHI and O. KHAN (eds.), *Islamophobia. Still a Challenge for Us All*, Runnymede, London, 2017, p. 42.

[85] CABINET OFFICE, *Counter-Extremism Strategy*, London 2015, available at https://assets.publishing.service.gov.uk/government/uploads/system/uploads/attachment_data/file/470094/51859_Cm9148_PRINT.PDF, last accessed 08.06.2018.

reveal when legislation might be expected. In May 2016, a Counter-Extremism and Safeguarding Bill was announced – but no detailed proposals emerged, and the bill was [and is] not published. On 21 June 2017, the Queen's Speech announced the establishment of a committee on the countering of extremism.[86] Again, at moment of writing, no further legislative or practical measures have come clear. The UK's Minister for Culture, Media and Sports, Ms Karen Bradley, announced that the latter counter-extremism approach was not part of counter-terrorism, as extremism was regarded a broader category than terrorism.[87] Yet the UK Parliamentary Joint Committee on Human Rights noted that the distinction between the two terms was critical, and that the Prevent approach, which still applied as part of a counter-terrorism strategy, also considered the term extremism.[88]

Overall, not only for the ECtHR but also for European jurisdiction, the boundary between extremism and/or religious fundamentalism on the one hand, and violence and/or the risk of violence on the other raises difficult questions. Needless to say, many of the adopted measures by Belgium, France and the United Kingdom were taken only recently in a period of unrest and insecurity about a new jihadist attack. It would be premature and unjust to conclude that human rights violations have occurred as a consequence of the counter-terrorism/counter-jihadism measures. Instead it would be interesting to follow the ECtHR in its future judgments on topics related to the human rights issues coming forth from such counter-terrorism measures. While most States emphasise the necessity to establish measures compatible with the ECHR, some of the strategies adopted might threaten the provisions enshrined in the ECHR. This illustrates the tension between maintaining the safety of citizens versus guaranteeing human rights for all individuals. It must be kept in mind that enlarging the authorities' mandate to take measures, which might inflict on certain rights and might be contrary to democratic values, will serve the goal of preventing the break-down of the democratic society through (the threat of) terrorism. But, paradoxically, neglecting human rights in the fight against terrorism could result in a potentially weaker democratic society, whereas human rights were originally meant to protect citizens in a democratically functioning state limited by the rule of law.

---

[86] J. Dawson and S. Godec, 'Counter-extremism policy: an overview', 23.06.2017, available at https://researchbriefings.parliament.uk/ResearchBriefing/Summary/CBP-7238, last accessed 07.06.2018.

[87] S. Wittendorp, R. de Bont, J. de Roy van Zuijdewijn et al., *Dealing with Jihadism. A Policy Comparison between the Netherlands, Belgium, Denmark, Germany, France, the UK, and the US (2010 to 2017)*, Leiden University, Leiden 2017.

[88] JOINT COMMITTEE ON HUMAN RIGHTS, Counter Extremism (2016–17 HL 39/HC 105), 2016.

5. CONCLUSION

One senses a strong tension between individual rights, even in the fight against terrorism, and the safety of the nation and the citizens both in the short and longer term. A tendency exists to generalise Islam, Shari'a and particularly Salafism as a dangerous ideology. But the legal tradition of Islam, Shari'a, and its sub-streams, such as Salafism, are not generalisable. The interpretation of Shari'a differs among Muslims and Muslim communities. The influence of legal scholars, imams and other influential Muslims, as well as the State's interpretation, over the course of centuries of development of the religion, have accounted for the wide variety of application and interpretation of the provisions of the Quran and Prophet Muhammad's habits and traditions.

This is true also for Salafism. As a long-established traditionalist, fundamentalist movement, Salafists appear well-organised and united in the pursuit of their goals. Indeed, they have adopted a singular approach towards Islam and Shari'a, creating a distinction between them and all other Muslims or 'non-believers' in society. However paradoxically, notwithstanding the singularity and unity emphasised by Salafists, the movement itself is strongly divided in the interpretation and application of Shari'a. Salafists can pursue goals either on an individual base, through political propaganda and empowerment, or through advocating for or using violence. Furthermore, on the understanding of certain key issues, such as the jihad, considerable variety exists among Salafists as not all would agree jihad indicates the necessity to use violence over other Muslims or non-Muslims to enforce the 'righteous Islam' upon them.

The judges of the ECtHR have deliberated several times on the issue between guaranteeing fundamental freedoms of all European citizens and the protection of the democratic society. Particularly Articles 9–11 and 17 of the ECHR are deemed relevant in the light of the ECtHR's case law and its application on the issue of Salafism in Europe. This is reflected in the cases of *Kalifatstaat v Germany*; *Hizb Ut-Tahrir v Germany*; *Kasymakhunov and Saybatalov v Russia*; and *Refah Partisi (the Welfare Party) and Others v Turkey*, but interesting conclusions were pulled also in *Gündüz v Turkey*. The ECtHR has dealt with 'extremist claims' in a way which tends to be general towards Islam as a whole. It has declared the pursuit of a worldwide Islamic regime based on Shari'a and the notion of legal pluralism incompatible with the fundamental democratic principles enshrined in the ECHR. The ECtHR has attributed a wide margin of appreciation for States to consider cases of (Islamic) fundamentalism in the light of their national traditions, but as a result thereof a grey area exists regarding defending, supporting and advocating for Shari'a (especially with political pretensions). In addition, the ECtHR has not taken opportunity to distinguish between advocating for the institution of Shari'a at the (national) political level and the institution of Shari'a for issues related to, but not limited to, family or heritage law – subjects which are typically under influence of Shari'a.

It would be profitable for all European societies if the ECtHR takes the opportunity to outline and clarify its perspectives on (religious) legal pluralism – not only where Islam is concerned but also for fundamentalist Jewish and Christian groups – as well as specify its approach towards non-violent, political Islamic manifestation. The ECtHR is in the position to answer to the difficulties on the boundary between defending or advocating for Shari'a and the liberty of religious thinking and manifestation of (Islamic) fundamentalists, in particular Salafists. Thereby should be taken into account that Salafism is just one among many religious fundamentalist groups, and thus that the ECtHR's judgments might have great impact on the occurrence and existence of religious fundamentalism in Europe.

Among certain Council of Europe Member States, a similar approach is noticeable within the context of the dilemma between human rights and public safety. The examples provided illustrate recently adopted counter-terrorism measures by Belgium, France and the United Kingdom, which might be interfering with citizens' rights protected by the ECHR. Usually it appears that the counter-terrorism measures are taken to protect democratic society and human rights from the threat of terrorism, but, paradoxically, they might break down on these same rights and fundamental principles. Human rights, instead, are meant to protect the citizens against the State, hence an increasing influence of the State on the downgrading of human rights could be detrimental to the future status of human rights in European societies. Terrorism itself uncovers an existing tension within the duties of the State to, on the one hand, protect individual fundamental freedoms, and on the other, protection of the society against (violent) threats. Jurisdictions under the ECHR taking measures against extremism, radicalism and/or (Islamic) fundamentalism are encouraged to take into full account the human rights and rule of law perspective as stipulated and developed by the Council of Europe, ECHR and ECtHR. A strong, human rights-based counter-terrorism approach will be fruitful in the future, not only to combat terrorism but also to prevent violent radicalism. Good practices are established by countries such as the Netherlands, Germany and Denmark.[89]

Human rights are the solution for future peaceful, sustainable democratic societies in which the fundamental freedoms as enshrined in the ECHR are guaranteed. However, the current dilemma Europe faces tends to direct Europeans to opt for either individual rights or national security. The democratic

---

[89] For a complete overview of counter-terrorism measures taken between 2010–2017 in the light of the Jihadist threat, by Belgium, Denmark, France, Germany, the Netherlands, the United Kingdom and the United States, it is suggested to consider S. WITTENDORP, R. DE BONT, J. DE ROY VAN ZUIJDEWIJN et al., *Dealing with Jihadism*, supra note 87.

society and rule of law principles as established in the ECHR are thus under pressure from the universalistic, theocratic pretentious of Salafists at one hand. But on the other, counter-terrorism measures taken by Council of Europe Member States as a result of the threat of Salafist-inspired terrorism pose a threat to the ECHR's values. The ECtHR has adopted a uniform approach towards Shari'a motivated by political pretensions. However, it would be interesting to follow future ECtHR case law on Shari'a for daily life legal purposes, e.g. without political insistence. Only this will clarify the ECtHR's stance on (non-)fundamentalist Islamic manifestation and Shari'a application. However, with due consideration of all the above, emphasis is put again on the necessity of guaranteeing human rights for all in the framework of counter-terrorism and democratic society, both by States, the ECtHR and European citizens.

DELAYS IN THE IMPLEMENTATION OF ECtHR JUDGMENTS

The Example of Cases Concerning Electoral Issues

Agnieszka SZKLANNA*

1. Introduction 446
2. Delays in the Implementation of ECtHR Judgments: The Existence
   of 'Pockets of Resistance' 448
3. Examples of Delays in Cases Concerning Electoral Issues 452
   3.1. *Hirst v the United Kingdom (No. 2)* and Other Similar
        Judgments 452
   3.2. *Paksas v Lithuania* 457
   3.3. *Sejdić and Finci v Bosnia and Herzegovina* and Other
        Similar Judgments 459
4. Conclusion 462

ABSTRACT

According to Article 46 paragraph 2 of the European Convention on Human Rights (ECHR), the Committee of Ministers is in charge of supervising the execution of judgments of the European Court of Human Rights (ECtHR). There are currently nearly 7,500 judgments pending before the Committee of Ministers and the implementation of some of them meet serious obstacles from the respondent States. As noted by the Committee of Ministers and the Parliamentary Assembly of the Council of Europe in their reports on this matter, the implementation of certain ECtHR judgments may reveal some 'pockets of resistance'. This article focuses on the ECtHR judgments concerning electoral issues: *Hirst v the United Kingdom (no. 2)*; *Paksas v Lithuania and Sejdic*; and *Finci v Bosnia and Herzegovina*, which have not been executed for several years. It is argued that, since these judgments touch upon serious

---

* The article reflects the author's personal opinions and does not engage the responsibility of the Council of Europe.

political issues, their implementation is complex, both legally and politically. When these judgments were delivered, the fact that some ECtHR judges had expressed their dissenting opinions was an early sign of the problems which were later encountered in their execution.

1. INTRODUCTION

Under the system of the European Convention on Human Rights (the Convention), two bodies – the European Court of Human Rights (ECtHR) and the Committee of Ministers (CM) – are responsible for the good operation of its human rights protection system. The ECtHR may receive individual or inter-State applications (see Articles 34 and 33 of the Convention). If it finds a violation of the Convention, its judgment is transmitted to the Committee of Ministers, the Council of Europe's statutory body, which supervises the implementation of its judgments under Article 46 paragraph 2 of the Convention. In fulfilling this role, the CM is assisted by its Secretariat and especially the Department for the Execution of Judgments of the ECtHR (in the Council of Europe's Directorate General Human Rights and Rule of Law – DGI). As of 31 December 2017, some 7,500 judgments of the ECtHR were pending before the CM.[1] Some of these judgments have been partially or almost fully implemented, while the execution of others is lagging behind; as long as the CM has not decided to close their supervision by adopting a final resolution, they are still pending before the CM, although they might be at various stages of execution. In case of non-execution, the Committee of Ministers may use diplomatic avenues such as adopting strong decisions and interim resolutions, sending letters by its Chair to the respondent States, examining cases at each of its Human Rights or ordinary meetings. When it comes to additional legal measures, the procedures foreseen in Article 46 paragraphs 3 and 4 of the Convention, as introduced by Protocol No 14 to the Convention, allow the CM to ask for the help of the ECtHR to interpret a judgment and to indicate whether it has or has not been implemented. The practical effects of these procedures are unknown so far. Thus, the follow-up that the Court will give to the CM's referral of the case of *Ilgar Mammadov v Azerbaidjan*,[2] decided under Article 46 paragraph 4 of the Convention on 5 December 2017, will be a genuine test for the Convention system.

---

[1] According to the 11th Annual Report of the Committee of Ministers, Supervision of the execution of judgments and decisions of the European Court of Human Rights 2017, published on 4 April 2018.
[2] ECtHR, *Ilgar Mammadov v Azerbaidjan*, no 15172/13, 22.05.2014.

Besides that, in case of failure to implement a judgment, the ultimate sanction that is available for the CM is Article 8 of the 1949 Statute of Council of Europe,[3] which provides that a Member State which has seriously violated Article 3 of the Statute (according to which a Member State shall respect rule of law and human rights) may be suspended from its rights of representation or even expelled from the organisation. So far this provision has not been used and it is often believed that its mere existence is sufficiently dissuasive. Without entering into a debate on the utility of this provision, the main aim of this article is to reflect on some cases in which protracted non-implementation of a judgment may hide political problems, including the absence of political will to comply with indications stemming from the Court's case law. In many of such cases, problems with ECtHR judgments' implementation are inherent to the thematic they are touching upon, i.e. issues which are of a political nature. Very often, the way in which a judgment has been adopted (i.e. by what majority of judges) and the existence of dissenting opinions are an indication that its implementation is likely to meet obstacles from the respondent State. In this context, it is worth recalling that in its 2002 opinion on the implementation of the Court's judgments, the European Commission for Democracy through Law ('Venice Commission') underlined the fact that the execution of judgments and its monitoring may not only be a legal but also a political problem.[4]

In the doctrine, certain authors try to make a distinction between 'principled' and 'dilatory' non-execution.[5] 'Principled' non-execution occurs (rarely) when States resist execution because of 'deep-seated politico-philosophical disagreements with the Court's interpretation of a particular provision, or with the concept of international supervision per se' (e.g. *Hirst v the UK (no. 2)*). 'Dilatory' non-execution covers a wider category of cases in which there is no dispute as to principle but rather 'problematic attitudinal and/or organisational resistance' to implementation and failure to organise the organs of the State in an 'effective, accountable, and rights-respecting way' (e.g. judgments against Azerbaijan).[6] This has been contested by other authors, as it is not always clear that non-execution is 'principled' and 'dilatory' non-execution can cover a large variety of cases, including those which have been partially executed.[7] Despite this debate, this article is not intended to further reflect on this theoretical issue, but

---

[3] Statute of the Council of Europe signed in London on 09.05.1949.
[4] VENICE COMMISSION, CDL-AD(2002)34, para. 50.
[5] F. DE LONDRAS and K. DZEHTSIAROU, 'Mission Impossible? Addressing Non-Execution Through Infringement Proceedings in the European Court of Human Rights', (2017) 66(2) *ICLQ (International and Comparative Law Quarterly)*, pp. 467–490.
[6] Ibid., pp. 474–480.
[7] A. DONALD, 'Tackling Non-Implementation in the Strasbourg System: The Art of the Possible?', *EJIL: Talk!*, 28.04.2017.

rather on determining the real reasons of non-execution at the earliest possible stage. Therefore, it will rather use the term 'delays' than 'non-execution', as under the process established by Article 46 paragraph 2 of the Convention the respondent States and the Committee of Ministers usually find a compromise concerning the scope of implementation of a judgment.[8] The term 'non-execution' refers to a specific lapse of time during which the respondent State does not take the measures required by the CM; the assumption is that the judgment will be executed. Any attempt to define the term 'non-execution' will have to respond at least to the two following questions: (1) how many years must have elapsed from the time when the judgment became final? (over 10 – like in many cases concerning structural problems or 17 years like in the case *Cyprus v Turkey*?);[9] (2) how to assess a case in which execution measures have been partially taken, but the respondent State is reluctant to take further measures required by the CM? For these reasons, this article will avoid entering a discussion on how to group different situations of 'non-execution' and how to define the latter term.

2. DELAYS IN THE IMPLEMENTATION OF ECtHR JUDGMENTS: THE EXISTENCE OF 'POCKETS OF RESISTANCE'

Delays in implementing ECtHR judgments are not negligible. As stressed by the Parliamentary Assembly of the Council of Europe (PACE or Assembly) in its Resolution 2178 (2011), there are more and more judgments which have not been implemented for more than ten years and which reveal serious structural problems. Most of these judgments have already been pinpointed in its previous resolutions, namely 1787 (2011) and 2075 (2015) of PACE.[10] This is particularly the case of certain judgments against Italy, the Russian Federation, Turkey, Ukraine, Romania, Hungary, Greece, Bulgaria, the Republic of Moldova and Poland.[11] In its Resolution 2178 (2017), the Assembly deplored the delays in the implementation of ECtHR judgments, the lack of political will to implement them and 'all the attempts made to undermine the Court's authority and the Convention-based human rights protection system'.[12]

---

[8] For examples of implementation of ECtHR judgments, see, in particular, *Impact of the European Convention on Human Rights in States Parties. Selected Examples*, Council of Europe, November 2016.
[9] ECtHR, *Cyprus v Turkey*, no 25781/94 [GC] 10.05.2001 and 12.05.2014.
[10] PACE, Resolution 2178 (2017), p. 6.
[11] See Appendix to the report of the PACE Committee on Legal Affairs and Human Rights (CLAHR), 'The Implementation of judgments of the European Court of Human Rights, Rapporteur Mr Pierre-Yves Le Borgn' (France, Socialist Group), Doc. 14340 of 12.06.2017 (also published by the Council of Europe, February 2018).
[12] PACE, Resolution 2178 (2017), p. 7.

The Assembly's resolution and the report of its Committee on Legal Affairs and Human Rights (CLAHR) speak about 'pockets of resistance', which concern 'particularly deeply-ingrained political issues'. According to the PACE, the difficulties in implementing this type of judgment are related not only to the question of adoption of general measures (i.e. measures aimed at preventing new violations of the Convention), but also of individual measures (i.e. measures aimed at ensuring the *restitution in integrum* for the applicants) and the payment of just satisfaction.[13] Speaking about 'pockets of resistance', PACE/CLAHR Rapporteur Pierre-Yves Le Borgn' (France, Socialist Group), has put emphasis on seven judgments/groups of judgments, stating that their execution 'raises complex political issues'.[14] These are: *Ilgar Mammadov v Azerbaijan*,[15] *Sejdić and Finci v Bosnia and Herzegovina*,[16] *Paksas v Lithuania*,[17] *Al Nashiri* and *Husayn v Poland*,[18] *Catan and Others v Russian Federation*,[19] *OAO Neftyanaya Kompaniya YUKOS v Russian Federation*[20] and *Hirst v United Kingdom (no. 2)*.[21]

The term 'pockets of resistance' comes from the CM 2015 Annual Report, in which the CM noted that it was increasingly confronted with difficulties related to this phenomenon. According to the 2015 Annual Report, these 'pockets of resistance' were linked to deeply-rooted prejudices of a social nature (for example toward Roma or certain minorities) or related to political or national security considerations or the situation in areas/regions of 'frozen conflict'. They require special effort from the respondent States, the CM and the Department for the Execution of ECtHR judgments.[22] Without going into a more detailed analysis of 'pockets of resistance', in its 2016 Annual Report, the CM listed four categories of non-implementation problems: (1) important and complex structural problems; (2) the absence of a common understanding of the scope of the execution measures required following developments of the Court's case law (in particular concerning interpretation of the concept of 'jurisdiction'); (3) slow or blocked execution as a result of disagreement between national institutions, or amongst political parties, as regards the substance of the reforms required and/or the procedure to be followed; and (4) refusal either to adopt, notwithstanding

---

[13] Ibid.
[14] PACE, CLAHR's report, *supra* note 11, Section 4.2.
[15] ECtHR, *Ilgar Mammadov v Azerbaidjan*, *supra* note 2.
[16] ECtHR, *Sejdić and Finci v Bosnia and Herzegovina*, no 27996/06 [GC] 22.12.2009.
[17] ECtHR, *Paksas v Lithuania*, no 34932/04 [GC] 06.01.2011.
[18] ECtHR, *Al Nashiri* and *Husayn v Poland*, nos. 28761/11 and 7511/13, 24.07.2014.
[19] ECtHR, *Catan and Others v Russian Federation*, no 43370/04, 19.10.2012.
[20] ECtHR, *OAO Neftyanaya Kompaniya YUKOS v Russian Federation*, no 14902/04, 20.09.2011 (on the merits) and 31.07.2014 (just satisfaction).
[21] ECtHR, *Hirst v United Kingdom (no. 2)*, no 74025/01 [GC] 06.10.2005.
[22] CM, 2015 Report on supervision of the execution of judgments and decisions of the European Court of Human Rights, published in April 2017, p. 10.

strong insistence from the CM, the individual measures required or to pay just satisfaction.[23] The report of the CLAHR provides for examples for each of the above-mentioned categories.[24]

As regards the first category of problems, i.e. 'important and complex structural problems', many of them have been listed in the CLAHR report with respect to the ten countries with the highest number of non-implemented judgments[25] (e.g. cases concerning excessive length of judicial proceedings in Bulgaria, Hungary, Italy, Poland, Romania and Ukraine or poor conditions of detention in Bulgaria, Hungary, the Republic of Moldova, Romania, the Russian Federation and Ukraine). Several of these judgments have not been implemented for more than ten years (examples concerning other countries might be found in the CM Annual Reports, including the one from 2017). One of the most illustrative examples in this context is that of the Ukrainian cases concerning non-execution of final domestic judgments (*Zhovner v Ukraine* group).[26] As no solution had been found at the domestic level to solve this structural problem and to prevent the increasing number of applications to the ECtHR, under Articles 19 and 46 of the Convention, the Court decided to send over 12,000 of them to the CM, for the examination of general measures (see the *Burmych v Ukraine* judgment).[27]

As regards 'the absence of a common understanding of the scope of the execution measures required following developments of the Court's case law', the *Catan and Others v Russian Federation*, concerning a violation of the right to education of numerous children from Latin-script schools located in the Transdniestrian region of the Republic of Moldova (violation of Article 2 of Protocol No 1), fits very well into this category of implementation problems. In this case, the Court and, subsequently, the Committee of Ministers pointed out that Russia incurred responsibility under the Convention, which the Russian authorities do not acknowledge.[28]

According to the CLAHR report, the judgments *Sejdić and Finci v Bosnia and Herzegovina*, *Paksas v Lithuania* and to a certain extent *Hirst v United Kingdom (no. 2)* – which will be examined in detail below – are representative of the third group of problems. As regards the fourth group, the *Ilgar Mammadov v Azerbaijan* and *OAO Neftyanaya Kompaniya YUKOS v Russian*

---

[23] Ibid., p. 13.
[24] PACE, CLAHR report, *supra* note 11, p. 24.
[25] Ibid., Section 2 and Appendix.
[26] ECtHR, *Zhovner v Ukraine* group, no 56848/00, 29.06.2004. See also ECtHR, *Yuriy Nikolayevich Ivanov v Ukraine*, no 40450/04, 15.01.2010.
[27] ECtHR, *Burmych v Ukraine* judgment, nos 46852/13, 47786/13, 54125/13 et al. [GC] 12.10.2017.
[28] CM, DH-DD(2017)976 (communication from the Russian authorities). The decisions adopted by the Committee of Ministers at its DH meetings and communications from the authorities can be consulted on the HUDOC-EXEC site.

Federation judgments, as well as those against Turkey concerning the northern part of Cyprus (*Cyprus v Turkey*,[29] *Varnava and Others v Turkey*[30] and *Xenides-Arestis v Turkey*[31] group of cases), are examples of 'outright refusal to execute'.[32] While in the case of *Mammadov v Azerbaijan* the respondent State has not released the applicant, which was required by the CM, in the remaining cases the respondent States refrained from paying to the applicants the just satisfaction awarded by the Court.

The CM's list of major problems in the implementation of ECtHR judgments contains a mixture of various situations ('slow or blocked execution') and reasons of non-implementation ('important and complex structural problems', 'a refusal to adopt measures' or 'the absence of common understanding as to the scope of the execution measures required'). It does not group in an exhaustive way the problems which may be at the origin of delayed execution (including 'slow or blocked execution'). Therefore, it seems that the formula of 'pockets of resistance' used in the CM 2015 Annual Report may be more useful to undertake a thorough analysis of the causes of delayed implementation or non-implementation. Unfortunately, a detailed analysis of the main examples falling into the fourth groups of 'pocket of resistance' would go beyond the scope of this article. Therefore, consideration will be given to three judgments/groups of judgments concerning electoral issues mentioned in the CLAHR report: judgments from the group *Hirst v the United Kingdom (no. 2)*, the *Paksas v Lithuania* judgment and judgments from the group *Sejdić and Finci v Bosnia and Herzegovina*. They are a good example of 'slow or blocked execution as a result of disagreement between national institutions, or amongst political parties, as regards the substance of the reforms required and/or the procedure to be followed'. Due to their problematic, they are anything but politically neutral. Although the Court has found violations of the Convention rights (under Article 3 of Protocol No 1 and Article 14) in very different factual circumstances, a reform of the electoral system is required as an execution measure (a general measure) for all these judgments; with respect to granting voting rights in the *Hirst (no. 2)* cases (active aspect of the right to vote) and – in the two other cases – with respect to the right to stand for election (passive aspect of this right). All these judgments have been pending on the agenda of the CM for many years: *Hirst (no. 2)* since October 2005, *Paksas* since January 2011 and *Sejdić and Finci* since December 2009.

---

[29] ECtHR, *Cyprus v Turkey*, supra note 9.
[30] ECtHR, *Varnava and Ohers v Turkey*, nos 16064/90 et al. [GC] 18.12.2009.
[31] ECtHR, *Xenides-Arestis v Turkey*, group of cases, no 46347/99, 22.12.2005 and 07.12.2006.
[32] The CLAHR's report also focuses on the *Al Nashiri* and *Husayn v Poland* judgments; however, it finds that they are quite distinct from these four groups.

3. EXAMPLES OF DELAYS IN CASES CONCERNING ELECTORAL ISSUES

3.1. *HIRST v THE UNITED KINGDOM (NO. 2)* AND OTHER SIMILAR JUDGMENTS

In *Hirst (no. 2)*, the ECtHR found a violation of Article 3 of Protocol No 1 to the Convention because of a blanket ban on all convicted prisoners voting in parliamentary elections (section 3 of the Representation of the People Act 1983). The Court noted that the restriction applied to all convicted prisoners in prison, irrespective of the length of their sentence and irrespective of the nature or gravity of their offence and their individual circumstances, and thus as 'a general, automatic and indiscriminate restriction on a vitally important Convention right' fell 'outside any acceptable margin of appreciation', which was 'large, but not all-embracing'.[33] The ban affected 48,000 prisoners. The Court left it to the UK legislature to 'decide on the choice of means for securing the rights guaranteed by Article 3 of Protocol No. 1'.[34] As no progress had been achieved in the implementation of this judgment despite several strong decisions of the CM and its Interim Resolution CM/ResDH(2009),[35] in November 2010, the Court delivered a 'pilot judgment' in a further case, *Greens and M.T. v the United Kingdom*,[36] concerning the applicants' ineligibility to vote in a general election and in the elections to the European Parliament (EP). The ECtHR found again that the blanket ban on voting of imprisoned convicted offenders was in violation of Article 3 of Protocol No 1 and that this was due to the non-implementation of the *Hirst (no. 2)* judgment.[37] It also noted that the blanket restriction imposed by the 1983 Act had been extended to elections to the EP[38] and that more than 70,000 prisoners were likely to have been affected by the ban since the *Hirst (no. 2)* judgment and might be potential applicants.[39] As there were 2,500 similar applications pending, the Court found that the UK's failure to introduce legislative proposals was 'not only an aggravating factor as regards the State's responsibility under the Convention for an existing or past state of affairs, but also represents a threat to the future effectiveness of the Convention machinery [...]'.[40] It stressed that a legislative amendment was required to render the electoral law compatible with the requirements of

---

[33] ECtHR, *Hirst v the United Kingdom (no. 2)*, *supra* note 21, para. 82.
[34] Ibid., para. 84.
[35] CM, Interim Resolution CM/ResDH(2009)160 adopted on 3 December 2009.
[36] ECtHR, *Greens and M.T. v the United Kingdom*, nos. 60041/08 and 60054/08, judgment of 23 November 2010.
[37] Ibid., pp. 78–79.
[38] By Section 8(1) of the European Parliamentary Elections Act 2002.
[39] ECtHR, *Greens and M.T. v the UK*, *supra* note 36, paras. 75 and 111.
[40] Ibid., para. 111.

the Convention and that it was for the Government to decide how to achieve this compliance.[41] Therefore, it decided to give a six-month deadline for the authorities to bring forward appropriate legislative proposals and to discontinue the examination of applications registered prior to the date of delivery of this judgment. The deadline was further extended till 23 November 2012,[42] following the Grand Chamber judgment in the case of *Scoppola v Italy (no. 3)*,[43] in which the Court had found no violation of Article 3 of Protocol No 1.

On 22 November 2012, the UK government submitted to Parliament a draft bill to amend the electoral legislation setting out three options, which were further considered by a joint committee of the two houses of Parliament.[44] On 18 December 2013, the Parliament's Joint Committee on the Draft Voting Eligibility (Prisoners) Bill published a report, in which it did not recommend re-enacting the existing blanket ban.[45] However, prisoners had not been allowed to vote in the general elections of May 2015 and June 2017. Although on 12 March 2013, the ECtHR decided to adjourn the examination of 2,300 applications concerning this problem, on 24 September 2013, it decided to resume their consideration.[46] Between August 2014 and February 2016, the Court handed down three judgments similar to *Hirst (no. 2)* and concerning very numerous applicants prevented from voting in general elections and/or elections to the EP *(Firth and Others, McHugh and Others* and *Millbank and Others)*.[47]

In its Interim Resolution CM/ResDH(2015)251 of December 2015,[48] the CM expressed its 'profound concern' that the blanket ban on the right to vote of convicted prisoners in custody remained in place and invited the UK authorities to continue high-level dialogue on this issue. The authorities pursued this dialogue with key stakeholders of the Council of Europe,[49] stressing that its purpose was to gather ideas and options on how to implement

---

[41] Ibid., paras. 112–114.
[42] CM, DH-DD(2011)679E of 5.09. 2011.
[43] ECtHR, *Scoppola v Italy (no. 3)*, no 126/05 [GC] 22.05.2012. The ECtHR has found no violation of Article 3 of Protocol No 1, because under Italian law only a very specific category of prisoners lost the right to vote. Following the submission by the UK, which acted as a third party in this case, the Court confirmed that each State had a wide discretion as to how it regulated the ban on voting.
[44] See *Voting Eligibility (Prisoners) Draft Bill* of 22.11.2012 and CM, DH-DD(2012)1106.
[45] Joint Committee of the House of Lords and the House of Commons, published on 18.12.2013, available at https://publications.parliament.uk/pa/jt201314/jtselect/jtdraftvoting/103/103.pdf, last accessed 22.05.2018.
[46] ECtHR, Press Release of 26.03.2013, and letter from the ECtHR Registry to the CM of 24.10.2013.
[47] ECtHR, *Firth and Others*, no 47784/09, 12.08.2014 (Chamber judgment); *McHugh and others*, no 51987/08, 10.02.2015 (Committee judgment) and *Millbank and others*, no 44473/14, 30.06.2016 (Committee judgment). The first one concerned 10 applications, the second one 1,015 and the third one 22.
[48] Adopted at its 1243rd meeting (DH) in December 2015.
[49] CM, DH-DD (2016)188, DH-DD(2016)734 and DH-DD(2016)1170.

the relevant judgments without amending section 3 of the Representation of the People Act 1983, as Parliament continued to oppose the passage of new legislation.[50]

Recently, progress seems to have been achieved. The UK authorities announced that they would give the right to vote to about 100 inmates in England and Wales released on 'temporary licence' and those released on home curfew.[51] If adopted, these new (administrative) measures would only give the right to vote to a small group of prisoners; nevertheless, it seems that it will be accepted and it will end a long battle over prisoners' voting rights between the UK authorities and the Council of Europe. As stressed by the UK authorities in their letter to the CM of November 2017, these measures 'have been developed to address the judgment and bring us within the margin of appreciation'.[52] They result from a 'fruitful dialogue' with other Member States of the Council of Europe and the Secretariat of the CM. According to the UK government, 'given that the custodial threshold in the UK is such that a custodial sentence is only given in the most serious offences and where it is appropriate and proportionate to do so, prisoners who reach that custodial threshold should not in general vote'.[53] Therefore, the UK government envisages taking administrative measures to give the right to vote to small a group of prisoners serving short sentences. Bearing in mind the fact that the applicant in the *Hirst (no. 2)* case had been sentenced to a discretionary life sentence (however, he had already been released from prison on licence when he complained to the ECtHR), it will be interesting to see how the CM will assess the measures proposed by the UK authorities. Will it accept a minimalistic and compromise solution in order to close a long-standing battle over the implementation of this judgment?

The answer will not be known until 1 September 2018 at the earliest (i.e. the deadline fixed by the CM to provide further information).[54] So far, the CM's reaction has been positive. The judgments in question were discussed by the Committee of Ministers at its 1,302nd (DH) meeting (5–7 December 2017), in the presence of the UK Secretary of State for Justice. In its decision taken at this meeting, the CM 'noted with satisfaction the package of administrative measures proposed by the authorities, in particular the changes in policy and guidance in relation to prisoners released on temporary licence and on home detention curfew', and considered that, 'in the light of the wide margin of appreciation in this area, these measures respond' to the ECtHR's judgments from this group.

---

[50] CM, DH-DD (2016)1201.
[51] BBC, 'Prisoner Voting Compromise Ends Dispute with European Court', 07.12.2017, available at http://www.bbc.com/news/uk-42271100, last accessed 22.05.2018.
[52] CM, DH-DD(2017)1229 of 02.11.2017, communication from the United Kingdom concerning the case of *Hirst v the United Kingdom (no. 2)*, 2.
[53] CM, DH-DD(2017)1229 of 02.11.2017, *supra* note 52.
[54] CM, decision taken at its 1302nd meeting (DH), December 2017.

On this basis, the CM encouraged the UK authorities to implement the proposed measures 'as soon as possible'.[55]

The issue of prisoners' voting rights is a political one and touches upon a State's right to organise its own electoral system. It is understandable that a complaint by a man, who like the applicant in the case of *Hirst (no. 2)* has been convicted for life prison for manslaughter, might have raised numerous controversies. In the said judgment, the ECtHR, on the basis of a survey provided by the UK government, noted that in thirteen Member States of the Council of Europe (including the UK) all prisoners were barred from voting or unable to vote[56] and that the law in the UK was 'less far-reaching than in certain other States'.[57] However, according to the Court, a blanket restriction on the right of prisoners to vote was imposed only in a 'minority of Contracting States' and 'even if no common European approach to the problem can be discerned, this cannot in itself be determinative of the issue'.[58] The fact that the Court did not pay much attention to the lack of consensus on this issue at the European level was raised by the five ECtHR judges who voted against the finding of a violation on this judgment. In their joint dissenting opinion, Judges Wildhaber, Costa, Lorenzen, Kovler and Jebens concluded that the legislation in Europe showed little consensus about whether or not prisoners should have the right to vote, the majority of Member States knew such restrictions (although not always blanket) and that the UK 'cannot be claimed to be in disharmony with a common European standard'.[59] According to these judges, 'taking into account the sensitive political character of this issue, the diversity of the legal systems within the Contracting States and the lack of a sufficiently clear basis for such a right in Article 3 of Protocol No. 1', it was not acceptable that 'it is for the Court to impose on national legal systems an obligation either to abolish disenfranchisement for prisoners or to allow it only to a very limited extend'.[60]

Concerns also appeared in the dissenting opinions of two judges in the judgment *Firth and Others*. Judges Nicolaou and Wojtyczek found that the conclusions of the Grand Chamber in the *Scoppola (no. 3)* judgment, in which the Court accepted that disenfranchisement might take effect on the basis of legislative provisions and without a judicial decision, had not been followed in this case.[61] Moreover, as to the admissibility criteria, Judge Nicolaou pointed

---

[55] See paragraphs 2 to 4 of the decision adopted in this case.
[56] ECtHR, *Hirst v the United Kingdom (no. 2)*, *supra* note 21, para. 33.
[57] Ibid., para. 81.
[58] Ibid.
[59] ECtHR, *Hirst v the United Kingdom (no. 2)*, *supra* note 21, joint dissenting opinion of Judges Wildhaber, Costa, Loreñen, Kovler and Jebens, para. 6.
[60] Ibid., para. 9.
[61] In the *Scoppola v Italy (no. 3)* judgment, the Court did not find a violation of Article 3 of Protocol No 1 with respect to the applicant's disenfranchisement, which was based on a law according to which only prisoners convicted of certain offences against the State or the

out that the applicants had given no details of their sentences and had not informed the Court whether they were still in detention (which was primordial for determining their status of victim). Judge Wojtyczek recalled, *inter alia*, that according to the *travaux préparatoires* to the Convention States kept a very broad scope of freedom in the domain of elections[62] and raised doubts as to the appropriateness of the use of the term 'blanket ban' in the context of *Hirst (no. 2)* (as it does not apply to persons in detention on remand) and applicability of Article 3 of Protocol No 1 to elections to the EP, in view of the 'democratic deficit' of the EU. Recalling the findings of the five dissenting judges in *Hirst (no. 2)*, he concluded that the ECtHR's case law on voting rights 'does not yield any clear answer as to what restrictions of voting rights are permissible and what restrictions are prohibited', and therefore should be revisited.[63]

Despite the doubts expressed by some of its judges in *Hirst (no. 2)*, the ECtHR followed its case law in a number of cases concerning other Member States of the Council of Europe, namely Austria (*Frodl*),[64] Bulgaria (*Kulinski and Sabev*),[65] the Russian Federation (*Anchugov and Gladkov*)[66] and Turkey (*Soyrel* and *Murat Vural*).[67] In *Frodl v Austria*, the impugned electoral legislation provided for a blanket ban on the vote of prisoners serving a term of imprisonment for more than one year for an offence committed with intent; following the ECtHR's judgment, the Electoral Code was amended accordingly in 2011 and the CM decided to close the supervision of the execution of this judgment.[68] The other cases pending before the CM supervision of execution are examined under the 'enhanced procedure'. They all concern an automatic disenfranchisement of convicted prisoners and, what is more, in the Bulgarian and Russian legal systems this restriction is clearly provided in the Constitution. The CM awaits information on implementation measures on these cases, although some progress has already been achieved in the Turkish cases (namely the Constitutional Court found unconstitutional Article 53 of the Turkish Criminal Code on the prisoners' right to vote).[69] Although the implementation of the Austrian case

---

judicial system, or sentenced to at least three years' imprisonment, lost the right to vote. The applicant sentenced to life imprisonment for a murder was automatically imposed a ban on public office, including permanent forfeiture of his right to vote. See ECtHR, *Scoppola v Italy (no. 3)*, *supra* note 43.

62   ECtHR, *Firth and Others*, *supra* note 47, dissenting opinion of Judge Wojtyczek, para. 3.
63   ECtHR, *Firth and Others*, dissenting opinion of Judge Wojtyczek, para. 8.
64   ECtHR, *Frodl*, no 20201/04, 08.04.2010.
65   ECtHR, *Kulinski and Sabev*, no 63849/09, 21.07.2017.
66   ECtHR, *Anchugov and Gladkov*, no 11157/04, 04.07.2013.
67   ECtHR, *Soyrel*, no 29411/07, 17.09.2013; ECtHR, *Murat Vural*, no 9540/07, 21.10.2014.
68   CM, Resolution CM/ResDH(2011)91 of 14.09.2011.
69   HUDOC-EXEC, Case description, *Söyler v Turkey*. Information on the state of execution in all these cases is available in the database HUDOC-EXEC, available at http://hudoc.exec.coe.int, last accessed 22.05.2018.

concerning this problematic has been quick, issues raised in the other judgments do not appear to be resolved speedily and might entail delays as in *Hirst (no. 2)*, despite the fact that, in the case of *Anchugov and Gladkov v Russia*, the Court stressed that a constitutional amendment was not indispensable to implement this judgment.[70]

3.2. PAKSAS v LITHUANIA

The judgment of *Paksas v Lithuania* is another example of flagrant delays in implementation. It concerns the former President of the Republic of Lithuania, Mr Rolandas Paksas, who was impeached from this office in April 2004 on gross violations of the Constitution found by the Constitutional Court (including unlawful granting of citizenship to a Russian businessman born in a Soviet military family). Following the impeachment, Mr Paksas was prevented from standing for elections to Parliament (Seimas), in accordance with the Constitutional Court's ruling of 25 May 2004 and the Law on Elections to the Seimas of 15 July 2004 adopted further to that ruling. The Court recalled that States enjoyed 'considerable latitude in establishing criteria governing eligibility to stand for election, and may impose stricter requirements in that context than in the context of eligibility to vote', but 'while the margin of appreciation is wide, it is not all-embracing'.[71] The Court pointed out that that Mr Paksas was permanently and irreversibly deprived of the opportunity to stand for election to Parliament and also from holding any other office for which it was necessary to take an oath in accordance with the Constitution. This restriction was based on a rule 'set in constitutional stone'.[72] According to the Court, a decision on barring a senior official from ever being a member of parliament was 'above all a matter for voters, who have the opportunity to choose at the polls whether to renew their trust in the person concerned'[73] and 'Lithuania's position in this area constituted an exception in Europe',[74] as in the majority of Council of Europe's Member States with a republican system impeachment had no effect on the electoral rights of the impeached person. The Court found that the 'permanent and irreversible nature'[75] of the applicant's disqualification from standing for elections was a disproportionate restriction and therefore violated Article 3 of Protocol No 1. Under Article 46 of the Convention, it urged the authorities to take steps to put an end to the violation and make all feasible reparation for its

---

[70] ECtHR, *Firth and Others*, supra note 47, dissenting opinion of Judge Wojtyczek, para. 111.
[71] ECtHR, *Paksas v Lithuania*, supra note 17, para. 96.
[72] Ibid., para. 110.
[73] Ibid., para. 104.
[74] Ibid., para. 106.
[75] Ibid., para. 111.

consequences, in such a way as to restore as far as possible the situation existing before the breach.[76]

Since this judgment became final in 2011, almost no progress has been achieved concerning the required individual and general measures (in this case, both types of measures are closely interrelated). Since 2004, Mr Paksas, who is currently a member of the European Parliament, has been unable to stand in the Seimas elections. Despite the ECtHR's judgment, he had been prevented from standing for the elections of October 2012 and October 2016. Although the CM was informed about several attempts to revise the Constitution,[77] there has not been any change of legislation which would have been an appropriate response to the judgment. In September 2012, a first attempt to modify the Seimas Electoral Act of 15 July 2004 was found unconstitutional by the Constitutional Court, which held that constitutional amendments were required to bring domestic law into line with Article 3 of Protocol No 1. In November 2012, a draft law proposing constitutional amendments was sent to the Seimas, but its adoption was postponed at the request of members from Mr Paksas's party; in the meantime, the Constitutional Court ruled that this draft law would be unconstitutional. Subsequently, following intervention of the UN Human Rights Committee,[78] an ad hoc investigation commission was established to examine the reasons for the non-implementation of this judgment. Another draft law was sent to the Seimas in March 2015, but it was rejected in December 2015 on its second reading (after members of Mr Paksas's party had again asked for postponement of its adoption). The applicant could not stand for the spring 2016 elections[79] and he was apparently involved in another corruption scandal. At their 1273rd meeting (DH) in December 2016, the CM expressed its deep concern over this turn of events, emphasised that the authorities were under an unconditional obligation to take steps to comply with the judgment, and took note of the authorities' continuing commitment to undertake all further efforts to ensure execution.[80] A few days later, on 22 December 2016, the Constitutional Court reaffirmed that a constitutional amendment was necessary to implement the ECtHR's judgment in this case. In March 2017, the authorities submitted again the previous version of the draft law,[81] but, due to the collapse of the coalition in September 2017, it was only debated for the first time in March 2018.[82] At its 1310th meeting (DH) in March 2018, the Committee of Ministers noted with 'grave concern' that 'no tangible progress has been achieved,

---

[76] ECtHR, *Paksas v Lithuania, supra* note 17, para. 119.
[77] CM, para 1. of the decision adopted at the 1310th meeting (March 2018).
[78] UN, CCPR/C/110/D/2155/2012.
[79] CM/Notes/1310/H46-10.
[80] CM, decision adopted at the 1273rd (DH) meeting (December 2016).
[81] CM, DH-DD(2016)884 and DH-DD(2018)20.
[82] CM, DH-DD(2018)20-add.

so that the situation found to be in breach of the Convention still persists'.[83] It regretted the stalemate which had existed in the Seimas since December 2015 and urged the authorities and political leaders to take all necessary action to comply with the judgment. The CM decided to examine this case again in December 2018 and to consider the adoption of an interim resolution, if the legislative process did not lead to tangible results.

While reflecting on the delays in the implementation of this judgment, it is interesting to recall the dissenting opinion by Judge Costa (joined by Judges Tsotsoria and Baka). He stressed that the case was political and unusual, because impeachment proceedings were rarely instituted in Europe and elsewhere in the world.[84] Considering that the case was inadmissible for formal reasons, Judge Costa stressed that although the penalty imposed on the applicant was severe, the allegations against him 'were not trivial either' and the impeachment took place following a high-court decision. Judge Costa concluded that 'in such a specific and delicate field as electoral law, and in a case involving the complex relations between the different public authorities, subject to the ultimate scrutiny of the electorate, and thus the sovereign people', he 'would advocate restraint; the State has a wide discretion, and therefore [...] the legitimate European supervision in this case should be restricted or limited'.[85]

3.3. SEJDIĆ AND FINCI v BOSNIA AND HERZEGOVINA AND OTHER SIMILAR JUDGMENTS

In *Sejdić and Finci v Bosnia and Herzegovina*,[86] the Court, for the first time, found that there has been a violation of Article 1 of Protocol No 12 prohibiting discrimination in the enjoyment of any right 'set forth by law'.[87] It found that the country's presidential election procedure was discriminatory, since it prevented the applicants (on the grounds of their Roma and Jewish origin) from standing in these elections due to their refusal to declare affiliation with a 'constituent people' (namely the Bosniacs, Croats or Serbs). The Constitution of Bosnia and Herzegovina made such a declaration of affiliation a condition of eligibility to stand for election for the Presidency and the House of Peoples (the second chamber of the State Parliament). The Court also found a violation of Article 14 taken in conjunction with Article 3 of Protocol No 1, as for the same reasons the applicants were prevented from standing in the elections to the House of Peoples. It concluded that their ineligibility lacked an objective and reasonable

---

[83] CM, Decision adopted at the 1310th (DH) meeting (March 2018).
[84] ECtHR, *Paksas v Lithuania*, supra note 17, dissenting opinion by Judge Costa, para. 2.
[85] Ibid., para. 12.
[86] ECtHR, *Sejdić and Finci v Bosnia and Herzegovina*, supra note 16.
[87] Only twenty Council of Europe's Member States have ratified this protocol (as of 26.03.2018).

justification and was discriminatory. Although at the time when the Dayton Agreement (including as one of the appendices the Constitution of the country) was approved in 1995, the approval of the 'constituent peoples' was necessary to ensure peace, there have been 'significant positive developments' since then.[88] By becoming a member of the Council of Europe, Bosnia and Herzegovina undertook to 'review within one year, with the assistance of the European Commission for Democracy through Law (Venice Commission), the electoral legislation in the light of Council of Europe standards, and to revise it where necessary'. A similar commitment was also accepted under the Stabilisation and Association Agreement with the European Union in 2008.[89]

The CM has been supervising the implementation of this judgment since December 2009. It has always considered that several amendments to the Constitution and the electoral legislation should be adopted to implement it (again, individual measures are interrelated with general ones). However, despite the elections of October 2010 and October 2014, the legislation has not been modified. The CM adopted three interim resolutions – CM/ResDH(2011)291, CM/ResDH(2012)233 and CM/ResDH(2013)259[90] – calling on the country's authorities and political leaders to ensure that the Constitution and legislation meet the requirements of the Convention. In these interim resolutions and its numerous decisions, the CM has also stated on a number of occasions that implementation of the judgment is a legal obligation for Bosnia and Herzegovina.

In July 2014 and May 2016, the Court found similar violations in two other cases: *Zornić v Bosnia and Herzegovina* (in which the applicant refused to declare affiliation with any of the 'constituent people') and *Šlaku v Bosnia and Herzegovina* (in which the applicant was of Albanian origin).[91] Referring to Article 46 of the Convention in both judgments, the ECtHR stated that the violations were 'the direct result of failure of the authorities to introduce measures to ensure compliance with the judgment in *Sejdić and Finci*'.[92] The failure to introduce the necessary constitutional and legislative proposals was considered as, like in *Greens and M.T. v the UK*, 'not only an aggravating factor as regards the State's responsibility under the Convention for an existing or past state of affairs', but also as 'a threat to the future effectiveness of the Convention machinery'.[93] Referring to the Dayton Agreement, the Court noted that 'eighteen years after the end of the tragic conflict, there could be no longer any reason for the maintenance of the contested constitutional provisions'. Therefore,

---

[88] ECtHR, *Sejdić and Finci v Bosnia and Herzegovina*, supra note 16, paras. 45 and 46.
[89] Ibid., para. 48.
[90] Adopted respectively on 02.12.2011, 06.12.2012 and 05.12.2013.
[91] ECtHR, *Zornić v Bosnia and Hewrzegovina*, no 3681/06, 15.07.2014; *Šlaku v Bosnia and Herzegovina*, no 56666/12, 26.05.2016 and *Pilav v Bosnia and Herzegovina*, no 41939/07, 09.06.2016.
[92] ECtHR, *Zornić*, para. 40, and *Šlaku*, para. 37.
[93] Ibid.

it 'expects that democratic arrangements will be made without further delay'.[94] In June 2016, the ECtHR delivered another judgment concerning this problem – *Pilav v Bosnia and Hercegovina*,[95] in which it found (only) a violation of Article 1 of Protocol No 12 (as the applicant, a Bosniac living in Republika Srpska was ineligible to stand for the presidential elections).

At its 1273rd meeting (DH) in December 2016, the CM noted with deep concern that no tangible progress had been made in this case since June 2015 (at the 1230th meeting). It also noted that that the authorities' efforts to launch the constitutional amendment process continued to be blocked as a consequence of the lack of consensus between the leaders of the political parties. Since the issue of the implementation of these judgments is being considered in the framework of the negotiations on Bosnia and Herzegovina's accession to the European Union,[96] the CM invited the Member States and the European Union to raise the issue of the execution of judgments in their contacts with Bosnia and Herzegovina.[97] The judgments were examined by the CM at its 1288th (DH) meeting (6–7 June 2017). Since no tangible information had been provided on the measures taken, the CM once again expressed its concern regarding this matter and recalled Bosnia and Herzegovina's obligation under Article 46 paragraph 1, to comply with the Court's judgments.[98]

The issue of implementation of this group of judgments is also being closely followed by other bodies of the Council of Europe, namely the Assembly and its Committee on the Honouring of Obligations and Commitments by Member States of the Council of Europe (Monitoring Committee). The Assembly has urged Bosnia and Herzegovina to implement the *Sejdić and Finci* judgment and to amend its Constitution without delay (see, in particular, its Resolutions 1701 (2010), 1725 (2010), 1855 (2012) and Recommendation 2025 (2013) concerning specifically this country; moreover, in Resolution 2149 (2017) on the progress of the monitoring procedure the Assembly once again called on Bosnia and Herzegovina to implement the said group of judgments). The European Committee against Racism and Intolerance has also strongly recommended that the authorities implement these judgments.[99]

In order to understand this stalemate, the arguments invoked by certain judges of the ECtHR at the time when the *Sejdić and Finci* judgment was delivered might shed some light on this issue. In his partly concurring and

---

[94] See *Zornić*, para. 43 and *Šlaku*, para. 40.
[95] ECtHR, *Pilav, supra* note 91.
[96] See, in particular, the European Parliament Resolution of 15.02.2017 on the 2016 Commission Report on Bosnia and Herzegovina and the Council conclusions on the application of Bosnia and Herzegovina for membership of the EU,Press Release, 20.09.2016.
[97] CM, decision taken at the 1273rd (DH) meeting (December 2016).
[98] See paragraphs 3 and 4 of its decision adopted at the 1288th (DH) meeting.
[99] ECRI, CRI (2017)2.

partly dissenting opinion Judge Mijović, joined by Judge Hajiyev, as well as Judge Bonello, in his dissenting opinion, considered that the Grand Chamber had failed to analyse the historical background and the circumstances in which the Bosnia and Herzegovina Constitution was imposed. Judges Mijović and Hajiyev considered that the Court entered 'a highly sensitive area'. Judge Bonello questioned the Court's finding that the situation in the country had changed, that the transitional period was over and that the 'delicate tripartite equilibrium', laboriously reached and based on an international treaty was no longer prevailing. In his view, it was not the Court's role to assess this situation but the national authorities'. Concerning the violation of Article 14 taken in conjunction with Article 3 of Protocol No 1, Judges Mijović and Hajiyev did not share the majority's view, contesting the applicability of the latter provision, mainly because members of the House of Peoples were appointed by the Entity Parliaments and not 'elected'. Therefore, there was no general right for anyone to stand for election to the House of Peoples, which had neither the characteristics nor the powers of a second chamber. Similarly, in his dissenting opinion to the judgment *Zornić v Bosnia and Herzegovina*, Judge Wojtyczek concluded that 'if Article 3 of Protocol No 1 allows a method of selecting the members of the second chamber other than through election by citizens, we can derive from this provision neither a subjective right to vote nor a subjective right to stand in elections to this chamber'; therefore, in his view, Article 14 was not applicable.

4. CONCLUSION

There are various situations in which political considerations delay the implementation of a judgment or even block it for many years. Cases concerning the right to vote or discrimination in its enjoyment have been on the agenda of the CM for many years (almost 13 years for *Hirst (no. 2)*, seven for *Paksas* and eight and a half for *Sejdić and Finci*), provoking a stalemate in the supervision process conducted by the CM due to an evident lack of progress. In all these cases, the Court and the CM have required that the respondent State take legislative measures in order to comply with the Court's judgments. The delays resulted from blockage in national parliaments and/or from the lack of agreement between leaders of main political groups. Therefore, the executive's will is not always sufficient and the CM action appears less efficient when implementation depends primarily on the decision and good will of the legislature.

Although there is some hope that the CM will close the examination of the cases from the *Hirst (no. 2)* group, if the authorities adopt the recently announced administrative measures, the closure of the two remaining cases/groups of cases seems to be more remote or perhaps even impossible at this stage. Moreover, if the proposal of the UK authorities to close the examination of the *Hirst (no. 2)* group is accepted by the CM, such a solution will raise doubts as to the effectiveness of the supervision system based on Article 46 paragraph 2 of the Convention. This would mean, it is suggested, that the CM has accepted administrative measures, while the Court has repeated on several occasions that the 1983 Act of the Representation of People needed to be amended. In this long-standing battle, on one hand, the UK authorities have consistently defended their own national system and their margin of appreciation. On the other hand, the ECtHR has made its case law evolve, by adjudicating in cases concerning similar issues in other States Parties to the Convention (Austria, Bulgaria, Italy, the Russian Federation and Turkey). Interestingly, in his dissenting opinion to *Firth and Others v the UK*, Judge Wojtyczek has concluded that this case law is not coherent and could perhaps be revisited, especially in the view of the nature of the issue at stake, which is at the heart of every electoral system. In this context, it will be also interesting to follow the CM's line in its supervision of the implementation of judgments concerning prisoners' voting rights in other States Parties. Will it take a firm stance and require constitutional and legislative amendments, or will it adopt a more minimalistic approach?

The *Paksas v Lithuania* case, in which the Seimas plays a key role, is a good example of the role of national parliaments in the implementation of ECtHR judgments. Due to political blockage and to the involvement of the Constitutional Court, several legislative initiatives have been dropped or suspended. The necessity of making the required legislative changes via constitutional amendments accentuates complexity to this case. The stalemate at the Seimas is due to various political considerations, including obstacles coming from the applicant's political party, whose members twice postponed the adoption of the draft law at stake. One can also conclude that the CM has been quite 'patient' as, besides the adoption of some stronger decisions following its DH meeting, it has not yet adopted any interim resolution in this case. As this case concerns the impeachment of a former President of the Republic, it is unique, and it is unlikely that similar cases, even against other States Parties, would reach the ECtHR.

One cannot examine the judgment of *Sejdić and Finci v Bosnia and Herzegovina* out of the context in which the State of Bosnia and Herzegovina was established. Nevertheless, despite all political considerations, the legal obligations stemming from this judgment are clear: the Constitution and the electoral laws must be amended. Since the end of 2009, no progress has been noted in that direction. It seems that the CM, which has already adopted three interim resolutions and several strong decisions, lacks ammunition in this respect. Within the Council of Europe, the case has been followed not only by the CM, but also by the PACE in the framework of the monitoring procedure with respect to Bosnia and Herzegovina, which shows that the implementation of this group of judgments has a clearly political dimension. Moreover, it is also important in the context of this country's relations with the European Union.[100]

One could argue about the correctness of the Court's finding of violations in the judgments in question. Some interesting arguments as to the political context or the scope of the rights enshrined in Article 3 of Protocol No 1 appear in the dissenting opinions of ECtHR judges. They explain, to a certain extent, the delays in execution. One could perhaps also argue that the CM (and especially its Secretariat) should pay attention to these opinions when it carries out its tasks based on Article 46 paragraph 2 of the Convention. Interestingly, despite the dissenting opinions of some judges, the ECtHR did not change its case law in dealing with further cases concerning similar problems – as in *Hirst* and *Sejdić and Finci*. It has reconfirmed its previous findings and referred to Article 46 of the Convention to underline the State's failure to take the required general measures. Although such (pilot or quasi-pilot) judgments might be useful for the CM in determining execution measures, the above-mentioned examples show that this has not been particularly the case in practice. Delays in execution became lengthier and political leaders did not pay much attention to the follow-up judgments. Therefore, even if the Court 'intervenes' in the execution process, by giving some indications as to the required execution measures, in cases which are politically sensitive, this does not considerably speed up this process.

---

[100] See, for example, B. HUSZKA, 'The EU's Changing Conditionality on Anti-Discrimination in Bosnia and Herzegovina', EYHR 2017 (European Yearbook on Human Rights), NWV, Vienna 2017, pp. 237–250.

PART IV
OSCE

ENHANCED STRUCTURE AND GEOGRAPHICAL BALANCE

Reforming the OSCE's Human Dimension Meetings

Jean P. FROEHLY

You have to try the impossible in order to achieve the possible

Hermann Hesse

1. Introduction 468
2. The OSCE Human Dimension and its Review Meetings
   in the Context of the OSCE's Comprehensive Security Concept......... 468
3. OSCE Human Dimension Meetings: The Need for Reform............. 470
4. Reform Proposals I: Duration of HDIM and 'Standing Agenda'......... 473
5. Reform Proposals II: Geographical Balance and Enhanced
   Structure of the Human Dimension Review........................ 474
6. Reform Proposals III: A Structured and Geographically Balanced
   OSCE Implementation Review Mechanism 476
7. Conclusion.. 478

ABSTRACT

Competing with other international and regional intergovernmental organisations in the area of fundamental freedoms and human rights, the review mechanism of the Organisation for Security and Co-operation in Europe (OSCE) Human Dimension is currently struggling for to maintain its relevance. The article provides an overview of the reform proposals concerning the review conferences of OSCE Human Dimension and advocates in favour of a comprehensive reform of the OSCE Human Dimension Meetings in order to rebuild trust and efficiency within the OSCE's human dimension of security. Different reform proposals presented in the past are analysed, followed by the presentation of a comprehensive reform proposal, suggesting a new 'OSCE Human Dimension Implementation Review Mechanism' (IRM).

1. INTRODUCTION

This article advocates in favour of a comprehensive reform of the OSCE Human Dimension Meetings in order to rebuild trust and efficiency within the OSCE's human dimension of security. The work in the OSCE's human dimension of security should be more structured, geographically balanced and more innovative in order to fulfil one of its main tasks, which is to identify and recommend areas of concrete political action for the OSCE participating States. Furthermore, the OSCE's human dimension of security should be of enhanced operational relevance for the political-military and the economic-environmental dimensions.

First, an overview of the review meetings of OSCE Human Dimension in the context of the OSCE's comprehensive security concept will be provided, followed by an outline of the urgent need for reform of these meetings. Furthermore, different reform proposals presented in the past will be analysed, to be followed by the presentation of a comprehensive reform proposal, introducing a new IRM.

2. THE OSCE HUMAN DIMENSION AND ITS REVIEW MEETINGS IN THE CONTEXT OF THE OSCE'S COMPREHENSIVE SECURITY CONCEPT

Since the adoption of the Helsinki Final Act in 1975, politically binding commitments in the field of human rights and fundamental freedoms as well as the regular review of their implementation by the participating States play a crucial role within the OSCE.

As the third pillar of the OSCE's 'comprehensive security concept', alongside its politico-military and economic-environmental dimensions, the so-called 'human dimension of security' is based on the understanding that sustainable, cooperative, equal and indivisible security and maintenance of peace are closely linked to the respect for human rights and fundamental freedoms. Thus, the OSCE is a security organisation with human rights and the promotion of democracy as a fundamental component. This was prominently reconfirmed by the heads of state of the OSCE's participating States during the OSCE summit in Astana in 2010, agreeing to work in favour of a 'free, democratic, common and indivisible Euro-Atlantic and Eurasian security community stretching from Vancouver to Vladivostok'.[1]

In practice, all three dimensions of the OSCE are dealt with by the Vienna-based decision-making bodies of the OSCE (e.g. by the Permanent Council, PC,

---

[1] For further analysis of the functioning of the OSCE and its current challenges see J. FROEHLY, 'The OSCE 40 years after Helsinki', (2016) 3(25) *The Polish Quarterly of International Affairs*, pp. 7–21.

and – in the case of the human dimension – its Human Dimension Committee), serving as a platform for dialogue among the OSCE participating States, as well as by the more assistance and programme-oriented OSCE executive structures (e.g. by the OSCE Secretariat or the OSCE field operations). Regarding the Human Dimension, three additional executive structures, the so-called 'OSCE institutions' of which the Warsaw-based Office for Democratic Institutions and Human Rights (ODIHR) is the most important one, offer assistance to the OSCE participating States through strong and autonomous mandates. Furthermore, the OSCE Parliamentary Assembly plays a crucial role in the Human Dimension through the work of its 'third committee' and its indispensable leading contribution to the OSCE's election observation efforts.

A series of annually organised conferences and seminars – the largest of which currently is the Human Dimension Implementation Meeting (HDIM) which has been held in Warsaw since 1993 – are usually referred to as the 'OSCE Human Dimension Meetings'. Besides the HDIM, there are three Supplementary Human Dimension Implementation Meetings (SHDIM) of one and a half days held in Vienna, as well as the two-day Human Dimension Seminar (HDS) which also takes place in Vienna. These meetings – the dates and agendas of which are to be adopted each year by consensus of all OSCE participating States – can be considered as the legacy of the process-oriented Conference on Security and Co-operation in Europe (CSCE) which began its negotiations in 1973 and, after the Helsinki Final Act in 1975, resulted in a series of follow-up and review conferences generally referred to as the 'Helsinki process'.

The OSCE Implementation meetings on Human Dimension issues have been institutionalised by decisions of the OSCE Helsinki summit in 1992:

> Every year [...] the ODIHR will organize a three-week meeting at expert-level of all participating States at its seat to review implementation of CSCE Human Dimension commitments. The meeting will perform the following tasks: [...] a thorough exchange of views on the implementation of Human Dimension commitments [...] as well as the consideration of ways and means of improving implementation [...] an evaluation of the procedures for monitoring compliance with commitments. [...] The implementation meeting may draw to the attention of the CSO measures to improve implementation which it deems necessary. [...] Implementation meetings will be organized to meet in formal and informal sessions. All formal sessions will be open. In addition, the participating States may decide, on a case-by-case basis, to open informal sessions. [...] Non-governmental organizations having relevant experience in the field of the Human Dimension are invited to make written presentations to the implementation meeting, e.g. through the ODIHR, and may be invited by the implementation meeting, on the basis of their written presentations, to address specific questions orally as appropriate.[2]

---

[2] CSCE, 'Helsinki Document 1992 – The Challenges of Change', 9–10 July 1992, available at https://www.osce.org/mc/39530?download=true, last accessed 29.05.2018.

The meetings are further regulated by decision no. 476 of the Permanent Council of 2002[3] in order to serve as a platform for exchange on the state of the implementation of States' commitments in the field of human rights among the OSCE participating States and the OSCE's Executive Structures. An important element of the events is that they are open to the participation of civil society representatives and non-governmental organisations (NGOs) by simple registration and without any prior accreditation or admission procedure. Thus, all interested NGOs and other civil society actors can seize the opportunity to address concerns about the actual implementation of OSCE human dimension commitments towards official representatives of the OSCE's participating States and make suggestions on how to solve problems, as reconfirms decision no. 476:

> All non-governmental organizations having relevant experience in the field of the human dimension will be invited to participate, subject to the provisions contained in Chapter IV, paragraph (16), of the Helsinki Document 1992, following registration with the ODIHR.[4]

3. OSCE HUMAN DIMENSION MEETINGS: THE NEED FOR REFORM

> The current practice regarding the overview of implementation of human dimension commitments to lengthy, poorly attended Human Dimension Implementation Meetings (HDIMs) in Warsaw needs to be changed.[5]

This quote, taken from a paper on the future of the OSCE, published by the OSCE Parliamentary Assembly in 2015, summarises well the growing sentiment among OSCE participating States, OSCE institutions and experts that some adjustments are needed to the way the OSCE Human Dimension meetings, designed back in 1990s, are organised. While there is no answer to question of what reforms would be necessary and how extensive these would need to be, most OSCE participating States delegations in Vienna however agree that there is a need to move the annual date of the HDIM from September to the first half of the year for it to better fulfil its mandated role to formulate recommendations to the OSCE Ministerial Council (which always takes place in December) and

---

[3] OSCE PERMANENT COUNCIL, 'Decision No. 476, Modalities for OSCE Meetings on Human Dimension Issues', 23.05.2002, https://www.osce.org/odihr/23982?download=true, last accessed 29.05.2018.

[4] OSCE PERMANENT COUNCIL, Decision No. 476, *supra* note 3; see J. FROEHLY (2016), 'The OSCE 40 years after Helsinki', *supra* note 1.

[5] OSCE PA, 'Helsinki +40: Building the OSCE of the Future', Helsinki +40 Project Final Report, July 2015, available at https://www.oscepa.org/documents/all-documents/helsinki-40/final-report/2949-helsinki-40-final-report/file, last accessed 29.05.2018.

to avoid constant overlap with the General Assembly of the United Nations in New York (let alone with the September session of the Human Rights Council in Geneva).

As the largest of the OSCE Human Dimension Meetings, the HDIM is at the centre of the debate: By pure statistical output the conference with its over 3,000 participants is still one of the largest annual gatherings in Europe in the field of human rights. However, OSCE participating States are increasingly struggling to send high level delegations from the capitals (with the notable exception of the Russian Federation and of the United States) due to lack of personnel and to the overlap with other international events in the field of human rights. Important international human rights NGOs or experts of international reputation often do not see an added value in attending the conference, mainly due to the limited speaking time within the working sessions (often restricted to three minutes) or to what is perceived as a lack of real debate within the session.

The conference still remains unknown to the wider public, despite great efforts made especially by former ODIHR Director Michael Georg Link to increase the visibility of HDIM by inviting high-level speakers, introducing live streaming and assuring broader social media coverage of the conference.

In December 2017, the 'Civic Solidarity Platform', an association of NGOs, stressed the need for reform from civil society's perspective:

> The HDIM is currently in crisis as each year its agenda is held hostage to politics. The decisions on the agenda often do not reflect the opinion of the majority but merely a 'lowest common denominator' compromise. HDIM currently competes with sessions of the UN Human Rights Council. Moreover, its dates in the second half September allow little time for follow-up before the Ministerial Council meeting takes place in early December. Moving the HDIM to April or May would be preferable, but this move should not be undertaken at the expense of sacrificing the content.[6]

Following the assessment of Wolfgang Zellner, Deputy Director of the Institute for Peace Research and Security Policy at the University of Hamburg (IFSH), Head of the IFSH's Centre for OSCE Research (CORE) and one of the leading experts of the OSCE Academic Network, it could even be argued, that the OSCE human dimension is undergoing a deep crisis of relevance, given the strength and added value of other international organisations in the field of reviewing human rights commitments:

> When the cycle of the OSCE's human dimension events was created in the early 1990s, it was unique among all other international organizations covering the same

---

[6] CIVIC SOLIDARITY PLATFORM, 'Civil Society Recommendations to the Participants of the OSCE Ministerial Council Meeting in Vienna', Adopted by the participants of the OSCE Parallel Civil Society Conference, Vienna, 5–6 December 2017, available at http://www.civicsolidarity.org/sites/default/files/recomendations_vienna_2017_3.12.pdf, last accessed 29.05.2018.

geographic area with respect to both its institutional set-up and its ability to review human dimension commitments in an effective manner. This situation has changed profoundly. Today, both the Council of Europe and the UN Human Rights Council provide human rights monitoring instruments that are at least at the same level of effectiveness as those of the OSCE, if not superior to them. Consequently, in a world where international organizations compete, including in the field of human rights and including international organizations with cross-cutting memberships, the OSCE is in a process of losing one of its key comparative advantages – its salient position in reviewing its human dimension commitments.[7]

Since 2013 another competitor to the OSCE human dimension has emerged, at least concerning the OSCE participating States which are also Member States of the EU: the EU's Fundamental Rights Agency (FRA) based in Vienna is covering similar activities as some of the OSCE institutions. In addition, FRA is organising a large-scale conference on an annual basis called the 'Fundamental Rights Forum' which – similar to the OSCE's HDIM – intends to serve as a platform for exchange between state actors and civil society: 'Building on the basic need for people to feel safe, secure and belong to a wider community, the Forum will bring together over 400 participants from human rights communities, the arts, business, international, national and local organisations to discuss new perspectives to pressing human rights issues and strategies.'[8]

W. Zellner considers the lack of structure and of geographical balance to be the main reasons for the OSCE human dimension's decreasing comparative advantage:

> The review process of the OSCE's human dimension commitments at the HDIMs is unstructured in several relevant aspects and falls short of the achievements of other international organizations covering the whole or large parts of the OSCE area. *First*, although the modalities for the HDIM outline the obligatory agenda items mentioned above, in which the implementation record must be reviewed, there is no stipulation at all that would provide for the review process to cover all participating States without exception. In practice, this means that the review process focuses more on the 'Eastern' states. Even if one does admit that the human dimension record in these countries is particularly worrisome, the current OSCE practice does not live up to the essential principle of equal treatment. What is equally important is that this practice probably does not live up to the monitoring standards achieved by both the Council of Europe and the UN Human Rights Council, which are much more detailed and cover, at least in the case of the UN Human Rights Council, all member states without exception. *Second*, in view of this point it is all the more worrisome that the substance of human

---

[7] W. ZELLNER, 'OSCE Human Dimension Events: Modalities, Duration and Effectiveness', Geneva DCFA, OSCE Focus Conference Proceedings, Geneva 2013, 19–20 October 2012, pp. 47–72.

[8] See FRA, 'Fundamental Rights Forum', available at http://fundamentalrightsforum.eu, last accessed 29.05.2018.

dimension monitoring processes of other international organizations, particularly the Council of Europe and the UN Human Rights Council, is not taken into account within the OSCE, at least not in a systematic manner. And *third*, there is no systematic link between the human dimension implementation review process in the HDIM and the one in the Permanent Council's Human Dimension Committee (HDC), which was mandated by the 2006 Brussels Ministerial Council (MC) meeting with the same task: 'Discuss human dimension issues, including implementation of the commitments of the OSCE participating States'.[9]

4. REFORM PROPOSALS I: DURATION OF HDIM AND 'STANDING AGENDA'

Already back in 2005, a Panel of Eminent Persons, mandated to make proposals for strengthening the effectiveness of the OSCE, had suggested shortening HDIM in light of the anticipated creation of the Human Dimension Committee as a sub-committee of the Permanent Council (which became effective in 2007). Furthermore, the Panel proposed not limiting the conference's venue to Warsaw:

> If a Human Dimension Committee is established, the Human Dimension Implementation Meeting (HDIM) could be reduced to a maximum of five days. Upon invitation, the HDIM could be held outside Warsaw every second year in order to raise its profile and increase the sense of ownership among participating States.[10]

Enhancing mainly the *effectiveness* of the OSCE Human Dimension meetings was also the cornerstone of the reform Efforts by the 2012 Irish Chairmanship of the OSCE (supported by an 'Informal Working Group on the Review of Human Dimension Events'), trying to link a reduction of the meetings (shortening of HDIM; abolition of the HDS) to the adoption of a so-called 'standing agenda' for the HDIM.[11] A standing agenda for the HDIM would have replaced annual negotiations on the topics of the conference by participating States and would thus have ensured a timely and orderly conference based on relevant human rights topics. Also, the standing agenda would not have been developed from scratch, as the main regulation on the human dimension events, Permanent Council Decision No. 476 adopted in 2002, already contains all important topics for the HDIM.

---

[9] W. ZELLNER (2013), 'OSCE Human Dimension Events: Modalities, Duration and Effectiveness', *supra* note 7.

[10] OSCE, 'Common Purpose – towards a more effective OSCE', Final Report and Recommendations of the Panel of Eminent Persons on Strengthening the Effectiveness of the OSCE, June 2005, available at https://www.osce.org/cio/15805?download=true, last accessed 30.05.2018.

[11] OSCE, Irish Chairmanship, 'Perception Paper on the Review of Human Dimension Events', 3 August 2012.

In the view of the Irish Chairmanship, a standing agenda for the HDIM would have paved the way for moving HDIM from the autumn period to earlier in the year. This would have provided for sufficient time for work to be taken forward on the recommendations emerging from HDIM, particularly those that might be the subject of Ministerial decisions at the following Ministerial Council. For the Irish Chairmanship, the event could then have been shortened to seven and a half days by omitting the so-called 'special days' (the topics of which are the object of tough negotiations each year among the OSCER participating States), which often seem to duplicate the subject matter of the standard working sessions. The Irish OSCE Chairmanship also proposed to delete HDIM's final plenary session, initially intended to host national human rights directors or senior officials from the capitals, and to replace it by a reinforced Permanent Council meeting some weeks after HDIM in Vienna with participation from the capitals.

Despite the pragmatic and balanced character of the proposal, no consensus for its adoption could be reached in 2012. It remains certainly relevant and can still be seen as a reform framework of reference, as the then ODIHR Director Michael Link put it in 2014: 'The Perception Paper by the Irish Chairmanship remains a robust and balanced point of departure for further discussion.'[12]

5. REFORM PROPOSALS II: GEOGRAPHICAL BALANCE AND ENHANCED STRUCTURE OF THE HUMAN DIMENSION REVIEW

The main attempt of the pragmatic 2012 Irish OSCE Chairmanship proposal was to enhance the efficiency of the meetings and to reshape the framework of the conferences. However, in focusing only on establishing a standing agenda for HDIM, the general *thematic approach* of the meeting – the division of working sessions according to specific fundamental freedoms and human rights – was supposed to remain untouched (and not to be replaced by a more *geographical or peer-review approach*). Therefore, the adoption of the Irish proposal could only have been a first step towards a more strategic and comprehensive approach towards the reform debate, which should focus on a comprehensive assessment of the existing OSCE review tools and take a critical look at the current human dimension implementation cycle as a whole.

Already back in 2005 and 2006, both, ODIHR and a Panel of Eminent Persons working on strengthening the Effectiveness of the OSCE had been suggesting reform of the *structural setup of how human rights commitments are*

---

[12] M. G. LINK, ODHIR Director 'Strengthening the Human Dimension and the Helsinki +40 Process', Speech, Warsaw, 23.09.2013, available at https://www.osce.org/odihr/124272?download=true, last accessed 30.05.2018.

reviewed in the OSCE Human Dimension and its meetings. While ODIHR was proposing that 'the OSCE should enhance the use of existing procedures and instruments, in particular by: [...] intensifying the use of peer review for more systematic review of implementation of human dimension commitments in the framework of the PC, thereby making full use of the expertise and assistance of the OSCE Institutions and structures',[13] the Panel of Eminent Persons suggested that 'criteria and methodology that ensure objectiveness, transparency and professionalism should be further developed and an approach taken that guarantees equal treatment of all participating States'.[14]

Bringing the work of the different platforms and actors within the OSCE Human Dimension closer to a more structured approach towards the review of implementation since then has been proposed from different actors/on different occasions. In 2010, on the occasion of the 'Copenhagen Anniversary Conference: Status and future perspectives',[15] organised by the Kazakh OSCE Chairmanship together with Denmark, recommendations were discussed on how the monitoring of the implementation of human dimension commitments could be strengthened (e.g. developing a peer review mechanism; introducing a Human Dimension commitments annual implementation report; ensuring systematic follow-up to ODIHR election related recommendations; developing an OSCE mechanism which would require the relevant OSCE institutions to gather objective information and prepare reports and recommendations for discussions in the Permanent Council).

More detailed contributions to the structural reform debate were made by the 'Civic Solidarity Platform' in 2013. A strong role for civil society and independent action by the OSCE Institutions was foreseen in these proposals for a more focused review approach:

> A more logical cycle of human dimension events, more focused on the assessment of the implementation of commitments, the adoption of recommendations for follow up action plans and their transmission for discussion and decisions in meetings of the Human Dimension Committee, the Permanent Council and the Ministerial Council. OSCE institutions and in particular ODIHR, with politically strengthened and financially supported mandates to monitor the implementation of commitment with more systematic input form civil society [...] The PC and the HDC paying particular attention to materials and recommendations presented by ODIHR and prepared during human dimension meetings and strengthening the system of voluntary reporting and peer-review by the participating States [...] appointing temporary representatives

---

[13] ODIHR, 'Common Responsibility: Commitments and Implementation', Report, 2006, available at https://www.osce.org/odihr/22681?download=true, last accessed 30.05.2018.
[14] OSCE (2005), 'Common Purpose', *supra* note 10.
[15] OSCE, '20 years of the OSCE Copenhagen Document: Status and future perspectives', Copenhagen, 10–11 June 2010. The programme and annotated agenda of the Conference available at https://www.osce.org/cio/69763, last accessed 29.05.2018.

of the CiO[16] for specific human dimension problems and the introduction of the self-assessment by the CiO, including voluntary pledges. ODIHR must be a leading institution in efforts to strengthen the OSCE's capacity to monitor implementation of human dimension commitments. In practical terms, the monitoring of the human dimension situation in the OSCE participating States and the implementation of commitments should be made more systematic and continuous and progressively cover an expanding scope of commitments. On-site observation of important human dimension events and situations is one of the key tools in ODIHR's monitoring of human dimension commitments. Direct ODIHR Observation should be progressively broadened.[17]

More recently, the 'Civic Solidarity Platform' presented detailed recommendations on how to reshape the debate of HDIM:

> To make HDIM more relevant, its procedures require modification. The chairs of sessions could allocate the first half an hour to a panel discussion, with questions to panellists and no statements. The questions should be short, and not provide an opportunity to make statements. Some delegations could be invited to prepare questions to speakers in advance. Currently, the moderator often gives quite a lengthy introduction which could be shortened, and official speaking time could be reduced. Some HDIM sessions could be organized in parallel break-out sessions with narrower focus requiring expert participation which could allow for more informed discussion on country situations. Some HDIM sessions could possibly be modelled on the UPR process to ensure an open peer discussion between States. The HDIM report is currently not used to maximum effect – as minutes of the sessions' are taken unevenly by the note-takers. ODIHR and/or the Chairmanship should think of producing a separate perception/ summary paper based on HDIM outcomes, outlining the most important issues and challenges.[18]

6. REFORM PROPOSALS III: A STRUCTURED AND GEOGRAPHICALLY BALANCED OSCE IMPLEMENTATION REVIEW MECHANISM

The following comprehensive proposal was developed by the then ODIHR Director Michael Link and his team in February 2015 and presented by Director Link during a hearing of the 'Panel of Eminent Persons on European Security

---

[16] CiO is the 'Chairmanship in Office'.
[17] CIVIC SOLIDARITY PLATFORM, 'Meeting Helsinki +40 Challenge: Strengthening Human Dimension Implementation through Systematic Monitoring, Voluntary Reporting and Follow-up Action', December 2013 available at https://civicsolidarity.org/sites/default/files/civil_society_recommendations_to_the_mcm_in_kiev_december_2013_final.pdf.
[18] Ibid.

as a Common Project'[19] in form of an unpublished paper.[20] It argues in favour of major changes to the way implementation review is organised within the OSCE and would offer new, systematic tasks to already existing OSCE executive structures as well as to the Human Dimension meetings. Also, the proposal would take the best out of the added value of the OSCE within the landscape of international organisations and agencies dealing with human rights, which is the expertise and input of strong OSCE institutions, of parliamentarians working in the OSCE Parliamentary Assembly from all over the OSCE region, and of civil society.

In order to rebuild trust and efficiency in the OSCE's human dimension of security, a new IRM should be introduced. The IRM should link in a systematic way the work of ODIHR, the Permanent Council's Human Dimension Committee and the annual conferences of the Human Dimension. It should also involve other OSCE executive structures. At the same time, the three dimensions of the OSCE's comprehensive approach to security should be more interconnected. This implies that the OSCE's human dimension of security should be of even more enhanced operational relevance for the political-military and the economic-environmental dimensions. Furthermore, the work in the OSCE's human dimension of security should be more structured, geographically balanced and more innovative in order to fulfil one of its main tasks, which is to identify and recommend areas for concrete political action for the OSCE participating States.

The IRM as the general human dimension review and monitoring instrument should be applied in a structured manner and equally to all participating States without exception. This instrument could be coordinated by ODIHR, also implying a role for other OSCE executive structures. It should prominently involve the OSCE Parliamentary Assembly, OSCE's decision-making bodies and the Human Dimension Committee (which reports to the Permanent Council), the OSCE field operations, as well as the several OSCE Human Dimension Meetings.

The review cycle of the new OSCE IRM could be composed of the following elements:

- Each year, the state of implementation of a certain number of participating States is reviewed by the IRM. If for example 10 States were to be reviewed every year, each of the OSCE's 57 participating States would be reviewed approximately every six years.

---

[19] The 'Panel of Eminent Persons on European Security as a Common Project', headed by the German Diplomat Wolfgang Ischinger, was established in 2014 on the initiative of the then Swiss OSCE Chairmanship in close co-operation with Serbia and Germany at the OSCE Ministerial Council 2014 in Basel on 4 December.
[20] OSCE, 'The Future of the OSCE's Human Dimension of Security', unpublished, file with the author.

- At the beginning of the review cycle (e.g. at the beginning of the calendar year), ODIHR submits a review implementation report for each of the States to be reviewed in a given year, based on the input of all of ODIHR's five programmes and of the other OSCE institutions, and taking into account already existing ODIHR and other institution's reports, e.g. preliminary and final report of the OSCE's Election Observation activities.
- The Human Dimension Committee would be the place where review discussion takes place among the OSCE participating States ('peer review'), with support of the OSCE institutions, based on the ODIHR reports and on the presentation of the participating States under review. Where applicable, OSCE field missions, operating in the state under review, could be invited to participate.
- The Human Dimension Implementation Meeting, to take place in the first half of the review cycle year, would be the moment for input from civil society to the IRM. One working session respectively would be dedicated to the OSCE participating State. If each year ten participating States are under review, this would mean, that one week of the HDIM is dedicated to the IRM. This procedure would take on board recommendations by civil society, suggesting that sessions at HDIM should be structured to ensure an open peer discussion between States as well as between States and civil society.[21]
- One of the sessions of the OSCE Parliamentary Assembly would also be dedicated to the participating States under review, eventually based either on the ODIHR report and/or on a report prepared by the OSCE Parliamentary Assembly's secretariat in Copenhagen. The session should include presentations of the parliamentary delegations of the States under review.
- A resuming report on the different stages of the implementation review, compiled and presented by ODIHR to the OSCE Ministerial Council in December, would complete the annual implementation review cycle of the IRM.

7. CONCLUSION

Increasingly competing with other international and regional intergovernmental organisations in the area of fundamental freedoms and human rights, the existing review mechanism of the OSCE Human Dimension is currently struggling for maintaining its relevance. While the OSCE Institutions, especially ODIHR, and other OSCE executive structures are delivering excellent monitoring, assistance and capacity building work to the OSCE participating States, the OSCE implementation review meetings are far from living up to the mandate given to

---

[21] CIVIC SOLIDARITY PLATFORM (2013) 'Meeting Helsinki +40 Challenge', *supra* note 17.

them by the OSCE heads of state and government more than 25 years ago. Only a strategic and comprehensive reform of the OSCE introducing a structured and geographically balanced approach to implementation review and taking advantage of the added values of the OSCE – the broad geographical scope and the comprehensive security concept – and its Human Dimension – the strong institutions and the involvement of civil society and parliamentarians – could restore the comparative advantage of the OSCE in this field – to the benefit of all 57 OSCE participating States.

THE CRISIS OF THE INTERNATIONAL PROTECTION OF HUMAN RIGHTS AND THE GEOPOLITICAL OSCE PERSPECTIVE

'The End of Human Rights', 'Shooting the Messenger' or Strengthening Cooperation?

Christian STROHAL

1. Introduction 482
2. Human Rights as an Essential Element of the OSCE's Comprehensive Security Concept 483
3. Key Underlying Factors for the Crisis 485
4. Current Manifestations of the Crisis, the 'Shrinking Space' and the Austrian Chairmanship 2017: A Success? 487
5. Shooting the Message, Too? or Developing 'Islands of Cooperation'? 491

ABSTRACT

'The end of human rights?' as a question against the background of the current geopolitical situation can be examined particularly well from the Organization for Security and Cooperation in Europe (OSCE) perspective – human rights, democracy and the rule of law have been established as key elements of a comprehensive security concept in the framework of the world's largest regional security organisation. The 'return of geopolitics' and the current crisis of the protection human rights results in a shrinking space especially for human rights defenders, non-governmental organisations (NGOs), and journalists, who are being targeted as carriers of a message of obligations and accountability. Austria's Chairmanship of the OSCE in 2017 has been affected in a number of ways by this situation but was brought to a relatively positive conclusion. In order to not only protect the messenger, but also the message, the year 2018 offers a special opportunity to strengthen the international human rights movement against the background of the 70th anniversary of the Universal Declaration of Human Rights and the 25th anniversary of the Vienna World Conference on Human Rights.

1. INTRODUCTION

'The End of Human Rights?' – when a US periodical,[1] specialised on foreign affairs, puts human rights on its cover, this is quite unusual in itself. It is even more unusual when it is done in this manner, implying a danger or even an end because of the current US administration's policies, breaking from decades of declared priorities. Following this implication, however, would mean to both under- and overestimate the importance of a US-centric perspective – the crisis has been developing over a number of years: its reasons are multifaceted, and it is not 'human rights' as such which are concerned, of course, but rather their protection, especially at the interface between the national level and multinational protection mechanisms. Where this becomes most visible, and urgent, is growing efforts trying to control the message, and the messenger, especially the messenger of criticism, be it human rights defenders and non-governmental organisations (NGOs), journalists or international institutions.

The Organization for Security and Cooperation in Europe (OSCE) provides a particularly appropriate framework to examine the current state of this crisis, as it has made, from its origins in the early 1970s, the protection of human rights one of the three key elements of its comprehensive security framework, together with political-military security issues and economic and environmental ones, called the three dimensions. This three-dimensional approach has made human rights, democracy and the rule of law essential not only as far as the overall security approach in this largest regional security organisation is concerned, but also essential to its normative, political, and operational basis, activities and outlook.[2]

Recently, manifestations of crisis have been coming more into the open in the organisation,[3] after having been simmering for a number of years, driven by increasing violations of its principles and commitments, but also by a growing

---

[1] D. RIEFF, 'The End of Human Rights', *Foreign Policy*, 09.04.2018, available at http://foreignpolicy.com/2018/04/09/the-end-of-human-rights-genocide-united-nations-r2p-terrorism/ last accessed 14.06.2018. The answer of its editor, J. TEPPERMAN, 'Down, but Not Out', Editor's Note, *Foreign Policy*, 09.04.2018, available at http://foreignpolicy.com/2018/04/09/down-but-not-out-3, last accessed 14.06.2018.

[2] This article is based on a number of years of direct experience in different functions with the organisation and with other international fora. Therefore, this is not a scientific article *strictu sensu*, but rather a personal appraisal of the current situation reflected through personal experience, and the notes are kept at a minimum. Overall see. www.osce.org, and the OSCE Yearbook published annually by the Institut für Friedensforschung und Sicherheitspolitik at Hamburg University, as well as, more recently, the Security and Human Rights Monitor, available at www.shrmonitor.org, last accessed 14.06.2018.

[3] The weekly meetings of the two main standing bodies of the organisation, the Permanent Council and the Forum for Security Cooperation provide the key opportunities for representatives of the 57 OSCE participant states to advance their positions; these meetings, however, are not public, albeit reflected in personal tweets by some participants.

unease in a number of governments about the organisation's activities precisely in this field: human rights, rule of law, and democracy – what is called, in OSCE jargon, the human dimension. Therefore, Austria's OSCE Chairmanship 2017 has also been affected by this crisis in several ways, most of which continue to hamper the full exercise of the organisation's objectives, let alone its potential.[4]

A key trigger in this development has been, of course, the illegal annexation of Crimea by Russia in 2014 and the continuing destabilisation of eastern Ukraine. However, the slow effect of growing centrifugal forces in the OSCE region has been simmering for longer. How did we get there?

2. HUMAN RIGHTS AS AN ESSENTIAL ELEMENT OF THE OSCE'S COMPREHENSIVE SECURITY CONCEPT

From the outset, the promotion and protection of human rights has been characterised by several specific features:

- Already throughout the Conference on Security and Co-operation in Europe (CSCE) process, before and after the adoption of the Helsinki Final Act,[5] human rights were dealt with, politically, as *quid pro quo*, as a necessary concession from the Soviet block to allow discussion of their interest in security and arms control. Subsequently, an extensive body of human rights related commitments was negotiated, not as a normative base additional to those of other international organisations, especially of the United Nations (UN) and the Council of Europe (CoE), but rather as specific political commitments, encompassing those legal obligations.[6]

---

[4] For a brief preview about the Chairmanship perspective see C. STROHAL, 'Die Zukunft der Europäschen Sicherheit und die Rolle der OSZE – einige Anmerkungen zur Ausgangslage vor dem Österreichischen Vorsitz 2017', *Wiener Blätter zur Friedensforschung* No.169, pp. 1–8. For a brief appreciation *ex post* see Wolfgang Richter, 'Die OSZE zwischen Konfrontation und "strukturiertem Dialog"', *SWP-Aktuell*, January 2018, pp. 1 et seq., available at https://www.swp-berlin.org/publikation/die-osze-zwischen-konfrontation-und-strukturiertem-dialog/, last accessed 19.06.2018.

[5] OSCE, Helsinki Final Act, 01.08.1975, available at www.osce.org/helsinki-final-act, last accessed 14.06.2018, adopted at the Helsinki Summit Conference 1975. See also M. REIMAA, '"Helsinki Catch – European Security Accords 1975" – A book presentation by former Finnish OSCE Ambassador Markku Reimaa', 14.11.2008, available at ww.finlande.nl/public/default.aspx?contentid=142535&nodeid=35916&culture=en-US, last accessed 14.06.2018.

[6] For a comprehensive collection, ordered both chronologically and thematically, OSCE, 'OSCE Human Dimension Commitments: Volume 1, Thematic Compilation (third edition)', 12.11.2012, available at https://www.osce.org/odihr/76894, last accessed 14.06.2018 and OSCE, 'OSCE Human Dimension Commitments: Volume 2, Chronological Compilation (third edition)', 12.11.2012, available at https://www.osce.org/odihr/76895, last accessed 14.06.2018.

- After the fall of the Berlin Wall and the demise of the Soviet Union, the implementation of these commitments on human rights – together with democracy and rule of law – was fully operationalised, in the course of the establishment of the OSCE as an organisation,[7] to become a key factor in the organisation's support for new democracies. This was particularly highlighted with the establishment of the Office for Democratic Institutions and Human Rights (ODIHR), the High Commissioner on National Minorities (HCNM) and the Representative on the Freedom of the Media (RFoM) as autonomous institutions within the overall OSCE framework; equally, this approach was also reflected in the mandates of the field missions established in many of the new democracies.[8]
- Subsequently,[9] with the gradual consolidation of autocratic structures in a number of post-Soviet states, human rights have increasingly been turned into an irritating factor, seen by these regimes as a means for interference in their affairs, if not even a tool for regime change.[10] Consequently, these countries have intensified efforts to roll back the operational capacities of the organisation in these fields.[11]

Under these circumstances, the international human rights regime, as determined by UN standards and procedures, has – as a first step – been integrated, explicitly and implicitly, into the OSCE. Instead of duplicating legal standards, the CSCE process and several dedicated OSCE conferences developed a detailed range of commitments,[12] as well as monitoring mechanisms and institutions for their comprehensive and long-term support, including in direct cooperation with the OSCE states. Thus, the achievements of these efforts and the activities of these institutions have been influencing positively the operationalisation of human rights protection through other international organisations as well.

---

[7] This process of institutionalisation started with the adoption of the 'Charter of Paris for a New Europe' at the Second CSCE Summit of Heads of State or Government, Paris, 19–21 November 1990; it is, however, not completed yet, as the OSCE lacks full legal personality.

[8] The Institutions and Field Missions include human dimension aspects in their work; operationally, they serve as key interface between the commitments and their implementation on the ground – cf. their respective websites.

[9] For a comprehensive overview see V.-Y. GHEBALI, *Le Rôle de l'OSCE en Eurasie, du Sommet de Lisbonne au Conseil Ministériel de Maastricht (1996–2003)*, Brussels, Brylant 2014.

[10] Regime change as an operational objective has been ascribed by the Kremlin and a few other governments in the post-Soviet space especially to the Open Society Foundation of George Soros, the U.S. government, and others.

[11] These efforts concentrate mainly on the three institutions and the field missions, which are mostly addressed by proposals to limit the operational budgets, or the mandates, or both. As the mandate of field missions – contrary to the institutions – is up for renewal annually, this allows for continuous pressures focusing mainly on their activities in the human dimension.

[12] OSCE (2012), 'OSCE Human Dimension Commitments: Volume 1' and OSCE, 'OSCE Human Dimension Commitments: Volume 2', both *supra* note 6.

This was particularly true for the integration of human rights, the rule of law and democracy into the broader *raison d'être* of the UN's *triade* of peace and security/human rights/development.[13]

More recently, however, this trend has been reversed: the OSCE framework has not been capable of encouraging its participating governments to continue to assume this role of *avant-garde*;[14] on the contrary, achievements made in other fora have increasingly been questioned by some of the post-Soviet governments, even if the same governments have accepted them explicitly in those other organisations.[15]

3. KEY UNDERLYING FACTORS FOR THE CRISIS

As indicated above, the crisis which this development has brought about has been slow in the making: essentially, it reflected a growing reluctance to accept accountability for the implementation of OSCE commitments, or rather the lack thereof, by a number of governments increasingly wary of having to stand up for their deficits in front of their peers, and of civil society representatives, especially in dedicated human dimension implementation meetings.[16]

This overall situation has been increasingly exacerbated by the unwillingness to resolve some of the so-called protracted conflicts in the OSCE region: Transnistria, Nagorno-Karabakh, and additional conflicts arising from the war between Russia and Georgia in the summer of 2008 and the subsequent occupation of Abkhazia and South Ossetia. Not only have these conflicts serious negative repercussions for the implementation of human rights commitments in those regions, they are also being used in the diplomatic and political activities to take hostage other issues treated in the organisation.

However, if one were to identify one specific area in which this reversal of human rights *avant-garde* has come to the fore most acutely and most typically

---

[13] UN, 'In Larger Freedom: Towards Development, Security and Human Rights for All', Report by the Secretary-General, 2005, available at http://www.un.org/en/events/pastevents/pdfs/larger_freedom_exec_summary.pdf, last accessed 14.06.2018.

[14] K. MÖTTÖLA (guest ed.), 'Helsinki + 40, the OSCE Under a Stress Test, Security and Human Rights', Special Issue, (2014) 25(2), *Security and Human Rights*.

[15] C. STROHAL, 'Closing the Implementation Gap: The OSCE and Added Value from Stronger Synergies Between Human Rights Organizations', in W. BENEDEK, F. BENOÎT-ROHMER, W. KARL, M.C. KETTEMANN and M. NOWAK, *European Yearbook on Human Rights (EYHR) 14*, NWV, Vienna/Graz 2014, pp. 395–403; so far, the comprehensive human rights protection cycle proposed there has not been materialising.

[16] This state of affairs is not helped by the reluctance among western countries to address shortcomings in their own region or to use some of the existing mechanisms to address severe violations of commitments, such as the Moscow Mechanism.

in an OSCE context, it is one of the key identifying capacities of the organisation: election observation.[17]

A number of decisions taken in the early 1990s created a solid foundation for election observation undertaken by professionals,[18] in conjunction with politicians, to allow a clear picture of fulfilling commitments in this area so crucial for democracy, the rule of law and human rights, and to provide a picture untainted by political considerations.

In creating and building the ODIHR, the OSCE states provided an excellent tool to implement this objective. With far over 300 individual observation missions, a globally unique expertise and methodology has been developed to ensure such observation, especially over the long term, and to put elections thus into the broader democratic, institutional and human rights context. It was precisely this success of election observation activities[19] which made it seemingly necessary, in the opinion of a few governments with less than appropriate records in the implementation of their commitments, to start questioning these activities.

As the deficits identified in ODIHR observation reports solidified in a number of countries, instead of being addressed effectively due to the fact that the reports and the opportunities provided for a systematic follow-up to their recommendations, criticism of the methodology was voiced by a small number of former Soviet countries, and efforts were undertaken to bring the ODIHR, its methodology and the observation results under the collective control of the OSCE governments.

The negative examples of presidential and parliamentary elections in Russia in 2007[20] and of parliamentary elections in Azerbaijan in 2015[21] provided the

---

[17] For an overview, OSCE, 'Elections', 25.06.2013, available at www.osce.org/odihr/elections, last accessed 14.06.2018 and the numerous publications and reports there, esp. the OSCE, *Election Observation Handbook* in its 6th edition, as well as C. STROHAL, 'More Must Be Done. The OSCE and the Protection of Human Rights after the Astana Summit', in IFSH (ed.), *OSCE Yearbook 2011*, Nomos, Baden-Baden 2011, pp. 241–255.

[18] The ODIHR was originally created in the Charter of Paris (*supra* note 7) as Office for Free Elections; subsequently, this denomination was changed to better reflect the necessary wider human rights context of democratic elections.

[19] Often described by representatives of pluralistic democracies as 'gold standard' of international election observation, while derided as lacking governmental control by some post-Soviet governments.

[20] OSCE/ODHIR, 'ODIHR unable to observe Russian Duma elections', Press Release, 16.11.2007, available at www.osce.org/odihr/elections/49175, last accessed 14.06.2018 – subsequently, however, Russian authorities refrained from trying to impose unacceptable conditions so that election observation missions could be deployed in 2011, 2012, 2016 and 2018.

[21] OSCE, 'Parliamentary Elections, 1 November 2015', available at www.osce.org/odihr/elections/azerbaijan/179226, last accessed 14.06.2018, for the presidential elections in 2018; however, a return to more normalcy was achieved with the deployment of a regular election observation mission by ODIHR.

most visible 'lowlights' of these developments, as these two cases forced ODIHR to decline observing, given the unacceptable and limiting conditions which would have been placed on the observation process.

However, OSCE countries continue to see their continuing invitations for election observation not only as implementing an OSCE obligation, but also as an important contribution to voter confidence and in helping them to address shortcomings in the conduct of elections and the broader democratic process.

4. CURRENT MANIFESTATIONS OF THE CRISIS, THE 'SHRINKING SPACE' AND THE AUSTRIAN CHAIRMANSHIP 2017: A SUCCESS?

Against this background, the outlook to the Austrian Chairmanship 2017 was somewhat bleak, especially as far as the human dimension is concerned:

- First, in some of the OSCE states negative developments prevailed as to a number of key human rights issues: freedom of speech, freedom of association and of assembly all saw serious curtailments, leading to a shrinking space for human rights organisations overall and compounded further by a growing clamp-down on journalists and human rights defenders.[22]
- At the same time, human rights issues became increasingly politicised and instrumentalised throughout the world, not only in the OSCE region: this became most visible in the context of armed conflict, migration flows, privacy rights versus the fight against terrorism, or growing intolerance against Muslims, Christians, and anti-Semitism, and, as a consequence, reflected in the OSCE also on the debate, and activities, in the framework of other international organisations, especially the CoE and the UN.
- In the OSCE context, the participating states had been unable, for three years in a row already, to agree on decisions on human dimension issues at the annual meetings of the Ministerial Council, given a lack of consensus regarding the drafts presented, or, more often, political preferences to link them to other issues on the agenda of ministers.
- And finally, the protracted lack of consensus among the OSCE foreign ministers to agree on the nomination for all four key leadership functions in the organisation over the course of 2016/17 – in addition to the Secretary-General: the High Commissioner on Minorities, the Director of ODIHR and

---

[22] S. BOKULIC, 'The OSCE and Human Rights Defenders: A Longstanding and Contentious Relationship', in W. BENEDEK et al (eds.), *EYHR 14, supra* note 15, pp. 429–440, on the long-term effort by ODIHR to support human rights defenders, *inter alia*, through the development of Guidelines on their protection.

the Representative on the Freedom of the Media – led to growing fears of impending and serious leadership vacuum and paralysation of the organisation as a result.[23]

These factors were further exacerbated by a number of developments within the human dimension process of the Permanent Council (PC):

- The decision some years ago to create three thematic committees of the PC, including one on the human dimension, did fulfil the expectations of allowing for a more regular and in-depth discussion of human rights issues among the delegations in Vienna, with the participation of representatives of the OSCE institutions and of specialists from capitals, including individual civil society representatives invited by the committee chair; however, the conflictual situation regarding preparations for the mandatory human dimension meetings, especially the annual Human Dimension Implementation Meeting, and their conduct did not improve:
    - The modalities established in the 1990s and reaffirmed 2002 in a PC decision[24] are increasingly being questioned, without a new consensus emerging;
    - As the choice of dates and special subjects (for the annual Human Dimension Implementation Meeting) need a consensus decision,[25] these were delayed through protracted negotiations over details, so as to make their timely organisation difficult, if not impossible;
    - In particular, the modalities regarding participation of civil society participants were increasingly challenged, with the perspective of giving governments a veto over individual participants, without, however, agreement over the precise implementation of existing modalities or new modalities emerging, with the effect of further exacerbating preparations of these meetings and their conduct.

---

[23] The nomination process is conducted by the Chairmanship based on proposals by the 57 governments; the coincidence of all four positions had not happened before. After conducting informal hearings, the German and subsequent Austrian Chairmanships were seeking consensus on the most widely supported candidates; this was originally refused by a very small number of delegations. The ensuing crisis developed because of an unwillingness of these delegations to accept the Chairmanship proposals; it was finally resolved only at the informal meeting of ministers organised by the Chairman-in-Office, Austria's Foreign Minister Sebastian Kurz in July 2017 in Mauerbach near Vienna.

[24] OSCE, 'Permanent Council Decision No. 476', 23.05.2002, PC.DEC/476, available at https://www.osce.org/pc/13198, last accessed 14.06.2018.

[25] Formally, this is not the case for the three yearly supplementary human dimension meetings where the final responsibility lies with the Chairmanship 'after consultations' with the participating states; however, Chairmanships are reluctant to decide against the explicit will of some delegations as this could open up 'hostage-taking' of other issues needing consensus decisions.

- And the decision regarding the annual budget of the organisation, including its institutions, has been delayed, as in past years, over the pretext of petty haggling over minor budget elements, in order to weaken planning and operational capacities.

Altogether, these factors contributed to the resolve of the Austrian Chairmanship to concentrate, in parallel with negotiating consensus approaches to all these issues, on specific Chairmanship initiatives especially in areas not requiring consensus decisions but only a general understanding. These priorities were conducted in the following overall context:

- First and foremost, the Chairmanship had to ensure the proper functioning of the organisation; in addition to the decision on the budget, the appointment of the four leading functions in the organisation had to be achieved, and was finally, at the informal meeting of foreign ministers in July.
- In parallel, and like every Chairmanship, Austria had to ensure the implementation of the full programme of the organisation: given the consensus principle, this required the daily balancing of managing the numerous issues on the table[26] and demonstrating leadership where necessary and possible, while maintaining a continuous consultative process with the other 56 participating states.
- As to substantive Chairmanship priorities, these were identified and pursued in all areas of the organisation, giving particular attention to the need to re-establish trust and confidence while being attentive to concrete realities on the wider security agenda.
- On the human dimension, these circumstances translated into pursuing priorities also through specific Chairmanship conferences,[27] on issues such as media and internet freedom, cyber security, or internally displaced persons, and more broadly, pursuing thematic priorities across the organisation's agenda relating to combating radicalisation and extremism, trafficking in human beings, and gender, and overall on rule of law and freedom of religion issues.

Taken together, the Chairmanship did achieve a number of key objectives and priorities, including holding a meaningful Ministerial Council in December, following up on the informal meeting of ministers in July. Under the circumstances, it is widely being seen as a successful Chairmanship.

---

[26] To illustrate the broad scope of issues dealt with by the organisation, it might be sufficient to point out that in the Austrian Chairmanship team, more than 100 issues were identified as being of sufficient importance to be assigned to a particular team member.

[27] For Chairmanship conferences, no formal consensus decision is necessary.

In this broader picture, beyond the human dimension as such, the following developments provide examples for a more optimistic general outlook:

- The creation of an improved focus on the situation in eastern Ukraine, especially concentrating on the humanitarian consequences of the conflict, through the Special Monitoring Mission (SMM) as well as the negotiations in the Trilateral Contact Group under the chair of Ambassador Martin Sajdik;[28]
- Improvements in the management of the Transnistrian conflict, especially through agreements, brokered by the Chairmanship's special representative, Ambassador Wolf-Dietrich Heim, over the opening of a bridge and related issues of schools, telecommunication and academic mobility in order to facilitate the integration of the population in Transnistria;
- The establishment of a new format for a focused dialogue on security challenges, the so-called Structured Dialogue, involving senior representatives from Foreign and Defence Ministries, and aiming at rebuilding trust, *inter alia*, through discussing diverging threat perceptions and addressing mechanisms to prevent military incidents;[29]
- In the human dimension proper, it was finally possible to hold the mandated meetings, under the protest of one participating state over participation of particular individuals,[30] while a consultation process was launched, in parallel, on the modalities of participation in the implementation and supplementary meetings. The special subjects for these meetings finally agreed upon were the following: access to justice; rights of the child; media freedom; equal participation in political and public life; economic, social and cultural rights as an answer to rising inequalities; tolerance and non-discrimination, and freedom of religion. At the same time, election observation activities proceeded relatively unhindered and were also facilitated through a strengthened cooperation between the ODIHR and the organisation's Parliamentary Assembly and its secretariat.

---

[28] Remarkable close cooperation between the SMM mandated by a decision of the PC and a political negotiation structure emanating from the so-called Normandy-Format (GER, F, UA, RF) and chaired by a personality appointed by the OSCE-chair.

[29] To address such issues in a separate forum had become necessary, in the view of many delegations, because of the continuing blockade of reforming the so-called Vienna Document on confidence- and security-building measures in the political-military field.

[30] Some participants registering for human dimension meetings were associated, in the opinion of the Turkish authorities, with the Gülen movement accused of masterminding the coup attempt of 2016; E. TAMKIN, 'Turkey Wants to Veto Civil Society Organizations at the OSCE', *Foreign* Policy, 20.04.2018, available at http://foreignpolicy.com/2018/04/20/turkey-wants-to-veto-civil-society-organizations-at-the-osce, last accessed 19.06.2018.

5. SHOOTING THE MESSAGE, TOO? OR DEVELOPING 'ISLANDS OF COOPERATION'?

In this rather mixed picture and the continuing difficult overall constellation, some observers and diplomats in Vienna are optimistic on several issues:

- Thematically, they see a growing potential for developing 'islands of cooperation'[31] on key overarching challenges to security in the Euro-Atlantic and Eurasian space, such as fighting terrorism or illegal migration, trafficking in human beings, cyber-crime, or extremism, which all have important human dimension aspects to them.
- Furthermore, the fact that a specific new format has been established for discussing military security challenges with the aim of rebuilding trust, through more dialogue, implementing confidence-building measures and more military-to-military contacts: the so-called Structured Dialogue decided at the Hamburg Ministerial Council in December 2016 and set up by the Austrian Chairmanship came up with a promising start, with the added expectation that the professional and high-level expert approach could somewhat 'spill over' into other areas.
- Structurally, there is hope in the leadership of the new Secretary-General and the Heads of the three Institutions to provide for more thematic and structural guidance and continuity.
- Finally, the growing uncertainties in the current geopolitical environment should encourage a more serious approach to security concerns, allowing the EU,[32] and others, to take a more strategic effort in engaging other governments for using fully the unique multilateral framework of the OSCE.

This more positive outlook overall could also mean better prospects for the human dimension, at least as its being taken hostage for other contentious

---

[31] A term coined originally in the context of the Final Report and Recommendations of the Panel of Eminent Persons on European Security, 'Back to Diplomacy', as a Common Project, nominated by the subsequent Swiss and German Chairmanships, and presented in November 2015. The report was not, however, dealt with formally in the OSCE context. On the human dimension, it recommended, *inter alia*, 'to establish a better ... review process along the lines of the UN and the Council of Europe practice'. See 'Back to Diplomacy', Final Report and Recommendations of the Panel of Eminent Persons on European Security, p. 16, available at https://www.osce.org/networks/205846?download=true, last accessed 19.06.2018. See also OSCE NETWORK OF THINK TANKS AND ACADEMIC INSTITUTIONS (eds.), *Road to the Charter of Paris – Historical Narratives and Lessons for the OSCE Today*, Vienna 2017, available at http://www.fes-vienna.org/fileadmin/user_upload/documents/The_Road_to_the_Charter_of_Paris.pdf, last accessed 19.06.2018.

[32] EUROPEAN UNION AGENCY FOR FUNDAMENTAL RIGHTS (FRA), 'Fundamental rights: a road sign at Europe's crossroad', Speech by the Director, 24.05.2018, available at http://fra.europa.eu/en/speech/2018/fundamental-rights-road-sign-europes-crossroad, last accessed 14.06.2018.

issues is concerned. Consequently, the operational scope of those human rights issues over which there is already broad agreement could be expanded. At the same time, however, one should not underestimate either the force of centrifugal developments if allowed unchecked, nor the real dangers of overall retreat of human rights on the global and regional, agenda, especially at the high political level. Therefore, it will have to be the civil society at large, including not only human rights organisations, but also institutions, parliamentarians, and academia, to push harder for the implementation of commitments, for clear accountability, but also for positive examples of concrete solutions to challenges and shortcomings.[33]

The year 2018 is the appropriate year for this. In addition to the geopolitical challenges outlined above, it provides the opportunity of the 70th anniversary of the adoption of the Universal Declaration of Human Rights and the 25th anniversary of the holding of the Vienna World Conference for Human Rights, a conference, which resulted, among other outcomes, in a strengthened global human rights movement.[34] That movement is now again under threat, throughout the world, because of the message they carry: human rights themselves are under threat, not only individual rights, but their application overall.[35] Their message is clear and well founded, but finds not enough echo with governments; on the contrary, the rise of populism and extreme political positions is creating a climate of 'shooting the messenger', be they representatives of NGOs, human rights defenders, or journalists – all too often literally.

---

[33] Specific and detailed recommendations are being formulated ahead of every Ministerial Council of the OSCE by the Civic Solidarity Platform, a platform of some 100 NGOs in the OSCE area, available at www.civicsolidarity.org, last accessed 14.06.2018.

[34] To commemorate these anniversaries and to help identify the way ahead, the Austrian government invited to a high-level expert conference, 'Vienna+ 25, Building Trust, Making Human Rights a Reality for All', in May 2018 and in cooperation with the Office of the High Commissioner for Human Rights of the UN, the City of Vienna and the Ludwig Boltzmann Institute for Human Rights, BUNDESMINISTERIUM FÜR EUROPA, INTEGRATION UND ÄUSSERES, 'Vienna+25', available at https://www.bmeia.gv.at/vienna-25, last accessed 14.06.2018; for the previous occasion see J. Kozma, A. Müller-Funk and M. Nowak (eds.), *Vienna + 20, Advancing the Protection of Human Rights – achievements, challenges and perspectives 20 years after the World Conference*, NWV, Vienna/Graz 2014, pp. 7–9.

[35] While covering essentially only the 47 member states of the CoE, interesting in this context are the reports published annually, for four years now, by its Secretary-General, on the state of democracy, the rule of law and human rights, for 2017, CoE, 'Secretary General's Annual Report of Democracy, Human Rights and the Rule of Law in Europe – Now released', 20.04.2017, available at https://www.coe.int/en/web/policy-planning/newsroom/-/asset_publisher/QGb00KhY3XFF/content/secretary-general-s-annual-report-on-state-of-democracy-human-rights-and-the-rule-of-law-in-europe-now-published, last accessed 14.06.2018, as well as those from the FRA, available at www.fra.europa.eu, especially FRA, 'Fundamental Rights Report 2018', June 2018, available at http://fra.europa.eu/en/publication/2018/fundamental-rights-report-2018.

The OSCE can no longer be seen as a clear, let alone quasi-automatic, *avant-garde* for such an approach, but it provides a strong institutional, political and diplomatic framework, which should be used to the full. It provides mechanisms for protection as well as for ensuring accountability. What is missing is adequate political will to use them. We must not allow the shooting of the messenger, let alone of the message.

HOW MULTILATERAL ORGANISATIONS CAN COMMUNICATE BETTER ABOUT HUMAN RIGHTS

Katarzyna GARDAPKHADZE and Gareth DAVIES

1. Introduction 496
2. Methodology 497
3. Human Rights Communication and its 'Elite', Highly Specialised and Inward-Looking Language................................. 498
4. The Architecture of Speaking 500
5. Confirming the Confirmation Bias in Human Rights Communication... 501
6. Human Rights Communication without a Human Face 503
7. Talking to Ourselves: Human Rights Echo Chambers 506
8. Embracing Decentralised Communications........................ 507
9. 'Know Thy Audience' 508
10. Harnessing New Communication Technologies 511
11. Building Contact with Journalists 513
12. Acting Locally, Thinking Globally 514
13. Conclusion: The Message and the Messenger.................... 515

ABSTRACT

Communication technologies and techniques are changing fast. This affects the way all of us create, share and consume knowledge in every sector of our lives. Yet, international organisations and institutions, including the OSCE Office for Democratic Institutions and Human Rights (ODIHR), are often seen to be falling behind in their efforts to adopt new ways of communicating about human rights and fundamental freedoms. Multilateral institutions are increasingly not heard. There are many reasons why: because of the hermetic language and old-fashioned means we use, because we fail to reach out beyond our echo chambers and tailor our messages to specific audiences, among others. Such challenges mean that we are not able to communicate about human rights in a way that makes people listen and changes lives. This creates a communication vacuum in which the opponents of human rights can shape a negative public narrative, undermining trust in laws and institutions and giving space to prejudiced, discriminatory and intolerant attitudes that threaten the security of our communities. To ensure that messages about human rights and fundamental freedoms heard and understood by everyday people, multilateral institutions, such as ODIHR, need to create and share these messages in ways that are fit for the realities of the 21st century. In this article, we discuss the urgent need and possible ways for international organisations to communicate more effectively, to be able to show ordinary people that human rights and fundamental freedoms are indispensable in their lives, and to strengthen public support for those rights and freedoms. We will also describe how we at ODIHR have begun to address this communication vacuum.

1. INTRODUCTION

International organisations and institutions are falling behind in their efforts to adopt new ways of communicating about the human rights and fundamental freedoms they are set up to promote. Multilateral organisations and institutions are increasingly not heard. There are many reasons for this; here, we discuss some of them, roughly grouped into two 'baskets' of issues.

The first basket relates to the way we frame our language and messages about human rights. We argue that multilateral organisations and institutions are increasingly failing to 'engage the disengaged' because of the hermetic, highly specialised, inward-looking language they use, their tendency to focus on the regression in human rights rather than on promoting the importance of rights for ordinary citizens and multiplying examples of success, and the inability of such organisations to reach beyond their own echo chambers.

The second basket of issues relates to communication tools and the methods we use to transmit those messages. Since the turn of the millennium the way messages are disseminated and consumed by people has changed significantly with the evolution of new technologies. Organisations promoting the importance of human rights need to embrace new technologies and find innovative ways of using them to engage their audiences. But beyond technology there are also other, practical, steps that international organisations can take to enhance the reach and resonance of their messaging.

Our point of departure is that international organisations and institutions need to regain, strengthen and sustain popular trust and support to be effective in promoting human rights and fundamental freedoms. This is especially important now, when such trust and support, for both international institutions and their human rights causes, seems to be in decline, and when some governments and public figures are turning away from human rights. In Pew Research Center's 2016 survey, for example, more than half of the surveyed

European public (an increase from previous studies) thought that improving human rights around the world should not be one of their countries' most important foreign policy goals.[1] By extension, we could expect that the human rights mandate of an intergovernmental organisation such as the Organization for Security and Co-operation in Europe (OSCE) – which, as a security-focused organisation, is intimately linked with foreign policy – would not be seen as a priority either. We recognise that 'general public' is a very broad and diverse group, including those who are strong proponents of human rights, those who oppose them, those who are undecided and those who rarely stand up for their own rights. Our argument is that to regain and sustain popular trust and support, multilateral human rights organisations need to be able to win the hearts and minds of the undecided and get better at giving voice to those who rarely stand up for their own rights.

We conclude that the current shortcomings in multilateral organisations' communication about human rights need to be addressed in a coherent, well-targeted and sufficiently resourced communication strategy that takes into account the audience, the means of communication, the message, and the messenger.

2. METHODOLOGY

Our methodological approach is primarily based on a critical review of literature in the spheres of human rights, communication theory and practice (in particular in the context of human rights organisations), and political and social psychology. We also look at available data from recent research and opinion polls insofar as they identify current attitudes and perceptions in those spheres. We have prioritised sources based on their relevance, incorporating both qualitative and quantitative information across those interrelated fields.

Our intention is to apply 'organic, creative and interpretive approaches to conducting reviews of complex literature',[2] rather than a conventional systematic review methodology. Our interpretative analysis and synthesis is subjectively biased because of our own empirical experience of working in an intergovernmental organisation (ODIHR). This bias is mitigated by

---

[1] B. STOKES, J. POUSHTER and R. WIKE, 'Europeans Face the World Divided Many question national influence and obligations to allies, but share desire for greater EU role in global affairs' (2016), *Pew Research Center*, available at http://www.pewglobal.org/files/2016/06/Pew-Research-Center-EPW-Report-FINAL-June-13-2016.pdf, last accessed 29.05.2018.

[2] M. DIXON-WOODS M, S. BONAS, A. BOOTH, D.R. JONES, T. MILLER, A.J. SUTTON, R.L. SHAW, J.A. SMITH and B. YOUNG, 'How can systematic reviews incorporate qualitative research? A critical perspective', (2006) 6(1) *Qualitative Research*, pp. 27–44.

demonstrating a growing recognition of similar gaps in communicating about human rights in other multilateral organisations such as the Council of Europe, the European Union's Fundamental Rights Agency and the United Nations.

As the discourse around such issues is new and good practice is scarce, we have not been able to draw on many good practice examples. But by bringing ideas together in new ways, this synthesis is designed to open up new possibilities for a broader, 'out-of-the-box' discussion about a problem that has only recently been recognised and voiced: ineffective communication about human rights by international organisations.

3. HUMAN RIGHTS COMMUNICATION AND ITS 'ELITE', HIGHLY SPECIALISED AND INWARD-LOOKING LANGUAGE

When talking about human rights, regardless of the audience, multilateral organisations and institutions often use a hermetic, 'elite' and highly specialised language.

In his 2009 book *Human Rights and Their Limits*, Professor Wiktor Osiatyński says:

> The idea of rights has seldom served the poor, destitute, dispossessed, and oppressed. Such people usually do not claim rights. [....] [R]ights have usually been claimed by those strong enough to demand them. [...] The challenge for every advocate of [...] human rights lies in restoring a sense of inclusion, dignity and self-respect to the millions of people who are considered 'useless' today.[3]

Time and again, studies have shown that the language used to communicate about human rights, often serves the 'elites' – those who understand and know how to use this language – and does not necessarily reflect and respond to the real needs of 'the poor, destitute, dispossessed, and oppressed'. For example, the Human Rights Perception Poll shows that among the surveyed populations, 'human rights language, people and activities are better established among elites than among society's lower echelons'. Unfortunately, this means that those who stand to benefit most from human rights norms – the poor, the powerless, and the oppressed – have less access to the human rights tools they need.[4] It also means, regrettably, that when elites use human rights language

---

[3] W. OSIATYNSKI, *Human Rights and their Limits*, Cambridge University Press, Cambridge 2009.

[4] J. RON (2017), 'The Human Rights Perception Polls', James Ron Blog <https://jamesron.com/hrpp/> accessed 29.03.2018.

to justify or act in violation of rights and freedoms, it undermines trust in these elites *and* in the language of human rights, causing 'collateral damage' that impacts the international institutions that have been set up to promote and protect those rights. The same side effect can result from populist and anti-establishment claims to speak for 'the people', presenting human rights as an obstacle to defending the majority against perceived threats.[5] In any case, the logic is the same: multilateral organisations are a part of the 'elite', and the 'elites' do not speak and act in the interest of 'the people', hence international institutions cannot be trusted.

Another issue is the 'over-specialisation' of multilateral organisations' output, which contributes to a perception problem regarding the universality of human rights. In communicating about human rights, the only qualifying factor should be being human, since universality means that all humans are entitled to the full realisation of all rights. Yet, we tend to speak about the rights of women, minorities, migrants and other specific groups as if they were distinct from the rights of non-women, non-minorities, non-migrants and others. By 'specialising' in human rights concerns for specific groups, multilateral organisations have created a perception that 'human rights belong only to certain vulnerable categories of the population'.[6] A civil society participant at the 2017 Fundamental Rights Agency meeting said 'We hear from the average man and woman: you only care about Roma and migrants – you don't care about us'.[7] We also tend to 'specialise' our messages around a particular right, such as non-discrimination, political participation, religion or belief, or any other, as if this right existed separately from other rights. The arguments of those holding opposing, relativist views (human rights being contingent upon traditional values, national sovereignty, the fight against terrorism or any other threat; or some human rights being more important than others) too easily fill the gap left by multilateral organisations' failure to effectively communicate the universality of human rights. Such voices are able to convince the people to 'take solace in the hazardous assumption that the selective enforcement of rights is possible – that the rights of others can be compromised while their own remain secure'.[8]

---

[5] K. ROTH, 'The Dangerous Rise of Populism: Global Attacks on Human Rights Values', *Human Rights Watch*, 2017, available at https://www.hrw.org/world-report/2017/country-chapters/dangerous-rise-of-populism, last accessed 29.05.2018.

[6] N. MUIŽNIEKS, '2nd Quarterly Annual Report 2017', Council of Europe Commissioner for Human Rights, 2017, available at https://rm.coe.int/2nd-quarterly-activity-report-2017-by-nils-muiznieks-council-of-europe/168073ec5f, last accessed 29.05.2018.

[7] EUROPEAN UNION AGENCY FOR FUNDAMENTAL RIGHTS, 'How to better communicate common values, fundamental rights and freedoms – Meeting report', 2017, available at http://fra.europa.eu/en/publication/2017/how-better-communicate-common-values-fundamental-rights-and-freedoms-meeting-report, last accessed 29.05.2018.

[8] K. ROTH (2017), 'The Dangerous Rise of Populism', *supra* note 5.

4. THE ARCHITECTURE OF SPEAKING

When writing this article, we asked a sample of people why they think the way international organisations talk about human rights does not appeal to 'the poor, destitute, dispossessed, and oppressed'. One of our respondents, a 'millennial' student, said: 'It is because your messages are either self-promotion, when you talk about how great your organisations are, or an abstraction, when your stories have no human face, or both. You are only interested in saying things, and you are not listening.' This response points to the findings of Daan Bronkhorst and others, who have noted the vertical and rigid nature of the terms of human rights discourse, and the fact that 'human rights communication has a strong tendency to be "autopoietic". That is, the terms of human rights discourse refer to themselves rather than to anything outside them.'[9]

Recent research shows that 'organizations construct and deploy an "architecture of speaking".[10] Even though we use all the correct keywords, such as 'engagement', 'dialogue' and 'consultation', on average 80% of resources that organisations produce in their public communications are used for one-way communication, that is, to distribute the organisation's information and messages – even on social media. In another study, almost half of respondents from civil society organisations felt that intergovernmental organisations do not even pretend to listen to them when it comes to developing their policies and programmes.[11] The study concluded that, beyond the 'two-minute plenary speeches' allocated to civil society organisations, there is no evidence that intergovernmental agencies take outreach to civil society seriously. Even the so-called 'consultative fora' that multilateral organisations so eagerly employ have been found to mostly engage the usual suspects: the same experts and representatives of the same international and civil society groups, 'with many individuals and groups ignored, or disengaged and silent',[12] and it is not always clear whether and how the results of these consultations influence policies

---

[9] D. BRONKHORST, 'Hard Times not Endtimes: The Case for Human Rights Defenders', in D. LETTINGA and L. VAN TROOST (ed.), *Debating the Endtimes of Human Rights: Activism and Institutions in a Neo-Westphalian World*, Amnesty International Netherlands, 2014, pp. 61–67, available at https://www.amnesty.nl/content/uploads/2016/12/debating_the_endtimes_of_human_rights.pdf, last accessed 29.05.2018.

[10] J. MACNAMARA, 'Creating an "Architecture of Listening" in Organizations: The Basis of Engagement, Trust, Healthy Democracy, Social Equity, and Business Sustainability', University of Technology Sydney, 2015, available at https://www.uts.edu.au/sites/default/files/fass-organizational-listening-report.pdf, last accessed 29.05.2018.

[11] CIVICUS, 'State of Civil Society: Intergovernmental Organisation Scorecard', available at http://civicus.org/images/SoCS_IGO_final3.pdf, last accessed 29.05.2018.

[12] J. MACNAMARA (2015), 'Creating an "Architecture of Listening"', *supra* note 10.

and the work of such intergovernmental organisations. We unintentionally reinforce the perception of the top-down, one-way communication when we speak about us (the communicators) and our target audience (the recipients). As a result of this 'architecture of speaking', multilateral organisations do not stimulate greater citizen engagement that could build a sense of belonging to the human rights cause among people. Such international organisations are not giving a strong enough voice to ignored and marginalised groups and are not effective in overcoming the lack of trust in institutions.

5. CONFIRMING THE CONFIRMATION BIAS IN HUMAN RIGHTS COMMUNICATION

When communicating about human rights, multilateral organisations and institutions can inversely reinforce the negative stereotypes and biased attitudes about human rights.

In his famous Ignorance Project, Dr. Hans Rosling observed that most of the surveyed people – students, general population and journalists alike – assumed a negative change in global trends and failed to acknowledge progress.[13] He concluded that it was a combined effect of personal bias, outdated facts and news bias that gives people a skewed view of information. And because we rely on our views to generalise about facts, our intuition works against us, giving us the illusion that we know the world is regressing. He noted that it would be easy to educate people who do not know anything, but it is very tough to teach a person who is ignorant or has ill-conceived ideas as a result of the 'illusion of knowledge', because it requires biased views to be erased first.[14]

The results of this study tell us that the communication approach multilateral organisations often use (*if we only present people with correct facts and hard data about human rights, they will understand and change their mind*) might be fundamentally incomplete, because it does not take into account the blend of personal bias (family and community beliefs people grow up with), outdated facts (as a result of inadequate education) and bias created by the news (which exaggerates the unusual).[15] This is not to say that facts and data are not important but rather that facts alone are not enough to overcome the confirmation bias, especially today when 'the very idea of "facts" has been shaken [and] by December 2016 the words "post-truth" were on the lips of commentators

---

[13] H. ROSLING, 'The Ignorance Project', *gapminder.org*, available at https://www.gapminder.org/ignorance, last accessed 29.05.2018.
[14] Ibid.
[15] H. ROSLING, 'The Ignorance Project', *supra* note 13.

around the world, eventually becoming the Oxford English Dictionary's word of the year'.[16] Multiple studies have shown that when presented with the same information, people receive and interpret it selectively in a way that confirms their preconceived beliefs (a phenomenon known as the 'confirmation bias').[17] Furthermore, as Charles G. Lord's study demonstrated, confirmatory evidence strengthens people's opinions – but, counter-intuitively, so does evidence contradictory to those opinions.[18] Attempts to bust a myth about human rights have the unintended effect that people remember the myth, rather than the corrective argument.

The choice of facts and data in communicating about human rights is also important. Multilateral organisations tend to focus more on the negative side of human rights (exposing the violations and highlighting challenges to human rights protection), rather than positive stories about achievements. In ODIHR public communication, for example, we rarely speak about human rights in a positive context. In our news items for the first quarter of 2018 alone, we used the word 'challenge' three times more than 'achievement' and we used 'problem' but never 'solution' or 'progress'.

While human rights violations around the world are very real, emphasising them is unlikely to engage more people to stand up for those rights. There are a few reasons why. First, 'we have entered a dangerous era of "human rights fatigue"',[19] and if we focus most of our communication on challenges and problems, we risk becoming the 'boy who cried wolf" and people will no longer pay attention. Second, echoing George Lakoff's conclusion that when we negate something, we evoke it; if we focus on the negative, we are inadvertently reinforcing the belief that things go from bad to worse in human rights, further undermining people's need for safety and hope, and eroding their trust in the ability of multilateral organisations to change things for the better.[20] Third, we tend to think that if we continue speaking out about violations and challenges to human rights, people will see that we are on the 'right side of history' so they will trust our message. But research shows that having better knowledge about human rights

---

[16] A. KRASODOMSKI-JONES, 'Talking to Ourselves: Political Debate Online and the Echo Chamber Effect', *Demos*, 2016, available at https://www.demos.co.uk/wp-content/uploads/2017/02/Echo-Chambers-final-version.pdf, last accessed 29.05.2018.

[17] See, for example esthermsmth, 'Confirmation Bias (Wason)', *Learning Theories*, 9 September 2017, available at https://www.learning-theories.com/confirmation-bias.html, last accessed 29.05.2018.

[18] C.G. LORD, L. ROSS and M.R. LEPPER, 'Biased Assimilation and Attitude Polarization: The Effects of Prior Theories on Subsequently Considered Evidence', (1979) 37 *Journal of Personality and Social Psychology*, pp. 2098–2109, available at https://nuovoeutile.it/wp-content/uploads/2014/10/BIASED-ASSIMILATION-AND-ATTITUDE-POLARIZATION.pdf, last accessed 29.05.2018.

[19] N. MUIZNIEKS (2017), '2nd Quarterly Annual Report 2017', *supra* note 6.

[20] G. LAKOFF, *Don't Think of an Elephant!: Know Your Values and Frame the Debate*, Chelsea Green Publishing, White River Junction, Vermont 2004.

problems does not automatically translate into a greater trust in human rights organisations.[21] Fourth, a 2015 study found that, rather than demonstrating how people use human rights ideas to address abuses, public discourse about human rights focuses on the most controversial examples of the abuses themselves.[22] The same can be said about the communications of multilateral organisations: we do not sufficiently multiply messages about progress in human rights, and we are not good enough at offering practical solutions that are capable of engaging people and giving them hope. The overwhelming pessimism in human rights communications can lead people to cynicism and inaction based on the belief that if everything is so bad, there is nothing anyone can do anymore.

6. HUMAN RIGHTS COMMUNICATION WITHOUT A HUMAN FACE

Celebrating the tenth anniversary of the Universal Declaration of Human Rights, Eleanor Roosevelt said:

> Where, after all, do universal human rights begin? In small places, close to home [...] [in] the world of the individual person. [...] Such are the places where every man, woman, and child seeks equal justice, equal opportunity, equal dignity without discrimination. Unless these rights have meaning there, they have little meaning anywhere.[23]

A 2012 study in the United Kingdom (UK) found that 22% of the population in England, Scotland and Wales was supportive of human rights, 26% opposed them and 11% were uninterested.[24] The largest group – 41% – expressed conflicted attitudes towards human rights. They could not see how human rights were relevant to their lives, but once the connection was made clear, their attitudes became more positive. One could – and perhaps should – ask how many of the 336 ODIHR public information pieces in 2017 conveyed a clear connection between human rights and the lives of ordinary people and how many other organisations succeed in delivering relatable messages.

---

[21] J. RON (2017), 'The Human Rights Perception Polls', *supra* note 4.
[22] R. KRYS, 'In the UK, public discourse undermines support for human rights', *Open Democracy*, 2015, available at https://www.opendemocracy.net/openglobalrights/rachel-krys/in-uk-public-discourse-undermines-support-for-human-rights, last accessed 29.05.2018.
[23] E. ROOSEVELT, 'The Great Question', excerpted in *Harpers Magazine*, 1958, available at https://harpers.org/blog/2007/12/roosevelt-on-human-rights-in-the-small-places, last accessed 29.05.2018.
[24] Equally Ours, 'Telling the Story of Everyone's Rights, Every Day', 2013, available at http://www.equally-ours.org.uk/blog/wp-content/uploads/2013/11/13-11-18-Briefing-1-vFinal-Approved.pdf, last accessed 29.05.2018.

This question is increasingly asked in multilateral organisations. For example, the Council of Europe Human Rights Commissioner recently noted that we are often satisfied by just quoting legal standards and international conventions and are not explaining why human rights are important and valuable.[25] Research shows that when communication about human rights uses individual stories it is highly effective in mobilising people to reject human rights violations and empowering people to take action to demand change.[26]

A breadth of research in political psychology confirms that people care about individuals, but the human mind is unlikely to connect to – and be empathetic about – issues that are presented in abstract jargon, or in large numbers. The larger the numbers, the less likely people are to demonstrate compassion (even if the numbers increase from one to two) – a phenomenon known as 'psychic numbing'.[27] Yet, multilateral organisations continue to use abstract jargon (*'Gender-sensitive multi-sectoral capacity building facilitates knowledge sharing and engages stakeholders in inclusive action'*) and large numbers (*OSCE participating States host more than 2.5 million refugees and asylum seekers; Millions remain exposed to racism*). Multilateral organisations generally do not use plain English, seldom attach an individual human story to their public communication about human rights, and rarely connect rights with everyday issues people care about.

The inability to link the human rights discourse with the lives of everyday people opens up fertile ground for those who attack the human rights framework. As the 2017 Edelman Trust Barometer[28] tells us, more than half of people around the world feel that the current system of institutions does not work for them. Those who attack human rights consistently make reference to ideas about 'restoring dignity' of 'everyday folk' and claim to represent an authentic voice of 'most people' – a message that gives people the impression that it is an issue that concerns them directly, whereas 'elite' institutions fail on this account.

As mentioned earlier, multilateral organisations tend to believe that countering negative stereotypes and biased attitudes about human rights requires simply presenting logical arguments to the contrary, backed by data and facts. The assumption that people will revert to rational behaviour when presented with logical arguments and data has been proven false, based on the

---

[25] N. MUIZNIEKS (2017), '2nd Quarterly Annual Report 2017', *supra* note 6.
[26] K.J. MCENTIRE, M. LEIBY and M. KRAIN, 'Human Rights Organizations as Agents of Change: An Experimental Examination of Framing and Micromobilization', (2015) 109 *American Political Science Review*, pp. 407–426.
[27] See various studies at Decision Research, 'Psychic Numbing and the Ongoing Genocide in Darfur', available at http://www.decisionresearch.org/psychic-numbing-and-the-ongoing-genocide-in-darfur, last accessed 29.05.2018.
[28] EDELMAN, '10 Trust Barometer Insights', 2017, available at https://www.edelman.com/10-trust-barometer-insights, last accessed 29.05.2018.

complex web of factors that influence human behaviour, including one of the most fundamental drivers: values.[29] This might pose a dilemma for multilateral organisations that often place human rights in opposition to commonly held values. And yet, a body of evidence from cognitive science points to the need of using the values framework when communicating about human rights. Studies by PRIC/Equinet tell us what kinds of values, metaphors and symbols can mobilise rather than repel public support for human rights.[30] They clearly demonstrate that while attitudes such as prejudice and inequality depend on how much importance people attach to certain values compared with others, values are not static and can be engaged and strengthened to promote support for human rights. Experts note that populists appeal to the entire framework of core human values (care, fairness, loyalty, authority/respect, sanctity/ purity, liberty) but international human rights institutions tend to appeal to only the first two, and seldom frame their communication in relation to more traditional concepts such as duty, honour, obligation and hospitality. Hence, they fail to build a broader base of support for human rights.[31]

In his recent book, John Bargh says that people's attitudes are shaped by reason and values, but they are also fundamentally – and often subconsciously – influenced by the most basic and powerful need for safety.[32] Research in the field of political psychology consistently shows that threats and fear are key factors in whether a person holds conservative or liberal attitudes.[33] However, international organisations seldom make a strong and understandable enough link between the protection of human rights and the safety of an individual, his/her family and community. Rather, we use language that highlights the risks and threats to security – which are undoubtedly present – but this choice of language, again, reinforces the perception that human rights are linked with problems rather than with opportunities and hope for a better, safer future. Our human rights discourse fails to connect emotionally with the people's need for safety. This leaves those most susceptible to feeling threatened or insecure easy targets of populist rhetoric that attempts to manipulate people's attitudes away

---

[29] See for example H. MERCIER and D. SPERBER, *The Enigma of Reason*, Harvard University Press, Harvard 2017.
[30] E. BLACKMORE, B. SANDERSON and R. HAWKINS, 'Valuing Equality: How equality bodies can use values to create a more equal & accepting Europe', European Network of Equality Bodies, 2014, available at http://www.equineteurope.org/IMG/pdf/valuing_equality.pdf, last accessed 29.05.2018.
[31] EUROPEAN UNION AGENCY FOR FUNDAMENTAL RIGHTS (2017), 'How to better communicate common values', *supra* note 7.
[32] J. BARGH, *Before You Know It: The Unconscious Reasons We Do What We Do*, William-Heinemann, London 2017.
[33] See, for example J.R. HIBBING, K.B. SMITH and J.R. ALFORD, 'Differences in Negativity Bias Underlie Variations in Political Ideology', (2014) 67 *University of Nebraska Faculty Publications: Political Science*, available at http://digitalcommons.unl.edu/poliscifacpub/67, last accessed 29.05.2018.

from human rights by appealing to the feelings of fear, whether of migrants, terrorists, minorities, religious groups, or simply of 'the others'.

7. TALKING TO OURSELVES: HUMAN RIGHTS ECHO CHAMBERS

The 2017 Edelman Trust Barometer shows that confidence in expert information is declining and that people have more trust in a person they feel they can identify with, regardless of any expert knowledge. This is an important indication for multilateral organisations that often do not reach out beyond their online and offline echo chambers, talking and communicating mostly with like-minded people, groups and institutions. We tend to stay within our comfort zones, partnering and speaking with the same experts, non-governmental organisations (NGOs), think tanks, academic institutions and organisations, preaching to the converted and rarely engaging in communication with those who have little interest in human rights or who openly oppose them.[34] This has multiple consequences: it limits our exposure to ideas that are alien or uncomfortable, and it reduces our ability to communicate with those who do not share our views, reinforcing the 'architecture of speaking'.

Among the key goals of multilateral organisations should be the imperative of building broad acceptance of our shared reality of human rights. But as long as we stay within our echo chambers, we will not be able to deliver on this goal. We also compromise our effectiveness because the human rights issues that we work to address, be it migrant integration, prevention of violence against women, or any other topic, need to be communicated to everybody who has a stake and can influence the advancement of rights; not just to those who already believe in the benefits of integrating migrants and agree that violence against women is a human rights issue.

While the long-term effects of speaking within echo chambers are not yet well documented, we suggest that this 'tribal' approach to human rights work is widening the gap between multilateral organisations (the 'expert elite') and the general population, which inadvertently adds to the growing polarisation of views about human rights. By staying within our echo chambers, we do not open ourselves up to hearing the legitimate grievances of those who do not share our views, or are undecided, allowing these grievances to be strategically appropriated by anti-rights discourses.

None of the human rights challenges of today can be effectively faced in isolation. And yet, the culture of segregated, silo operations, both within and

---

[34] N. MUIZNIEKS (2017), '2nd Quarterly Annual Report 2017', *supra* note 6.

outside of individual multilateral organisations, often makes us view other organisations working in the same field with suspicion, thinking of them as competitors for resources and recognition, and pushing back when we think they trespass on the territory of our mandates. This is also reflected in communication – or 'sub-chambers' within our echo chambers, where each multilateral organisation is focusing on promoting itself and its work, rather than creating and communicating a common vision of human rights, effectively 'basking in the historic respect for an organisation's reputation, and failing to address the tough questions about how best to achieve change in a changing world'.[35]

8. EMBRACING DECENTRALISED COMMUNICATIONS

We have discussed how multilateral human rights institutions need to amend their message to engage the disengaged and promote respect for human rights. But how should they go about doing that? It is important for multilateral organisations to also think about how they actually disseminate messages to effectively reach beyond their echo chambers and be heard by the general public. This is a key question for human rights institutions, which need to escape from their echo chambers and engage a broadly defined 'general public'. To think about what means organisations have at their disposal for transmitting their messages it is necessary to understand the contemporary media landscape.

Since the turn of the millennium communications technologies have evolved almost beyond recognition. Once, multilateral institutions would disperse their messages via press releases, direct contact with journalists and through the reporting of journalists in regular print, radio and television media. The highly centralised media landscape of the past, in which the authority to communicate such issues was held by a relatively small group of elites and outlets, no longer exists in its traditional form. Today, we live in a world of decentralised communications where anyone has the ability to disseminate messages and has the opportunity to be heard. In many ways, the media landscape of today is more democratic than it was in the past, since a greater number of people are able to express themselves and present alternative narratives through social media. But this also causes problems for large organisations who not only have to vie for space in an increasingly 'online'

---

[35] S. CRAWSHAW, 'Neo-Westphalia, So What?', in D. LETTINGA and L. VAN TROOST (eds.), *Debating the Endtimes of Human Rights: Activism and Institutions in a Neo-Westphalian World*, Amnesty International Netherlands, 2014, pp. 61–67, available at https://www.amnesty.nl/content/uploads/2016/12/debating_the_endtimes_of_human_rights.pdf, last accessed 29.05.2018.

media landscape, but also face the challenge of fighting the phenomenon of 'fake news' or of countering negative narratives that undermine the work of such organisations. As Peter Levine says, without a central regulating authority 'these media work for good and for ill – as instruments of enlightenment and emancipation and also as tools of propaganda and division'.[36]

For multilateral organisations to be able to amplify their voices in this new and decentralised media landscape it is necessary to understand how people consume media today. Data by research firm Zenith shows that the average US citizen now spends 455.8 minutes per day consuming media, which is more than ever before.[37] This means there is a greater opportunity to communicate directly with people via the internet, bypassing the traditional methods of coverage through traditional media. But it is not just the volume of media we consume that is changing; the methods of accessing such media have changed and continue to change. The latest media consumer survey by consulting firm Deloitte, shows that people are increasingly accessing content via smartphones and tablets. The study also points to the increasingly blurred line between social content, news and entertainment.[38] If multilateral institutions are to be heard in this busy landscape, their communications need to adapt to the reality of how people are consuming media – focusing on engaging creatively via social media and adapting their products to be accessible on smartphones and tablets.

9. 'KNOW THY AUDIENCE'

It is unreasonable to believe that all of the messages we convey will be received in the same way by every member of society they reach. Therefore, it is necessary for multilateral human rights institutions to target their messages to their audiences. Too often in our human rights communications we unconsciously assume that we are speaking to people like us, who will receive messages in the same way as we do and who have the same sympathies and concerns as us. This can strengthen the perception that human rights concerns are somehow elitist and enforce the idea that multilateral institutions are only in dialogue with one another and are therefore not relevant to ordinary citizens. Without a solid understanding of the audience it is difficult to convey any message effectively.

---

[36] P. LEVINE, 'Media Literacy for the 21st Century', (2015) 23 *Democracy and Education*, available at https://democracyeducationjournal.org/home/vol23/iss1/15, last accessed 29.05.2018.
[37] Statista, 'Media Use – Statistics and Facts', available at https://www.statista.com/topics/1536/media-use, last accessed 27.05.2018.
[38] M. GUEST and M. COOPER, 'Media Consumer 2015: The Signal and the Noise', *Deloitte LLP*, 2015, available at http://www.deloitte.co.uk/mediaconsumer/assets/pdf/Deloitte_Media_Consumer_2015.pdf, last accessed 25.03.2018.

The key to any effective communications strategy is rooted in comprehensive understanding of the audience and research into what messages will resonate best with particular subgroups in society.

It is therefore important that multilateral institutions take the time to reflect on who their audience is and what messages work best. A self-reflective communications strategy should take into account whether expert or simple language is used, whether the message is one of fear or of hope, and give adequate thought to how messaging will be received by the target audience. The first step to better understanding the audience should be to analyse website and social media statistics, not only to understand the demographic of those accessing content, but also to identify which messages are most popular and which are least popular. From this point, content can be adapted to those audiences. No matter who the audience is, one thing that should be kept in mind for all human rights communications is that it must be written in simple, jargon-free language that is comprehensible by the broadest possible range of individuals. We often make the mistake of believing that human rights communication efforts are all about what we are saying to the outside world, when in fact, they are more about what people hear.

Multilateral institutions dealing with human rights issues spend a significant portion of their time working on issues directly affecting a minority group within the population. It is rarely the dominant group in society that experiences the most egregious human rights violations. So, part of the challenge lies in convincing the dominant group in society to care about the stories of the minority group or groups. In such scenarios human rights organisations should focus their efforts on building empathy between groups. Empathy can be built through contact and through speaking about human rights issues of a minority group in terms that the majority group understands and recognises in themselves. In its public communications strategy, Amnesty International sets out a series of common and universal ideas that can be mobilised to evoke empathetic responses in audiences. They include talking about building consensus around what is 'fair', helping people to realise that the rights minority groups seek to claim are the rights that the majority group themselves enjoy without even questioning them, and that human rights are part of a legal framework that protects us all, so by protecting human rights we are protecting the rule of law.[39] These are all useful points that should guide human rights communications.

It is counter-productive to employ a 'one size fits all' communications strategy for the broad range of issues that multilateral organisations, including ODIHR, deal with and the broad range of interlocutors we want to engage with.

---

[39] AMNESTY INTERNATIONAL, 'More People: The Amnesty International UK Communications Strategy – 2016–2020', available at http://edenstanley.co.uk/wp-content/uploads/2017/03/More-People-Short-Presentation-Version.pdf, last accessed 29.05.2018.

Numerous campaigns strategists stress the importance of thinking about who the key audience is for a specific issue and targeting it using all of the analytical tools that an organisation has at its disposal – whether through websites or social media. Given the rise in the number of people using social media sites as a news source (45% of United States of America (US) adults now report using Facebook as a news source)[40] it is important that multilateral institutions utilise these networks and, if needed, promote material to specific audiences. If poorly tailored messages reach citizens who are apathetic towards or conflicted about human rights, those messages may enforce established negative stereotypes about human rights and have the opposite effect to that intended, as outlined in Charles G. Lord's aforementioned study.[41]

Opinion polling expert Laurence Janta-Lipinski suggests approaching human rights communications by segmenting the audience according to four categories: those who are pro human rights (already convinced of their importance), those who are anti human rights (who openly reject any positives), those who are conflicted (can see the good and the bad), and finally, those who are apathetic (who have no strong views for or against human rights). Analysing data about our audiences and effectively segmenting users may help to ensure that more of our messages hit their mark. Segmentation is crucial because 'the messages needed to persuade the apathetic person and the conflicted person will be quite different'.[42] Too often, we do not take a segmented approach when we develop our communications strategies, but instead focus broadly on how one message can resonate with all people, on the assumption that support for human rights is something we have in common. This leads us into a situation where, once more, we are speaking within an echo chamber. Segmentation is the first step towards developing a communications strategy capable of effectively moving beyond our established audience and speaking to the anti, conflicted and apathetic portions of society.

As part of our efforts to move away from 'one-way' communication, professionals working in multilateral institutions may consider bringing in people who self-identify as anti-human rights or are conflicted or apathetic about them. We should not be afraid of speaking to human rights sceptics and should actively engage with them to understand their rationale. Having an honest discussion about their views and what messages resonate with them would help

---

[40] E. SHEARER and J. GOTTFRIED, 'News Use Across Social Media Platforms 2017', *Pew Research Center*, 2017, available at http://www.journalism.org/2017/09/07/news-use-across-social-media-platforms-2017, last accessed 29.05.2018.

[41] C.G. LORD, L. ROSS and M.R. LEPPER, 'Biased Assimilation', *supra* note 18, pp. 2098–2109.

[42] L. JANTA-LIPINSKI, 'Know thy audience: effective messaging in human rights campaigns', *Open Democracy*, 2015, available at https://www.opendemocracy.net/openglobalrights/laurence-janta-lipinski/know-thy-audience-effective-messaging-in-human-rights-campa, last accessed 29.05.2018.

to mitigate any institutional blindness we may suffer from and pay dividends when thinking about how to approach communications campaigns in the future.

10. HARNESSING NEW COMMUNICATION TECHNOLOGIES

Advances in technology over the past 20 years have created the opportunity for human rights organisations to communicate their messages in many different ways. However, whether due to funding constraints, a lack of time, or established and bureaucratic ways of doing things, multilateral human rights organisations are rarely the first to embrace such new technologies.

With the advent of new technologies, the line between social content, entertainment and news has become blurred, with many people consuming non-social content, such as news, on social channels, such as Facebook and Twitter.[43] Due to the changing media landscape, it is no longer sufficient for multilateral organisations to simply send out press releases and post updates on their websites and expect them to be read by the general public. Instead, if such organisations want to reach out and improve their digital footprint, it is necessary to harness new technologies to engage people in a disruptive and attention-grabbing way. But technology is only one part of the equation. The other part is compelling content. As Trevor Thrall and Diana Sweet state:

> Technology [alone] will not transform […] communication ability because it can never resolve the central problem of global communication: the zero-sum nature of attention. To win attention […] requires having the organisational resources necessary to create newsworthy and compelling information for both media and public audiences.[44]

Technology is a powerful tool for amplifying our message, but only if the message is inspiring, resonant and positive in the first place.

Multilateral human rights organisations should not be shy about looking at how private sector companies are reformulating their own communications to reach a broader audience, since they often have the resources to be industry leaders in that regard. Specifically, it is useful to look at how newspapers and other online news outlets have adapted to the changing media landscape and how they have innovated to create new platforms and products to engage

---

[43] M. GUEST and M. COOPER (2015), 'Media Consumer 2015', *supra* note 38.
[44] T. THRALL, D. SWEET and D. STECULA, 'May We Have Your Attention Please? Human Rights NGOs and the Problem of Global Communication', (2014) 19(2) *International Journal of Press/Politics*, available at http://journals.sagepub.com/doi/abs/10.1177/1940161213519132, last accessed 29.05.2018.

in effective and empathy-building story-telling. Products such as interactive articles focusing on the human side of serious stories, the likes of which have been created by the Guardian, among others, grab people's attention by presenting them with something they have not seen before.[45] While the internet makes it easier to speak, the decentralised nature of communications today makes it more difficult to be heard. Indeed, human rights organisations face a difficult task in being heard, since most of them 'lack the organisational resources to compete effectively for either traditional news coverage or for public attention'.[46]

To win over the attention of audiences in an increasingly crowded media landscape, numerous newspapers, NGOs and think-tanks have adopted new strategies of engagement. One key strategy evident across the board is a tendency to use data visualisation or image-heavy social media posts that can cut through the noise and grab people's attention. Indeed, ODIHR has begun to project key messages from statements or events by using media rich posts that include photos with key quotes from the Director or other experts, on the basis that these are more eye-catching and accessible.[47] Eye-tracking studies have shown that readers pay close attention to images that carry information and that when images are relevant to the content, users spend more time looking at the image and its text than they would reading text alone on a page.[48] By the same token, in one experiment, tweets with images were shown to be shared (retweeted) 150% more than tweets without images.[49] Multilateral organisations may, therefore, want to consider moving away from text alone, and begin telling stories and reaching out to people through text-image and text-video combinations.

Social media posts are useful to multilateral organisations because they act as a hook into our websites. Social media posts are the bait that we put out into the world, which should be enticing enough to ensure that readers click and are redirected to our websites, where the bulk of our activities can be explored

---

[45] One of the earliest examples of such effective digital storytelling is the Guardian's investigation of human stories surrounding the problem of wildfires in Australia. See 'Firestorm', *The Guardian*, 29.05.2013, available at https://www.theguardian.com/world/interactive/2013/may/26/firestorm-bushfire-dunalley-holmes-family, last accessed 29.05.2018.

[46] T. THRALL, D. SWEET and D. STECULA (2014), 'May We Have Your Attention Please?', *supra* note 44.

[47] For example, see OSCE/ODIHR, 'As millions remain exposed to #racism, #equality bodies must be strengthened, say heads of European #humanrights institutions on International Anti-Racism Day', Twitter, 2017, available at https://twitter.com/osce_odihr/status/976432581599252480, last accessed 29.05.2018.

[48] J. NIELSEN, 'Photos as Web Content', Nielsen Norman Group, 2010, available at https://www.nngroup.com/articles/photos-as-web-content, last accessed 29.05.2018.

[49] B.B. COOPER, 'How Twitter's Expanded Images Increase Clicks, Retweets and Favorites [New Data]', *Buffer*, 2016, available at https://blog.bufferapp.com/the-power-of-twitters-new-expanded-images-and-how-to-make-the-most-of-it, last accessed 29.05.2018.

in more detail. Such posts provide a way for organisations to win attention in a crowded environment, to promote the main messages we want to disseminate and to entice people into our websites. Today, social media is the main way we amplify our voices and research shows that 92% of global NGOs have a Facebook page and 72% have a Twitter page.[50]

As part of efforts to project a message of hope rather than one of fear, human rights organisations should also consider borrowing tools from journalism to tell positive stories about the work they do. Multilateral organisations often maintain a neutral face in their communications with the outside world, reporting factually on their activities in a broadly emotionless manner. There is little incentive for anyone beyond the community of human rights practitioners and those already interested in the work of such organisations to engage with this kind of content. Multilateral institutions should consider embracing the blurred line between social, entertainment and news to create products that people want to engage with and which project our key messages. It is crucial that such products tell human stories about our work and its positive impact in order to build an emotive connection with the audience.

11. BUILDING CONTACT WITH JOURNALISTS

It is an illusion that multilateral organisations hold a monopoly over the means to shape public opinion about their activities. Certainly, we have a degree of control, but there are also external actors who are capable of shaping narratives about the work we do. Chief among those external actors are journalists. Despite the changing media landscape, news outlets still command the most authority and the largest readership among our target audiences. Therefore, the way we are represented in the media is important if we are to protect our reputation and project the messages we want to.

Multilateral organisations cannot (and indeed do not want to) control what journalists write, but one thing we can help to improve is the accuracy of reporting about our activities and mandates. Organisations like the OSCE, of which ODIHR is just one executive institution, have complex structures and their work is rooted in numerous commitments that can be found in various international documents. In order to improve the quality of reporting about such organisations it may be a good idea to invite key journalists covering international affairs to training courses on the origin, purpose, structure and mission of the given institution – in our case, the OSCE. This would not only

---

[50] C. MANGLES, 'Global NGOs social media usage and effectiveness', *Smart Insights*, 2017, available at https://www.smartinsights.com/social-media-marketing/social-media-platforms/global-ngos-prefer-use-facebook-instagram, last accessed 29.05.2018.

help to ensure that journalists report on our activities with accuracy but may also lead them to engage more with our work.

Having face-to-face contact in the form of training events would help to build networks between the international journalist community and the OSCE, which may encourage journalists to reach out to us for press comment on a more regular basis, and by extension increase our coverage in the press. It is important that any such initiative to train journalists on the activities and mandate of the OSCE, for example, brings in professionals from across the political spectrum, including from both tabloid and broadsheet newspapers. Multilateral organisations could also consider providing internships for young media professionals to 'follow our story' or invite established journalists into our organisation to accompany us on specific trips to meet local communities. Such a scheme would also be a learning opportunity for staff who work within multilateral organisations and who can benefit from the communications expertise of journalists.

Very few, if any, international organisations or NGOs currently run training activities for journalists, despite the immense power they have to shape opinion about institutions. In 2009, the European Union Directorate General for Communications funded a website for journalists covering the EU, which provided journalists with key information about how the EU works and all the details of relevant press contacts in the institutions. However, the website no longer exists.

12. ACTING LOCALLY, THINKING GLOBALLY

In the current political environment, with rising populism and an increasingly sovereigntist agenda in parts of Europe, large multilateral organisations are struggling to win the trust of ordinary people. Our current political moment is characterised by waning trust in elites and in businesses, media, government and NGOs.[51] Large organisations such as the OSCE need, therefore, to justify their relevance to ordinary people. To shatter the image of bureaucracy it is necessary to show people that we are working with local communities on the ground and are networked into their regions. The OSCE Special Monitoring Mission's Instagram page is a positive step in this direction, since it includes photos from the frontline in eastern Ukraine and shows OSCE officials directly helping local communities.[52] The Special Monitoring Mission is constantly working in the field, so it has many opportunities to broadcast the local side of its work.

---

[51] EDELMAN (2017), '10 Trust Barometer Insights', *supra* note 28.
[52] The OSCE Special Monitoring Mission's, *Instagram*, available at https://www.instagram.com/oscesmm, last accessed 29.05.2018.

Most of ODIHR's seminars and training events do engage with different local communities, and with policymakers and practitioners in the 57 countries in the OSCE region. To enhance perceptions of relevance among local people across the OSCE region we should be working harder to broadcast the work we do with local communities. Our narratives should tie local issues to global themes, to build a discourse that local activities contribute to global change. We should actively focus on building such narratives. There are a few ways we can do this: one way is to include testimony from local interlocutors who have benefited from activities or workshops and using partnerships with grassroots NGOs to link into networks on the ground and increase awareness of our organisations among ordinary people in small communities.

13. CONCLUSION: THE MESSAGE AND THE MESSENGER

To have the messages of human rights and fundamental freedoms heard and understood by ordinary people, multilateral organisations need to create and share these messages in ways that are fit for the realities of the 21st century. There is an urgent need for international organisations to communicate more effectively, to be able to show to ordinary people that human rights and fundamental freedoms are indispensable in their lives, and to strengthen public support for those rights and freedoms. What can multilateral organisations do to address this communication vacuum?

The analysis of the problems gives us a clear indication of what should be done. Multilateral organisations should:

- Develop an effective 'architecture of listening';
- Simplify the language in communications materials, avoiding jargon where possible;
- Focus on the universality of rights, while demonstrating clear links between human rights and the lives of everyday people and individualising human rights messages – giving them a human face;
- Use the entire repertoire of positive communication (data and facts, not contradicting others' anti-rights arguments but consistently presenting our own, transmitting and multiplying messages about progress);
- Link with the values frameworks that have proven effective to promote attitudes supportive of human rights; give hope, not fear; and
- Get out of their comfort zones to reach out beyond echo chambers, abandon tribal attitudes and work with others to create and communicate a common vision of human rights.

All of these steps should happen simultaneously, which is obviously easier said than done, not least because it means that multilateral organisations should start behaving differently than they are used to when it comes to communicating about human rights. But there is enough research and knowledge out there, including on what is important for people and where there are the gaps in human rights communication, for us to craft new approaches.

Multilateral organisations are increasingly looking at their communication strategies to regain the shrinking trust and support of the general public for human rights. In his 2017 quarterly report, the Council of Europe's Human Rights Commissioner called for stronger efforts to demonstrate the universality of human rights, their benefit for each person, and their relevance to addressing contemporary challenges.[53] The Commissioner wrote that the Council of Europe should do this 'by being creative, increasingly visual, and appealing not only to people's minds, but their emotions as well', by supplementing 'long texts and reliance on traditional media with astute use of social media and other new technologies', and by escaping pro-human rights echo chambers and engaging 'in active debates with those who oppose human rights or believe they are irrelevant'.[54] In March this year, the Council of Europe's and the United Nations' Commissioners for Human Rights joined the European Union Fundamental Rights Agency and others in a public statement of commitment to improve their public communication to successfully promote and protect human rights; in the document, they commit to take a critical look at their own communication, get better at listening, including to the critics and the indifferent, and reach out of their own communication bubble.[55] Recognising that a fragmented and siloed culture in international organisations undermines trust and credibility, the United Nations developed a 'Delivering as One' slogan, representing the entire 'UN development system that delivers together across mandates, sectors and institutional boundaries', and including the 'Communicating as One' guidance for its staff that notes the need to emphasise the shared values.[56] Throughout 2017, the European Union Fundamental Rights Agency organised several discussions on improving communication about common values, fundamental rights and freedoms, in which ODIHR also took part, and produced several interesting

---

[53] N. MUIZNIEKS (2017), '2nd Quarterly Annual Report 2017', *supra* note 6.
[54] Ibid.
[55] K. GILMORE, N. MUIZNIEKS, M. O'FLAHERTY, L. VIDOVIC and F. SIMBIRI-JAOKO, 'Joint Statement: International organizations commit to building broader support for human rights', European Network of Equality Bodies, available at http://www.equineturope.org/IMG/pdf/geneva_event_joint_statement_final.pdf, last accessed 29.05.2018.
[56] UNITED NATIONS DEVELOPMENT GROUP, 'Guide to communicating as one', 2014, available at https://undg.org/wp-content/uploads/2016/09/Guide-to-Communicating-as-One-edited-1.pdf, last accessed 29.05.2018.

publications on the topic.[57] Even though one cannot escape the impression that these efforts still remain in the same echo chambers (just like this article), it is critically important that debates about effective human rights communication are gaining momentum and that multilateral organisations join forces in these debates. If the organisational silos become more permeable, more platforms can emerge to support such cooperation and collective action.

One way to reach beyond our echo chambers, and increase our relevance and effectiveness, is to redirect resources to build an 'architecture of listening'. The number of stakeholders for multilateral organisations – whether employees, experts, representatives of governments and civil society, or citizens generally – is large, so the organisations 'need to be capable of *large-scale* listening' that recognises, acknowledges and pays attention to others' views, and interprets those views to act towards advancing the message of human rights. This requires having money and engaging professional staff with expertise in public communication. Both can be achieved, Professor Macnamara points out, by prioritising and redirecting existing resources to enhance communication about human rights.[58] We believe that multilateral organisations need to prioritise and reallocate resources to communications if they are serious about building trust and support for human rights among the general public. At ODIHR, we already know how to listen to our beneficiaries to make our training programmes and reports contextually relevant; now we need to take this knowledge forward to develop our ability to engage in '*large-scale* listening'.

We need to be clearer about the desired result of our communication. If we want people to adapt attitudes and behaviours in favour of human rights, we need to rethink how we structure our messages. Research shows that attitudes and behaviours are influenced by the values that people hold most strongly. The values can be engaged by what people see, read, hear and experience, and when one value is engaged, other values close to it are also engaged while the opposing ones are suppressed.[59] For example, for people to be concerned about the safety of minority groups, the discussion needs to be framed around the values of human needs, care and protection; if it is based on security values, it will likely evoke nationalism and discrimination.[60] The values frames multilateral organisations use are thus critically important because people will react differently depending on which values we engage. We need to invest – engaging experts and using

---

[57]   EUROPEAN UNION AGENCY FOR FUNDAMENTAL RIGHTS (2017), 'How to better communicate common values', *supra* note 7.
[58]   J. MACNAMARA (2015), 'Creating an "Architecture of Listening"', *supra* note 10.
[59]   PIRC/COUNTERPOINT/EQUALLY OURS, COUNTERPOINT, 'Building Bridges: Connecting with values to reframe and build support for human rights', 2014, available at http://counterpoint. uk.com/wp-content/uploads/2016/06/Building-Bridges.pdf, last accessed 29.05.2018.
[60]   E. BLACKMORE, B. SANDERSON and R. HAWKINS (2014), 'Valuing Equality', *supra* note 30.

the 'architecture of listening' – in developing and consistently repeating human rights messages framed around values that change public attitudes and build support for human rights. At ODIHR, we have been working on reframing our human rights education methods so they can influence people's behaviour in favour of human rights. These experiences could well be expanded and applied to our public communication activities.

Audience research tells us that communication about human rights cannot be about fear. To be effective, it needs to evoke hope. As discussed earlier, communication that fuels fear encourages closed-minded and defensive thinking, and is a strong demotivator. The opposite is also true: messages of hope provide inspiration and stimulate collective action.[61] So we need to rethink the predominantly negative language we use to speak about human rights.

The founding documents of human rights – the Universal Declaration (70 years old this year) and the Charter of Paris for a New Europe – give us exceptional examples of this language of vision and hope. In the first lines of the Declaration's Preamble, we are told that: 'recognition of the inherent dignity and of the equal and inalienable rights of all members of the human family is the foundation of freedom, justice and peace in the world'.[62] While the Charter of Paris that gave birth to ODIHR opens with the inspirational message that: 'The courage of men and women, the strength of the will of the peoples and the power of the ideas of the Helsinki Final Act have opened a new era of democracy, peace and unity in Europe. Ours is a time for fulfilling the hopes and expectations our peoples have cherished for decades: steadfast commitment to democracy based on human rights and fundamental freedoms [...]'.[63] Multilateral organisations need to 'go back to the basics' of these inspirational founding acts and communicate about human rights in a way that fosters people's aspirations and hopes, not their fears.

We also need to get better at using facts and positive emotions together. For example, why are we mostly lamenting the shrinking space for civil society, but are not equally vocal when it comes to praising the resilience, dedication and good work of civil society organisations, giving them the recognition they deserve and sharing the inspiration they offer? We could seek inspiration in wildly popular projects such as 'Humans of New York',[64] with its slogan ('New York City, one story at a time'). The project reaches more than 20 million followers on social media and showcases many uplifting stories of ordinary

---

[61] PIRC and EQUINET, 'Communication Handbook for Equality Bodies: Framing Equality', 2017, available at http://www.equineteurope.org/Framing-Equality-Communication-Handbook-for-Equality-Bodies, last accessed 29.05.2018.
[62] UN Universal Declaration of Human Rights 1948.
[63] OSCE, Charter of Paris for a New Europe 1990, available at https://www.osce.org/mc/39516, last accessed 29.05.2018.
[64] 'Humans of New York', available at http://www.humansofnewyork.com, last accessed 30.03.2018.

people from the city. It is not difficult to imagine a similar joint project by several multilateral organisations: 'advancing human rights, one story at a time'.

Cognitive science teaches us that the messenger is as important as the message. Multilateral organisations often lack the credibility and recognition needed to change public perception into one favourable of human rights. But there are others who are closer to the communities and the people who might be better placed to deliver the key messages on our behalf. Steve Crawshaw brings the example of Helsinki Foundations that 'took a dry inter-governmental process – the Helsinki Final Act, full of apparently empty verbiage – and made it their own. […] Backed by an international human rights movement, they created the possibilities of extraordinary change […]'.[65] In today's world, the number of grassroots organisations, social movements, online activists, artists, bloggers and many others who stand up for human rights is truly extraordinary. At ODIHR, we have seen that when we gave a human face and voice to human rights discourse – for example when we invited a youth grassroots activist to the otherwise rather rigid Human Dimension Implementation Meeting to speak about her own experiences interacting with Syrian refugee children – people not only listened but were also genuinely moved and inspired. One lesson for multilateral organisations is that their 'human rights messengers' should not always be diplomats and experts from within their own institutions and surrounding echo chambers, but also those who can share personal experiences that everyday people can identify with and become inspired by. We need to link with and support effective human rights messengers, even if they are not within our traditional networks.

ODIHR's experience shows that when we engage with people from various fields, such as digital communications, psychology, new media, marketing, open-source and data-driven investigations techniques and design, we help human rights activists better communicate about human rights and mobilise public support – and we learn ourselves. To achieve lasting change in the way multilateral organisations 'win hearts and minds' for human rights, we not only need to mobilise resources and engage experts, we also need to seek strategic partnerships with civil society organisations and companies that work at the intersection of human rights, social change and communications, and learn from their successes in changing public attitudes about human rights.[66]

Paraphrasing Rachel Krys, multilateral organisations need 'a new shorthand', because how people feel about and understand human rights not only guides how they use them, but also how they react when their rights are under threat.[67]

---

[65] S. CRAWSHAW (2014), 'Neo-Westphalia, So What?', *supra* note 35.
[66] See for example Stanford Social Innovation Review, 'Making Ideas Move', available at https://ssir.org/making_ideas_move, last accessed 29.03.2018.
[67] R. KRYS (2015), 'In the UK', *supra* note 22.

RISING POPULISM AND ITS IMPACT ON WOMEN'S RIGHTS

Selected Cases from the OSCE Region

Ajla van HEEL and Jacopo LEONE

1. Populism and Gender. 522
2. The Five Star Movement and the League in Italy 525
3. The Front National in France 530
4. Law and Justice in Poland 533
5. Party for Freedom in the Netherlands. 537
6. Conclusion. 540

ABSTRACT

The rise of populism as a political phenomenon in recent years poses a new set of challenges to our democracies across the Organization for Security and Cooperation in Europe (OSCE) region. In their political agendas, populist parties symbolise a profound dilemma for democratic regimes, to some extent challenging the very system of liberal values and human rights which came to define Western Liberal democracies over the last decades. In doing so, populist parties tend to position 'the people' against 'the elite', portraying themselves as true representatives of an homogeneous people, abandoned by a corrupt and conspiring elite (political, economic, cultural). Additionally, some populist parties partly or entirely reject the long-standing foundations of democratic institutions, i.e. separation of powers, transparency, rule of law, and non-discrimination. Resting on the profusion of analyses available on the revamp of populism, this article will specifically try to assess the impact populist parties and their agendas have on gender equality and women's rights across the OSCE region. Are populist parties more inclined to adopt a critical stand towards gender equality and women's rights? What type of alternative political narrative, if any, do they promote in the gender relations within our societies? Looking at selected populist political parties across the OSCE region, the present analysis will compare their political agendas and narratives on gender equality and women's rights issues, with the aim of identifying consistent patterns, possibly highlighting concerns and recommendations to be taken into consideration in future efforts to promote more inclusive and equal democratic societies.

1. POPULISM AND GENDER

Over the last decade, and to a greater extent during recent years, populism has become a prominent feature of political party systems across the OSCE region,[1] with populist actors appearing to gain significant political relevance and representing large sectors of our societies. Although still lacking a shared definition and conceptual clarity, populism is often used to describe a rather negative political phenomenon, currently posing one of the greatest challenges and threats to liberal democracies and their underlining values of pluralism, rule of law and inclusion. Already in 2010, in an interview with the Frankfurter Allgemeine Zeitung, the European Union (EU) President Herman von Rompuy declared populism 'the greatest danger for Europe'.[2]

Data that has been gathered over recent years seems to support the growing attention populism is receiving. The Timbro Authoritarian Populism Index,[3] a Europe-wide comprehensive study that aims to shed light on raising populist political actors, analysing electoral data from 1980 to the summer 2017, shows populism asserting itself as a main political force, gathering the support of a fifth of the European electorate, or around 55.8 million people during each European country's latest general elections. Similarly, according to a recent analysis produced by the Tony Blair Institute for Global Change,[4] the populist vote in an EU state was, on average, 85% in 2000, growing to 24.1% in 2017. Moreover, a growing number of mainstream political parties are accepting populist actors into forming governing coalitions, with a resulting substantial influence over the political direction of these OSCE participating states.

However, defining populism remains notoriously subjective. In this context, in the attempt to better understand and delineate what ultimately defines populism, populist political movements, as well as populist rhetoric, an extensive amount of scientific analyses and academic research has been produced on the subject. The challenge of defining populism is at least partially due to the fact that the term has been used to describe political movements, political parties, ideologies, and leaders across different geographical, historical, and ideological contexts.

---

[1] The OSCE has 57 participating states from Europe, Central Asia and North America.
[2] The EUOBSERVER, 'EU President issues stark warning against nationalism', 10.11.2010, available at https://euobserver.com/institutional/31240, last accessed 28.05.2018.
[3] TIMBRO, 'Timbro Authoritarian Populism Index 2017', 04.01.2018, available at https://timbro.se/allmant/timbro-authoritarian-populism-index2017, last accessed 28.05.2018.
[4] M. EIERMANN, Y. MOUNK and L. GULTCHIN, 'European Populism: Trends, Threats and Future Prospects', Tony Blair Institute for Global Change, 29.12.2017, available at https://institute.global/insight/renewing-centre/european-populism-trends-threats-and-future-prospects, last accessed 28.05.2018.

As a matter of simplification and in broader terms, three different approaches to defining populism have emerged: populism as an ideology, populism as a discursive style and populism as a political strategy.[5]

Referencing the existing research and analysis, the present article will avoid entering the conceptual debate over the nature and definition of populism. To the benefit of its limited scope, this article will use the largely accepted understanding of populism as a set of ideas characterised by an antagonism between the people and the elite, as well as the primacy of popular sovereignty, whereby the virtuous general will is placed in opposition to the moral corruption of elite actors. Cas Mudde, one of the most renowned experts on political extremism and populism, defines populism in these terms: 'a thin-centered ideology that considers society to be ultimately separated into two homogenous and antagonistic groups, "the pure people" versus "the corrupt elite", and which argues that politics should be an expression of the volonté générale (general will) of the people.'[6]

Thin-centred ideologies are to be understood as not full ideologies and so must attach themselves to other ideologies. This liquid concept of populism seems to imply that instead of a homogenous and coherent populist ideology, what we are presented with is rather various political actors with different resulting ideologies and political options.[7] For this reason, a distinction between left-wing oriented forms of populism and more right-wing oriented forms has been presented.[8] While left-wing populists are more inclined to pay attention to social inequality and economic exclusion, right-wing populist parties tend to promote instead sentiments of nationalism, and emphasise the mutually exclusive contraposition between groups in society and cultural identities. Whatever its form, a populist vote remains largely an expression of discontent. Moreover, populism has also been closely related to political polarisation that under some conditions may push party systems to the verge of collapse.[9] Following the same approach, others consider populism as a virus that infects party systems across Europe with epidemic effects.[10]

---

[5]   B. MOFFITT and S. TORMEY, 'Rethinking Populism: Politics, Mediatisation and Political Style', (2014) 62(2) *Political Studies Association*, pp. 381–397 and T. PAUWELS 'Measuring Populism: A Quantitative Text Analysis of Party Literature in Belgium', (2011) 21(1) *Journal of Elections, Public Opinion and Parties*, pp. 97–119.

[6]   C. MUDDE, 'The Populist Zeitgeist', (2004) 39(4) *Government and Opposition*, pp. 541–563.

[7]   S. ALONSO and C.R. KALTWASSER, 'Spain: No Country for the Populist Radical Right?', (2015) 20(1) *South European Society and Politics*, pp. 21–45.

[8]   H. KRIESI, 'The Populist Challenge', (2014) 37(2) *West European Politics*, pp. 361–378.

[9]   T. PAPPAS, 'Populist Democracies: Post – Authoritarian Greece and Post-Communist Hungary', (2013) 49(1) *Opposition and Government*, pp. 1–23.

[10] S. BARTOLINI, 'Political Parties, Ideology and Populism in the Post-Crisis Europe' (2011), Poros Conference, 7–10 July 2011.

Despite the breadth and depth of inquiries into populism, its definition and main characteristics, its relationship with gender equality and particularly women's rights remains a widely understudied topic. A number of studies have demonstrated that compared to almost all other parties, populist parties on the right side of the political spectrum draw more votes from men than from women.[11] These studies go further to suggest that socio-economic policies and programmatic attitudes, most notably those on anti-immigration as well as law and order, are the factors at the base of explaining why women are less likely to be attracted by these populist parties.

Wishing to expand understanding on populist political movements and their implication on gender equality and women's rights, referencing the studies already produced in this respect in recent years, the present article will offer a gender analysis of populist political party platforms in selected countries. In this regard, recent work has been done by Professor Akkerman,[12] offering a useful comparison on the issues here analysed over the years. By contributing towards looking at how a number of prominent populist political parties are framing and promoting the issue of women and gender equality, as well as what role women play within populist parties and in social and political life according to their party platforms and policy proposals, the present article will assess whether the growing political relevance of populist political narrative across the OSCE region might have substantial consequences on gender equality and women's rights. As noted,[13] and given the European focus of the selected political parties here analysed, there is an implicit acknowledgement that systematic analyses of populist parties and movements that are not only challenging the EU project and EU policies but also fighting to be represented at EU level, are still lacking in the European and international contexts.

A number of studies argue specifically that populist movements are curbing women's rights, with party programmes that include concrete steps against gender equality and human rights, creating a strong anti-feminist bias and taking action to the detriment of already achieved rights.[14] While some employ

---

[11] E. HARTVELD, W. VAN DER BRUG, S. DAHLBERG and A. KOKKONEN, 'The Gender Gap in Populist Radical-Right Voting: Examining the Demand Side in Western and Eastern Europe', (2015) 49 (1–2) *Patterns of Prejudice*, pp. 103–134 and T. IMMERZEEL, 'Voting for a Change: The Democratic Lure of Populist Radical Right Parties in Voting Behaviour' (2015), unpublished dissertation, Utrecht University and N. SPIERINGS and A. ZASLOVE, 'Gendering the Vote for Populist Radical-Right Parties', (2015) 49(1–2) *Patterns of Prejudice*, pp. 135–162.

[12] T. AKKERMAN, 'Gender and the Radical Right in Western Europe: a Comparative Analysis of Policy Agendas', (2015) 1–2(49) *Patterns of Prejudice*, pp. 37–60 and T. AKKERMAN and A. HAGELUND, 'Women and Children First! Anti-immigration Parties and Gender in Norway and the Netherlands', (2007) 2(41) *Patterns of Prejudice*, pp. 197–214.

[13] G. LAZARIDIS, G. CAMPANI, and A. BENVENISTE, *The Rise of the Far Right in Europe Populist Shifts and 'Othering'*, Palgrave Macmillan, Basingstoke 2016.

[14] I. BALABANOVA-STOYCHEVA, M. KADIEVA and T. KRUMOVA, 'Women's Rights and Right-Wing Populism – New Tools for Development of Democratic and Social Values', Friedrich

the '"backlash" narrative of women's emancipation, which sees nations making linear progress towards equality, interrupted by setbacks that can be overcome by joint action': Peto and Grzebalska argue that if progressive groups do not understand the new challenges posed to women's rights by the illiberal states of Central Europe, future progress may be elusive.[15]

The article will look specifically, due to its limited scope, at the policies and political platforms of the League and the Five Star Movement in Italy, Law and Justice in Poland, Front National in France, and the Party for Freedom in the Netherlands, in the attempt to offer a balanced geographical coverage. How are women represented in these populist parties? Are these parties more inclined to adopt a critical stand towards women's rights? What type of alternative political narrative, if any, do they promote in the gender relations within our societies? The present analysis offers a comparison of political agendas and narratives on gender equality and women's rights issues, with the aim of identifying consistent patterns, possibly highlighting concerns and recommendations to be taken into consideration in future efforts to promote more inclusive and equal democratic societies. Finally, a short conclusion will offer a brief analysis of the main findings, exploring possibilities for future research to expand the scope of the present analysis.

2. THE FIVE STAR MOVEMENT AND THE LEAGUE IN ITALY

The recent Italian parliamentary elections on 4 March 2018 proved to be a dramatic turning point for the Mediterranean country since the founding of the republic following the Second World War. With politicians and commentators hailing the beginning of a new 'third republic',[16] following the so-called 'second republic' which resulted from the Mani Pulite political scandal and the collapse of the prior political party systems between 1992 and 1994, this time it was a populist wave to split the country in two and redefine the political party spectrum in Italy. The Five Star Movement (FSM – *Movimento Cinque Stelle*) and the League (*Lega*) imposed themselves as the true political winners: the

---

Ebert Stiftung Sofia, June 2017, available at https://www.womenlobby.org/IMG/pdf/pravata-na-jenite-eng-all.pdf, last accessed 28.05.2018.

[15] A. PETO and W. GRZEBALSKA, 'How Hungary and Poland have silenced women and stifled human rights', *Huffington Post*, 06.12.2017, available at https://www.huffingtonpost.com/the-conversation-global/how-hungary-and-poland-ha_b_12486148.html, last accessed 28.05.2018.

[16] The HUFFINGTON POST, 'Di Maio: "Inizia la Terza Repubblica, quella dei cittadini"', 05.03.2018, available at https://www.huffingtonpost.it/2018/03/05/di-maio-daremo-un-governo-allitalia_a_23377149, last accessed 28.05.2018.

FSM becoming the first party in Italy with 33% of the vote and gaining the entire Italian South and Sicily, the League campaigning with its right-wing nationalist leader Matteo Salvini to earn almost 18% of the centre-right coalition vote and outstrip Silvio Berlusconi of his leadership of the conservative Italian block.

Despite evident differences in their political ideals and electorate support, both political parties, the FSM and the League, have been properly identified as examples of European populism and populist political parties. In fact, a number of studies looking at the rise of populism in Europe often suggest the FSM as the prime example of a highly successful populist party.[17]

The FSM has repeatedly drawn a clear line between itself and established political parties, and its rapid rise in recent Italian elections has been considered a challenge for political science and electoral research.[18] While the party was founded only in 2009, it already gained a considerable appeal in the 2010 regional and the 2012 local elections, and this breakthrough was further consolidated in the 2013 national elections. This electoral success has been explained by invoking a number of elements.[19] First, and maybe most importantly, is the appeal of the charismatic leader of the party, Beppe Grillo, who succeeded in turning his strong popular profile into a political and electoral movement, mobilising a large portion of voters. Part of this success is due to the fact that Grillo and his party managed to use the internet and other electronic media much more effectively than other political parties in Italy.

Indeed, the incredible success of Grillo's political satire in the early 2000s led to the opening of his highly influential personal blog (beppegrillo.it), symbolic and legal headquarters of the FSM, and the launch of a series of initiatives to address the failures of Italy's party system and establishment politics, combining horizontal communication between and among citizens with a diffuse anti-establishment aversion, environmentalist and anti-globalist sentiments, with the willingness to protect and promote the common good. The resulting liquid organisational structure of the FSM, accompanied by the lack of a well-developed internal party machine rather preferring its focus on the personal role of Grillo, has been mentioned as a key element for the electoral success of the party.[20] The bold use of political rhetoric also partly explains why

---

[17] M. ROODUIJN, S. DE LANGE and W. VAN DER BRUG, 'A Populist Zeitgeist? Programmatic contagion by populist parties in Western Europe', (2012) 20(4) *Party Politics*, pp. 563–575.
[18] See generally, F. BORDIGNON and L. CECCARINI, 'Five Stars and a Cricket. Beppe Grillo Shakes Italian Politics', (2013) 18(4) *South European Society and Politics*.
[19] L. CARUSO, 'Il Movimento 5 Stelle e la fine della politica', (2015) 56(2) *Rassegna Italiana di Sociologia*, pp. 315–340.
[20] R. VIGNATI, 'The Organization of the Movimento 5 Stelle: A Contradictory Party Model', in F. TRONCONI (ed.), *Beppe Grillo's Five Star Movement. Organisation, Communication and Ideology*, Farnham, Ashgate 2015, pp. 29–52.

the FSM managed to attract a large proportion of voters in a relatively short period, mostly among young and first-time votes, winning the support of 31% of those aged 18–22 and 35% of those aged 23–28 during the recent 2018 elections.[21]

The resulting political platform of the FSM appears as the direct consequence of its peculiar structure. By proposing an idea of direct democracy where the popular sovereignty is opposed to an allegedly corrupt and parasitic elite, typical of every populist party, the FSM also implements these ideas through an extensive system of web tools that allow grassroots participation. As explained by one of the leaders of the FSM following the positive result at the parliamentary elections last March, 'citizens everywhere are calling for real democracy, to express their voices directly and to no longer be held back by the establishment', vindicating how 'direct democracy, made possible by the Internet, has given a new centrality to citizens and will ultimately lead to the deconstruction of the current political and social organizations. Representative democracy – politics by proxy – is gradually losing meaning'.[22] As Beppe Grillo famously declared in 2013, the FSM wants '100% of Parliament, not 20% or 25% or 30%. When the movement gets to 100%, when the citizens become the state, the movement will no longer need to exist'.[23]

In these terms, the FSM does not seem to fit in the pattern of either right-wing populism, like the kinds in Austrian, the Netherlands, or France, no left-wing populism as documented for example in Latin America, Spain or Greece. A similar absence of ideological positioning appears to be confirmed also by the tendencies of the FSM voters, who do not seem to have a specific preference with regard to left-right divisions.[24] During an interview in 2013, Beppe Grillo stated that the FSM will not take a position on fascism, observing that such 'question does not concern me', and that 'the FSM is an ecumenical movement'.[25]

Given its refusal to locate itself in any ideological framework, what remains is a strongly issue-oriented political party, where the political platform rather than

---

[21] SKYTG24, 'Elezioni 2018, sondaggio Quorum: M5s primo partito tra i giovani', 16.02.2018, available at http://tg24.sky.it/politica/photogallery/2018/02/15/Elezioni-2018-sondaggi-m5s-primo-partito-giovani.html#7, last accessed 28.05.2018.

[22] D. CASALEGGIO, 'A top leader of Italy's Five Star Movement: Why we won', *The Washington Post*, 19.03.2018, available at https://www.washingtonpost.com/news/theworldpost/wp/2018/03/19/five-star/?utm_term=.16172f07d34e, last accessed 28.05.2018.

[23] S. FARIS, 'Italy's Beppe Grillo: Meet the Rogue Comedian Turned Kingmaker', *Time*, 07.03.2013, available at http://world.time.com/2013/03/07/italys-beppe-grillo-meet-the-rogue-comedian-turned-kingmaker, last accessed 28.05.2018.

[24] M. HOOGHE, and J. OSER, 'The Electoral Success of the Movimento 5 Stelle: An Example of a Left Populist Vote?', (2015) 44 *Austrian Journal of Political Science*, pp. 25–36.

[25] CORRIERE DELLA SERA, 'Grillo e casa Pound: «Non sono un fascista ma il Movimento 5 Stelle è ecumenico»' 13.01.2013, available at http://www.corriere.it/politica/13_gennaio_13/grillo-casa-pound_9767dc68-5d98-11e2-8540-81ed61eeac0a.shtml, last accessed 28.05.2018.

its ideological foundations is considered as a sacred text. In particular, there are five specific themes (the five stars in the name: public water, sustainable transport, sustainable development, free Internet access, and environmentalism) that guide the political action of the party as the cardinal points, triggering a total overlap between the party and the programme.

How does this translate in terms of the FSM's support for specific gender equality policies and the promotion of women in the Italian society? Due to its post-ideological stance, its issue-oriented approach, and rejection of conventional political labels as mentioned above, such a question does not appear to have clear and straight answers. Looking at the names of the FSM (due to its peculiar structure, the party does not have traditional party organisms), as with other populist parties across Europe, its leaders and most representative figures have always been male: Beppe Grillo, Gianroberto and Davide Casaleggio, Luigi Di Maio, Alessandro Di Battista, Roberto Fico, Enrico Maria Nadasi.

The numbers resulting from the recent elections offer a more optimistic picture for the women within FSM. In a context of improved representation of women in the Italian parliament which moved from 17.2% of women elected in 2006 to 34.6%, primarily due to a new electoral law requiring parties to place 40% of women candidates on their lists, the FSM came out as the most inclusive political force, with 39.34% of women elected in its lists, better than any other political party.

However, when moving beyond numbers and analysing the political program and platform of the FSM, a general lack of attention towards the promotion of gender equality and women's rights appears evident. As mentioned, gender equality considerations do not appear in the five stars, the five funding priorities, of the FSM. Furthermore, the electoral platform presented by the FSM on the occasion of the recent March elections does not place women on the list of priorities. Made up of 20 points, the FSM's electoral platform mentioned women only in 'point 10' and 'point 11', pledging for the extension of a more favourable retirement scheme for women on the one hand, and several welfare measures in support of mothers on the other, with deductions on kindergarten services and bonuses to pay for diapers and day-care.[26] Confirming a vision of the woman as primarily a mother, the FSM leader Di Maio, on the occasion of the International Women's Day and few days after the elections, stated how the party will use its strong political victory to 'achieve real parity between men and women in the job market, starting by introducing measures that will help

---

[26] DIPARTIMENTO PER GLI AFFARI INTERNI E TERRITORIALI, 'Programma Elettorale Movimento 5 Stelle', 18.01.2018, available at http://dait.interno.gov.it/documenti/trasparenza/Doc/4/4_Prog_Elettorale.pdf, last accessed 28.05.2018.

women to reconcile family and work, and a welfare system which will support them when bringing a child in the world'.[27]

The other populist winner of the recent Italian elections, the League, does not differ substantially from the FSM in relation to its promotion of gender equality and women's rights. Despite the attempt to re-brand the party from a pro-independence ideology of northern Italy, with the consequent dropping of the 'Northern' in the name of the party, to embrace a wider national audience on the model of a nationalist, right-wing, *lepenist* political party, the League continues to base its political success in the northern regions of Italy. It is primarily in these regions that the League and its leader Matteo Salvini managed to gain almost 18% of the national votes, ousting Silvio Berlusconi to take the leadership of the centre-right coalition.

Formed in the 1980s, the Northern League (as it was known at the time) was an example of early populism in Europe, feeding on the collapse of the Italian party system during Mani Pulite, and embracing from the very start a confrontational attitude towards corrupt elites based in Rome and migrants, at the time represented by fellow Italians coming to the north from the south of the country to find better opportunities.

Under the leadership of Matteo Salvini since December 2013, the League has reinforced its populist traits, positioning itself in the known model of other radical right populist parties like Fidez in Hungary, Party for Freedom in the Netherlands, Law and Justice in Poland, and Front National in France, adopting a strong anti-European Union rhetoric and most importantly a vocal nativism making immigration its signature issue, targeting over the years the uncontrolled migration of Roma, Albanians, North Africans, and refugees from Middle Eastern countries at different points in time. Invoking slogans like 'Italians first', the League portrays an Italy as invaded by migrants and subjugated by the European Union autocratic policies, calling for a regaining of national sovereignty and pride.

Under these circumstances, it cannot be surprising than the League largely disregard the promotion of greater gender equality in society and women's rights. Indeed, the League appears to champion traditional models of femininity and the 'natural family' as the fundamental base of social order, often also framing the anti-immigration rhetoric in gender terms, with gender-specific roles for men (caring fathers, protectors of the nation's mothers from outsiders) and women (caring mothers of the nation who are assigned the role of biologically and socially reproducing the national community).[28]

---

[27] L. Di Maio, 'Per una vera parità sul lavoro tra uomo e donna #8Marzo', *Il Blog delle Stelle*, 08.03.2018, available at https://www.ilblogdellestelle.it/2018/03/per_una_vera_parita_sul_lavoro_tra_uomo_e_donna_8marzo.html, last accessed 28.05.2018.

[28] F. Scrinzi, 'A Relational Approach to the Study of Gender in Radical Right Populism', in S. Magaraggia and G. Vingelli (eds.), *Genere e Partecipazione Politica*, Franco Angeli, Milan 2015, pp. 82–94.

Moreover, like most radical right populist parties, women in the League are traditionally a minority among members and elected representatives. Only 30.8% of candidates elected from the party list during the last March elections are women. Out of 30 members of its party board with voting rights, currently only two are women. The leadership of the party, with Matteo Salvini, Umberto Bossi, Roberto Calderoli and Giulio Cementero, remains completely male-dominated.[29]

Moving to the election platform presented by the League ahead of the March 2018 elections, women are not women, but rather mothers. Similar to what was described for the FSM, the League addresses women only in one point of the party platform, under the chapter 'More support to families', calling for an extraordinary deal to promote birth rates, with child-care benefits, financial support for each child, and gender equality provisions in the pension scheme to benefit mothers (but not all women).[30] In line with the League's strong nativism, all these measures are confined to Italian mothers and children only.

In this sense, despite deep differences in the political substance of the two parties, both the FSM and the League present three main characteristics in relation to gender and women's rights. First, both populist parties fail to make gender equality issues and the role of women in society a political priority. Only one point of their respective political platforms is dedicated to the issue, accompanied by a rather narrow understanding of the role women play in society. In fact, and secondly, both the FSM and the League promote a traditional view of gender roles, where women are first and foremost mothers, in need of receiving welfare benefits and social protection because of their role in the family as child-bearer. Lastly, both parties also show a poor picture in the promotion of women inside their party structures and elected representatives, although the FSM appears to fare better in this regard.

3. THE FRONT NATIONAL IN FRANCE

The Front National (FN) has now been a significant political force in French politics for over two decades, and arguably one of the most successful of all populist parties in Western Europe. As observed with regard to the FN, the

---

[29] LEGA NORD, 'Memberi del Consiglio Federale', available at https://www.leganord.org/il-movimento/organi-federali/15-il-movimento/consiglio-federale/20-membri-del-consiglio-federale, last accessed 28.05.2018.

[30] LEGA NORD, 'Salvini Premier, la Rivoluzione del Buon Senso – Programma di Governo Elezioni 2018', available at https://www.leganord.org/component/phocadownload/category/5-elezioni?download=1514:programma-lega-salvini-premier-2018, last accessed 28.05.2018.

party can be seen as a magnifying glass of the far right's evolution in Western Europe (Nonna Mayer, 2013). Characterised by a combination of fervent nationalism, opposition to immigration, and a populist hostility to the political establishment' (Eatwell, 2000), the FN has offered an early model to other radical right populist parties in Europe, embracing a strong nativism and xenophobia against immigration and Islam, demands for a regained national sovereignty over the European Union and globalisation processes, together with the return to traditional French values (Mazzoleni, 2003).

Since 2011, when Marine Le Pen took over from her father Jean-Marie Le Pen as president of the party, FN has engaged in an attempt of modernisation of its public image, ultimately with the announced intention to re-brand the party under a new name.[31] The strategy seemed to bring positive results during the last French presidential elections in spring 2017, when the FN achieved 21.3% of the vote in the first round, the second biggest political force in France behind En Marche! of Emmanuel Macron, which took 24% of the national vote, and ahead of the Republican party with 20%.[32] Despite this positive result, the second phase of the elections proved severe for the FN, losing the presidential race with 33.9% of the total votes.[33] In the following legislative elections in June 2017, the FN ran out of steam and only managed to obtain 8.7% of the votes, translating into a mere eight elected representatives at the National Assembly.[34]

Despite these numbers, FN remains a mainstream political party in France, rising in consensus, and with a clear vocation to govern. From a gender perspective, this has become more visible in recent years, with the attempt by Marine Le Pen to move the party from traditional towards more modern-traditional discourses and policies on gender. This new gender approach of the FN focuses on selective policy issues, like employment, welfare services and other forms of social protection. More precisely, the party discourse has also moved from celebrating traditional models of gender, represented

---

[31] K. WILLSHER, 'Marine Le Pen sparks row over new name for Front National', *The Guardian*, 12.03.2018, available at https://www.theguardian.com/world/2018/mar/12/marine-le-pen-row-new-name-front-national-rassemblement-national, last accessed 28.05.2018.

[32] CONSEIL CONSTITUTIONNEL, 'Déclaration du 26 avril 2017 relative aux résultats du premier tour de scrutin de l'élection du Président de la République', 26.04.2017, available at http://www.conseil-constitutionnel.fr/conseil-constitutionnel/francais/les-decisions/acces-par-date/decisions-depuis-1959/2017/2017-169-pdr/decision-n-2017-169-pdr-du-26-avril-2017.148939.html, last accessed 28.05.2018.

[33] CONSEIL CONSTITUTIONNEL, 'Proclamation des résultats de l'élection du Président de la République', 26.04.2017, available at http://www.conseil-constitutionnel.fr/conseil-constitutionnel/francais/les-decisions/acces-par-date/decisions-depuis-1959/2017/2017-171-pdr/decision-n-2017-171-pdr-du-10-mai-2017.148982.html, last accessed 28.05.2018.

[34] MINISTÈRE DE L'INTÉRIEUR, 'Résultats des élections législatives 2017', 18.06.2018, available at https://www.interieur.gouv.fr/Elections/Les-resultats/Legislatives/elecresult__legislatives-2017/(path)/legislatives-2017//FE.html, last accessed 28.05.2018.

by the ideal of the 'mothers of the nation', to a focus on 'modern' femininity, defined by the working women/mothers dichotomy and the relationship between private life and career.

This revised approach to gender issues and women's role in society, intended to accommodate common understanding of gender issues in today's France and as well as to save the party from accusation of misogyny recurrent in the past, has also been reflected in a partial modification of its policies and political platform on issues of gender, sexuality and family. This has resulted in a more strategic and pragmatic approach to sensitive issues like abortion and same-sex marriage. As Marine Le Pen stated in an opinion piece published in 2016, 'I am revolted today by the unacceptable silence and, therefore, tacit consent of the French Left in the face of these fundamental attacks on the rights of women. I am scared that the migrant crisis signals the beginning of the end of women's rights'.[35] A twice divorced single mother herself, Le Pen describes herself as 'almost a feminist', recalling the period when, after her divorce, she struggled to combine her job and political role with caring for her children (Le Pen, 2006).

Nevertheless, at least two main contradictions result from this attempt to adopt more modern-traditional policies on gender. The first one is represented by the uneasy balance between a rhetoric upholding traditional models of society and family with a discourse on the promotion of women's rights, where also immigration is often associated with sexual violence and conservatism in the matter of gender relations. The second contradiction rested in the connection between women and household on one side, and the acceptance of women included in the labour market on the other. Moreover, while women appear to need support and tailored policies to reconcile private 'family' life and professional 'career' life, men are absent from this scenario as well as the idea of a burden-sharing between men and women.

More importantly, the revised approach to gender and women's rights promoted by Marine Le Pen appear to fail to substantially inform the FN's political platform and its policy proposals. Looking at the recent party document '144 Engagements Presidentiels', (144 Presidential Commitments) functioning as the FN platform for the 2017 French Presidential Elections, the word 'women' appears only twice throughout its 24 pages. Specifically, Commitment 9 titled *'Defending women's rights'* spells out the securitisation of gender issues as seen also by other radical right populist parties, with the pledge on the one hand to fight against the 'islamisation' of society responsible for undermining the

---

[35] L'OPINION, 'Marine Le Pen : « Un référendum pour sortir de la crise migratoire »', 13.01.2016, available at https://www.lopinion.fr/edition/politique/marine-pen-referendum-sortir-crise-migratoire-94568, last accessed 28.05.2018.

fundamental freedoms of women, while on the other hand pledging for reducing the gender pay-gap and fight against professional and social insecurity.[36]

In conclusion, FN appears to well fit in the model of other radical right populist parties, with an emphasis on traditional political issues like immigration, anti-EU sentiments, and protectionism, among others. At the same time, however, under the leadership of Marine Le Pen a number of contradictions have emerged from the attempt to reconcile a slight openness to an evolved role of the woman in society and labour market with a traditional set of values that see women first and foremost as mothers and home-makers. More generally, the defence of women's rights appears to remain mainly in the framework of the fight against immigration and in terms of cultural clashes.

4. LAW AND JUSTICE IN POLAND

Prawo i Sprawiedliwość (PiS), Law and Justice Party is the ruling party in Poland, sweeping to power in October 2015 by winning a parliamentary majority with 37.5% of the vote. It is a solidarist and mildly Eurosceptic party, characterised by a combination of nationalism and anti-immigration views, similar to other populist parties, such as Hungary's Fidesz or France's Front National. Despite being often seen as a nationalist party, its leadership claims their views to be patriotic rather than nationalistic, as 'nationalism is evil'.[37] The party has faced tremendous criticism from the West, which 'accused it of dismantling democracy with policies designed to limit civil liberties, control media, politicise the civil service and neuter judicial independence'.[38] Despite international criticism, PiS remains the most popular political force in Poland today, with various surveys estimating that the party enjoys as much as 47% of public support, in comparison to 16% support for the main opposition party, the Civil Platform.[39] PiS patriotic revolution and return to traditional values has brought support for 'families of women and men, with children' at the expense of women's rights.[40]

---

[36] M. LE PEN, '144 Engagements présidentiels', 2017, available at http://www.frontnational.com/pdf/144-engagements.pdf, last accessed 28.05.2018.

[37] PAP, 'Prezydent L. Kaczyński: nacjonalizm jest złem', 30.09.2008, available at https://wiadomosci.wp.pl/prezydent-l-kaczynski-nacjonalizm-jest-zlem-6036779525371009a, last accessed 28.05.18.

[38] R. ADEKOYA, 'Xenophobic, authoritarian – and generous on welfare: how Poland's right rules', *The Guardian*, 25.10.2016, available at https://www.theguardian.com/commentisfree/2016/oct/25/poland-right-law-justice-party-europe, last accessed 28.05.18.

[39] R. ADEKOYA, 'Why Poland's Law and Justice Party Remains So Popular', *Foreign Affairs*, 03.11.2017, available at https://www.foreignaffairs.com/articles/central-europe/2017-11-03/why-polands-law-and-justice-party-remains-so-popular, last accessed 28.05.2018.

[40] FREEDOM, 'Polish Government's War on Women', 26.11.2017, available at https://freedomnews.org.uk/polish-governments-war-on-women, last accessed 28.05.2018.

In turn, it comes as no surprise that the internal structure of the Prawo i Sprawiedliwość (PiS), Law and Justice Party of Poland is male-dominated. The party is chaired by a man and the Presidency of the party includes seven persons, including one woman, an equivalent of 14.3% women. The Political Council of PiS consists of 117 persons, including nine women, an equivalent of 7.7%. The Political Committee of PiS consists of 33 persons, including seven women, an equivalent of 21.2% women.[41] Public sources indicate that men account for about two-thirds of the party's members, while it is unclear from the party's website whether the party has a database of members and whether it is sex-disaggregated.[42]

The representation of PiS women deputies is generally below the overall women's representation in Polish legislature and the European Parliament, and significantly below the representation of women deputies from the main opposition party. In terms of women's representation in the lower house of the Polish parliament, out of 237 PiS deputies in the Polish Sejm, around 26% are women.[43] This is below the 28% of the overall women's representation in the Sejm and well below the 39% of women deputies of the main opposition party, Civic Platform.[44] The upper house of the Polish parliament presents a similar picture with women making up 14% of the PiS senators, same level as the 14% overall representation of women in the Senate, and slightly below the 16% of women senators of the main opposition party, Civic Platform.[45] In the European Parliament, women make up 37% of the Parliament, 25% of Polish MEPs, 21% of PiS MEPs, and 39% of the Civic Platform MEPs.

Data on women's representation demonstrates that PiS women candidates may often be placed in unwinnable seats. The overall higher representation of Polish women deputies in the Sejm and in the European Parliament, in comparison to the Polish Senate, can be explained by the existence of legislated candidate quotas for the lower house and the sub-regional level. As specified in the amendments to the Election Code introduced in January 2011, 'the number of candidates who are women cannot be less than 35% of all candidates on the list […] (and that) the number of candidates who are men cannot be less than

---

[41] PRAWO I SPRAWIEDLIWOŚĆ, 'Wladze, ludzie', available at http://pis.org.pl/partia/wladze-ludzie, last accessed 28.05.2018.

[42] M. Molenda, 'Tylko w Fakt24.pl: Tak wygląda armia PiS', Fackt 24, 17.10.2016, available at http://www.fakt.pl/wydarzenia/polityka/tak-wyglada-armia-pis/svbfps6, last accessed 28.05.2018.

[43] SEJM RZECZYPOSPOLITEJ POLSKIEJ, 'Klub Parlamentarny Prawo i Sprawiedliwość', available at http://www.sejm.gov.pl/sejm8.nsf/klub.xsp?klub=PiS, last accessed 28.05.2018.

[44] INTER-PARLIAMENTARY UNION, 'Women in National Parliaments', 01.01.2018, available at http://archive.ipu.org/wmn-e/arc/classif010118.htm, last accessed 28.05.2018. And SEJM RZECZYPOSPOLITEJ POLSKIEJ, 'Klub Parlamentarny Platforma Obywatelska', available at http://www.sejm.gov.pl/sejm8.nsf/klubposlowie.xsp?klub=PO, last accessed 28.05.2018.

[45] SENAT RZECZYPOSPOLITEJ POLSKIEJ, Senatorowie, available at https://www.senat.gov.pl/sklad/senatorowie, last accessed 28.05.2018.

35% of all candidates on the list'.[46] Similarly, the Election Code (2011) prescribes the same quota for the sub-national level, while also specifying placement rules as follows: 'For lists that include 3 candidates, there must be at least one candidate of each gender.'[47] Legislated quotas without placement rules for candidates' lists to the Polish Sejm demonstrate that all parties contesting the election had to propose 35% of candidates of either gender, but the candidates' ultimate success in the election would, *inter alia*, be affected by the position on the list allocated to them. The fact that out of 35% PiS women candidates, women make up 26% of PiS Members of Parliament may demonstrate that women were likely placed towards the bottom of the PiS candidates' list, thus in unwinnable seats.

The statute of PiS does not refer to women's participation within the party, nor does it mention women's rights or gender equality in any parts of the 35 page text. It covers the party's objectives and specifies in great detail the roles and responsibilities of party members, elected officials, and various party structures. As one of its objectives, it refers to 'strengthening the role of the family as the basic social unit' and supporting it with a friendly state policy.[48] The statute further specifies the role of the 'Forum of Young People' of the party, though it does not refer to other traditionally under-represented groups, such as young women or women more broadly.[49] The statute also lists rules for candidacy selection and re-election by the party for the posts of Members of Parliament, Senate or the European Parliament, specifying that 'compliance with the voting discipline' of the party will, *inter alia*, be considered as a basic criterion.[50]

The ideological basis of PiS party program lies 'in the respect for the inherent and inalienable dignity of every human being', (with the) elementary rights of the human person being 'the right to life, the right to freedom and the right to equality'.[51] Analysing this ideology from a perspective of gender equality and women's rights leads to a broader discussion on family life, marriage, divorce, and reproductive rights, many of which affect women specifically. For example, PiS notion of equality broadly refers to economic and social equality and mentions 'equality of citizens' and abolishment of 'restrictions for women'

---

[46] ACE ELECTORAL KNOWLEDGE NETWORK, 'Poland 2011 Election Code: An English translation of Poland's 2011 Election Code', 31.01.2011, available at http://aceproject.org/ero-en/poland-2011-election-code/view, last accessed 28.05.2018.

[47] INTERNATIONAL IDEA, 'Gender Quotas Database, Country Data, Poland', available at https://www.idea.int/data-tools/data/gender-quotas/country-view/242/35#sources, last accessed 27–28.05.2018.

[48] PRAWO I SPRAWIEDLIWOŚĆ, 'Dokumenty: Statut Prawa i Sprawiedliwości', article 4(5), available at http://pis.org.pl/dokumenty, last accessed 28.05.2018.

[49] Ibid., article 38.

[50] Ibid., Attachment: Rules for Re-Election, article 1(3).

[51] PRAWO I SPRAWIEDLIWOŚĆ, 'Dokumenty: Program Prawa I Sprawiedliwości 2014', available at http://pis.org.pl/dokumenty, last accessed 28.05.2018.

though with reference to the historic successes of the Second Polish Republic at the beginning of 20th Century.[52] Gender equality of today or tomorrow are not mentioned.

PIS program refers to the right to life as 'protecting life from conception'.[53] On a policy level, this protection of life is generally provided by limiting women's reproductive rights. Paradoxically, it appears that a life protected from conception may not necessarily include a women's life to be protected. 'It is widely acknowledged that in countries in which abortion is restricted by law, women seek abortions clandestinely, often under conditions that are medically unsafe and therefore life-threatening.'[54] In turn, multiple human rights instruments protecting the right to life call upon states to ensure that women do not have to undergo life-threatening abortions.[55]

PiS further defines family as a 'lasting relationship between a woman and a man [...], in which children are born', thus defining the type and duration of a family, while framing a woman in a role of lasting wife and mother.[56] This role of woman as a mother is further to be strengthened though special measures, such as improving the 'care for mother and child', promoting 'reproductive health', and public financing of medical care for pregnant women and for childbirth.[57] In PiS program, women's reproductive health does not refer to or include women's reproductive rights. Extended maternity and parental leave, along with free kindergarten, are also being proposed by PiS. PiS introduced child benefit payments for people with two or more children, while those with a single child need to be means tested. Since a third of children are raised by single parents, mainly women, and it is mainly single parents that have only one child, one can conclude that the child benefits are not aimed at supporting single mothers. Parental leave, free childcare, and child benefits can be seen as positive social benefits, as long as they also include paternity leave, do not prevent women's return to the labour market after giving birth, and do not discriminate against those outside traditional families.

Over the past few years, the public and legislative debate on women's rights in Poland has repeatedly revolved around attempts to tighten the abortion law. Poland already has one of the most restrictive abortion legislations in the OSCE region, which bans all abortions except for cases of rape or incest, severe damage

---

[52] Ibid., p. 9.
[53] Ibid., p. 7.
[54] CENTER FOR REPRODUCTIVE RIGHTS, 'Safe and Legal Abortion is a Woman's Human Right', available at https://www.reproductiverights.org/sites/crr.civicactions.net/files/documents/pub_fac_safeab_10.11.pdf, last accessed 28.05.2018.
[55] CCPR, General Comment No. 28: Equality of rights between men and women, UN Doc. CCPR/C/21/Rev.1/Add.10, 29.03.2000, para. 10.
[56] PRAWO I SPRAWIEDLIWOŚĆ, 'Dokumenty: Program Prawa I Sprawiedliwości 2014', p. 8, available at http://pis.org.pl/dokumenty, last accessed 28.05.2018.
[57] Ibid., p. 10.

to foetus or if the pregnancy threatens the mother's life. The Polish parliament, where PiS holds the majority of seats, attempted in 2016 to introduce a total abortion ban, including proposed jail sentences for doctors participating in abortions as well as for women who terminated pregnancy. In October 2016, this led to 100,000 women taking to the streets across Poland in Black Protest, the largest women's strike in Polish history and one that prompted solidarity events across the world. In turn, the ruling PiS party scrapped the proposal. In January 2018, the abortion agenda was back in the Parliament, on the one hand a citizens' initiative proposed by the 'Stop Abortion' committee, calling for a ban on abortions even when the foetus is deformed, and on the other hand an initiative 'Let's Save Women 2017' that aimed to liberalise the law. A wave of demonstrations erupted with 'pro-choice demonstrators wearing black as a sign of mourning for their reproductive rights, which have come under threat under the ruling conservative Law and Justice Party'.[58]

5. PARTY FOR FREEDOM IN THE NETHERLANDS

The organisation of the Party for Freedom (PVV) is largely centralised and, in the absence of internal party structures, male-dominated. The PVV has no members, or more specifically, the only member of the association Party for Freedom is a man, Geert Wilders. The party does not have any local organisations or departments and is ineligible for the Dutch public funding for political parties. Founded in 2005 by Geert Wilders under the name Association Group Wilders, it operates as a one-man fraction.

The representation of PVV women deputies is below the overall women's representation in Dutch legislature and the European Parliament, and significantly below the representation of women deputies from other parliamentary parties in the Netherlands. In terms of women's representation in the Tweede Kamer, the lower or second house of the Dutch parliament, out of 20 PVV deputies, five are women, an equivalent of 25%.[59] This is significantly below the overall 34% women's representation in the Tweede Kamer or the women's representation in other parliamentary parties. For the sake of comparison, People's Party for Freedom and Democracy (VVD) has 30% women deputies in the lower chamber of parliament, Christian Democratic Appeal (CDA) 32%,

---

[58] L. SMITH, 'Poland abortion ban: Thousands of women take to streets across country to demand reproductive rights', *The Independent*, 17.01.2018, available at https://www.independent.co.uk/news/world/europe/poland-women-abortion-ban-march-strike-protest-reproductive-rights-polish-government-latest-a8163281.html, last accessed 28.05.2018.

[59] TWEEDE KAMER DER STATEN GENERAAL, 'Partij voor de Vrijheid (PVV)', available at https://www.tweedekamer.nl/kamerleden_en_commissies/fracties/partij_voor_de_vrijheid, last accessed 28.05.2018.

Democrats 66 (D66) also 32%, Greenleft (GL) 57%, Socialist Party (SP) 29%, and Labour Party (PvdA) 56%.[60]

PVV women representatives in the upper house of Dutch parliament or at the sub-national level are significantly less represented in comparison with other parties, if represented at all. In the Senate, the upper or first house of the Dutch parliament, women's representation among PVV senators is significantly below women's representation of any other party, with as much of a 39% difference. PVV has nine representatives, of which one is a woman, equalling 11%. Interestingly enough, the PVV woman senator is also the leader of the PVV fraction. For the sake of comparison, women make up 35% of the overall senators, 46% of VVD senators, 42% of CDA senators, 30% of D66 senators, 33% of SP senators, 50% of PvdA senators and GL senators.[61] In the European Parliament, PVV has four seats, all occupied by men, while women make up 38% of overall Dutch MEPs. The PVV delegation in the European Parliament is part of the Europe of Nations and Freedom Group (ENF), including representatives of the Front National in France and Italy's Northern League. The ENF is composed of 32% women, of which none come from PVV.

Moving beyond quantitative representation within PVV to its ideology, one can observe extreme contradictions in the party's political ideology. PVV is considered a populist party, with a combination of conservative and liberal, right and left-oriented views.[62] On certain issues such as healthcare or elderly care, the PVV can be seen as left and social, though exclusive in the sense that these benefits shall support mainly Dutch citizens, while development aid abroad shall be cut. On issues of immigration, culture and religion, the party is nationalistic and xenophobic, claiming that Judeo-Christian views should be seen as dominant cultures in the Netherlands, while Quran should be banned and all mosques in the Netherlands shut. Similar to other populist parties in Europe, such as Fidesz in Hungary or PiS in Poland, PVV stands strongly against immigration, national and Brussels elites, thus arguing that the Netherlands must become politically, culturally and economically independent again. While initially claiming that he dislikes far-right parties like Front National of France, Wilders and his PVV joined with Front National and Italian League, the Europe of Nations and Freedom Group at the European Parliament, with two common pillars: Islamophobia and Europhobia.[63]

---

[60] TWEEDE KAMER DER STATEN GENERAAL, 'Fracties', available at https://www.tweedekamer.nl/kamerleden_en_commissies/fracties, last accessed 28.05.2018.
[61] Ibid.
[62] PARLEMENTAIR DOCUMENTATIE CENTRUM, 'Parlement and Politiek, Partij voor de Vrijheid (PVV)', available at https://www.parlement.com/id/vhnnmt7m4rqi/partij_voor_de_vrijheid_pvv, last accessed 28.05.2018.
[63] J.P. Heinisch, 'ENF: the New Right-Wing Force in the European Parliament and how to Deal with It', Heinrich Boll Stiftung, 14.01.2016, available at https://eu.boell.org/en/2016/01/14/enf-new-right-wing-force-european-parliament-and-how-deal-it, last accessed 28.05.2018.

Looking at gender and women's rights aspects within PVV's ideology, one can similarly not escape a sense of contradiction and twisted ideologies. In 2008, friends of the PVV commissioned and produced a short film by Geert Wilders called Fitna, where it is argued that Islam motivates its followers towards hate and encourages acts of violence against women. The film resulted in many Muslims protests across the globe, including Muslim women, claiming that the movie wrongfully presents Islam as a religion of hate and thus offends Muslim believers across the globe.[64] 'As per PVV, the Quran prescribes behaviors, which conflict with our rule of law, such as [...] discrimination of women.' It is a contradicting ideology that argues against violence against women, by simultaneously arguing for restrictions of religious freedoms of Muslims, including Muslim women, as demonstrated by PVVs proposal to 'forbid the burqa and the Qur'an, and tax headscarves'.[65]

In its Election Programme 2010–2015, PVV's 60-page document makes extensive references to women and women's issues, stating that it aims to defend the essential elements of Dutch culture: freedom of the LGBT community, as well as assured equality of men and women, which Islam may challenge. 'PVV chooses for the rights of homosexuals and women', it states.[66] When warning against the dangers of Islamisation of Europe as related to the health and care sector, PVV makes examples of 'Muslim women who refuse treatment by male doctors or do not want to be washed by their male brothers'.[67] Furthermore, female genital mutilation should be heavily punished, as per PVV, in line with international standards, which generally consider female genital mutilation (FGM) as a human rights violation, torture, and an extreme form of violence and discrimination against girls and women.[68] PVV's 1-page Election Programme for 2017 makes only one reference to women, arguing for a ban on Islamic headscarves in public functions.[69]

PVV's ideology is mainly based on Islamophobia, which in itself is problematic particularly in democratic and multi-religious societies such as

---

[64] MEMRI, 'Protests Continue in Pakistan over Geert Wilderss's "Anti-Koran" Film "Fitna", Danish Newspapers Reprinting of Muhammad Cartoons', 10.04.2008, available at https://www.memri.org/reports/protests-continue-pakistan-over-geert-wilderss-anti-koran-film-fitna-danish-newspapers, last accessed 28.05.2018.

[65] PARTIJ VOOR DE VRIJHEID, 'De agenda van hoop en optimisme – Een tijd om te kiezen: PVV 2010–2015', pp. 13 and 15, available at https://www.parlement.com/9291000/d/2010_pvv_verkiezingsprogramma.pdf, last accessed 28.05.2018.

[66] Ibid., p. 6 and p. 33.

[67] Ibid., p. 6.

[68] EQUALITY NOW, 'International Law on FGM', available at https://www.equalitynow.org/international-law-fgm, last accessed 28.05.2018.

[69] PARTIJ VOOR DE VRIJHEID, 'Nederland weer van ons! – Concept Verkiezingsprogramma PVV 2017–2021', available at https://www.pvv.nl/images/Conceptverkiezingsprogrammma.pdf, last accessed 28.05.2018.

the Netherlands. However, within the framework of its extreme Islamophobia, PVV originally argued against Islam as a way of preventing violence against women, ensuring equality between women and men, protecting rights of homosexuals and women, and punishing female genital mutilation. All these are indeed important rights, if only they were applied to all women without discrimination and if they did not infringe on religious rights of Muslim women. However, PVV's latest Election Programme barely makes any reference to equality of women and men, or women's emancipation, possibly in an attempt to avoid large discrepancies with similar populist parties, such as Polish PiS or the Italian League, whose standpoints are very far from protecting women's rights.

6. CONCLUSION

Gender equality and women's issues are broad concepts that can and do span into all aspects of life. Yet, it appears quite impressive to observe to what extent the various populist political parties across Europe have been able to almost fully harmonise their platforms as regards their views on gender equality and women's issues. Certainly, recognising slight variations and a few exceptions, populist parties in Italy, France, Poland, and the Netherlands have many common characteristics as related to women's role within their structures as well as in terms of policy offer.

First, and most visibly, the concept of gender equality and the word 'gender' do not feature in any of the platforms of the parties analysed. Reference to women is mainly made in relation to traditional roles of a woman as a mother or in relation to the traditional family of men and women with children. In turn, most electoral platforms and policies of the populist political parties analysed argue for an increased support to families, child-care benefits, favourable retirement schemes for women, and in a number of cases promotion of birth rate at the expense of women's reproductive rights. Interestingly enough, other issues such as women's political participation, women's participation in the labour market, violence against women, or sharing of care responsibilities among women and men do not feature prominently in any of the platforms or policies of the analysed populist parties.

As noted in a recent study, the cultural dimension of gender and family issues is often perceived to be the most important by radical right populist parties. Indeed, the present analysis confirms that these parties share convictions about the so-called 'traditional' model of the family as the preferred model, promoting the protection of the family as a political issue which demands political intervention. This allows for the identification of a pattern in the instrumental use of gender and family issues, which are either presented as means to secure the welfare state, or as means for solving problems with regard to the family crisis, demographic sustainability, and protecting the national values.[70]

Secondly, framed in the context of strong anti-immigration sentiments, these populist parties often portray the migrant crisis as the end of women's rights, creating an evident paradox. Namely, populist parties on the one hand aim to uphold traditional models of society, family, and women's roles, while on the other hand arguing for women's emancipation under attack from immigration and Islamisation. In this context, gender lies at the heart of the analysed populist parties. This appears to confirm the recent findings on the rise of so-called *'femonationalism'*, that is the exploitation of feminist ideas by anti-Islam and xenophobic campaigns, describing the practice and claims that, by characterising Muslim men as oppressors and by emphasising the need to rescue Muslim women, this results in the use of gender equality to justify prejudice.[71] In the current context of rising hostility towards Muslims, the theme of gender equality is indeed mobilised in instrumental ways by the analysed parties, seeking to legitimise their claims and attract women's votes; new female leaders are transforming the image of these parties, making them appear more acceptable and less stigmatised, as with the FN in France; in some countries the traditional gender gap among their voters is narrowing.

Thirdly, it comes as no surprise that populist parties are, with a few exceptions, mainly male-dominated. Similarly, it comes as no surprise that these male-dominated parties would be proposing traditional roles for women. Male-dominated party structures, low female representation in elected office and frequent placement of female candidates in unwinnable positions demonstrates that women do not have strong formal influence in the decision-making and policies of populist parties, both internally within parties or externally as party's representatives in legislatures. However, as male-dominated as they are, these political parties often do have strong stands on issues related to gender equality and women's rights. This dichotomy demonstrates the danger that populist parties pose to women's rights, resulting in mainly men debating and introducing policies affecting mainly women.

The fact that the internal structures of these parties is male-dominated may be seen as a factor determining their views and policies on women's rights and gender equality, though it may also be seen simply as a reflection of overall

---

[70] B. Siim, A. Krizsan, D. Gruziel and A. Nissen, 'Report of Case Studies on Gender Equality as a Focus Point of National and Nativist Discourses', *BEUCITIZENS*, 01.07.2016, available at http://beucitizen.eu/wp-content/uploads/Report-9-7-Version-16-06-2016.pdf, last accessed 28.05.2018.

[71] S. Farris, 'In the Name of Women's Rights: The Rise of Femonationalism', Duke University Press, 2017.

political landscapes and party organisations in these countries and generally across the OSCE region. As a general observation, while women's representation in elected offices varies, internal party structures in most countries of the OSCE region are with a few exceptions male-dominated. On average, women make up only about 27% of legislators in the OSCE region.[72]

To conclude, while it would be possible to argue that populist parties are curbing gender equality, women's rights and women's political participation in Europe, it is also necessary to look at mainstream parties to seek for more comprehensive answers. While the ideologies of populist parties on women's issues can be seen as a backlash to women's rights, it is also the politics and decision-making of all political actors that need to translate their words into action and strengthen efforts towards not only *de facto* but *de jure* gender equality and promotion of women's rights.

---

[72] INTER-PARLIAMENTARY UNION, 'Women in National Parliaments', *supra* note 44.

THE IMPACT OF #METOO ON WOMEN'S RIGHTS IN THE OSCE REGION

Ewa Sapiezynska and Johanna Pruessing*

Empowering women to know and demand their rights is essential to tackling violence perpetrated against them. The more women speak out, as we have seen most recently, for example, in the #MeToo campaign, the greater their power and ability to use legal and other means available to confront the perpetrators.

OSCE/ODIHR Director Ingibjörg Sólrún Gísladóttir

1. Introduction 544
   1.1. Theoretical Framework 546
   1.2. Methodology. 548
2. The Power Structure is Shaking 549
   2.1. Politics 549
   2.2. Justice System 552
   2.3. Religious Communities. 553
   2.4. International Organisations 554
3. The OSCE and #MeToo 554
   3.1. The OSCE before #MeToo: Relevant OSCE Commitments
        and Work on Violence against Women. 555
   3.2. The Impact of #MeToo within the OSCE Structures
        and Institutions. 556
4. Changes in Attitudes and Reporting Levels 559
5. Changes in Legal Framework and Policies 563
6. Istanbul Convention. 566
7. Conclusion: Challenges and Opportunities Ahead 567

---

* The opinions expressed in this article are authors' own, and do not necessarily reflect the policy and position of ODIHR. The authors are grateful to peer reviewers for their comments on the earlier version of the article.

ABSTRACT

All across the region covered by the Organization for Security and Co-operation in Europe (OSCE) #MeToo sparked public debates about abuse of power and sexual violence against women perpetuating gender inequality. These debates carried serious consequences on both individual and structural levels: powerful perpetrators were forced to resign and biased power structures were questioned. We argue that the campaign provides a perfect case to study how a digital social movement can give agency to the victims and impact the structural level. On basis of an extensive press coverage review of the #MeToo movement conducted in 12 languages and covering the period of six months between October 2017 and March 2018, complemented with legal and document reviews, we analyse the impact the #MeToo campaign has had on women's human rights in the OSCE region, both *de facto* and *de jure*. We conclude that in many of the OSCE participating States a renewed push for ratification of the Istanbul Convention has been observed and five of them have ratified the treaty since the #MeToo movement started. Furthermore, several States are revising their laws on sexual harassment; many noted a sharp increase in the number of cases of sexual assaults formally reported; and in some there is already evidence of attitude change towards sexual harassment and sexism as an immediate result of the #MeToo movement. There is also evidence suggesting that #MeToo contributed to the current surge in numbers of women candidates running for elections in the US.

1. INTRODUCTION

On 5 October 2017, *The New York Times* broke a story of Ashley Judd and Rose McGowan alleging decades of sexual harassment and assault by Hollywood mogul Harvey Weinstein. Following this incident, unprecedented numbers of women in Hollywood and other industries came forward sharing their experiences of sexual harassment and assault, while calling out male perpetrators in powerful positions. Reacting to these revelations on 12 October 2017, actress Alyssa Milano tweeted 'If all women who have been sexually harassed or assaulted wrote "Me Too" as a status, we might give people a sense of the magnitude of the problem'.[1] Within 20 minutes, the post had 10,000 replies and quickly turned into a movement under the hashtag #MeToo.

The #MeToo hashtag (henceforth #MeToo) achieved global reach with over 1 million tweets in 48 hours and more than 12 million posts, comments,

---

[1] A. MILANO, 'If you've been sexually harassed or assaulted write "me too" as a reply to this tweet', *Twitter*, 15.10.2017, available at https://twitter.com/Alyssa_Milano/status/919659438700670976, last accessed 11.06.2018.

and reactions on Facebook in under 24 hours.[2] According to Facebook US, 45% of Facebook users had friends posting the hashtag #MeToo within this time period.[3] The hashtag also sparked debates in various national translations and interpretations such as #BalanceTonPorc (Denounce your pig) in France, #MoiAussi (me too) in Canada, #ЯТоже (me too) in Russian speaking countries, #YoTambién (me too) in Spanish speaking countries, #QuellaVoltaChe (The Time When) in Italy, #СегаКажувам (Now Telling) in Macedonia and #stilleføropptak (Silent Until Recorded) in Norway. All across the OSCE region #MeToo opened a platform where victims' voices were heard and survivors' stories were believed, leading to serious consequences going beyond the individual level: powerful perpetrators were forced to resign and biased power structures were questioned.

The phrase 'MeToo' was originally coined by Tarana Burke in New York in 2006, as the name of her activist group supporting survivors of sexual violence, mainly composed of young women of colour, and raising awareness about the scale, impact and consequences of sexual assault. When Alyssa Milano took the 'MeToo' movement to Twitter in the context of the Weinstein allegations, she tapped into a momentum in time, successfully giving visibility to a shocking prevalence of sexual violence and discrimination against women worldwide. The digital nature of the movement was able to draw a global picture of the pervasiveness of the phenomenon and its structural character. 'Its power lies in its simplicity: the whole poisonous spectrum of misogyny covered in two mundane words.'[4]

The success of the #MeToo movement builds on the achievements of various preceding national and regional campaigns advocating for women's rights and demanding an end to violence and discrimination against women. Notable movements include the hashtag #яНеБоюсьСказать (I am not afraid to say) trending on Russian and Ukrainian social media in 2016 and shedding light on experiences of sexual harassment and violence;[5] the South American wide protest movement 'Ni Una Menos' following the brutal rape of a girl in

---

[2] E. GALLAGHER, '#MeToo hashtag network visualization', *Medium*, 20.10.2018, available at https://medium.com/@erin_gallagher/metoo-hashtag-network-visualization-960dd5a97cdf, last accessed 11.06.2018.

[3] CBS NEWS, 'More than 12M "Me Too" Facebook posts, comments, reactions in 24 hours', 17.10.2017, available at https://web.archive.org/web/20171024095757/https://www.cbsnews.com/news/metoo-more-than-12-million-facebook-posts-comments-reactions-24-hours, last accessed 11.06.2018.

[4] A. SCHWARTZ, '#MeToo, #ItWasMe, and the Post-Weinstein Megaphone of Social Media', *The New Yorker*, 19.10.2017, available at https://www.newyorker.com/culture/cultural-comment/metoo-itwasme-and-the-post-weinstein-megaphone-of-social-media, last accessed 11.06.2018.

[5] S. WALKER, 'Russian and Ukrainian women's sexual abuse stories go viral', *The Guardian*, 08.07.2016, available at https://www.theguardian.com/world/2016/jul/08/russian-ukrainian-women-sexual-abuse-stories-go-viral, last accessed 11.06.2018.

Argentina in 2015;[6] and the massive Women's marches of January 2017 against the then incoming administration of Donald Trump (the 'Gropper-in-Chief').[7] Since the story broke in October 2017, #MeToo has become an integral part of the worldwide efforts in ending sexual harassment and violence against women.

On the occasion of the 70th anniversary of the Universal Declaration of Human Rights (UDHR), #MeToo also showcased significant shortcomings in the effective implementation of national laws as well as of international human rights treaties such as the UDHR itself (1948),[8] the Convention on the Elimination of All Forms of Discrimination against Women (CEDAW, 1979),[9] the Inter-American Convention on the Prevention, Punishment and Eradication of Violence against Women (1994), the Istanbul Convention (2011), and Organization for Security and Cooperation in Europe (OSCE) commitments further outlined below. Recent research conducted by the World Health Organization (WHO) provides further evidence of the limited implementation of international standards by showing that 'Violence against women – particularly intimate partner violence and sexual violence – is a major public health concern and a violation of women's human rights'.[10] The WHO numbers demonstrate that almost one in three women (35%) experience sexual violence in their lifetime and as many as 38% of murders of women are committed by a male intimate partner.[11]

1.1. THEORETICAL FRAMEWORK

The article inscribes itself in the critical realism as represented by Margaret Archer,[12] analysing – on basis of empiric cases – how agency can reshape or transform the structure. The notion of agency is chosen as central also because it bears an additional, specific meaning in the feminist movement where it denominates an act of speaking publically of an experience of assault, an act which requires 'incredible strength of mind and sense of self-possession in order

---

[6] P. Mlabo-Ngcuka, 'Executive Director's blog series: "Ni Una Menos" (Not One Less) – Fulfilling the promise to end femicide for women and girls', *UN Women*, 2017, available at http://www.unwomen.org/en/news/stories/2017/11/op-ed-ed-phumzile-16days-day5, last accessed 11.06.2018.

[7] D. Zarkov and K. Davis, 'Ambiguities and Dilemmas around #MeToo: #ForHowLong and #WhereTo?', (2018) 25(I)(3–9) *European Journal of Women Studies*, pp. 3–9.

[8] Universal Declaration of Human Rights, 1948, United Nations, 217 (III) A, Paris, Art. 1.

[9] Convention on the Elimination of All Forms of Discrimination against Women, 1979, A/RES/34/180.

[10] WHO MEDIA CENTRE, 'Violence against women', 2017, available at http://www.who.int/mediacentre/factsheets/fs239/en, last accessed 11.06.2018.

[11] Ibid.

[12] M. Archer, *Structure, Agency and the Internal Conversation*, Cambridge University Press, Cambridge 2003.

to remain a person, and not be reduced to, or by, the acts of violence'.[13] Even the movement's name #MeToo can be interpreted as linking the individual agency level ('me') with the social context, the structure ('too').[14]

Women's rights movement's voice means, in theoretical terms, the ability to generate publics.[15] As Nancy Fraser argues, in past centuries women, while excluded from the mainstream political debate, have created alternative publics.[16] In this article, we see online feminist activism as a new space for debate, new alternative publics and a chance for global and local women's movements to 'turn up the volume from whisper to voice'.[17] This is because digital feminist activism creates not only a renewed and widespread consciousness of issues like sexual harassment and violence, it also promotes a dynamic new engagement on these topics.[18]

Online and offline interactions of structure and agency are not considered in the article as separate analytical spaces but are understood as integrated social practices. There is a growing body of research on the political impact of online social movements[19] as well as on how online feminist practice[20] and gender-related hashtags in particular can lead to a real world change.[21] Candi Olson concludes, already on the basis of studies anterior to the unprecedented reach of #MeToo, that the 'so called hashtag activism has been particularly effective at driving attention to issues of importance to the international

---

[13] D. ZARKOV and K. DAVIS (2018), 'Ambiguities and Dilemmas', *supra* note 7, p. 4.

[14] J. HEARN, 'You, Them, Us, We, too? … Online-offline, Individual-collective, Forgotten-remembered, Harassment-violence', (2018) 25(2) *European Journal of Women Studies*, pp. 228–235.

[15] H. KNAPPE and S. LANG, 'Between Whisper and Voice: Online Women's Movement Outreach in the UK and Germany', (2014) 21(4) *European Journal of Women Studies*, pp. 361–381.

[16] N. FRASER, 'Rethinking the Public Sphere: A Contribution to the Critique of Actually Existing Democracy', in C. CALHOUN (ed.), *Habermas and the Public Sphere*, Cambridge University Press, Cambridge 1992.

[17] H. KNAPPE and S. LANG (2014), 'Between Whisper and Voice', *supra* note 15, p. 362.

[18] H. BEAR, 'Redoing Feminism: Digital Activism, Body Politics, and Neoliberalism', (2016) 16(1) *Feminist Media Studies*, pp. 17–34; S. THRIFT '#YesAllWomen as Feminist Meme Event', (2014) 16(6) *Feminist Media Studies*, pp. 1090–1092.

[19] M. CASTELLS, *Network of Outrage and Hope: Social Movements in the Internet Age*, John Wiley & Sons, Boston 2012; M.A. POLITY, Z. TUFEKCI and C. WILSON, 'Social Media and the Decision to Participate in Political Protest: Observations from the Tahrir Square', (2012) 62 *Journal of Communication*, pp. 363–379.

[20] S. NUNEZ PUENTE, D. FERNANDEZ ROMERO and S. VAZQUEZ CUPEIRO, 'Online Feminist Practice, Participatory Activism and Public Policies against Gender-Based Violence in Spain', (2017) 13(3) *Feminist Theory*, pp. 299–321.

[21] H. BAER (2016), 'Redoing Feminismm', *supra* note 18, pp. 17–34; S. BERRIDGE and L. PORTWOOD-STACER, 'Introduction: Feminism, Hashtags and Violence against Women and Girls', (2015) 15(2), *Feminist Media Studies*, pp. 341–344; K. MENDES, J. RINGROSE and J. KELLER, '#MeToo and the Promise and Pitfalls of Challenging Rape Culture through Digital Feminist Activism', (2018) 25(2) *European Journal of Women Studies*, pp. 236–246; C.C. OLSON, '#BringBackOurGirls: Digital Communities Supporting Real-World Change and Influencing Mainstream Media Agendas', (2016) *Feminist Media Studies*.

women's movement'.²² Jeff Hearn, on the other hand, raises the concern that policy changes which #MeToo-type campaigns bring about might finally not be enforced²³ by what Callerstig called feminist implementation.²⁴ This article strongly shares this concern. This is why the article pays special attention to the ratification and implementation of one of the key legally binding instruments on violence against women, namely the Istanbul Convention in the studied period, as further discussed in section 6.

1.2. METHODOLOGY

The research question guiding the article has been whether the #MeToo campaign has had an impact on the structural level in the OSCE participating States and the organisation itself. For the sake of this research we defined the structural level as (1) power structures (understood here as the realm of politics, the justice system, religious communities, and international organisations – subtopic which opens for a detailed analysis of the case of the OSCE); (2) attitudes and reporting levels; and finally (3) the legal framework and policies.

It is an exploratory study of a topic that has barely been researched due to its recent emergence. Research projects on the movement's impact are thus only beginning.²⁵ This article is also the first attempt to systematise the impact of the movement in the broad and diverse OSCE region spanning over 57 States. The campaign started in one of the OSCE participating States, namely the United States, and spread across the region. Taking into account that the movement targeted sexual harassment in labour settings, we also deemed relevant to capture the possible impact on the OSCE structures and institutions themselves.

A triangulation of methods was used. The first method was an extensive press coverage review of the #MeToo movement in 12 languages, including all the six official OSCE languages: English, French, German, Italian, Russian and Spanish. The others six languages reviewed were Danish, Norwegian, Polish, Portuguese, Slovak and Swedish. Attention was paid to reach English or Russian language press in cases of OSCE participating States whose languages are not among the 12 listed above. The search words were the different translations and spellings of '#MeToo'. The press review covered the period between the start of the movement, October 2017 and the moment of writing of the first version of

---

22   Ibid., p. 3.
23   J. HEARN (2018), 'You, Them, Us, We, too?', *supra* note 14, pp. 228–235.
24   A.C. CALLERSTIG, *Making Equality Work: Conflict, Ambiguities and Change Actors in the Implementation of Equality Policies in Public Sector Organisations*, Linkoping University, Sweden 2014.
25   See for example UNIVERSITY OF GUELPH, Prof Investigates Global Impact of #MeToo Movement, available at https://news.uoguelph.ca/2018/03/prof-investigates-global-impact-metoo-movement, last accessed 11.06.2018.

the article, March 2018. The information collected in this way was cross-checked with other sources (and if there were publications in English on a particular issue, these are the ones quoted in the footnotes for the ease of reference). However, some inaccuracies may still remain due to the nature of sources used and the absence of a peer reviewed research body on the movement.

The press review was complemented with a legal review of the progress of the ratification and implementation of the Istanbul Convention, as well as a review of the existing academic studies on sexual harassment, assault incidence levels and the most recent changes in reporting levels. The third method, used as the principal one when looking at the impact on OSCE structures and institutions, was a document review.

Nonetheless, the list of cases presented in the article serves merely an illustrative function and is by no means exhaustive. And what might seem an over-representation of the cases from the United States is due to the fact that the movement started there and its impact in the country has been more widespread and better described by the media and analytical bodies than anywhere else.

2. THE POWER STRUCTURE IS SHAKING

Originating in Hollywood and the US media, the #MeToo spread to several power structures, through the political world, the justice sector, religious communities, and to international organisations. Throughout these sectors powerful men were losing their positions and held accountable. In some, women were already starting to ascend.

2.1. POLITICS

Several female members of the European Parliament (EP) shared their sexual harassment experiences during a special #MeToo inspired debate and demanded more measures to be taken, including an external audit of the situation of sexual harassment in the EP, establishment of a new dedicated committee on the topic as well as mandatory training for all staff to ensure the zero-tolerance approach becomes the norm. All these proposals were passed as a part of the EP resolution of 26 October 2017 on combating sexual harassment and abuse in the EU. The text called on all politicians to act 'as responsible role models in preventing and combating sexual harassment in parliaments and beyond'.[26]

---

[26] Procedure 2017/2897(RSP), European Parliament resolution of 26 October 2017 on combating sexual harassment and abuse in the EU, 26 October 2017, available at http://www.europarl.europa.eu/sides/getDoc.do?type=TA&reference=P8-TA-2017-0417&language=EN&ring=P8-RC-2017-0576, last accessed 11.06.2018.

In Norway, #MeToo shook the political scene with politicians stepping down from their functions and apologising publicly after complains of inappropriate sexual behaviour. The most notable case was Trond Giske, an influential figure in Norwegian politics for more than 20 years. He had held several ministerial posts in previous governments and was the deputy leader of the main opposition Labour Party until January 2018. On the conservative side of the political spectrum, Kristian Tonning Riise resigned as leader of the Conservative Party's youth group after being accused of harassment against young women and Ulf Leirstein stepped down as legal affairs spokesman for his populist Progress Party after reports that he had sent pornographic images to under-aged boys.[27]

The #MeToo wave reached the Russian political sphere as well, when in March 2018 the well-known Russian Foreign Ministry Spokeswoman Maria Zakharova accused the chairman of the Duma's International Affairs Committee, Leonid Slutsky, of sexual harassment. Zakharova was the fourth and most famous political figure to accuse Slutsky after the three journalists Yekaterina Kotrikadze, a deputy editor at RTVI television, Darya Zhuk producer at Dozhd TV producer, and BBC Russian Service correspondent Farida Rustamova had already come forward.[28] Slutsky initially threatened to sue the accusers for defamation but apologised later for his behaviour. The case was briefly investigated by the ethics committee, but Slutsky did not face any further consequences nor did the incident lead to any structural changes.

#MeToo has also resulted in a reshuffling of the UK cabinet. In November 2017, the Defence Secretary Sir Michael Fallon resigned following revelations he 'lunged' at a female journalist trying to kiss her. He also admitted that his past behaviour towards women had 'fallen short'. In December 2017, Prime Minister Theresa May made Damian Green resign as First Secretary of State after a Cabinet Office investigation found that he had misled the public and MPs over his knowledge about pornography found on an office computer. The British Prime Minister did not grasp the crisis as a chance to promote gender equity in her government and did not appoint women for these two vacancies.[29]

The Canadian political establishment was affected by three resignations following accusations of sexual misconduct in January 2018: Kent Hehr,

---

[27] Please note that the accused all stayed on as MPs, partly because the constitution makes it almost impossible for lawmakers to give up their seat before their term expires. A. GURZU, '#MeToo hits Norway's woman-dominated politics', *Politico*, 02.02.2018, available at https://www.politico.eu/article/trond-giske-kristian-tonning-riise-ulf-leirstein-metoo-hits-norways-woman-dominated-politics, last accessed 11.06.2018.

[28] 'Russian Foreign Ministry Spokeswoman Accuses Alleged "Sex Pest" Deputy', *Radio Free Europe/Radio Liberty*, 11.03.2018, available at https://www.rferl.org/a/russia-sexual-harassment-zakharova-slutsky/29091085.html, last accessed 11.06.2018.

[29] T. MCTAGUE, 'Theresa May misses her opportunity, again', *Politico*, 03.11.2017, available at https://www.politico.eu/article/theresa-may-gavin-williamson-michael-fallon-misses-her-opportunity-again, last accessed 11.06.2018.

the Minister of Sport and Persons with Disabilities stepped down, as did leaders of the Progressive Conservatives in Ontario and in Nova Scotia. In particular, the resignation of the Ontario leader, Patrick Brown, threw his party into disarray only some months before the provincial elections, which he was likely to win. Several of his top aides also resigned.[30]

In the United States, similar resignations did not reach a higher political level. Two White House staffers stepped down over domestic abuse allegations, the staff secretary Rob Porter and speechwriter David Sorensen.[31] Nonetheless, in December 2017, the White House dismissed calls for a congressional investigation of allegations against Donald Trump who had allegedly sexually harassed several women before running for president.[32] In the meantime, the former President George H.W. Bush publicly apologised after being accused of groping actress Heather Lind from his wheelchair some years earlier. His spokesman said Bush occasionally 'patted women's rears in what he intended to be a good-natured manner'.[33]

Analysts also noticed that as a result of #MeToo an unprecedented number of women have signed up to run for the highest elected offices than ever before in the United States – 472 women have entered the race for the House in 2018 and 57 women have filed or were likely to file their candidacies for the Senate as of April 2018. The most relevant comparison would be the year 2012, which marked the last big wave of female candidates, with 298 women running for the House and 36 for the Senate. Even though at the moment of writing, women held only six out of 50 governorships, the number of women likely to run for governor in 2018, 78, was record high. And in the 36 gubernatorial races to take place this year, 35 were expected to have female candidates.[34]

---

[30] C. PORTER and I. AUSTEN, 'Ontario's Opposition Leader Quits Over Sexual Misconduct Allegations', *The New York Times*, 25.01.2018, available at https://www.nytimes.com/2018/01/25/world/canada/patrick-brown-ontario-sexual-misconduct.html, last accessed 11.06.2018.

[31] A. RESTUCCIA, 'Second White House staffer resigns amid abuse allegation', *Politico*, 10.02.2018, available at https://www.politico.eu/article/white-house-domestic-abuse-david-sorensen-staffer-resigns-allegation, last accessed 11.06.2018.

[32] 'Donald Trump rejects congressional sexual harassment probe', *Deutsche Welle*, 12.12.2017, available at http://p.dw.com/p/2pBFo, last accessed 11.06.2018.

[33] K. PHILLIPS and E. ROSENBERG, 'George H.W. Bush "has patted women's rears" but never meant to offend, spokesman says', *The Washington Post*, 26.10.2017, available at https://www.washingtonpost.com/news/arts-and-entertainment/wp/2017/10/25/george-h-w-bush-apologizes-for-attempt-at-humor-after-actress-accused-him-of-groping, last accessed 11.06.2018.

[34] CENTER FOR AMERICAN WOMEN AND POLITICS, 'Elections: Data and analysis for current and past races with women candidates, by election year', 2018, available at http://cawp.rutgers.edu/facts/elections/election_watch, last accessed 11.06.2018; H. CAYGLE, 'Record-breaking number of women run for office', *Politico*, 08.03.2018, available at https://www.politico.com/story/2018/03/08/women-rule-midterms-443267, last accessed 11.06.2018, M. TALBOT, 'The Women Running in the Midterms During the Trump Era', 18 April 2018,

2.2. JUSTICE SYSTEM

The justice sector is internally known for its hierarchical power structures. It is thus hardly surprising that the sector faced its own #MeToo movement. In the United States the prominent Federal Appeals Court Judge Alex Kosinski announced his retirement in December 2017, following sexual harassment allegations by more than 15 women. Kosinski, who was first appointed by President Ronald Reagan in 1985, served for 32 years as Federal Judge and had already faced similar allegations in the past.[35]

A recent investigation highlights, however, that the above-mentioned case is only the tip of the iceberg. The analysis found that sexual harassment and assault are rampant in the US justice system and showed that 'None of the actual complaints (more than 1,000 are filed annually) are made public. In public judicial orders, claims are sparingly summarized, and accused judges' names rarely appear. Some orders refer to "corrective action" by a judge without specifying what exactly happened'.[36] As a result, Supreme Court Chief Justice John Robert announced in December 2017, that 'The judiciary will begin 2018 by undertaking a careful evaluation of whether its standards of conduct and its procedures for investigating and correcting inappropriate behaviour are adequate to ensure an exemplary workplace for every judge and every court employee'.[37] While a substantial reform will depend on an amendment and a thorough implementation of appropriate policies, #MeToo did manage to shed light on the insufficient handling of harassment complaints and set in motion a process of change.

When similar revelations shook the legal industry in Sweden, women lawyers started their own movement under the hashtag #medvilkenrätt (with what right) and almost 6,000 women legal professionals immediately signed a petition demanding a zero-tolerance stance on sexual abuse and highlighting that representing the law also requires defending it.[38]

---

available at https://www.newyorker.com/news/news-desk/2018-midterm-elections-women-candidates-trump, last accessed 11.06.2018.

[35] N. CHOKSHI, 'Federal Judge Alex Kozinski Retires Abruptly After Sexual Harassment Allegations', *The New York Times*, 18.12.2017, available at https://www.nytimes.com/2017/12/18/us/alex-kozinski-retires.html, last accessed 11.06.2018.

[36] J. BISKUPIC, 'CNN Investigation: Sexual misconduct by judges kept under wraps', *CNN*, 25.01.2018, available at https://edition.cnn.com/2018/01/25/politics/courts-judges-sexual-harassment/index.html, last accessed 11.06.2018.

[37] PUBLIC INFORMATION OFFICE, '2017 Year-End Report on the Federal Judiciary', 31.12.2017, available at http://cdn.cnn.com/cnn/2017/images/12/31/2017.year-end.report[1].pdf, last accessed 11.06.2018.

[38] '6,000 female lawyers are calling out sexual abuse in the Swedish legal industry – and it's just the tip of the iceberg', *Business Insider*, 16.11.2017, available at https://nordic.businessinsider.com/6000-swedish-female-lawyers-are-calling-out-sexual-abuse-in-their-industry--and-its-just-the-tip-of-the-iceberg-2017-11, last accessed 11.06.2018.

#MeToo has also resulted in strengthening women's capacity to fight sexual harassment all over the United States with the support of 'Time's Up Legal Defence Fund'. The TimesUp initiative was established by the very same Hollywood actresses, initially leading the #MeToo movement. In January 2018 an open letter[39] announced the initiative will use Hollywood's privilege to fight for working women everywhere by setting up a legal defence fund which not only provides financial support to victims but also matches their cases with local attorneys. The fund is administered through National Women's Law Center[40] and has already raised $21 million. As of March 2018, 1,800 women have already requested support.[41]

2.3. RELIGIOUS COMMUNITIES

Potentially one of the most exemplifying signs of #MeToo's impact on existent powers structures are voices criticising the discrimination and harassment of women in religious communities, especially if the criticism comes from within the community itself. In the Unites States, more than 140 evangelical Christian women published a statement featuring the hashtag #SilenceIsNotSpritual calling on churches to end their silence and to support victims of harassment and violence. As of March 2018, 5,773 people had signed the statement including Lynne Hybels, co-founder of one of the US's largest churches.[42]

Even the Vatican itself started to experience its #MeToo moment, when the March 2018 edition of the monthly Women's magazine 'Women Church World' of the Vatican newspaper *L'Osservatore Romanofo* denounced the treatment of nuns like 'indentured servants by cardinals and bishops, for whom they cook and clean for next to no pay'. The magazine publicly exposed conditions of 'underpaid labour and unappreciated intellect of religious sisters' challenging the long-lasting status quo.[43]

---

[39] TIMESUP, 'Dear Sisters', 21.12.2017, available at https://assets.documentcloud.org/documents/4339359/Womenhollywood.pdf, last accessed 11.06.2018.
[40] NATIONAL WOMEN'S LAW CENTRE, 'Time's Up Legal Defense Fund', available at https://nwlc.org/times-up-legal-defense-fund, last accessed 11.06.2018.
[41] 'Here's How The Time's Up Legal Defense Fund Actually Works', *NPR*, 11.03.2018, available at https://www.npr.org/2018/03/11/592307856/heres-how-the-time-s-up-legal-defense-fund-actually-works, last accessed 11.06.2018.
[42] '#SilenceIsNotSpiritual Breaking the Silence on Violence Against Women and Girls', *Statement*, available at http://www.silenceisnotspiritual.org/statement, last accessed 11.06.2018.
[43] P. PULLELLA, 'Stop exploiting nuns for cheap Church labor, Vatican magazine urges', *Reuters*, 01.03.2018, available at https://www.reuters.com/article/us-pope-nuns-stop-exploiting-nuns-for-cheap-church-labor-vatican-magazine-urges-idUSKCN1GD5S8, last accessed 13.06.2018.

2.4. INTERNATIONAL ORGANISATIONS

Finally, the #MeToo has also shaken the aid sector and other international organisations. In February 2018, a journalistic investigation revealed that the charity Oxfam, which receives more than £300 million a year from the British government and public donations, covered up the use of prostitutes by senior aid workers.[44] Another journalistic investigation, published in January 2018, described a widespread culture of silence surrounding sexual harassment and assault at the UN, with employees feeling unable to report complaints for fear of losing employment. Three alleged victims said they had lost their jobs, or been threatened with termination of contract, after reporting sexual harassment or assault. Two cited concerns with investigations, and said there had been errors in transcripts, or that key witnesses had not been interviewed. Alleged perpetrators were allowed to remain in senior positions – with the power to influence proceedings – throughout investigations.[45]

At the same time, several international organisations, including the UN, quickly understood the significance and the impact #MeToo was starting to have on a global, national and local level. UN roundtable of experts before the International Women's Day on 8 March 2018 stated:

> This is a transformative moment, a liberating and an empowering moment. By speaking out at this scale, women are shaking centuries-old established discriminatory norms which normalise, accept and justify sexual violence against women and have constrained women in well-defined roles of inferiority and subordination. This is what is so significant about the moment. It is no longer just about individuals, it is about society. It is not about so-called morals and honour; it is about women's rights as human rights. It is the system of the concentration of power and domination that is being challenged.[46]

3. THE OSCE AND #METOO

Staying within the realm of international organisations, this section first summarises OSCE commitments and efforts on violence against women, and then examines the impact of #MeToo within the OSCE structures and institutions.

---

[44] 'Oxfam Haiti allegations: How the scandal unfolded', *BBC*, 21.02.2018, available at https://www.bbc.com/news/uk-43112200, last accessed 11.06.2018.

[45] R. RATCLIFFE, 'Sexual harassment and assault rife at United Nations, staff claim', *The Guardian*, 18.01.2018, available at https://www.theguardian.com/global-development/2018/jan/18/sexual-assault-and-harassment-rife-at-united-nations-staff-claim, last accessed 11.06.2018.

[46] OHCHR, 'International Women's Day Statement by United Nations Women's Human Rights Experts', 06.03.2018, available at http://www.ohchr.org/EN/NewsEvents/Pages/DisplayNews.aspx?NewsID=22759&LangID=E, last accessed 11.06.2018.

3.1. THE OSCE BEFORE #METOO: RELEVANT OSCE COMMITMENTS AND WORK ON VIOLENCE AGAINST WOMEN

OSCE's comprehensive concept of security spans three interlinked dimensions: the politico-military, the economic and environmental dimension and the human rights dimension, recognising that the security of women, men, girls and boys is indivisible from the other aspects of security. The OSCE Gender Action Plan, adopted in 2004, encouraged the participating States to 'ensure that existing national legislation on violence against women is enforced, and that new legislation is drafted where necessary'.[47] Subsequently, two key OSCE Ministerial Council Decisions (MC.DEC.), documents reached by consensus of all the 57 participating States, stressed the importance of enhanced efforts on preventing and combating violence against women.

The MC. DEC. number 15/05 from Ljubljana urged the OSCE participating States 'To adopt and implement legislation that criminalizes gender-based violence and establishes adequate legal protection'. It also noted that 'violence against women and girls often remains unreported and unrecorded and is therefore not adequately reflected in statistics', and encouraged participating States 'to support efforts to raise awareness; to make significant additional efforts to collect, analyse and disseminate comparable data'.[48] In the MC. DEC. number 7/14 from Basel, the OSCE participating States unanimously declared to be 'Deeply concerned by the persistence of violence against women as one of the most pervasive human rights violations in the OSCE area, manifested as physical, sexual, and psychological violence' and reiterated 'the particular need to take more vigorous measures in preventing and combating violence against women, to which gender inequality can be among the major contributing factors'.[49]

In July 2016, the then German Chairmanship of the OSCE and the Gender Section of the OSCE Secretariat organised a regional conference in Vienna to discuss concrete steps to combat gender-based violence more effectively. In June 2017, the 2nd OSCE-wide Gender Equality Review Conference, organised by the Austrian Chairmanship, the OSCE Office for Democratic Institutions and Human Rights (ODIHR), and the Gender Section of the OSCE Secretariat, provided additional best practices and lessons learnt on the topic. It also resulted

---

[47] OSCE, 'Ministerial Council Decision No. 14/04, 2004 OSCE Action Plan for the Promotion of Gender Equality', 07.12.2004, 0042, available at https://www.osce.org/mc/23295?download=true, last accessed 11.06.2018.

[48] OSCE, 'Ministerial Council Decision No. 15 on preventing and combating violence against women', 06.12.2005, 0004ii, available at https://www.osce.org/mc/17451, last accessed 11.06.2018.

[49] OSCE, 'Ministerial Council Decision No. 7/14 on preventing and combating violence against women', 05.12.2014, 0009, available at www.osce.org/cio/130721, last accessed 11.06.2018.

in an update of the 2016 publication 'Combating violence against women in the OSCE region: a reader on the situation in the region, good practices and the way forward'.[50]

Several OSCE structures assist OSCE participating States in their work on prevention and addressing of gender-based violence (GBV): ODIHR, the Gender Section of the OSCE Secretariat and OSCE field operations. The Gender Section is currently preparing a survey on GBV in several participating States which were not covered by recent the EU Fundamental Rights Agency (FRA) survey on the topic.[51] OSCE field operations work closely with the authorities in their respective countries supporting them in closing the gaps between the *de jure* and *de facto* freedom from violence for women and girls.

ODIHR's efforts to prevent and combat sexual and gender-based violence include strengthening legal and policy frameworks, through expert advice given to participating States by the Legislative Support Unit of the Office. And ODIHR's 'Human Rights, Gender and Security' programme has built a track record working on a gender-sensitive security delivery and gender-responsive security sector reform. It gives expert advice to decision-makers, builds the capacities of security sector representatives from all across the OSCE region as well as raises awareness on gender-based violence through publications, workshops, conferences and roundtables. In 2017 ODIHR's 'Human Rights, Gender and Security' programme focused its efforts on Ukraine with a series of capacity building events for the National Police, its police academies and its oversight body, all aimed at enhancing police responses to sexual and gender-based violence.

3.2. THE IMPACT OF #METOO WITHIN THE OSCE STRUCTURES AND INSTITUTIONS

The movement has impacted mostly the organisational discourse, but first policy changes have also taken place. Since the #MeToo campaign started, ODIHR Director Ingibjörg Sólrún Gísladóttir has referenced it systematically in her public statements. For example, in a joint OSCE statement for the 16 Days of Activism against Gender-based Violence on 24 Nov 2017 Gísladóttir said:

> Empowering women to know and demand their rights is essential to tackling violence perpetrated against them, whether it is of physical, psychological, economic or political nature. The more women speak out, as we have seen most recently, for example, in the #MeToo campaign, the greater their power and ability to use legal and other means

---

[50] OSCE, 'Combating violence against women in the OSCE region', 08.2017, available at https://www.osce.org/secretariat/286336?download=true, last accessed 11.06.2018.

[51] OSCE, 'OSCE Survey on the Well-being and Safety of Women', available at https://www.osce.org/projects/survey-on-the-well-being-and-safety-of-women, last accessed 11.06.2018.

available to confront the perpetrators.' She also emphasised, just like the leaders of the #MeToo movement, that 'violence against women is most often based on the power, privilege and entitlement of perpetrators. To counter this, it is also important that men and boys participate in this conversation, including with each other, and become part of the solution.[52]

The ODIHR Director also chose #MeToo as the topic of her statement ahead of the Human Rights Day celebrated on 10 of December:

> In the last few months, we have witnessed millions of women virtually joining hands in a world-wide act of solidarity demanding justice, inspiring courage and calling for action. The #MeToo campaign has generated an unprecedented impetus to speak up at all times about sexual harassment, assault and violence suffered by women all over the world. Breaking the silence has become a powerful and rights-affirmative denunciation of tolerance towards violence.

She further stressed the relevance of the issue as a breach of human rights:

> Security of the person is one of the first rights spelled out in the Universal Declaration, and violence against women, including sexual violence and harassment, is the most basic violation of that right.[53]

As the only speaker before the OSCE Permanent Council on 8 March 2018, the ODIHR Director mentioned the #MeToo movement:

> in light of International Women's Day, let me refer to the extraordinary and forceful #MeToo campaign which has taken place in the past few months across the OSCE region. The campaign has created a momentum for all of us to reinforce our efforts to demonstrate to women that we will take measures to ensure that their working environment, in all sectors, is free from sexual harassment and other gender based violence. At ODIHR we will […] continue our efforts to promote a professional working environment, including in our election observation activities.[54]

The last sentence refers to the impact on policy level – the establishment of an ODIHR working group on the prevention of sexual harassment and to the new leaflet of ODIHR's Election Department 'Promoting a Professional Working Environment on Election Observation Activities'. The leaflet explains

---

[52] OSCE, 'OSCE marks 16 Days of Activism against Gender-based Violence – calls on States to step up efforts to end violence against women and girls', 24.11.2017, available at https://www.osce.org/secretariat/358756, last accessed 11.06.2018.

[53] ODIHR, 'Ahead of Human Rights Day, ODIHR Director calls on states to leverage current momentum to address gender-based violence, sexual assault, harassment', 08.12.2017, available at https://www.osce.org/odihr/361666, last accessed 11.06.2018.

[54] Address by Ingibjörg Sólrún Gísladóttir, Director of ODIHR, 1178th Meeting of the Permanent Council, Vienna, 08.03.2018, p. 3, available at https://www.osce.org/odihr/374815?download=true, last accessed 12.06.2018.

the mechanisms in place to report misbehaviour and to address violations of the professional working environment, including sexual harassment. It was envisaged both as a preventive tool and an informational material to facilitate access to remedies. It is distributed to all members of ODIHR's election observation missions, including the local staff. For that purpose, it has already been translated from English into Azeri, Hungarian, Italian, Montenegrin, Russian and Turkmen. Additionally, the Election Department has integrated elements of the leaflet into standard presentations for both long-term and short-term observers.

Furthermore, the Human Resources Office of the OSCE Headquarters in Vienna stepped up its focus on sexual harassment in the working environment. As part of the global 16 Days of Activism, Human Resources organised a presentation for all staff on sexual harassment, which was attended and watched online by approximately 100 staff from across the OSCE. The recording is also available to all staff on the Learning Management System. #MeToo has been at the centre of ODIHR's attention since it organised, together with UN Women, United Nations Office for Drugs and Crime (UNODC), Equality Now and CAT-W, a side event at the Commission on the Status of Women (CSW) in New York in March 2018 under the title: '"#MeToo", Say Survivors: Human Rights, Gender and Trafficking in Human Beings.' The event built on the Sustainable Development Target 5.2.: 'eliminate all forms of violence against all women and girls in public and private spheres, including trafficking and sexual and other types of exploitation' and pointed to the fact that 96% of victims trafficked for sexual exploitation are women and girls.[55] It was also rooted in the first #MeToo campaign started by Tarana Burke who saw 'MeToo' as 'a catch phrase to be used from survivor to survivor to let folks know that they were not alone and that a movement for radical healing was happening and possible'. In her opening remarks, before giving the floor to several survivors of trafficking who shared their stories and political messages, the ODIHR Director stressed the 'global power of the recent #MeToo campaign and the impact it is having in breaking the silence and ending the impunity'.[56]

The next section will analyse the relation between the perceptions of – and attitudes towards – sexual harassment and assault on one hand, and the levels of reporting on the other. It will further show what impact #MeToo has had on the perceptions, attitudes and victims' readiness to report in some of the OSCE participating States.

---

[55] UNODOC, 'Global Report on Trafficking in Persons', United Nations Publication, 2016, p. 27, available at https://www.unodc.org/documents/data-and-analysis/glotip/2016_Global_Report_on_Trafficking_in_Persons.pdf, last accessed 11.06.2018.

[56] '#MeToo Say Survivors: Human Rights, Gender and Trafficking in Human Beings' (CSW62 Side Event), 15.03.2018, available at http://webtv.un.org/search/metoo-say-survivors-human-rights-gender-and-trafficking-in-human-beings-csw62-side-event/5752063068001/?term=CSW62&lan=english&sort=date&page=2, last accessed 11.06.2018.

4. CHANGES IN ATTITUDES AND REPORTING LEVELS

One of the key aspects when working on prevention of and when addressing gender-based violence are the perceptions about what constitutes different forms of such abuse, including sexual harassment and assault. The perceptions about which behaviours amount to sexual harassment vary widely by gender, age and across OSCE participating States, as shown by recent studies. One example is the survey done by YouGov among a representative group of men and women in Germany, Britain, France, Denmark, Sweden, Finland and Norway. Different situations, like for example a man whistling at a woman, sex jokes told by men to women at work or groping, were generally less likely to be seen as harassment by men than by women and less likely to be evaluated as such by older than by younger women.[57] These discrepancies in perceptions vary also significantly from country to country and, as a result, make us aware of how challenging it is to obtain comparable data on the prevalence of sexual harassment across the OSCE area.

Perceptions of social and cultural norms, including the question of what behaviour amounts to harassment or assault, tend to draw their legitimacy and impact from an inter-subjective nature shaping a collective awareness of what is right or wrong. The vast scale of #MeToo has not only challenged the legitimacy of widely held beliefs and behaviours impacting women's human rights but also helped shed light on country-specific perceptions of harassment and assault and illustrated a vast discrepancy between women's rights as defined in the international framework and women's everyday experiences.

These perceptions and attitudes are among the factors that may impact negatively the readiness of victims to report sexual abuse to the police or even their readiness to talk about past assaults. Global data shows remarkably low numbers of reported cases of sexual harassment and assault, compared to the high prevalence of such behaviours very clearly illustrated by the #MeToo movement. The phenomenon of low reporting rates of crimes such as domestic violence, sexual assault and rape is well known and makes it impossible to rely only on the number of police reported cases when assessing how widespread the phenomenon is. This is why other methods, like anonymous surveys, are seen as a better data source. Yet, surveys also have their shortcomings as discussed below.

A survey on violence against women conducted by FRA in 2014 shows that half of all women in Europe had at some point in their lives been victims of sexual harassment, one in 10 women experienced some form of sexual violence

---

[57] 'Over-friendly or sexual harassment? It depends partly on whom you ask', *The Economist*, 17.11.2017, available at https://www.economist.com/blogs/graphicdetail/2017/11/daily-chart-14, last accessed 11.06.2018.

since the age of 15, with one in 20 having been raped.[58] It also indicates that only 14% of women reported the most serious incidents of intimate partner violence, with 13% reporting the most serious incidents of non-partner violence to the police.[59] Surprisingly for many, even though not based on numbers of formally reported cases but a survey, the FRA study shows Denmark, Finland and Sweden as countries with the highest frequency of violence against women in Europe, while Sweden and France receive the highest scores on the prevalence of sexual harassment. This is explained, however, by a greater willingness of victims in these countries to speak about their experiences of harassment and assault to the researchers conducting the survey, arguably reflecting a culture with lower stigma and taboo than in other parts of Europe.

The reasons for under-reporting globally involve patriarchal power structures, deep-rooted gender roles, and corresponding concepts of honour and guilt. As a result, victims frequently find themselves in a position where the emotional and social costs of reporting are significantly higher than the potential benefits of pursuing justice. Victims frequently report on feelings of shame and humiliation and the fear of stigmatisation and retaliation, such as losing their job, when reporting and seeking justice. A study from the United States conducted in 2003, found that 75% of employees who spoke out against workplace mistreatment were confronted with some form of retaliation.[60] In a culture where blame is frequently put on the victims,[61] just moving on with their lives is likely to be the easiest way out of the situation. With the burden of proof on the victim's side, victims who might want to pursue legal charges for sexual harassment or assault, have to undergo lengthy reporting processes that not only put their right to privacy at risk, but also force them to relive their experiences repeatedly, increasing the risk of re-traumatisation.

In addition, despite efforts on the international level and various national laws in place criminalising sexual harassment and assault,[62] the past decades have been characterised by a climate of impunity for perpetrators across all

---

[58] FRA, 'Challenges to women's human rights in the EU: Gender discrimination, sexist hate speech and gender-based violence against women and girls', Contribution to the third Annual Colloquium on Fundamental Rights, November 2017, p. 11, available at http://fra.europa.eu/en/publication/2017/colloq-womens-rights, last accessed 11.06.2018.

[59] Ibid.

[60] L.M. CORTINA and V.J. MAGLEY, 'Raising Voice, Risking Retaliation: Events Following Interpersonal Mistreatment in the Workplace', (2003) 8(4) *Occupational Health Psychology (OCP)*, pp. 247, 255.

[61] K. ROBERTS, 'The Psychology of Victim-Blaming', *The Atlantic*, 05.10.2016, available at https://www.theatlantic.com/science/archive/2016/10/the-psychology-of-victim-blaming/502661, last accessed 12.06.2018.

[62] P. TAVARES and Q. WODON, 'Global and Regional Trends in Women's Legal Protection against Domestic Violence and Sexual Harassment', *World Bank*, 03.2018, available at http://pubdocs.worldbank.org/en/679221517425064052/EndingViolenceAgainstWomenandGirls-GBVLaws-Feb2018.pdf, last accessed 12.06.2018.

sectors as touched upon in section 2. Reporting of harassment and assault cases only rarely results in justice for victims, as demonstrated by the low numbers of convictions or the frequent absence of appropriate investigations.[63] This climate of impunity may well explain the low levels of victims' trust in formal institutions, contributing to low reporting rates.

Support, protection, and justice for victims of harassment and assault depends thus, *inter alia*, on the interdependencies between perceptions, awareness, reporting levels and an appropriate response of the justice system in place. The women and men coming forward and pursuing legal action in the context of the #MeToo movement have significantly contributed to challenging existing perceptions, to raising awareness, to starting public debates about the definition of sexual harassment as well as to fighting the climate of impunity regarding sexual harassment and assault. Depending on the country, the #MeToo movement has also succeeded in questioning whether the legal system in place is actually designed to support victims, as further outlined in section 5.

#MeToo's impact on perceptions around assault and harassment resulted in a global awareness of the extent and the patterns of abusive power systems in place, opened debates on what behaviour exactly constitutes harassment and abuse, broadened the definition of sexual harassment and violence by introducing a debate on the need for explicit consent, and arguably also reduced some of the stigma and barriers faced by victims. This general trend can be exemplified by a recent survey providing evidence for a change in attitudes towards sexual harassment in the United States as an immediate result of the #MeToo movement.[64] It was conducted on a representative sample of voters in the United States and showed that 44% of the surveyed now think that sexism is a 'big problem' compared to only 30% in December 2016, while 73% of voters stated that stories of sexual harassment and assault made them think more generally about sexism in society (up from 40% in December 2016). Furthermore, 72% reported that they spoke to a friend or family member about questions pertaining to gender equality, which represents a major increase since December 2016 when only 49% of voters reported the same. Finally, the survey

---

[63] R. DOOLITTLE, 'Why the police dismiss 1 in 5 sexual assault claims as baseless', *The Global and Mail*, 03.02.2017, available at https://www.theglobeandmail.com/news/investigations/unfounded-sexual-assault-canada-main/article33891309, last accessed 12.06.2018; L. BATES, 'How the police are letting sexual assault victims down', *The Guardian*, 21.11.2014, available at https://www.theguardian.com/lifeandstyle/womens-blog/2014/nov/21/police-letting-rape-victims-down-too, last accessed 12.06.2018.

[64] PERRY UNDEM RESEARCH/COMMUNICATION, 'What a Difference a Year Makes: Polling Update on Sexism, Harassment, Culture and Equality', *Perry Undem Report*, 06.12.2017, p. 16, available at https://www.scribd.com/document/366406592/PerryUndem-Report-on-Sexism-Harassment-Culture-And-Equality-compressed?irgwc=1&content=27795&campaign=VigLink&ad_group=3045&keyword=ft500noi&source=impactradius&medium=affiliate, last accessed 12.06.2018.

showed that the stories about harassment and assault have prompted 43% of male voters to questions their own behaviour towards women in the past.[65]

A similar trend becomes apparent when looking at changing reporting patterns following the #MeToo revelations. The Rape, Abuse & Incest National Network (RAINN) in the United States reported a surge of calls of 25% in November 2017 and 30% in December 2017 when compared to 2016. RAINN also reported that the total number of calls in 2017 was the highest in one year since the foundation of the network in 1993. The DC Rape Crisis Centre experienced similar changes with not only more people reaching out for help but also an increase in donations following the #MeToo stories.[66] Unsurprisingly, the trend is not limited to the United States. The Swiss police reported a 10% increase in reporting[67] while the German Army stated that in 2017, 80% more cases of sexual harassment and assault were reported compared to the year 2016.[68] The Sexual Violence Centre in the Netherlands informed that the numbers of reports by victims of sexual violence had 'skyrocketed as a result of the #MeToo discussion'.[69]

Even though the movement has sparked controversy for having generated 'trial by the media',[70] it has in fact also prompted prosecutors increasingly to investigate allegations of sexual assault holding perpetrators accountable.[71] In Belgium, a criminal court convicted a man of 'Sexism in the Public Space' for the first time and fined €3,000 'for verbally abusing a female police officer who tried to question him after he was seen jaywalking'.[72]

In conclusion, awareness, perceptions, and reporting levels are closely linked and #MeToo is now leading to significant changes in the balance between these processes globally. While the results are very different from country to country, the majority of OSCE participating States have witnessed and are witnessing

---

[65] Ibid., p. 5.
[66] L. LAMBERT, '#MeToo effect: Calls flood U.S. sexual assault hotlines', Reuters, 17.01.2018, available at https://www.reuters.com/article/us-usa-harassment-helplines/metoo-effect-calls-flood-u-s-sexual-assault-hotlines-idUSKBN1F6194, last accessed 12.06.2018.
[67] M. BRINER, 'Mehr Anzeigen wegen Belästigung', Tagblatt, 03.12.2017, available at http://www.tagblatt.ch/nachrichten/schweiz/mehr-anzeigen-wegen-belaestigung;art505763,5157643, last accessed 12.06.2018.
[68] '234 Verdachtsfälle bei der Bundeswehr', Zeit Online, 27.01.2018, available at http://www.zeit.de/gesellschaft/zeitgeschehen/2018-01/bundeswehr-sexuelle-uebergriffe, last accessed 12.06.2018.
[69] J. PIETERS, 'Sexual Violence Reports Skyrocket after #MeToo', NL Times, 16.11.2017, available at https://nltimes.nl/2017/11/16/sexual-violence-reports-skyrocket-metoo, last accessed 12.06.2018.
[70] D. ZARKOV and K. DAVIS (2018), 'Ambiguities and Dilemmas', supra note 7, pp. 3–9.
[71] J. HEYMANN and R. VOGELSTEIN, 'Commentary: When Sexual Harassment Is Legal', Fortune, 17.11.2017, available at http://fortune.com/2017/11/17/sexual-harassment-legal-gaps, last accessed 12.06.2018.
[72] M. SCHREUER, 'Belgian Man Convicted of "Sexism in the Public Space", a First', New York Times, 06.03.2018, available at https://www.nytimes.com/2018/03/06/world/europe/belgium-sexism-fine.html, last accessed 12.06.2018.

debates on women's human rights, incidence of gender-based violence and its definitions. The overall societal discourse is being changed already, simply by more women coming forward and reporting. In such a context, tolerance for abusive behaviours is likely to decrease further making it impossible for perpetrators to continue to rely on the established power dynamics to silence their victims without fearing any consequences. #MeToo empowered women's voices and provided an entry point for lawmakers, activists and women's rights movements to advocate for legislative changes with the aim to bring about social change as further discussed below.

5. CHANGES IN LEGAL FRAMEWORK AND POLICIES

In some of the OSCE participating States legal changes are already on the way as a result of the #MeToo movement. In Sweden in December 2017, the government proposed new legislation – to go into effect in July 2018 – changing its rape law so that people would have to get explicit consent before sexual contact.[73] So even though the rape concept has been debated in Sweden for some years already, the legislative change has been speeded up in the aftermath of #MeToo.[74] Iceland amended its legislation in March 2018 – the parliament unanimously passed a law that requires an explicit consent before a sexual act.[75] Also in Austria in March 2018, the parliament started working on a new motion to prevent sexual harassment and support victims.[76]

In France new legislation regarding sexual abuse including street harassment has been proposed by the gender equality minister Marlène Schiappa. Until now street harassment has had no legal definition making it difficult to file a police report or complaint about it. The bill will extend the deadline for reporting sexual assault and establish fines for public harassers. The law will also set an

---

[73] GOVERNMENT OFFICE OF SWEDEN, 'New sexual offence legislation based on consent', Press Release, 21.12.2017, available at https://www.government.se/press-releases/2017/12/new-sexual-offence-legislation-based-on-consent, last accessed 12.06.2018.

[74] J. HEARN (2018), 'You, Them, Us, We, too?', *supra* note 14, pp. 228–235; S. STRID, '#talkaboutit: Talking about Consent and Coercion', in S. WALBY, P. OLIVE and J. TOWERS et al. (eds.), *Stopping Rape*, Policy Press, Bristol 2015.

[75] P. FONTAINE, 'Iceland Unanimously Passes Landmark Law on Sexual Consent', *The Reykjavik Grapevine*, 23.03.2018, available at https://grapevine.is/news/2018/03/23/iceland-unanimously-passes-landmark-law-on-sexual-consent, last accessed 12.06.2018; ALTHINGI, 'Frumvarp til laga, um breytingu á almennum hegningarlögum, nr. 19/1940, með síðari breytingum (kynferðisbrot)', 148. Legislative Assembly 2017–2018, available at http://www.althingi.is/altext/148/s/0010.html, last accessed 12.06.2018.

[76] PARLAMENT REPUBLIK ÖSTERREICH, 'Parlamentskorrespondenz Nr. 183. Parlament: Clearingstelle für Fälle sexueller Belästigung und Machtmissbrauch nimmt Arbeit auf', 02.03.2018, available at https://www.parlament.gv.at/PAKT/PR/JAHR_2018/PK0183/index.shtml, last accessed 12.06.2018.

age – 15 – under which it will be presumed that the individual in question has not agreed to have sex with someone aged 18 or more. This change will facilitate rape prosecutions.[77] The bill was still to go through the parliamentary debate at the time of writing.

Canada is revising its Labour Code to enhance protections against workplace harassment and violence, including sexual harassment, in the federally-regulated workplaces.[78] The Bill C-65, tabled in November 2017, was at the Committee stage at the time of writing. If passed, it would require employers to investigate and report on any incidents brought to their attention. The government wants to couple the legislation with awareness-raising campaigns, education and training tools for employers and employees, as well as with a helpline for employers with questions regarding the introduction of anti-harassment policies in their workplaces.[79]

The United States have seen several legislative initiatives appear in the aftermath of #MeToo. Since November 2017, the Congress has worked on reforming the Congressional Accountability Act of 1995 so that the taxpayers would no longer pay for sexual harassment settlements involving members of Congress. Until now, any settlement payments were paid using federal taxes and it was reported that within a decade, $15 million of taxpayers' money had been spent settling harassment and discrimination complaints.[80] The reform also introduced more transparency compared to the old system, where complaints regarding the legislative branch required complete confidentially throughout the process. It also took months of counselling and mediation before a complaint could actually be filed. The new legislation would make the process quicker, more effective and give more rights to the victims. The bill would allow the victims to work away from the presence of the alleged harasser. For the first time, the same protections would also apply to unpaid workers, including fellows and interns. 'What we want to do is create – and I think we're seeing it already – a sea change

---

[77] ASSEMBLÉE NATIONALE 'Project de loi. Renforçant la lutte contre les violences sexuelles et sexists', 21.03.2018, available at http://www.assemblee-nationale.fr/15/projets/pl0778.asp, last accessed 12.06.2018.

[78] PARLIAMENT OF CANADA, 'Bill C-65', 2017, House of Commons of Canada, available at http://www.parl.ca/DocumentViewer/en/42-1/bill/C-65/first-reading, last accessed 12.06.2018.

[79] GOVERNMENT OF CANADA, 'Government of Canada takes strong action against harassment and sexual violence at work', News Release, 07.11.2018, available at https://www.canada.ca/en/employment-social-development/news/2017/11/government_of_canadatakesstrongactionagainstharassmentandsexualv.html, last accessed 12.06.2018.

[80] H.R. 4458: To amend the Congressional Accountability Act of 1995 to prohibit the use of public funds for the payment of a settlement or award under such Act in connection with a claim arising from sexual harassment committed by a Member of Congress, and for other purposes, available at https://www.govtrack.us/congress/bills/115/hr4458/text/ih, last accessed 12.06.2018; H.R. 4396: ME TOO Congress Act, 15.11.2017, available at https://www.govtrack.us/congress/bills/115/hr4396/summary, last accessed 12.06.2018.

in the culture in the members and the staff', said Gregg Harper, head of the House Administration Committee about the legislation's aim.[81] The bill passed the House in February 2018.

The US House of Representatives also approved a resolution amending the parliamentary Code of Conduct to specifically ban sexual relations between members of Congress and staffers they supervise. If the resolution passes, it would require each office to adopt an anti-harassment and anti-discrimination policy. It would also result in setting up the Office of Employee Advocacy to help staffers who complain about sexual harassment to navigate the process.[82]

In parallel, already in December 2017, a new US tax law disallowed a corporate tax deduction for any settlement, pay-out or attorney fees related to sexual harassment or sexual abuse if such payments are subject to a confidentiality agreement.[83]

Also on the State level there has been a visible push for new legislation in the midst of the #MeToo movement. A group of Michigan lawmakers came together in February 2017 aiming to pass new laws that will bolster the prevention and combat of sexual harassment and violence, especially on college campuses, increase funding for education programmes on the issue, better protect assault survivors and offer more accountability.[84] In the meantime, Oregon passed a gun control law which makes it harder for convicted domestic abusers to buy arms. Already since 1996, federal law has largely prohibited people with domestic abuse misdemeanours from accessing guns. Nonetheless, the new State bill closes a gap in the federal statute, by expanding the definition of domestic partner to also include 'intimate partner'. Under the new law in Oregon, a domestic abuse

---

[81] L.A. CALDWELL, 'House unveils landmark sexual harassment overhaul bill', *NBC News*, 18.01.2018, available at https://www.nbcnews.com/politics/congress/house-unveils-landmark-sexual-harassment-overhaul-bill-n838436, last accessed 12.06.2018.

[82] House Resolution 724, Resolution requiring each employing office of the House of Representatives to adopt an anti-harassment and anti-discrimination policy for the office's workplace, establishing the Office of Employee Advocacy to provide legal assistance and consultation to employees of the House regarding procedures and proceedings under the Congressional Accountability Act of 1995, and for other purposes, 02.02.2018, available at https://docs.house.gov/billsthisweek/20180205/HRES___.pdf, last accessed 12.06.2018.

[83] J. VEIT, '#MeToo: new tax law impacts the deduction of legal settlement amounts', 2018, *DLA PIPER*, available at https://www.dlapiper.com/en/belgium/insights/publications/2018/02/metoo-new-tax-law-impacts-the-deduction-of-legal-settlement-amounts, last accessed 12.06.2018.

[84] Senate Bill 871, Criminal procedure; statute of limitations; statute of limitations for certain criminal sexual conduct violations; modify. Amends sec. 24, ch. VII of 1927 PA 175 (MCL 767.24)., 27.02.2018, available at http://legislature.mi.gov/doc.aspx?2018-SB-0871, last accessed 12.06.2018; Senate Bill 0880, Criminal procedure; sentencing guidelines; penalty for not reporting child abuse; increase. Amends sec. 15g, ch. XVII of 1927 PA 175 (MCL 777.15g). TIE BAR WITH: SB 0874'18, 27.02.2018, available at http://legislature.mi.gov/doc.aspx?2018-SB-0880, last accessed 12.06.2018.

convict who only dated their victim cannot buy or own a gun. The gun ban extends to those under a restraining order or convicted of stalking.[85]

Finally, in the aftermath of #MeToo major changes on policy and practice levels occurred in the private sector all over the world. The extent of these transformations and actions would however require a separate thorough analysis which goes beyond of the scope of this article which focuses on #MeToo's impact on OSCE participating States and the organisation itself.

6. ISTANBUL CONVENTION

#MeToo has given strength to a renewed push for the ratification and implementation of the Council of Europe (CoE) Convention on preventing and combating violence against women and domestic violence (the so-called Istanbul Convention). The States that ratify the Convention must criminalise psychological violence, stalking, physical and sexual violence (including rape, which definition explicitly covers all engagement in non-consensual sexual acts). The Convention states that sexual harassment – not restricted in the treaty to the field of employment – must be subject to 'criminal or other legal sanction' (Latcheva 2017).

Even though the Convention stemming from 2011, has been signed by 46 CoE Member States plus the EU, it had only been ratified by 24 countries before the eruption of #MeToo. The long-awaited ratification by Germany finally took place on 12 October 2017 when the #MeToo movement was born. It was followed by the ratification by Estonia on 26 October 2017, Cyprus in November, Switzerland in December 2017 and the former Yugoslav Republic of Macedonia, which in March 2018 became the 29th State to ratify the document.[86]

However, there were also unsuccessful attempts to ratify the document in several other countries during the studied period. In February 2018, Bulgaria's ruling party withdrew the treaty from parliament in the face of opposition by its allies in the government and by religious groups.[87] Slovakia followed right after,

---

[85] M. SEVCENKO, '"Boyfriend loophole": backlash after Oregon joins 23 states in curbing guns', *The Guardian*, 21.03.2018, available at https://www.theguardian.com/us-news/2018/mar/21/oregon-boyfriend-loophole-bans-convicted-domestic-abusers-from-buying-guns, last accessed 12.06.2018.

[86] CoE, 'Chart of signatures and ratifications of Treaty 210', Status as of 12/06/2018, available at https://www.coe.int/en/web/conventions/full-list/-/conventions/treaty/210/signatures, last accessed 12.06.2018; also Iceland ratified the Convention in April 2018, after the first version of the article was handed in. CoE, '"The former Yugoslav Republic of Macedonia" ratifies the Istanbul Convention', *Newsroom*, 23.03.2018, available at https://www.coe.int/en/web/istanbul-convention/-/-the-former-yougoslav-republic-of-macedonia-ratifies-the-istanbul-convention, last accessed 12.06.2018.

[87] A. KRASIMIROV, 'Bulgaria rejects treaty to combat violence against women', *Reuters*, 15.02.2018, available at https://www.reuters.com/article/us-bulgaria-treaty/bulgaria-rejects-treaty-to-combat-violence-against-women-idUSKCN1FZ0FJ, last accessed 12.06.2018.

bowing to opposition from a junior coalition partner and religious groups.[88] At the time of writing, the Croatian government was urging the parliament to ratify the Istanbul Convention sparking street protests of conservative and religious groups.[89] In Ukraine, after years of debate and preparations, the Istanbul Convention was finally not ratified due to controversies sparked by the definition of gender included in the treaty, namely: "'gender" shall mean the socially constructed roles, behaviours, activities and attributes that a given society considers appropriate for women and men'.[90] In December 2017, the Ukrainian parliament passed a new law on domestic violence, which does not, however, mention the concept of 'gender'.

Moreover, with an impetus strengthened by the #MeToo momentum women's rights organisations in Hungary have been lobbying for ratification of the Convention already signed by the country in 2014 but encountered harsh criticism from the government.[91] All in all, the studied period has seen a sharp increase in the rhythm of ratification of the Istanbul Convention in the OSCE region.

7. CONCLUSION: CHALLENGES AND OPPORTUNITIES AHEAD

The #MeToo movement has been a reminder that women's rights are human rights in the very year of the 70th anniversary of the Universal Declaration of Human Rights (UDHR). And even though some researchers were quick to criticise #MeToo for 'a moralizing discourse'[92] and pushing women into the traditional role of victims,[93] this article argues that the movement has in fact empowered women to take possession of their narratives and experiences allowing them to

---

[88] 'Slovakia rejects treaty combating violence against women', *Reuters*, 22.02.2018, available at https://www.reuters.com/article/us-slovakia-treaty/slovakia-rejects-treaty-combating-violence-against-women-idUSKCN1G620F, last accessed 12.06.2018.

[89] 'Croatians protest against European treaty they say threatens traditional family', *Reuters*, 24.03.2018, available at https://www.reuters.com/article/us-croatia-protests/croatians-protest-against-european-treaty-they-say-threatens-traditional-family-idUSKBN1H00GW, last accessed 12.06.2018.

[90] CoE, 'Treaty 210: Council of Europe Convention on preventing and combating violence against women and domestic violence', Istanbul, 11.V.2011, available at https://www.coe.int/fr/web/conventions/full-list/-/conventions/rms/090000168008482e, last accessed 12.06.2018.

[91] S. DRAKULIĆ, '#MeToo East and West: A matter of history and conditioning', *Eurozine*, 26.01.2018, available at https://www.eurozine.com/where-to-for-metoo, last accessed 12.06.2018.

[92] D. ZARKOV and K. DAVIS (2018), 'Ambiguities and Dilemmas', *supra* note 7, pp. 3–9.

[93] Ibid., pp. 3–9.; L.Y. GARFIELD-TENZER, '#MeToo, Statutory Rape Laws and the Persistence of Gender Stereotypes', *SSRN Journal*, 08.02.2018, available at https://papers.ssrn.com/sol3/papers.cfm?abstract_id=3120348, last accessed 12.06.2018.

become agents of change. This agency – arising from publicly sharing one's story (where #MeToo provided a digital vehicle) – builds on the 'strength of mind and sense of self-possession'[94] needed to overcome the experience of sexual assault. The movement contributed thus to a gradual reduction of the stigma faced by the victims as a consequence of speaking up. This new agency of victims, combined with the extent of global solidarity generated by the campaign, led to a domino effect and turned single voices into a collective demand to believe the victims, to end sexual harassment and violence, and to transform gender power relations.

In that sense, the #MeToo campaign provides an ideal case to study how a digital social movement can give agency to the victims and impact the structural level. While many cases were still unfolding, and revelations were continuously coming up during the time of writing, the article has aimed at summarising the resonance of the movement in the OSCE region and the impact it has had until now. As demonstrated, #MeToo already has had long-lasting consequences with raising awareness levels regarding the prevalence of sexism and the effect it has on women's exercise of their rights; and a sharp increase in sexual abuse reporting levels in the United States, Germany, Netherlands and Switzerland. At the same time, the power structure is changing through women ascending into influential positions as illustrated, for example, by a historic number of women running for public office in the Unites States.

#MeToo now has also an opportunity to achieve a lasting structural impact through legislative initiatives born in the midst of the movement all across the OSCE area, with new sexual harassment legislation under way in France, Canada and Austria, new rape laws in Sweden and Iceland, a new law on domestic violence in Ukraine, as well as several proposed bills related to sexual harassment and abuse in the United States. Furthermore, the ratification rate of the Istanbul Convention has increased since the global rise of the #MeToo hashtag, with ratifications by Germany, Estonia, Cyprus, Switzerland and the former Yugoslav Republic of Macedonia. The challenge in this respect lies, nonetheless, in the implementation of the new (as well as the existing) legal instruments, as also noted by Hearn and Callerstig.[95] As shown in a recent report by Amnesty International, Poland, which ratified the Istanbul Convention in 2015, has still not made any progress in adapting Polish laws and public services for victims to international standards as required by the treaty.[96]

---

[94] D. Zarkov and K. Davis (2018), 'Ambiguities and Dilemmas', *supra* note 7, p. 4.
[95] J. Hearn (2018), 'You, Them, Us, We, too?', *supra* note 14, pp. 228–235; A.-C. Callerstig, *Making Equality Work: Conflict, Ambiguities and Change Actors in the Implementation of Equality Policies in Public Sector Organisations*, Doctoral Thesis, Linköping University Electronic Press, Sweden 2014.
[96] AMNESTY INTERNATIONAL POLAND, 'Polska: Bierność władz wobec przemocy wobec kobiet i przemocy domowej', 13.02.2018 available at https://amnesty.org.pl/polska-biernosc-wladz-wobec-przemocy-wobec-kobiet-i-przemocy-domowej, last accessed 12.06.2018.

#MeToo seems to be changing many societies to their core, while in others its impact is weaker or still to be assessed. For example, in Turkey, the Russian Federation and several Central Asian countries, #MeToo has had little influence on the public discourse on women's rights and the gendered relations of power so far, and virtually no impact on the legislative framework. Also, the aforementioned renewed push for the ratification of the Istanbul Convention has met – in several OSCE participating States – a backlash from conservative and religious groups. That is why the intended ratification of the convention did not take place in Bulgaria, Slovakia or Ukraine and is also very improbable in Hungary. The case of Hungary also exemplifies the danger of the movement being used in populist rhetoric to justify xenophobia and racism – a recurring topic in this volume. The Prime Minister Viktor Orbán has in fact suggested from the floor of the parliament that the best way to combat violence against women is by preventing migration.[97]

#MeToo will still have to pass the test of time 'offline' – articulating its policy and legislation demands. If this is not the case, the movement might miss its momentum and fail to translate the newly gained awareness into lasting structural change. In addition, the movement's long-term success will also depend on the movement's ability to further transform perceptions on women's human rights regardless of a woman's class, racial and religious background.[98] Data collected in the United States, for example, show that women of colour tend to face higher levels of harassment and abuse.[99] Yet, despite having its origin in a movement of women of colour, #MeToo has not really succeeded so far in turning the spotlight on their experiences of racialised sexual harassment.[100] The movement should also pay more attention to trafficked women and girls and prostitutes by questioning deep-rooted fallacies such as that 'a prostitute cannot be assaulted'. The reality paints a somewhat darker picture and shows that 'prostituted women have the highest rate of rape of any women on the planet. Sex buyers' behaviours are a model for sexual harassment and sexual predation. [...] Women in prostitution are seen as a legitimate target for men's violence'.[101]

---

[97] J. SPIKE, 'Orbán: preventing migration is the best way to combat violence against women', *The Budapest Beacon*, 28.11.2017, available at https://budapestbeacon.com/orban-preventing-migration-best-way-combat-violence-women, last accessed 12.06.2018.

[98] D. ZARKOV and K. DAVIS (2018), 'Ambiguities and Dilemmas', *supra* note 7, pp. 3–9.

[99] WOMEN OF COLOR NETWORK, 'Facts & Stats: Domestic Violence in Communities of Color', 06.2006, available at http://www.doj.state.or.us/wp-content/uploads/2017/08/women_of_color_network_facts_domestic_violence_2006.pdf, last accessed 12.06.2018.

[100] K. GISCOMBE, 'Sexual Harassment and Women of Colour', *Catalyst*, 13.02.2018, available at http://www.catalyst.org/blog/catalyzing/sexual-harassment-and-women-color, last accessed 12.06.2018.

[101] M. FARLEY, '#MeToo must Include Prostitution', (2018) 3(1) *Dignity: A Journal on Sexual Exploitation and Violence*, available at http://digitalcommons.uri.edu/cgi/viewcontent.cgi?article=1113&context=dignity, last accessed 12.06.2018.

Generally, we anticipate that the debate on sexual harassment and assault will soon move into a discursive mainstream thanks to #MeToo. At the current moment it is also safe to say that the unprecedented scope of the movement allowed the global society to get a snapshot of the state of women's right to freedom from violence. Further systematic data collection would help the movement itself in articulating its demands, as well as support researchers and decision-makers in getting this picture right in order to advance on the path of gender equality.

PART V
OTHERS

THE ROLE OF THE UKRAINIAN PARLIAMENT COMMISSIONER FOR HUMAN RIGHTS IN THE FIELD OF EQUALITY AND NON-DISCRIMINATION

Monika MAYRHOFER

1. Introduction 574
2. The Ukrainian Parliament Commissioner for Human Rights:
   A National Human Rights Institution 576
3. Legal Framework Regarding Equality and Anti-Discrimination
   in Ukraine 580
4. The Role of the Ukrainian Parliament Commissioner for Human
   Rights as an Equality Body 587
5. Critical Evaluation of the Work of the Commissioner in the Field
   of Equality and Anti-Discrimination. 595

ABSTRACT

The Ukrainian legal framework for the protection against discrimination has been considerably expanded over recent years. In the course of this process, the mandate of the Ukrainian Parliament Commissioner for Human Rights has also been extended. This body, which is accredited as an A-Status National Human Rights Institution, also fulfils the role of an equality body as required, for example, by European Union equality legislation. This article focuses on the role of the Ukrainian Parliament Commissioner for Human Rights with regard to the advancement of equality and anti-discrimination in Ukraine. In order to get a better understanding of the body, the article will start by giving a general introduction to the institution and briefly describe its mandate, competences and composition. The next section will briefly outline the national equality legislation in Ukraine as it provides the legal framework for the work of the Ukrainian Parliament Commissioner for Human Rights in this area. Subsequently, the role of the Commissioner as an equality body will be outlined and analysed. The article concludes with a short evaluation of the work of the Commissioner in the field of equality and anti-discrimination.

1. INTRODUCTION

Discrimination and different forms of inequality are a serious and systematic problem in Ukraine. Discrimination on grounds of gender,[1] sexual orientation and gender identity,[2] colour of skin and ethnic origin,[3] disability,[4] Human Immunodeficiency Virus (HIV) Status,[5] nationality and citizenship, language,[6] religious or other belief[7] and discrimination against internally displaced persons (IDPs)[8] are frequently reported to be of major concern. In order to address these issues, the Ukrainian legal and institutional framework for the protection against discrimination and the promotion of equality has been considerably improved and expanded in recent years. The adoption of the Law of Ukraine 'On Principles

---

[1] See for example, COMMITTEE ON THE ELIMINATION OF DISCRIMINATION AGAINST WOMEN (CEDAW), Concluding observations on the eighth periodic report, UN Doc. CEDAW/C/UKR/CO/8, 9.03.2017.

[2] See for example, NASH MIR CENTER, 'The Face of Hatred. Crimes and incidents motivated by homophobia and Transphobia in Ukraine in 2014–2017', Kiev 2018, available at http://gay.org.ua/en/blog/2018/02/12/the-face-of-hatred-crimes-and-incidents-motivated-by-homophobia-and-transphobia-in-ukraine-in-2014-2017-the-second-edition-corrected-and-enlarged/, last accessed 08.06.2018; INDEPENDENT ADVISORY GROUP ON COUNTRY INFORMATION, 'Country Policy and Information Note. Ukraine: Sexual orientation and gender identity', London 2017, available at https://assets.publishing.service.gov.uk/government/uploads/system/uploads/attachment_data/file/626236/Ukraine_-_SOGI_-_CPIN_-_v2_0__July_2017_.pdf, last accessed 08.06.2018.

[3] See for example, ECRI, Report on Ukraine (fifth monitoring cycle), CRI(2017)38, Strasbourg 2017; Уповноваженого Верховної Ради України з прав людини про стан дотримання прав і свобод людини і громадянина в Україні, ПРАВА ЛЮДИНИ, ЩОРІЧНА ДОПОВІДЬ, КИЇВ 2018, pp. 532–540.

[4] See, for example, COMMITTEE ON THE RIGHTS OF PERSONS WITH DISABILITIES, Concluding observations in relation to the initial report of Ukraine, UN Doc. CRPD/C/UKR/CO/1, 4 September 2015.

[5] See for example, I. Demchenko et al., 'The People Living with HIV Stigma Index', Kyiv 2014, available at http://www.stigmaindex.org/sites/default/files/reports/Ukraine%20Stigma%20Index_Report2014_ENG.pdf, last accessed 08.06.2018.

[6] See for example, Уповноваженого Верховної Ради України з прав людини про стан дотримання прав і свобод людини і громадянина в Україні, ПРАВА ЛЮДИНИ, ЩОРІЧНА ДОПОВІДЬ, КИЇВ 2018, pp. 532–540.

[7] See for example, ECRI (2017), Report on Ukraine, *supra* note 3; Уповноваженого Верховної Ради України з прав людини про стан дотримання прав і свобод людини і громадянина в Україні, ПРАВА ЛЮДИНИ, ЩОРІЧНА ДОПОВІДЬ, КИЇВ 2018, pp. 540–546.

[8] See for example, OSCE, 'Conflict-related Displacement in Ukraine: Increased Vulnerabilities of Affected Populations and Triggers of Tension within Communities', Special Monitoring Mission to Ukraine 2016, available at https://www.osce.org/ukraine-smm/261176, last accessed 08.06.2018. For an overview of the situation of discrimination against various grounds, see EQUAL RIGHTS TRUST, 'In the Crosscurrents. Addressing Discrimination and Inequality in Ukraine', London 2015, pp. 27–218, available at http://www.equalrightstrust.org/ertdocumentbank/In%20the%20Crosscurrents%20Addressing%20Discrimination%20and%20Inequality%20in%20Ukraine.pdf, last accessed 08.06.2018.

of Prevention and Combating Discrimination in Ukraine'[9] (hereinafter the Anti-Discrimination Act) in 2012 marked a big step towards aligning the Ukrainian legal framework with European and international equality and anti-discrimination standards. The process has been considerably influenced and propelled by international stakeholders – especially by the European Union (EU) – but also by non-governmental organisations (NGOs) that repeatedly voiced their concerns about prevalent forms of discrimination and pointed out protection gaps in the legal framework.

The Ukrainian Parliament Commissioner for Human Rights (hereinafter the Commissioner) plays an increasingly important role in this context. The Commissioner[10] was established in 1998 and accredited as a B-status National Human Rights Institution (NHRI) by the former International Coordinating Committee of National Institutions for the Promotion and Protection of Human Rights in 2008. Being upgraded to an A-status institution in 2009, the Commissioner is now a multi-mandated institution which also fulfils the role of an equality body as required, for example, by European equality law. This article will focus on the role of the Ukrainian Parliament Commissioner for Human Rights concerning the advancement of equality and anti-discrimination in Ukraine. In order to understand the functioning of the Commissioner as an institution the article will start with a general introduction of the Commissioner as a NHRI and shortly provide an overview of its general mandate, competences and composition. Although the Commissioner's mandate is mainly spelled out in a specific law, the Law of Ukraine 'On the Ukrainian Parliament Commissioner for Human Rights'[11] (hereinafter the Law on the Commissioner), the work of the body in the field of equality and anti-discrimination is significantly shaped by the general national legal framework that regulates the field of equality and anti-discrimination in Ukraine. Therefore, in section 3 the article will briefly outline the legal equality and anti-discrimination framework in Ukraine, its evolution over the years and will summarise its key points as well as its most problematic gaps and shortcomings. The subsequent section will concentrate on the role of the Commissioner as an equality body and delineate and analyse the most important tasks and competences of the Commissioner in this regard. The article will conclude with evaluating the work of the Commissioner in the field of equality and anti-discrimination. The findings of the article are based on an analysis of legal and policy documents as well as on publications

---

[9] For an English translation of the Act see http://www.twinning-ombudsman.org/wp-content/uploads/2017/03/LAW-OF-UKRAINE-on-prevention-and-combating-discrimination-in-Ukraine-amended.docx, last accessed on 08.06.2018.

[10] The Term 'Commissioner' refers to both the institution and the ombudsperson.

[11] For an English translation of the Act see http://www.twinning-ombudsman.org/wp-content/uploads/2017/03/EN_Law-of-Ukraine-on-the-Ukrainian-Parliament-Commissioner-for-Human-Rights.pdf, last accessed on 08.06.2018.

by academics and other stakeholders (such as international human rights bodies, reports of EU bodies and analytical reports by international civil society organisations) and on interviews conducted with representatives of the Commissioner.

2. THE UKRAINIAN PARLIAMENT COMMISSIONER FOR HUMAN RIGHTS: A NATIONAL HUMAN RIGHTS INSTITUTION

As mentioned above, the Ukrainian Parliament Commissioner for Human Rights is accredited as an A-Status NHRI by the Global Alliance of National Human Rights Institutions (GANHRI, the former International Coordinating Committee of NHRIs). This means it is fully compliant with the Paris Principles relating to the Status of National Institutions.[12] The Paris Principles lay down that NHRIs shall be endowed with 'the competence to promote and protect human rights' and they should 'be given as broad a mandate as possible, which shall be clearly set forth in a constitutional or legislative text'.[13] The Commissioner was established on basis of Articles 55, 85, 101 and 150 of the 1996 Constitution of Ukraine.[14] According to Article 101 of the Constitution, the Commissioner shall conduct 'parliamentary control over observance and protection of human and citizen's constitutional rights and freedoms' and submit annual reports on 'the state of affairs' in this field to the parliament (Article 85). The Constitution further lays down that everyone has the right to appeal for the protection of his or her rights to the Commissioner (Article 55). The Commissioner is also entitled to apply to the Constitutional Court of Ukraine in order to resolve issues of compliance with the Constitution of Ukraine concerning law and legal acts of the Parliament, acts of the President of Ukraine, acts of the Cabinet of Ministers and legal acts of the Verkhovna Rada of the Autonomous Republic of Crimea (Article 150).

The exact mandate as well as the organisation and composition of the Commissioner are laid down in the Law on the Commissioner that was passed on 23 December 1997 and entered into force on 15 January 1998. Article 3 defines the purposes of the parliamentary control exercised by the

---

[12] GANHRI, 'Chart of the Statues of National Institutions, accredited by the Global Alliance of National Human Rights Institutions, Accreditation status as of 21 February 2018', available at https://nhri.ohchr.org/EN/AboutUs/GANHRIAccreditation/Documents/Status%20 Accreditation%20Chart.pdf, last accessed 08.06.2018.
[13] UNGA, Principles relating to the Status of National Institutions (The Paris Principles), UN Doc. A/RES/48/134, 20.12.1993.
[14] For an English translation of the Constitution of Ukraine see https://rm.coe.int/constitution-of-ukraine/168071f58b, last accessed 08.06.2018.

Commissioner. These include the protection of human and citizens' rights and freedoms envisaged by the Constitution of Ukraine, the laws of Ukraine and international treaties of Ukraine, the observance of, respect for and prevention of violation of these rights and 'the facilitation of the process of bringing legislation of Ukraine on human and citizens' rights and freedoms in accordance with the Constitution of Ukraine and international standards in this area'. Additional fields of competence laid down in Article 3 are the improvement and further development of international cooperation in this area, the prevention of any form of discrimination in relation to the fulfilment of human rights and freedoms and 'the promotion of legal awareness of the population and protection of confidential information about a person'. In order to fulfil these purposes, the Commissioner is endowed with a broad range of powers,[15] including, for example, comprehensive competences concerning the carrying out of inquiries, inspections, observations, the obtaining of information and documents and the monitoring of compliance with human and citizen's rights or the power to appeal to the Constitutional Court of Ukraine and the right to make proposals for the improvement of legislation.

The Commissioner is an ombudsperson type of NHRI[16] with a principle mandate to deal with human rights and headed by a single person with several representatives. The ombudsperson is supported by a secretariat. An important competence of the Ukrainian Commissioner is to receive and consider appeals of citizens of Ukraine, foreigners, stateless persons or persons acting in their interests concerning the violation of their rights.[17] The work of the office of the Commissioner is to a large extent committed to receiving and processing individual appeals. Some 80% of the work is dedicated to reacting to these appeals and only 20% is available for doing pro-active work which would also be an important part of the mandate of the Commissioner.[18] In 2015, the Commissioner received and reviewed about 19,000 appeals associated with more

---

[15] See Law of Ukraine on the Ukrainian Parliament Commissioner for Human Rights, Articles 13–19.

[16] The OHCHR differentiates between six different models of NHRIs: human rights commissions, human rights ombudsman institutions, hybrid institutions, consultative and advisory bodies, institutes and centres and multiple institutions, see OHCHR, *National Human Rights Institutions. History, Principles, Roles and Responsibilities*, United Nations Publications, New York and Geneva 2010, pp. 16–19. The European Union Agency for Fundamental Rights (FRA) mentions three different types of NHRIs: commissions, ombudsman institutions and institutions, see FRA, *National Human Rights Institutions in the EU Member States. Strengthening the Fundamental Rights Architecture in the EU*, Publication Office of the European Union, Luxembourg 2010, pp. 26–28. See also M. NOWAK, 'National Human Rights Institutions in Europe: Comparative, European and International Perspectives', in J. WOUTERS and K. MEUWISSEN (eds.), *National Human Rights Institution in Europe, Comparative, European and International Perspectives*, Intersentia, Antwerp 2013, pp. 15–16.

[17] See Law of Ukraine on the Ukrainian Parliament Commissioner for Human Rights, Article 17.

[18] Interview with representatives of the staff of the Commissioner in February 2017.

than 48,000 human rights violations. About 94% of complaints were submitted by citizens of Ukraine, foreigners, stateless persons or their representatives, 5% by legal entities, 1% by People's Deputies of Ukraine and less than 1% were initiated by the Commissioner. The appeals concerned violations of civil (55%), personal (14%) and social (14%) rights.[19]

As laid down in Article 85 of the Constitution of Ukraine and in Chapter II of the Law on the Commissioner, the Verkhovna Rada (the Ukrainian Parliament) is entitled to appoint and remove the Commissioner. Articles 5–9 of the Law on the Commissioner contain detailed stipulations on the appointment of the Commissioner, including the requirements for the potential candidates for the post, the term of office, the procedure for nominating the candidates, criteria concerning incompatibilities, termination of authority and dismissal of the Commissioner from the post. The first office holder, Nina Karpachova, was elected by the Ukrainian Parliament on 14 April 1998. She was succeeded by Valeriya Lutkovska on 27 April 2012. On 15 March 2018, the Ukrainian Parliament voted for Lyudmyla Denisova, a former Member of Parliament and member of the Ukrainian right-wing party People's Front, to be appointed as the third Commissioner. The appointment of the latter attracted much criticism not only because it was a lengthy process and, thus, exceeded the timeframe laid down by Article 6 of the Law on the Commissioner. It also raised questions concerning specific details of the nomination and voting process. In particular, with regard to using either secret ballot votes, which is envisaged by the Law on the Commissioner, or open votes, which is suggested by the Law of Ukraine 'On Constitutional Court of Ukraine'[20] which amended Article 208 of the Parliament's Rule and Procedures in 2017, the Verkhovna Rada was divided on which law to apply. Although the Law on the Commissioner was not amended, the parliament decided to use an open vote.[21] The decision as well as the process was criticised by human rights activists and international human rights organisations.[22] For example, in May 2017, the European

---

[19] B. LIEGL et al., 'Analysis and Assessment of the Efficiency of Activities of the Ombudsperson on Elimination of Detected Human Rights Violations, Control Procedures over Fulfilment of Ombudsperson's Recommendations, Response to the Ombudsperson's Acts of Submission to the State and Local Self-Government Bodies, their Officials, on Elimination of Detected Human Rights Violations, Activity 2.2.1. Mission Report', Kiev 2017, available at http://www.twinning-ombudsman.org/wp-content/uploads/2017/03/EN_Mission-Report-2.2.1.-14.12.2017.pdf, last accessed 26.03.2018.

[20] Excerpt from the Law of Ukraine 'On Constitutional Court of Ukraine', available at http://www.twinning-ombudsman.org/wp-content/uploads/2017/03/EN_Law-of-Ukraine-On-Constitutional-Court-of-Ukraine.pdf, last accessed on 08.06.2018.

[21] For a detailed analysis, see A. LOVIN, 'Ukraine's Political Maneuvering: Parliament does not Appoint an Ombudsman', (2017) 3 *DRI Legal News*, available at http://democracy-reporting.org/stuck-in-the-quicksand-of-ukraines-political-maneuvering-parliament-does-not-appoint-an-ombudsman, last accessed 08.06.2018.

[22] See ibid.; see also, H. COYNASH, 'Political Shenanigans to the End: Ukraine's Parliament elects their own MP as "Human Rights Ombudsman"', *Human Rights in Ukraine*, Information

Network of National Human Rights Institutions (ENNHRI) wrote a letter to the Chair of the Parliament and the Minister of Foreign Affairs of Ukraine and urged the addressees 'to ensure broad consultation and participation of civil society representatives throughout the selection and appointment process of the Commissioner for Human Rights'[23] and warned against risking the independence of the Commissioner and the possibility of downgrading the accreditation status of the Commissioner by the GANHRI's Sub-Committee on Accreditation. The Ukrainian Helsinki Human Rights Union appealed to the Ukrainian President 'to stop manipulation with the Parliament's voting regarding the procedure for the election of the Human Rights Ombudsperson'.[24] The parliament, however, did not heed these interventions and followed through with this highly controversial process. In order to comply with the stipulations defined by Article 8 of the Law on the Commissioner, which lays down that the post of a Commissioner is incompatible with being a member of a political party or having a representative mandate, the new Commissioner, Ms. Lyudmyla Denisova, terminated her party membership.

Under the second Commissioner, an advisory board was established in 2012. The main reason for setting up the advisory board[25] was to improve transparency and independence of the Commissioner and her office. The first Ombudsperson and her office was regarded as a politicised institution and had a problematic reputation among civil society organisations (CSOs).[26] In order to address these problems, public discussions with CSOs and human rights defenders were started and broadcast on the internet. Furthermore, the office invited Evgen Zakharov – a widely esteemed human rights defender – to be the head of a working group entrusted with the task to specify criteria for the formation, activities and the rights and duties of the members of the advisory board. The Statute of the advisory board was signed by the Commissioner in

---

Website of the Kharkiv Human Rights Protection Group, 15.03.2018, available at http://khpg.org/en/index.php?id=1521149517, last accessed 08.06.2018.

[23] See ENNHRI letter to Mr. Andriy Parubiy, Chair of the Parliament of Ukraine, 08.05.2017, available at http://ennhri.org/IMG/pdf/ennhri_ltr_chair_of_parliament_ukraine.pdf, last accessed 08.06.2018 and ENNHRI letter to Mr. Pavlo Klimkin, Minister of Foreign Affairs of Ukraine, 8 May 2017, available at http://ennhri.org/IMG/pdf/ennhri_ltr_mfa_ukraine.pdf, last accessed 08.06.2018.

[24] UKRAINIAN HELSINKI HUMAN RIGHTS UNION, 'Statement to the President of Ukraine concerning manipulations with the Parliament's voting concerning the procedure for the election of the Ukrainian Parliament Commissioner for Human Rights', 21.07.2017, available at https://helsinki.org.ua/en/appeals/statement-to-the-president-of-ukraine-concerning-manipulations-with-the-parliament-s-voting-concerning-the-procedure-for-the-election-of-the-ukrainian-parliament-commissioner-for-human-rights, last accessed 08.06.2018.

[25] Although the Law on the Commissioner allows for the establishment of an advisory board, the institutionalisation of such a body is not obligatory.

[26] Interview with representatives of the staff of the Commissioner in February 2017.

July 2012. Based on the Statute, six thematic expert groups were introduced. The advisory board provides for external monitoring of the work of the Commissioner and her office by independent human rights defenders.[27] The latter demonstrates that Valeriya Lutkovska, the second Commissioner, has put much work in building trustworthy relationships with civil society organisations. It is yet unclear, what damage the problematic appointment process of the third Commissioner has caused to these relationships.[28]

The Law on the Commissioner further regulates the organisation of the activity of the Commissioner in Chapter III. Article 11 of this chapter provides the Commissioner with the right to appoint representatives. Currently, the Commissioner has seven representatives in different thematic areas, including a representative responsible for children's rights, non-discrimination and gender equality. However, due to an ongoing reorganisation of the office in the wake of appointing a new Commissioner the competences and composition of the office are to be restructured.[29]

3. LEGAL FRAMEWORK REGARDING EQUALITY AND ANTI-DISCRIMINATION IN UKRAINE

The work of the Commissioner in the field of equality and anti-discrimination is not only determined by the Law on the Commissioner, it is also strongly shaped by the international and national equality legislation. On the one hand, this legislation defines the legal foundation of the work of the Commissioner in this thematic field and, thus, also determines limitations of the Commissioner's work in this area. On the other hand, it also empowers the Commissioner as – in addition to the Law on the Commissioner – it lays down further competences of the institution in this field and allows for the Commissioner to influence and improve the national legal framework. Thus, it is important to have a closer look at this legal context before moving on to the exact role and competences of the Commissioner as an equality body in the next section.

The Ukrainian legal and policy framework on equality and anti-discrimination is multi-layered and extensive. Ukraine is State party to all

---

[27] Statute of the Advisory Board as of 14 March 2014 (in Ukrainian), available at http://www.ombudsman.gov.ua/ua/page/secretariat/docs/dokumenti/171214-jd-polozhennya-pro-konsultativnu-radu-pri-upovnovazhenomu-verxovnojii-rad.html, last accessed 08.06.2018.
[28] See for example, H. COYNASH (2018), 'Political Shenanigans to the End: Ukraine's Parliament elects their own MP as "Human Rights Ombudsman"', 'Human Rights in Ukraine', *supra* note 22.
[29] According to information obtained during interviews with representatives of the staff of the Commissioner in May 2018, the thematic fields of children's rights on the one hand and non-discrimination and gender equality on the other hand will be separated in two units and headed by two representatives.

major UN human rights treaties, including those focusing on equality and non-discrimination such as the Convention on the Elimination of All Forms of Racial Discrimination (CERD), the Convention on the Elimination of All Forms of Discrimination against Women (CEDAW) or the Convention on the Rights of Persons with Disabilities (CRPD). In addition, Ukraine has ratified or acceded to important regional human rights instruments such as the European Convention on Human Rights and Fundamental Freedoms, the European Social Charter, the European Charter for Regional or Minority Languages, the Framework Convention for the Protection of National Minorities and the European Convention on Nationality.

On a national level, the Ukrainian legal and policy framework relevant for equality and anti-discrimination has been significantly extended over the past years. The process was considerably influenced by the EU-Ukraine Visa Dialogue, which started in October 2008 and led to the adoption of the Action Plan on Visa Liberalisation (VLAP) on 22 November 2010. Block four of the VLAP with the heading 'External relations and fundamental rights' envisages the adoption and implementation of comprehensive anti-discrimination legislation and policies in order to comply with international and European human rights standards. It also lays down the implementation of an Action Plan to fight against discrimination as well as the launching of general awareness-raising campaigns against racism, xenophobia, anti-Semitism and other forms of discrimination, and the strengthening of competent bodies for anti-discrimination policies and for combating racism, xenophobia and anti-Semitism. In addition, it stipulates the provision of specific training to law enforcement officials, prosecutors and judges potentially involved in the prosecution of hate crimes.[30] Furthermore, the Association Agreement between the EU and Ukraine that fully entered into force on 1 September 2017 requires Ukraine to adjust its anti-discrimination and equality legislation to EU legislation within three to four years.[31] The negotiation process for the conclusion of this agreement started more than ten years earlier and was concluded in 2012. Political upheavals in Ukraine and problems with ratification in EU Member States hampered the full implementation of the Agreement. However, most parts of the Agreement have already been provisionally applied since 1 September 2014.[32]

---

[30] COUNCIL OF THE EUROPEAN UNION, EU-Ukraine Visa Dialogue – Action Plan on Visa Liberalisation, 17883/10 (2010), available at http://data.consilium.europa.eu/doc/document/ST-17883-2010-INIT/en/pdf, last accessed 12.06.2018.

[31] PUBLICATIONS OFFICE OF THE EUROPEAN UNION, Association Agreement between the European Union and its Member States, of the one part, and Ukraine, of the other part, Annex XL to Chapter 21, OJ L 161/3, 29.05.2014.

[32] See EUROPEAN COUNCIL/COUNCIL OF THE EUROPEAN UNION, 'Ukraine: Council adopts EU-Ukraine association agreement', Press Release, 11.07.2017, available at http://www.consilium.europa.eu/en/press/press-releases/2017/07/11/ukraine-association-agreement, last accessed 08.06.2018.

The 1996 Constitution of Ukraine contains several articles on equality and non-discrimination. The most important provision is Article 24, that says that there 'shall be no privileges or restrictions based on race, color of skin, political, religious and other beliefs, sex, ethnic and social origin, property status, place of residence, linguistic or other characteristics.' The third paragraph of this article focuses on equal opportunities and specific measures to be carried out by the State to promote equality:

> Equality of the rights of women and men shall be ensured by providing women with opportunities equal to those of men in public, political and cultural activities, in obtaining education and in professional training, in work and remuneration for it; by taking special measures for the protection of women's health and occupational safety; by establishing pension benefits; by creating conditions that make it possible for women to combine work and motherhood; by adopting legal protection, material and moral support of motherhood and childhood, including the provision of paid leave and other privileges to pregnant women and mothers.

The Equal Rights Trust pointed out that all five special measures (also understood as positive action) listed in this paragraph are problematic, because, firstly, the formulation of 'providing women with opportunities equal to those of men' is not laid down to be a requirement. However, international human rights law requires States to take such positive measures in order to improve equality. Secondly, some measures suggested by this constitutional provision contain discriminatory formulations, for example, the proposal of special measures for protecting women's health and occupational safety suggests that women per se 'have [...] particular occupational safety requirements that men do not have, or vice versa'.[33] Thirdly, the paragraph contains stereotypical and other problematic notions, for example, the exclusive focus on motherhood suggests that it is first and foremost women who are responsible for the upbringing of children and that men do not have difficulties in combining parenthood and work or that specific measures with regard to pregnancy are 'privileges'.

The problematic and potentially discriminatory wording of Article 24 of the Ukrainian Constitution has serious consequences when policy and legal measures proposing special measures are reviewed if they are in line with the provisions of the Constitution as required by the Anti-Discrimination Act. That means, that 'provisions of legislation which would otherwise be considered as discriminatory on the basis of sex have been considered unproblematic, in part because they are arguably measures which fall within the third paragraph of Article 24'.[34] An additional shortcoming of Article 24 of the Constitution

---

[33] EQUAL RIGHTS TRUST (2015), 'In the Crosscurrents', *supra* note 8, p. 241.
[34] Ibid., p. 242.

is the limitation of 'special measures' to promote equality on the grounds of gender. Other characteristics, as would be required by international human rights law, are not covered by this paragraph on providing positive action.

Concerning ordinary legislation, the two central laws are the Law of Ukraine 'On Principles of Prevention and Combating Discrimination in Ukraine', mentioned above, and the Law of Ukraine 'On Equal Rights and Opportunities for Women and Men'[35] (hereinafter the Gender Equality Act). The Anti-Discrimination Act entered into force on 7 September 2012 for the purpose of complying with one of the requirements laid down by the EU-Ukraine VLAP. The Act was criticised because of a number of gaps, flaws and non-compliances with European and international standards and, as a consequence, was considerably amended in May 2014. Although the amended law provides for a very comprehensive protection against discrimination, some problems concerning non-compliance with EU standards remain, such as the lack of providing for measures to protect individuals from victimisation or not including multiple discrimination and discrimination by association in the law. Draft Law No. 3501 'On amendments to certain legislative acts of Ukraine (regarding the harmonization of the legislation in the sphere of prevention and combating discrimination with the European Union law)'[36] of 20 November 2015 would remedy some of these issues, although, the proposal has not been adopted by the Verkhovna Rada so far. The current valid version of the Anti-Discrimination Act lists five forms of discrimination in Article 5, including direct discrimination, indirect discrimination, incitement to discrimination, assistance in discrimination and harassment. The scope of the law is laid down in Article 4 and covers 'relations between the legal entities of public and private law, which are registered at the territory of Ukraine, as well as persons who are on the territory of Ukraine'. According to this provision the law applies to areas of public relations such as social and political activities, public service and services provided by bodies of local self-government, justice, labour relations including the application of the principle of reasonable accommodation by the employer, health protection, education, social protection, housing, access to goods and services, and other areas of public relations. The Ukrainian Anti-Discrimination Act contains an open list of discrimination grounds. In Article 1(2) several grounds are explicitly mentioned including race, colour of skin, political, religious and other beliefs, sex, age, disability, ethnic or social

---

[35] For an English translation of the law see http://www.twinning-ombudsman.org/wp-content/uploads/2017/03/EN_Law-of-Ukraine-On-Ensuring-Equal-Rights-of-Women-and-Men.pdf, last accessed on 08.06.2018.

[36] I. GERASCHENKO, I. KLYMPUSH-TSINTSADZE, M. IONOV et al., 'The Law of Ukraine, introduced by people's deputies of Ukraine' (draft), 2017, available at http://www.twinning-ombudsman.org/wp-content/uploads/2017/03/DRAFT-LAW-3501_On-harmonization-of-legislation-in-the-sphehere-of-prevention-and-combating-discrimination.docx, last accessed on 08.06.2018.

origin, nationality, family and property status, place of residence and language. The list is concluded with the formulation 'and other traits' which makes it possible for individuals to claim their rights in case they are discriminated on the basis of other grounds. Although different national and international stakeholders repeatedly demanded the explicit inclusion of sexual orientation and gender identity in the law, these grounds are not mentioned in the law.[37] However, the Highest Specialised Court of Ukraine on Civil and Criminal Cases has issued a ruling that confirms that sexual orientation is implicitly included in existing legislation.[38] Yet, this statement is not binding on other courts.[39] The 2015 amendment of the Labour Code of Ukraine prohibits discrimination at the workplace and explicitly refers to a broader list than the Anti-Discrimination Act. The grounds of sexual orientation and gender identity were explicitly included in this Act in order to comply with the requirements of the VLAP.[40]

The Law of Ukraine 'On Equal Rights and Opportunities for Women and Men' was adopted by the Ukrainian Parliament in 2005 and entered into force on 1 January 2006. The law was criticised for several reasons, including the failure to define different forms of discriminations. Compared to the Anti-Discrimination Act, the Gender Equality Act is a much less comprehensive text and the duality of texts with differences in scope and definitions has attracted criticism.[41] For example, the CEDAW Committee voiced its concern that the difference in the definition of discrimination 'results in a contradictory interpretation of the term discrimination at the practical level'.[42] Yet, it has also been pointed out that some of the provisions of the Gender Equality Act 'have no equivalent in the broader anti-discrimination law, such as the requirement to carry out gender-based assessment of legislation, and thus retain their utility'.[43] Besides these two main pieces of legislation, there are a range of other laws that are relevant in the area of equality and non-discrimination, for example, the Law of Ukraine 'On the Fundamentals of Social Protection of Disabled

---

[37] See I. GERASCHENKO, I. KLYMPUSH-TSINTSADZE, M. IONOV et al. (2017), 'The Law of Ukraine, introduced by people's deputies of Ukraine', *supra* note 36, pp. 61–87.
[38] EUROPEAN COMMISSION/HIGH REPRESENTATIVE OF THE EUROPEAN UNION FOR FOREIGN AND SECURITY POLICY, Implementation of the European Neighbourhood Policy in Ukraine Progress in 2014 and recommendations for actions, Joint Staff Working Document, SWD(2015) 74 final, Brussels, 25.03.2015, p. 8.
[39] EQUAL RIGHTS TRUST (2015), 'In the Crosscurrents', *supra* note 8, p. 265.
[40] I. FEDOROVYCH, 'Equal Employment Opportunities in Ukraine – Is There Still Discrimination and How Should We Tackle it?', Policy Brief, International Renaissance Foundation/Open Society Foundations, Kyiv 2016a, p. 3, available at http://rpr.org.ua/wp-content/uploads/2017/02/Renaissance_A4_2Equal-employment.pdf, last accessed 08.06.2018.
[41] See J. PAUŽAITĖ-KULVINSKIENĖ et al., 'Analytical Report on the Existing Regulatory and Legal Framework Governing the Activities of the Ombudsperson', Kiev 2017, available at http://www.twinning-ombudsman.org/wp-content/uploads/2017/03/EN_Mission-report-1.1-Consolidated-2.pdf, accessed 08.06.2018.
[42] CEDAW (2017), Concluding observations, *supra* note 1, para. 20.
[43] EQUAL RIGHTS TRUST (2015), 'In the Crosscurrents', *supra* note 8, pp. 272–273.

Persons in Ukraine', the Law of Ukraine 'On National Minorities in Ukraine', the Law of Ukraine 'On Freedom of Conscience and Religious Organizations' and specific provisions included in other legal fields such as Criminal Law, Family Law, Employment Law or Immigration Law. Ukraine has also reacted to wide-spread discrimination against IDPs and inserted a non-discrimination clause (Article 14) into the Law of Ukraine 'On ensuring of rights and freedoms of internally displaced persons'.

Ukraine has also adopted a National Human Rights Strategy and as required by the VLAP an Action Plan to be implemented by 2020. The strategic areas relating to discrimination and equality are under the headings 'Preventing and combating discrimination', 'Ensuring equal rights for women and men' and 'Ensuring the rights of national minorities and indigenous peoples'. Envisaged outcomes in the section on preventing and combating discrimination include, for example, a comprehensive and consistent legislation in this area, awareness-raising programmes, access to efficient legal protection from discrimination, appropriate and timely positive actions and the commitment to effectively investigate crimes motivated for reasons of racial, national, religious and other intolerance and hold the perpetrators accountable. Concerning gender equality, the Strategy expects outcomes ranging from transposing international standards to implementing comprehensive measures to combat gender discrimination including gender stereotypes. The section on the rights of national minorities and indigenous peoples intends, for example, to establish an effective mechanism to protect the rights of and ensure equal participation of representatives of national minorities and indigenous peoples.[44] Although, the National Human Rights Strategy and the corresponding Action Plan are ambitious policy programmes, their implementation is problematic in practice. The Commissioner pointed out in its 2018 Annual Report that the main objectives spelled out in the section on 'Preventing and combating discrimination' remain unfulfilled.[45] Also civil society actors report 'slow and uneven progress' concerning the implementation process:

> Some tasks are not accomplished due to lack of coordination and cooperation among ministries, some are openly ignored by the authorities, and others cannot be accomplished due to ignorance from the side of the Parliament. [...] Another concern about successful implementation of the Action Plan is its lack of backing from the State Budget. [...] Many activities are run by the CSOs with the help of international

---

[44] DECREE OF THE PRESIDENT OF UKRAINE #501/2015 on Approval of the National Human Rights Strategy of Ukraine of 25 August 2015, translated by UN OHCHR in Ukraine, pp. 8–11.

[45] Уповноваженого Верховної Ради України з прав людини про стан дотримання прав і свобод людини і громадянина в Україні, *ПРАВА ЛЮДИНИ*, ЩОРІЧНА ДОПОВІДЬ, КИЇВ 2018, p. 515.

donors. For example, awareness-raising campaigns on gender equality and prohibition of discrimination are run by the CSO with support of the National Equality Body and financing from international donors. The State does not provide intellectual expertise, social advertisement quotas or any other resources to support such work, despite the fact that informational and educational campaigns are one of the tasks in the Action Plan.[46]

To briefly sum up: Although the Ukrainian legal framework concerning equality and anti-discrimination has been significantly extended over past years and provides for comprehensive protection against discrimination, there are also several shortcomings, the most important of which are: firstly, the different legal texts with different scopes, definitions and grounds of discrimination create 'a lack of legal certainty and consistency'.[47] In addition, some legal texts, for example the Constitution but also other legislation, still contain discriminatory provisions, especially in the area of gender equality, and thus are in conflict with international human rights obligations.[48] Secondly, the implementation and enforcement of anti-discrimination laws are poor. The legal framework has 'not yet translated into a significant reduction in discrimination in practices'.[49] In addition, redress procedures are not very effective as the law 'does not provide for easily accessible judicial and/or administrative proceedings'.[50] Thirdly, Ukraine's anti-discrimination policies lack an effective pro-active approach. Although the instrument of positive action is laid down in several acts and the Constitution, the law does not require the State to take positive action but merely permits it.[51] In addition, although positive action programmes, plans and initiatives have been launched in the past (for example, the National Human Rights Strategy and the corresponding Action Plan or specific gender action plans) there is a 'lack of implementation in practice'.[52] As the Commissioner

---

[46] I. FEDOROVYCH, 'Anti-Discrimination Legislation in Ukraine – Box Ticking for the EU or Real Reforms to Ensure Equality for Ukraine's Citizens?', International Renaissance Foundation/Open Society Foundations, Kiev 2016b, p. 5, available at http://rpr.org.ua/wp-content/uploads/2017/02/Renaissance_A4_1Discrimination.pdf, last accessed 08.06.2018.
[47] Ibid., p. 1.
[48] EQUAL RIGHTS TRUST, 'Shadow Report submitted to the 66th Session of the Committee on the Elimination of All Forms of Discrimination against Women in Relation to the eighth Periodic Report of Ukraine', London 2017, available at http://tbinternet.ohchr.org/Treaties/CEDAW/Shared%20Documents/UKR/INT_CEDAW_NGO_UKR_26372_E.pdf, last accessed 11.06.2018.
[49] EQUAL RIGHTS TRUST (2015), 'In the Crosscurrents', supra note 8, p. XVII.
[50] ECRI (2017), Report on Ukraine, supra note 3, p. 13.
[51] EQUAL RIGHTS TRUST (2015), 'In the Crosscurrents', supra note 8, p. 275.
[52] CEDAW (2017), Concluding observations, supra note 1, para. 25; see also I. FEDOROVYCH (2016a), 'Equal Employment Opportunities in Ukraine', supra note 40 and I. FEDOROVYCH (2016b), 'Anti-Discrimination Legislation in Ukraine', supra note 46; EQUAL RIGHTS TRUST (2015), 'In the Crosscurrents', supra note 8.

highlights with regard to gender action plans, the 'activities are not adequate [sic!] funded and are of declarative nature rather than result-based'.[53]

4. THE ROLE OF THE UKRAINIAN PARLIAMENT COMMISSIONER FOR HUMAN RIGHTS AS AN EQUALITY BODY

Over the last years, the Commissioner has developed and established mechanisms and competences in order to fulfil the role of an equality body. This process was influenced by several international and European developments which will be briefly discussed here. Equality institutions were initially established in the United States in the context of civil rights legislation in the 1960s. They then experienced a 'chain of legal transfers'[54] starting in the US and moving eventually to all parts of Europe. EU equality legislation played a crucial role in this process. It obliges Member States and States with specific agreements with the EU to set up judicial and/or administrative procedures that allow individuals to enforce their rights under the so-called equality directives.[55] In order to comply with its obligation under the VLAP and especially the EU-Ukraine Association Agreement, Ukraine also had to establish an equality body that complies with EU law. The Racial Equality Directive (2000/43/EC) and the Gender Equality Directives (2006/54/EC recast and 2004/113/EC) explicitly provide for the setting up of bodies for the

---

[53] UKRAINIAN PARLIAMENT COMMISSIONER FOR HUMAN RIGHTS, 'Shadow Report (Submission) on Implementation of the Convention on the Elimination of all Forms of Discrimination against Women by Ukraine', Ukraine 2017a, p. 4, available at https://www.ecoi.net/en/file/local/1408348/1930_1497437078_int-cedaw-ifn-ukr-26216-e.pdf, last accessed 11.06.2018.

[54] B. DE WITTE, 'New Institutions for Promoting Equality in Europe: Legal Transfers, National Bricolage and European Governance', (2012) 60(49) *The American Journal of Comparative Law*, pp. 51–53.

[55] See Council Directive 2000/78/EC of 27 November 2000 establishing a general framework for equal treatment in employment and occupation (Employment Equality Directive), Art. 9(1); Directive 2006/54/EC of the European Parliament and of the Council of 5 July 2006 on the implementation of the principle of equal opportunities and equal treatment of men and women in matters of employment and occupation (recast) (Gender Equality Directive) (2006/54/EC) recast, Art. 17(1); Council Directive 2004/113/EC of 13 December 2004 implementing the principle of equal treatment between men and women in the access to and supply of goods and services (Gender Goods and Services Directive), Art. 8(1); Council Directive 2000/43/EC of 29 June 2000 implementing the principle of equal treatment between persons irrespective of racial or ethnic origin (Racial Equality Directive), Art. 7(1).

promotion of equal treatment with almost identical clauses. For example, the Racial Equality Directive (2000/43/EC) lays down in Article 13(2) that:

> Member States shall ensure that the competences of these bodies include:
>
> - […] providing independent assistance to victims of discrimination in pursuing their complaints about discrimination,
> - conducting independent surveys concerning discrimination,
> - publishing independent reports and making recommendations on any issue relating to such discrimination.

Only the Gender Equality Directive on Employment (2006/54/EC recast) contains a further stipulation enabling these bodies to exchange available information with corresponding European bodies such as the European Institute for Gender Equality. Subsequently, so-called equality bodies were established in all EU Member States and beyond. As the provisions on setting up equality bodies in the respective directives are rather vague – the three functions are 'only mentioned and not defined',[56] there is a broad variety concerning the histories, structures and exact mandate of equality bodies. Some of them are predominantly tribunal-type equality bodies, which means they are 'impartial institutions which spend the bulk of their time and resources hearing, investigating and deciding on individual instances of discrimination brought before them'.[57] Others are predominantly promotion-type equality bodies that have their focus on a wider range of activities including the enhancement of good practice in organisations, raising awareness concerning rights, developing a knowledge base on equality and anti-discrimination and providing legal advice and assistance to victims of discrimination.[58]

The proliferation of equality bodies all over Europe was preceded by a number of other important developments, *inter alia*, the 'Europe-wide diffusion of the Nordic ombudsman tradition' and 'the international movement for the creation of human rights institutions'.[59] This provided favourable conditions for the establishment of equality bodies as it 'helped to diffuse the view that the effectiveness of fundamental rights may be hampered by individuals'

---

[56] B. DE WITTE (2012), 'New Institutions for Promoting Equality in Europe: Legal Transfers, National Bricolage and European Governance', *supra* note 54, p. 66.

[57] M. AMMER, N. CROWLEY, B. LIEGL, E. HOLZLEITHNER, K. WLADASCH and K. YESILKAGIT, 'Study on Equality Bodies set up under Directives 2000/43/EC, 2004/113/EC and 2006/54/EC', Human European Consultancy in partnership with the Ludwig Boltzmann Institute of Human Rights, Utrecht/Vienna 2010, available at https://publications.europa.eu/en/publication-detail/-/publication/815d7d06-c009-4208-89d7-c6edcdc0cc5b/language-en, last accessed 08.06.2018, p. 43.

[58] Ibid., p. 44.

[59] B. DE WITTE (2012), 'New Institutions for Promoting Equality in Europe: Legal Transfers, National Bricolage and European Governance', *supra* note 54, p. 54.

inability to invoke them in court'.[60] However, it also contributed to increase the diversity of equality bodies in terms of mandate and structure. Some equality bodies are institutions of their own, others are merged with either NHRIs or ombudsperson's institutions or both.[61] Indeed, some authors see a tendency towards integrating equality bodies into NHRIs which usually have a much broader mandate than equality bodies.[62] The respective equality directives explicitly allow for such a merging of institutions as they lay down, for example, in Article 13(1) of the Racial Equality Directive that equality bodies 'may form part of agencies charged at national level with the defence of human rights or the safeguard of individuals' rights'. These merged institutions mostly constitute a third type of equality body. They are 'a combination of tribunal-type and promotion-type bodies. They hear, investigate and decide on cases of discrimination, but also implement a range of activities to raise awareness, support good practice and conduct research'.[63] The mandate of the Ukrainian Parliament Commissioner for Human Rights in the field of equality and non-discrimination accommodates both dimensions and, thus, represents such a combined type of equality body.

A further institutional framework that has to be mentioned in the context of equality bodies as it is also relevant for Ukraine is the European Commission against Racism and Intolerance (ECRI). ECRI is an independent monitoring body established in 1993 and monitors activities and problems in relation to racism and intolerance in the 47 Member States of the Council of Europe. In ECRI General Policy Recommendation No. 2 from June 1997, ECRI recommends Member States to set up specialised institutions 'to combat racism, xenophobia, antisemitism and intolerance at national level' and suggests basic principles including functions and responsibilities, statutes and style of operation of such bodies. These stipulations were considerably extended, specified and refined in December 2017.[64]

The mandate of the Ukrainian Parliament Commissioner for Human Rights in the field of equality and non-discrimination is, first, laid down in the Law on

---

[60] Ibid., p. 60.
[61] See EQUINET, 'Enhancing the Impact of Equality Bodies and Ombudsperson Offices: Making Links', European Network of Equality Bodies, Brussels 2017, available at http://www.equineteurope.org/IMG/pdf/ebombud_final_web.pdf; last accessed 11.06.2018.
[62] N. CROWTHER and C. O'CINNEIDE, 'Bridging the Divide? Integrating the Functions of National Equality Bodies and National Human Rights Institutions in the European Union', Nuffield Foundation 2013, available at https://www.ucl.ac.uk/laws/sites/laws/files/btd-report.pdf, last accessed 08.06.2018.
[63] EQUINET, 'The Bigger Picture: Equality Bodies as Part of the National Institutional Architecture for Equality – An Equinet Perspective', Brussels 2014, p. 6, available at http://www.equineteurope.org/IMG/pdf/institutional_architecture_eng_with_cover.pdf, last accessed 11.06.2018.
[64] ECRI, General Policy Recommendation No. 2: Equality Bodies to Combat Racism and Intolerance at National Level, CRI(2018)06, adopted on 7 December 2017, Strasbourg 2018.

the Commissioner and, secondly, in other laws that explicitly focus on equality and anti-discrimination. According to the Law on the Commissioner, among the central purposes of the parliamentary control exercised by the Commissioner are the 'protection of human and citizens' rights and freedoms envisaged by the Constitution of Ukraine, the laws of Ukraine and international treaties' (Article 3(1)) and the facilitation of the 'the process of bringing legislation of Ukraine on human and citizens' rights and freedoms in accordance with the Constitution of Ukraine and international standards in this area' (Article 3(4)). This means that the Commissioner's mandate does covers not only equality and anti-discrimination clauses in the Constitution but also relevant stipulations in international and European human rights treaties, including specialised human rights instruments such as the CERD, the CEDAW and the CRPD. The Law on the Commissioner also explicitly defines the 'prevention of any forms of discrimination in relation to fulfilment of person's rights and freedoms' (Article 3(1)) as one of the purposes of the work of the Commissioner and the exercise of 'control over [...] ensuring equal rights and opportunities for women and men' as a specific right of the Commissioner (Article 13(13)). The Commissioner has several priority areas, one of which is the prevention and combating of discrimination.[65]

The two national laws with a specific focus on equality and anti-discrimination that further define the role of the Commissioner in this field are the Anti-Discrimination Act and the Gender Equality Act, discussed above. The Gender Equality Act explicitly defines in Article 7 that the Commissioner is an institution vested with powers in the field of ensuring equal rights and opportunities for women and men. The Act further lays down that all agencies, institutions and organisations vested with powers in this field can apply positive action in their activity in order to achieve the objective of the law. Article 9 of this law determines the specific mandate of the Commissioner in the area of ensuring equal rights and opportunities for women and men including: the power to exercise control over observance of equal rights and opportunities for women and men in the context of monitoring of the observance of human and civil rights and freedoms; the authority to consider complaints on cases of discrimination based on sex; and the obligation to highlight the issue of observance of equal rights and opportunities for women and men in the annual report. In addition, Article 22 stipulates that:

> the person who thinks that there was a discrimination against him/her on the basis of sex or he/she became the object of sexual harassment, has the right to submit a

---

[65] Other priority areas are access to information, rights of the child, personal data protection, social, economic and humanitarian law and the National Preventive Mechanism under the Optional Protocol to the Convention against Torture.

complaint to [...] the Ukrainian Parliament Commissioner for Human Rights [...] according to the procedure provided by law.

The Law of Ukraine 'On Principles of Prevention and Combating Discrimination in Ukraine' defines in Article 9(1) the Ukrainian Parliament Commissioner for Human Rights as one of the bodies provided with the authority to prevent and combat discrimination and – similar to the Gender Equality Act – provides for the possibility to utilise positive action to achieve the objectives of the law. The specific powers of the Commissioner concerning the prevention and combating of discrimination are laid down in Article 10. Accordingly, the Commissioner is entrusted with the competence:

- to carry out the control over the observance of the principle of non-discrimination in various areas of public relations, in particular in the private sphere;
- to appeal to the court with statements on discrimination in order to protect public interests and personally or through a representative be involved in the judicial process in cases and according to the procedure established by law;
- to conduct monitoring and summarise the results of the observance of the principle of non-discrimination in various areas;
- to consider the applications of persons and/or groups of persons on discrimination;
- to keep record and summarise the cases of discrimination in various areas;
- to make proposals on the improvement of legislation with regard to preventing and combating discrimination and the application and termination of positive actions;
- to give opinions in cases of discrimination at the court's request;
- to highlight the issue of preventing and combating discrimination and the observance of the principle of non-discrimination in the annual report;
- to cooperate with international organisations and the relevant authorities of foreign countries on compliance with international standards of non-discrimination; and
- to carry out other tasks defined by the Constitution and the laws of Ukraine.

In addition, Article 14 of the Anti-Discrimination Act gives every person who thinks that there was a discrimination against him/her the right to submit a complaint to various State institutions including the Commissioner, according to the procedure provided by law. The range of different legal competences reveals that the Commissioner, as an equality body, is entrusted with a mandate that combines tasks of promotional-type equality bodies (such as monitoring the right to equality and non-discrimination and carrying out positive measures) as well as tasks predominately carried out by tribunal-type equality bodies (such as receiving, investigating and responding to individual discrimination complaints). Thus, as previously indicated, it constitutes a body that, according to its legal foundation, is a combination of both types.

From 2014–2017, the Ukrainian Parliament Commissioner for Human Rights implemented a Strategy and an Action Plan for Preventing and Combating Discrimination in Ukraine. The aims and objectives of the Strategy was the compliance of the national legal framework and case law on equality and non-discrimination with international and European standards, the effective monitoring for public and private sector bodies' compliance with equality and non-discrimination legal standards, effective response to incidents of individual and systemic discrimination and due redress, effective promotion of equality and non-discrimination by elucidating and raising awareness of the issue and the operation of strategic networks with relevant national and international stakeholders to promote equality and non-discrimination.[66]

To sum up, the Commissioner is an A-rated NHRI that also has the function of an equality body. According to Equinet, the cooperation and links between NHRIs and equality bodies is taking place on a broad spectrum, ranging from mere exchange of information to a full merger, 'where a single body has a mandate in relation to both human rights and equality'.[67] The Ukrainian Commissioner represents the merger type, as it is a multi-mandated body that is responsible for the whole human rights catalogue, including a specific focus on equality and non-discrimination.

Looking at the different competences an equality body has to fulfil according to EU equality law (as discussed at the beginning of this article) most of the actual work of the Commissioner concentrates on the first dimension of providing assistance to victims of discrimination in pursuing their complaints about discrimination.[68] The number of appeals with regard to non-discrimination and equality varies enormously from year to year. In 2013, the body received 2,051 applications linked to discrimination. The vast majority of these complaints concerned discrimination on grounds of religious or other beliefs (1,768 or about 86% of the total number).[69] In 2014, the number dropped

---

[66] UKRAINIAN PARLIAMENT COMMISSIONER FOR HUMAN RIGHTS, 'Strategy for Preventing and Combating Discrimination in Ukraine 2014–2017', available at http://www.ombudsman.gov.ua/files/documents/foreing/Eng/CommissionersEqualityStrategicPlan_ENG_FINAL.pdf, last accessed 11.06.2018; 'Action Plan toward the implementation of the Strategy for Preventing and Combating Discrimination in Ukraine for 2014–2017 (order of the Ukrainian Parliament Commissioner for Human Rights of November 15, 2013 No. 23/02–13)', available at http://www.ombudsman.gov.ua/files/documents/foreing/Eng/2014-01-20_Action-Plan-2014.pdf, last accessed 11.06.2018.

[67] See EQUINET (2017), 'Enhancing the Impact of Equality Bodies and Ombudsperson Offices', *supra* note 61, pp. 7–8.

[68] This was confirmed during interviews conducted in February 2017 and May 2018.

[69] Щорічна доповідь Уповноваженого Верховної Ради України з прав людини про стан дотримання прав і свобод людини і громадянина, КИЇВ, 2014, p. 375.

to 609 applications (including 154 applications concerning discrimination on grounds of religious belief and 113 applications on grounds of gender discrimination).[70] The data presented in the subsequent annual reports do not include discrimination on grounds of gender (although the reports contain chapters on gender equality). In 2015, the Commissioner received 359 and, in 2016, 303 applications concerning cases of discrimination.[71] According to the Annual Report 2018, in 2017 the Commissioner received 373 applications concerning incidents of discrimination and violations of the principle of equality.[72] This number, however, does also not include discriminations on grounds of gender. According to the data published on the Commissioner's website, the total number of appeals concerning the right to equality amounts to 741 applications in 2017.[73] This constitutes 2.09% of the total number of applications to the Commissioner.

Concerning the legal framework on receiving complaints, it is disputed if the legal competences in this regard defined by the Law on the Commissioner, the Anti-Discrimination Act and the Gender Equality Act are completely in line with the required competences of equality bodies laid down in the EU equality directives. All three acts stipulate the obligation of the Commissioner to 'consider' complaints on cases of discrimination. The equality directives, however, require an equality body to have the competence of 'providing independent assistance to victims of discrimination in pursuing their complaints'.

Furthermore, the competence of 'conducting independent surveys concerning discrimination' is not incorporated in the three laws in exactly this wording. However, it could be argued that this is included in the monitoring function that is explicitly laid down in the Anti-Discrimination Act and, implicitly, also in the two other laws (the Gender Equality Act and the Law on the Commissioner).[74] In practice, the Commissioner and her Secretariat are already involved in carrying out surveys on different topics in the field of

---

[70] Щорічна доповідь Уповноваженого Верховної Ради України з прав людини про стан додержання та захисту прав і свобод людини і громадянина в Україні, КИЇВ 2015, pp. 272–273.

[71] Щорічна доповідь Уповноваженого Верховної Ради України з прав людини про стан дотримання прав і свобод людини і громадянина, КИЇВ, 2016, p. 147, and Щорічна доповідь Уповноваженого Верховної Ради України з прав людини про стан дотримання прав і свобод людини і громадянина, КИЇВ, 2017, p. 92.

[72] Уповноваженого Верховної Ради України з прав людини про стан дотримання прав і свобод людини і громадянина в Україні, *ПРАВА ЛЮДИНИ*, ЩОРІЧНА ДОПОВІДЬ, КИЇВ 2018, p. 510.

[73] See UKRAINIAN PARLIAMENT COMMISSIONER FOR HUMAN RIGHTS, 'Statistics', available at http://www.ombudsman.gov.ua/ua/page/applicant/statistics/, last accessed 08.06.2018.

[74] See also, J. Paužaitė-Kulvinskienė et al., 'Recommendations Aimed at Bringing the National Regulatory and Legal Framework in Accordance with the Best EU Practices in the Human Rights Area', Kiev 2017, pp. 35–36, available at http://www.twinning-ombudsman.org/wp-content/uploads/2017/09/EN_Mission-report-1-3.pdf, last accessed 11.06.2018.

anti-discrimination.[75] In 2017, the institution was furthermore involved in developing manuals on discrimination issues.[76]

Also concerning the third competence explicitly mentioned by the EU equality directive, the publishing of independent reports and the making of recommendations on any issue relating to discrimination, the Commissioner is increasingly carrying out pro-active work. For example, the Commissioner has started to submit shadow reports to UN bodies that monitor human rights compliance of Ukraine with their international human rights obligations.[77] Furthermore, the Commissioner publishes an annual report analysing the situation concerning discrimination and equality in Ukraine as well as recommendations on how to remedy shortcomings concerning the legal framework and on how to improve the specific situation of and eliminate discrimination against members of specific groups. In particular, the monitoring of the legal framework constitutes an important part of the pro-active work of the Commissioner. In 2017, in the field of anti-discrimination and equality, the Commissioner and her staff initiated amendments to 19 laws in order to remove discriminatory provisions, they participated in the development of proposals concerning changes to eleven draft laws and submitted six appeals to the Constitutional Court of Ukraine regarding the discriminatory nature of specific legal norms and their non-compliance with the Constitution of Ukraine.[78] In addition, the Commissioner also carries out training and seminars related to anti-discrimination.[79]

Another issue was raised by ECRI. Although ECRI notes in its last monitoring report on Ukraine that powers to prevent and combat discrimination that are

---

[75] For example, in partnership with the Centre for Political Studies and Analysis, the Secretariat of Ukrainian Parliament Commissioner for Human Rights carried out a survey on gender awareness raising of 166 authorities. Another example is a survey of problems faced by the Roma community that was carried out in cooperation with the International Charity Fund 'Roma Women's Fund Chirikli' in the context of the UNDP Democratization, Human Rights and Civil Society Development Programme in Ukraine in 2014. For further information, see UKRAINIAN PARLIAMENT COMMISSIONER FOR HUMAN RIGHTS (2017a), 'Shadow Report (Submission) on Implementation of the Convention on the Elimination of all Forms of Discrimination against Women by Ukraine', *supra* note 53.

[76] Уповноваженого Верховної Ради України з прав людини про стан дотримання прав і свобод людини і громадянина в Україні, *ПРАВА ЛЮДИНИ, ЩОРІЧНА ДОПОВІДЬ*, КИЇВ 2018, p. 513.

[77] See UKRAINIAN PARLIAMENT COMMISSIONER FOR HUMAN RIGHTS, 'Shadow Report of the Ukrainian Parliament Commissioner for Human Rights on the Status of Implementation of Recommendations made to Ukraine under the Universal Periodic Review', Ukraine 2017b, available at https://uprdoc.ohchr.org/uprweb/downloadfile.aspx?file name=4242&file=EnglishTranslation, last accessed 11.06.2018; UKRAINIAN PARLIAMENT COMMISSIONER FOR HUMAN RIGHTS (2017a), 'Shadow Report (Submission) on Implementation of the Convention on the Elimination of all Forms of Discrimination against Women by Ukraine', *supra* note 53.

[78] Уповноваженого Верховної Ради України з прав людини про стан дотримання прав і свобод людини і громадянина в Україні, *ПРАВА ЛЮДИНИ, ЩОРІЧНА ДОПОВІДЬ*, КИЇВ 2018, p. 512.

[79] Ibid.

almost fully in line with its General Policy Recommendations have been granted to the Commissioner, it highlights investigation powers as the only missing element.[80]

5. CRITICAL EVALUATION OF THE WORK OF THE COMMISSIONER IN THE FIELD OF EQUALITY AND ANTI-DISCRIMINATION

The Ukrainian Parliament Commissioner for Human Rights' mandate on equality and non-discrimination has been continually extended over past years. The Gender Equality Act and especially the Anti-Discrimination Act entrusted the Commissioner with competences that are crucial for the functioning of an equality body. The Commissioner so far enjoys a high reputation which is reflected by the high number of individual applications brought before the body. The Commissioner is also commended for advancing the rights of groups that face particular disadvantage and discrimination. For example, the Commissioner has included information on discrimination against and persecution of LGBTIQ+ persons in its annual reports since 2013. Furthermore, the institution has carried out an educational campaign and made several legislative proposals on preventing and combating discrimination based on sexual orientation. However, these proposals have not been supported by the Parliament so far.[81] Recently, a petition that was published on the President's official website was removed on request of the Commissioner. The petition had 'asked for measures to be taken to stop propaganda of homosexuality and to defend family values'.[82] The Commissioner also pushes forward legal reforms in the field of anti-discrimination and equality and monitors the media and the public discourse on complying with anti-discrimination and equality law. The Commissioner has not only made a significant contribution to enhancing the national legal framework on equality and improving the protection against discrimination, the body has also continuously worked towards the strengthening and enhancement of its own competences. The Commissioner is also increasingly involved in raising awareness among officials, civil society and the public at large, for example, by providing anti-discrimination training for civil servants and human rights defenders. The body also contributes to the monitoring activities of international human rights bodies by submitting shadow reports on the issues of equality and non-discrimination.

---

[80] ECRI (2017), Report on Ukraine, *supra* note 3, pp. 13–14.
[81] See ECRI (2017), Report on Ukraine, *supra* note 3, pp. 33 and 70–71.
[82] Quoted after H. COYNASH, 'Ukraine's Ombudsman takes unprecedented and contentious step in defence LGBT rights', 05.04.2018, available at http://khpg.org/en/index.php?id=1522808546, last accessed on 11.06.2018.

On the downside, there are still some problematic points that concern the work of the Commissioner in the field of non-discrimination. Firstly, the Commissioner operates on the basis of a legal framework that, although considerably improved over the last decade, is still characterised by inconsistencies and sometimes even discriminatory provisions (as discussed above). Secondly, the Commissioner's work in general and in the field of non-discrimination in particular still follows a rather reactive approach. The major part of the work is dedicated to following up individual applications to the Commissioner. Although, legally the Commissioner is entitled to carry out 'tribunal' functions as well as 'promotional' activities, only a small part of the work is dedicated to pursuing a pro-active agenda and to enhance positive action. The reaction to individual applications and the provision of support and independent assistance is, of course, an important task of an equality body. In order to achieve substantive equality a purely complaints-led model – which in case of discrimination requires an individual person to lodge a complaint at a court or another competent body, such as equality bodies or ombud institutions, in order to establish a violation of her or his rights not to be discriminated against – is important but not sufficient.[83] Discriminatory attitudes and structures are often deeply embedded in society and thus, a focus on addressing complaints or appeals may only 'be capable of bringing about a limited amount of social change'.[84] Closely connected with the last point is the issue of resources. In light of the high number of individual complaints it is doubtful whether the Commissioner is equipped with adequate resources to fulfil satisfactorily all the tasks that are laid down in the legal framework. Thirdly, concerning individual cases of discrimination it is criticised that the Commissioner does not have the power to issue binding decisions and impose sanctions. The body can only give recommendations.[85] Fourthly, as discussed in the previous section, it is not entirely sure if the legal framework that is in place now fulfils the standards of equality bodies laid down in EU equality law. The Draft Law No. 3501 of 2015 mentioned above would remedy the last two shortcomings and also equip the Commissioner with investigative powers, as recommended by ECRI. However, this law has not yet been adopted. Despite these problematic points, it is important to stress that the Commissioner plays an increasingly important role in promoting equal rights and combating discrimination in Ukraine. Should Draft Law No. 3501 be adopted this role will be considerably enhanced in the future.

---

[83] S. Fredman, 'Making Equality Effective: The Role of Proactive Measures', European Network of Legal Experts in the Field of Gender Equality. European Commission. Directorate-General for Employment, Social Affairs and Equal Opportunities, Brussels 2009, p. 1, available at http://ec.europa.eu/social/BlobServlet?docId=4551, last accessed 11.06.2018.

[84] C. O'Cinneide, 'Positive Action', 2014, available at http://www.era-comm.eu/oldoku/SNLLaw/04_Positive_action/2014_April_Cinneide_Paper_EN.pdf, last accessed on 08.06.2018.

[85] I. Fedorovych (2016a), 'Equal Employment Opportunities in Ukraine', *supra* note 40, p. 6.

PART VI
BOOK REVIEWS

Christian BREITLER

Katja S. Ziegler, Elizabeth Wicks and Loveday Hodson (Eds.)

The UK and European Human Rights – A Strained Relationship?

Oxford, Hart Publishing, Paperback Edition 2018, 525 pages, £39.99

Is the relationship between the United Kingdom (UK) and European human rights law a 'strained' one? As the title might suggest, this is the question to be answered in this 525 page compendium. However, as the preface makes clear, the question the volume tries to answer is not so much *if* the relationship is strained, but rather what the *causes* of this strained relationship are. The assertion that the relationship is 'not relaxed or friendly' (Oxford Learner's Dictionary) is essentially more of an underlying presumption than the research subject *per se*.

The book that was first published in 2015 in hardback contains contributions from 23 authors and predominantly originates from a conference at the University of Leicester in May 2014. As such, it fills a gap in existing literature by offering a comprehensive and interdisciplinary view on the tensions between British legal traditions and the European human rights framework. Although there are practitioners among the authors, most contributions come from academia. Consequently, the addressed readership are primarily scholars and interested students in the field of law and related subjects.

The compendium is divided into an introduction followed by five parts and a conclusion.

Part I, which examines the relationship between the UK and the European Court of Human Rights (ECtHR) in general, is by far the most enlightening regarding the legal dimension. While *Paul Mahoney*, former British judge at the ECtHR, emphasises the cooperation model between the Strasbourg court and domestic courts through 'judicial dialogue', former Justice *Lord Kerr* questions the very existence of such a dialogue. *Kerr*, like *Richard Clayton* in his chapter, devotes much attention to the so-called *Ullah* principle and the question as to what effect judgments by the ECtHR have under the Human Rights Act (HRA). *Clayton* and *Kerr* seem to agree that the *Ullah* principle has been modified in a way that makes the term 'mirror principle' no longer accurate. Not only do authors in this compendium reflect about the way Strasbourg jurisprudence is to be considered by British courts, but also whether the HRA might be replaced altogether. *Ed Bates* adopts a historical view and seeks to show that concerns regarding national sovereignty are by no means new developments but have been present from the very beginning in the relationship between the UK and the ECtHR. He argues that UK courts must in any case continue to consider the case law of the ECtHR in order to maintain a cooperation mode with Strasbourg based on subsidiarity. *Brice Dickson* suggests that British courts should put a stronger emphasis on common law approaches to human rights.

Part II considers specific sensitive issues in the UK-Strasbourg relationship: Voting eligibility, counter-terrorism, immigration and application of the European Convention on Human Rights (ECHR) in situations of armed conflict are discussed in this part. As *Reuven Ziegler* and *Helen Fenwick* show, sensitive cases as in the fields of counter-terrorism and voting require a careful balance between the ECtHR's living instrument doctrine on the one hand and subsidiarity and margin of appreciation on the other hand.

Part III shifts the focus to the triangular relationship of national law, ECHR and European Union (EU) law. The EU Charter of Fundamental Rights is no less subject to scepticism in the UK. However, as *Sionaidh Douglas-Scott* demonstrates, by functioning as a counterweight to EU powers, the Charter preserves citizen's rights and national sovereignty.

Part IV starts with an introduction on compliance with ECtHR judgments followed by chapters about experiences in France, Italy, Germany, and two chapters about the role of the ECHR in Russia. Although the aim of Part IV is to provide a perspective that contrasts the different experiences, unfortunately only one author – *Julia Rackow* in her chapter about Germany – fully attempts to draw a comparison. Most other authors only touch upon the UK's experience, while one author – *Oreste Pollicino* – does not even refer to the UK once.

Finally, Part V addresses the role of the media. While *Robert Uerpmann-Wittzack* elaborates on the media as a public watchdog, *David Mead* and *Lieve Gies* show in their chapters that certain sections of the infamous British press are often not watchdogs but rather fighting dogs in their coverage of European human rights law. Undoubtedly, the media has contributed to a distorted image of the ECHR in the UK.

While the compendium is an excellent resource about the UK's relationship with European human rights law, it is clearly a shortcoming that the publisher did not issue a revised re-edition instead of an unmodified paperback edition, as it does not take into account the 2016 Brexit referendum or any subsequent developments. Therefore, calls for embracing the EU Charter of Fundamental Rights seem a bit outdated. Nonetheless, this is not to detract from the fact that the compendium provides a comprehensive insight into what will likely continue to be a 'strained relationship'.

Moritz DEINHAMMER

Emily Reid
Balancing Human Rights, Environmental Protection and International Trade – Lessons from the EU Experience
Oxford, Hart Publishing, 2017, 313 pages, €29

The book *Balancing Human Rights, Environmental Protection and International Trade – Lessons from the EU Experience* arose from doctoral research undertaken by Emily Reid, Associate Professor for European Union Law at Southampton University. The text provides a thorough examination of possible ways to reconcile interests of 'non-economic' nature with trade liberalisation.

This academic publication is particularly concerned with the conflict inherent in the simultaneous pursuit of human rights and environmental protection on the one hand and economic interests on the other. This selection of interests is explained by the need to address contemporary issues, such as climate change and the emerging aspiration of sustainable development. In analysing the current international legal system as well as the conduct of trade liberalisation regimes, the author assesses the potential and limits of the existing international regulatory framework to accomplish the said reconciliation.

The book is divided into two parts: the first part focuses on the approach of the European Union (EU) to protect non-economic interests, namely human rights and environmental protection, as well as the development of these interests, as objectives in themselves. It also analyses the extent to which the EU has succeeded in balancing these non-economic interests and its initial purpose of economic liberalisation. In the following part, Reid turns to the World Trade Organization (WTO), where the relationship between economic and non-economic interests is presently being developed and she examines in detail the diverging approaches to environmental protection and human rights issues in the WTO.

The author argues that in the EU, the development of both human rights and environmental protection were initially driven by economic concerns. Their evolution towards objectives as an end in themselves was due to a combination of Member State and Court of Justice action, followed by institutional action and amendment of the treaties. For this development, the pre-existing common consensus in terms of values within the EU has been of particular importance.

Providing an in-depth analysis of relevant EU case law, Reid notes that, despite the Court's approach in the case *PreussenElektra*, there is no hierarchy between social, environmental and economic interests but that these interests must be weighed against one another. In doing so, the Court adopted in *Schmidberger* a 'two-way proportionality test' and endorsed this approach in subsequent cases. The author characterises this proportionality-based approach as an 'operationalization of the principle of sustainable development'.

Regarding the EU's external relations, Reid observes that the EU has pursued the inclusion of human rights and environmental commitments in its agreements with third states since the 1980s. This overarching concept of sustainable development can be seen as a necessary means to ensure that the EU does not breach its internal obligations. However, the negotiation experience in the past has demonstrated a degree of inconsistency where significant EU interest had been at stake and a consensus with the partner state could not be found. Furthermore, the EU has been criticised as exporting its values in an imperialistic fashion by imposing human rights or environmental conditionality in its agreements. Despite all the criticism, the author points out that the EU is promoting social and environmental interests in international trade regulation by placing non-economic interests on the agenda when cooperating with third states.

In contrast to the legal framework of the EU, the WTO rules remain first and foremost concerned with the promotion of free trade and the removal of restrictions on trade. Even though the WTO constitutes the only international body which can adjudicate on the balance to be drawn between economic and non-economic interests, Reid states that the WTO has not yet adjusted to the contemporary issues and therefore remains ill-equipped to fulfil this important role. As it seems to be impossible to separate the protection of the environment or the pursuit of human rights and the negatively viewed regulation or restriction of trade, the problem of regulation is political. The author raises the questions why trade liberalisation is still prioritised and why the pursuit of economic development does not imply long-term interests in terms of sustainable development. Reid concludes that, dependent upon electoral support, governments may be reluctant to support necessary reforms. Therefore, it is for the WTO panels and the Dispute Settlement Body (DSB) to decide how non-economic interests should be protected. However, an action to protect the environment is not held to breach the General Agreement on Tariffs and Trade (GATT) as long as it satisfies the conditions of Article XX (or similar provisions in other WTO agreements). Furthermore, there is no reference to human rights, nor an exception applicable to the protection of human rights to be found in the WTO Agreement. Moreover, a body of human rights with universal recognition within the WTO framework is still to be identified. The author's analysis of the GATT and WTO case law further indicates that even though an environmental measure has not yet been held to be a legitimate restriction on trade, this is due to the fact that those measures that were subject of complaint have had 'an air of protectionism rather than genuine environmental concern'.

Reid argues that the legal framework of the WTO should adopt a more holistic approach and be reconceptualised with special regards to sustainable development. She reiterates that in relation to reconciliation of economic and non-economic interests, consensus, as to the values to be pursued, and political foresight are of the essence. The book provides an exceptionally detailed analysis of the standing of human rights and environmental protection within international trade law. Referencing a large number of cases, treaties and agreements it illustrates complex rules and procedures in a comprehensible manner. Although concrete answers and solutions on this matter cannot be expected, the book points out overdue next steps in the process of integrating human rights and environmental protection in international trade law.

Philipp Alexander DILLINGER

Nicole Bürli
Third-Party Interventions before the European Court of Human Rights

Cambridge, Intersentia, 2016, 214 pages, €79

As the title of this book indicates, this is a technical book on the specific role of third-party interveners in proceedings before the European Court of Human Rights (ECtHR). The fact that the book is available only in hardcover edition, contributes to the rather elevated price-level of the book. The publication deals with interventions of non-governmental organisations on the one hand and with member state interventions, and amicus curiae interventions on the other. The book's main intended audience is a readership interested in technical reflections on complex proceedings before the ECtHR, since general knowledge of the proceedings before the ECtHR as well as of the European Convention on Human Rights are presumed by the author. Thus, the book is not advisable for someone who is not familiar with basic knowledge on the proceedings before the ECtHR, as the author does not focus on the elaboration of this basic information. The experienced reader profits from an in-depth examination of complex issues.

The book, which is not part of a series, reflects on the special topic of proceedings before the ECtHR and the interventions of third parties, by providing extensive insight and analyses cases with third-party interventions between the years 1979 and 2016. More specifically, the potential influence of those third-party interventions on the reasoning and decision-making of the ECtHR is analysed. Moreover, the book includes a table of cases, which provides a complete overview of all cases before the ECtHR that entailed third-party interventions in the aforementioned period. This table of cases provides the reader with information on the specific type of third-party intervention. In addition, the cases are arranged in alphabetical order within each year of the period between 1979 and 2016. Thus, the reader is offered the possibility to gain a general overview on all third-party interventions on the one hand, and the opportunity of specific information on single cases with third-party interventions on the other. In addition, the table of cases is interlinked logically with the book's table of contents, as well as the index, so that the reader can navigate easily through complex issues dealt with in the book, even if he/she is only interested in certain sections of it.

The book is divided into five chapters, beginning with the introduction which gives an overview of the whole subject and the applied methods. The conclusion at the end provides the reader with a valuable summary of the author's insights. The three main chapters follow a clear structure, each of them including preliminary observations, notion and origin of the respective chapter's issue and a conclusion to sum up the main findings of the respective chapter before gathering the findings in the main conclusion at the end of the book. The first main chapter is dedicated to the 'amicus curiae interventions' which represents the most elaborated issue of this book. Starting from the actual development of these amicus curiae interventions from their historic roots, the issue of amicus curiae interventions is examined closely in this chapter. The chapter on the 'amicus curiae interventions' focuses in detail on the role of non-governmental organisations and other international organisations in third-party interventions. The difference between interventions of non-governmental organisations and international organisations is clearly elaborated and underlined in this chapter. The second main chapter is concerned with member state interventions, circumventing diverse interventions in proceedings before the European Court of Human Rights of member states to the Council of Europe. The third main chapter examines actual third-party interventions, which originate from civil disputes between private parties, since the Court has increasingly decided on cases on purely civil disputes.

The book's structure build around three main chapters, offers the reader a logical guide through the complex issue of third-parties intervening in diverse ways in proceedings before the ECtHR, completing its task in the summarising and reflective conclusion at the end of the book.

As the book aims at examining all cases before the European Court of Human Rights that involved interventions of third-parties, it must be criticised, that there is neither a concrete definition nor an explicit explanation for those specific cases chosen by the author as the subject of discussion in the book.

Christina SEEWALD

Stijn Smet and Eva Brems (Eds.)
When Human Rights Clash at the European Court of Human Rights – Conflict or Harmony?

Oxford, Oxford University Press, 2017, 288 pages, €79.49

Some cases at the European Court of Human Rights (ECtHR, the Court) appear to be impossible to be justly resolved: Should the Court either deny maternity, by deciding to destruct the frozen embryos against the wishes of the woman who contributed her ovum, or force paternity against the will of the applicant's former partner? The ECtHR dealt with this question in the *Evans v The United Kingdom case*, which entails a conflict between human rights, namely a 'conflict between the Article 8 rights of two private individuals' (para. 73). Also, *Ladele v The United Kingdom*, *Axel Springer AG v Germany* and *Fernández Martinez v Spain* are just some additional examples of cases at the Court which encompass conflicts between Convention Rights. However, there is little literature covering possible human rights conflicts and the existing literature with its different approaches is widely scattered, making it difficult for practitioners to get a profound overview. The book *When Human Rights Clash at the European Court of Human Rights: Conflict or Harmony?*, composed of contributions by different renowned authors, with the editors Stijn Smet and Eva Brems leading the way, is a compelling compendium of various approaches to tackle not only the resolution of human rights conflicts but also the very possibility of their existence. The book is divided into two parts, with the first part (pp. 23) setting out different theoretical approaches and the second part (pp. 75) resolving the four cases, mentioned at the beginning of this review, which form the 'analytical backbone' of the book (p. 2). While some might criticise that this work is a mere collection of separate papers by different contributors, it must be emphasised that it is a coherent whole with the four cases running like a common thread through all the separate chapters. In the second part of the book, each of the four cases is discussed in two chapters from a different angle by two authors, which leaves the reader the impression of a comprehensive resolution of the human rights conflict each case entails. Furthermore, it must be noted here that the 'contributors truly build on and substantively debate each other's arguments' resulting in a perfectly rounded overall image (p. 19).

It is also noteworthy that most chapters of this book originate from the symposium '(How) Should the European Court of Human Rights Resolve Conflicts between Human Rights?', organised by the Human Rights Centre of Ghent University in 2014. The chapters from the symposium, however, were revised and enriched with the feedback from (former) judges at the ECtHR, who acted as commentators and shaped the contours of the book and contents of its chapters (p. 18).

With only 288 pages, this compendium comes handy to provide a first overview of the different approaches in literature and the inconsistent human rights practice of the Court. However, due to the books rather short scope, one cannot expect to acquire all knowledge covering the 'entire range of views on this topic in contemporary human rights scholarships' (p. 242).

Three characteristic features of this work should be highlighted: first, this publication stands out among other literature on human rights conflicts at the ECtHR due to the debate on whether or not human rights can even conflict with one another or if the Convention rights should be understood in terms of their harmonious compatibility. The majority of existing literature focuses on the resolution of human rights conflicts and ignores the question of the very existence of such conflicts. The reviewed book, however, offers a unique approach in this discussion, especially highlighted in Leto Cariolou's contribution (pp. 171), as she consistently writes of 'purported' conflicts and therefore 'appears to deny the existence of human rights conflicts' (p. 3). Secondly, this book shows well the interplay of the 'twin notions of subsidiarity and the margin of appreciation' and conflicting rights and therefore this work is not restricted only to the substantive resolution of human rights conflicts but also examines so called 'procedural checks' (p. 17). Thirdly, the book attracts attention due to its unusual cover, as the hardcover is wrapped with a paper cover depicting the Judgment of Solomon, taken from a stained glass window of the church of Saint-Gervais-Saint-Protais in Paris. Overall, this book might be overlooked due to its short scope, but there is more to it than expected: (academic) readers can quickly familiarise themselves with the various approaches of conflicts between Convention rights, which are conveniently collected in this coherent whole. The systematic composition of this compendium, build around the four cases, which serve as the analytical backbone of the book, is convincing and contributes to a pleasant reading.

Ulrike BRANDL

Violeta Moreno-Lax
Accessing Asylum in Europe, Oxford Studies in European Law

Oxford, Oxford University Press, 2017, 624 pages, €107

The book is dedicated to one of the central factual and legal problems refugees have been facing for many years when they intend to seek asylum in Europe or – according to the author's terminology – exercise the EU 'right to flee' (pp. 393f., 474f.). They need to get access to the territory or – to be more precise – to the jurisdiction of a Member State of the European Union (EU) in order to submit their claim for international protection. The monograph analyses in a comprehensive and illustrative way the development of various kinds of measures created with the intention to deny or limit this access.

The book written by *Violeta Moreno-Lax* is divided into two main parts. Each part consists of five chapters. Part 1 covers the various types of EU pre-border and extraterritorial border control systems and their implications for access to protection in Europe. These measures include, *inter alia*, visa obligations, sanctions against carriers who transport persons not holding valid entry papers and also pre-emptive controls in maritime areas. Part II starts with an examination of legal obligations of Member States when they carry out extraterritorial acts. The other chapters of Part II are dedicated to the tension between these measures and obligations under the *fundamental rights acquis* of the EU.

The problems are not new in general, but the increase of persons seeking access to asylum procedures in the last three years and the reactions of Member States added new legal questions to the already existing ones concerning their human rights compatibility. Even between the publication of the present monograph and the writing of the review new measures were created to limit the options to reach Europe via the Mediterranean Sea or even to restrict the possibilities to leave the ports or territorial waters of countries of departure.

In Part I the author starts with a clarifying reconstruction of the externalisation of border control measures. She lucidly points to the emergence of the concept of 'Integrated Border Management' and the various regimes, which may be summarised under this heading. The creation and development of the Schengen system, the nearly uniform visa regime and the delegation of powers to liaison officers are scrutinised in detail.

The chapters of Part I provide an in depth-analysis of the first set of measures designed to control access already in the country of origin or departure country, with a combination of visa requirements for nationals of certain third countries, with sanctions imposed against carriers and with the externalisation of border controls to liaison officers. These officers support carriers, airline personnel and also state officials with the performance of visa and document controls.

These measures led to the current situation, where only a very limited or even negligible number of persons in need of protection who reach Europe is in possession of valid entry documents. The numbers of persons arriving by plane or with an official carrier are rather low as well. Most of them either cross borders illegally by themselves or they are supported by smugglers either on land or on sea. This is a consequence of the lack of legal possibilities to access asylum in Europe. With the exception of selected resettlement programs carried out by some Member States, no such options exist.

Chapter 6 is particularly interesting as Frontex joint-maritime operations and pre-emptive controls undertaken by these missions are described and their functions are analysed with regard to their immediate and long-term consequences. The establishment of these controls forms the underlying aim of the various stages of Frontex missions (p. 189ff.). The author concludes from her analysis and also based on empirical data that 'more controls have not translated into more deterrence' (p. 198).

Part II explores how the *fundamental rights acquis* limits the execution of such measures. The author examines whether pre-entry controls are compatible with 'EU rights of refugees and forced migrants'. This is a legitimate introduction to this core question as access to the EU is scrutinised. In order to elaborate a fully comprehensive answer, the analysis should have started with a clarification of whether public international law obligations allow such measures. The author however only briefly refers to the public international background. After a few pages the author turns to EU law and identifies a transformation of human rights into 'fundamental rights' within the EU legal order (p. 214). She then continues to examine obligations under EU law and does not further analyse the public international law obligations, their scope and interpretation. If small points of criticism may be expressed, this underlying corollary and the euro-centred focus should be mentioned. The author identifies the core aim of the study. The aim is to determine the content of the specific responsibilities of the EU Member States in the context of extraterritorial entry control, thereby identifying the legal limits to this approach. These legal limits have their origin in public international, in constitutional law obligations of Member States and also in EU law.

It is a pleasure to read the origins and the current status of pre-entry controls in the Member States with the precise statements and the clear analysis with regard to human rights compatibility provided by *Violeta Moreno-Lax*. The book is an excellent example for a legal analysis of techniques invented by States to avoid that possible applicants for protection get access to their jurisdiction.

The author formulates valuable conclusions at the end, which summarise the development and the negative implications of the measures adopted. The first part of the Conclusions is entitled 'The Sein', 'The Sollen' is the heading of the second part. The author summarises the obligations and creates common standards called EU non-refoulement and the right to (leave to seek) asylum in the Charter of Fundamental Rights of the EU, which is named the EU 'right to flee'.

Amaia Azkorra Camargo and Sara Vassalo Amorim

Mark Dawson
The Governance of EU Fundamental Rights

Cambridge, Cambridge University Press, 2017, 230 pages, €102.99

Mark Dawson's *The Governance of EU Fundamental Rights* provides a comprehensive overview of how the European Union (EU) is protecting and enforcing fundamental rights. Highlighting the central role that fundamental rights have acquired in the political debate on the EU's action and evolution, Dawson aims to critically explain the evolution of EU fundamental rights in the past 10 years.

For this purpose, the author starts by framing the theoretical debate surrounding EU fundamental rights, underlining the *suis generis* nature of this legal order. Dawson makes an interesting point on the important proactive role of the EU institutions on the protection and fulfilment of the fundamental rights across the EU.

This study is followed by the analysis of the performance of the EU's institutions in the fundamental rights field. After a comprehensive and very valuable study, the author points out that the institutional diversity within the EU could be a double-edged sword: there are too many deficiencies in relation to the fundamental rights performance of some institutions, but, at the same time, the interaction (and even competition) between these institutions can limit the impact of measures seeking to restrict fundamental rights.

Finally, the author presents some case studies related to two policy fields – social rights and the protection of the rule of law. Hungary and Romania are the two scenarios chosen by the author to depict the crisis of the rule of law in the EU. Those are two useful examples for the reader in order to understand the reality and challenges that EU's rule of law is facing. Greece, Portugal and Ireland are later studied to illustrate the deep hole that the 'Euro crisis' exposed in the EU's constitutional framework. These three countries are a clear example of how their citizens' fundamental rights were severely affected by the austerity measures that the EU, with its coercive power, imposed. The choice of a case of the recent past that had such strong repercussions for the citizens' rights and that uncovered strong divides in the construction of the European project proves to be a very interesting and useful one. However, even if it is understood that the author analyses the case from a legal point of view, the conclusion appears to be somewhat superficial, since some key economic aspects were not taken into consideration. Fundamental rights are not to be understood as an isolated legal order, but need to be integrated in the overall social, economic and political context in which they are to be applied. Therefore, the reader is only given a partial and incomplete picture of the overall scenario.

Throughout the analysis, the author refers to concrete examples of the Court of Justice of the European Union's (CJEU) case law to illustrate the reality of fundamental rights in the EU. This brings fluidity and a scholarly aspect to the book, which proves beneficial to the reader.

Dawson concludes the book with the idea that the EU's fundamental rights challenges are manifold, and that these need to be addressed by the Member States as well. Ultimately, the effective implementation of EU fundamental rights is a political game. In this sense, Dawson presents a rather bleak picture regarding the EU's fundamental social rights in post-'Euro-crisis' Europe.

Dawson's study is interesting, albeit limited. As the author himself acknowledges, the case studies are exemplary, and not exhaustive. Nonetheless, this choice is understandable considering the scope of the study. Furthermore, the overarching analysis of the EU's institutions is an interesting academic exercise, which can be particularly practical for readers who are not acquainted with the EU institutional framework, such as fundamental rights students. However, more experienced readers may find that some of the ideas presented could use further development.

On a technical level, it is surprising that, despite the extensive references throughout the text, the book has a final index regarding its most significant concepts and CJEU cases, but does not encompass a final bibliography or a list of references. This would be a valuable addition, especially considering the book's potential scholarly audience.

Despite the overall distraught tone that prevails in his writing, Mark Dawson offers his audience an instrument to better understand the current position of EU's institutions and its Member States that could certainly prove useful.

Florian HASEL

Philip Leach
Taking a Case to the European Court of Human Rights, 4th Edition

Oxford, Oxford University Press, 2017, 699 pages, €140.19

The European Convention on Human Rights from 1953 has played a very important role in the development and awareness of human rights across Europe. Without doubt, the European Court of Human Rights (ECtHR, the Court) in Strasbourg can be considered as the cornerstone of the Convention system. Nevertheless, the Court currently faces a backlog of over 55,000 cases.[1] Additionally it is being confronted with renewed challenges of its legitimacy, which is exemplified by the Draft Copenhagen Declaration from February 2018,[2] which was initiated by the Danish Chairmanship of the Council of Europe and has triggered again a political and academic debate on the role of the ECtHR.

Philip Leach does not directly enter into that debate with his new book, but rather provides a comprehensive handbook for lawyers, who intend to lodge an application with the ECtHR. However, his publication can still be seen as an important contribution in strengthening the Convention system as Tim Eicke, judge at the ECtHR, points out in his foreword, since the quality of the arguments advanced before the ECtHR is essential in ensuring the protection of the rights protected under the Convention (p. viii). Indeed, Leach's fourth edition *Taking A Case to the European Court of Human Rights* will not only support practitioners in their work, but also is an invaluable help for academics and students in gaining a better understanding of the Strasbourg system.

The book generally follows the structure of the previous three editions and starts with a short introduction on the history of the Council of Europe and the Convention and its Protocols. Leach continues with a detailed overview of the pre-judgement phase before the Court and describes how the practice of judgement and enforcement is regulated. An excellent summary of the underlying Convention principles is given in the fifth chapter. Most pages of his

---

[1] See ECtHR Website, available at https://www.echr.coe.int/Documents/Stats_pending_month_2018_BIL.pdf, last accessed 26.06.2018.
[2] Draft Copenhagen Declaration, 05.02.2018, available at https://menneskeret.dk/sites/menneskeret.dk/files/media/dokumenter/nyheder/draft_copenhagen_declaration_05.02.18.pdf, last accessed 26.06.2018.

book (pp. 210–589) are dedicated to detailed commentary of the substantive rights of the Convention and its Protocols. For Articles 8–11, which are all similarly structured and often require that a balance between different rights is to be struck, Leach provides a very good overview of how the Court addresses this issue of conflicting rights (pp. 400–403). After a short chapter on the issue of derogation and reservation, Leach concludes with an analysis of the redress in form of pecuniary and non-pecuniary compensation that is available from the ECtHR. Throughout the book, the expertise of the author becomes evident time and again. Leach brings to the task not only his rich experience as a Professor of Human Rights Law at Middlesex University and Director of the European Human Rights Advocacy Centre, but also his insights as a lawyer with more than 20 years of experience in practicing before the ECtHR.

This publication is currently the only one on the market that focuses on the practice and the procedure of taking a case before the ECtHR, which also includes an in-depth analysis of the admissibility criteria (pp. 119–185). This makes this book a unique and much-needed resource. Considering the very low 'success rate' of applications, the practical advice from an experienced lawyer that is provided in this book will be extremely valuable for practitioners who want to take a case before the Strasbourg court successfully.[3] The index at the end of the book will help everyone who is looking for a specific issue that has been dealt with by the Court in the past. Therefore, Leach's book should be a standard reference work for academics and students alike who will benefit greatly from the commentary on the Convention system, which primarily portrays the Court's interpretation of the Convention (and its Protocols). While the price of the hardcover version is rather high (€140.19), fortunately a much more affordable softcover version is available for only €56.06.[4]

The 4th Edition includes the procedural developments that have been adopted since the publication of the 3rd Edition, such as the introduction of the obligatory application form in 2014 and the revised process of Rule 47. Furthermore, it also includes the newly-established case law, e.g. concerning the restrictions on in vitro fertilization, same-sex partnerships or asylum procedures and migrants at sea. One may criticise that Leach refrains from referring to any academic discussion about the Court's case law and related issues throughout his book – with only one exception referring to an article in the Heidelberg Journal of International Law (HJIL) (p. 601) – but since the book is

---

[3] 81% of the applications were declared inadmissible or struck out in 2017, see the statistics provided on the ECtHR website, European Court of Human Rights, Statistics 2017, available at https://www.echr.coe.int/Documents/Stats_annual_2017_ENG.pdf, last accessed 26.06.2018.

[4] Oxford University Press Website, available at https://global.oup.com/academic/product/taking-a-case-to-the-european-court-of-human-rights-9780198755418?cc=at&lang=en&, last accessed 15.08.2018.

intended to be more of a practitioner's guide, rather than a critical commentary, this should come as no surprise. However, these minor deficiencies should not detract from the fact that *Taking a Case to the European Court of Human Rights* will be the standard guide for questions related to the procedure before the ECtHR. As such, it is a seminal contribution that will help promote human rights in Europe.

Melanie Helene SCHINAGL

Sionaidh Douglas-Scott and Nicholas Hatzis (Eds.) Research Handbook on EU Law and Human Rights

Cheltenham, Edward Elgar Publishing, 2017, 584 pages, €214

Human rights are pronounced as one of the European Union's (EU) founding principles in Article 2 Treaty on European Union (TEU) and the Charter of Fundamental Rights of the European Union (CFR, Charter) holds the same legal value as the Treaties of the EU, constituting primary EU law (Article 6 TEU). Scholars have exhaustively discussed the role of fundamental rights within the Union for decades. This research handbook provides a compilation of the latest research, ideas, practices and critical insights regarding the position of human rights within the EU. It is made up of 23 articles by distinguished professionals in the field and aims at contributing to current debates on this issue. It is available in hardcover and as an e-book.

The handbook starts with an introduction by the editors and is then divided into three parts. The first part, which is titled 'The Framework', addresses the evolution of the human rights protection system within the EU. Stijn Smismans opens by critically analysing the emergence of four fundamental rights narratives, which retrospectively claim that the main purpose of the European Union/European Economic Community was to ensure peace and unification in Europe. These narratives imply that human rights were foundational for the Union and thus act as its *raison d'être*, even though the original treaties did not mention human rights and the Court of Justice of the European Union (CJEU) was indifferent towards them initially. Civil society and political institutions believed and acted upon these political myths nonetheless and they even shaped how the EU came to see itself. The author discusses current policies, which put these narratives to the test.

Several essays proceed to assess the scope of application and contribution of the Charter and question whether it could widen the competences of the EU.

Angela Ward evaluates the judicial enforceability of EU fundamental rights. Other authors examine particular freedoms, such as the right to good administration in Art 41 CFR or the freedom of movement for EU citizens, in more detail. Alison Young aims to provide a theory of human rights adjudication for the CJEU. She highlights the unique difficulty of ruling on human rights violations over actions of both the Union and its Member States and calls for uniformity, diversity and dialogue in this regard.

The second part of the book, 'Beyond the European Union', centres on the external relations of the Union with regard to human rights. Several authors examine the correlation of EU law and the European Convention on Human Rights (ECHR). The prospect of EU accession to the ECHR and the position the Union would have relating to the European Court of Human Rights (ECtHR), is assessed by several authors, who argue that the ECtHR would become the final authority of human rights protection in the EU, by having to review EU activities.

The CJEU's objection to the accession agreement in Opinion 2/13 is examined in multiple contributions. Several authors argue that the Court's main objective was to maintain the autonomy and jurisdiction of EU law in its entirety. Tobias Lock however asserts that the CJEU would retain the primary jurisdiction for human rights in spite of the accession, given that the review by the ECtHR is only subsidiary. It would simply place the CJEU in the same position as the supreme courts of the Member States and thereby exhibit the Union's maturity.

Lastly, the third part of the book is titled 'EU Action and New Directions in Fundamental Rights'. It discusses the Charter's impact on the Union's human rights system and its influence on current areas of action.

The contribution by Sionaidh Douglas-Scott and Nicholas Hatzis, for instance, examines the issue of social rights protection under the Charter. According to them, the utility of social rights is limited, given their classification as 'principles' as opposed to 'rights'. Massimo Fichera investigates the role of human rights in the European Arrest Warrant (EAW). He criticises the CJEU's principle of mutual recognition in criminal cases and argues that the Union cannot necessarily act on the assumption that all members guarantee the same level of human rights protection. He highlights the need for constructive dialogue between different levels and organs in the EU. James Fraczyk's contribution analyses EU fundamental law in the financial crisis. He condemns the CJEU for refusing to apply the Charter to several financial instruments that originated from the crisis and offers some ideas for future use of the Charter.

Other topics covered in this part include the freedom to conduct business, the enforcement of competition law, the right to privacy and data protection, the freedom of expression in the digital age, immigration and asylum law, the internal market and the Charter's environmental provisions.

To conclude, this research handbook on EU law and human rights offers a wide-ranging study on the position of fundamental rights within EU law. This book is not, nor does it claim to be, a structured textbook on human rights in the EU and will not be an easy read for those unfamiliar with the topic in question. This handbook however constitutes a valuable resource for practitioners, policymakers and scholars of European and human rights law, who want to be up to date with current research, latest thinking and critical insights, regarding the state of the law and future developments within this field.

Reinmar NINDLER

Lauri Mälksoo and Wolfgang Benedek (Eds.)
Russia and the European Court of Human Rights – The Strasbourg Effect

Cambridge, Cambridge University Press, 2018, 399 pages, €104.06

For this book, several renowned international experts join forces to address one of the most notorious topics of the contemporaneous European human rights landscape, which is the (strained) relationship between Russia and the European Court of Human Rights (ECtHR). To that outcome, the editors Lauri Mälksoo and Wolfgang Benedek bring together an international assembly of experts, willing to tackle the book's subject matter from a variety of different perspectives.

The diversity amongst these contributors is indeed noteworthy, given their different regional, academic and professional backgrounds. Russian authors contribute as well as Western scholars; articles of political scientists put the contributions of legal experts into perspective and the thoughts of scholars are joined by the voices of those who have seen actual legal practice – that is two former judges at the ECtHR.

But what exactly is the question this publication deals with? In the preface, the editors quite flatly state that the 'book deals with the question of what has been the impact of Russia's almost twenty years under the jurisdiction of the European Court of Human Rights' (p. xiii). While that seems broad, the subtitle *The Strasbourg Effect* hints at the main thrust of the book's analytical focus: a play on the notion of the 'Helsinki effect', the supposed positive effect that the Helsinki Final Act of 1975 had for the dissident movement in the then Union of Soviet Socialist Republics. However, as Lauri Mälksoo phrases it, the editors, when 'raising the question of the Strasbourg effect on Russia', present the phrase 'Strasbourg effect' with 'a certain question mark and not as a triumphant exclamation' (p. 24). As a methodological approach, the 'socialization theory' is tested for its relevance to the case of Russia.

To shed a light on Russia's relation with the ECtHR, the book is divided into four principal parts. The first part, which is fittingly called 'Setting the scene' consists of two contributions outlining the publication's background. Lauri Mälksoo analyses the alleged 'paradox' of a human rights backlash in Russia during its time under ECtHR jurisdiction, while Petra Roter deals with 'Russia's à la carte participation' (p. 55) in the Council of Europe (CoE) and therefore embedding an analysis of Russia's interaction with the larger institutional framework behind the ECtHR.

Parts II and III of the publication form its analytical backbone. Part II, which is by far the largest single part of the book, explores the broad topic of the '[i]nteraction between the ECtHR and Russian courts' with six contributions. An article by Anton Burkov looks into the use of European human rights law in Russian courts, including lower courts. Two further contributions then focus on the relation between the Russian Constitutional Court and the ECtHR, one of them from a legal, the other one from a political science perspective. Furthermore, Bill Bowring weighs in with a piece on the implementation of Russia's ECtHR cases. Finally, two former ECtHR judges provide the reader with their opinion on how Russia has impacted the Strasbourg system.

Part III then follows up with three articles dealing with case studies about specific rights and violations. This part deals with egregious human rights violations in Chechnya, property rights in Russia and lesbian, gay, bisexual, and transgender rights in Russia.

Finally, in Part IV, Benedikt Harzl and Wolfgang Benedek undertake the task of trying to provide a certain explanation for the state of Russia's relation with the ECtHR and to answer the questions discussed in the publication, as well as providing an assessment of what the 'Strasbourg effect' has been on Russia.

Overall, this book is a mandatory read for everyone who is interested in the topic of human rights in Russia, but also a valuable source of knowledge and new insights for academics who deal with the impact of the ECtHR on the countries under its jurisdiction.

This publication has the potential to foster mutual understanding between Western scholars and decision makers and their Russian counterparts and is therefore a contribution to a strengthening of the European human rights system.

INDEX

2012 Strategic Framework and Action Plan 194

A
A.S. v Slovenian Republic 112, 127
access to housing and healthcare 88–94
accountability 214
Al Skeini 378
ambiguity 214
Anchugov 330
anti-discrimination 573
Aranovskiy (Judge), opinion of 326
Austria 300–301
autochthonous 190

B
Belgium 301–303
best interests of the child 396
Blue Card Directive 113
border control 138

C
C.K. and Others v Slovenia 126
carrier sanctions 375
Catan 380
Charter of Fundamental Rights of the European Union 320, 344
CHEZ 186
clean hands 51
coherent policy 215
Committee of Ministers of the Council of Europe 260, 291, 337, 446
Committee of the Permanent Representatives of the Governments of the Member States to the EU (COREPER) 199
Committee on the Rights of the Child 397
Common European Asylum System (CEAS) 48
 deficiencies of the CEAS 105
Common Foreign and Security Policy (CFSP) 66
communication strategy 497
communication technologies 495
confirmation bias 501
corresponding rights 320, 344
Court of Justice of the European Union (CJEU) 175, 185
criminal law 72–74

D
data protection 60, 62
detention 345, 392

dignity 82
dilatoriness 320, 338
diplomatic representations 121
Directive 2004/38/EC (Racial Equality Directive) 50, 175, 191
discrimination 62–65
diversity 168
doctrine of mutual trust 125
Dublin III 107
durable solutions 76

E
echo chambers 495
effective implementation of human rights guarantees 171
elites 498
Energy Charter Treaty 323
equality 168, 573
equality body 573
EU Foreign Affairs Council 200
EU Framework for National Roma Integration Strategies up to 2020 168
EU Fundamental Rights Agency 171
EU Guidelines on Freedom of Religion or Belief 193, 201
 commitments 209
 implementation of 200
 review of implementation 203
EU Visa Code 52
European Citizens' Initiative 54
European Convention on Human Rights (ECHR) 288, 419
 Article 17 420
 limitation on use of restrictions on rights (Article 18) 258–259
 no punishment without law (Article 7) 243
 Protocol 16 288, 296, 315
European Court of Human Rights (ECtHR) 229–265, 288, 320, 344, 419, 446
European external borders 138
ever closer Union 191
execution 446
execution of judgments 260–262
expectations 76
external action 209
external dimension of the EU migration policy 376
externalisation of border controls 394
externalisation of migration 138
extraterritorial asylum processing centres 114

Intersentia 623

Index

F
Facebook 510
Fedasil 76
Five Star Movement 525
France 525
freedom of association 420
freedom of expression 248–249, 420
freedom of movement 256–258
freedom of religion and belief 246–248, 420
　Special Envoy for the promotion of FoRB outside the EU 197
freedom of the press 250
freedom to receive and impart information 250–251
Front National 525
fundamental freedoms 496

G
gender 544
　gender-based violence 556
　gender equality 521
general measures to prevent new violations of ECHR 449
Geneva Convention relating to the Status of Refugees 49
Germany 303–304
　Constitutional Court 339
good faith 291, 297, 299, 315, 317

H
Handbook for Schengen Visa 117
hashtag activism 547
human and minority rights 169
Human Dimension Implementation Meeting (HDIM) 469
humanitarian visa 53–54, 115
Human Rights Council (HRC) 211
human rights standards 214
human security 139

I
Iceland 304–305
Illascu 380
inclusion 169
in-depth documentation 225
infringement 105, 109, 180
Instagram 514
international agreement 55–56, 58, 60
interpretive authority 294–297, 316
irregularly crossed 129
Islamic fundamentalism 420
Islamic headscarves 62–65
Islamic State 420
Istanbul Convention 544
Italy 305–307, 525
　Constitutional Court 333
　The League 520

J
jihadi-Salafism 420
judgment 446

jurisdiction 375
just satisfaction 259–260

K
Khadija Jafari and Zainab Jafari (Jafari) 127
Koushkaki 117

L
Latvia 307–308
law and justice 525
legal certainty 112
liberal democracies 521
Libya 383
long-term visa 120

M
#MeToo 544
M.S.S. v Belgium and Greece 124, 392
margin of appreciation 452
maritime interdictions 375
Mediterranean 137
Mengesteab 131
Mengozzi, Advocate General 119
migration crisis 138
minority 54, 169
monitoring 202
multilateral institutions 496
mutual trust 71–72

N
N.S. v Secretary of State for the Home Department 124
Netherlands 308, 525
　Party for Freedom 525
network analysis 267, 270, 275, 277
neutrality 64–65
new technologies 496
non-discrimination 521
non-refoulement 120, 345, 375, 378
nulla poena sine lege 72, 74

O
open societies and inclusiveness 168
OSCE 521, 544
　human dimension 468
　meetings 468
　reform 468
　Office of Democratic Institutions and Human Rights (ODIHR) 555

P
pacta sunt servanda 324
Parliamentary Assembly of the Council of Europe 448
passenger name record 58
Permanent Court of Arbitration 323
Poland 525
political psychology 504
populism 521
populist parties 521
positive obligations 51
prescription 72

Index

principled disobedience 320, 338
prohibition of collective expulsion of aliens 258
prohibition of discrimination 251–254
prohibition of forced labour 236
prohibition of inhuman and degrading treatment 235–236
proportionality 393
protected entry procedures 114

R
Racial Equality Directive, see Directive 2004/38/EC
reception conditions 131
refoulement, see *non-refoulement*
refugees 136
  Syrian refugees from Lebanon 76
refugee status 50
Regina v Immigration Officer at Prague Airport 378
religion 62–65
religious extremism 419
repetitive case 267–268, 271, 273
reporting and monitoring system 224
res interpretata 294
resettlement 76, 115
  awareness 78
restrictive measures 66–67, 69
right not to be tried or punished twice 258
right to a fair trial 237–243
right to an effective remedy 71
right to correspondence 245
right to education 80
right to family life 244
right to free elections 255–256
right to leave 374
right to liberty 237
right to life 233–235
right to private life 243–246
right to property 255
right to vote 453
right to work 80
Romani
  action plan on improving the situation of Roma and Sinti 173
  Austrian Romani initiatives 188
  National Roma Integration Strategies 178
  Romanes 188
  Romani studies 170
  Romano Centro 190
Russia 289, 308–310
  Constitutional Court 320
  Ministry of Justice of Russia 324

S
salafism 419–433
sanctions 69–70
second Action Plan on Human Rights and Democracy 195
security of person 80
sexism 544
sexual harassment 544
sexual violence 544
Shari'a 419
Sharpston, Advocate General 129
slavery 392
socio-economic (vulnerable) group 176
Spain 310
Stamose v Bulgaria 384
standard of protection 320, 344
state necessity 56
structural problems 448
supervision 446

T
terrorism 50–51, 58–61
transparency 209
Treaty on the Functioning of the EU 195
trust 496
Twitter 511

U
Ukraine 312, 573
Ukrainian Parliament Commissioner for Human Rights 573, 575, 587–595
ultra vires 341
United Kingdom 288, 311
United Nations
  United Nations Charter 50–51
  United Nations Convention on the Rights of the Child 396
  United Nations High Commissioner for Human Rights (OHCHR) 183
  United Nations High Commissioner for Refugees (UNHCR) 76
  United Nations Security Council 50
  United Nations Special Rapporteur on freedom of religion or belief 203

V
Vienna Convention on the Law of Treaties 411
  Article 27 328
Visa Code 116
visas 345, 375
  admissibility criteria 117
  limited territorial validity (LTV) 116
  long-term 120

W
West Balkan Route 127
women 525, 544
women's rights 521, 545

X
X and X v Belgium 112

Y
Yaroslavtsev (Judge), dissenting opinion of 326
Yukos 320–321